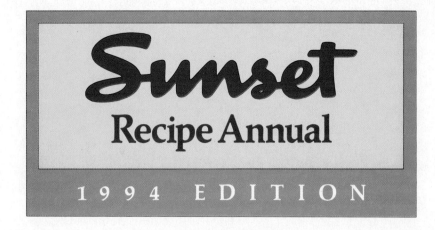

Sunset
Recipe Annual

1994 EDITION

Every *Sunset Magazine* recipe and
food article from 1993

By the *Sunset* Editors

NORMAN A. PLATE

Italian Fisherman's Salad (page 248)

Sunset Publishing Corporation ■ Menlo Park, California

Join Our Annual Feast

For the seventh year we offer our annual banquet—the *Sunset Recipe Annual*—our traditional salute to another year of splendid eating. As in past editions, this collection contains all the food articles and recipes from the previous year's issues of *Sunset Magazine*.

What's new from 1993? Another ample platter for your selection, with choices ranging from citrus to crayfish to Central American specialties. You'll find some of our all-time Western classics as well as edible treats from Latin America, Europe, and Asia. Cooks from around the West share their specialties—breakfast favorites from Portland, inspired creations from tailgate chefs, spicy chile recipes from New Mexico, rib-sticking trail fare from cowboy cooks.

For fresh ideas on casual entertaining we explore the kitchens of wine country cooks, investigate football parties at several Western colleges, and visit with masters of Texas barbecue. You'll also find plenty of suggestions for spur-of-the-moment parties as well as seasonal holiday feasts.

No *Sunset Recipe Annual* would be complete without our popular regular features—*Sunset's Kitchen Cabinet* and *Chefs of the West,* which showcase recipes from our readers; *Menus,* featuring casual meals for family and friends; and the newest, *Why?,* which answers our readers' questions about food and cooking.

Slim Red and Green Pasta (page 150)

PETER CHRISTIANSEN

Material in this book originally appeared in the 1993 issues of *Sunset Magazine*.

Sunset Recipe Annual was produced by *Sunset Books*.

Front cover: Summer Fruit Shortcakes (recipe on page 158). Photography by Kevin Sanchez. Design by Susan Bryant. Food and photo styling by Susan Massey.

Back cover: Baked Fennel with Gorgonzola (recipe on page 235). Photography by Norman A. Plate.

Sunset Magazine
    Editor: William R. Marken

Sunset Books
    Editor: Elizabeth L. Hogan

First printing March 1994

Contents

A Letter from Sunset

DEAR READER,

You might be surprised to learn how much you influence what goes into *Sunset*. All year long, you let us know what's on your mind: you write, you call, and occasionally you even stop by. You send us your favorite dishes or request a copy of a *Sunset* recipe; you need our help solving a problem, you have a bone to pick, or you just want to say you like what we do.

What do your recipes tell us? Plenty! We discover what you like to cook, how much time you have, and how your tastes are changing. We find out about your health concerns. We learn about the ingredients you use—both those that have become standbys and those you're experimenting with. Many of the recipes you send appear in our two reader-only features, *Kitchen Cabinet* and *Chefs of the West*. And sometimes your creations are the stars of a story—as for Nanaimo Bars in May and dried persimmons in October.

Your cooking problems and concerns also give us ideas for stories. We developed the feature *Why?* expressly to answer reader questions. This year, we've discussed—among other things—why braised meat sometimes turns gray and soupy (March) and why meringues go flat (July).

Your requests and complaints are treated seriously. You want less fat, so we've continued to emphasize low-fat cooking techniques—as long as the results are as good as or better than those achieved by traditional methods. And if the richer dish really is the tastier one, we've at least reduced temptation by making lavish treats smaller, as in January's "They're grand desserts, but down-sized"!

You've asked for more vegetarian dishes, so we're moving them into the limelight; our October issue, for example, presented a selection of party-perfect vegetable casseroles. You want sugarless recipes, and we've complied with a March feature on jellies and jams made with fruit concentrates.

Because we do print so many reader contributions, we thought you'd like to know how your recipes get into *Sunset*. We start by

FOOD WRITERS *and editors gather regularly to evaluate staff and reader recipes: (front row) Bernadette Hart, Elaine Johnson, Linda Anusasananan, Barbara Goldman; (back row) Betsy Bateson, Jerry Di Vecchio, and Christine Weber Hale.*

KEEPSAKE EDITIONS *of Sunset recipes include* The Best of Sunset *in 1987 and six editions of the* Sunset Recipe Annual, *each containing all the past year's food articles and recipes from* Sunset Magazine.

1987   1988   1989   1990   1991   1992   1993

selecting dishes that seem most timely and appealing. Next, we prepare each recipe for a taste panel of *Sunset* staff members (a different group each time). Always in attendance are several of our food writers; the entire group is shown with me in the photo at left, at a taste panel on our entertaining patio.

Once the dishes are sampled and the ballots filled in, we tally the results. Recipes that score well move on into story files. The food writer assigned to the story translates the recipe into *Sunset* format, then tests it until she's satisfied that the results are consistently excellent and the instructions easy to follow. Along the way, she adjusts the recipe as needed, perhaps reducing fat or simplifying techniques. Finally, to make sure the directions are absolutely clear, the dish is made again in our test kitchens by one of our on-call retesters—someone who likes to cook but isn't a professional.

The recipes that make it through this rigorous process—and into our magazine and this book—are all winners, wonderful dishes for family meals, simple entertaining, and grand parties. Enjoy them!

Looking forward to hearing from you,

Jerry DiVecchio

Senior Editor (Food and Entertaining)
Sunset Magazine

TO USE OUR NUTRITION INFORMATION

Sunset recipes contain nutrition information based on the most current data available from the USDA for calorie count; grams of protein, total fat (including saturated fat), and carbohydrates; and milligrams of sodium and cholesterol.

This analysis is usually given for a single serving, based on the largest number of servings listed for the recipe. Or it's for a specific amount, such as per table-spoon (for sauces) or by a unit, as per cookie.

The nutrition analysis does not include optional in-gredients or those for which no specific amount is stated (salt added to taste, for example). If an ingredient is listed with an alternative, the figures are calculated using the first choice or a comparable food. Likewise, if a range is given for the amount of an ingredient (such as ½ to 1 cup butter), values are figured on the first, lower amount.

Recipes using regular-strength chicken broth are based on the sodium content of salt-free homemade or canned broth. If you use canned salted chicken broth, the sodium content will be higher.

January Menus

QUICK, SEASONAL,
BUDGET-WISE...
FOR FAMILY AND
FRIENDS

Cozy ambience, warm meals, and friendly gatherings with good conversation are effective antidotes to winter's chilly blasts and gloomy skies. Simple, familiar dishes fit these menus.

For a casual get-together some afternoon or evening, serve a chili buffet. With its built-in flavor flexibility, it suits a range of tastes and ages. Another day, do fish-and-chips with a neater, leaner twist: oven-fried and crisp.

CHILI BUFFET (at right)
Tailor chili and beans to taste: add toppings of choice to bowls. Follow with make-your-own sundaes.

FISH-AND-CHIPS SUPPER (page 8)
Lighter, leaner, easier fish-and-chips (with potato wedges, zucchini slices) are baked, not deep fried.

THE DETAILS

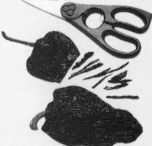

Extra Chili Flavor

Thinly snip mellow dried chilies, like the ancho, and toast crisp in hot oil.

Chili Toppings

Fresh choices include lettuce, cheese, celery, tomatoes, and carrots.

Shapely Cornbread

Bake cornbread in individual molds: corn-shaped pans, madeleine pans, muffin pans.

Build a Sundae

Offer dessert sauces, nuts, and whipped cream for personalized sundaes.

PETER CHRISTIANSEN

7

A day ahead, you can cook beans and chili, and bake cornbread (from a mix or favorite recipe) in corn-shaped or other decorative pans. For dessert, top ice cream with your choice of nuts, sauces (caramel, choco-late, fruit), granola, fruit, and whipped cream.

Gloria's Add-on Chili with Beans

2 pounds *each* boned beef chuck and pork shoulder or butt, fat trimmed

3 large (about 1¾ lb. total) onions, chopped

8 large garlic cloves, minced or pressed

2 cups regular-strength beef broth

2 bottles (12 oz. each) tomato-based chili sauce

1 tablespoon dried oregano leaves

1 teaspoon *each* anise seed, cumin seed, and crushed dried hot red chilies

Beans (recipe follows)

Chili toppings (suggestions follow)

Cut beef and pork into ¾- to 1-inch cubes. Put meat in a 5- to 6-quart pan; add ½ cup water, cover, and bring to a boil. Simmer 30 minutes. Uncover and boil on high heat until liquid evaporates and drippings in pan sizzle and are dark brown; stir of-ten. Add ⅓ cup water; stir to release drippings. Add on-ions, garlic, and ½ cup wa-ter. Stir often until liquid evaporates and browned bits stick in pan. Add ½ cup wa-ter and stir browned bits free. Boil until browned bits stick again.

Add broth, chili sauce, oregano, anise, cumin, and crushed chilies; stir browned bits free. Simmer, covered,

PETER CHRISTIANSEN

CRUNCHY CORNMEAL *coats crisp baked fish-and-chips; season with malt vinegar and tartar sauce.*

until meat is very tender when pierced, about 1½ hours. (If making ahead, cool, cover, and chill up to 1 day; reheat.) Ladle chili and beans into bowls; add top-pings as desired. Serves 8 to 10.—*Gloria Ciccarone-Nehls, The Big Four Restaurant, San Francisco*

Per serving without toppings: 485 cal. (18 percent from fat); 43 g protein; 9.9 g fat (3.2 g sat.); 58 g carbo.; 1,022 mg sodium; 89 mg chol.

Beans. Sort debris from 1 pound **dried black beans** (about 2⅓ cups); rinse and drain beans.

Combine beans and 2 quarts **water** in a 5- to 6-quart pan. Cover and bring to a boil on high heat; re-move from heat and let stand 1 hour or up to 1 day.

Drain and discard bean liquid. To beans add 1½ quarts *each* **regular-strength beef broth** and **water;** 1 large (about 10 oz.) **onion,** chopped; and 1 tablespoon **dried thyme leaves.** Bring to a boil on high heat; cover and simmer until beans are tender to bite, about 1½ hours. (If making ahead, let cool; cover and chill up to 2 days. Reheat.) Makes about 6 cups.

Chili toppings. Wipe dust

from 2 medium-size (about ¾ oz. total) **dried ancho,** Cali-fornia, or New Mexico **chil-ies;** cut into thin strips. Dis-card seeds and stems.

In an 8- to 10-inch frying pan over medium-high heat, stir chili strips in 2 teaspoons **salad oil** until chilies are crisp and smell toasted; about 2 minutes; drain on towels. (If making ahead, store airtight up to 1 day.)

In separate dishes, ar-range chilies, 3 cups finely shredded **iceberg lettuce,** and 2 cups *each* shredded **carrots,** chopped **tomatoes,** sliced **celery,** and shredded **cheddar cheese.**

While vegetables and fish bake, make the salad.

Baked Fish-and-Chips

1½ cups yellow cornmeal

2 teaspoons sugar

1 teaspoon pepper

About ½ teaspoon salt

3 large egg whites

2 large (about 1½ lb. total) potatoes, scrubbed and each cut into 8 wedges

2 large (about 1 lb. total) zucchini, ends trimmed, each cut lengthwise into 6 slices

3 tablespoons salad oil

4 pieces (4 to 6 oz. each) skinned and boned, firm, white-flesh fish such as rockfish or orange roughy

Malt or cider vinegar

Tartar sauce (optional)

Salt

Mix cornmeal, sugar, pep-per, and ½ teaspoon salt in a shallow dish.

In another shallow dish, lightly beat egg whites until slightly frothy.

Dip potato wedges and zucchini slices, 1 piece at a time, into egg white; roll in cornmeal mixture. Lay pieces in a single layer.

Rub 1 tablespoon oil in bottom of each of 2 pans, 10 by 15 inches. Place pans in a 450° oven for 3 minutes. Lay potato and zucchini pieces slightly apart in separate pans. Bake zucchini until crust is crisp, about 25 min-utes; bake potatoes until they are tender when pierced, about 40 minutes. After 15 minutes of baking, turn vege-tables with a spatula.

Meanwhile, dip fish into egg white and turn to coat with cornmeal mixture; lay in a single layer. With spatula, transfer cooked zucchini to a platter and keep warm.

Add remaining 1 table-spoon oil to pan; lay fish slightly apart in pan. Bake until crusty and golden on bottom, about 4 minutes. Turn fish with spatula and bake until bottom is golden and flesh is opaque but still moist-looking in thickest part (cut to test), about 6 minutes longer.

If fish is done before pota-toes, keep warm on platter.

Season fish and vegeta-bles to taste with vinegar, tartar sauce, and salt. Makes 4 servings.

Per serving: 549 cal. (21 percent from fat); 33 g protein; 13 g fat (1.9 g sat.); 74 g carbo.; 126 mg sodium; 40 mg chol. ∎

By Betsy Reynolds Bateson

BLACK POPPY, *pale sesame, and tan cumin seed make bold pattern, crunchy crust on crisp breadsticks. The bread can be made ahead and reheated.*

Swiss twists

They're crisp and crunchy breadsticks coated with seeds

A TRIO OF SEEDS—sesame, cumin, and poppy—coats these twisted breadsticks with a flavorful and crunchy armor. The handsome twists, called *chnuspi,* are a specialty of Brothuus Zoller, a bakery in Basel, Switzerland.

To duplicate, begin with a whole-wheat yeast dough. Cut it into strips, brush with egg white, roll strips in seeds, twist, and bake. Chnuspi make a delicious companion for soups and salads.

Basel Seeded Wheat Twists (Chnuspi)

1 package active dry yeast

1 cup warm water (about 110°)

2 tablespoons salad oil

1 tablespoon honey

½ teaspoon salt

2 cups whole-wheat flour

1 to 1¼ cups all-purpose flour

⅓ cup sesame seed

3 tablespoons *each* cumin seed and poppy seed

1 large egg white

Sprinkle yeast over water in a large bowl; let stand about 5 minutes to soften. Stir in oil, honey, and salt. Add whole-wheat flour and beat until stretchy and sticky, about 5 minutes. Stir in 1 cup all-purpose flour.

To knead with a dough hook, beat at medium speed until dough pulls cleanly from bowl, 5 to 7 minutes. If dough still sticks, add all-purpose flour, 1 tablespoon at a time, until dough pulls free.

To knead by hand, scrape dough onto a lightly floured board. Knead until smooth and elastic, adding just enough flour to prevent sticking, about 5 minutes. Return dough to bowl.

Cover bowl with plastic wrap. Set in a warm place. Let dough rise until doubled, about 1 hour. Punch dough down; knead briefly on a lightly floured board to release air. Roll or pat dough into a 6- by 9-inch rectangle. Cover rectangle with plastic wrap and let stand until puffy, 20 to 30 minutes. Cut dough into 10 equal 6-inch-long strips.

On waxed paper (about 14 in. square), mix sesame, cumin, and poppy seed. Brush 1 dough strip all over with egg white. Hold both ends and stretch strip evenly to a length of 12 inches. Roll in seeds to coat all over. Set strip on 1 of 2 greased 12- by 15-inch baking sheets; still holding ends, twist strip 3 or 4 times. Repeat to make remaining strips; place about 2 inches apart on pans.

Bake in a 375° oven until browned and crusty, 25 to 30 minutes. (If using 1 oven, switch pan positions halfway.) Transfer bread to racks. Serve warm or cool. If made ahead, cool and store airtight up to a day; freeze up to 3 weeks. Recrisp to serve: lay sticks (thawed, if frozen) on pan. Place in a 350° oven until warm, 8 to 10 minutes. Makes 10.

Per stick: 215 cal.; 7 g protein; 7.2 g fat (0.9 g sat.); 33 g carbo.; 121 mg sodium; 0 mg chol. ■

By Linda Lau Anusasananan

'Melogold'
grapefruit-pummelo
hybrid

'Rio Red'
grapefruit

'Moro'
blood orange

'Variegated Pink'
lemon

'Lane Late'
navel orange

'Wekiwa'
tangelolo

'Page'
mandarin

Citrus

Here are new varieties to try

Breakthroughs

'Oroblanco'
grapefruit-pummelo
hybrid

By Lauren Bonar Swezey,
Linda Lau Anusasananan

LEMONS WITH PINK FLESH, ORANGES WITH RUBY red flesh and a mouth-tingling flavor that hints of raspberries, and tangelolos that look like miniature grapefruits: these are some of the new (and not so new, but lesser-known) citrus—trees and fruits—now coming from growers in the citrus belts of California, Arizona, and Texas. Some, such as 'Melogold' and 'Oroblanco' grapefruit-pummelo hybrids and 'Wekiwa' tangelolo, are new types of citrus. Others, such as 'Encore' mandarin, 'Rio Red' grapefruit, and 'Variegated Pink' lemon, are new varieties of more familiar citrus. Here and on the next two pages, we describe these citrus surprises and suggest ways to use them in sweet and savory dishes ranging from a refreshing pasta salad to a tangy open faced dessert tart.

The chart on page 12 lists more than a dozen kinds of citrus fruits selected for their distinctive flavor. You can buy many of the citrus fruits discussed here in specialty markets and grocery stores that offer unusual produce. In citrus-growing areas of the West and Southwest, some may be offered seasonally in farmers markets.

They're usually available between late fall and early spring. If you don't find them, you can substitute standard market varieties. But remember, every time you make a substitution, flavor, color, or tartness may be slightly different based on the substituted variety's characteristics.

As our recipes show, these special citrus fruits are

SANDRA WILLIAMS

FRESHLY PICKED *'Oroblanco' is a breakfast treat for Claire and David Guggenheim.*

CITRUS GALAXY

From grapefruit hybrids without bitterness to green-striped, pink-fleshed lemons, new citrus varieties add zing to breakfast juice. Or add citrus to dishes, such as the spicy black bean chili with orange slices pictured at right. Garnish with sour cream, cilantro, and citrus peel.

NORMAN A. PLATE

also versatile. You can accent our spicy Black Bean Chili not only with seedless oranges, but also with such intriguing relatives as mandarins or tangelolos, and with more familiar tangelos.

Segments of either red-fleshed grapefruit or sweet-tart grapefruit-pummelo hybrids make juicy topping for Pasta and Grapefruit Salad.

Squeeze any variety of citrus juice to combine with sparkling wine for the bubbly apéritif we call Citrus Wine Splashes.

Candied Citrus Peel Marmalade, a classic French garnish for a dessert of fresh orange slices, can be made with the citrus fruit of your choice—grapefruit, oranges, mandarins, tangelolos, tangelos, or lemons.

Tart Lemon Tart

  Butter pastry (recipe follows)
3 large eggs
1 cup granulated sugar
1 teaspoon grated lemon peel
⅓ cup lemon juice
¼ cup all-purpose flour
¾ teaspoon baking powder
  Powdered sugar

6 very thin lemon slices, cut in half crosswise and seeds discarded

Press pastry evenly over bottom and sides of a 10½- to 11-inch tart pan with removable rim. Bake in 325° oven until pale gold, about 25 minutes.

In a small bowl, beat eggs with a mixer at high speed until foamy. Gradually add granulated sugar, beating until mixture is thick and lighter in color. Add lemon peel, lemon juice, flour, and baking powder; beat until smooth.

Pour mixture into baked crust. Bake in a 325° oven until filling no longer jiggles when gently shaken, 20 to 25 minutes. Let cool on a rack. If making ahead, cover when cool and hold up to 1 day.

Remove pan rim and lightly sift powdered sugar onto tart. Garnish with lemon slices. Cut tart into wedges; wipe knife blade clean after each cut. Makes 12 servings.

Per serving: 242 cal. (35 percent from fat); 4.1 g protein; 9.5 g fat (5.3 g sat.); 36 g carbo.; 128 mg sodium; 92 mg chol.

Butter pastry. In a food processor or bowl, mix 1½ cups **all-purpose flour,** ¼ cup **sugar,** and 1 teaspoon **grated lemon peel.** Add ½ cup **butter** or margarine, cut into small pieces; whirl or rub with your fingers until fine

Type of citrus	Looks? Taste?	When available?
GRAPEFRUIT AND GRAPEFRUIT HYBRIDS		
'Melogold' grapefruit-pummelo hybrid	Large, 6- to 7-inch yellow fruit with medium-thick rind. Sweet with minimal tartness, no bitterness.	Mid-December to March.
'Oroblanco' grapefruit-pummelo hybrid	Large, yellow 5- to 6-inch fruit with thick rind; few seeds. Sweet-tart; often more flavorful than 'Melogold'.	Early November to March.
'Rio Red' grapefruit	Yellow 5- to 6-inch fruit with pink blush, red flesh; no seeds. Mild, sweet with tang.	January to May or longer.
MANDARINS		
'Encore' mandarin	Small (2 to 3 inches), light orange fruit; seedy; peels easily. Sweet-tart; complex flavors.	March to July or later.
'Page' mandarin	Small, 2- to 3-inch fruit with deep orange flesh and skin; has few seeds, thin skin. Very sweet and juicy.	December to March or later.
'Pixie' mandarin	Small, 2- to 3-inch yellowish orange fruit; no seeds. Bumpy rind, irregular fruit. Very sweet and flavorful; low acid.	March to June or July.
LEMON		
'Variegated pink' lemon (also called 'Pink Lemonade')	Small, 3-inch-long lemons with green stripes and light pink flesh. Typical tart, highly acid lemon flavor.	November to April or later.
ORANGES		
'Lane Late' navel **'Spring'** navel	Medium, 3- to 4-inch orange fruit; no seeds. Flavor similar to other navels. 'Spring' is dark orange and sweet.	December to June or later.
'Moro' blood orange	Medium, 3- to 4-inch fruit with deep burgundy flesh, reddish orange rind. Sweet-tart, with raspberry undertones, juicy.	December to March or April.
'Sanguinelli' blood orange	Small to medium, 3½- to 4-inch oblong fruit; flesh orange with red streaks. Sweet-tart flavor; juicy.	December to April or May.
'Tarocco' blood orange	Medium to large, 4½-inch fruit; internal red color unreliable. Sweetest, most flavorful blood orange.	December to April or May.
TANGELOLO		
'Wekiwa' tangelolo (lavender gem, pink tangelo)	Looks like mini-grapefruit (3 to 4 inches wide) with pinkish flesh. Sweet, mild grapefruit taste; very juicy.	November to February or later. Not widely available.

crumbs form. Add 1 **large egg;** whirl or stir with a fork until dough holds together. Pat into a smooth ball.

Black Bean Chili with Oranges

2 large (about 1 lb. total) onions, chopped

2 cloves garlic, pressed or minced

1 tablespoon salad oil

2 quarts regular-strength chicken broth

1 pound (about 2⅓ cups) dried black beans, sorted for debris and rinsed

1 tablespoon coriander seed

1 teaspoon whole allspice

1 teaspoon dried oregano leaves

¾ teaspoon crushed dried hot red chilies

6 cardamom pods, hulls removed (¼ teaspoon seed)

About 2½ pounds (4 to 6) oranges, mandarins, tangelolos, or tangelos

Sour cream

Fresh cilantro (coriander) sprigs

Salt

In a 5- to 6-quart pan, combine onions, garlic, and oil. Stir often over high heat until onions are tinged with brown, about 8 minutes. Add broth, beans, coriander seed, allspice, oregano, chilies,

and cardamom. Bring to a boil on high heat; cover and simmer until beans are tender to bite, 1½ to 2 hours.

Meanwhile, finely shred enough peel from citrus to make 2 teaspoons. Ream juice from enough fruit to make ½ cup. Cut peel and white membrane from remaining fruit. Thinly slice fruit crosswise; pick out and discard the seeds.

Uncover beans and boil over high heat until most of the liquid evaporates, 10 to 15 minutes; reduce heat and stir occasionally as mixture thickens. Stir in 1 teaspoon peel and the ½ cup juice. Ladle beans into bowls; top equally with fruit slices. Add sour cream, cilantro sprigs, and salt to taste. Garnish with remaining peel. Makes 6 or 7 servings.

Per serving: 356 cal. (13 percent from fat); 18 g protein; 5.1 g fat (1 g sat.); 62 g carbo.; 67 mg sodium; 0 mg chol.

Pasta and Grapefruit Salad

8 ounces dried tiny bow tie (tripolini) or other small pasta

1 package (1 lb.) frozen petite peas, thawed

1 cup chopped celery

½ cup thinly sliced green onions

⅓ cup chopped fresh mint leaves

3 large (about 3½ lb. total) grapefruit

RED-FLESHED 'RIO RED' GRAPEFRUIT *segments add juicy tart-sweetness to bow-tie pasta salad.*

NORMAN A. PLATE

½ teaspoon grated lemon peel

2 tablespoons lemon juice

½ to 1 teaspoon minced fresh hot chili

Fish sauce (*nuoc mam* or *nam pla*) or salt

8 or 10 large butter lettuce leaves, rinsed and crisped

½ pound thinly sliced cooked ham

Fresh mint sprigs

In a 5- to 6-quart pan, bring about 3 quarts water to a boil on high heat. Add pasta and cook, uncovered, just until barely tender to bite, about 5 minutes. Drain; immerse pasta in cold water. Drain pasta when cool.

In a large bowl, combine pasta, peas, celery, onions, and chopped mint.

Cut peel and white membrane from grapefruit. Over another bowl, to catch juice, cut between membrane to remove fruit segments; add segments to pasta mixture. Squeeze membrane over juice bowl. Measure collected juice; you'll need about ½ cup. Save extra for other uses. Add lemon peel and juice to the ½ cup grapefruit juice. Add juice mixture, chili, and fish sauce to taste to pasta mixture; mix gently.

PETER CHRISTIANSEN

BLOOD ORANGE JUICE *mixes with Asti Spumante to make a bubbly spritzer.*

Arrange lettuce leaves on 4 or 5 dinner plates. Spoon pasta mixture equally onto lettuce. Roll ham slices and set on plates. Garnish with mint sprigs. Makes 8 cups, 4 or 5 servings.

Per serving: 371 cal. (13 percent from fat); 22 g protein; 5.4 g fat (1.6 g sat.); 60 g carbo.; 831 mg sodium; 27 mg chol.

Citrus Wine Splashes

About ⅓ cup chilled Asti Spumante or brut or extra-dry champagne

About ⅓ cup freshly squeezed grapefruit, orange, mandarin, tangelolo, or tangelo juice

Pour wine into a wineglass; add juice. Serves 1.

Per serving: 85 cal. (1 percent from fat); 0.5 g protein; 0.1 g fat (0 g sat.); 8.1 g carbo.; 4.7 mg sodium; 0 mg chol.

Candied Citrus Peel Marmalade

Serve candied peel over ice cream, or citrus segments, or on toast with cream cheese.

3 pounds grapefruit, oranges, mandarins, tangelolos, tangelos, or lemons

2 cups orange juice (only if using lemons)

½ cup sugar

With a vegetable peeler, cut colored part only from the fruit. Cut peel into very thin slivers.

Ream fruit to extract juice (if using lemons, ream 2 and use with the 2 cups orange juice; reserve remaining lemons for another use).

In a 2- to 2½-quart pan, cover peel with water; bring to a boil. Drain; repeat step and drain again.

Add juice and sugar to peel. Boil, uncovered, on high heat until most of the liquid evaporates and peel looks translucent, 25 to 35 minutes; as mixture thickens, watch closely, stir often, and reduce heat to prevent scorching. Serve, or cover and chill up to 2 months. Makes 1 to 1½ cups.

Per tablespoon: 38 cal. (2.4 percent from fat); 0.3 g protein; 0.1 g fat (0 g sat.); 9.3 g carbo.; 0.5 mg sodium; 0 mg chol. ■

They're grand desserts . . . but downsized

They're also easier to prepare

FAVORITE DESSERTS—*turtle pecan pie with caramel sauce, chocolate*

T HESE SCALE-MODEL desserts are classics that satisfy a yearning for their delectable tastes, but they've been trimmed in size to eliminate tempting leftovers. They make two, three, or four servings, as consciences permit.

For the pie and decadence, you need a 6-inch-wide cake or tart pan with a removable rim; you'll find these pans in cookware stores and cookware sections of department stores.

Because you are working with smaller amounts, preparation and cleanup are actually easier—enough to rate considering these desserts for midweek entertaining.

Turtle Pecan Pie

- ½ cup all-purpose flour
- About ⅓ cup sugar
- About 3 tablespoons butter or margarine, cut into chunks
- 1 large egg
- ¼ cup corn syrup
- 1 teaspoon vanilla
- 3 tablespoons whole or chopped pecans
- 3 tablespoons semisweet chocolate baking chips
- Caramel sauce (recipe follows)

In a small bowl, rub flour with 4 teaspoons sugar and 3 tablespoons butter to make coarse crumbs. With a fork, stir in 1 teaspoon water. Squeeze dough into a ball, then press it over bottom and ¾ inch up sides of a buttered 6-inch-wide cake or tart pan (1 to 1½ in. deep) with a

removable rim.

Bake in a 350° oven until pastry is golden brown and firm when pressed, about 20 minutes.

Meanwhile, in the bowl, use fork to blend remaining ¼ cup sugar, egg, corn syrup, vanilla, pecans, and chocolate. Pour into warm crust. Bake until filling is set when pan is gently shaken, about 30 minutes. Let stand until cool, at least 30 minutes longer. Serve, or cover airtight and keep at room temperature up to 1 day. Remove rim; cut into wedges and accompany with warm caramel sauce. Serves 3 or 4.

Per serving: 479 cal. (43 percent from fat); 4.3 g protein; 23 g fat (12 g sat.); 66 g carbo.; 168 mg sodium; 101 mg chol.

Caramel sauce. In a 1- to 1½-quart pan over high heat,

combine 1 tablespoon **butter** or margarine and 5 tablespoons **sugar;** shake pan frequently to mix until sugar is melted and amber in color, about 3 minutes; watch carefully. Off the heat, add ¼ cup **whipping cream** (mixture sputters); stir until caramel is smoothly mixed with cream. Serve warm. If making ahead, cover and chill up to 1 week; reheat, stirring. Makes about 5 tablespoons.

Chocolate Decadence

- About ¼ cup (⅛ lb.) butter or margarine, cut into chunks
- ¼ cup semisweet chocolate baking chips
- 2 large eggs
- 1 tablespoon *each* sugar and unsweetened cocoa

PETER CHRISTIANSEN

decadence with berries, and tiramisu—look full-size but are scaled down to serve two to four.

¼ cup raspberries, rinsed and drained (optional)

Raspberry sauce (recipe follows)

In a 1- to 1½-quart pan over low heat, stir ¼ cup butter, chocolate, and 2 tablespoons water until smooth. Let cool. Add eggs, sugar, and cocoa; beat until mixed.

Butter a 6-inch-wide cake or tart pan (1 to 1½ in. deep) with removable rim. Set pan on 2 sheets of heavy foil, each about 10 inches square. Lift foil edges and press firmly against pan, with edges extending above pan rim; set in a larger pan. Pour batter into cake pan.

Set nested pans in a 350° oven; pour ½ inch boiling water into outer pan. Bake until center of cake feels set when gently touched, about

30 minutes. Lift with foil onto a rack. When cake is cool, remove foil; cover dessert airtight and chill at least 30 minutes or up to 1 day.

Remove rim. Decorate cake with raspberries; cut into wedges and accompany with sauce. Serves 3 or 4.

Per serving: 239 cal. (68 percent from fat); 4.3 g protein; 18 g fat (10 g sat.); 19 g carbo.; 154 mg sodium; 139 mg chol.

Raspberry sauce. In a blender or food processor, whirl 1½ cups fresh or frozen unsweetened **raspberries** with 2 teaspoons **sugar.** Rub sauce through a fine strainer into a bowl; discard seeds. Add more sugar to taste.

Tiramisu

6 double ladyfingers (1½ oz. total), each about 3 inches long, split

Espresso (recipe follows)

Rum cream (recipe follows)

About 1 tablespoon grated semisweet chocolate

Arrange ladyfingers, overlapping slightly if needed, over bottom and up sides of a shallow 2- to 3-cup bowl; moisten cookies evenly with hot espresso.

Spoon rum cream over cookies. Cover and chill until cool, at least 30 minutes or up to 1 day. Sprinkle with chocolate. Scoop out portions. Serves 2 or 3.

Per serving: 248 cal. (51 percent from fat); 5.6 g protein; 14 g fat (7.8 g sat.); 21 g carbo.; 116 mg sodium; 152 mg chol.

Espresso. Use ½ cup **freshly made espresso cof-**

fee, or mix 1½ teaspoons instant espresso coffee powder (or 1 tablespoon instant coffee powder) with ½ cup boiling water. Use hot.

Rum cream. In the top of a double boiler over (not in) simmering water, or in a round-bottom zabaglione pan over high electric or medium gas heat, whisk 1 **large egg,** 2 tablespoons **sugar,** and 1 tablespoon **rum** until mixture is thick enough to mound slightly for a few seconds, 4 to 5 minutes.

Cover mixture and chill until cool, at least 30 minutes or up to 1 hour.

In a small bowl, smoothly blend 1 small (3-oz.) package **cream cheese** with 1 tablespoon **rum.** Add chilled rum mixture; gently fold the mixtures together. ■

By Karyn I. Lipman

PETER CHRISTIANSEN

SKI PICNIC *travels light. Sandwich makings of hummus with carrot slaw, relishes, and cookies are packed in plastic bags.*

For a winter picnic, pack light

This meal travels well and satisfies

H IGH-ENERGY FOODS, designed to pack and tote on a picnic, will satisfy the ravenous appetites of skiers or hikers.

The menu combines a flavorful mix of complex carbohydrates packed in heavy plastic food bags for minimum bulk and weight.

The meal holds up well in a backpack or fanny packs without insulation for 4 to 5 hours on a cool winter day.

Black Bean Hummus and Carrot Slaw Sandwiches

2 cans (about 15 oz. each) black or white (any kind) beans, rinsed and drained

⅓ cup roasted, salted almonds, finely chopped

¼ cup lemon juice

1 clove garlic, minced or pressed

½ teaspoon ground cumin

1 can (7 oz.) whole green chilies or 1 jar (7 oz.) roasted red bell peppers, drained

4 or 5 pocket breads (6 to 7 in. wide)

Carrot slaw (recipe follows)

In a bowl, mash beans, nuts, lemon juice, garlic, and cumin with a potato masher or fork until hummus is cohesive enough to spread.

To transport, spoon hummus into a 1-quart zip-lock plastic freezer bag, press out air, and seal. Put in another bag of the same size, press out air, and seal.

In separate, same-size bags, seal chilies and bread, pressing out air. Fit each into another plastic bag and seal. If making ahead, chill foods up to 1 day.

To eat, spread hummus on bread; top with slaw and chilies. Serves 4 or 5.

Per serving without slaw: 389 cal. (20 percent from fat); 16 g protein; 8.8 g fat (0.8 g sat.); 63 g carbo.; 1,043 mg sodium; 0 mg chol.

Carrot Slaw

1½ pounds carrots, peeled and shredded

1 teaspoon grated lime peel

⅓ cup lime juice

2 tablespoons distilled vinegar

2 tablespoons honey

1 tablespoon Dijon mustard

1 teaspoon caraway seed

¼ teaspoon crushed dried hot red chilies

Salt

In a 1-quart zip-lock plastic freezer bag, combine the carrots, lime peel, juice, vinegar, honey, mustard, caraway seed, and chilies. Squeeze bag to mix ingredients; add salt to taste.

Press air from bag; seal. Seal in another bag of the same size. Chill up to 2 days. Just before departure, drain dressing from slaw; reseal bags. Serves 4 or 5.

Per serving: 88 cal. (5.1 percent from fat); 1.4 g protein; 0.5 g fat (0 g sat.); 21 g carbo.; 136 mg sodium; 0 mg chol.

Brownie Bars

1 cup all-purpose flour

1 teaspoon baking powder

1 cup semisweet chocolate baking chips

½ cup raisins

½ cup roasted peanuts

About ⅓ cup (⅛ lb.) butter or margarine

½ cup firmly packed brown sugar

1 large egg

2 teaspoons vanilla

In a small bowl, mix flour, baking powder, chocolate baking chips, raisins, and peanuts.

In a large bowl, beat ⅓ cup butter (in chunks), sugar, egg, and vanilla until well mixed. Beat in flour mixture. Spread batter in a buttered 9-inch square pan. Bake in a 325° oven until mixture feels firm in center when pressed, 40 to 45 minutes. Let cool in pan on a rack. Cut into 8 to 10 pieces.

To transport, seal bars in zip-lock plastic bags, 1 or 2 per bag. If making ahead, hold at room temperature up to 3 days; freeze to store longer. Makes 8 to 10.

Per piece: 316 cal. (43 percent from fat); 4.6 g protein; 15 g fat (7.2 g sat.); 44 g carbo.; 177 mg sodium; 38 mg chol. ∎

By Karyn I. Lipman

TENDER SHREDS *of brisket and sauce in tortillas make birria burritos.*

DARROW M. WATT

After 4 hours unwatched

Moist-cooked beef becomes birria

I N THE MOUNTAINS OF Zacatecas, a sheep-raising state in central Mexico, young lamb is traditionally used to make *birria*, a well-known stew of the area. But due in part to the accessibility of cattle raised on nearby plains, beef versions of the dish have also evolved. Fresh brisket, the base of this birria, takes especially well to moist, slow, and untended oven cooking with mild chilies, seeds and spices, vinegar, and onions.

Tear tender meat into shreds and serve in its own sauce. If you like, spoon birria into flour tortillas to make burritos.

Birria-style Brisket

4 dried California or New Mexico chilies, or ¼ cup chili powder

2 small dried hot red chilies

1½ cups dry red wine

¼ cup wine vinegar

6 cloves garlic

1½ teaspoons ground cumin

1½ teaspoons dried oregano leaves

½ teaspoon ground cinnamon

1 piece (2½ to 3 lb.) center-cut beef brisket, surface fat trimmed

4 large (about 1¾ lb. total) onions, thinly sliced

Fresh cilantro (coriander) sprigs

Lime wedges

Sour cream

Warm flour tortillas (optional)

Remove and discard stems and seeds from California and hot chilies. Rinse chilies, then put in a 2- to 3-quart pan and add 1 quart water. Bring to a boil over high heat. Remove from heat, cover, and let stand until softened, 45 minutes to 1 hour; drain. In a blender or food processor, whirl the chilies, wine, vinegar, garlic, cumin, oregano, and cinnamon until smoothly puréed.

Lay meat in a 12- by 15-inch roasting pan; top with chili mixture and onions. Seal pan tightly with foil. If making ahead, chill up to 1 day.

Bake, covered, in a 350° oven until brisket is very tender when pierced, about 4 hours. With 2 forks, shred meat; mix with onions and juices. (If making ahead, cover and chill up to 2 days. To reheat, cover and bake in a 350° oven until hot, about 45 minutes.) Serve meat with cilantro, lime, and sour cream to add to taste; roll mixture in tortillas, if desired. Makes 6 to 8 servings.

Per serving: 281 cal. (35 percent from fat); 32 g protein; 11 g fat (3.6 g sat.); 13 g carbo.; 118 mg sodium; 87 mg chol. ■

By Christine B. Weber

Start with golden apples

L URE THE FAMILY TO breakfast some quiet weekend morning with the aroma of apples, raisins, and cinnamon bubbling beneath crunchy oatmeal pastry. Serve cobbler plain or with scoops of frozen vanilla yogurt.

Breakfast Cobbler

⅓ cup firmly packed brown sugar

2 tablespoons quick-cooking tapioca

1 teaspoon cinnamon

1 tablespoon lemon juice

¼ cup water

4 large (about 2 lb. total) Golden Delicious apples, peeled, cored, and sliced

⅓ cup raisins

Oat crunch (recipe follows)

In a shallow 1½- to 2-quart casserole, mix sugar, tapioca, and cinnamon. Add lemon juice and water; stir to mix. Let stand at least 15 minutes to soften; stir several times. Mix in apples and raisins.

Bake in a 375° oven for 15 minutes. Stir well; crumble oat crunch onto fruit. Bake until the oat topping is well browned, 35 to 40 minutes. Spoon into bowls. Serves 4 or 5.

Per serving: 411 cal. (29 percent from fat); 3.5 g protein; 13 g fat (7.7 g sat.); 74 g carbo.; 131 mg sodium; 33 mg chol.

Oat crunch. Rub together until crumbly ⅓ cup (⅙ lb.) **butter** or margarine, ¾ cup **all-purpose flour**, ⅓ cup **regular rolled oats**, and 3 tablespoons **sugar**. Press into lumps. ■

By Karyn I. Lipman

PETER CHRISTIANSEN

WARM APPLE COBBLER *suits breakfast.*

LOW-FAT SPAGHETTI WITH MEATBALLS *makes a hearty main dish for dinner.*

PETER CHRISTIANSEN

Trimming a family classic

Spaghetti and meatballs usually conceals a lot of fat and calories. This version doesn't

THE ALL-TIME FAMILY favorite, spaghetti and meatballs, often has high counts of fat and calories. You can easily trim this classic by making the meatballs from very lean beef mixed with soaked bulgur (cracked wheat). The grain absorbs juices from the meat, making the meatballs moist and tender; it also makes them expand. Oven-browning, instead of frying, is another lean step.

Because the meatballs will continue to soak up liquid, heat them only briefly in the sauce, then serve on pasta.

Low-fat Spaghetti and Meatballs

¾ cup bulgur (cracked wheat)

¾ pound fat-trimmed beef top round (or ground beef with 15 percent or less fat)

1 large (about ½ lb.) onion, chopped

4 cloves garlic, minced or pressed

1 teaspoon dried oregano leaves

¼ teaspoon pepper

Salt

½ pound mushrooms, rinsed and sliced

1 tablespoon dried basil leaves

¼ tablespoon crushed dried hot red chilies

About 1¼ cups regular strength beef broth

1 large can (28 oz.) crushed tomatoes

1 pound dried spaghetti

Chopped parsley

Grated Parmesan cheese

In a bowl, mix bulgur with 1½ cups boiling water. Let stand until grains are tender to bite, about 15 minutes.

Cut beef into ½-inch cubes. Coarsely grind in a food processor or food chopper; mix beef, onion, 2 cloves garlic, oregano leaves, pepper and ½ teaspoon salt. Drain soaked bulgur; mix well with beef mixture. Shape into ¼-cup-sized balls; place slightly apart in a lightly oiled 10- by 15-inch pan. Bake in a 425° oven until balls are well browned, 25 to 30 minutes.

As meat cooks, in 5- to 6-quart pan combine mushrooms, remaining garlic, basil, chilies, and ¼ cup water. Stir often over high heat until juices evaporate and vegetables begin to brown, about 10 minutes. To deglaze, add ¼ cup broth; stir to free browned bits. Stir often until browned again. Repeat deglazing once or twice more, using ¼ cup broth with each step, until mushrooms are browned. Add tomatoes. Cover and simmer 10 minutes. Add meatballs; cover and simmer about 5 minutes. (If sauce sticks, stir in a little broth.)

Also, in a covered 5- to 6-quart pan on high heat, bring about 3 quarts water to a boil. Add spaghetti; cook, uncovered, just until barely tender to bite, 7 to 10 minutes; drain. In pan bring ⅓ cup broth to a boil; add pasta and pour into a wide bowl. Top with sauce and parsley. Add salt and cheese to taste. Serves 5 or 6.

Per serving: 469 cal. (7.7 percent from fat); 28 g protein; 4 g fat (1g sat.); 82 g carbo.; 257 mg sodium; 32 mg chol. ∎

By Linda Lau Anusasananan

Husky muffins, with big hats, bulging with fiber

Snack without guilt; it's practically a sacrament

By Richard Dunmire, Joan Griffiths

MUFFIN BEGAT blueberry muffin, and from their lineage sprang—during the '80s—a host of other muffins in a gratifyingly broad range of flavors. And these muffins were different from their progenitors—husky, with big hats, and bulging with minimum daily requirements of practically everything, especially fiber. Snacks without guilt, they made you feel positively good about having a midmorning indulgence in something sweet.

This being the case, eating one of Albert Fossat's fiber-rich oat bran whole-wheat muffins is not an indulgence—it's practically a sacrament.

Oat Bran Whole-Wheat Muffins

3 cups oat bran
1 cup whole-wheat flour
1 teaspoon ground cinnamon
1 tablespoon baking powder
1 teaspoon baking soda
¼ teaspoon salt
½ cup firmly packed brown sugar
1 cup raisins
½ cup chopped walnuts
4 large egg whites
½ cup honey
1¾ cups nonfat milk
½ cup applesauce
¼ cup salad oil
1 teaspoon vanilla

In a large bowl, stir together oat bran, flour, cinnamon, baking powder, baking soda, and salt. Stir in sugar, raisins, and nuts until well blended.

In another bowl, beat to blend egg whites, honey, milk, applesauce, oil, and vanilla. Add egg mixture to dry ingredients and stir just until evenly moistened.

Spoon batter into greased or paper-lined 2½-inch muffin cups, filling to rim.

Bake in a 400° oven until muffins are browned and tops spring back when lightly touched, 20 to 25 minutes. Serve hot or cool; when cool, store airtight up to 2 days. Makes about 2 dozen.

Per piece: 153 cal. (28 percent from fat); 4.5 g protein; 4.8 g fat (0.6 g sat.); 29 g carbo.; 132 mg sodium; 0.4 mg chol.

Albert J. Fossat

Helper, Utah

FROM CAMANO Island, Washington, Dick Sturza sends the following recipe for cheese and sausage pie.

He assembled it one night from the only ingredients he could find in the refrigerator. How fortunate for him (and for us) that these were precisely the ingredients one needs for a quiche. Oops! Cheese pie! Sturza denies eating quiche. Old vocabularies die hard.

Although the original quiche lorraine was an appetizer, a slice of it, or of cheese and sausage pie, makes a hearty lunch accompanied by a green salad and crusty rolls.

Cheese and Sausage Pie

¾ pound pork sausage links
Unbaked 9-inch pie shell, at least 1¼ inches deep
½ cup chopped onion
1 clove garlic, minced or pressed
⅓ cup chopped red or green bell pepper
1½ cups (6 oz.) shredded sharp cheddar cheese
1 tablespoon all-purpose flour
2 large eggs
1 cup evaporated milk
1 tablespoon chopped parsley
¼ teaspoon pepper

In a 10- to 12-inch frying pan over medium-high heat, cook sausage until well browned, 10 to 15 minutes; drain on towels. Discard all but 1½ teaspoons drippings.

At the same time, bake pie crust on bottom rack of a 375° oven for 10 minutes.

To frying pan, add onion, garlic, and bell pepper; stir often over medium-high heat until limp, about 5 minutes.

Cut sausages into ½-inch lengths into a bowl; add onion mixture, cheese, and flour. Mix well and scrape into hot crust.

In the same bowl, beat eggs to blend with milk, parsley, and pepper. Pour over sausage mixture. Bake pie on the bottom oven rack until filling is set when gently shaken, 30 to 35 minutes. Let stand at least 15 minutes to firm. Serve hot or cold, cut into wedges. Makes 6 to 8 servings.

Per serving: 347 cal. (65 percent from fat); 15 g protein; 25 g fat (11 g sat.); 16 g carbo.; 580 mg sodium; 102 mg chol.

Dick Sturza

Camano Island, Washington

Sunset's Kitchen Cabinet

Creative ways with everyday foods—submitted by *Sunset* readers,
tested in *Sunset* kitchens, approved by *Sunset* taste panels

Mussels and Millet in Curry Sauce

Emily Bader, Bothell, Washington

1 tablespoon salad oil

1 large (½ lb.) onion, thinly sliced

1 tablespoon minced fresh ginger

Curry spice (recipe follows)

3 cups regular-strength chicken broth

2 small (about 5 oz. each) tomatoes, cored and chopped

1 cup millet

1½ pounds mussels, scrubbed

Salt and pepper

Unflavored yogurt

In a 5- to 6-quart pan, stir oil, onion, and ginger over medium-high heat until onion is limp, 6 to 8 minutes. Stir in spice mixture; add broth and tomatoes, and bring to boiling.

In a fine strainer, rinse and drain millet; add to pan. Cover and simmer 15 minutes. Add mussels, cover, and simmer until millet is tender to bite and mussels pop open, 7 to 9 minutes. Ladle into bowls; add salt, pepper, and yogurt to taste. Serves 3.

Curry spice. Combine 1 teaspoon **mustard seed,** 1 teaspoon **ground coriander,** ½ teaspoon **ground cumin,** ½ teaspoon **cayenne,** and ¼ teaspoon **ground turmeric.**

Per serving: 429 cal. (23 percent from fat); 19 g protein; 11 g fat (1.8 g sat.); 62 g carbo.; 258 mg sodium; 19 mg chol.

STEAM MUSSELS *in curry, ginger, and tomato-seasoned broth with millet.*

Onion Herb Batter Bread

Janet Risi Field, Santa Rosa, California

1 package active dry yeast

1½ tablespoons sugar

½ cup warm (110°) water

½ cup milk

1 tablespoon butter or margarine

2 tablespoons dried minced onion

½ teaspoon dried or 1 teaspoon chopped fresh rosemary

½ teaspoon dried or 1 teaspoon chopped fresh dill weed

2¼ cups all-purpose flour

In a large bowl, combine yeast, sugar, and warm water; let stand until yeast softens, about 5 minutes.

In a 1- to 1½-quart pan, heat milk and butter just until mixture is 110°.

Add to bowl the milk mixture, onion, rosemary, dill, and flour. With a heavy-duty mixer or a heavy spoon, beat until batter is very sticky and stretchy. Cover with plastic wrap. Let rise in a warm place until dough triples, 45 minutes to 1 hour. Punch dough down and scrape into an oiled 4½- by 8½-inch loaf pan; spread batter to level it. Cover with plastic wrap; let stand in a warm place until puffy, about 15 minutes.

Bake in a 350° oven until a rich brown color, about 45 minutes. Cool bread in pan 10 minutes; invert onto a rack. Serve warm or cool. Makes 1 loaf, about 1 pound.

Per ounce: 82 cal. (12 percent from fat); 2.3 g protein; 1.1 g fat (0.6 g sat.); 15 g carbo.; 12 mg sodium; 3 mg chol.

ROSEMARY, DILL, AND ONION *flavor yeast batter bread. Serve with soup or salad.*

Turkey and Pea Soup

Naneen Karraker, Berkeley, California

1 pound ground turkey

⅓ cup fine dry bread crumbs

1 large egg

⅓ cup finely chopped onion

½ teaspoon ground cinnamon

¼ teaspoon ground allspice

2 tablespoons chopped fresh or crumbled dried mint leaves

About ½ teaspoon salt (optional)

1½ quarts regular-strength chicken broth

1 bag (1 lb.) frozen petite peas

Mix turkey well with crumbs, egg, onion, cinnamon, allspice, 1 tablespoon mint, and ½ teaspoon salt.

In a 3- to 4-quart pan, bring the broth to a boil on high heat. Form turkey mixture into about 1-inch balls. Drop the balls, as formed, into the boiling broth. Cover and simmer until meatballs are no longer pink in center (cut to test), about 8 minutes. Stir in peas; cook just until hot, about 2 minutes. Sprinkle with remaining 1 tablespoon mint. Ladle into a tureen or bowls. Add salt to taste. Serves 4.

Per serving: 339 cal. (35 percent from fat); 31 g protein; 13 g fat (3.4 g sat.); 23 g carbo.; 417 mg sodium; 136 mg chol.

GROUND TURKEY *and peas float in mint-scented soup for quick, light supper.*

Polenta with Sausage Sauce

Nancy Gils Carbó, Foster City, California

1 pound mild Italian sausages

1 large (about ½ lb.) onion, chopped

1 cup dry white or red wine

1 can (6 oz.) tomato paste

1 teaspoon dried oregano leaves

¾ teaspoon dried thyme leaves

1½ cups polenta or yellow cornmeal

1 cup milk

Salt and pepper

Grated parmesan cheese

Remove and discard casings from sausages. Crumble sausages into a 10- to 12-inch frying pan. Stir often over high heat until browned and crumbly, 5 to 7 minutes; discard fat. Add onion; stir until lightly browned, about 5 minutes. Add wine, 1 cup water, tomato paste, oregano, and thyme. Simmer, uncovered, until reduced to 3 cups, about 10 minutes; stir occasionally.

Meanwhile, in a 3- to 4-quart pan, smoothly mix polenta, 4½ cups water, and milk. Bring to a boil, stirring, on high heat. Reduce heat to low; stir often until polenta is thick and creamy, 8 to 10 minutes. Spoon polenta into bowls; top with sauce. Add salt, pepper, and cheese to taste. Serves 4 or 5.

Per serving: 475 cal. (38 percent from fat); 20 g protein; 20 g fat (7.1 g sat.); 46 g carbo.; 910 mg sodium; 59 mg chol.

SPOON TOMATO-SAUSAGE SAUCE *over soft, creamy polenta; serve as a main dish.*

Sweet Potato and Apple Salad

Geri Hupp, Brookeland, Texas

4 small (about 2 lb. total) sweet potatoes or yams

½ cup walnuts

2 tablespoons honey

1 teaspoon grated lemon peel

1 tablespoon lemon juice

¾ teaspoon ground ginger

½ teaspoon ground cinnamon

1 cup unflavored nonfat yogurt

2 small (about 1 lb. total) red apples

¾ cup thinly sliced celery

Salt

In a 5- to 6-quart pan, simmer potatoes in water to cover just until barely tender when pierced, 20 to 30 minutes. Drain; let cool.

Place nuts in a 9-inch-wide pan. Bake in 350° oven until light gold under skin, 10 to 15 minutes. Let cool.

In a large bowl, mix honey, lemon peel, juice, ginger, cinnamon, and yogurt until blended. Peel cool potatoes and cut into ¾-inch cubes. Core apples and cut into ¾-inch cubes. Add potatoes, apples, ⅓ cup nuts, and celery to yogurt dressing; mix gently. Add salt to taste. Transfer to serving bowl. Garnish with remaining nuts. Serves 8 to 10.

Per serving: 160 cal. (23 percent from fat); 3.4 g protein; 4.1 g fat (0.4 g sat.); 29 g carbo.; 35 mg sodium; 0.5 mg chol.

MIX DICED APPLES *with sweet potatoes, walnuts, celery, and yogurt for salad.*

Mint Sandies

Katherine A. Emmons, Scottsdale, Arizona

½ cup (¼ lb.) butter or margarine

1 cup plus 3 tablespoons all-purpose flour

6 tablespoons granulated sugar

6 tablespoons firmly packed dark brown sugar

½ teaspoon vanilla

½ teaspoon baking soda

½ teaspoon salt

1 large egg

1 cup (about 6 oz.) coarsely chopped mint-flavor green-tinted white chocolate or thin chocolate-mint wafer candies

In a large bowl, combine butter, flour, granulated and brown sugars, vanilla, baking soda, and salt. With an electric mixer, beat on medium speed just until mixture is blended and crumbly. Lightly beat egg and add to flour mixture; stir just until mixture is evenly moistened. Stir in chocolate.

Drop rounded tablespoonfuls about 2 inches apart on ungreased 12- by 15-inch baking sheets. Bake in a 350° oven until lightly browned, about 12 minutes. Cool cookies on pans about 5 minutes, then transfer to racks. Serve warm or cool. Makes about 2 dozen.

Per cookie: 123 cal. (45 percent from fat); 1.3 g protein; 6.2 g fat (2.4 g sat.); 16 g carbo.; 111 mg sodium; 20 mg chol.

Compiled by Linda Lau Anusasananan

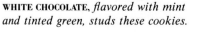

WHITE CHOCOLATE, *flavored with mint and tinted green, studs these cookies.*

February Menus

QUICK, SEASONAL,
BUDGET-WISE . . .
FOR FAMILY AND
FRIENDS

Chocolate and Valentine's Day—a winning team, but for breakfast? The opulent touch of chocolate works if you want to pamper someone very special on this February Sunday with an easily prepared breakfast in bed. Although the menu is a lavish way to start the day, you can meet your nutritional goals with lighter meals for lunch and dinner. Well suited are both of the menus that follow—a low-fat soup supper based on turkey sausages, and a satisfying vegetable casserole suitable for guests.

VALENTINE BREAKFAST (at right)
Bed trays bear whimsical treats for chocolate fans—curls for hot beverage and chocolate-almond muffins.

HEARTY SOUP SUPPER (page 24)
Warm the family with turkey-sausage soup. It's filling and lean, and takes about an hour to simmer.

CASUAL COMPANY DINNER (page 25)
Vegetable-cheese casserole, started ahead, and salad are a reliable duo for weeknight entertaining.

THE DETAILS

Nosegay Holders

Tiny vase, demitasse cup, shot glass, or sake carafe are scaled to tray bouquets.

Spoons or Curls

Cloak spoons with chocolate, or make chocolate curls. Stir into mocha au lait.

Sugar Twist

To sweeten beverage, try white or raw sugar cubes, or brown sugar crystals.

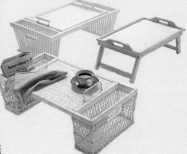

Bed Trays

Lap trays with sturdy legs make cozy breakfasts-in-bed comfortable.

PETER CHRISTIANSEN

23

Ruby Grapefruit

Strawberries

Chocolate Macaroon Muffins

Mocha au Lait

Chocolate is the dominant flavor of this indulgent breakfast. Muffins, with almond paste and cocoa, are equally good baked the day before if you don't want their aroma to give away your morning surprise.

On individual breakfast trays, arrange 1 or 2 muffins, a big cup filled with hot strong coffee and frothed hot milk flavored with more chocolate. Accompany with a chocolate-coated spoon for stirring mocha au lait, or a little cup of chocolate curls to stir into the cup.

For less chocolate, serve coffee with hot frothed milk and offer unusual sweeteners like unrefined sugar cubes, crystalline lumps of brown sugar, or rock candy swizzle sticks (sold in candy and liquor stores).

Segmented grapefruit are luxurious, but if time is precious, simply serve the fruit in halves along with several fresh strawberries, if available, on individual plates.

Chocolate Macaroon Muffins

About ¼ cup (⅛ lb.) butter or margarine

½ cup sugar

1 teaspoon vanilla

2 large eggs

¾ cup all-purpose flour

¼ cup unsweetened cocoa

¾ teaspoon baking powder

Macaroon filling (recipe follows)

In a large bowl, beat to blend ¼ cup butter, sugar, and vanilla until fluffy. Beat in eggs, 1 at a time, until blended.

In another bowl, combine flour, cocoa, and baking powder; stir into butter mixture until well mixed.

Equally divide ½ the batter among 8 buttered or

PETER CHRISTIANSEN

WARMING SOUP, *full of lean sausage, vegetables, and barley, gets a kick from mustard and horseradish added to taste.*

paper-lined muffin cups (2- to 2½-in. diameter). To each cup, add an equal portion of ½ of the macaroon filling. Next, add equal portions of remaining chocolate batter, then top equally with the remaining macaroon filling.

Bake in a 350° oven until muffins spring back when gently pressed and macaroon filling is lightly browned, about 25 minutes. Let muffins cool in pan 10 minutes, then transfer to a rack to cool. Serve warm or cool. If making ahead, let cool, package airtight, and hold at room temperature up to 1 day, or freeze to store longer. Makes 8.

Per muffin: 345 cal. (39 percent from fat); 7.2 g protein; 15 g fat (5.7 g sat.); 48 g carbo.; 112 mg sodium; 69 mg chol.

Macaroon filling. In a food processor or bowl, whirl or beat ¾ cup (7 oz.) **almond paste** and ½ cup **sugar** until mixture forms coarse crumbs. Add 2 **large egg whites,** 1 at a time; whirl or beat until smooth. Stir in ¼ cup **sweetened flaked dried coconut.**

Mocha au Lait

1½ cups nonfat, extra-light (1 percent), or light (2 percent) milk

2 tablespoons sweetened ground chocolate

1½ cups hot espresso or hot strong coffee

Chocolate spoons or curls (directions follow)

Pour milk and chocolate into a 1- to 1½-quart pan; stir to mix well. Place on medium heat and stir until liquid is steaming. To froth, whip in pan on heat with a mixer at high speed, or pour into a blender and whirl.

Pour hot espresso equally into 2 large cups or mugs (each at least 1½ cups), then add milk and foam. Offer with chocolate spoons to stir mocha, or spoon chocolate curls, to taste, into cups and mix with plain spoons. Serves 2.

Per serving without chocolate spoons or curls: 122 cal. (30 percent from fat); 6.8 g protein; 4 g fat (2.4 g sat.); 16 g carbo.; 101 mg sodium; 3.7 mg chol.

Chocolate spoons. In the top of a double boiler over hot (not boiling) water, melt 3 ounces (about ½ cup) **semisweet chocolate baking chips;** stir often until smooth.

Dip bowls of 2 soup-spoons, 1 at a time, into chocolate, thickly coating cupped and back sides of

spoon and about ½ inch of the handle. Lift spoon from chocolate; let it drip briefly, then set on a sheet of waxed paper or foil. Chill until firm, at least 15 minutes. Repeat to make a thicker coating, if desired. If making ahead, package spoons airtight and chill up to 1 week.

Chocolate curls. Use **semisweet, bittersweet, milk,** and **white chocolate,** or just 1 kind of chocolate; you need the equivalent of 1 plain chocolate bar (3 to 4 oz.) at least ¼ inch thick.

Working with 1 bar at a time, unwrap chocolate and place, smooth side up, on a square of cooking parchment or waxed paper.

Warm in a microwave oven at full power (100 percent) for 5-second intervals (or warm in a 150° oven for 1½ to 2 minutes) until bar gives faintly when gently pressed. If chocolate gets too soft, let cool a few minutes.

Pull a vegetable peeler toward you over top of the softened chocolate, using firm and even pressure to cut curls. If chocolate splays out instead of curling, gently neaten and curl with fingers. Transfer curls to a flat surface to firm. Serve curls, or store in an airtight container up to 1 week. Save chocolate scraps for another use. A 3-ounce bar makes 1½ to 2 cups curls (1¾ to 2¼ oz.), or 2 servings.

Per ounce semisweet chocolate: 135 cal. (56 percent from fat); 1.2 g protein; 8.4 g fat (5 g sat.); 18 g carbo.; 3.1 mg sodium; 0 mg chol.

Sausage-Barley Soup with Swiss Chard

Soft Pretzels

Crisp Vegetables

Baked Apples

Vanilla Frozen Yogurt

Dark Beer

Chilled Apple Cider

The soup cooks in about an hour, but it can be started a day ahead. Refreshingly lean, it helps bring balance to a day when you've had a rich lunch or breakfast, such as the Valentine's Day treat, preceding.

Chewy pretzels and crisp raw vegetables—such as radishes, cucumber sticks, bite-size flowerets of broccoli and cauliflower—are also low in fat.

Bake apples as the sausage-barley soup simmers; serve the fruit, hot or cool, and top portions, if you like, with scoops of low-fat vanilla frozen yogurt.

Sausage-Barley Soup with Swiss Chard

1 pound turkey kielbasa sausage, cut into ¼-inch slices

1 large (about ½ lb.) onion, chopped

2 large (about ½ lb. total) carrots, thinly sliced

10 cups regular-strength beef broth

1 cup pearl barley

1 tablespoon minced fresh or 1 teaspoon crumbled dried oregano leaves

½ pound Swiss chard, rinsed and drained

Prepared horseradish and Dijon mustard

In a 5- to 6-quart pan over medium heat, combine sausage, onion, and carrots. Stir often until sausage and vegetables are lightly browned, about 15 minutes. Spoon off and discard any fat in pan.

To pan, add broth, barley, and oregano. Bring to a boil over high heat; reduce heat, cover, and simmer until barley is tender to bite, about 30 minutes. If making ahead, cool, cover, and refrigerate up to 1 day. Reheat to continue.

Trim and discard discolored stem ends of chard. Coarsely chop leaves and stems; stir into soup. Simmer, uncovered, until leaves are limp and bright green, about 10 minutes. Ladle into wide bowls. Add horseradish and/or mustard to taste. Makes 6 servings.

Per serving: 283 cal. (21 percent from fat); 19 g protein; 6.7 g fat (2.1 g sat.); 39 g carbo.; 776 mg sodium; 52 mg chol.

While the cheese-topped vegetable casserole (ideal for friends who eschew meat) bakes, make a green salad, warm the rolls, and peel and slice oranges for dessert.

Pepper, Rice, and Cheese Casserole

4 large (about 2 lb. total) red, yellow, or green bell peppers

1 large (about ½ lb.) onion, chopped

2 cloves garlic, minced or pressed

1 cup regular-strength chicken broth

4 cups cooked rice

4 large eggs

About 2 cups (15-oz. container) part-skim ricotta cheese

¾ cup grated parmesan cheese

Rinse, stem, seed, and slice or chop peppers. In a 5- to 6-quart pan over high heat, combine peppers, onion, garlic, and ¼ cup of the broth.

Stir often until broth evaporates and browned bits stick to pan. Add ¼ cup broth, and stir to scrape bits free.

Stir rice into vegetables. Spread mixture in a deep 3-quart casserole.

In a bowl, beat to blend remaining broth, eggs, ricotta, and half the parmesan; spread over vegetable mixture. Sprinkle with remaining parmesan.

Bake in a 375° oven until the cheese mixture is golden brown on top, about 45 minutes. Serves 6.

Per serving: 424 cal. (28 percent from fat); 22 g protein; 13 g fat (6.6 g sat.); 54 g carbo.; 332 mg sodium; 172 mg chol. ■

By Christine B. Weber

POUR HOT *pie filling into crust; chill to firm.*

NORMAN A. PLATE

Lemon pie in a microwave

LEMON PIE FILLING cooked in a microwave oven may not be much faster, but it requires less attention—just a stir every few minutes.

You have two ways to finish; top while warm with meringue and bake briefly. Or chill and top with whipped cream. The meringue is less rich, but whipped cream bypasses egg-safety concerns.

Microwave Lemon Pie

About 1 cup sugar

About 1 cup water

1 tablespoon butter or margarine

2 teaspoons grated lemon peel

¼ cup cornstarch

⅓ cup lemon juice

3 large egg yolks

1 baked pastry shell for a single-crust 9-inch pie

3 large egg whites and ¼ teaspoon cream of tartar (optional)

1 cup whipping cream (optional)

In a 2- to 3-quart microwave-safe bowl, combine ¾ cup sugar, 1 cup water, butter, and peel. Heat at full power (100 percent), uncovered, in microwave oven until sugar dissolves, 3 to 4 minutes.

Mix cornstarch with lemon juice; stir into bowl. Cook until mixture boils; stir every 2 minutes. Beat yolks with 2 tablespoons water. Stir into bowl. Cook until glossy and thick enough to mound briefly, 2 to 3 minutes; stir every 1½ minutes. Pour into crust.

For meringue, whip whites and cream of tartar at high speed in a large bowl until foamy. Gradually whip in ¼ cup sugar until whites hold stiff, glossy peaks. Swirl over warm filling and against pastry. Bake in 400° oven until meringue is tinged with gold, 3 to 5 minutes. Chill, uncovered, about 2 hours.

For cream topping, whip cream until it holds soft peaks, sweeten to taste, and swirl over chilled filling. Serve, or cover without touching the topping and chill up to 10 hours. Serves 8 to 10.—*Shirley Suhrer, Pacifica, California*

Per serving with meringue: 239 cal. (37 percent from fat); 3.4 g protein; 9.8 g fat (3 g sat.); 35 g carbo.; 160 mg sodium; 75 mg chol. ■

By Paula Smith Freschet

Ultimate barbecued steak

"Have coals hot enough to sear meat quickly . . . and get nice browned edges outside. No garnish is necessary!!!"—Judy Murphy

NOTHING MAKES a stronger statement about how Westerners like to barbecue than our year-round love affair with cooking on the grill. Come rain or come shine, we use fire and smoke to work magic on foods. One of the favorite grilling candidates is beef steak because it benefits from the hot glowing coals; beef also takes well to an imaginative spectrum of seasonings, such as this robust tequila marinade.

Tequila Beef Steaks

4 New York strip steaks (each 8 to 10 oz., cut 1 to 1½ in. thick), fat trimmed
½ cup tequila
2 tablespoons olive oil
1 tablespoon pepper
2 teaspoons grated lemon peel
1 clove garlic, pressed or minced
Salt

With a damp paper towel, wipe steaks; put meat in a 1-gallon plastic food bag. Add tequila, oil, pepper, lemon peel, and garlic; seal bag, and turn to mix seasonings. Set bag in a bowl; chill at least 1 hour or up to 1 day; turn bag over occasionally.

Drain steaks and place on a grill 4 to 6 inches above a solid bed of hot coals (you can hold your hand at grill level only 2 to 3 seconds, or set gas barbecue at this heat).

Turn steaks to brown evenly; for medium-rare (cut to test), cook 12 to 14 minutes. Transfer meat to plates; season to taste with salt. Serves 4.— *Judy Murphy, Foster City, California*

Per serving: 385 cal. (44 percent from fat); 49 g protein; 19 g fat (6.6 g sat.); 0.7 g carbo.; 116 mg sodium; 129 mg chol. ■

By Linda Lau Anusasananan

DAVID BROAD

Grill-seared steak—saturated with marinade of tequila, pepper, and lemon peel—combines volatile liquor and spiciness.

PETER CHRISTIANSEN

Margarita champions... with choices

Sour or sweet, slushy or not, even tequila or not

Classic margarita, icy cold in a salt-rimmed glass, combines tequila, fresh lime juice, and orange-flavor liqueur.

ELVIS SIGHTINGS and claims to the best margarita occur with similar frequency and equal conviction. The difference is, you can put a margarita to the test. When we asked *Sunset* readers to share their best margarita recipes, little did we anticipate such spirited reactions. Battle lines are a bit fuzzy, but these points demand consideration:

The tequila—should it be clear or golden?

Do you have to use tequila? Surprisingly, giving up the basic ingredient doesn't seem to hinder enthusiasm—even for nonalcoholic margaritas.

The citrus juice, fresh or otherwise? Fresh lime juice is classic; a die-hard faction insists on fresh lemon juice. Soft drink fanciers, attuned to sweeter tastes, push handy frozen limeade.

The orange-flavor liqueur most mentioned is triple sec, but readers concede they use any orange-flavor liqueur, from Cointreau to curaçao—even nonorange-flavor liqueurs, or no liqueur at all.

Ice in or out? For most intense flavor, strain out the ice. For thick, chilling drinks, whirl in the ice.

Salt-rimmed glasses are a margarita signature, and certainly a zingy component. But they are optional—and some makers use sugar instead.

Which version to choose? Here are options: the first, smooth and tart; the second, sweeter and less intense; the third, cool and nonalcoholic.

Salt-rimmed glasses. Rub rims of glasses (each about 1 cup) with a **lime** or lemon **wedge,** or moist shell of a reamed lime or lemon. Have **coarse salt** on a flat plate. Dip lime- or lemon-moistened glass rim into salt. Chill until serving time.

Classic Margarita

¾ cup (6 oz.) lime juice
¾ cup (6 oz.) tequila
½ cup (4 oz.) orange-flavor liqueur
3 cups coarsely crushed ice
  Salt-rimmed glasses (see preceding)
4 lime slices or wedges

Shake in a covered container or whirl in a blender until slushy the lime juice, tequila, liqueur, and ice. Pour into glasses (if mixture is shaken, you can pour drink through a strainer and discard ice); garnish with lime slices. Serves 4.

Per serving: 199 cal.; 0.2 g protein; 0 g fat; 13 g carbo.; 0.9 mg sodium; 0 mg chol.

Convenience Margarita

1 large (12 oz.) can frozen limeade concentrate
  About 3 cups crushed ice
½ cup (4 oz.) tequila or beer
¼ cup (2 oz.) orange-flavor liqueur
  Salt-rimmed glasses (see preceding)
4 lime wedges or slices

In a blender or food processor, whirl limeade concentrate, 3 cups ice, and (if space permits) tequila and liqueur until ice is very finely crushed. Pour into salt-rimmed glasses (add any remaining tequila or orange liqueur equally); add more ice if desired. Garnish with lime wedges. Serves 4.—*David Patton, Vancouver, Washington*

Per serving: 315 cal. (0.3 percent from fat); 0.2 g protein; 0.1 g fat (0 g sat.); 58 g carbo.; 0.3 mg sodium; 0 mg chol.

Frozen Virgin Margarita

1 large (12 oz.) can frozen limeade concentrate
  About 2 cups coarsely crushed ice
1 can (12 oz., 1½ cups) nonalcoholic beer
  Salt-rimmed glasses (see preceding)
6 lime wedges or slices

In a blender or food processor, whirl limeade concentrate and ice until ice is very finely crushed.

Add beer (if space in blender is limited, add only part of the beer). Pour into salt-rimmed glasses (add any remaining beer equally to each) and garnish with lime wedges. Serves 6.—*Nancy Hymer, Fox Island, Washington*

Per serving: 146 cal. (1 percent from fat); 0.3 g protein; 0.1 g fat (0 g sat.); 38 g carbo.; 1 mg sodium; 0 mg chol. ∎

By Karyn I. Lipman

PETER CHRISTIANSEN

COLORFUL SALADS, *oven-braised brisket go with savory broth in which meat cooks.*

Cozy and inviting, a beef dinner from Alsace

Calming, satisfying, and make-ahead

W ITH THE GLUT OF fancy food during the holidays, diners (and cooks) often yearn for a home-cooked meal with plain, simple flavors. This beef brisket dinner, typical of Alsace and based on one we sampled at the Taverne du Vigneron in Gueb-

willer, provides such a meal, worthy of family or friends.

Slowly oven-braise a beef brisket with broth and seasonings until tender. As the meat cooks unattended, make an assortment of vegetable salads, all with a mustard vinaigrette. Once the beef is done, its cooking broth becomes a rich-flavored soup to sip with the meal.

Meat and salads can be prepared up to a day ahead; or assemble salads as the meat cooks.

With the meal, you might serve a Pinot Noir, such as Domaines Schlumberger from Alsace or one from Oregon or Washington.

Alsatian Beef Brisket with Broth

1   beef brisket (4 to 4½ lb.)
1   large (8 oz.) onion, thinly sliced
2   dried bay leaves
2   cloves garlic
1   teaspoon black peppercorns
½   teaspoon dried thyme leaves
½   teaspoon whole cloves
1   small dried hot red chili
6   sprigs parsley
    About 3 quarts regular-strength beef broth
    Coarse salt
    Prepared horseradish
    Dijon mustard

Trim surface fat from beef. In a 12- by 14-inch roasting pan (at least 2½ in. deep), combine beef, onion, bay leaves, garlic, peppercorns, thyme, cloves, chili, parsley, and 3 cups broth.

Cover tightly with foil. Bake in a 325° oven until very tender when pierced, 3½ to 4 hours. (If making ahead, cool, cover, and chill up to a day. Lift off and discard fat. Reheat meat, tightly covered, in a 325° oven until hot, about 45 minutes.)

Lift out meat and place on a platter; keep warm. Pour pan juices, a portion at a time, through a fine strainer into a 1- to 2-quart glass measure. Skim off fat. Measure juices and pour into a 4- to 5-quart pan; add broth to make 10 to 12 cups total. Bring broth to a boil. To serve, pour into an attractive tea kettle, pitcher, or tureen.

Slice beef across grain. Offer salt, horseradish, and mustard to add to taste. Makes 8 to 10 servings.

Per serving: 302 cal. (40 percent from fat); 39 g protein; 13 g fat (4.7 g sat.); 3.8 g carbo.; 149 mg sodium; 113 mg chol.

Marinated Vegetable Platter

4   or 5 large (about 2 lb. total) leeks
    Dijon dressing (recipe follows)
    About 2 pounds (about 3 large) celery root
¼   cup reduced-calorie or regular mayonnaise
3   cups (about 10 oz.) shredded carrots
1   large (about 1¼ lb.) European cucumber, thinly sliced
1   teaspoon salt
1   large (16 oz.) and 1 small (8¼ oz.) can julienne beets, drained
1   tablespoon chopped parsley

Trim root ends and dark green tops off leeks. Split leeks in half lengthwise; rinse well. In a 10- to 12-inch frying pan on high heat, bring about 1 inch water to a boil. Add leeks and simmer, uncovered, until tender when pierced, 5 to 8 minutes. Drain and immerse in cold water. When cold, drain. Place in a rimmed dish. Moisten with 3 tablespoons of the Dijon dressing.

Trim stems and peel celery root; rinse well. Mix mayonnaise with 6 tablespoons dressing. Coarsely shred enough celery root to make 3 cups; at once, mix with mayonnaise mixture (exposed to air, root quickly discolors).

Mix shredded carrots with ½ cup dressing.

Thinly slice cucumber. Mix

cucumber with salt; let stand until limp, about 30 minutes. Rinse and drain well. Mix with ¼ cup dressing.

Mix beets with ¼ cup dressing.

(If making ahead, cover and chill salads, separately, up to a day.) Arrange on a platter; sprinkle celery root with parsley. Serves 8 to 10.

Per serving: 197 cal. (63 percent from fat); 2.3 g protein; 14 g fat (2 g sat.); 18 g carbo.; 417 mg sodium; 1.7 mg chol.

Dijon dressing. Stir together ⅔ cup **olive oil,** ⅔ cup **white wine vinegar,** 1 tablespoon **Dijon mustard,** ¼ teaspoon **pepper,** and 1 clove **garlic,** pressed or minced.

Oranges in Brandy

6   large (about 4¾ lb. total) oranges
½   cup sugar
1   teaspoon coriander seed, crushed
1½ cups pitted prunes
1   cup plum brandy or regular brandy

Finely shred enough peel from oranges to make 1 tablespoon; set aside.

With a sharp knife, cut peel and white membrane from oranges. Over a bowl, cut between membranes to remove segments; squeeze juice from membranes into bowl. Drain juice from oranges into a 1½- to 2-quart pan. Cover; chill segments.

To pan add peel, sugar, coriander, and 1 cup water. Stir over high heat to dissolve sugar. Add prunes. Cover; simmer 5 minutes. Remove from heat; add brandy. Cool. Gently mix orange segments with prunes. Serve, or cover and chill up to a day. Serves 8 to 10.

Per serving: 237 cal. (1.9 percent from fat); 1.8 g protein; 0.5 g fat (0 g sat.); 51 g carbo.; 1.1 mg sodium; 0 mg chol. ∎

By Linda Lau Anusasananan

FOR DESSERT, *oranges and prunes steep in brandy and coriander-flavored syrup.*

PETER CHRISTIANSEN

HEARTY BREAKFAST *combines hot wild rice, sautéed apple and banana, warm milk, and brown sugar.*

You can tame wild rice

Three convenient ways to cook four flavorful dishes, including breakfast

ULTIVATED WILD rice is a paradox, but a reality. This native of the northern Great Lakes area has been transplanted to the Sac-ramento and San Joaquin valleys of California. And whereas the yield from wild rice gathered in its native habitat is quite sparse, 13,000 California acres are now producing about 3,500 tons of wild rice annually.

Even so, the product is not exactly flooding the market. Regular rice yields about 5,100 pounds of grain per acre; cultivated wild rice produces about 600 pounds.

Grains of cultivated wild rice are larger than the truly wild, but both have a rich, nutty flavor and a firm, chewy texture. Cultivated rice is more affordable.

Wild rice takes 2 to 3 times longer to cook than white rice and, unlike white rice, cannot be sautéed before it's cooked in liquid—the grains become hard and will no longer absorb liquid. We detail three convenient ways to cook wild rice: simmering, quick-simmering, and microwaving. The time that it takes wild rice to become tender to bite varies with the size of the grain and its relative freshness; use times given as guides, then check and adjust as needed. Cooked wild rice stores and reheats well.

The flavorful dishes that follow offer a range of ways to use wild rice: a hearty pilaf, a main-dish soufflé, a robust breakfast combination, and a baked dessert.

Wild Rice and Barley Pilaf

1   small onion, minced
½   pound mushrooms, sliced
1   garlic clove, minced
1   cup wild rice

3½   cups regular-strength chicken broth
½   cup pearl barley
    Salt and pepper

In a 12-inch frying pan or 2- to 3-quart pan, combine onion, mushrooms, garlic, and ½ cup water. Cook, uncovered, on high heat until liquid evaporates and a brown film forms in pan, about 15 minutes; stir often. Add 2 or 3 tablespoons water and stir to free the brown film; cook until the film forms again. Repeat this step 4 or 5 times until onions are richly browned, about 15 minutes.

Rinse and drain rice. Mix with broth in pan. Bring to a boil on high heat; cover, and simmer 30 minutes. Rinse and drain barley. Add to rice; simmer until grains are tender to bite but just slightly chewy, about 20 minutes longer. Season with salt and pepper to taste. Makes 5 or 6 servings.

Per serving: 184 cal. (7.3 percent from fat); 7.8 g protein; 1.5 g fat (0.7 g sat.); 217 g carbo.; 36 mg sodium; 0 mg chol.

Wild Rice Soufflé

1   tablespoon butter or margarine
½   cup minced parsley
1   teaspoon dried tarragon leaves
¼   teaspoon ground nutmeg
¼   cup all-purpose flour
1   cup nonfat milk
2   tablespoons dry sherry or dry white wine
1¼   cups (about 5 oz.) shredded gruyère cheese
3   large eggs, separated
1   cup cooked wild rice (cooked in broth; instructions follow)
¼   teaspoon cream of tartar

In a 1½- to 2-quart pan over medium-high heat, stir butter with parsley, tarragon, and nutmeg until butter melts. Add flour and stir until it begins to brown slightly, 2

DARK, SLENDER GRAINS *of raw wild rice swell and split when cooked in liquid to reveal creamy interior.*

or 3 minutes.

Remove pan from heat and smoothly stir in milk and sherry. Stir over high heat until boiling. Add 1 cup cheese; off the heat, stir until cheese melts. Stir yolks into sauce, then mix in rice.

In a deep bowl, beat egg whites and cream of tartar with an electric mixer on high speed until whites form soft, moist peaks. Stir about ⅓ of the whites into rice mixture, then gently fold in remaining whites.

Pour mixture into a buttered, straight-sided 1½- to 2-quart soufflé dish or deep casserole. Sprinkle evenly with remaining cheese. Bake in a 350° oven until top is richly browned, 40 to 45 minutes. Serve immediately. Makes 4 to 6 servings.

Per serving: 237 cal. (53 percent from fat); 14 g protein; 14 g fat (4.3 g sat.); 14 g carbo.; 163 mg sodium; 143 mg chol.

Cooked Wild Rice

Rinse **wild rice** with cool **water** in a fine strainer. Cook by any of the following methods. Drain and serve hot, seasoned with **salt** to taste; use in these recipes; or use cold (as in salads).

Cooked, 1 cup wild rice makes about 3 cups (it fluffs as it cools, and measures a bit more). If rice is cooked ahead, chill airtight up to 1 week; freeze to store longer.

Per 1 cup: 191 cal. (2.4 percent from fat); 7.9 g protein; 0.5 g fat (0.1 g sat.); 40 g carbo.; 3.7 mg sodium; 0 mg chol.

To simmer, bring 1 cup rinsed **wild rice** and 2 cups **water** or regular-strength chicken or beef broth to boil in a 1½- to 2-quart pan on high heat. Cover; simmer until grains begin to split and are tender to bite, yet slightly chewy, about 40 minutes.

To quick-simmer, bring 2 cups **water** or regular-strength chicken or beef broth to boiling in a 1½- to 2-quart pan; add 1 cup rinsed **wild rice.** Cover; remove from heat and let stand 4 to 12 hours. Bring to a boil and simmer, covered, until grains begin to split and are tender to bite, yet slightly chewy, 10 to 25 minutes.

To microwave, put 1 cup rinsed **wild rice** in a 1½- to 2-quart microwave-safe deep bowl. Add 2 cups **water** or regular-strength chicken or beef broth. Cover; bring to a boil in a microwave oven at full power (100 percent), about 8 minutes.

Reduce power to medium (50 percent) and cook until wild rice grains begin to split and are tender to bite, yet slightly chewy, about 30 minutes. Let stand 10 minutes.

To reheat in the oven, put 1 recipe's worth **cooked wild rice** in a 3- to 4-cup casserole, cover, and bake at 375° until hot, about 15 minutes (25 minutes if frozen).

To reheat in a microwave oven, put rice in a 3- to 4-cup microwave-safe dish; cover. Heat at full power (100 percent) until hot, 2 to 3 minutes (3 to 4 minutes if frozen).

Wild Rice Breakfast

1 tablespoon butter or margarine

At least 2 tablespoons firmly packed brown sugar

1 teaspoon ground cinnamon

1 large (about ½ lb.) Golden Delicious apple, peeled, cored, and thinly sliced

1 medium-size (about 5 oz.) ripe banana, peeled and sliced

1 recipe's worth hot cooked wild rice (preceding)

About 1½ cups warm milk

In a 10- to 12-inch frying pan over medium heat, melt butter with 2 tablespoons sugar and cinnamon. Add apple; turn fruit as needed until translucent, 3 to 4 minutes. Add banana and heat until warm, about 3 minutes; turn slices once. Spoon rice into bowls, top with fruit, and add milk and sugar to taste. Serves 4 to 6.

Per serving with ⅓ cup milk: 211 cal. (22 percent from fat); 6.9 g protein; 5.1 g fat (3 g sat.); 37 g carbo.; 63 mg sodium; 17 mg chol.

Wild rice breakfast with bananas. Follow preceding directions for **wild rice breakfast,** but omit apple and use 2 medium-size ripe **bananas** (about ⅔ lb. total).

Add ½ teaspoon **coconut extract** to milk.

Per serving with ⅓ cup milk: 216 cal. (21 percent from fat); 7 g protein; 5.1 g fat (3 g sat.); 38 g carbo.; 63 mg sodium; 17 mg chol.

Wild Rice Pudding

4 cups milk

1 cup cooked wild rice (cooked with water, preceding)

½ cup sugar

1 teaspoon vanilla

Softly whipped cream

Mix milk with rice, sugar, and vanilla in an 8- to 9-inch square pan. Bake, uncovered, in a 350° oven for 45 minutes; stir crust into rice. Bake, stirring 3 or 4 times, until most of the milk is absorbed, about 1½ hours longer. Spoon into bowls and serve hot or cool, topped with whipped cream. If making ahead, cover and chill up to 1 day. Serves 4 or 5.

Per serving: 237 cal. (25 percent from fat); 8 g protein; 6.6 g fat (4.1 g sat.); 37 g carbo.; 97 mg sodium; 27 mg chol. ∎

By Christine B. Weber

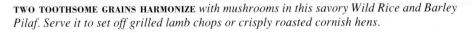

TWO TOOTHSOME GRAINS HARMONIZE *with mushrooms in this savory Wild Rice and Barley Pilaf. Serve it to set off grilled lamb chops or crisply roasted cornish hens.*

CHOCOLATE LOVERS *share thick chocolate (or mocha espresso) shake from dark chocolate sack; eat sack when empty, or rinse and devour later.*

PETER CHRISTIANSEN

Chocolate Sack and Shake

6 ounces bittersweet or semisweet chocolate, coarsely chopped

   Mold for chocolate sack (see preceding)

   Chocolate shake (recipe follows)

Place chocolate in top of a double boiler over hot, but not simmering, water; stir often until smooth. Remove from heat; leave over water.

Open bag and smooth interior. With a stiff-bristled pastry brush, paint chocolate inside bag thickly and evenly up to, but not over, bag rim. Coat corners and creases generously; if thin, they tend to crack first.

Set bag upright; chill until chocolate is hard, about 2 hours. Remelt chocolate in double boiler; paint a second layer, using all but 1 to 2 tablespoons chocolate. Chill until hard, about 2 hours. To unwrap chocolate sack, snip through fold on bottom of paper bag; gently peel and snip paper from chocolate. Touch sack as little as possible to avoid melting.

Check for cracks (sack has to be leakproof); look through bag toward a strong light or shine a flashlight into it. To patch cracks or thin spots, tear a piece of waxed paper that is larger than the weak area; hold paper against weak spot on outside of sack. Coat on inside with remaining remelted chocolate. Chill until firm, about 20 minutes; peel off paper.

If sack breaks, melt pieces and start again. If making ahead, chill sack airtight up to 1 week. Set sack on a small flat plate, pour in shake; serve with straws. Eat bag as emptied, or rinse with cold water, drain dry, and eat later. The empty sack weighs about 5 ounces; filled, it serves 2 generously.

Per serving: 846 cal. (61 percent from fat); 16 g protein; 57 g fat (34 g sat.); 90 g carbo.; 206 mg sodium; 98 mg chol.

Chocolate shake. In a blender, whirl until smooth 3 cups **chocolate ice cream**, ½ cup **milk**, and 3 tablespoons **instant espresso powder** (optional). Use at once. ∎

By Elaine Johnson

A chocolate sack–shake for your valentine

Even the container is edible—very edible

BAG YOUR VALENTINE with this end-all chocolate milkshake served from an edible chocolate sack. The project takes minimal artistic skills—you paint the inside of a paper bag with melted chocolate. When chocolate has hardened, peel off bag.

Mold for chocolate sack. For each sack, you need a small, clean, unwrinkled food-safe (as follows) paper bag about 1½ by 3 inches at the base and 6 inches tall; trim to this height if taller. (In reality, you need two or three bags in case chocolate breaks when you tear off the bag.)

Either shape a bag from cooking parchment, using plastic tape to make interior seams smooth, or buy food-grade, plastic-lined ½-pound coffee bags at a coffee shop.

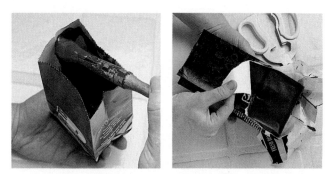

TO MAKE SACK, *heavily paint paper bag interior with two coats of melted chocolate; chill chocolate between coats. Tear off paper; if chocolate breaks, remelt and try again.*

PETER CHRISTIANSEN

SWEET-TART THAI *flavors mingle in rich brown glaze clinging to chicken wings.*

Bake, uncovered, in a 400° oven until browned and crisp, about 1 hour and 15 minutes; turn occasionally. Drain off fat. If making ahead, cool, cover, and chill up to 1 day. Reheat, uncovered, in a 350° oven until hot, about 15 minutes.

With a slotted spoon, transfer wings to warm garlic sauce; mix well. To serve, pour wings onto a platter; scatter with basil and red pepper. Eat hot or cold. Makes 4 to 6 main-dish servings, or 8 to 12 appetizer servings.

Per appetizer serving: 240 cal. (41 percent from fat); 13 g protein; 11 g fat (2.8 g sat.); 21 g carbo.; 41 mg sodium; 36 mg chol.

Thai sweet garlic sauce. In a bowl, mix 1 cup *each* **regular-strength chicken broth** and **sugar,** ¼ cup **fish sauce** (*nam pla* or *nuoc mam*) or soy sauce, 2 tablespoons **cider vinegar,** 1 tablespoon **cornstarch,** and 2 teaspoons **paprika;** set aside.

Set a 4- to 5-quart pan or wok over high heat. When pan is hot, add 1 tablespoon **salad oil,** ⅓ cup minced **garlic,** and 3 tablespoons minced **fresh jalapeño chilies** (and seeds). Stir-fry until garlic is tinged gold and fragrant, about 4 minutes. Add broth mixture; stir often until sauce boils. Boil, stirring, until reduced to about 1¼ cups, 10 to 15 minutes. Use, or cover and chill up to 1 day. Reheat to use.

Transparent basil leaves. Rinse 1 cup **fresh basil leaves.** Spread out on towels to dry thoroughly. In a deep 3- to 4-quart pan, heat 1 inch **salad oil** to 370°. Fry a few leaves at a time (oil spatters if leaves are damp) until they turn bright green and somewhat transparent, 5 to 20 seconds. Take care not to scorch. Transfer leaves from oil with a slotted spoon; drain on towels. Leaves are more transparent when cool. Use or, if making ahead, store airtight in a towel-lined container up to 3 days. ∎

By Karyn I. Lipman

Heavenly chicken wings

Crisp and sticky, sweet and spicy

ONE OF THE MOST popular dishes chef Chaiwatt Siriyarn and his wife, May, prepare at their San Francisco restaurant, Marnee Thai, is chicken wings.

Even though this recipe has several preparatory steps, the wings aren't difficult to make. We bake the wings (Chaiwatt fries them), then mix them with the garlic sauce. The fried basil leaves are optional.

Spiced Angel Wings

3 pounds chicken wings

Thai sweet garlic sauce (recipe follows)

Transparent basil leaves (recipe follows) or about ½ cup slivered fresh basil leaves

Red bell pepper strips (optional)

Rinse wings and pat dry. Cut apart at joints; reserve wing tips for other uses. Place wings in 1 layer in a 10- by 15-inch pan.

DARROW M. WATT

SOUP IN MINUTES. *Plunge noodles into boiling broth with shrimp; steep, then add peas.*

Quick soup: the secret is steeping

Declining heat does the cooking, preserves delicate flavor

THE GENTLE HEAT OF steeping (cooking foods in hot liquid off the heat) is an effective way to preserve the delicate texture of shrimp and liver. Steeped in seasoned broth, they quickly make very lowfat main-dish soups.

Gingered Shrimp Soup

1 package (10 oz.) frozen petite peas

6 cups regular-strength chicken broth

2 tablespoons minced fresh ginger

¾ pound extra-large (26 to 30 per lb.) shrimp, shelled, deveined, and rinsed

1 package (about 2 oz.) dried bean threads (*saifun* or cellophane noodles)

½ cup thinly sliced green onions

Fish sauce (*nam pla* or *nuoc mam*), oyster sauce, or soy sauce

In a colander, rinse peas with hot water; set aside.

In a 5- to 6-quart pan, combine broth and ginger. Cover and bring to a rolling boil over high heat. Add shrimp and bean threads, cover, and at once remove from heat. Let stand 4 minutes. (Do not uncover while steeping.) At 4 minutes, check shrimp for doneness (opaque but moist-looking in center of thickest part; cut to test). If shrimp are still translucent, cover and let stand until done; check at 2-minute intervals. Add peas to pan, cover, and let stand to warm, about 3 minutes. Add onions and ladle soup into bowls; season with fish sauce. Serves 4.

Per serving: 221 cal. (15 percent from fat); 21 g protein; 3.8 g fat (0.9 g sat.); 24 g carbo.; 280 mg sodium; 105 mg chol.

Liver and Onion Soup

3 large (1½ lb. total) onions, thinly sliced

4 cloves garlic

¾ pound beef liver, rinsed and drained

4 cups regular-strength beef broth

¼ cup port

¼ cup minced parsley

½ teaspoon caraway seed

Unflavored nonfat yogurt

Beet-flavored prepared horseradish

In a 5- to 6-quart pan over high heat, occasionally stir onions with ¼ cup water until liquid evaporates and browned bits stick in pan. Add ¼ cup water and garlic; stir to free browned bits. Stir often until liquid evaporates and browned bits form again. Repeat step, using ¼ cup water at a time, until onions develop rich brown color, about 30 minutes total.

Meanwhile, trim any membrane or tubes from liver, then cut liver into ¼-inch-thick slices, each about 2 inches long.

Add broth, port, parsley, and caraway to onions. Cover and bring to a rolling boil over high heat. Add liver and at once cover and remove from heat; let stand 4 minutes. (Do not uncover while steeping.) At 4 minutes, check liver for doneness (no longer pink in center of slice; cut to test). If liver is still pink, cover pan and let stand until done; check at 2-minute intervals. Ladle into bowls; add yogurt and horseradish to taste. Serves 4.

Per serving: 199 cal. (17 percent from fat); 20 g protein; 3.7 g fat (1.3 g sat.); 21 g carbo.; 74 mg sodium; 301 mg chol. ■

By Karyn I. Lipman

These Asian spices are lively secrets

Sichuan peppercorns and sansho add zip and aromatic flavor to your cooking

PRICKLY ASH ISN'T A name that invites culinary experimentation. But what if you called it Sichuan peppercorn or sansho? The dried berries of these two species of prickly ash (*Zanthoxylum*) add aromatic flavor and a zingy sensation to fish, meats, popcorn, and other foods.

You may have encountered the woody, spicy-sweet flavor of Sichuan peppercorns (*Z. simulans*) in dishes from their namesake region of China. Japanese favor the lemony taste of sansho (*Z. piperitum*), sometimes called Japanese pepper. Neither is hot like black pepper (nor are they related to it botanically). The berries are pleasantly tingly, rather than hot, on the tongue.

Asian markets sell sansho ground and ready to use. You'll find whole reddish brown Sichuan peppercorns sold in plastic bags; to release their fragrance, toast them briefly before grinding or crushing.

To grind Sichuan peppercorns, discard any thorny stems from 3 tablespoons peppercorns (a combination of split husks and seeds). Shake in a 6- to 8-inch frying pan over medium-low heat until they start to smoke, 3 to 4 minutes. Grind finely in a mortar and pestle, electric grinder, or blender. Use, or store airtight up to 3 months. Makes 2 tablespoons.

Using sansho and Sichuan peppercorns

Try either ground spice sprinkled lightly on scrambled eggs and simply cooked chicken. Sichuan peppercorns are especially good with beef. Sansho makes a fresh accent for fish. Or combine the peppers with other ingredients, as follows.

With popcorn. Sprinkle sansho and salt to taste over popcorn. Or sparingly sprinkle Sichuan peppercorns (ground as directed, preceding) over popcorn with Oriental sesame oil, cayenne, and salt to taste.

With tofu. Slice soft tofu and fan on small plates. Season to taste with sliced green onions, sansho or Sichuan peppercorns (ground as directed, preceding), and equal parts of rice vinegar (or cider vinegar) and soy sauce.

With cucumber. Peel and thinly slice cucumber; combine with thinly sliced red bell pepper. Season to taste with rice vinegar (or cider vinegar), sugar, salt, and sansho or Sichuan peppercorns (ground as directed, preceding). ∎

By Elaine Johnson

GLENN CHRISTIANSEN

GOLDEN GROUND SANSHO *(top left) and red-brown Sichuan peppercorns (whole in center band, ground in lower triangle) brighten flavor of salmon and other foods.*

Our favorite barbecued chicken

A lemon-rosemary marinade flavors this easy poultry entrée

WHEN WE ASK readers to nominate their all-time favorite *Sunset* barbecue recipes, a perennial winner is this chicken seasoned with rosemary and lemon.

Lemon-Rosemary Barbecued Chicken

1 broiler-fryer chicken (about 3½ lb.); discard fat lumps and cut chicken into pieces

3 large (about 1 lb. total) lemons

¼ cup olive oil or salad oil

½ cup fresh or 3 tablespoons dried rosemary leaves

6 cloves garlic, pressed or minced

Fresh rosemary sprigs

Lemon wedges

Salt and pepper

Rinse chicken and pat dry.

Cut lemons in half and ream juice to make about ¾ cup. In a large plastic food bag, combine the reamed lemon shells, lemon juice, oil, rosemary, and garlic. Add chicken to bag and seal. Turn bag to coat chicken with marinade. Set bag in a bowl. Cover and chill at least 4 hours or up to 1 day; turn bag over occasionally.

Lift chicken from the bag; pour marinade into a small bowl and save. Arrange chicken pieces on a grill 4 to 6 inches above a solid bed of medium coals (you can hold your hand at grill level only 3 to 4 seconds), or set a gas barbecue at this heat. As chicken browns, turn to cook evenly. During the first 15 minutes, brush chicken occasionally with marinade; discard remaining marinade.

If fire flares up, use a spray bottle of water to extinguish, or transfer chicken pieces to other parts of grill. Cook chicken until meat at thigh bone is no longer pink (cut to test), 25 to 35 minutes.

Transfer chicken to a platter; garnish with rosemary sprigs and lemon wedges. Add salt and pepper to taste. Makes 4 or 5 servings.—*Jan Whitehouse, Napa, California*

Per serving: 395 cal. (57 percent form fat); 38 g protein; 25 g fat (6.1 g sat.); 2.8g carbo.; 116 mg sodium; 123 mg chol. ∎

By Linda Lau Anusasananan

From a Mogul emperor to Marin County

Shahi Korma is a delectable and spicy Indian stew

INDIAN-BORN HARISH LAL hails from Delhi, where he trained to become a chef, a trade he now plies in Mill Valley, California. His repertoire of dishes includes some favorites handed down from a precolonial Mogul emperor famous for his interest in subtle and complex dishes. Shahi Korma, a delectable, spicy lamb stew thickened with ground cashews, stems from this source.

Chef Lal's stew is nicely exotic even without the seasonings he has made optional for your convenience. But he suggests that cooks willing to trek to a well-stocked Indian food store (his favorite—in Berkeley, California—is as good as ones back home, he reports) will find it rewarding to make the dish as recorded by the emperor. Items that you may not have on hand are garam masala, a spice blend with many variations (pick one that smells good to you); methi, or fenugreek (a

seed, ground and often included in curry powder blends and in Moroccan dishes); and aromatic black cardamom, which is used whole.

Shahi Korma

2 large (about 1 lb. total) onions
1 clove garlic
1 tablespoon salad oil
1 tablespoon minced fresh ginger
½ teaspoon cardamom seed
½ teaspoon cumin seed
¼ teaspoon black peppercorns
2 whole cloves
1 to 1½ pounds boned and fat-trimmed lamb shoulder, cut into about 1-inch cubes
¼ cup golden raisins
1 tablespoon garam masala or curry powder
1½ teaspoons methi (ground fenugreek, optional)
1 whole black cardamom pod (optional)
¼ teaspoon saffron threads (optional)
1 cup unflavored yogurt
½ cup whipping cream
½ cup salted, roasted cashews
6 cups hot cooked rice
About ¼ cup minced fresh cilantro (coriander)

Chop onions and put in a 5- to 6-quart pan with garlic, salad oil, ginger, cardamom seed, cumin seed, peppercorns, and cloves. Cover and simmer over medium heat, stirring occasionally, until onions are limp, about 15 minutes. Uncover and turn heat to high. Stir until onions are slightly browned, about 15 minutes longer.

In a blender or food processor, whirl onion mixture until smoothly puréed. Return to pan and add lamb, raisins, garam masala, methi, black cardamom pod, saffron, yogurt, and cream. Bring to boil on high heat; cover and simmer gently until meat is very tender when pierced, about 50 minutes.

As meat cooks, whirl about ¼ cup of the cashews

into a fine powder in a blender or food processor.

When meat is tender, stir ground and whole cashews into the pan. Ladle onto cooked rice; sprinkle with cilantro. Makes 4 to 6 servings.

Per serving: 593 cal. (32 percent from fat); 25 g protein; 21 g fat (8 g sat.); 76 g carbo.; 154 mg sodium; 77 mg chol.

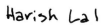

Mill Valley, California

SCOTT MALCOLM CALLS his one-person, one-dish fish dinner Ruffy Simplisticado. We think of it, in our faux Spanish, as Roughy Sophisticado. The fish, simply sautéed, is cradled by romaine and onion warmed with cream. Not-so-strange bedfellows are carrots and basmati rice.

We're flattered to be numbered among those who re-

"SIMPLY PREPARED orange roughy is cradled by romaine and onion."

ceive Malcolm's sporadic circular letter titled The J/Scott Food-A-Month Club, the source of this recipe.

Ruffy Simplisticado

¼ cup chopped onion

2 small (4 to 6 oz. total) carrots, thinly sliced

1 teaspoon olive oil

1 fillet (about 7 oz.) orange roughy, rinsed and patted dry

2 tablespoons whipping cream

About ¾ cup finely slivered rinsed and crisped romaine leaves

About 1 cup hot cooked basmati rice

Chopped parsley

About 1 tablespoon finely chopped roasted, salted macadamia nuts (optional)

Salt and pepper

In an 8- to 10-inch frying pan, combine onion and 2 tablespoons water. Stir onion often over medium-high heat until water in pan evaporates; pour the onion into a small bowl.

In pan, combine carrots and ¼ cup water. Stir often over medium-high heat until water evaporates; pour carrots into another small bowl.

Place frying pan over medium-high heat; add oil. When oil is hot, lay roughy fillet in pan and cook until edges turn opaque. Turn with a wide spatula and continue to cook until fish is

opaque but still moist-looking in center of thickest part (cut to test), about 9 minutes total. Transfer fish to a plate and keep warm.

Wipe pan clean, set on high heat, and add carrots and 1 tablespoon water; stir until carrots are hot. Pour beside fish.

To pan on high heat, add onion and cream; when cream boils, stir in romaine until wilted. Spoon rice beside fish and pour vegetable mixture over both. Sprinkle with parsley and nuts; season to taste with salt and pepper. Makes 1 serving.

Per serving: 728 cal. (36 percent from fat); 38 g protein; 29 g fat (6.8 g sat.); 78 g carbo.; 184 mg sodium; 73 mg chol.

Newport Beach, California

By Richard Dunmire, Joan Griffiths

A lighter, whiter chili

PALED BY THE TREND toward eating lighter, this chili uses poultry in place of red meat, and white beans (canned for convenience) instead of red ones. It simmers with green chilies.

White Chili

1 broiler-fryer chicken (3½ to 4 lb.), cut up

2 cups regular-strength chicken broth

1 tablespoon salad oil

2 large (about 1¼ lb. total) onions, sliced

1 clove garlic, minced or pressed

1 cup dry white wine

2 cans (15 oz. each) cannellini beans, rinsed and drained

¼ cup lime juice

1 can (4 oz.) diced green chilies

1 small fresh jalapeño chili, stemmed, seeded, and minced

¼ cup minced fresh cilantro (coriander)

1 teaspoon dried oregano leaves

½ teaspoon ground cumin

¼ teaspoon ground cinnamon

1 cup (¼ lb.) shredded jack cheese

Condiments (choices follow)

Discard chicken skin and fat; rinse meat. Bring broth and 2 quarts water to boiling in a 5- to 6-quart pan over high heat. Add chicken legs, thighs, and backs; cover and simmer 5 minutes. Add breast and wings; simmer until the thickest part of the breast is no longer pink (cut to test), about 15 minutes longer.

Drain chicken, saving broth. When chicken is cool enough, tear off meat in chunks; discard bones. Meanwhile, boil broth in pan on high heat, uncovered, until reduced to 2 cups, about 25 minutes. Put into a bowl.

Wipe pan clean. Pour in oil and place over medium-high heat. Add onions and garlic; stir often until onions are golden and taste sweet, about 20 minutes.

Add the 2 cups broth, wine, beans, lime juice, green chilies, jalapeño, cilantro, oregano, cumin, and cinnamon. Bring to a boil over high heat; cover and simmer 15 minutes. Stir

in chicken and cheese; heat until hot. Ladle into bowls and add condiments to taste. Serves 6.

Per plain serving: 394 cal. (32 percent from fat); 41 g protein; 14 g fat (1.8 g sat.); 26 g carbo.; 514 mg sodium; 105 mg chol.

Condiments: diced **Roma-type tomatoes,** shredded **jack cheese,** sliced **ripe olives, fresh cilantro sprigs.** ∎

By Christine B. Weber

DARROW M. WATT

LADLE CHICKEN CHILI *into bowls and add condiments.*

Sunset's Kitchen Cabinet

Creative ways with everyday foods—submitted by *Sunset* readers,
tested in *Sunset* kitchens, approved by *Sunset* taste panels

Marie-Paule's Coffee Cake

Marie-Paule Hajdu, Palo Alto, California

FOR BRUNCH *or coffee break, this moist, moderately sweet cake is appealing.*

Flavored yogurt—coffee or vanilla—contributes to this cake's moist, tender texture. Enjoy it plain or with a light dusting of powdered sugar.

- 2 cups all-purpose flour
- 1 teaspoon baking powder
- 1 teaspoon baking soda
- About ½ cup (¼ lb.) butter or margarine, cut into chunks
- 1 cup granulated sugar
- 1 cup coffee- or vanilla-flavor low-fat yogurt
- 2 large eggs
- ¾ cup raisins
- Powdered sugar (optional)

In a small bowl, combine flour, baking powder, and baking soda; set aside.

In a large bowl, beat ½ cup butter, granulated sugar, yogurt, and eggs until blended. Add flour mixture and raisins; beat until evenly moistened.

Butter and flour-dust a 9-inch (12-cup) tube pan; pour batter into pan.

Bake in a 350° oven until cake is well browned and begins to pull from pan sides, and center springs back when lightly pressed, about 55 minutes. Set pan on a rack for about 10 minutes. Run a thin knife between cake and rim; invert cake onto a rack or a platter. Sift powdered sugar over cake. Cut into wedges. Serves 10 to 12.

Per serving: 264 cal. (31 percent from fat); 4.5 g protein; 9 g fat (5.2 g sat.); 42 g carbo.; 207 mg sodium; 57 mg chol.

Risotto with Mushrooms

Carmela M. Meely, Walnut Creek, California

MUSHROOMS, ONION, *parmesan cheese, and wine flavor rice for risotto.*

- 2 teaspoons olive oil
- 1 clove garlic, minced or pressed
- 1 cup coarsely chopped onion
- 1 cup short-grain white rice (such as arborio or pearl)
- 2¼ cups regular-strength chicken broth
- ½ pound mushrooms, rinsed, drained, and thinly sliced
- ¼ cup grated parmesan cheese
- 2 tablespoons dry white wine
- Parsley sprigs

In a 10- to 12-inch pan over medium heat, combine oil, garlic, and onion; stir often until limp, about 5 minutes. Add rice; stir until grains are opaque, 3 to 4 minutes.

Mix broth and mushrooms into pan. Bring to a boil on high heat, stirring often. Reduce heat; simmer, uncovered, until rice is tender and most of the liquid is absorbed, about 25 minutes; stir occasionally, oftener as mixture thickens.

Remove rice from heat; mix in cheese and wine. Pour into a serving dish and garnish with parsley. Serves 4 to 6.

Per serving: 183 cal. (17 percent from fat); 5.5 g protein; 3.4 g fat (1 g sat.); 31 g carbo.; 85 mg sodium; 2.6 mg chol.

Curried Shrimp Salad

Kimberly Scharf, Santa Barbara, California

DILL-SEASONED *shrimp salad includes dried tomatoes, cucumber, and corn.*

This quick-to-make salad goes well as a luncheon main dish. If you want to make a lower-fat version, use sour cream instead of mayonnaise.

- 1 to 1¼ pounds shelled cooked tiny shrimp, rinsed and drained
- 1 package (10 oz.) frozen corn kernels, thawed
- 1 cup coarsely chopped cucumber
- ⅓ cup dried tomatoes packed in oil, drained, coarsely chopped
- Dill dressing (recipe follows)
- 4 large butter lettuce leaves, rinsed and crisped
- Salt

In a bowl, gently mix shrimp with corn, cucumber, ¾ of the tomatoes, and dill dressing.

Place lettuce leaves on 4 plates and mound salad equally in leaves. Top with remaining chopped tomatoes. Add salt to taste. Serves 4.

Per serving: 280 cal. (35 percent from fat); 27 g protein; 11 g fat (2 g sat.); 20 g carbo.; 859 mg sodium; 228 mg chol.

Dill dressing. Mix 3 tablespoons **regular** or reduced-calorie **mayonnaise** or sour cream, 1 tablespoon **Dijon mustard,** ½ teaspoon **grated lemon peel,** 1 tablespoon **lemon juice,** 1 teaspoon **dried dill weed,** ½ teaspoon **curry powder,** and ½ teaspoon **pepper.**

Sweet-Hot Mustard

Mrs. Bruce Farrington, Valier, Montana

- 3 tablespoons dry mustard
- 3 tablespoons distilled white or white wine vinegar
- 2 tablespoons water
- 1 tablespoon all-purpose flour
- 3 tablespoons sugar
- 3 tablespoons butter or margarine, cut into small chunks

In a 1- to 1½-quart pan, mix mustard, vinegar, and water; let stand 1 hour.

Combine flour and sugar. Add to mustard mixture along with butter. Stir over medium-high heat just until boiling. Serve hot, warm, or cool.

If making ahead, cover mustard when cool, and refrigerate up to 1 month. Makes about ¾ cup.

Per tablespoon: 47 cal. (63 percent from fat); 0.5 g protein; 3.3 g fat (1.8 g sat.); 4 g carbo.; 29 mg sodium; 7.8 mg chol.

SWEET AND HOT MUSTARD *enlivens sandwiches, makes welcome gifts.*

Mean Lean Vegetable Chili

Susan Ball, Seattle

- 3 large (about ¾ lb. total) carrots, peeled and chopped
- 1 large (about ½ lb.) onion, coarsely chopped
- 1 can (28 oz.) tomatoes
- 1 can (about 1 lb.) *each* black beans, pinto beans, and kidney beans (or 3 cans of 1 kind)
- 3 tablespoons chili powder
  About ½ cup sour cream or unflavored yogurt
  Crushed dried hot red chilies

In a 4- to 5-quart pan over high heat, combine carrots, onion, and ½ cup water. Stir often until liquid evaporates and vegetables begin to brown and stick in pan, about 10 minutes.

Add tomatoes (break up with a spoon) and their liquid, beans and their liquid, and chili powder. Bring to a boil, then reduce heat and simmer, uncovered, to blend flavors, about 15 minutes. Ladle chili into wide bowls; add sour cream and crushed chilies to taste. Makes 6 to 8 servings.

Per serving: 228 cal. (17 percent from fat); 11 g protein; 4.3 g fat (2 g sat.); 39 g carbo.; 863 mg sodium; 6.3 mg chol.

ALL-VEGETABLE CHILI *is a tasty mix of canned beans, tomatoes, and carrots.*

Malted Brownies

Roxanne Chan, Albany, California

The deep, rich flavor of these morsels depends on malted milk and chocolate. The dark chocolate glaze stays deliciously soft, so don't stack the brownies.

- 1⅓ cups all-purpose flour
- 1 cup sugar
- ¾ cup malted milk powder
- 1 teaspoon baking powder
- 1½ cups (9 oz.) semisweet chocolate baking chips
  About ½ cup (¼ lb.) butter or margarine
- 3 large eggs, separated
- 2 teaspoons vanilla
  Chocolate glaze (recipe follows)
  About 20 pecan halves (optional)

In a bowl, mix flour, ½ cup sugar, malted milk powder, and baking powder; set aside.

In a 2- to 3-quart pan over low heat, stir ½ cup chocolate chips and ½ cup butter until melted. Remove from heat. Add flour mixture, egg yolks, and vanil-la, beating to blend. Stir in remaining 1 cup chocolate chips.

In a deep bowl, whip egg whites with an electric mixer on high speed until foamy. Gradually beat in remaining ½ cup sugar, 1 tablespoon at a time, until whites hold stiff, moist peaks. Stir ⅓ of the whites into chocolate mixture, then gently fold in remainder.

Butter and flour-dust a 7- by 11-inch or 9-inch-square pan. Pour batter into pan; smooth top. Bake in a 325° oven until the top looks dry and brownie begins to pull from pan sides, about 45 minutes. Set on a rack and spread with chocolate glaze. When cool, cut brownie into 20 pieces and top each with a pecan. Serve, or wrap airtight up to 2 days. Makes 20.

Per piece: 270 cal. (43 percent from fat); 3.9 g protein; 13 g fat (7.6 g sat.); 37 g carbo.; 145 mg sodium; 51 mg chol.

Chocolate glaze. In a 1- to 1½-quart pan over low heat, stir 1 cup (6 oz.) **semisweet chocolate baking chips** with ⅓ cup **whipping cream** and 2 teaspoons **vanilla.** Use warm.

Compiled by Karyn I. Lipman

PECAN HALVES *stud glossy glaze on chocolate and malted milk brownies.*

March Menus

March teases with signs of spring—fragrant blossoms, blooming bulbs, warming days. Let these sensory temptations draw you outdoors to enjoy the season.

Enhance the pleasures further with meals to take with you. Enjoy the perfume of flowering trees along with a sushi salad lunch. For cool- or warm-weather dining, serve refreshingly light braised cabbage rolls. On a balmy afternoon, tote a simplified version of Grandmother's Sunday chicken dinner outside to eat on a sheltered patio.

BLOSSOM BENTO BOX LUNCH (at right)
A spring garden is the setting for sushi makings of vinegared rice, condiments, and nori wrappers.

LEBANESE SUPPER (page 44)
Cigar-shaped cabbage rolls, spiced with mint, headline a casual, make-ahead supper from Lebanon.

SPRING CHICKEN DINNER (page 45)
Handsome dinner for four features roast chicken and vegetables; the meal unfurls with impressive ease.

THE DETAILS

Asian Carriers

Stacked baskets, covered bento (lunch) boxes make handsome food containers.

Japanese Crisps

Supermarkets and Asian food stores offer savory-sweet crackers and cookies.

Pickled Vegetables

For appetizers, purchase a selection of colorful pickles at a Japanese market.

Plum Wine Coolers

Mix equal portions Japanese plum wine and sparkling water for refreshing coolers.

PETER CHRISTIANSEN

43

Several hours ahead, cook and season rice for sushi (it's best eaten on the day it's made) and assemble the saladlike sushi condiments.

Carry lunch to a favorite spot in the garden. Nibble crisp rice crackers and salty Japanese pickled vegetables with plum wine coolers as you contemplate the flowers—and sushi combinations.

California Sushi Salad

1½ cups short- or medium-grain white rice

½ cup finely chopped carrots

¼ cup seasoned rice vinegar (or ¼ cup rice vinegar and 1 tablespoon sugar)

1 cup finely diced cucumber

⅓ cup thinly sliced green onion

5 or 6 large butter lettuce leaves, rinsed and crisped

About 4 dozen toasted nori (seaweed) squares, about 4-inch size

Condiment tray (directions follow)

In a 2- to 3-quart pan, rinse rice with water until water runs clear; drain. Add 1½ cups water to rice. Cover; bring to a boil over high heat. Reduce heat to low and cook 10 minutes.

Sprinkle carrots over rice. Cook, covered, until rice is tender to bite, about 5 minutes. Stir vinegar into rice and spread out in a 10- by 15-inch pan. Turn rice often with a wide spatula until no longer steaming, then let cool. Mix cucumber and onion with rice. If making ahead, cover up to 3 hours.

Divide the sushi rice among 5 or 6 lettuce-lined plates. Spoon the rice on nori or lettuce, add condiments to

FRANÇOISE DUDAL KIRKMAN

SQUEEZE LEMON WEDGES *and spoon minted yogurt over slender Middle Eastern cabbage rolls.*

taste, and wrap to eat. Serves 5 or 6.

Per serving without condiments: 208 cal. (1.7 percent from fat); 4.8 g protein; 0.4 g fat (0.1 g sat.); 46 g carbo.; 269 mg sodium; 0 mg chol.

Condiment tray. Snap tough ends off ¾ pound **asparagus.** In a 10- to 12-inch frying pan over high heat, cook asparagus in 1½ inches water, uncovered, until barely tender to bite, 3 to 5 minutes; drain. Immerse in ice water until cold. Drain; cut asparagus into 3-inch pieces.

On a tray, arrange the asparagus, ½ pound **shelled cooked crab;** ½ pound **shelled cooked tiny shrimp;** 1 small (about 6-oz.) firm-ripe **avocado,** peeled, pitted, thinly sliced, and coated with **rice** or white wine **vinegar;** ½ cup sliced **pickled ginger;** and about 1 cup (2 oz.) **daikon sprouts** (optional).

Make a paste of 1 tablespoon **wasabi powder** and about 2 teaspoons **water;** form into a cone.

Place wasabi cone and a small bowl of **soy sauce** on condiment tray. If making ahead, cover and chill up to 3 hours.

Up to 1 day ahead, you can tightly roll the mint-seasoned lamb-rice filling in wilted cabbage leaves and keep cold. Start the thick version of the yogurt sauce at the same time.

Bake the cabbage rolls and serve them with yogurt sauce and sliced cucumbers.

Lebanese Cabbage Cigars

1 large (about 2¼-lb.) head savoy or regular green cabbage

1 pound ground lean lamb

⅔ cup long-grain white rice

1 small (6-oz.) onion, chopped

6 cloves garlic, pressed or minced

6 tablespoons chopped fresh mint leaves

About ½ teaspoon salt

¼ teaspoon pepper

2 cups regular-strength chicken broth

¼ cup lemon juice

Lemon wedges

Fresh mint sprigs

Yogurt sauce (recipe follows)

Cut out cabbage core and discard. Gently separate leaves. In a 5- to 6-quart pan, bring about 3 quarts water to a boil on high heat. Plunge leaves, about ¼ at a time, into boiling water; cook until wilted, about 2 minutes. With a slotted spoon, lift out leaves and immerse in cold water. Repeat with remaining leaves; drain leaves.

Thoroughly mix lamb, rice, onion, 4 cloves garlic, 3 tablespoons chopped mint, salt, and pepper. Trim thickest part of rib from back of cabbage leaves.

About 1 inch from stem end of each leaf, place a ½-inch-thick band of lamb mixture across width of leaf. (To use smaller leaves, overlap several of them, and use as a large leaf.) Roll leaf around filling, shaping like a cigar. Stack rolls in a 9- by 13-inch pan. (If making ahead, cover and chill up to 1 day.)

Add broth and cover casserole tightly. Bake in a 350° oven until lamb in center rolls is firm (cut to test; meat may be quite pink), about 1 hour. With a slotted spatula, put rolls on a platter.

Skim and discard fat from juices. Boil juices over high heat until reduced to ½ cup, about 5 minutes. Add lemon juice and remaining garlic and chopped mint; spoon over rolls. Garnish with lemon wedges and mint sprigs; serve with yogurt sauce. Serves 4.

Per serving: 433 cal. (35 percent from fat); 28 g protein; 17 g fat (6.6 g sat.); 44 g carbo.; 428 mg sodium; 76 mg chol.

Yogurt sauce. (If time is limited, season undrained yogurt and serve; sauce is thinner.) Stir 2 cups (1 lb.) **unflavored nonfat yogurt** and spoon ½ of it into a cloth-lined strainer set over a deep bowl. Cover airtight and chill at least 6 hours or up to 1 day. Spoon drained yogurt into a bowl with remaining yogurt; mix with ¼ cup chopped **fresh mint leaves,** and **salt** to taste. Makes 1½ cups; serves 4.

Per serving: 52 cal. (1.7 percent from fat); 5.5 g protein; 0.1 g fat (0.1 g sat.); 6.6 g carbo.; 63 mg sodium; 1.1 mg chol.

SPRING CHICKEN DINNER

Artichoke-Celery Salad

Orange Roast Chicken with Peas

Lemon Ice or Sorbet

Coconut Macaroons

Dry Chenin Blanc or Sparkling Water

This attractive meal will impress in-laws, yet is easy enough for the new cook. Chicken and potatoes roast together; make flambéed gravy from the drippings, then quickly heat peas in the roasting pan.

Because raw artichoke salad darkens quickly, make it just before serving—or start with cooked artichokes and a dipping sauce.

Artichoke-Celery Salad

5 tablespoons lemon juice

1 large (about 1-lb.) artichoke

3 tablespoons extra-virgin olive oil

1 to 2 ounces parmesan cheese

2 cups very thinly sliced celery

Salt and pepper

In a bowl, mix 3 tablespoons lemon juice and 3 cups water. Trim off artichoke leaves (save for other uses, if desired), cut out fuzzy center, and trim stem. Dip artichoke bottom in lemon water. Using a vegetable peeler, cut artichoke bottom into paper-thin slices directly into the lemon water.

Drain artichoke and mix with remaining lemon and oil. With a cheese slicer or vegetable peeler, shave at least ½ the cheese onto artichoke. Add celery; mix gent-

PETER CHRISTIANSEN

ROASTED CHICKEN *and potatoes served with succulent peas, fragrant orange on a rustic table take on a country look.*

ly and mound onto 4 plates. Shave remaining cheese onto salads. Add salt and pepper to taste. Serves 4.— *Gianfranco Audieri, Fior d'Italia, San Francisco*

Per serving: 157 cal. (75 percent from fat); 4.9 g protein; 13 g fat (2.9 g sat.); 8.5 g carbo.; 231 mg sodium; 5.6 mg chol.

Orange Roast Chicken with Peas

1 broiler-fryer chicken (about 4 lb.)

1 small (about 6-oz.) onion, diced

1 small (about 6-oz.) unpeeled orange, rinsed and diced

5 sprigs (each about 4 in.) fresh rosemary or 1 teaspoon dried rosemary leaves

12 small (each about 2-in. diameter, about 1½ lb. total) thin-skinned potatoes, scrubbed and cut in half

About ½ cup regular-strength chicken broth

½ teaspoon grated orange peel

¼ cup orange-flavor liqueur or orange juice

⅓ cup orange juice

1 tablespoon cornstarch

1 package (1 lb.) frozen petite peas, thawed

Orange wedges

Remove chicken neck and giblets; reserve for other uses. Discard lumps of fat. Rinse chicken inside and out; pat dry. Fill body cavity with onion, diced orange, and 2 sprigs rosemary or 1 teaspoon dried rosemary. Place chicken, breast down, on a rack in a 12- by 15-inch roasting pan. Place potatoes in pan around chicken.

Bake, uncovered, in a 400° oven for 30 minutes. Turn chicken over and stir potatoes. Bake until a thermometer inserted in thickest part of thigh reaches 185° or until meat at thigh bone is no longer pink when cut, 40 to 45 minutes longer.

Transfer chicken and potatoes to a large platter; keep warm. Skim and discard fat from pan drippings. Measure drippings; add broth to make ⅔ cup. Add orange peel and

liqueur to pan; warm over medium heat. Ignite liqueur (not under an exhaust fan or near flammable items). When flames subside, add broth. Stir to free browned bits. Mix orange juice and cornstarch; add to pan. Stir until boiling; pour into bowl.

Add peas to pan; stir over high heat until hot, about 3 minutes. Pour peas around chicken. Garnish chicken with remaining rosemary sprigs and orange wedges. Add sauce to taste. Serves 4.

Per serving: 828 cal. (41 percent from fat); 65 g protein; 38 g fat (11 g sat.); 52 g carbo.; 363 mg sodium; 204 mg chol. ■

By Linda Lau Anusasananan

Light Chocolate Mousse

Serve this lowfat mousse after an ample dinner.

1 envelope (2 teaspoons) unflavored gelatin

⅓ cup granulated sugar

About ⅓ cup unsweetened cocoa

½ cup water

½ cup canned evaporated nonfat (skim) milk

2 teaspoons vanilla

In 1- to 1½-quart pan, mix gelatin, sugar and ¼ cup of the cocoa, and ½ cup water. Place over high heat; stir until boiling. Pour into a deep metal bowl (about 2 qt.); mix in milk. Freeze, covered, until mixture is firm, about 45 minutes.

With a mixer at high speed, whip frozen mixture until fluffy and thick enough to hold peaks, about 3 minutes; stir in vanilla. Pour into small (½ cup) ramekins or bowls; spread tops smooth. Serve or cover without touching mousse and chill up to 1 day. Uncover; dust with remaining cocoa. Serves 4.— *Donna Newberry, Davis, California*

Per serving: 121 cal. (10 percent from fat); 5.1 grams protein; 1.4 g fat (0.8 g sat.); 24g carbo.; 39 mg sodium; 1.3 mg chol. ■

By Karyn Lipman

WESTERN CLASSICS

One is Italian, by way of San Francisco. Two have roots in Mexico

Western classic dishes, indigenously or ethnically rooted by ingredients or people, are appealing enough to transcend trend and time. Which are the all-time favorites? We put the question to a vote of our readers as part of the search for *Sunset's Best of the West,* an all-new publication premiering on newsstands this spring.

Our readers chose these Western classics: cioppino, Caesar salad, and salsa. Many variations exist, but the following versions are noteworthy.

1. CIOPPINO

Italian immigrant fishermen in San Francisco get credit for creating cioppino, a stew made with local fish and shellfish. Why it's called cioppino is the subject of learned, heated, and often humorous debate.

Of the many cioppino recipes we received, a number were almost identical. To our surprise, they appear to come from a 1960 *Sunset* recipe. In it, seafood is layered with a tomato-chard-herb sauce and simmered.

Layered Cioppino

- 2 cans (26 oz. each) tomatoes
- 1 can (6 oz.) tomato paste
- 1 cup dry white wine
- ¼ cup olive oil
- 2 teaspoons pepper
- 1 quart (about 10 oz.) coarsely chopped Swiss chard
- 2 large (about 1 lb. total) red bell peppers, stemmed, seeded, and chopped

California cioppino: clams, Dungeness crab, shrimp, and fish chunks bathed by tomato-wine broth laced with Swiss chard and a bouquet of herbs. Soak up flavorful broth with sourdough bread.

NORMAN A. PLATE

½ cup chopped parsley

¼ cup chopped fresh or 1 tablespoon dried basil leaves

2 tablespoons *each* chopped fresh marjoram leaves, rosemary leaves, thyme leaves, and sage leaves; or 2 teaspoons of each dried herb

3 dozen small hard-shelled clams suitable for steaming

3 dozen extra-jumbo (about 2 lb. total, 16 to 20 per lb.) shrimp

2 large (about 2 lb. each) cooked Dungeness crab, cleaned and cracked

2 pounds firm white-flesh fish such as rockfish, rinsed and cut into 2-inch chunks

Salt

In a large bowl, coarsely mash tomatoes. Stir in tomato paste, wine, oil, pepper, chard, bell peppers, parsley, basil, marjoram, rosemary, thyme, and sage.

Scrub clams. Discard gaping ones that won't start to close when touched; they're dead. To devein shrimp, insert tip of a slender skewer under vein between segments of shell along back and gently pull up. Repeat on each shrimp; rinse well.

Arrange clams in the bottom of a heavy 12- to 14-quart pan. Spoon ¼ of the tomato mixture over clams. Layer shrimp, ¼ of tomato mixture, crab, ¼ of tomato mixture, fish, and remaining tomato mixture (a 12-qt. pan may be full to rim). Cover tightly and bring to a boil over high heat, 10 to 20 minutes. Simmer gently until fish is opaque but still moist-looking in thickest part (cut to test), 15 to 20 minutes. Ladle into wide bowls; dig deep to scoop from each layer. Add salt to taste. Serves 12.

Per serving: 290 cal. (25 percent from fat); 40 g protein; 8.2 g fat (1.2 g sat.); 14 g carbo.; 633 mg sodium; 165 mg chol.

Flavor options. To tomato mixture, add 2 to 4 (2-in.-long) **fresh red chilies,** stemmed, seeded, and minced, and 1 cup chopped **onion** or green onion.

Replace fish chunks with 2 pounds **sea scallops,** rinsed and drained.

2. CAESAR SALAD

A chef in Tijuana presented this salad, named in his own honor, to the world sometime in the first half of this century.

Many a stained, well-used "personally" written recipe ascribed to Caesar's hand has been copied and sent to us through the years. Most were simi- lar; none were identical. Perhaps Caesar never ceased inventing. Basics include crisp romaine lettuce; croutons; parmesan cheese; soft, warm egg; olive oil; and lemon juice.

Arguments start with anchovies. The first Caesar salad *Sunset* published, in 1945, didn't have anchovies. The party-size Caesar salad, at the end of our traditional recipe, does, plus other extras that have gained favor over time in this classic.

Egg-safe options follow if you want to replace the coddled egg.

Caesar Salad

1 clove garlic

6 tablespoons olive oil or salad oil

1 cup ¾-inch cubes day-old French bread

1 large egg

3 quarts rinsed and crisped bite- size pieces romaine

Freshly ground pepper

2 tablespoons lemon juice

3 or 4 canned anchovy fillets, chopped

¼ cup freshly grated parmesan cheese

To make garlic oil, crush garlic in a small bowl. Add oil and let stand for at least 1 hour or up to 8 hours.

To make croutons, coat bread cubes with 2 tablespoons garlic oil; spread out in a 9-inch-wide pan. Bake in a 325° oven until browned, 20 to 25 minutes; stir occasionally.

To coddle egg, immerse in boiling water to cover for exactly 1 minute; use egg warm or cool.

Place romaine in a large bowl with a few croutons and pepper. Add

Caesar salad: crisp romaine and crunchy croutons await dressing of ground pepper, garlic-flavor olive oil, lemon juice, freshly grated parmesan cheese, coddled egg, and the debated anchovies.
NORMAN A. PLATE

Mexican salsa: tomatoes, hot chilies, tart tomatillos, onions, and lime juice create the most popular dip of the decade.
NORMAN A. PLATE

remaining garlic oil and mix.

Break coddled egg over salad, sprinkle with lemon juice, and lift with a salad fork and spoon to mix well. Add anchovies and cheese; mix again. Add remaining croutons; mix gently. Serve at once. Makes 5 or 6 servings.

Per serving: 191 cal. (75 percent from fat); 5.7 g protein; 16 g fat (2.9 g sat.); 6.6 g carbo.; 204 mg sodium; 40 mg chol.

Flavor options. Add to salad any or all of the following: 1 to 2 tablespoons **white** or red **wine vinegar;** ¼ to ½ teaspoon **Worcestershire sauce;** 2 tablespoons chopped, drained **oil-packed dried tomatoes;** 2 tablespoons **crumbled blue cheese.**

Egg-safe Caesar. Omit coddled egg; use 3 tablespoons **egg substitute** or mayonnaise. Or mix 1 large egg white with lemon juice; cover and chill at least 48 hours or up to 4 days.

Altman's Caesar salad. Use 6 quarts rinsed, crisped bite-size pieces **romaine.** Make croutons (preceding) using 2 cups **bread cubes** and ¼ cup unseasoned **olive oil.**

In a large salad bowl, mix ½ cup **olive oil** with ¼ cup **freshly grated parmesan cheese;** 1 **coddled egg** (preceding); 2 tablespoons **red wine vinegar;** 1½ tablespoons **lemon juice;** 1 tablespoon **Dijon mustard;** 1 teaspoon **Worcestershire sauce;** 2

canned **anchovy fillets,** drained and minced, or 2 teaspoons anchovy paste; 1 teaspoon drained **canned capers;** and 2 cloves **garlic,** pressed or minced. Add the romaine and croutons; mix well. Serves 10.
—*Bernie Altman, Los Angeles*

Per serving: 209 cal. (78 percent from fat); 4.7 g protein; 18 g fat (2.9 g sat.); 7.9 g carbo.; 191 mg sodium; 24 mg chol.

3. SALSA

When Spanish explorers came north from Mexico, the indigenous foods of Mexico followed, and so began our Western love affair with Mexican foods in general, and chilies in particular.

No dish better exemplifies this devotion than salsa. It's ubiquitous as a staple—the catsup of the '90s.

In salsa's simplest form chilies, mild to hot, are combined with tomatoes, onions, lime juice, and cilantro—then the seasonings take off in all directions. *Fresca* means the ingredients are mostly raw; favored present-day alternatives are canned chilies and canned tomatoes.

Salsa Fresca

1 large (about ¾-lb.) ripe tomato

2 large tomatillos (about 6 oz. total) or 1 small (6-oz.) ripe tomato

¼ cup chopped fresh cilantro (coriander)

⅓ cup chopped onion or green onions

2 tablespoons lime juice

2 to 6 tablespoons minced fresh or canned hot chilies

   Salt

Core and coarsely chop tomato. Husk and chop tomatillos. Combine tomato, tomatillos, cilantro, onion, lime juice, and chilies and salt to taste. Makes 2½ to 3 cups.

Per ¼ cup: 12 cal. (7.5 percent from fat); 0.5 g protein; 0.1 g fat (0 g sat.); 2.5 g carbo.; 3 mg sodium; 0 mg chol.

Flavor options. Instead of fresh tomatoes and tomatillos, use 1 can (28 oz.) **ready-cut tomatoes.**

Instead of lime juice, use 3 to 4 tablespoons **red wine vinegar.**

Add 1 clove minced **garlic.** ∎

By Linda Lau Anusasananan

PLANTAINS, *a Central American staple, look like bananas but are cooked and served like a vegetable. The skin turns black when ripe.*

PETER CHRISTIANSEN

Central American

surprises

These distinctive dishes offer fresh and basic tastes. They're part of a cultural shift that is enriching the West

DIVERSE CLIMATES, MANY NATIONAL BOUNDARIES, A complex blend of indigenous and European cultures, native foods, and lively interplays of ingredients and seasonings all contribute to the different cuisines of countries that collectively form Central America.

As people from these countries have settled in large numbers in the West in recent years, particularly in and around Los Angeles and San Francisco, they've brought many appealing foods that are quite distinctive from those of Mexico.

With the proliferation of Central American restaurants and markets, and supermarket availability of many foods important to Central American cookery, we felt the time was right to seek out some good home cooks and learn how they make a few of their favorite dishes. The result is this sampler of well-flavored, inviting dishes—some simple and quick, some complex and rewarding—to enrich your menus for everyday and for entertaining.

Ingredients and flavors Central American cooks work with aren't unusual, and many of their basics are native foods also familiar to North American cooks: corn, beans, squash, and potatoes. They also make frequent use of the prosaic-looking, widely available but less well known native roots malanga and yuca. European and African ties are reflected in ingredients such as rice, wheat, plantains, citrus, ñame, many spices, and most meats.

NICARAGUA

"Nacatamales are a big project!" admits Myriam Paiz, partly because each one is big enough to fill a dinner plate and make a meal.

Like smaller Mexican tamales, nacatamales are based on masa, but the dried corn dough is merely a foundation for a full-meal assortment of toppings.

One flavorful taste verifies why nacatamales are among Nicaragua's best-loved dishes. Snugly wrapped in banana leaves and cooking parchment, the huge tamales sim-

PLATE-SIZE *nacatamales are joint effort of Myriam Paiz and family. Fold back wrapper to reveal a meal.*

GUATEMALA FRUIT AND CHICKEN:
Chicken, chayotes, and raisins simmer in a fragrant fruit-flavored broth called chicha.

DARROW M. WATT

HONDURAS, BELIZE FINE FISH:
Pan-browned fish goes with yuca cooked in savory-sweet coconut milk.

GLENN CHRISTIANSEN

EL SALVADOR GRAND PUPUSAS:
Cheese-filled masa cakes, pan-toasted, go with crisp cabbage relish.

Magnificent tamales, earthy stews, tropical flavors, tangy

mer in water. You can make them ahead, even freeze them, and reheat. Myriam Paiz tackles their involved production by gathering the ingredients (many steps can be spread over several days), and arranging them in order of use, much like an assembly line. With her daughters or friends to help, a chore becomes a party.

Cooking parchment is sold in well-stocked supermarkets; some Latino markets sell the parchment already cut into the size of pieces you need.

Paiz suggests cold chocolate milk with nacatamales; it's a surprisingly refreshing combination. Serve fruit for dessert.

Nacatamales

If you can't get banana leaves, use 3 layers of cooking parchment or just 1 piece of foil.

12 pieces cooking parchment or heavy foil, each 12 by 18 inches
    Banana leaves (directions follow)
    Señora Paiz's masa (recipe follows)

Filling ingredients (directions follow)
    Marinated pork (recipe follows)
3   cups lightly packed, rinsed and drained fresh mint sprigs
    Sliced vegetables (directions follow)
12 pieces cotton string, each about 4 feet long

For each tamale, put 1 piece parchment on a flat surface; set 1 piece banana leaf on parchment. Spoon ¾ cup masa onto center of leaf;

pat masa to flatten slightly. Add filling ingredients, starting with ¼ cup rice. Push 5 or 6 potato slices, on a narrow edge, into perimeter of masa and make a wall around rice. Push 1 chili, 1 prune, and 6 olives through rice into masa; top with 1 tablespoon raisins.

With a slotted spoon, lift ¹⁄₁₂ of the pork from marinade and put on rice. Stir marinade; spoon 1 tablespoon onto meat. (When nacatamales are assembled, discard remaining marinade.)

Put ¼ cup mint on meat;

BANANA LEAF on parchment is nacatamal foundation (1); masa with potato wall holds fillings (2). Wrap and tie (3).

stack 1 slice each of onion, tomato, and bell pepper onto the mint.

Snugly fold parchment and banana leaf, together, over nacatamal to enclose; fold ends under. Securely wrap packet lengthwise and crosswise with string; tie tightly. Repeat to assemble each nacatamal. If making ahead, set nacatamales in a rimmed pan (to catch drips) and chill up to 1 day.

Stack nacatamales in 1 very large pan (at least 21 qt.) or 2 large pans (each at least 12 qt.). Set a heatproof plate on top of the tamales (to keep them from floating); cover tamales with water. Cover pan and bring water to a boil over high heat, about 45 minutes. Simmer for 1 hour. Lift tamales from pan with slotted spoons or tongs, draining well. Serve hot; or, if making ahead, let nacatamales cool, then cover and chill them up to 1 day. Package airtight to freeze up to several months; thaw overnight in refrigerator. To reheat, immerse in simmering water to cover until hot in center, about 25 minutes.

Place each nacatamal on a plate, snip string, and fold back wrappers. Makes 12;

STEPHEN CRIDLAND

PANAMA TROPICAL BEEF: *Beef rib stew, in full-flavored broth, is laden with rounds of corn, chunks of ñame, malanga, and yuca.*

relishes, creamy plantains

each serves 1 or 2.—*Myriam Paiz, Los Angeles*

Per nacatamal: 923 cal. (41 percent from fat); 29 g protein; 42 g fat (15 g sat.); 110 g carbo.; 863 g sodium; 88 mg chol.

Banana leaves. Stack 1 pound **fresh** or thawed frozen **banana leaves;** fold loosely to fit into a 6- to 8-quart pan. Fill pan halfway with **water;** bring to a boil over high heat. Simmer leaves, uncovered, until olive green, about 12 minutes. Occasionally push floating leaves beneath water; turn bundle over after 6 minutes.

Drain leaves and rinse with cool water; let cool. Trim leaves to make 12 rectangles, each about 9 by 15 inches (if needed, overlap scraps to make rectangles of this size as placed on cooking parchment).

Señora Paiz's masa. Peel 5 large (about 1¾ lb. total) **russet potatoes** and cut into 2-inch chunks. Place in a 5- to 6-quart pan; add **water** to cover. Bring to a boil over high heat; cover and simmer until tender when pierced, about 15 minutes. Drain potatoes well; in pan, mash until smooth with a potato masher or electric mixer.

To pan, add 4 cups **dehydrated masa flour** (corn tortilla flour), 1 cup **orange juice,** 1 cup **regular-strength beef broth** or water, ½ cup **liquid from Spanish-style olives** (see filling ingredients, following), ⅓ cup **lime juice,** and 3 tablespoons **catsup.** Mix until evenly moistened.

In a 10- to 12-inch frying pan, combine 2 cups **lard** or salad oil; 2 large (about 1 lb. total) unpeeled **onions,** thickly sliced; and 1 head unpeeled **garlic,** separated into cloves. Stir often over medium-high heat until onions are very brown, about 35 minutes. Carefully pour hot fat into a fine strainer over masa, pressing vegetables to extract as much oil as possible. Discard vegetables. Stir masa mixture until blended. Season to taste with **salt.** If making ahead, chill airtight up to 3 days.

Filling ingredients. Place 1 pound (2½ cups) **long-grain white rice** in a bowl; add cool water to cover by 1 inch. Let stand at least 6 or up to 24 hours; drain.

Peel 2¼ pounds (about 6 medium-size) **russet potatoes;** cut into ¼-inch-thick rounds. Immerse in water; use within 2 hours.

You will also need 12 drained **canned hot yellow chilies,** 12 **dried pitted prunes,** about 72 (2 cups) **small pitted** or pimiento-stuffed **Spanish-style olives** (reserve liquid for masa, preceding), and ¾ cup **raisins.**

Marinated pork. At the market, have 1 pound **pork back ribs** (optional) sawed crosswise into 2-inch lengths. At home, rinse meat and cut between ribs to separate.

Trim and discard fat from 3 pounds **boned pork shoulder** or butt; cut meat into 1- by 2-inch chunks.

In a large, noncorrodible bowl, mix 3 cups **distilled white vinegar,** 1 package (4 oz.; 110 g) **achiote paste** (or achiote substitute, following), 1 teaspoon **pepper,** and 1 teaspoon **salt** (optional). Add meat; mix. Cover and chill 1 to 3 days.

PETER CHRISTIANSEN

COSTA RICA JUICY PORK, CREAMY PLANTAINS: *Braise pork chops with garbanzos and capers; serve with browned plantain slices, rice, cabbage and tomato salad.*

Achiote substitute. Mix 3 tablespoons **paprika** with 2 tablespoons **distilled white vinegar;** 1½ teaspoons **dried oregano leaves;** 3 cloves **garlic,** minced or pressed; and ½ teaspoon **ground cumin.**

Sliced vegetables. Peel 2 large (about 1 lb. total) **onions,** core 2 large (about 1 lb. total) firm-ripe **tomatoes,** and stem and seed 2 medium-size (about ¾ lb. total) **green bell peppers.** Cut each vegetable into 6 equal, crosswise slices.

GUATEMALA

Like all Central Americans, the people of Guatemala enjoy a variety of meat and vegetable stews. Marta Troche often makes one with

Special ingredients from Latino markets

Well-stocked supermarkets sell many of these Central American foods. Latino markets provide the rest

TAMARIND POD (*tamarindo*) adds refreshing sweet-sour tang to stews (page 56), soups, and drinks. Brittle shells expose sticky brown fruit that coats smooth seed. Pull off the shell.

ACHIOTE PASTE is a mild seasoning mixture based on red annatto seed. Use to color and flavor foods (page 53), particularly rice and meats. Buy or make substitute achiote paste (page 53).

PLANTAINS (*plátanos*) look like bananas, but you eat them cooked. Green-skinned unripe fruit is dense, starchy; boil like potatoes (page 57). Yellow-skinned fruit is riper; black skin indicates ripest, sweetest fruit with creamy texture. You can brown slices of both in butter (page 57).

To use plantains, cut off ends and score peel lengthwise and pull off.

ÑAME (*yam*) is a tuber with brown skin that looks much like a russet potato—which it also resembles in taste and texture when cooked (page 57). It is cylindrical or squat with round protrusions, and may be as small as 1 pound, but grows much larger; store may cut in pieces.

Raw, the white or cream-colored interior is wet and sticky. Tubers should be hard, with no soft or brown spots or mold. Store ñame up to one week at room temperature.

To use fresh ñame, cut off skin and any brown spots; rinse and cut ñame into 1-inch chunks. (Frozen ñame is peeled.) As alternatives, use potatoes, malanga, or yuca.

BANANA LEAVES, used to wrap foods like nacatamales (page 52), are sold fresh or frozen; heat to make more flexible. If leaves are unavailable, use cooking parchment or foil.

COCONUT MILK, canned, frozen, or freshly made with graded coconut, is a popular cooking ingredient (page 56) on the Caribbean coast of Central America.

COTIJA is a sharp, salty, crumbly cheese used to sprinkle on foods for seasoning (page 56). Similar-tasting parmesan cheese can be used in place of cotija.

MALANGA (*yautia*, often confused with smaller taro) is covered with soft, barklike skin and shaggy hairs. Malanga flesh is speckled beige, pink, or yellow (scratch to check). Pink ones turn mauve when cooked. The roots weigh ½ to 2 pounds and are usually shaped like a fat carrot, but they can be squat and bulbous. Malanga's moist, slightly sticky texture becomes dense and drier when cooked (page 57). Its flavor is mild. Choose roots with no soft spots or mold. Store up to 1 week at room temperature.

To use malanga, trim ends and peel, and trim out brown spots; rinse and cut into 1-inch chunks. (Frozen malanga is peeled.) Potatoes, yuca, or ñame can be used instead of malanga.

DEHYDRATED MASA FLOUR is made of dried corn treated with slaked lime, ground, dried again, and pulverized. To use, rehydrate flour; season to make dough for nacatamales (page 52) and pupusas (page 56).

YUCA (*cassava, manioc*) is always eaten cooked (pages 56 and 57). The root's barklike skin is usually wax coated to reduce spoilage. Flesh just beneath skin is pink. Yuca is dense, waxy, and fibrous; the taste is very mild with a faint tang.

Fresh roots ½ to 3 pounds in size should be very hard, covered with skin, and have pure white flesh. Store up to 1 week at room temperature.

To use fresh yuca, cut crosswise into 3-inch chunks; cut off skin and any brown spots. Rinse chunks, quarter lengthwise; trim and discard ropelike core. (Frozen yuca is peeled; use frozen.) As an alternative, use malanga, ñame, or potatoes.

CHAYOTE is a green or white pear-shaped squash with smooth skin or soft spines. Peel if skin is spiny or tough. Cooked chayote has a delicate flavor, and the edible seed tastes like sweet corn. Cook like tender squash (page 56). Pattypan squash can be used instead.

RAW CANE SUGAR (*panocha*) comes in brown cones, disks, or chunks. It has a faint molasses flavor. Melt into sauces (page 56) or grate to use dry. Or use brown sugar.

chicken for Sunday dinner. It takes its name from the liquid base, *chicha*, made of fermented pineapple peel, tamarind, and other ingredients. Our simplified version, using beer with the peel and tamarind, requires no fermentation; save the pineapple for dessert.

Serve rice with the stew.

Chicha Chicken Stew

1 cut-up broiler-fryer chicken (3½ to 4 lb.), fat discarded; rinsed

1½ teaspoons salad oil
Chicha (recipe follows)

2 chayotes (about ¾ lb. each; peel if skin is tough); or 1½ pounds pattypan squash, cut into 1-inch chunks

½ cup raisins

1 large (about ½-lb.) firm-ripe tomato, cored, peeled, and chopped
Thin slices fresh serrano or jalapeño chilies (optional)
Salt

Pat chicken dry. In a 5- to 6-quart pan over medium-high heat, brown chicken pieces in oil without crowding; set aside as browned. Discard oil. Return chicken, except breast pieces, to pan along with chicha, chayotes, and raisins. Bring to a boil over high heat; cover and simmer 20 minutes.

To pan, add tomato and breast pieces; simmer until thighs are very tender when pierced, 10 to 15 minutes longer. Add chilies and salt to taste. Serves 6 to 8.—*Marta Troche, San Francisco*

Per serving: 443 cal. (43 percent from fat); 27 g protein; 21 g fat (5.9 g sat.); 39 g carbo.; 108 mg sodium; 101 mg chol.

Chicha. Cut off and discard crown from a 3- to 4-pound **pineapple.** Rinse the fruit and cut off peel. Put half the peel in a 3- to 4-quart pan; discard remainder. Save fruit for other uses.

To pan, add 1 quart **water,** ¼ cup **distilled white vinegar,** ¾ cup **beer,** 1 **cinnamon stick** (about 3 in.), 4 **cloves,** and a ¼-pound piece **raw cane sugar** or ⅓ cup firmly packed dark brown sugar. Peel shells from 5

large (4- to 5-in.-long) **tamarind pods** (or use 3 tablespoons lemon juice); add to pan. Bring to a boil; cover and simmer for 2 hours.

Pour chicha through a fine strainer into a large bowl, pressing to extract liquid; discard seasonings. Use or, if making ahead, cover and chill up to 2 days.

HONDURAS AND BELIZE

These two countries share tropical produce, the sea's bounty along the Caribbean coast, and, particularly, the use of coconut.

When Marie L. Andrews of Honduras and Ruby Sylvester of Belize described traditional fish stews, the dishes' similarities were striking. Andrews' version is called *tapado;* Sylvester's is *serey.* Our simplified version, quick enough for weeknights, combines tangy yuca simmered in coconut milk with pan-browned fish.

Coconut Yuca with Fish

1 small (about 3-oz.) onion, chopped

1 large clove garlic, minced

3 tablespoons salad oil

1 teaspoon ground cumin

1 teaspoon pepper

1½ pounds fresh or frozen yuca or peeled thin-skinned potatoes

1 can (14 to 16 oz.) coconut milk

¼ cup all-purpose flour

4 pieces (5 to 6 oz. each) boned and skinned firm white-flesh fish such as rockfish or lingcod, rinsed

2 tablespoons minced fresh cilantro (coriander)
Fresh cilantro sprigs
Raw vegetable relish (recipe follows)
Salt

In a 3- to 4-quart pan over medium-high heat, stir onion and garlic often in 1 tablespoon oil until onion is limp, 5 to 10 minutes. Add ½ teaspoon *each* of cumin and pepper; stir for 1 minute.

Meanwhile, prepare fresh yuca as directed on page 177, or cut potatoes into 1½-inch chunks. (If using frozen yuca, cut up after cooking.)

Stir coconut milk into pan and bring to a boil over high heat. Add yuca; cover and simmer, turning several times, until tender when pierced, 40 to 50 minutes (20 to 25 minutes for potatoes).

Meanwhile, mix remaining cumin and pepper with flour. Coat fish with flour mixture, shaking off excess.

Pour remaining oil into a 10- to 12-inch frying pan over medium-high heat. When oil is hot, add fish and brown evenly; cook until no longer opaque but still moist-looking in center (cut to test), 10 to 12 minutes total, depending on thickness.

With a slotted spatula or spoon, transfer fish and yuca to plates and keep warm. Pour oil from frying pan and

discard. Scrape coconut sauce mixture into frying pan; stir to free browned bits. Skim off and discard fat on sauce; pour sauce into a small bowl. Sprinkle foods with minced cilantro; garnish plates and sauce with cilantro sprigs. Accompany with vegetable relish; add salt to taste. Serves 4.—*Marie L. Andrews*

Per serving: 519 cal. (43 percent from fat); 33 g protein; 25 g fat (17 g sat.); 42 g carbo.; 110 mg sodium; 50 mg chol.

Raw vegetable relish. Mix ½ cup coarsely chopped **onion,** ⅔ cup coarsely chopped **bell pepper,** ¼ cup **lemon juice,** 3 tablespoons **water,** 1 tablespoon **salad oil** (optional), and **salt** and **pepper** to taste. Let mixture stand at least 2 hours or cover and chill up to 3 days. Makes about 1¼ cups.

Per tablespoon: 2.8 cal. (0 percent from fat); 0.1 g protein; 0 g fat; 0.6 g carbo.; 0.8 mg sodium; 0 mg chol.

EL SALVADOR

Pupusas are El Salvador's equivalent of tacos, and *pupuserias* (pupusa shops) are quite common in Latino sections of Western cities. Instead of a cooked tortilla, masa dough is sealed around a filling, then toasted on a griddle until speckled with brown and hot in the center.

Once you get a feel for shaping the masa, pupusas are easy to make for snacks or a light meal. Monique Jerreda's family likes pupusas with melted cheese centers; she fills the dough with a mixture of cheeses. For dinner, she serves pupusas with the traditional accompaniments: refried beans, sour cream, guacamole, and *curtido,* a crisp cabbage relish that keeps up to a week.

Cheese Pupusas

2 cups dehydrated masa flour (corn tortilla flour)

¼ pound jack cheese

1 small package (3 oz.) cream cheese

6 ounces cotija or parmesan cheese

In a bowl, stir masa with a fork, gradually adding 1¼

TO SHAPE PUPUSAS, *make balls of masa and cheese filling (1), flatten masa (2), pinch around cheese (3), and pat into cakes.*
PETER CHRISTIANSEN

cups water until moistened and dough holds together.

As you shape pupusas, you need to moisten your hands frequently, so have a bowl of water available. Moisten hands; shape dough into 12 equal balls; cover.

Cut jack cheese, cream cheese, and cotija into chunks. Whirl smooth in a food processor. (Or finely shred jack and grate cotija. Stir with cream cheese until well mixed.) Moisten hands and shape cheese mixture into 12 equal balls; cover.

Pat 1 ball of masa between moistened hands to make a 4-inch round. Put 1 cheese ball in center; fold masa around cheese. Roll ball in palms to smoothly seal in cheese. Pat between palms to make a smooth 4-inch round; if masa cracks, moisten to smooth. If cheese breaks through, cover with a pinch of masa. If making ahead, stack pupusas with pieces of plastic wrap between them; seal in a plastic bag and chill up to 1 day.

Place a nonstick griddle or 2 nonstick frying pans, each 10 to 12 inches, over medium heat. (Or heat an electric griddle or frying pan to 350°.) When griddle is hot, lay pupusas slightly apart on it. Cook until brown on bottom; turn and brown other side, 8 to 12 minutes total. Serve hot, or keep warm until all are cooked. Makes 12, or 4 to 6 servings.—*Monique Jerreda, West Covina, California*

Per pupusa: 178 cal. (50 percent from fat); 8.2 g protein; 9.8 g fat (1.7 g sat.); 15 g carbo.; 320 mg sodium; 27 mg chol.

Curtido

3 cups finely slivered green or red cabbage, or a combination

½ teaspoon dried oregano leaves

⅓ cup chopped onion

1 fresh hot chili such as guerito (wax), Fresno, or jalapeño, stemmed and minced (optional)

1 dried bay leaf

1 small (about 2-oz.) carrot, cut diagonally into thin slices

⅓ cup distilled white vinegar

Salt (optional)

Mix cabbage, oregano, onion, and chili; put in a tall 1-quart glass or plastic container. Tuck bay leaf and carrot slices between glass and cabbage mixture. Mix vinegar, 1 teaspoon salt (if desired), and 1¾ cups water; pour over vegetables. Cover and chill at least 4 hours or up to 1 week. Serve with a slotted spoon. Makes about 3½ cups.

Per ¼ cup: 8.3 cal. (0 percent from fat); 0.3 g protein; 0 g fat; 2.1 g carbo.; 4.3 mg sodium; 0 mg chol.

PANAMA

"Our seasonings are very simple," says Annette Reynolds. She uses just cilantro, oregano, salt, and pepper in this beef stew with starchy root vegetables, including some native to Central America. The vegetables have become increasingly available in American markets.

As Panama is the bridge between two continents, it's not surprising that Panamanian foods, like the stew, reflect influences from north and south. The Caribbean imprint is also strong; one example is the use of pigeon peas. To go with the stew, combine cooked rice with hot canned pigeon peas (they're sold in Latino markets as *gandules*).

Beef Short Rib and Vegetable Stew

Although yuca, malanga, and ñame each has a distinctive taste and texture, you can simplify the stew by using just one of them—a total of 3 pounds. Or use 3 pounds potatoes, peeled and cut into 1½-inch chunks; cook as directed for ñame.

2 pounds beef short ribs, cut into 2-inch lengths, fat trimmed; or 1½ pounds boned beef short ribs, fat trimmed, cut into 2-inch chunks

2 quarts regular-strength beef or chicken broth

1 large (about ½-lb.) onion, cut into 1-inch chunks

2 medium-size (about ⅓ lb. total) Roma-type tomatoes, cored and thickly sliced

1 medium-size (6- to 7-oz.) green bell pepper, stemmed, seeded, and sliced

¼ cup chopped fresh cilantro (coriander)

1 teaspoon dried oregano leaves

1 large (about ¾-lb.) green plantain

1 pound fresh or frozen yuca

1 pound (about 3 medium-size) fresh or frozen malanga

1 pound fresh or frozen ñame

2 large (1½ lb. total) ears corn, silk and husks removed

Cilantro sprigs

Salt and pepper

Rinse meat and put in a 6- to 8-quart pan. Add broth, onion, tomatoes, bell pepper, chopped cilantro, and oregano; bring to a boil over high heat. Cover and simmer for 2 hours.

Meanwhile, prepare plantain, yuca, malanga, and ñame as directed on pages 176 and 177. Cut plantain into 1-inch lengths. Cut each corn ear into 4 equal pieces.

To pan, add plantain, yuca, malanga, and corn (add ñame later). Return to a boil over high heat; simmer, covered, for 15 minutes. Add ñame and simmer until meat and vegetables are tender when pierced, 20 to 30 minutes longer. Skim and discard fat. (If making ahead, cool, cover, and chill up to 2 days; reheat.) Garnish portions with cilantro sprigs and season to taste with salt and pepper. Serves 8.—*Annette Reynolds*

Per serving: 370 cal. (23 percent from fat); 22 g protein; 9.6 g fat (3.7 g sat.); 50 g carbo.; 83 mg sodium; 50 mg chol.

COSTA RICA

"Our Spanish heritage strongly influences Costa Rican food," says Marlen Campain. In her pork chop recipe, Spanish touches are the addition of garbanzos, capers, and olive oil. Worcestershire is frequently used in Costa Rica, particularly to season meats. Fried plantains are

well liked and often served with meals, filling the same menu role as potatoes.

But native ingredients—tomatoes and green pepper—hold their own. Tomatoes in cabbage salad and sautéed bell peppers with rice are popular in Costa Rica and throughout Central America.

Pork Chops, Spanish-style

6 center-cut pork chops (2¾ lb. total; each ¾ inch thick), fat trimmed

2 tablespoons Worcestershire

1 tablespoon olive oil

½ cup water

1 tablespoon drained canned capers

1 can (15 oz.) low-salt garbanzos, drained

Salt and pepper

In a bowl, rub pork with Worcestershire. In a 10- to 12-inch frying pan over medium-high heat, brown chops in oil, without crowding; discard oil. Return meat to pan and add water. Simmer, covered, for 10 minutes. Turn chops; add capers and garbanzos. Simmer, covered, until meat is no longer pink at bone (cut to test), about 5 minutes. Add salt and pepper to taste. Serves 6.—*Marlen Campain, Los Angeles*

Per serving: 307 cal. (38 percent from fat); 34 g protein; 13 g fat (3.7 g sat.); 13 g carbo.; 319 mg sodium; 86 mg chol.

Fried Ripe Plantains

3 medium-size ripe plantains (about 1½ lb. total; skin mostly black)

5 tablespoons butter or margarine

Peel plantains (see page 176); cut into ¾-inch-thick diagonal slices. In a 10- to 12-inch frying pan over medium heat, brown half the slices in half the butter, turning once, 5 to 8 minutes total; repeat to brown remaining slices. As cooked, keep warm on a platter in a 150° oven up to 45 minutes. Serves 6.

Per serving: 175 cal. (51 percent from fat); 1.1 g protein; 9.9 g fat (6 g sat.); 24 g carbo.; 101 mg sodium; 26 mg chol. ■

By Elaine Johnson

Manual slicers
for precision cuts

These cutting tools produce
ruffles, shreds, slices, strips

ARMED WITH THESE cutting tools, anyone can slash up a zucchini—and much more—with the speed and dexterity of Zorro. Slicing boards, boxes, and rotary slicers give you fine control for making slices equal to those found in Japanese and other fine restaurants. Turn zucchini into noodles, carrots into ruffles, and potatoes into waffle chips.

True, you can do the same with a knife, provided you have the patience and skill. But these tools don't just speed the job: for most of us, they make it possible.

These tools are fueled by hand power rather than electricity—you glide foods repeatedly over a blade or,

1 STAINLESS STEEL MANDOLINE. *Cadillac model of classic slicer comes from France. Adjustable blades, built into cutting platform, make julienne, waffle, zigzag, and smooth slices. About $150.*

2 PLASTIC MANDOLINE. *Simpler version of the French classic has three removable blades and a guard. Makes thick or thin slices, shreds, or julienne. Blades store under cutting platform. Costs $25 to $30.*

3 JAPANESE SLICING BOARDS. *Plastic version fits over bowl, has four removable blades and a notched end for zigzag cuts; $12 to $15. Wooden model has two built-in thick and thin julienne blades; about $6.*

PETER CHRISTIANSEN

sometimes, turn a handle. The design of the blade determines the shape of the results; in some cutters, you can make mechanical adjustments to control thickness. The Japanese rotary slicers produce a single continuous slice or strand as you rotate the vegetable—held in place above the stationary blade.

The length of a cut is often determined by the food itself. Choose sides: slice a carrot lengthwise for long strands, from an end for short pieces.

These tools are priced from $3 to $150. Depending on needs, some cooks will find the least expensive just as useful as the most costly. Some slicers make only one kind of cut, while others make more with different blades. Some can be adjusted, some have guards to protect fingers, and, certainly, some are more durable than others.

You will find these slicers where specialty cooking equipment is sold, including department and hardware stores. Japanese cutters are also sold in Japanese hardwares or food markets. ∎

By Linda Lau Anusasananan

4 BOX CUTTER. *Compactly holds four blades and a vegetable peeler in a plastic box. The cut foods collect in box. About $17.*

5 ROTARY SLICER. *Japanese model turns food over stationary blade to produce continuous ruffly slices or strands. Costs $40 to $125.*

6 CUTTING BOARDS. *Set of three boards has four hammer-tempered blades to slice, grate, coarse-shred, or fine-shred. About $10.*

7 ROTARY CUTTER. *French model presses food against rotating blade to cut. Has three blades. About $15.*

8 STANDARD BOX CUTTER. *Basic model has different-texture cutting surface on each side. Costs $3 to $14.*

Southwest beans

ENJOY THEIR
GOOD LOOKS
AND GOOD
TASTE

Beans native to the American Southwest and Mexico are finding their way into markets, onto restaurant menus—and now into home kitchens. These are bean varieties that date back hundreds or even thousands of years, with such descriptive names as 'Anasazi', once grown by cliff dwellers of ancient New Mexico, and 'Montezuma Red Twiner', said to be discovered in 3,000-year-old Mayan tombs.

Long touted by nutritionists for their low fat and high protein, fiber, and mineral content, dried beans like these Southwest natives are also gaining status for their delicious versatility.

You may come upon these fancifully named and often eye-catching dried beans in a specialty market. After you bring them home, store them in an airtight container until you're ready to cook them. To kill any weevils or eggs that can come in on beans (especially if sold in bulk), place beans in a freezer overnight.

Mail order sources for many of the beans are listed on page 62.

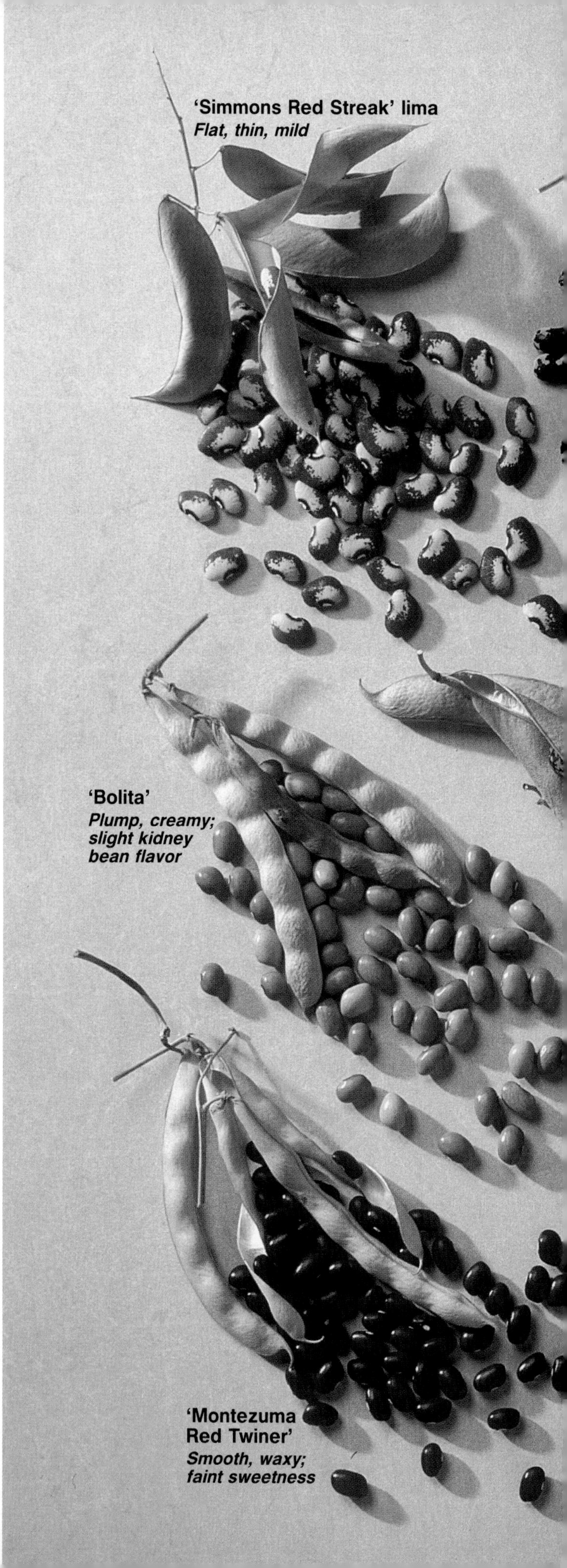

'Simmons Red Streak' lima
Flat, thin, mild

'Bolita'
Plump, creamy; slight kidney bean flavor

'Montezuma Red Twiner'
Smooth, waxy; faint sweetness

'New Mexico Appaloosa'
Smooth, creamy, mild

'Anasazi'
Creamy, smooth; cooks quickly

'Hopi Red' lima
Mealy, mild; peppery skin; cooks up plump

'Aztec Dwarf White'
Plump; mashed potato texture

'Mitla Black'
Small, firm, dense, creamy, mild

'Aztec Scarlet Runner'
Meaty, firm; chestnut-like flavor

'Blue Speckled' tepary
Small, firm, dry, mild

MAIL-ORDER SOURCES

These three catalogs offer beans for cooking.

The Bean Bag, 818 Jefferson St., Oakland, CA 94607; (800) 845-2326. 'Anasazi', 'New Mexico Appaloosa', 'Hopi White' lima, scarlet runner, and brown and white tepary.

Gallina Canyon Ranch, 144 Camino Escondido, Santa Fe, NM 87501; (505) 982-4149. 'New Mexico Appaloosa', scarlet runner.

Phipps Ranch, Box 349, 2700 Pescadero Rd., Pescadero, CA 94060; (415) 879-0787. 'Anasazi', 'New Mexico Appaloosa', 'Bolita', scarlet runner, 'White Aztec' (pueblo), brown and white tepary.

COOKING DRIED BEANS

If you soak dried beans, cooking time is reduced by about half. Some feel soaking reduces factors that cause indigestion and gas as well.

Soaked dried beans. Sort and discard foreign matter from 1 pound (2 to 2¾ cups) **dried beans**. Rinse beans and place in a 5- to 6-quart pan; add 2½ quarts **water**. Let stand at least 8 hours or up to 12 hours; drain and rinse. To speed the process, bring beans and water to a boil; boil 2 to 3 minutes. Cover; cool at least 1 hour or up to 4 hours. Drain and rinse.

Cooked Southwest soaked beans. To a 5- to 6-quart pan, add 3 quarts **water** for each pound (dry weight) **soaked dried beans** (directions precede). Bring to a boil; simmer, covered, until beans are tender to bite (add more water to cover if necessary), 25 minutes to 2 hours. Time depends on how long beans have been stored (those older than a year may never soften) and how they were soaked. Drain. Use, store airtight in refrigerator up to 3 days, or freeze up to 3 months. Each pound of dried

beans yields 6 to 7 cups cooked.

Use one kind of bean or a mixture in the following recipes. To maintain their shape, cook each bean variety separately, then mix in recipe. If shape doesn't matter (as in the taco filling), cook a variety of beans together; some may fall apart. Many beans change color when cooked.

You can substitute pinto, lima, small white, red, pink, or black beans from your supermarket.

Bean and Tomato Salad

⅓ cup orange juice

¼ cup balsamic vinegar

1 tablespoon extra-virgin olive oil

2 tablespoons chopped fresh or 1 tablespoon dried basil leaves

4 cups cooked, cooled Southwest beans (directions precede)

4 large (about 10 oz. each) firm-ripe tomatoes, cored

Fresh basil sprigs (optional)

Salt and pepper

In a bowl, mix together the orange juice, vinegar, olive oil, chopped basil, and cooked beans.

Thinly slice tomatoes crosswise. Divide tomatoes equally among six plates. Mound bean mixture equally

on tomatoes. Garnish with basil sprigs; add salt and pepper to taste. Serves 6.
—David Tanis, Cafe Escalera, Santa Fe

Per serving: 225 cal. (14 percent from fat); 11 g protein; 3.4 g fat (0.5 g sat.); 40 g carbo.; 21 mg sodium; 0 mg chol.

Bean and Hominy Stew

1 teaspoon salad oil

1 teaspoon cumin seed

1 large (about ½-lb.) onion, chopped

2 cloves garlic, minced or pressed

2 tablespoons all-purpose flour

1 quart regular-strength chicken broth

2 cans (7 oz. each) diced green chilies

6 to 7 cups cooked Southwest beans (directions precede)

1 can (14½ oz.) golden hominy, drained

⅓ cup chopped fresh cilantro (coriander)

Cilantro sprigs (optional)

Salt

In a 4- to 5-quart pan, combine oil, cumin, onion, and garlic. Stir over medium heat until onion is limp, about 7 minutes. Stir in flour to coat onion. Gradually stir in broth until blended; stir until broth boils. Mix in chilies, beans, and hominy. Cover and simmer until hot, about 15 min-

utes. Stir in chopped cilantro. Ladle into bowls or a tureen. Garnish with cilantro sprigs; add salt to taste. Serves 7 or 8.

Per serving: 283 cal. (8 percent from fat); 15 g protein; 2.5 g fat (0.5 g sat.); 51 g carbo.; 445 mg sodium; 0 mg chol.

Soft Tacos with Beans

12 corn tortillas (5- to 6-in. size)

1 large (about ½-lb.) onion, chopped

¼ cup ground New Mexico or California chilies

1 tablespoon all-purpose flour

1 teaspoon ground coriander

1 cup regular-strength chicken broth

3 to 3½ cups cooked Southwest beans (cooking directions precede)

2 cups shredded lettuce

1 cup (¼ lb.) shredded cheddar or jack cheese

¾ cup sour cream (optional)

Lime wedges

Salt

Lightly brush tortillas with water and stack. Wrap tortillas in foil and place in a 325° oven until hot and steamy, about 20 minutes.

In a 3- to 4-quart pan, stir onion in 2 tablespoons water over medium-high heat until onion is limp and tinged with brown, about 10 minutes. Stir in chilies, flour, and coriander. Gradually blend in broth. Stir until mixture boils. Reduce heat; add beans. Simmer, covered, until beans are hot, about 5 minutes; stir occasionally. Remove 1 cup beans from pan and coarsely mash; return to pan.

Present beans, tortillas, lettuce, cheese, sour cream, and lime wedges in separate bowls. To make tacos, fill tortillas with beans, lettuce, cheese, and sour cream; add lime juice and salt to taste and roll up to eat. Makes 4 servings.

Per serving: 573 cal. (24 percent from fat); 28 g protein; 15 g fat (6.2 g sat.); 87 g carbo.; 434 mg sodium; 30 mg chol. ■

By Lauren Bonar Swezey, Linda Lau Anusasananan

NORMAN A. PLATE

MULTIHUED BEANS *star in a salad with tomatoes and a citrus dressing. Use one or several bean varieties.*

ONE DOUGH *is the quick route to three very different breads: from left, rosemary and garlic fougasse, poppy seed bow ties, oat-speckled triangles.*

DARROW M. WATT

Yeast rolls, from mixing bowl to table in an hour

We give ways to speed up the process, and choices of seasonings and shapes

HOT, AROMATIC YEAST rolls made from scratch in just an hour? They're reality when you speed up the process by doubling the yeast, using hot liquid, kneading dough in seconds in a food processor (with the choice of a longer hand-kneading alternative), and letting dough rise only once.

For versatility, you have three ways to season and shape the dough.

One-hour Dinner Rolls

About 2¼ cups all-purpose flour

½ cup cornmeal

2 packages active dry yeast

1 tablespoon sugar

½ teaspoon salt

¾ cup milk

1 tablespoon butter or margarine

1 large egg

Seasonings and shapes (directions follow)

In a food processor, whirl 2¼ cups flour, cornmeal, yeast, sugar, and salt. (Or mix in a bowl.) Heat milk and butter to 130°; use microwave-safe bowl in a microwave oven at full power (100 percent), or a 1- to 1½-quart pan on medium-high heat.

With motor running, pour milk mixture, then egg, into processor. Whirl until dough pulls cleanly from container, about 1 minute. If dough is sticky to touch and clings to container, whirl in more flour, 1 tablespoon at a time. (Or add hot liquid to flour mixture, beat thoroughly, and add egg. Beat with a spoon until dough is stretchy.)

On a floured board, knead dough briefly to form a smooth ball. (Or knead by hand until smooth and elastic, 8 to 10 minutes.) Season and shape in any of the 3 following ways. Cover lightly with plastic wrap. Let dough rise in a warm place (80° to 90°) until puffy, 15 to 20 minutes; uncover.

Bake rolls in a 400° oven until well browned, 15 to 20 minutes; serve hot or cool. If making ahead, cool on racks and store airtight up to 1 day. Freeze to store longer. Makes 12 servings fougasse, 16 poppy seed bow ties, or 12 rolled-oat triangles.

Per serving fougasse: 159 cal. (25 percent from fat); 4.4 g protein; 4.5 g fat (1.4 g sat.); 25 g carbo.; 115 mg sodium; 22 mg chol.

Per bow tie: 111 cal. (19 percent from fat); 3.6 g protein; 2.3 g fat (0.9 g sat.); 19 g carbo.; 88 mg sodium; 23 mg chol.

Per triangle: 158 cal. (15 percent from fat); 5.3 g protein; 2.7 g fat (1.2 g sat.); 28 g carbo.; 117 mg sodium; 30 mg chol.

Seasonings and shapes.

Fougasse. In a 6- to 8-inch frying pan over medium-high heat, stir 2 tablespoons **olive oil,** 1 large clove minced **garlic,** and 2 teaspoons **dried rosemary leaves** until garlic is pale gold, about 2 minutes.

Roll dough on floured board to make a 9- by 12-inch oval; spread with garlic mixture. With a floured 2-inch-wide biscuit cutter, cut 6 rounds, 1 inch apart, and 1 inch from rim of oval. Transfer dough oval to an oiled 12- by 15-inch baking sheet. Fit rounds onto pan around oval, without touching oval. Let rise and continue as directed, preceding.

Poppy seed bow ties. You'll need 1½ tablespoons beaten **egg** and 2 tablespoons **poppy seed.**

Shape dough into a 12-inch log. Brush all over with egg, then pat poppy seed onto dough to cover.

With a sharp knife, cut dough into ¾-inch-thick rounds. Hold each round on opposite sides and twist ½ over to form a bow. Place bows slightly apart on an oiled 12- by 15-inch baking sheet. Let rise and continue as directed, preceding.

Rolled-oat triangles. You'll need 1½ tablespoons beaten **egg** and ⅔ cup **regular rolled oats.**

On floured board, roll dough into a 5- by 12-inch rectangle. Brush with egg, then sprinkle with oats; turn rectangle over and repeat.

With a sharp, floured knife, cut across narrow width of dough, making 3 equal sections.

Through each section, make 2 diagonal cuts (from the corners) to create 4 triangles. Lay triangles slightly apart on an oiled 12- by 15-inch baking sheet. Let rise and continue as directed, preceding. ■

By Elaine Johnson

Quick and colorful soup and salad

You build them around beans, canned and convenient

AVING SOARED FROM humble to healthful in the public eye, beans are making more menu appearances these days, and justly so. Not only do they offer fiber, protein, and little fat, but they also come canned and ready to use in quick, nutritious, and good-tasting dishes.

Both the two-tone soup and the colorful salad are striking to look at. The soup gets its hues from purées of canned black beans and canned white cannellini beans, poured deftly to preserve their identities. The salad combines the cannellini with chicken breasts and tomatoes for a main dish.

Black and White Bean Soup

1 large (½ lb.) onion, chopped

1 clove garlic

3½ cups regular-strength chicken broth

⅓ cup (2 oz.) drained oil-packed dried tomatoes, minced

4 green onions, ends trimmed, minced

¼ cup dry sherry

BOLDLY CONTRASTING COLORS *and flavors of seasoned black beans and white cannellini beans dramatically hold their places but blend as eaten in first-course soup.*

NORMAN A. PLATE

2 cans (15 oz. each) black beans, rinsed and drained

2 cans (15 oz. each) cannellini (white kidney) beans, rinsed and drained

Slivered green onion (optional)

Place onion and garlic in a 5- to 6-quart pan over high heat. Add ½ cup water; stir often and boil until liquid evaporates and browned bits stick in pan. Add 2 tablespoons broth and stir to release browned bits; stir often until liquid evaporates and browned bits form again. Repeat step with 2 more tablespoons broth. Scrape browned bits free with ½ cup broth; pour mixture into a blender or food processor.

In the same pan, combine tomatoes and minced green onions over high heat. Stir until onions are wilted, about 2 minutes. Add sherry and stir until liquid evaporates; remove from heat.

To onion and garlic mixture add black beans; whirl, gradually adding 1¼ cups broth until smoothly puréed. Pour into a 3- to 4-quart pan.

Rinse blender or food processor; add cannellini beans and whirl, gradually adding remaining 1½ cups broth until smoothly puréed. Stir into pan with tomato mixture. Set both pans of soup on medium-high heat; stir often until steaming.

From pans (or 2 lipped containers such as 1-qt. measures or pitchers, which are easier to handle), pour soups simultaneously into opposite sides of a wide, 1½- to 2-cup soup bowl so mixtures flow together but do not mix. Repeat to fill 5 more bowls. Garnish with slivered green onion. Serves 6.

Per serving: 260 cal. (23 percent from fat); 15 g protein; 6.5 g fat (0.9 g sat.); 36 g carbo.; 725 mg sodium; 0 mg chol.

White Bean, Chicken, and Bacon Salad

½ cup malt or cider vinegar

¼ cup regular-strength chicken broth

2 tablespoons extra-virgin olive oil or salad oil

2 tablespoons minced fresh or 1 teaspoon crumbled dried sage leaves

1 teaspoon sugar

2 cans (15 oz. each) cannellini (white kidney) beans, rinsed and drained

4 boned and skinned chicken breast halves (about 1 lb. total)

6 to 8 large leaves leaf lettuce, rinsed and crisped

1¼ pounds Roma-type tomatoes, cored and thinly sliced

4 slices bacon, cooked and crumbled

Fresh sage sprigs (optional)

Salt and pepper

Mix together vinegar, broth, oil, sage, and sugar. Place beans in a bowl and add ⅓ cup of the dressing; mix well. If making ahead, cover and chill bean mixture and remaining dressing up to 1 day. Bring to room temperature to use.

Rinse chicken and pat dry. Bring 2 quarts water to boiling in a 4- to 5-quart pan over high heat. Add chicken and remove pan from heat at once; cover and let stand undisturbed until you're ready to check chicken for doneness, about 20 minutes. Cut a small slit in center of thickest part of chicken; if no longer pink, remove from water. If pink, return to hot water and let stand until meat is white in center; check every 5 minutes.

Let chicken cool (to speed this step, immerse in ice water until cold, then drain and pat dry). Cut chicken diagonally into ½-inch-thick slices. Arrange lettuce on a platter. Spoon bean salad onto 1 section of platter; arrange chicken in another space and tomato slices in yet another. Spoon remaining dressing over tomatoes and chicken, then sprinkle salad with bacon, garnish with sage, and add salt and pepper to taste. Serves 4.

Per serving: 408 cal. (29 percent from fat); 40 g protein; 13 g fat (2.6 g sat.); 33 g carbo.; 453 mg sodium; 71 mg chol. ■

By Christine B. Weber

DARROW M. WATT

POUR HOT DRESSING *flavored with Dijon mustard and dill over shrimp and spinach.*

Cool salads, warm dressings

These two are main dishes, using cabbage or spinach and shrimp

CRISP, COOL GREENS mixed with a hot dressing create a main-dish salad that seems more substantial than its calorie count suggests.

A popular old standby, wilted spinach and bacon salad, is the inspiration for these two recipes, one using tender napa cabbage, the other spinach leaves. But they differ with a purpose: the dressings are very low in fat, and leaner shrimp replace the bacon. If you want to get a head start, arrange salad greens and shrimp in a serving bowl, cover, and chill for several hours. You can also measure dressing ingredients.

Warm Cabbage and Shrimp Salad

- 1 large (about 2½ lb.) napa cabbage, rinsed and drained
- ¾ pound shelled cooked tiny shrimp, rinsed and drained
- ¼ cup regular-strength chicken broth or water
- 3 tablespoons smooth peanut butter
- 3 tablespoons rice vinegar
- 2 tablespoons berry jelly
- 1 teaspoon soy sauce
- 1 clove garlic, minced or pressed
- 4 green onions, ends trimmed, thinly sliced

Cut cabbage crosswise into ¼-inch-wide strips. Put in a wide, shallow bowl; top with shrimp. Chill airtight up to 4 hours or continue.

In a 1- to 1½-quart pan over medium-high heat, stir broth, peanut butter, vinegar, jelly, soy sauce, and garlic until bubbling. Pour hot dressing over cabbage and shrimp; mix well. Sprinkle with onions and serve at once. Makes 6 to 8 servings.

Per serving: 118 cal.; 13 g protein; 3.9 g fat (0.7 g sat.); 9.6 g carbo.; 182 mg sodium; 83 mg chol.

Spinach and Shrimp Salad with Warm Mustard Dressing

- 12 cups (about 2¼ lb.) firmly packed rinsed and drained spinach leaves
- ¾ pound shelled cooked tiny shrimp
- 1 teaspoon cornstarch
- 1 tablespoon sugar
- 1 tablespoon rice vinegar
- ¼ cup regular-strength chicken broth or water
- ⅓ cup Dijon mustard
- 2 tablespoons minced fresh dill or 1½ teaspoons dried dill weed

Cut spinach into about ⅜-inch-wide strips. Put spinach in a wide, shallow bowl; top with shrimp. Chill airtight up to 4 hours or continue.

In a 1- to 1½-quart pan, mix cornstarch and sugar. Smoothly mix in vinegar, broth, and mustard. Over high heat, stir until boiling; add dill. Pour hot dressing over salad. Mix well and serve at once. Makes 6 to 8 servings.

Per serving: 91 cal.; 13 g protein; 1.6 g fat (0.2 g sat.); 7.8 g carbo.; 495 mg sodium; 83 mg chol. ∎

By Karyn I. Lipman

Why?

Why does meat brown? Why brown it? Why does it sometimes get gray and soupy?

WHEN DAYS ARE brisk, warming stews, braised dishes, and soups that depend on meat for flavor and substance are appealing. But in making these dishes, questions about browning meat invariably pop up. Answers to three very common questions follow.

NORMAN A. PLATE

FORCE MEAT *(left) to ooze juices; boil dry to brown residue (right), then braise.*

Why does meat brown?

Heat makes meat brown by setting in motion chemical changes that develop color and flavor compounds not present when the meat is raw. Meat is composed of protein and fat, with 75 percent water interspersed among the protein fibers. Heated protein starts to coagulate (firm) and shrink, squeezing out the liquid and melting some of the intramuscular fat.

Heat also evaporates meat juices, and their residue undergoes color and flavor changes much like meat does. If cooked enough, the residue turns a very dark brown and develops a mellow, sweet flavor as it caramelizes. If you're overly cautious about scorching or burning, the sauce won't get the full, rich color the residue can give.

If you are going to cook meat in liquid, why brown it first?

Browning contributes rich flavor and appetizing color changes to the meat. Also, the browned residue of evaporated meat juices, rinsed free by the cooking liquid, adds a dark color and richly flavored essence that is absorbed by the meat and other foods cooked with it.

Why does pan-browned meat sometimes end up in a soupy gray mess?

Meat browns quickly if there is enough heat and if the pan isn't too crowded for the juices to evaporate.

As meat continues to cook, juices flow (claims that searing holds in meat juices have long been disproved). If you rush and overload the pan, the pan cools down and juices accumulate. In short order, you switch from browning to boiling; the meat ceases to brown and turns gray.

Can you still get a browned flavor when this happens?

Yes. If you continue to cook the mixture, uncovered, on medium-high to high heat, the liquid will evaporate and its residue will brown.

How to sweat and deglaze meat

The most typical way to brown chunks of meat is to dust them with flour, then brown them in small batches in a little fat over relatively high heat. Generally, all you can brown effectively at one time in a 10- to 12-inch-wide pan is ⅓ to ½ pound of meat.

The drawbacks? You have to add fat, and the flour and meat both absorb some of it. You have to turn the chunks. As meat juices seep, they spatter wildly in the fat— broadcasting a greasy film.

In *Sunset*'s test kitchens, we've developed another way to brown meat. It's a two-step process we call sweat-deglazing. You'll find these steps used in many *Sunset* recipes because they produce more succulent results, develop richer flavor than flour-browned meat, take less effort, make less mess, and need no fat. These steps can actually help you reduce fat in a dish.

You can use the procedure (following) in any dish that calls for browning meat before simmering in liquid— including soups and sauces.

Sweat-deglazing. Instead of fighting meats' natural tendency to ooze, take advantage of it. Force the meat to sweat—squeeze out juice as heat shrinks the protein.

Place meat chunks in a pan (they can be stacked). Add just enough liquid (water, broth, wine) to make ¼ to ½ inch in pan bottom. Cover and cook over medium to medium-high heat until meat is very juicy and juices are boiling rapidly, about 30 minutes for 2 to 3 pounds of meat.

Uncover and cook over medium-high to high heat, stirring often, until juices evaporate, turn dark brown, and either stick to pan or mostly on meat (when using a nonstick pan). Discard fat.

To deglaze (free the browned materials), add to pan 3 to 4 tablespoons water or the liquid used in recipe; scrape film or bits free.

To intensify color and flavor, boil again, uncovered, until the brown film forms; deglaze. For more concentrated flavor, repeat this step several times. The meat may look gray, but the liquid will be very dark brown.

If your recipe calls for browned chopped vegetables (onions, garlic, celery), add raw chopped vegetables to pan now, along with 3 to 4 tablespoons liquid. Cook uncovered, stirring often, until liquid evaporates and vegetables begin to brown.

Add liquid and seasonings, as your recipe directs. Simmer, covered, until the meat is very tender when pierced; by now it will have absorbed brown color.

More questions?

If you encounter other cooking mysteries and would like to know why they happened, send your question to Why?, *Sunset Magazine,* 80 Willow Rd., Menlo Park, Calif. 94025. With the help of Dr. George K. York, extension food technologist at UC Davis, *Sunset* food editors will find the solutions. ∎

By Linda Lau Anusasananan

PETER CHRISTIANSEN

STREW CARAMELIZED *sugar-coated nuts over buttery, lemon-scented crumbs in pan. Baked (right), the crumbs and nuts fuse to make a crumbly, shortbread-textured cookie. Serve wedges with cappuccino or espresso.*

Not a pizza, it's a cookie torte

It's crunchy with candied nuts

ANDIED ALMONDS, pistachios, and pine nuts emblazon this crunchy cookie torte. It goes together quickly and easily—either mixed by hand or in a food processor.

Candied Nut Cookie Torte

¾ cup sugar

2 tablespoons plus ½ cup blanched almonds

3 tablespoons shelled pistachios

3 tablespoons pine nuts

1⅓ cups all-purpose flour

½ teaspoon grated lemon peel

About ½ cup (¼ lb.) butter or margarine, cut into small chunks

1 tablespoon lemon juice

In an 8- to 10-inch frying pan over medium-high heat, shake 3 tablespoons sugar often until it melts and turns golden, 5 to 7 minutes. Remove from heat and add 2 tablespoons almonds, the pistachios, and pine nuts. Quickly stir to coat nuts with melted sugar; pour mixture onto a sheet of buttered foil and let cool.

Meanwhile, whirl remaining ½ cup almonds in a blender or food processor until finely ground. To nuts in the processor, add ½ cup sugar, flour, and lemon peel; whirl to mix. (Or pour nuts from blender into a bowl; mix with ½ cup sugar, flour, and peel.) Add ½ cup butter and whirl or rub with your fingers to make fine, even crumbs. Sprinkle lemon juice over mixture and mix to blend well.

Spread crumbs evenly in a 9-inch-diameter cake pan with removable rim. Break apart the candied nuts and scatter them over crumbs, then press nuts lightly into crumbs. Sprinkle torte evenly with the remaining 1 tablespoon sugar.

Bake in a 325° oven until cookie is a rich golden color, 45 to 50 minutes. Let cool in pan at least 10 minutes; remove rim. Either serve torte from pan bottom or slide spatula between torte and pan, and slip torte onto a flat plate. Serve warm or cool. If making ahead, let cool, wrap airtight, and store up to 1 week. Cut into wedges. Makes 8 servings.

Per serving: 351 cal. (54 percent from fat); 6 g protein; 21 g fat (8.2 g sat.); 38 g carbo.; 120 mg sodium; 31 mg chol. ∎

By Linda Lau Anusasananan

LOOK FOR *fruit juice concentrates that have no added sugar. Make small batches of jelly; store in refrigerator.*

Tangy jams and jellies start with concentrates

NO SUGAR ADDED jams and jellies often have a base of fruit concentrate. When juice is concentrated, liquid is removed and the fruit's natural sugar, fructose, becomes intense enough to sweeten preserves.

To make your own no-sugar preserves, start with frozen apple juice concentrate—plain, flavored with another fruit concentrate or mint, or mixed with fruit. You also need packaged pectin designed for low- or no-sugar preserves to get thick, spoonable jams and jellies.

Do you save calories? No. But the preserves have a refreshing, faintly tart fruit flavor, and, for some people, fructose is more digestible than sucrose.

All-Apple or Apple-Raspberry Jelly

2 cans (12 oz. each) unsweetened frozen apple juice or apple-raspberry juice concentrate

1 package (2 oz.) dry pectin for jams and jellies made with little or no sugar

Partially thaw concentrate and add enough water to make 1 quart; pour into a 5- to 6-quart pan. Add pectin; stir until dissolved, about 10 minutes. Scrape the pan sides often.

On medium-high heat, stir until boiling. On high heat, bring to a rolling boil that can't be stirred down; boil exactly 1 minute. Off the heat, skim off foam. Pour hot liquid into 1- to 2-cup jars to within ½ inch of rims.

Wipe rims clean, then cover with lids. Let jelly cool; serve or chill up to 3 months. Makes 4 cups.

Per tablespoon: 25 cal. (0 percent from fat); 0.1 g protein; 0 g fat; 6.1 g carbo.; 3.4 mg sodium; 0 mg chol.

Apple-Mint Jelly

Follow recipe for **all-apple jelly** (preceding) but flavor apple juice concentrate and water with 1 cup firmly packed **fresh mint leaves.** Heat to boiling. Cover; let cool. Pour through a strainer into a bowl; discard leaves.

Rinse pan, then add liquid and pectin; continue as directed. Or, instead of boiling the fresh mint, add ¼ teaspoon **mint extract** after skimming the hot liquid.

Per tablespoon: 25 cal. (0 percent from fat); 0.1 g protein; 0 g fat; 6.1 g carbo.; 3.4 mg sodium; 0 mg chol.

Apple-Blueberry Jam

Follow recipe for **all-apple jelly** (preceding), adding 1 package (12 to 16 oz.) **frozen unsweetened blueberries** to juice concentrate and water.

Boil on high heat, uncovered, until reduced to 1 quart; stir often. Let cool, then add pectin; continue as directed.

Per tablespoon: 28 cal. (3.2 percent from fat); 0.1 g protein; 0.1 g fat (0 g sat.); 6.8 g carbo.; 3.3 mg sodium; 0 mg chol. ■

By Karyn I. Lipman

APPLE JUICE CONCENTRATE *gives jams and jellies their sweetness and mildly tart flavor; pectin thickens them.*

Stellar make-ahead dessert

Strawberries and frothy sabayon sauce top star-shaped meringues

THIS DRAMATIC dessert is the creation of pastry chef Emily Luchetti. In the combination of individual almond meringues, strawberries, and a frothy sauce she captures some of the same magic she displays at Stars, one of San Francisco's liveliest restaurants.

You can make the meringues, berry sauce, and champagne sabayon (a French version of Italian zabaglione) in advance, then dazzle your guests by assembling the components before their appreciative eyes.

Almond Meringue Stars with Berries and Champagne Sabayon

4   large egg whites
½   teaspoon cream of tartar
1   cup sugar
3   tablespoons finely minced toasted almonds

Champagne sabayon (recipe follows)

Strawberry sauce (recipe follows)

3   cups sliced strawberries

To make meringues. Line 2 baking sheets, each 12 by 15 inches, with cooking parchment; or butter and dust sheets with flour. On each sheet trace 3 stars, each about 6 inches across (use knife tip on floured sheets).

In large bowl of an electric mixer, beat egg whites and cream of tartar at high speed until foamy. Gradually add the sugar (about 1 tablespoon every 45 seconds), scraping the side of the bowl occasionally. Beat until meringue holds straight, very stiff peaks when beaters are lifted. Fold in almonds. If using parchment, glue corners to pans with a little meringue.

Spoon meringue into a pastry bag fitted with a ½-inch plain or fluted tip (or use a spoon instead of pastry bag). Pipe or spoon meringue about ½ inch thick onto baking sheets to evenly cover star shapes. About ½ inch from edges of each star, pipe or spoon on additional meringue into a rim about ½ inch thick and ½ inch wide.

Bake stars in a 225° oven until centers are firm to touch and meringues just begin to turn very pale gold, about 2 hours; switch pan positions halfway through baking. Turn off oven and let meringues stand until cool, 2 to 2½ hours. Gently release meringues. If making ahead, store airtight up to 3 days.

To assemble desserts. Place each meringue on a plate. Spoon a little of the champagne sabayon in center of stars and partway around them. Then spoon a little strawberry sauce in empty space around stars. Spoon strawberries onto meringues. Accompany with additional sabayon and sauce. Makes 6 servings.

Per serving 356 cal. (30 percent from fat); 6.4 g protein; 12 g fat (5.1 g sat.); 56 g carbo.; 51 mg sodium; 164 mg chol.

Champagne sabayon. In a large metal bowl whisk 4 large **egg yolks,** ¼ cup **sugar,** and ⅓ cup slightly sweet (extra-dry or sec) **champagne,** or brut or extra-dry sparkling wine. Fill another bowl, large enough to contain the first bowl, ¼ full of ice water; set aside.

Nest sabayon bowl in a pan over 1 inch simmering water. Vigorously whisk until sabayon thickens and mounds slightly, 4 to 6 minutes; if overcooked, the sabayon may curdle.

Immediately nest sabayon bowl over bowl of ice water; whisk until sabayon is cold, about 5 minutes.

In another bowl, beat ½ cup **whipping cream** until it holds soft peaks; fold into sabayon. If making ahead, chill airtight up to 3 hours.

Strawberry sauce. In a blender, whirl 3 cups hulled **strawberries** until puréed. Rub through a fine strainer over a bowl; discard seeds. Stir in 1 tablespoon **sugar** and 1 teaspoon **lemon juice.** If making ahead, chill airtight up to 1 day. ∎

By Elaine Johnson

Whisk sabayon over hot water until it's thick and mounding slightly.

Beat meringue until it holds straight, very stiff peaks when beater is lifted.

Pipe meringue rim ½ inch from star edges.

DESIGNED TO DAZZLE, *star-shaped almond meringues are topped with sliced strawberries and champagne sabayon. Meringues can be made ahead; store airtight up to 3 days.*

Ham and eggs pizza— for breakfast

Or could we interest you in dried tomato canapé spread?

PIZZA FOR BREAKFAST? Why not, especially if it contains ham and eggs? This showy pizza, its crust formed by a purchased Italian bread shell, is an impressive way to serve breakfast or brunch at a family gathering. Remember when scrambling the eggs that they will continue to cook under the broiler as the cheese topping melts— so you may want the eggs a tad soft when you put them in the bread shell.

Gardner Cook's recipe does not call for additional toppings, but if you set out ripe black olives, chopped tomatoes, marinated artichoke hearts, or whatever, they will mysteriously disappear.

Breakfast Pizza

10 large eggs
½ cup thinly sliced green onions, including tops
¾ cup coarsely chopped turkey ham
1 tablespoon butter or margarine
1 large (12-in.-wide, 1-lb.) refrigerated or frozen baked Italian bread shell
1 cup *each* (¼ lb. each) shredded jack cheese and shredded sharp cheddar cheese

In a bowl, beat eggs to blend with onions and ham. In a 10- to 12-inch frying pan over medium heat, melt butter; add egg mixture. As eggs cook, lift cooked portions to allow uncooked eggs to flow underneath. Cook until eggs are set but still very moist on top.

Meanwhile, set bread shell on a 12- by 15-inch baking sheet. Sprinkle shell with jack cheese. Broil about 4 inches from heat until cheese melts, 1 to 2 minutes.

Spoon egg mixture evenly onto melted cheese; sprinkle eggs with cheddar cheese and broil until it melts, about 1 minute. Cut into wedges. Makes 8 servings.

Per serving: 386 cal. (49 percent from fat); 24 g protein; 21 g fat (6 g sat.); 26 g carbo.; 702 mg sodium; 308 mg chol.

Sausalito, California

MERLE ALEXANDER shares with us this recipe. It combines two of his family's favorite desserts (Mom's apple pie and Aunt Hattie's pecan pie). The result is praline apple pie, and it is a no-holds-barred, take-no-prisoners, devastatingly rich finish to a special meal. The apple portion of the filling is straight- *(Continued on page 197)* forward classical apple pie.

The praline is not the powdered nut brittle of classical French cooking but a spiritual descendant combining sugar, corn syrup, eggs, and flavoring to create a dark, rich custard like that of a traditional pecan pie. The pecans display themselves on the top of the apple layer.

Praline Apple Pie

2 pounds tart apples, such as Newtown, Pippin, or Granny Smith

1 tablespoon butter or margarine

2 tablespoons granulated sugar

1 tablespoon lemon juice

½ teaspoon ground nutmeg

Pastry for a single-crust 9-inch pie

2 large eggs

½ cup firmly packed brown sugar

¾ cup light corn syrup

½ teaspoon vanilla

¼ teaspoon maple flavoring

1 cup coarsely chopped pecans

Peel, core, and thinly slice apples. In a 10- to 12-inch frying pan over medium heat, stir butter and granulated sugar until butter melts. Add apples, lemon juice, and nutmeg. Turn apples often with a spatula just until limp, about 10 minutes; let cool.

Meanwhile, roll out pastry on a floured board to fit a 9-inch pie pan. Put pastry in pan and flute rim. Pour apples into pastry and press gently to make an even, compact layer.

In a small bowl, beat eggs to blend with brown sugar, syrup, vanilla, maple flavoring, and pecans; pour this praline mixture onto apples.

Set pie on a larger baking sheet to catch any boilover. Bake on a lower rack in a 375° oven until pastry is a rich golden brown and nut topping is set when gently shaken, 50 to 60 minutes. Let stand until lukewarm or cool, at least 1 hour. If making ahead, cover and chill up to

a day. Cut into wedges. Makes 8 or 9 servings.

Per serving: 394 cal. (39 percent from fat); 3.7 g protein; 17 g fat (3.5 g sat.); 59 g carbo.; 193 mg sodium; 51 mg chol.

Hoquiam, Washington

FOR A FULL ACCOUNT of the origins of the Mexican sauce called mole, see pages 100 through 104 of the March 1992 issue of *Sunset.* There you will find detailed instructions for making mole poblano, the best known of Mexico's chocolate-shaded sauces. This go-for-broke recipe contains 21 ingredients, including four kinds of chilies, and requires much roasting, toasting, and puréeing, as well as a number of pans. Todd Christoffel's Ground Turkey Chili Mole contains somewhat fewer ingredients and requires only one pan.

Although chocolate is present (in the form of cocoa), chilies, oddly enough, are not; their place is taken by yet another form of chili, liquid hot pepper seasoning. The flavor is still mole, and you will still say olé!

Ground Turkey Chili Mole

1 medium-size (about 5-oz.) onion, chopped

1 pound ground turkey

2 cloves garlic, minced or pressed

1 can (8 oz.) tomato sauce

1 can (15 oz.) stewed tomatoes

1 can (about 15 oz.) kidney beans, rinsed and drained

1 tablespoon molasses

¼ teaspoon liquid hot pepper seasoning

1 tablespoon cocoa

1 teaspoon *each* paprika and ground cumin

½ teaspoon *each* dried oregano leaves and dried basil leaves

Tortilla or corn chips

In a 4- to 5-quart pan over high heat, combine onion and ¼ cup water. Boil, uncovered, until liquid evaporates and onion begins to stick. Add another ¼ cup water, stir to free browned bits, and boil dry again. Add ¼ cup water and repeat step.

Add turkey and garlic; stir, crumbling meat and cooking until it's no longer pink and juices have cooked away.

Stir in tomato sauce, tomatoes, beans, molasses, hot pepper seasoning, cocoa, paprika, cumin, oregano, and basil. Bring to a boil, reduce heat, cover, and simmer until flavors are well blended, about 30 minutes.

Spoon into bowls; serve with tortilla chips. Makes 4 or 5 servings.

Per serving: 254 cal. (28 percent from fat); 22 g protein; 7.8 g fat (2 g sat.); 25 g carbo.; 691 mg sodium; 66 mg chol.

Seattle

DIFFERENCE OF OPINION, it is said, is what makes horse racing interesting. The same might be said of tapenade, the canapé spread sometimes called niçoise caviar. Differences of opinion lie in the choice of ingredients and their proportions. The original formula contained anchovies, tuna, olives, capers, and seasonings. (Tapeno is Provençal for caper.) Some cooks add garlic, some mustard; some add olive oil, others do not. One revolutionary recipe omits capers, which seems a deliberate flouting both of history and of etymology.

Among these variations, the use of black olives has been a constant. But a light bulb went on over the head of Gary Danko, chef at The Ritz-Carlton Hotel in San Francisco, as he contemplated a jar of dried tomatoes in oil. There is, he thought, also red caviar; why not red tapenade? So history is made. Serve this sharp-sweet spread on crisp toast rounds or unsalted

crackers, topped, perhaps, with a little fresh chèvre. Enjoy the combination with salad or beverages.

"THERE IS, he thought, red caviar; why not red tapenade?"

Dried Tomato Tapenade

1 jar (about 8 oz., 1 cup) drained dried tomatoes packed in oil

½ cup drained canned capers

1 can (2 oz.) anchovy fillets, drained and chopped

1 tablespoon minced or pressed garlic

1 tablespoon chopped parsley

2 tablespoons extra-virgin olive oil

2 teaspoons brandy (optional)

1½ teaspoons Dijon mustard

In a food processor or blender, coarsely purée tomatoes, capers, anchovies, garlic, parsley, olive oil, brandy, and mustard. Serve, or cover and chill up to 1 week. Makes about 1⅓ cups.

Per tablespoon: 42 cal. (64 percent from fat); 1.3 g protein; 3 g fat (0.4 g sat.); 3.2 g carbo.; 179 mg sodium; 1.2 mg chol.

San Francisco

By Richard Dunmire, Joan Griffiths

Sunset's Kitchen Cabinet

Creative ways with everyday foods—submitted by *Sunset* readers,
tested in *Sunset* kitchens, approved by *Sunset* taste panels

ORANGE PEEL *and grapefruit juice taste like marmalade in date muffins.*

Citrus Muffins

Yvonne Visteen, Portland

    1   cup all-purpose flour
    1   cup quick-cooking rolled oats
    ¼   cup 7-grain cereal (or more
        rolled oats)
    2   teaspoons baking powder
    ½   teaspoon baking soda
        About ¼ cup (⅛ lb.) butter or
        margarine, in chunks
    ¼   cup sugar
    5   tablespoons grated orange peel
    1   large egg
    ¾   cup grapefruit or orange juice
    1   cup chopped pitted dates

In a bowl, combine flour, oats, cereal, baking powder, and soda.

In another bowl, combine butter, sugar, and orange peel. Beat until smoothly mixed. Add egg; beat to blend.

Stir grapefruit juice and dates into butter mixture. Add flour mixture and stir just until evenly moistened.

Spoon batter equally into 10 buttered muffin cups (2½ to 2¾ in. wide). Bake in a 400° oven until muffins are deep golden brown, 18 to 20 minutes. Serve hot or cool. Makes 10.

Per muffin: 231 cal. (29 percent from fat); 4.1 g protein; 7.4 g fat (3.9 g sat.); 39 g carbo.; 194 mg sodium; 37 mg chol.

ROSY PAPRIKA SAUCE *with eggs on toast makes a quick breakfast or supper.*

Hungarian Eggs on Toast

Ann Bartos Rushton, Denver

    ¼   cup minced onion
    1   cup low-fat milk
    ¼   cup all-purpose flour
    1   cup regular-strength chicken
         broth
    1½   tablespoons hot or mild
         Hungarian paprika, or regular
         paprika
    4   large hard-cooked eggs, shelled
         and thinly sliced
    6   slices hot whole-wheat toast
    ½   cup diced red bell pepper
         Parsley sprigs

In a 3- to 4-quart pan over high heat, boil onion with ¼ cup water until pan is dry and onion begins to brown and stick, about 3 minutes; stir often. Add ¼ cup water, stir to release browned bits, and boil until pan is dry and onion begins to brown again, about 2 minutes.

Meanwhile, in a bowl, mix a little milk smoothly with flour; add remaining milk and the broth.

When onion is browned, add paprika and stir about 10 seconds. Stir in milk mixture; stir until boiling. Add eggs, remove from heat, and mix gently.

Cut toast into triangles; set on 4 plates; spoon egg sauce onto toast. Top with bell pepper and parsley. Serves 4.

Per serving: 238 cal. (31 percent from fat); 14 g protein; 8.2 g fat (2.4 g sat.); 29 g carbo.; 327 mg sodium; 216 mg chol.

CELERY ROOT, *broccoli, other vegetables are appetizers with blue cheese dip.*

Celery Root Antipasto Salad

Rosemary H. Milburn, Wickenburg, Arizona

    ¾   pound celery root, rinsed
    1¾   cups broccoli flowerets
    1   tablespoon distilled white
         vinegar
         Butter lettuce leaves
    1   cup cherry tomatoes
    1   jar (7½ oz.) baby corn, drained
    1   jar (6 oz.) marinated artichoke
         hearts, drained
         Blue cheese dip (recipe follows)

Peel celery root and cut into ½- by 3-inch sticks; set aside. In a 2- to 3-quart pan, bring 1½ inches water to a boil over high heat.

Add broccoli to boiling water and cook, covered, until tender-crisp to bite, about 1 minute. Lift from water with a slotted spoon; immerse in ice water until cool. Add celery root and vinegar to pan; simmer, covered, until root is tender-crisp to bite, about 10 minutes. Drain and let cool; drain broccoli.

Line a platter with lettuce; arrange celery root, broccoli, tomatoes, corn, and artichoke hearts separately on leaves. Accompany with dip. Serves 6.

Per serving: 113 cal. (40 percent from fat); 6.4 g protein; 5 g fat (1.7 g sat.); 13 g carbo.; 332 mg sodium; 7.3 mg chol.

Blue cheese dip. Mix ¾ cup **unflavored low-fat yogurt,** 2 teaspoons **red wine vinegar,** ½ teaspoon minced **garlic,** ½ teaspoon **dill weed,** and ⅓ cup crumbled **blue cheese.** Spoon into bowl and sprinkle with more dill weed.

Stir-fried Pork and Asparagus

Kimiko Bigelow, San Jose, California

1 pound boned pork loin, fat trimmed

¼ cup reduced-sodium soy sauce

1 tablespoon sake (rice wine)

2 teaspoons ground ginger

1½ pounds slender asparagus (tough ends trimmed), in 3- to 4-inch lengths

2 teaspoons salad oil

1 tablespoon sliced green onion

Cut pork into thin strips. In a bowl, mix pork, soy, sake, and ginger; let stand 5 to 30 minutes.

Place asparagus and ½ cup water in a wok or 10- to 12-inch frying pan over high heat; cover. Stir occasionally until asparagus is tender-crisp to bite, 2 to 4 minutes. Drain asparagus, put on a platter, and keep warm.

Add oil to wok on high heat. With a slotted spoon, lift meat from marinade. Stir-fry in pan until meat is no longer pink in center (cut to test), 2 to 3 minutes. Add marinade and 2 tablespoons water; stir gently until boiling. Pour over asparagus; garnish with onion. Serves 4.

Per serving: 246 cal. (40 percent from fat); 30 g protein; 11 g fat (3.2 g sat.); 7.3 g carbo.; 678 mg sodium; 72 mg chol.

CUT PORK STRIPS *and marinate briefly. Cook asparagus, stir-fry meat in wok.*

Baked Lentils with Honey and Chutney

Teresa E. Cassetta, Capitola, California

6 slices (¼ lb.) bacon, chopped; or 1 tablespoon salad oil

¾ cup sliced green onions

1¾ cups (12 oz.) lentils, sorted of debris, and rinsed

⅓ cup chopped Major Grey chutney

⅓ cup honey

2 teaspoons dry mustard

Salt and pepper

Lime wedges

In a 3- to 4-quart pan over medium-high heat, stir bacon until crisp; drain on towels. Discard all but 1 tablespoon fat

from pan (or add oil).

Reserve 2 tablespoons onions; add remainder to pan. Stir until onions are limp, about 5 minutes. Add lentils and 1 quart water. Bring to a boil over high heat; simmer, covered, for 20 minutes. Stir in chutney, honey, and mustard.

Pour mixture into a shallow 2-quart casserole, 8 to 9 inches wide. Bake, uncovered, in a 350° oven until most of liquid is absorbed, 35 to 45 minutes; stir several times. Mix in bacon, sprinkle with reserved onions, and add salt, pepper, and lime to taste. Serves 6.

Per serving: 345 cal. (13 percent from fat); 18 g protein; 5.1 g fat (1.5 g sat.); 59 g carbo.; 259 mg sodium; 6 mg chol.

SWEET-SPICY LENTILS *need a squeeze of lime juice to balance their seasonings.*

Rhubarb Angel Pie

Gisela M. Brabb, Palo Alto, California

4 large egg whites

½ teaspoon cream of tartar

1⅔ cups sugar

¼ cup water

2 teaspoons grated lemon peel

8 cups rhubarb, in ½-inch slices

3 tablespoons cornstarch

In a deep bowl, whip whites and cream of tartar on high speed until foamy. Beating, gradually add 1 cup sugar; whip until whites hold stiff peaks.

Oil and flour-dust a 12- by 15-inch baking sheet. Scoop out 1 cup meringue and divide into 6 equal mounds, well apart, on baking sheet.

Oil and flour-dust a 9-inch nonstick pie pan, and scrape remaining meringue into it; spread evenly, making a high rim on sides. Bake meringues in a

250° oven until crisp and pale golden, about 1 hour. Let cool; if making ahead, store airtight up to 3 days.

In a 4- to 5-quart pan, combine remaining ⅔ cup sugar, 2 tablespoons water, peel, and rhubarb. Cover and bring to simmering over medium heat; stir occasionally until the rhubarb is tender when pierced, 7 to 10 minutes. Smoothly mix remaining water and cornstarch; add to rhubarb. Stir often until boiling, about 1 minute. Chill until cold, about 2 hours.

Spoon rhubarb mixture into meringue shell; top with meringue mounds. Cover and chill at least 2 or up to 8 hours. Spoon out portions. Serves 6.

Per serving: 275 cal. (1 percent from fat); 3.8 g protein; 0.3 g fat (0 g sat.); 67 g carbo.; 44 mg sodium; 0 mg chol.

Compiled by Elaine Johnson

PUFFS OF MERINGUE *crown rhubarb filling in tender meringue shell.*

April Menus

QUICK, SEASONAL, BUDGET-WISE . . . FOR FAMILY AND FRIENDS

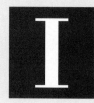

Inspired by the traditions of Russian Easter, we propose kulich and paskha for this relaxed Easter brunch. The tall, cakelike yeast kulich and the sweet, fresh cheese paskha must both be started well ahead, leaving little to do at the last minute, except, perhaps, to hunt for eggs.

Light meals are also needed to match light spirits that come with spring. The other two menus, which focus on vegetables, fit the bill extremely well. The first has a baked vegetable flan with salad, the second a green soup with shrimp.

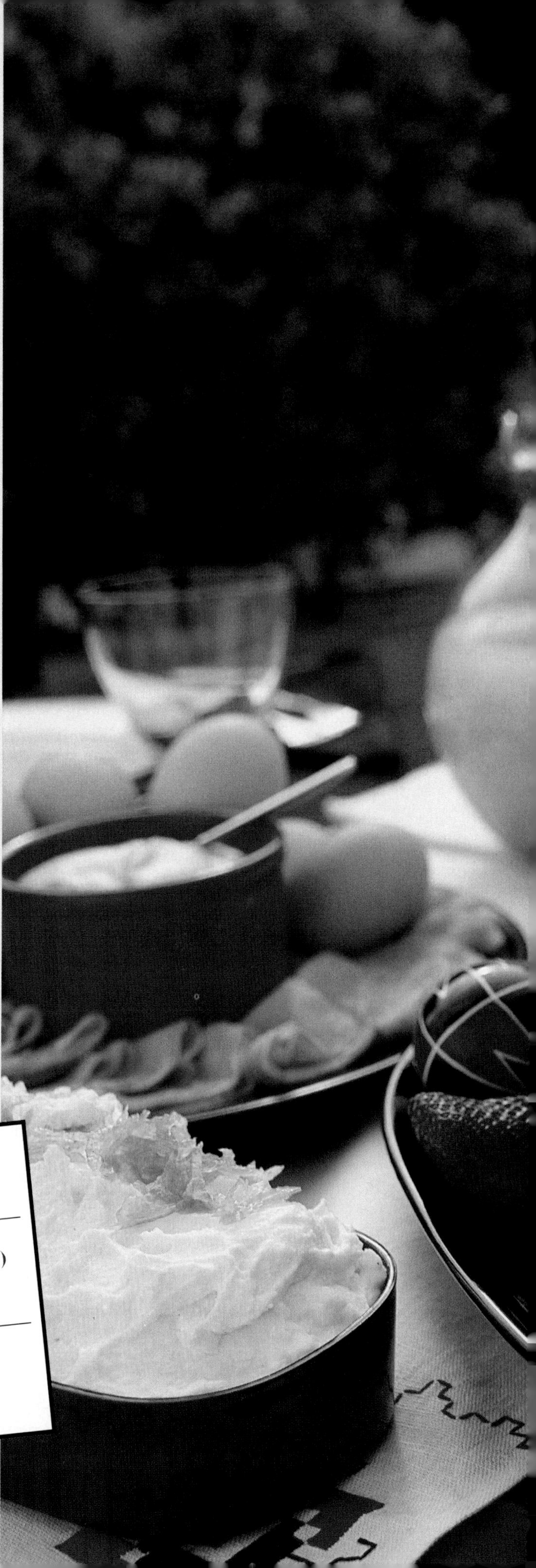

EASTER BRUNCH (at right)
Highlight is sweet Russian bread to eat with ricotta spread and candied orange peel—which flavors both.

PEPPER FLAN AND SALAD LUNCH (page 77)
Mellow red bell pepper purée is base of baked custard; serve hot or cool with black bean salad.

SPRING SOUP SUPPER (page 77)
Wonderfully fresh-tasting, quick soup is laden with asparagus, petite peas, diced carrots, and tiny shrimp.

THE DETAILS

Petite Bouquets

Use egg cups or tiny vases to hold flowers and set a bouquet at each place.

Russian Decor

Russian table runner and lacquer spoons are authentic accessories for meal.

Intricate Eggs

Complex Ukrainian-style decorated eggs enhance the Easter decor.

It's in the Bag

For tall loaf, bake sweet bread in double-thick brown paper lunch bags.

PETER CHRISTIANSEN

Start the paskha up to 3 days before it is to be served; the kulich dough can be chilled up to 24 hours, so you can bake and serve it warm for brunch. Fresh candied orange peel goes into and with bread and cheese.

Ricotta Paskha

If you use seed from a vanilla bean to flavor paskha and kulich, store the pod in a tightly covered jar of sugar to make vanilla sugar.

1 piece (3 to 4 in. long) vanilla bean, or 2 teaspoons vanilla

¼ cup milk

1 container (15 oz., about 2 cups) low-fat or part-skim ricotta cheese

1 pint (2 cups) nonfat small-curd cottage cheese

¼ cup sugar

1 teaspoon candied orange peel (see kulich, following)

Split vanilla bean lengthwise; with a knife, scrape out seeds and put in a blender or food processor. Add milk, ricotta, cottage cheese, and sugar; smoothly purée.

Line a strainer with a single layer of muslin or a double layer of cheesecloth. Set strainer over a deep bowl (strainer base should be at least 2 in. above bottom of bowl). Spoon cheese mixture into cloth. Fold cloth over cheese and set a plate just smaller than strainer top on cheese; set a 1-pound weight (such as a can of food) on plate. Cover entire bowl airtight; chill at least 12 hours or up to 24 hours.

Remove weight, fold back cloth, and spoon paskha into a bowl. Serve, or cover and chill up to 2 days. Garnish cheese with candied orange peel. Makes 2¾ cups, 6 to 8 servings.

PETER CHRISTIANSEN

COMPLEMENT RED PEPPER *flan, in individual ramekins, with salad of black beans, jicama, cilantro, and lime.*

Per tablespoon: 26 cal. (25 percent from fat); 2.7 g protein; 0.7 g fat (0.4 g sat.); 2.3 g carbo.; 49 mg sodium; 2.8 mg chol.

Kulich with Candied Orange Peel

1 vanilla bean (6 to 8 in. long), or 2 teaspoons vanilla

1 tablespoon vodka or brandy

8 tablespoons (¼ lb.) butter or margarine

About 2¼ cups all-purpose flour

¼ cup milk

3 large eggs

1 package active dry yeast

2 tablespoons warm water

½ cup sugar

¼ teaspoon salt

2 tablespoons finely chopped candied orange peel (recipe follows)

2 brown paper lunch bags with 3½- by 5-inch bases

Glaze and rosebuds (directions follow)

Split vanilla bean lengthwise; with a knife, scrape out seeds and mix with vodka. Discard pod.

In a 1- to 1½-quart pan over medium-high heat, melt 1 tablespoon butter. Off the heat, smoothly mix in 2 tablespoons flour and milk; return to heat and stir until mixture is very thick, about 1 minute. Remove from heat. Separate 1 egg and add yolk to pan; stir until thoroughly blended. Let cool until just slightly warm to touch.

Meanwhile, in a bowl stir yeast, warm water, and ½ teaspoon sugar; let stand until yeast is moistened, about 5 minutes. Add to cooked mixture and beat to blend; cover and let stand in a warm place until about doubled and very foamy, about 15 minutes.

In a bowl, beat 6 tablespoons butter with remaining sugar and salt until well blended. Add yeast mixture, vodka mixture, egg white, remaining 2 eggs, 2 cups flour, and candied orange peel; stir until thoroughly moistened.

With a dough hook or mixer, beat on high speed until

dough is very stretchy and shiny, and pulls from side of bowl. Lightly touched, the dough should not be sticky; if it is, beat in flour, 1 tablespoon at a time, as required.

With a heavy spoon, beat dough until stretchy, about 4 minutes. Then, with oiled hands, rapidly pull handfuls of the very soft dough from the bowl and forcefully throw back; repeat until dough pulls free from bowl in a single lump, about 25 minutes. If it still sticks, add flour, 1 tablespoon at a time, as required.

Cover dough in bowl with plastic wrap. (If making ahead, put kneaded dough in the refrigerator up to 24 hours.)

Let rise in a warm place until almost doubled, about 1 hour (longer, if chilled).

Fit 1 paper bag into the other. Fold tops neatly down together to make a bag 5½ inches tall; gently pull bag open to straighten sides. Melt remaining 1 tablespoon butter; brush it over interior of bag. Set bag upright in a 4-by 8-inch loaf pan.

Stir soft dough vigorously to expel air. Shape into a ball with oiled hands and drop into bag. Cover with plastic wrap and set in a warm place until dough has risen about 3 inches in bag, 20 to 30 minutes (longer if dough is cold).

Bake on lowest rack of a 325° oven until richly browned and a long, slender wooden skewer inserted into center comes out clean, about 1 hour. Cool loaf in pan about 10 minutes. Tear off bag. Spread glaze on top of loaf, letting excess drip down sides. Set roses in glaze. Serve kulich warm or cool; cut vertically into thin slices. Makes 1 loaf, about 1½ pounds. Serves 6 to 8.

Per ounce: 124 cal.; 36 percent from fat; 2 g protein; 5 g fat (2.9 g sat.); 18 g carbo.; 71 mg sodium; 37 mg chol.

Candied orange peel. With a vegetable peeler, cut colored part only from 3 large **oranges** (about ½ lb. each); cut peel into slivers. Ream fruit to extract juice.

In a 2- to 3-quart pan, cover peel with **water;** bring to a boil. Drain; repeat step.

Add ¼ cup **sugar** and

juice to drained peel. Boil, uncovered, on high heat until liquid is almost gone and syrup forms big bubbles, 10 to 15 minutes. Stir often; watch closely to avoid scorching. Serve, or chill airtight up to 2 months. Makes about ⅓ cup.

Per teaspoon: 11 cal. (0 percent from fat); 0 g protein; 0 g fat; 2.7 g carbo.; 0 mg sodium; 0 mg chol.

Glaze and rosebuds. Smoothly blend 1 cup unsifted **powdered sugar** with about 1 tablespoon **water** to make a mixture that is just thick enough to spread. Decorate bread with 2 or 3 **fresh tiny rosebuds** (pesticide-free, or candied rose petals) and **fresh citrus leaves** (pesticide-free), rinsed and drained.

Handy canned mild red peppers and beans give this light menu a quick start; everything can be made ahead if you'd like to serve a cool lunch. Purchase crisp breadsticks, and buy brownies, or bake them, using your favorite recipe.

Red Pepper Flan with Bean Salad

2 cans (7 oz. each, or 1 cup) roasted red bell peppers, drained and patted dry

3 large eggs

⅓ cup regular-strength chicken broth

  Bean salad (recipe follows)

4 to 8 large butter lettuce leaves, rinsed and crisped

  Fresh cilantro (coriander) sprigs

In a blender or food processor, smoothly purée peppers, eggs, and broth. Pour mixture equally into 4 small ramekins or baking dishes (each ¾ cup and 2 in. deep).

THIN ASPARAGUS *slices, tiny peas, and diced carrots swim in steaming broth; add shrimp seasoned with onion and parsley.*

PETER CHRISTIANSEN

Set ramekins, side by side, in a larger pan (at least 2 in. deep). Set pan on center rack of a 325° oven.

Pour boiling water into pan up to level of pepper mixture. Bake until flan no longer jiggles in center when gently shaken, 25 to 35 minutes. Lift ramekins from water. Serve hot or cool; if making ahead, cool flan; cover and chill up to 1 day.

Set flan on plates; serve bean salad on lettuce leaves alongside. Garnish with cilantro. Serves 4.

Per serving: 233 cal. (27 percent from fat); 14 g protein; 6.9 g fat (2.6 g sat.); 30 g carbo.; 573 mg sodium; 167 mg chol.

Bean salad. Drain 1 can (about 15 oz.) **black beans.** In a bowl, combine 1 cup finely chopped **jicama,** ¼ cup crumbled **feta cheese,** 3 tablespoons **lime juice,** ⅓ cup minced **fresh cilantro** (coriander), 2 tablespoons chopped **green onion,** 2 teaspoons **honey,** and ¼ teaspoon **crushed hot dried red chilies.** Mix well. Serve; or if making ahead, cover and chill up to 8 hours.

The soup is ready almost as quickly as the broth base comes to boiling; the soup not only tastes fresh and light, but also is very low in fat. For dessert, dunk dense biscotti cookies into the strong coffee.

Spring Vegetable and Shrimp Soup

6 cups regular-strength chicken broth

2 cups diced carrots

2 cups thinly sliced asparagus

1 package (10 oz.) frozen petite peas

1½ pounds shelled cooked tiny shrimp, rinsed

½ cup chopped green onions

¼ cup minced parsley

In a 5- to 6-quart pan over high heat, combine broth and carrots; bring to boiling. Add asparagus and peas; simmer until asparagus is just tender to bite, about 2 minutes. Meanwhile, in a small bowl, combine shrimp, onions, and parsley. Ladle soup into bowls and add shrimp mixture. Serves 8.

Per serving: 155 cal. (13 percent from fat); 23 g protein; 2.3 g fat (0.6 g sat.); 10 g carbo.; 244 mg sodium; 166 mg chol. ∎

By Karyn I. Lipman

Crayfish or

Whatever . . . Westerners

LUCY I. SARGEANT

ROCKY KNETEN

This crustacean takes a licking—food and craft booths sell everything from suckers to crayfish étouffée makings.

And they're off—sort of. Crayfish races are a popular, if poky, event at Bridge City, Texas, festival.

Bug-eyed 'n' bow-tied crayfish roams Napa, California, fair.

Cajun dancing is served up along with crayfish at many festivals.

crawfish?

really know how to enjoy them

By Lora J. Finnegan and Linda Lau Anusasananan

Fiddling around with Cajun music is often on the menu at festivals during crayfish season.

The rubboard, or frattoir, adds its zip to zydeco music at many crayfish fairs.

WILLIAM MERCER McLEOD

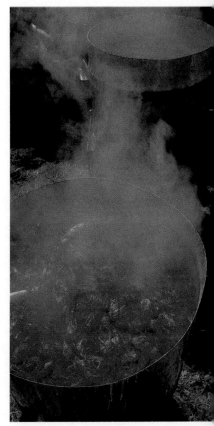

Turning red, crayfish (or crawfish, depending on who's minding the pot) cook in a spicy broth.

Like some Rodney Dangerfield of the crustacean world, crayfish don't always get much respect, certainly not compared with their cousins, shrimp and lobster. In many parts of the world, they're considered a delicacy. Here, the unconverted may scoff that the best way to use a crayfish is as bait.

Granted, they can't get by on their looks. These 10-legged, pincered, eyes-on-stalks bottom dwellers look rather creepy. But once you taste them—in a spicy Cajun stew or dipped into a delicate sauce—you'll understand what all the excitement is about.

You may still be in doubt as to what to call them. In California's Sacramento–San Joaquin Delta, where these crustaceans make up the state's largest freshwater catch (up to 500,000 pounds per year), fishermen usually call them crayfish. In Texas and Louisiana, where the critter also constitutes a major industry, Southern slang softens the name to crawfish or crawdads.

The harvest is well under way now in Texas; in the Sacramento Delta, the main season runs from May through October. From spring into summer, festivals in California, Texas, and Oregon celebrate this crustacean with silly parades, spicy dishes, and sometimes with hot Cajun music and dancing from the culture that so loves this creature.

The name for the lobsterlike creature derives from the French *écrevisse*. According to one fanciful tale, when the French-speaking Acadians (who became Cajuns) were forced from Maritime Canada down to Louisiana, lobsters went with them. Legend says the journey was so long and exhausting that, when the lobsters arrived, they'd lost so much weight they were reduced to crayfish. Regardless of the creature's true origins, Cajuns have used crayfish in spicy dishes ever since their arrival in the South.

And crayfish are catching the fancy of Western cooks. Indeed, crayfish thrive all over the West in freshwater streams, rivers, and lakes. Worldwide, there are more than 500 species of crayfish (existing everywhere but the polar regions). Though there are more kinds here, in the West we commercially harvest just two—the signal crayfish (*Pacifastacus leniusculus*), harvested in the Sacramento Delta and abundant in the wild throughout California, Washington, and Oregon; and the Louisiana red or red swamp crayfish (*Procambarus clarkii*) found in Texas (and some California rice fields and irrigation ditches, where it's considered a pest).

Jeff Skeele, general manager of Jake's Famous Crawfish Restaurant in Portland, explains a key difference. ''The Louisiana red crayfish have a slightly muddier taste than the signal crayfish [which don't burrow and do live in cleaner-flowing streams and lakes]. Some Southerners think ours actually taste too clean.'' Others can't taste any difference.

Once you start looking for crayfish, you'll be surprised how common they are—scuttling about in streams and lakes, hiding under rocks and logs. They're most active at night, feeding on snails, larvae, and tadpoles. They can grow to 7 inches (the Louisiana red is smaller).

Crayfish are easy and fun to catch. The season is year-round, and you may not need a license (check with your state fish and game department). Often you can catch them by hand (watch out for their strong front pincers) or by baiting a hook with cheese, chicken, or bacon. Friends we know go crayfishing by dropping a small crab pot or trap (baited with a can of dog food with holes punched in it) over the side of their houseboat at night; in the morning, they pull the trap up and reap the easy pickings.

Once you taste your crayfish bounty, you'll understand why otherwise intelligent people spend an inordinate

amount of time patiently peeling mounds of steaming red crayfish for the tiny morsels each contains.
(Continued on page 82)

Celebrating Crayfish 1993

CALIFORNIA
Napa, April 24 and 25. Cajun Gumbo Ya Ya and Crayfish Festival, Napa Fairgrounds.

Vallejo, May 15 and 16. Crayfish Festival, Vallejo Waterfront.

Roseville, June 12 and 13. The Tardy Mardi Gras, Roseville Fairgrounds.

All of the above festivals have food booths, Cajun music, and dancing lessons. Roseville has a parade. Admission: $7 ages 12 and over. For hours, call (916) 361-1309.

Isleton, June 18, 19, and 20. Isleton Crawdad Festival, on the town's main streets. There are more than a hundred booths, crayfish races, and live music. Free admission. For hours, call (916) 777-5880.

OREGON
Tualatin, August 14. Tualatin Crawfish Festival. Food booths, crafts, crayfish-eating contest, and parade. Free admission. For hours, call (503) 692-0780.

TEXAS
Bridge City, March 27 and 28. Texas Crawfish and Saltwater Crab Festival. Crayfish races, food booths, crayfish-eating contest, Cajun music, and dancing. Admission: $1, 50 cents ages 12 and under. For hours, call (409) 379-3560.

Alvin, April 3. The Rice and Crawfest, National Oak Park. Craft, food booths; rice cook-off; carnival. Free admission. For hours, call (713) 331-1882.

Mauriceville, April 16, 17, and 18. Mauriceville Crawfish Festival, Mauriceville Fairgrounds. Food booths, crayfish races, eating contests, and parade. Admission: $2, 50 cents for students. For hours, call (409) 745-3777.

Old Town Spring, April 30, May 1 and 2. Texas Crawfish Festival, Preservation Park. Cajun food booths, and zydeco, Cajun, and reggae music. Admission is $3, free for ages 12 and under. For hours, call (800) 653-8696.

Dig in! It's a crayfish feast. On newspaper-lined table, crayfish lovers attack mounds of shellfish marinated in a spicy brine.

WILLIAM MERCER McLEOD

There's a right way to eat crayfish

LUCY I. SARGEANT

1. Twist tail and body in opposite ways; pull apart.

2. Pinch in tail sides to crack ridges along inside of tail.

3. Pull sides of tail back to crack shell; loosen meat.

4. Pull tail meat from cracked shell to eat.

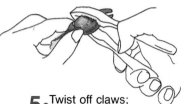

5. Twist off claws; crack shells; dig out meat.

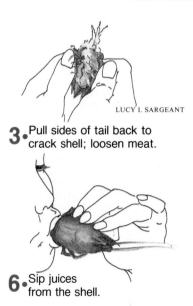

6. Sip juices from the shell.

PETER CHRISTIANSEN

A mound of rice tempers explosive spiciness of étouffée made with peeled crayfish tails.

Enjoying the catch

Whether you catch crayfish or buy them, simply boil them briefly for a delicious hands-on meal. Then serve them hot—or marinate in a spicy bath to enjoy cold. To eat, peel the tails and crack the claws (if large) for morsels of sweet meat (see page 135). If you're daring, suck the body cavity for delicious juices, the green- to gold-colored "butter," and red eggs (in females).

If you don't want to spend time peeling the tails, consider buying peeled, cooked ones to use much like shrimp in recipes.

Crayfish sources

Check your fish market. Many markets can order live crayfish. Some also sell whole cooked crayfish, but freshly cooked live shellfish is far superior. Depending on the season, some markets have a minimum order and may require up to a week's notice. Frozen peeled crayfish tails are more difficult to find; you can substitute shrimp.

Three sources ship crayfish to your home or nearest airport. It usually costs less per pound to order enough for a party. You need at least 1 pound whole live crayfish per serving, more if it constitutes the whole meal.

Bayou-To-Go Seafood, Inc., Box 20104, New Orleans, La. 70141; (800) 541-6610. Live crayfish (November to July 15, 40-pound minimum), cooked seasoned whole crayfish, frozen peeled cooked crayfish tails (5-

pound minimum).

Jake's Famous Crawfish and Seafood, Box 97, Clackamas, Ore. 97015; (503) 657-1892. Live crayfish (April to October), frozen cooked whole crayfish, cooked seasoned whole crayfish, frozen peeled cooked tails. No minimum.

Louisiana Cajun Lady, 6355 Scarlett Court, Suite 5, Dublin, Calif. 94568; (800) 982-2586. Frozen cooked whole crayfish (10-pound minimum), frozen peeled cooked crayfish tails (5-pound minimum).

ROCKY KNETEN

"Handle with care" appears to be the watchword of this young fairgoer.

Crayfish recipes

The following recipes for Crayfish with Spicy Court Bouillon and Crayfish Étouffée come from chef Marcel Lahsene, of Jake's Famous Crawfish Restaurant in Portland. At Jake's they serve the spicy chilled marinated shellfish in a bowl with the broth accompanied by crusty bread to sop up the juices.

Crayfish with Spicy Court Bouillon

If you don't have a 14- to 16-quart kettle, use an 8- to 12-quart one; half-fill it with water, and cook crayfish in two batches.

- 3   large (about 1½ lb. total) onions, chopped
- 1¼ pounds celery, chopped
- ¾   cup pickling spice
- ¾   cup Worcestershire
- ⅓   cup liquid hot pepper seasoning
- 1   tablespoon salt
- 3   tablespoons malt vinegar
- 3   tablespoons crushed dried hot red chilies
- 3   tablespoons black peppercorns
- 3   cinnamon sticks (each about 3 in. long)
     About 10 pounds live crayfish

In a 10- to 12-quart pan on high heat, bring 1¼ gallons water to a boil with onions, celery, pickling spice, Worcestershire, hot pepper seasoning, salt, vinegar, chilies, peppercorns, and cinnamon sticks. Cover and simmer 30 to 40 minutes.

If pan is not corrosion resistant, transfer mixture to 1 or 2 large noncorrodible containers (at least 12 qt. total). Let spiced broth cool; cover and chill up to 1 day.

Rinse crayfish with cool water. Discard limp ones that don't move; they're dead.

In a 14- to 16-quart pan (such as a canning kettle) over high heat, bring about 2½ gallons of water to a boil. Drop the crayfish into the water. Cover and cook on high heat (boil may not resume) until tail meat is firm and opaque in the center (pull off a tail to test), 7 to 8 minutes. Drain.

Immerse crayfish in pans

of chilled, spiced broth. Cover; chill at least 4 hours or up to 1 day, stirring occasionally. Ladle crayfish and broth into wide bowls; or, with a slotted spoon, transfer crayfish to a newspaper-lined table or large platter. Peel crayfish to eat. Makes 8 to 10 servings.

Per serving: 114 cal. (8 percent from fat); 13 g protein; 1 g fat (0.2 g sat.); 14 g carbo.; 1,146 mg sodium; 76 mg chol.

Crayfish Étouffée

Serve this spicy stew with hot cooked rice.

- ¼   cup salad oil
- ½   cup all-purpose flour
- 1   cup finely diced onion
- ½   cup finely diced celery
- ½   cup *each* finely diced red and green bell peppers
     Spice mixture (recipe follows)
- 2   cups regular-strength fish or chicken broth
- 1   pound (3 cups) peeled cooked crayfish tails (thawed, if frozen), or uncooked peeled and deveined medium-size shrimp (43 to 50 per lb.)
     Salt

Pour oil into a 5- to 6-quart pan on high heat. When oil is hot, add flour all at once; stir until flour turns a dark caramel color, 4 to 5 minutes. Remove roux from heat and, all at once, stir in onion, celery, bell peppers, and spice mixture. Stir often on low heat until vegetables soften slightly, 2 to 3 minutes. Stirring, gradually add broth to pan. Cover and simmer until flavors blend, 15 to 20 minutes; stir occasionally.

Add crayfish; stir often until hot, 1 to 2 minutes. (If using shrimp, cook until they are opaque in thickest part, 3 to 4 minutes; cut to test.) Add salt to taste. Serves 4.

Per serving: 355 cal. (41 percent from fat); 31 g protein; 16 g fat (2.3 g sat.); 20 g carbo.; 120 mg sodium; 202 mg chol.

Spice mixture. Combine 2 teaspoons **paprika,** 1½ teaspoons **dried basil leaves,** 1¼ teaspoons **dried thyme leaves,** ½ teaspoon **cayenne,** ½ teaspoon **ground white pepper,** and ½ teaspoon **pepper.** ■

PETER CHRISTIANSEN

Italian Greens Risotto

¾ pound asparagus, tough ends snapped off

¾ pound rapini (broccoli rabe) or Chinese broccoli (*gai laan*), tough stem ends trimmed off and yellowed leaves discarded

2 tablespoons olive oil

1 large (about ½-lb.) onion, finely chopped

1 cup short- to medium-grain white rice such as pearl or arborio

3 cups regular-strength chicken broth

½ cup dry white wine

1 cup (¼ lb.) shredded parmesan cheese

Rinse and drain asparagus and rapini (cut in half lengthwise stems that are thicker than ⅜ in.). Chop or thinly slice half the asparagus and rapini.

In a 10- to 12-inch frying pan over medium-high heat, combine sliced asparagus, chopped rapini, and 1 tablespoon oil. Stir until vegetables are just tender to bite, about 4 minutes. Remove from pan and set aside.

Add ½ cup water and whole asparagus and rapini to pan. Cover; cook, turning vegetables often with a wide spatula, until just tender to bite, about 4 minutes. Lift from pan and set aside.

In the same pan, combine remaining oil and onion; stir often until onion is faintly browned, 5 to 8 minutes. Add rice and stir until it is opaque, 2 to 3 minutes. Stir in broth and wine and bring to a boil. Boil rice gently, uncovered; stir often until tender to bite, 15 to 20 minutes. Reduce heat and stir often to develop creaminess, about 5 minutes. Stir in chopped vegetables and ½ cup cheese. Spoon onto a warm platter. Add whole vegetables; sprinkle with remaining cheese. Makes 4 to 6 servings.

Per serving: 296 cal. (40 percent from fat); 13 g protein; 13 g fat (4 g sat.); 33 g carbo.; 359 mg sodium; 13 mg chol. ■

By Betsy Reynolds Bateson

Northern Italians like their risotto green

STIR COOKED GREEN *vegetables into rice when the grains are tender and creamy.*

THE SATISFYING foundation for this spring main dish, typical of what home cooks serve in northern Italy, is creamy risotto. The rice balances the delicate taste of asparagus against the contrasting, slightly bitter flavor of a less well known green, rapini.

Italian cooks prize rapini (also called broccoli rabe) for its intriguing bite. But unless you've looked specifically for the green, you may not have noticed it, even if it's in your market. Rapini looks like skinny, leafy broccoli, with tiny green flower buds at the tips of its multiple stalks, and is easily confused with widely available Chinese broccoli. Because Chinese broccoli has similar flavor and cooks at the same rate, you can use either green in this dish.

It takes very little effort or time to create a menu around risotto to serve for either lunch or a light supper. Here is one easily managed plan.

Offer amaretti (the petite version of the crunchy, purchased Italian almond macaroons) with strong coffee and, if you like, bowls of fresh strawberries.

GREENS CELEBRATION

Italian Greens Risotto

Green Salad

Dry Sauvignon Blanc or Orvieto

Amaretti

Espresso

Although the main dish is designed to combine tepid whole vegetables and hot risotto, you can easily present it with both elements hot. Put risotto and vegetables on a microwave-safe platter; heat on full power (100 percent) until vegetables are just hot, 2 to 3 minutes.

This centerpiece is cool paella

You can have it ready and waiting for a big party

EFFECTIVE STRATEGIES for carefree entertaining, the party-giver's dream, are often much simpler than end results indicate. Two that work best are advance preparation and a menu trimmed down to just one great dish.

This party paella salad meets these criteria. The salad can be made completely ahead and served cold; it's a showy, whole-meal entrée presented from a large platter. When serving time arrives, all you need to do is set out the salad. Guests serve themselves.

Another plus of this salad is that one big pan performs a multitude of chores. In it, you steep seafood in a wine broth,

about 3 minutes. With a slotted spoon, transfer scallops to bowl with shrimp.

Return broth to a boil. Add clams; cover and simmer until shells pop open, 5 to 10 minutes. With a slotted spoon, transfer clams (discard unopened ones) to bowl with shrimp and scallops; set seafood aside.

Pour broth into a 2-quart glass measure, leaving behind gritty sediment. Rinse pan. If needed, add water or boil broth, uncovered, to make 7½ cups. Add 1 cup broth to the dressing. Reserve remaining broth.

Add 1 cup dressing to seafood; mix. Cover; chill until cold, about 2 hours or up to 1 day. Stir occasionally.

To the rinsed pan, add oil, onions, and garlic. Stir often over medium-high heat until onion is very limp, about 10 minutes. Add rice and stir until grains turn opaque, about 5 minutes. Add reserved 6½ cups broth and saffron. Boil gently, uncovered, until most of the liquid evaporates, 8 to 10 minutes. Cover tightly and cook over very low heat until rice is tender to bite, about 15 minutes. Uncover rice and cool; gently stir several times.

To rice, add artichokes, olives, red bell peppers, and remaining dressing. Mix gently. If making ahead, cover and chill up to 1 day.

Up to 6 hours before serving, gently stir tomatoes and peas into rice. If desired, line a large platter with romaine leaves. Mound rice onto lettuce. With a slotted spoon, transfer seafood onto rice; spoon dressing in bowl over salad. If making ahead, cover and chill up to 6 hours. Makes 10 to 12 servings.

Per serving: 539 cal. (28 percent from fat) 30 g protein; 17 g fat (2.4 g sat.); 66 g carbo.; 594 mg sodium; 112 mg chol.

Dressing. Mix 1 cup **white wine vinegar,** 1 cup **broth from seafood** (see preceding), ½ cup **olive oil,** 3 tablespoons drained **capers,** 1 tablespoon minced **fresh oregano leaves** or 1 teaspoon dried oregano leaves, ¾ to 1 teaspoon **crushed dried hot red chilies,** and 2 cloves **garlic,** pressed or minced. Makes 2½ cups. ∎

By Linda Lau Anusasananan

TRANSFORM INGREDIENTS
for paella—rice, shellfish, vegetables, saffron, and dried chilies—into a handsome make-ahead party salad for 10 to 12 guests.

then cook the rice in the richly flavored broth with saffron. Add lots of vegetables and a caper-chili dressing to the pan of rice. Meanwhile, marinate the seafood in more of the same dressing.

You can cook the rice and the seafood up to a day ahead. If your refrigerator is large enough, assemble the salad up to 6 hours before serving. If chilling space is restricted, you can quickly transfer the elements to the platter at serving time.

For predinner nibbles, offer warm almonds with dry sherry. To accompany the salad, serve crusty bread and a white wine such as dry Sauvignon Blanc or dry Chenin Blanc. Crescents of cool honeydew, Persian melon, or cantaloupe accented with whole strawberries end the meal simply.

Party Paella Salad

3 cups regular-strength chicken broth

1½ cups dry white wine

1 dried bay leaf

2 pounds large shrimp (31 to 35 per lb.), shelled and deveined

1 pound bay scallops, rinsed

2 to 3 dozen small clams in shells, suitable for steaming, scrubbed

Dressing (recipe follows)

3 tablespoons olive oil

2 large (1 lb. total) onions, chopped

2 cloves garlic

4 cups long-grain white rice

⅛ teaspoon powdered saffron or ground saffron threads (grind with a mortar and pestle)

2 packages (9 oz. each) frozen artichoke hearts, thawed

1 jar (5 oz.) or ½ cup drained Spanish-style olives

2 large (about 1 lb. total) red bell peppers, stemmed, seeded, and chopped

1 pound (about 2 cups) cherry tomatoes, stemmed, rinsed, and cut in half

1 package (1 lb.) frozen petite peas, thawed

Romaine lettuce leaves, rinsed and crisped (optional)

In a 5- to 6-quart pan, combine broth, wine, bay leaf, and 3 cups water. Bring to a boil; stir in shrimp. Cover tightly and remove from heat; let stand just until shrimp is opaque in thickest part (cut to test), about 3 minutes. With a slotted spoon, put shrimp in a large bowl.

Return broth to a boil; stir in scallops. Cover tightly and remove from heat; let stand until scallops are opaque in thickest part (cut to test),

DARROW M. WATT

85

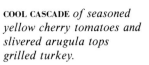

COOL CASCADE *of seasoned yellow cherry tomatoes and slivered arugula tops grilled turkey.*

add the endive strips, minced mint and basil, vinegar, and pepper; mix well. Wrap endive leaves and barley salad separately and airtight; chill until cold, at least 1 hour or up to 1 day.

The meat. Place lamb chops on a lightly greased grill 4 to 6 inches above a solid bed of hot coals (you can hold your hand at grill level for only 2 to 3 seconds). Cook, turning once, until meat is browned but still pink in the center (cut to test), 7 to 9 minutes .

To serve. On 4 dinner plates, arrange lettuce leaves and top equally with barley salad. Set 2 chops on each salad. Garnish with reserved endive leaves and basil sprigs. Serves 4.

Per serving: 500 cal. (22 percent from fat); 41 g protein; 12 g fat (4.1 g sat.); 57 g carbo.; 133 mg sodium; 101 mg chol.

PETER CHRISTIANSEN

Main-dish salads from the barbecue

Meats, hot from the grill, team with grain, vegetables, fruit

THE CONTRAST OF HOT and cold plays a role equal to the seasonings in creating the character of these main-dish salads. Meats hot off the grill rest on top of cool salads. As you cut the meat, juices seep into the ingredients below, and as you eat, the warm moistness of the meat is a foil for the salad textures.

The first salad features lamb loin with minted barley. Turkey breast slices are teamed with tomatoes and arugula. And pork tenderloin mingles with apple slices.

Grilled Lamb Chops with Barley Salad

1¼ cups pearl barley, rinsed and drained

2½ cups regular-strength chicken broth

1 clove garlic, minced or pressed

1 head (4 to 5 oz.) Belgian endive, rinsed and drained

¼ cup minced fresh or 2 tablespoons dried mint leaves

¼ cup minced fresh or 2 tablespoons dried basil leaves

¼ cup seasoned rice vinegar (or rice vinegar plus 1 teaspoon sugar)

½ teaspoon coarsely ground pepper

8 boned loin lamb chops (about 1⅓ lb. total), cut about 1 inch thick, fat trimmed

4 large butter lettuce leaves, rinsed and crisped

Fresh basil or mint sprigs (optional)

The salad. Combine barley, broth, and garlic in a 3- to 4-quart pan over high heat. Cover, bring to a boil, and simmer until barley is tender to bite, about 30 minutes. Pour barley into a bowl; stir often until cool.

Reserve 8 endive leaves. Cut remaining endive into thin strips. To the cool barley,

Grilled Turkey with Two-tone Tomato Salad

¼ cup balsamic or red wine vinegar

2 tablespoons salad oil

2 tablespoons Dijon mustard

3 cups (about 1 lb.) yellow cherry tomatoes, stemmed and rinsed

2 cups lightly packed (about 2 oz.) arugula or fresh basil leaves, rinsed and drained

4 boned, skinned turkey breast slices (about ¾ lb. total), ¼ to ⅓ inch thick

3 large (about 1⅓ lb. total) firm-ripe tomatoes, rinsed

3 tablespoons shredded parmesan cheese

Salt

The salad. In a large bowl, mix vinegar, oil, and mustard; set aside 3 tablespoons. Cut cherry tomatoes in half and mix with dressing. Cut arugula into fine slivers. If making ahead, wrap tomatoes and arugula separately and airtight, and chill up to 1 day.

The meat. Rinse turkey and pat dry; brush with some of the reserved dressing. Set meat on a grill 4 to 6 inches above a solid bed of medium coals (you can hold your hand at grill level for only 4 to 5 seconds). Cook, turning once and brushing with remaining dressing, until slices are white in thickest part (cut to test), about 4 minutes.

To serve. Slice large tomatoes equally onto 4 dinner plates. Mix cherry tomatoes and arugula. Set turkey on sliced tomatoes; top with cherry tomato mixture and cheese; add salt to taste. Serves 4.

Per serving: 242 cal. (39 percent from fat); 25 g protein; 11 g fat (2.2 g sat.); 14 g carbo.; 394 mg sodium; 56 mg chol.

Grilled Pork with Greens and Apple

1 pork tenderloin (about ¾ lb.), fat trimmed

¼ cup cider vinegar

2 tablespoons extra-virgin olive oil or salad oil

½ teaspoon coarsely ground pepper

8 to 10 cups (about ½ lb.) rinsed, crisped bite-size pieces mixed salad greens (mesclun)

⅔ cup packed Roquefort or other blue cheese, crumbled

1 large (about ½-lb.) red apple

1 tablespoon lemon juice
   Salt

The meat. Ignite about 60 charcoal briquets on firegrate in a barbecue with a lid. When coals are well covered with gray ash, about 30 minutes, push half to each side of firegrate. Let burn until coals are medium-hot (you can hold your hand at grill level for only 3 to 4 seconds).

Lay meat in center of grill (not over coals); cover barbecue and open vents. After 10 minutes, turn meat over. Cook until meat in center registers 155° or is no longer pink (cut to test), 10 to 15 minutes longer.

The salad. Meanwhile, in a large bowl, combine vinegar, oil, and pepper; beat until well blended. Add salad greens and crumbled blue cheese; mix gently and pour onto a large platter.

Core and cut apple into thin wedges and mix with the lemon juice to coat well. Arrange slices alongside the salad greens, at one side or both ends of the platter.

To serve. Cut pork into ¼-inch-thick slices and arrange in center of platter; pour juices from pork over meat. Season to taste with salt. Serves 4.

Per serving: 294 cal. (52 percent from fat); 25 g protein; 17 g fat (6.2 g sat.); 11 g carbo.; 435 mg sodium; 81 mg chol. ■

By Christine B. Weber

GRILLED PORK *and crisp apple slices accompany blue cheese-accented mixed greens.*

PETER CHRISTIANSEN

GRILLED LAMB CHOPS *stuffed with blue cheese and pine nuts create a showy but simple entrée. Serve with sliced tomatoes and couscous.*

Easy but dressy dinner ideas

They're lamb or pork chops . . . with a pocket of cheese

SPOON CHEESE FILLING *into pocket of soy-marinated lamb chop, then grill.*

TUCKED INSIDE THESE chops lies a pocket of pungent cheese. In the first recipe, blue cheese and toasted pine nuts fill soy-marinated lamb chops. Tangy chèvre cheese goes into sherry-infused pork chops for another choice. Both make easy-to-prepare, dressy dinner entrées.

To make the pockets, slit chops horizontally to the bone. Marinate the chops for extra flavor, then stuff the pockets with cheese. Grill the chops to brown the meat and warm the filling.

Lamb Chops with Blue Cheese Pockets

8 small lamb rib chops (about 2 lb. total), cut 1 inch thick

½ small onion (3-oz. piece), cut into chunks

¼ cup soy sauce

2 tablespoons firmly packed brown sugar

2 tablespoons lemon juice

1 large clove garlic

Blue cheese filling (recipe follows)

Trim fat off lamb. With a sharp knife, cut a horizontal 1½-inch-wide pocket in each lamb chop, from meaty side to the bone; set chops aside.

In a blender or food processor, whirl onion, soy sauce, brown sugar, lemon juice, and garlic until smoothly puréed. Pour into a heavy plastic food bag. Add lamb chops. Seal bag; rotate to mix well. Chill at least 30 minutes or up to 6 hours; turn occasionally.

Lift out chops and drain, reserving marinade. Using a spoon, stuff ⅛ of the cheese filling deep into the pocket of each chop.

Place chops on a greased grill 4 to 6 inches above a solid bed of hot coals (you can hold your hand at grill level only 2 to 3 seconds).

Cook, basting twice with marinade and turning once, until meat is done to your liking in thickest part (cut to test), 6 to 8 minutes total for medium-rare. Serves 4.

Per serving: 316 cal. (54 percent from fat); 27 g protein; 19 g fat (6.4 g sat.); 12 g carbo.; 1,251 mg sodium; 75 mg chol.

Blue cheese filling. In a 6- to 8-inch frying pan, stir ⅓ cup **pine nuts** or slivered almonds often over medium heat until golden, 3 to 5 minutes. Pour the nuts into a small bowl and mix with ⅓ cup crumbled **blue cheese.** Add **pepper** to taste.

Pork Chops with Chèvre Pockets

4 center-cut pork loin chops (about 2 lb. total), cut 1 inch thick

½ cup cream sherry

2 tablespoons lemon juice

2 ounces chèvre cheese

Lemon wedges

Trim fat off pork. With a sharp knife, cut a horizontal 1½-inch-wide slit in each chop, from meaty side to bone; widen it near bone. Set chops in a heavy plastic food bag. Add sherry and lemon juice. Seal bag; rotate to mix. Chill at least 30 minutes or up to 6 hours; turn occasionally. Lift out chops and drain, reserving marinade. Stuff ¼ of cheese deep into each pocket. Place chops on a greased grill 4 to 6 inches above a solid bed of medium coals (you can hold your hand at grill level only 4 to 5 seconds). Cook, basting with marinade and turning once, just until meat is no longer pink in thickest part (cut to test), 10 to 14 minutes total. Offer lemon wedges to squeeze onto meat. Serves 4.

Per serving: 338 cal. (40 percent from fat); 37 g protein; 15 g fat (3.9 g sat.); 4.5 g carbo.; 228 mg sodium; 106 mg chol. ∎

By Karyn I. Lipman

Why?

Why cook meat ? What precautions are necessary in handling raw meat?

ONE REASON IS TO give meat the look, taste, texture, and aromas that develop when heat sets off certain chemical changes.

But another vital benefit is that heat destroys the bacteria that, if present in meat (here defined as beef, lamb, pork, game, poultry, and fish), can make you sick and may cause death. Even *Escherichia coli*, the culprit recently found in fast-food hamburgers, is killed by sufficient heat.

How do bacteria get on meat?

Our environment is teeming with bacteria—the vast majority of which are harmless. For the most part, we coexist with them without problems. Harmful bacteria come from animal and human wastes, infectious wounds, and the soil; they are transferred by contact. In moderate to large numbers, they can multiply to dangerous levels in a few hours—in or out of your body.

How can you make sure harmful bacteria aren't present?

Since bacteria are too tiny to see without a microscope, food-safe practices start with the assumption that harmful ones are present.

Proper handling and storage are the first steps toward controlling them. Use the "Keeping clean" section at far right as a guide.

Next, you need to cook the meat for at least 4 minutes at 140°, the minimum temperature at which you can kill non-spore-forming bacteria,

including the dangerous ones, *Campylobacter, Escherichia coli, Salmonella,* and *Staphylococcus.* It takes less time to kill them at higher temperatures. Even if food is heavily contaminated, heat will kill the bacteria.

Once bacteria are killed, food has to be recontaminated by contact with more bacteria before there is a problem. If food is recontaminated—for example, if cooked meat comes into contact with uncooked meat or its juices—more heat will kill new bacteria and the food will be safe to eat.

For any meat, the cook concerned about quality and safety will find an accurate food thermometer invaluable. The thermometer should register at least 212°, and you should check its accuracy regularly by immersing the stem in boiling water. At sea level, the thermometer will read 212° at boiling.

Cuts of beef or lamb are often served rare.

Is this dangerous? Bacteria are on surfaces, not within the muscle and solid fat of meat, unless a gash permits entry. When a roast, steak, or chop is cooked to rare (about 135°) internally, it's hotter on the surface, and surface bacteria are destroyed.

If you cook in a microwave oven, check meat temperature throughout.

Why is rare ground meat a greater risk?

When meat is ground, any surface bacteria present are distributed throughout.

What is a safe way to cook a hamburger patty?

The way to cook commercially ground meat is now under scrutiny. The USDA and FDA may soon recommend thoroughly cooking meat to an internal temperature of 155°, even 160°, as the fail-safe approach. Some fast-food restaurants already use 155° to compensate for variables involved in large-scale commercial cooking.

If you like meat less well done, cook it until it maintains 140° internally for 4 minutes. Use a thermometer to check thick patties, or use the following technique for ones ½ inch thick or less.

Cook patties on one side until they're well browned. Turn them over and cook until the other side is well browned and a few bubbles of juice break through the top surface; the meat may be slightly pink in the center.

But what if I want really rare beef or to eat beef or fish raw?

Eating raw meat is not recommended for young children, the elderly, or pregnant women. Anyone with an immune system compromised by medication or disease should also refrain from consuming raw meat because their risk of illness or death is greater. The USDA and FDA discourage consuming meat raw.

If you love raw or rare beef, you'll have the most quality control if you grind or cut your own. If you choose to grind or cut meat at home, start with a solid chunk and

use the cleanliness guidelines that follow.

If you want to be certain that harmful surface bacteria are dead before starting preparations, immerse the piece of meat in boiling water for 5 to 10 seconds.

For such raw fish preparations as sashimi, seviche, or gravlax, use fish that has been frozen at 0° for at least a week.

Keeping clean

1. Wash your hands thoroughly with soap and water after handling any raw meat and before touching any other foods, especially those that aren't going to be cooked.

2. Always put raw meat on a clean surface (washed with detergent and water, then rinsed); use clean tools for cutting and chopping.

3. Avoid cross-contamination. Never let meat or its juices touch food that won't be cooked (such as salad greens and other raw vegetables) or put those foods on surfaces touched by meat or its juices. Wash cutting boards between uses for meats and other foods.

4. Keep foods in the refrigerator. If perishable moist foods are held at room temperature for 4 hours or more, bacteria can grow to numbers high enough to cause illness. Refrigerator temperatures permit only very slow growth of some types of bacteria. Freezing stops bacterial growth but doesn't destroy significant numbers.

Growth of surface bacteria resumes when frozen or refrigerated foods reach room temperature.

More food questions?

Send your questions about food to Why?, Sunset Magazine, 80 Willow Rd., Menlo Park, Calif. 94025. Dr. George K. York, extension food technologist at UC Davis, and Sunset food editors will find the solution. ∎

By Linda Lau Anusasananan

BRIGHT BANDS *of carrot dress up baked gefilte fish loaf.*

NORMAN A. PLATE

Winning Passover dishes

For cooks of all persuasions

L IKE THANKSGIVING'S roast turkey, dishes prepared for the Jewish Passover celebration are appealing for other meals as well. Gefilte fish, baked in a terrine, makes a delicious fish loaf that's lower in calories and fat than a meat counterpart. By any standard, the matzo tart is a fine dessert.

Gefilte Fish Terrine

Tilapia, swordfish, and regular salt are not suitable to use in Jewish religious dishes for Passover.

2½ pounds boned and skinned white-flesh fish such as pike, carp, tilapia, or swordfish (or a combination), cut into ½-inch chunks

1 large (about ½-lb.) onion, chopped

2 large eggs

¼ cup matzo meal

2 teaspoons sugar

1 teaspoon kosher or regular coarse salt

½ teaspoon white pepper

About ⅓ cup prepared horseradish

2 cups finely chopped carrots

12 large butter lettuce leaves, rinsed and crisped

Fresh dill sprigs

In a food processor or blender, smoothly purée half the fish, onion, and eggs with 2 tablespoons water. Scrape into a bowl. Repeat step. Stir in matzo meal, sugar, salt, pepper, and 1 tablespoon horseradish.

Line bottom of an oiled 5-by 9-inch loaf pan with foil or cooking parchment cut to fit; oil lining. Spoon ⅓ of fish mixture into pan; spread smooth. Sprinkle with ½ the carrots. Repeat with layers of fish, carrots, and fish. Tap pan sharply against counter to settle mixture.

Set loaf pan in a larger pan at least 2 inches deep. Set pans on center rack in a 325° oven. Pour 1½ inches boiling water into outer pan. Bake until loaf feels firm when pressed in center, about 45 minutes. Lift loaf pan from water. Let cool, then chill until cold, at least 6 hours or up to 1 day. Slide a knife between loaf and pan sides; invert loaf onto a platter tapping pan to release. Peel off lining and discard. Slice loaf; present slices on lettuce with dill garnish. Add horseradish to taste. Makes 12 servings.

Per serving: 128 cal. (11 percent from fat); 20 g protein; 1.6 g fat (0.4 g sat.); 7.5 g carbo.; 184 mg sodium; 72 mg chol.

Matzo Tart with Orange Curd

1 cup sugar

¼ cup potato starch

1 tablespoon grated orange peel

¾ cup orange juice

¼ cup lemon juice

2 large eggs

Matzo meal crust (recipe follows)

2 cups fresh or frozen unsweetened blueberries, rinsed and drained

In a 1½- to 2-quart pan, mix sugar with potato starch. Stir in peel, orange juice, and lemon juice. Stir over high heat until boiling. Off the heat, whisk in eggs. Return to heat and stir just until mixture bubbles. Let cool at least 10 minutes. (If making ahead, cool, cover, and chill up to 1 day. If clear liquid separates from mixture, whisk on medium-high heat until bubbling; let cool 10 minutes.)

Spread warm filling into tart shell; top with the blueberries. Cut tart, warm or cool, into wedges. Makes 8 to 10 servings.

Per serving: 297 cal. (33 percent from fat); 3.6 g protein; 11 g fat (2 g sat.); 47 g carbo.; 130 mg sodium; 64 mg chol.

Matzo meal crust. In a food processor or a bowl, whirl or rub with your fingers 1 cup **matzo meal,** ⅓ cup **sugar,** and ½ cup (¼ lb.) **margarine** or butter, in pieces, until well mixed. Add 1 large **egg** and 3 tablespoons **water;** whirl or stir until the dough holds together. Dip fingers in more matzo meal and press the soft dough evenly over the bottom and sides of a 9-inch tart pan with removable rim.

Bake in a 325° oven until crust is darker brown and feels firm when pressed in center, 30 to 40 minutes. Use warm or cool; if making ahead, wrap crust airtight up to 1 day. ■

By Karyn I. Lipman

They are Easter cookie eggs

You shape dough in half-egg plastic molds

A TREAT FOR ANY AGE: *Icing-glazed cookie eggs, sandwiched together with more icing, are tied with slender ribbons. Attach decors while icing is moist.*

GLENN CHRISTIANSEN

RUNCHY EGG-SHAPED cookies, iced and festively decorated, make a pretty addition to Easter baskets. Shape dough in half-egg plastic molds that are sold in cookware and bakery supply stores; the molds come in a range of sizes.

Chocolate Cookie Eggs

½ cup unblanched almonds

¾ cup (⅜ lb.) butter or margarine

About ½ cup granulated sugar

2 teaspoons vanilla

½ cup chocolate baking chips

2 cups all-purpose flour

Whole blanched almonds (optional)

About 4 cups sifted powdered sugar

About ¼ cup water

Candy decors (optional)

In a food processor or with a knife, mince nuts. Whirl or beat nuts with butter, ½ cup granulated sugar, and vanilla until blended.

In a 1- to 1½-quart pan

over low heat, stir chocolate just until smoothly melted. Add to nut mixture; whirl or beat. Add flour gradually; whirl or mix until dough holds together.

Rub half-egg plastic molds (2-teaspoon- or 1-tablespoon-size) with salad oil, then sprinkle liberally with granulated sugar; shake out excess. If desired, lay a whole blanched almond (or several) in each mold. Pack dough firmly into molds; scrape surface smooth; reuse scraps. Chill dough until firm to touch, 5 to 15 minutes.

Invert molds on ungreased 12- by 15-inch baking sheets; tap briskly to release dough. Use tip of a small knife to coax a bit. Repeat until pans are filled with cookies spaced slightly apart. Bake in a 300° oven until lightly browned, 20 to 30 minutes for 2-teaspoon-size cookies, 30 to 40 minutes for tablespoon size. If using 1 oven, switch pan positions halfway through baking.

Put the cookies, flat side down, on racks to cool thoroughly.

In a bowl, mix 4 cups powdered sugar with ¼ cup water until smooth. Icing needs to be thin enough to pour thickly from a spoon—add a little more sugar or water if needed.

Place a clean baking sheet or waxed paper under racks. With a spoon, ladle icing evenly over cookies. Scrape icing on sheet into a bowl; cover and set aside. While icing is damp on eggs, attach decors as desired. Let icing dry until firm to touch, about 3 hours.

Spread flat side of 1 cookie with reserved icing; sandwich against flat side of same-size cookie. Press until they hold together, then let dry on rack until icing is firm, about 2 hours. Serve, or store airtight up to 4 days. Makes about 42 small whole eggs (4-teaspoon size) or 28 large whole eggs (2-tablespoon size).

Per small whole-egg cookie: 118 cal. (37 percent from fat); 1.1 g protein; 4.8 g fat (2.1 g sat.); 18 g carbo.; 34 mg sodium; 9 mg chol. ■

By Karyn I. Lipman

PACK DOUGH *into half-egg molds. Chill; pop from molds onto pan to bake.*

ENLIST TINY HANDS *to help secure colorful ribbons around cookie eggs.*

In a small bowl, beat egg yolks and cream together. Stir some hot soup into eggs, then stir as you pour egg mixture into soup.

Add diced artichoke bottoms; stir until steaming. Ladle into bowls and garnish with green onions. Season to taste with salt and pepper. Serves 5 or 6.

Per serving: 204 cal. (66 percent from fat); 5.5 g protein; 15 g fat (8.2 g sat.); 14 g carbo.; 161 mg sodium; 109 mg chol.

El Segundo, California

EVERETT ADAMS, WISHING to impress his mother-in-law on the occasion of her Easter visit, prepared a crown roast of pork on the barbecue. She was impressed; we were, too, when our kitchen repeated his performance.

You don't approach this show lightly. In the first place, you'll need to have your butcher prepare the roast for you. Properly cut, it will really resemble a crown, with the ribs arching upward and outward in a circle. When you bring the finished roast to the table, let it stand for 10 minutes before carving, not only to firm it up for the knife but also to give the guests time to admire it before you demolish it.

Barbecued Pork Crown Roast

1 medium-size (5- to 6-oz.) onion, chopped

2 cloves garlic, minced or pressed

2 tablespoons minced fresh ginger

1 teaspoon dry mustard

¼ teaspoon pepper

½ cup *each* olive oil, bourbon, and soy sauce

2 tablespoons balsamic vinegar

Pork crown roast (6¾ to 7 lb.) with 12 ribs

In a bowl, stir together onion, garlic, ginger, mustard, pepper, oil, bourbon, soy

Getting to the essence of artichokes

Cream soup is a big effort, but justifiable

EATING AN ARTICHOKE involves a bit of effort, but it's worth it. Making artichoke cream soup involves even more effort, but it's justifiable. You and your guests get the artichoke's flavor (enriched by cream and egg) without the bother of stripping pulp from the leaves or teasing out the choke.

Artichoke Cream Soup

4 medium-size (about 2 lb. total) artichokes

2 leeks (12 to 14 oz. total)

3 tablespoons butter or margarine

3 tablespoons all-purpose flour

3½ cups or 2 cans (14½ oz. each) regular-strength chicken broth

2 large egg yolks

½ cup whipping cream

Thinly sliced green onions

Salt and pepper

Cut off top ⅓ of each artichoke; rinse artichokes well.

Set upside down in a round 9-inch-wide microwave-safe dish. Add ½ cup water and cover with microwave-safe plastic wrap. Cook in a microwave oven on full power (100 percent) until stem ends are tender when pierced, 13 to 15 minutes; rotate dish ¼ turn every 5 minutes. Let stand, covered, for 5 minutes.

With a small spoon, scrape and reserve tender pulp from leaves; discard leaves. Scrape and discard fuzzy choke from artichoke bottoms; dice bottoms and set aside.

Trim tough green leaves and roots from leeks. Split leeks lengthwise; rinse well and thinly slice.

Melt butter in a 2- to 3-quart pan over medium heat; add leeks. Cover and stir occasionally until leeks are limp, 8 to 10 minutes. Add flour and stir until bubbly and well blended. Gradually add broth, stirring until mixture bubbles. Add artichoke pulp, cover, and simmer for 15 minutes. Pour mixture, a portion at a time, into a blender and whirl until smooth. Return to pan.

*"**HE WISHED** to impress his mother-in-law on the occasion of her visit."*

Y OU WILL FIND BREAD pudding on down-home dining tables and in the grandest restaurants, especially those that claim New Orleans as a spiritual ancestor. The pudding is a shining example of how the simplest ingredients can be combined for stunning effect. (What are diamonds but carbon in a special configuration?)

Why is this bread pudding different from all other bread puddings? For one thing chef Meely, like chef Adams, favors burbon for flavoring. Mixed with sugar, butter, and egg to make a bubbling broiled-on sauce, it glazes the baked pudding with distinction.

sauce, and vinegar.

Place roast in a heavy plastic food bag (about 2 gal.); pour in onion mixture and seal bag. Tilt to coat meat with marinade. Set bag in a rimmed pan and chill 4 to 24 hours; turn bag over several times to allow marinade to coat all surfaces.

Ignite 50 to 60 charcoal briquets on firegrate in a barbecue with a lid. When coals are well spotted with gray ash, in about 30 minutes, push coals equally to opposite sides of firegrate.

Set a drip pan in center firegrate. Add 4 briquets to each mound of coals; repeat this step every 30 minutes to maintain steady heat.

Place grill 4 to 6 inches above firegrate; lightly oil grill. Lift roast from marinade; drain briefly, reserving marinade. Set meat, largest side down, on grill over drip pan, not coals.

Cover barbecue, open vents, and cook until a meat thermometer inserted at bone in thickest part of roast registers 155°, about 2 hours. Baste frequently during the first hour with reserved marinade.

Place roast on a platter and let stand for 10 minutes, then cut down between the ribs. Makes 10 to 12 servings.

Per serving: 478 cal. (73 percent from fat); 28 g protein; 39 g fat (12 g sat.); 2.5 g carbo.; 755 mg sodium; 104 mg chol.

Reno

Bourbon Bread Pudding

- 1 loaf (1 lb.) day-old French bread
- 5 large eggs
- 3 cups sugar
- 2 teaspoons vanilla
- 4 cups milk
- 1 cup raisins

  About ¼ cup (⅛ lb.) unsalted butter or margarine
- ½ cup bourbon

  Vanilla ice cream (optional)

Cut French bread into ½-inch cubes.

In a large bowl, beat 4 eggs to blend with 2 cups of the sugar, the vanilla, and the milk. Add bread and raisins; let stand at least 10 minutes. Stir often to saturate bread with milk mixture.

Spoon mixture into a buttered 9- by 13-inch pan. Set pan in a slightly larger pan that is at least 2 inches deep. Put pans in a 350° oven and pour about 1 inch boiling water into larger pan. Bake until pudding feels firm in center when lightly touched, about 1 hour.

Melt ¼ cup butter in a 1- to 1½-quart pan over medium-high heat. Add the remaining 1 cup sugar and the bourbon; stir until the sugar dissolves.

In a small bowl, beat re-maining egg to blend. Stir a little of the hot butter mixture into the egg, then return egg mixture to pan and stir bourbon sauce about 1 minute.

Pour hot bourbon sauce over warm pudding. Broil about 8 inches from heat until top of pudding is glazed and sauce bubbles. Scoop into bowls and top with vanilla ice cream. Makes 12 to 14 servings.

Per serving: 400 cal. (19 percent from fat); 7.8 g protein; 8.4 g fat (4.3 g sat.); 72 g carbo.; 247 mg sodium; 95 mg chol.

(signature)

Walnut Creek, California

*"**ROOT VEGETABLES** held a more important place in our diets."*

I N EARLIER TIMES, BEFORE refrigeration and rapid transport made fresh fruits and vegetables available throughout the year, root vegetables held a more important place in our diets. Hardy to cold and easily stored, they were the winter vegetables par excellence.

That they are no longer a necessity is no reason to abandon them to the root cellar. As Louise Galen prepares them, parsnips and sunchokes (Jerusalem artichokes) mashed together make a richly flavored alternative to potatoes, rice, or noodles.

The sunchoke (*Helianthus tuberosus*) is native to the continental United States. For some strange reason, it has long been known as the Jerusalem artichoke. Perhaps it's because the Italian word for sunflower, *girasole*, sounds a bit like Jerusalem.

But since it's a species of sunflower, produce dealers encourage the logical use of sun in this vegetable's name.

Mashed Parsnips and Sunchokes

- 3 tablespoons vinegar or lemon juice
- 1½ pounds sunchokes (Jerusalem artichokes)
- 2 cups regular-strength chicken broth
- 2 pounds parsnips, peeled and cut into 1-inch chunks
- ¼ teaspoon *each* ground nutmeg and white pepper
- 1 tablespoon butter or margarine
- 2 tablespoons sour cream or whipping cream

  Chopped parsley
  Salt

In a bowl, combine vinegar and 1 quart water. Peel sunchokes and cut them into ½-inch cubes; immediately immerse cubes in the acid-water to prevent browning.

In a 3- to 4-quart pan over high heat, combine broth, drained sunchokes, parsnips, nutmeg, and pepper. Cover and bring to a boil; boil gently until parsnips are soft enough to mash easily, about 35 minutes. Uncover and boil on high heat until liquid is absorbed; as liquid reduces, stir often and watch mixture carefully to avoid scorching it.

With an electric mixer or a potato masher, beat vegetables until smoothly mashed (sunchokes may retain a little texture).

Add butter and cream. Sprinkle with parsley. Season to taste with salt. Makes about 5 cups, 5 or 6 servings.

Per serving: 195 cal. (18 percent from fat); 4.1 g protein; 3.8 g fat (2 g sat.); 38 g carbo.; 53 mg sodium; 7.3 mg chol.

(signature) Louise Galen

Los Angeles

By Richard Dunmire, Joan Griffiths

SUNSET'S KITCHEN CABINET

Creative ways with everyday foods—submitted by *Sunset* readers,
tested in *Sunset* kitchens, approved by *Sunset* taste panels

WHIRL WHOLE-WHEAT *flour, eggs, and broth in blender to make popovers.*

Whole-wheat Popovers

Helen Robinson, Clifton, Texas

These crisp popovers are made with broth instead of the usual milk; whole-wheat flour adds its toasty flavor. Enjoy them hot for breakfast, lunch, or dinner.

    3 large eggs
    1 cup regular-strength chicken
       broth
    ⅔ cup whole-wheat flour
    ⅓ cup all-purpose flour

Butter 6 nonstick muffin cups or popover cups (each 2 to 2½ in. wide).

In a blender, whirl to smoothly mix the eggs, chicken broth, whole-wheat flour, and all-purpose flour. At once, pour the batter equally into the buttered cups.

Bake in a 375° oven until the popovers are very well browned and firm to the touch, 45 to 50 minutes. Run a knife between each cup and popover; invert and serve hot. Makes 6 popovers.

Per popover: 113 cal. (25 percent from fat); 6 g protein; 3.1 g fat (0.9 g sat.); 16 g carbo.; 41 mg sodium; 106 mg chol.

TARRAGON *dressing seasons slivered Belgian endive, radishes, and bacon.*

Belgian Endive and Radish Salad

Marilyn Swartz, Los Angeles

    3 large (each about 5 oz.) heads
       Belgian endive, leaves
       separated, rinsed, and crisped
    1 cup thinly sliced red radishes
    1 large hard-cooked egg, finely
       chopped
    6 slices crisp cooked bacon,
       drained and crumbled
    ¼ cup minced parsley
       Tarragon dressing (recipe
       follows)

On each of 6 salad plates, arrange 4 endive leaves in a fan. Slice remaining leaves crosswise into ¼-inch-wide strips. Combine sliced endive, radishes, egg, bacon, and parsley. Spoon mixture equally onto plates at base of leaves, and spoon dressing over salads. Makes 6 servings.

Per serving: 128 cal. (77 percent from fat); 3.9 g protein; 11 g fat (2.2 g sat.); 4 g carbo.; 172 mg sodium; 41 mg chol.

Tarragon dressing. In a small bowl, whisk together 3 tablespoons **tarragon-flavor vinegar** or white wine vinegar, 3 tablespoons **salad oil,** 2 teaspoons **Dijon mustard,** 1 clove minced or pressed **garlic,** ½ teaspoon **pepper,** and 1 teaspoon minced **fresh** or ½ teaspoon dried **tarragon leaves.**

Citrus-Shrimp Salad

Mrs. L. K. Ross, Elk Grove, California

    ½ cup thawed frozen orange juice
       concentrate
    ½ cup dry sherry (optional)
    1 teaspoon dried rosemary leaves
    ½ teaspoon dried coriander seed
    1 pound large (25 to 32 per lb.)
       shrimp, shelled, deveined, and
       rinsed
    2 teaspoons toasted sesame seed
    1 medium-size (about ¾-lb.) head
       red leaf lettuce, rinsed and
       crisped
    2 large (about 2⅓ lb. total)
       grapefruit
    2 large (about 1¼ lb. total) oranges
       Citrus cream dressing (recipe
       follows)

In a 1½- to 2-quart pan on high heat, bring to boiling 2 cups water, orange juice concentrate, sherry, rosemary, and coriander. Add shrimp; cover pan and remove from heat. Let stand 20 minutes. Drain and chill shrimp.

Dry pan. Add sesame seed and stir over medium heat until golden, about 3 minutes; pour from pan.

Tear lettuce into bite-size pieces into a wide, shallow bowl. With a sharp knife, cut peel and white membrane from grapefruit and oranges. Hold fruit over greens and cut between inner membranes to free segments; scatter fruit onto greens. Top salad with shrimp, sesame seed and dressing; mix gently. Makes 4 main-dish servings.

Per serving: 281 cal. (11 percent from fat); 25 g protein; 3.3 g fat (0.6 g sat.); 40 g carbo.; 304 mg sodium; 141 mg chol.

Citrus cream dressing. In a small bowl, combine 1 cup **unflavored nonfat yogurt,** 2 tablespoons thawed **frozen orange juice concentrate,** 1 tablespoon **Dijon mustard,** 2 teaspoons **prepared horseradish,** and 2 finely chopped **green onions.**

STEEPED SHRIMP *with grapefruit and orange sections make a colorful salad.*

Asparagus and Pasta Stir-fry

Diana K. Estey, Portland

  6 ounces dried vermicelli

  1 pound asparagus, tough ends trimmed

  2 teaspoons salad oil

  1 clove garlic, minced or pressed

  1 teaspoon minced fresh ginger

  ½ cup diagonally sliced green onions

  2 tablespoons soy sauce

  ⅛ teaspoon crushed dried red hot chilies

In a 4- to 5-quart pan, bring 3 quarts water to a boil on high heat. Add pasta; cook, uncovered, just until tender to bite, 6 to 8 minutes. Drain well.

Meanwhile, diagonally slice asparagus into 1½-inch pieces. Place a wok or 10- to 12-inch frying pan over high heat. When pan is hot, add oil, garlic, ginger, asparagus, and onions. Stir-fry until asparagus is tender-crisp, about 3 minutes. Add soy sauce and chilies; stir-fry 1 minute longer. Add drained pasta to pan; stir-fry until hot. Serves 4 to 6.

Per serving: 134 cal. (13 percent from fat); 5.3 g protein; 2 g fat (0.3 g sat.); 24 g carbo.; 347 mg sodium; 0 mg chol.

STIR-FRIED ASPARAGUS *and vermicelli are seasoned with fresh ginger and garlic.*

Crusted Lamb and Potatoes

Mrs. W. Shultz, Blaine, Washington

Half a leg of lamb is ideal for a quick, small dinner; it cooks faster than the whole leg.

    Upper thigh half (3 to 3½ lb.) of 1 leg of lamb

  3 pounds russet potatoes, peeled and sliced ¾ inch thick

  1½ cups regular-strength chicken broth

    Seasoning paste (recipe follows)

    Salt and pepper

Trim and discard surface fat from lamb. Cover bottom of a 12- by 15-inch roasting pan with potato slices; add broth and set lamb on potatoes.

Roast, uncovered, in a 400° oven for 45 minutes. Spread paste evenly over lamb and potatoes. Continue roasting until crust on meat is well browned and until a thermometer inserted in thickest part of lamb at bone registers 145° for medium-rare, about 25 minutes longer. Transfer lamb, potatoes, and any juices to a platter. Season portions to taste with salt and pepper. Serves 6.

Per serving: 467 cal. (25 percent from fat); 36 g protein; 13 g fat (6 g sat.); 49 g carbo.; 349 mg sodium; 108 mg chol.

Seasoning paste. In a bowl, mash together 3 cloves **garlic**, minced; 1 small (¼-lb.) **onion,** minced; 3 tablespoons minced **parsley;** 1 cup **seasoned stuffing mix;** 3 tablespoons **butter** or margarine, at room temperature; 1 tablespoon grated **lemon peel;** and 2 tablespoons **lemon juice.**

PAT SEASONING *paste of garlic, lemon, and parsley onto lamb and potatoes.*

Chocolate Double-dip Strawberries

Heather Sager, Carlsbad, California

Dipped berries look and taste best if served within a few hours.

  12 large (2- to 2½-in.-wide) strawberries with stems

  ¾ cup (4½ oz.) semisweet chocolate baking chips

  ½ cup (3 oz.) white chocolate baking chips for dipping

Rinse strawberries; do not remove stems. Drain dry on towels.

Place semisweet chocolate in a double boiler top or bowl nested over hot (not simmering) water; stir occasionally until chocolate is smoothly melted, about 8 minutes. (Or heat for 5-second intervals in a microwave-safe bowl in a microwave oven; stir often.) Remove pan top from heat.

Dip strawberries, tips down, into semisweet chocolate. Rotate each berry to coat about ⅔ of the tip end. Set strawberries well apart on a 12- by 15-inch waxed paper–lined baking sheet (or embed toothpicks well apart in plastic foam, then impale each berry, tip up, on a toothpick). Chill until chocolate is firm, about 15 minutes.

In another bowl or pan, melt white chocolate as directed for semisweet chocolate. Dip each strawberry tip into white chocolate, rotating to coat about half the dark chocolate at strawberry tip. Chill at least 10 minutes or up to 8 hours. Hold stems to eat. Makes 12.

Per berry: 84 cal. (47 percent from fat); 0.9 g protein; 4.4 g fat (2.5 g sat.); 12 g carbo.; 6.7 mg sodium; 0.1 mg chol.

Compiled by Paula Smith Freschet

STRAWBERRIES, *double chocolate-dipped, make an elegant, refreshing dessert.*

May Menus

What's for dinner? Since the early '30s, menus geared to offer an inviting response to this daily query have been among the regular features in *Sunset*. The focus now, as it was then, is on ways to serve family and friends interesting, attractive meals that make good use of seasonal foods and discriminating use of time and effort.

This month is no exception. Tamale pie gets a fresh, quicker, lighter take; pizza moves to breakfast; and Asian seasonings enliven chicken salad.

PETER CHRISTIANSEN

TAMALE PIE FOR THE '90S (at right)
Make-ahead turkey-tortilla casserole with nacho topping is a great family meal with green salsa, salad, and jicama.

PIZZA FOR BREAKFAST (page 98)
Fruit, ricotta cheese, and a little sugar and spice on a ready-bake crust give pizza a breakfast personality.

ASIAN SALAD SUPPER (page 99)
Chicken and pineapple with salad greens and fried noodles contrast crisp and juicy, warm and cool, sweet and spicy.

TAMALE PIE, AN ENDURING FAVORITE

Tamale Pudding, Sunset's first version of tamale pie, appeared in 1920. It had a cornmeal crust, meat and tomato filling, and quasi-Mexican seasonings.

Of the many variations that followed, none resembled an authentic Mexican dish. In 1944 (above), the filling was in a ring of cornmeal mush. Cowgirl, below, offers a 1959 concoction with ham and cornbread.

TERI SANDISON

In Yucatán, we discovered a hotel cook who decided to bake tamales in a pan, inadvertently creating a true Mexican tamale pie. We published her delicious innovation, well laced with lard, in 1980. Our current tamale pie, at left, captures similar flavors with tortillas and turkey, but no lard.

97

The tamale pie and fruit sauce hold if you want to prepare them a day ahead. Wake up appetites with crisp radishes and jicama slices to dip into chili-seasoned salt. To give white jicama slices a fresh look, dip narrow edges in some of the chili salt. Purchase the salsa and frozen yogurt.

Turkey Tamale Pie with Nacho Crust

2   pounds (2 large) turkey thighs or (about 6) chicken thighs, skin and fat removed

1   quart regular-strength chicken broth

3   tablespoons ground dried California or New Mexico chilies, or regular chili powder

1½ teaspoons dried oregano leaves

2   large (about 1 lb. total) onions, each cut into 8 wedges

1   can (14½ oz.) unsalted or salted stewed tomatoes

18 corn tortillas (6½-in. size; about 21 oz. total)

1   cup drained pimiento-stuffed Spanish-style olives

1   tablespoon cornstarch

1   package (10 oz.) thawed frozen corn

½   cup raisins

½   cup chopped fresh cilantro (coriander)

1   cup (¼ lb.) grated sharp cheddar cheese

Fresh cilantro sprigs

In a 4- to 5-quart pan over high heat, bring thighs, broth, chilies, and oregano to

PETER CHRISTIANSEN

MORNING PIZZA *is topped with grapes (instead of olives) and nectarines. Bubbly drink is sparkling juice—not beer.*

a boil. Cover and simmer for 10 minutes; turn thighs over and add onions. Return to simmer and cook until thighs are no longer pink at bone (cut to test), about 20 minutes longer for turkey (15 minutes for chicken). With a slotted spoon, lift out thighs and onions; set onions aside. Let meat cool, then tear from bones into ½-inch-wide strips; discard bones.

Meanwhile, add tomatoes with their liquid to broth; boil, uncovered, over high heat until reduced to 3¾ cups, about 15 minutes. Dunk 12 tortillas, 1 at a time, into hot liquid to soften, about 10 seconds. Line a well-oiled shallow 3- to 3½-quart casserole with sauce-dipped tortillas, overlapping to cover bottom and sides, flush with rim.

Arrange onions, turkey, and all but ⅓ cup of the olives on tortillas. Mix cornstarch smoothly with 1 tablespoon water; stir into broth mixture along with corn, raisins, and chopped cilantro. Pour broth mixture over ingredients in casserole. (If

making ahead, let cool, then cover and chill up to 1 day; also wrap remaining tortillas and olives airtight and chill.)

Cover casserole tightly with foil. Bake in a 425° oven for 30 minutes (40 minutes, if chilled). Meanwhile, stack remaining tortillas and cut stack into 8 wedges.

Uncover casserole and scatter tortilla wedges and cheese over filling. Turn oven to 475° and bake casserole, uncovered, until cheese melts and tortillas are crisp, 10 to 12 minutes. Slice reserved olives; scatter olives and cilantro sprigs over tamale pie. Scoop out portions. Serves 6 to 8.

Per serving: 441 cal. (27 percent from fat); 25 g protein; 13 g fat (4.6 g sat.); 60 g carbo.; 734 mg sodium; 63 mg chol.

Mangoes and Raspberries with Frozen Yogurt

2   medium-size (about 1¼ lb. total) soft-ripe mangoes

½   teaspoon anise seed

1   quart vanilla frozen yogurt

1½ cups raspberries, rinsed and drained

Slide a sharp knife lengthwise down each side of mango pits to cut fruit free. Cut peel from fruit, and any remaining fruit from pits. Cut a few mango slices and set aside. Smoothly whirl remaining fruit and anise in a blender or food processor. If making ahead, chill airtight up to 1 day.

Scoop frozen yogurt into 6 to 8 bowls. Pour mango sauce over yogurt and top with raspberries and mango slices. Serves 6 to 8.

Per serving: 143 cal. (8.2 percent from fat); 4.5 g protein; 1.3 g fat (0 g sat.); 29 g carbo.; 56 mg sodium; 5 mg chol.

Tequila or Orange Sours

⅓   cup sugar

⅔   cup water

1⅓ cups lime juice

1⅓ cups tequila or orange juice

1½ quarts ice cubes

Lime wedges

In a 1- to 1½-quart pan over high heat, bring sugar and water to a boil, stirring until sugar is dissolved; let cool. If making ahead, cover and chill syrup up to 1 week. Mix syrup, lime juice, and tequila. Pour into ice-filled glasses; garnish with lime wedges. Serves 6 to 8.

Per serving: 133 cal. (0.7 percent from fat); 0.1 g protein; 0.1 g fat (0 g sat.); 11 g carbo.; 7 mg sodium; 0 mg chol.

A ready-to-cook refrigerated pizza crust, the base for the breakfast pastry, makes morning baking a snap. In addition to the fruit pastry, offer more fresh grapes and nectarines for munching. Serve sparkling apple juice and hot tea: Lapsang souchong has a distinctive smoky flavor.

Quick Fruit and Ricotta Pizza

1   package (10 oz.) refrigerated pizza crust dough

2   ounces paper-thin slices prosciutto

8   ounces (1 cup) part-skim ricotta cheese

2   teaspoons grated lemon peel

2   medium-size (⅔ lb. total) nectarines or peeled peaches, pitted and thinly sliced

¾   cup dark seedless grape halves

2   tablespoons sugar

¼   teaspoon ground cinnamon

Unroll dough and press evenly into an oiled 14-inch pizza pan (or 10- by 15-in. pan). Bake on bottom rack in a 425° oven until crust is well browned, about 8 minutes.

Cut enough prosciutto into ¼-inch strips to make ¼ cup; set remainder aside. Mix ricotta and peel; drop in 1-tablespoon portions over crust. Arrange nectarines, grapes, and prosciutto strips on crust. Combine sugar and cinnamon; sprinkle over pizza. Bake until fruit is hot to touch, about 5 minutes longer. Accompany with remaining prosciutto. Cut into wedges. Serves 6.

Per serving: 234 cal. (22 percent from fat); 11 g protein; 5.6 g fat (2.5 g sat.); 35 g carbo.; 487 mg sodium; 17 mg chol.

ASIAN SALAD SUPPER

Sweet and Spicy Asian Chicken Salad

Coconut Cream Pie

Ale

Fried bean threads make an intriguing base for this salad; or you can use the no-frying alternative.

Sweet and Spicy Asian Chicken Salad

1   medium-size pineapple (3½ lb. with crown and peel, 1½ lb. without)

PETER CHRISTIANSEN

CHICKEN BREAST *in pineapple-sesame sauce nestles on tangle of crisp bean threads with greens, pineapple alongside.*

2   tablespoons coarsely chopped fresh ginger

⅓   cup reduced-sodium soy sauce

1   tablespoon Oriental sesame oil

½   teaspoon crushed dried hot red chilies

1   teaspoon anise seed, crushed

6   boned, skinned chicken breast halves (2 lb. total), rinsed and drained

3   quarts (about 8 oz.) rinsed and crisped mesclun salad mix (or lettuce pieces)

¾   cup shredded carrots

⅓   cup finely cut shreds fresh mint leaves
    Fried noodles (directions follow)

Peel pineapple; quarter lengthwise and core. Cut half the fruit into slender spears and set aside. Cut remaining pineapple into chunks. In blender or food processor, smoothly purée pineapple chunks, ginger, soy, sesame oil, chilies, and

anise. Pour into a 9- by 13-inch pan. Turn chicken pieces in sauce and arrange in a single layer. Bake in a 425° oven until breasts are no longer pink in thickest part (cut to test), 15 to 20 minutes.

Meanwhile, mix mesclun with most of the carrots and mint; arrange mixture around rim of a large platter. When chicken is cooked, lay pineapple spears on mesclun, put noodles in center, and lay chicken pieces on noodles; sprinkle with remaining carrot and mint. Pour chicken juices into a small bowl; ladle sauce onto portions of salad. Serves 6.

Per serving: 407 cal. (33 percent from fat); 37 g protein; 15 g fat (2.1 g sat.); 31 g carbo.; 637 mg sodium; 88 mg chol.

Fried noodles. Inside a bag, pull apart 3 ounces **dried bean thread noodles** (cellophane noodles, *sai fun*) in sections no more than ½ inch wide. Pour 1 inch **salad oil** (2 to 5 cups) into a wok or deep 5- to 6-quart pan. Bring to 400° over medium heat. Add threads, 1 handful at a time, pushing into oil with

tongs. Noodles swell immediately. When crackling noise stops, in 3 to 5 seconds, turn threads over and cook until crackling stops again, about 5 seconds longer. Transfer with a slotted spoon to drain on towels. Repeat to cook remaining noodles. Use hot or cool; when cool, you can wrap noodles airtight and hold up to 1 day.

(Or omit fried bean threads and use noodles from 5 packages, 3 oz. each, instant Oriental noodle soup mix; break noodles into big chunks. Save seasoning for other foods.) ∎

By Elaine Johnson

Salad of Leaves and Fruit

With no oil in the honey-sweetened dressing, this salad is almost fat free.

1   large (about ¾ lb.) orange

1   medium size (about ½-lb.) head butter lettuce, leaves rinsed and crisped

1   small (about 3-oz.) head radicchio or Belgian endive, rinsed and crisped

1   cup raspberries or seedless red grapes, rinsed and drained
    Citrus dressing (recipe follows)
    Salt

Cut peel and membrane from orange. Cut beside membrane to release segments; discard seeds.

Break lettuce and radicchio into pieces; mix. Equally mound leaves on 4 salad plates; top with orange segments and berries. Add dressing and salt to taste. Serves 4.
—Carol Clouse, Watsonville, California

Per serving: 66 cal. (6.8 percent from fat); 1.8 g protein; 0.5 g fat (0 g sat.); 16 g carbo.; 4.9 mg sodium; 0 mg chol.

Citrus Dressing. Mix together ¼ cup **orange juice,** 2 tablespoons **raspberry** or red wine **vinegar,** and ½ teaspoon **honey.**

By Karyn I. Lipman

COWBOY

Food fashions come and go, but there's nothing

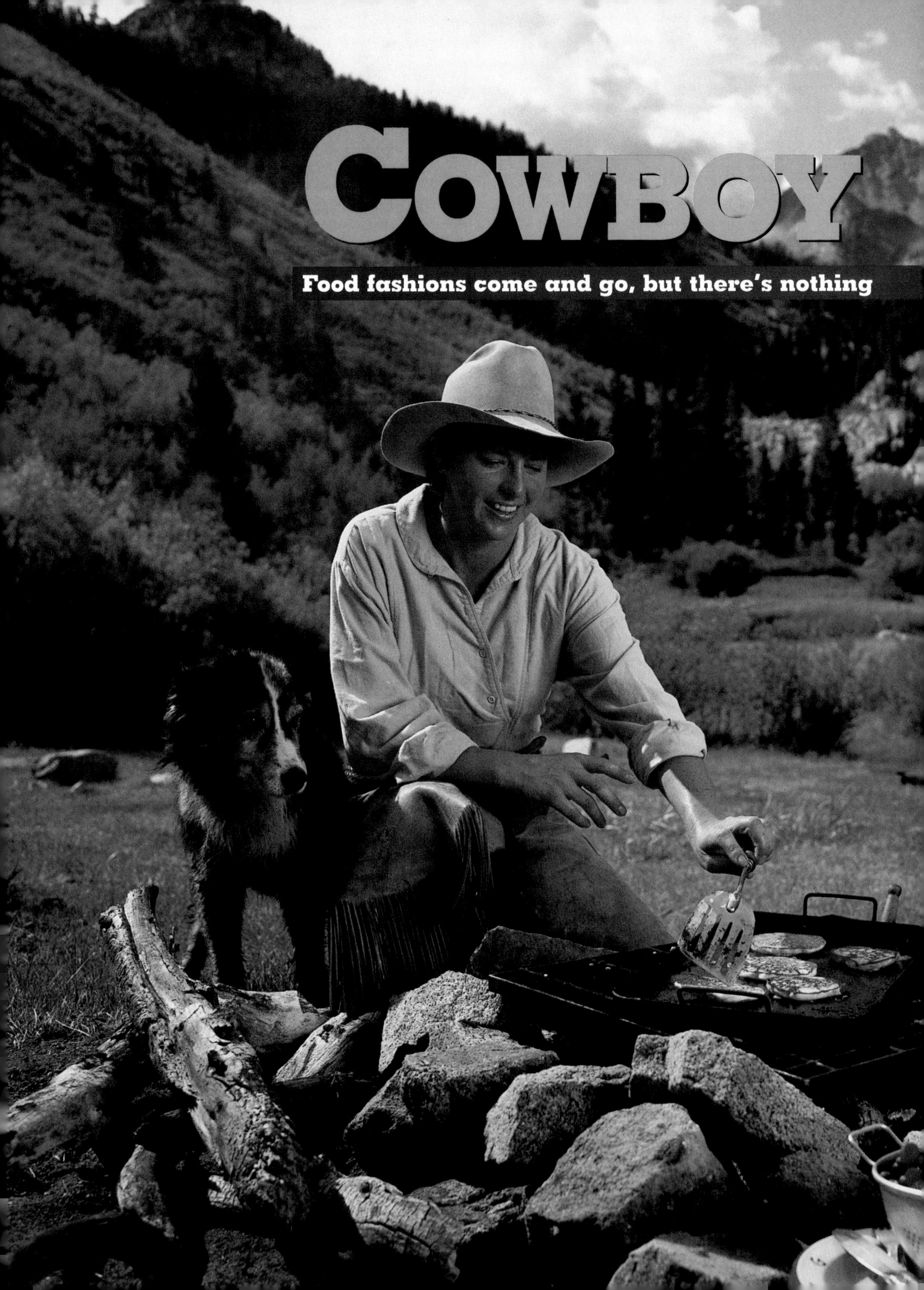

COOKING

like these hearty, classic Western dishes

By Linda Lau Anusasananan

"Sour dough flapjacks work better in the open, particularly in the high mountains. When you bring them down to civilization they pine away like a sheep dog."
—Sunset Magazine, July 1943

THIS WAS COWBOY COOK PHILOSOPHY EXPOUNDED a half-century ago, and it hasn't changed. Food fashions come and go, but good "chuck"— plain, honest, rib-sticking food—is still appealing (and surprisingly compatible with current rules of healthy eating). Today's city slickers yearn for that taste of the Wild West as they flock to dude ranches, pack stations, and cattle drives, eager to play cowboy. They savor the homespun flavors and comfortable simplicity of rough-and-ready meals cooked outdoors.

Whether you're on the trail or in your backyard, you can enjoy good chuck. We asked the cowboy cooks featured on these pages—from California ranchers to Oregon pack trip leaders and Wyoming dude ranch cooks—to share their favorite recipes (see page 108). Keep in mind, a good part of the magic that makes these foods taste mighty good is fresh air and hunger bred by strenuous labor.

McGee Creek Pack Station Sierra Breakfast

AS JENNIFER ROESER GREW UP AT HER FAMILY'S MCGEE CREEK Pack Station in the California Sierra near Mammoth Lakes, she learned the art of trail cooking. She now applies this training skillfully while transporting guests to the High Sierra.

Her specialty is sourdough baking. "I have a sourdough starter that was given to me by a good friend," she says. "It had been started by the ranch owner's great-great-grandmother in Kansas in the 1870s. It has quite a distinctive flavor, slightly sweet and buttery. It makes the best bread, biscuits, and pancakes."

Sourdough Pancakes (recipe on page 108)
Fresh Berries
Crisp Bacon and Sourdough Sausages
Cowboy Coffee

GARY MOSS

To a cowboy, food means survival. On the trail, he might get only two meals—one well before dawn, and supper after the day's work was done.

Today's cowboy cooks are perpetuating the Western role of "Cookie," the cook who accompanied the cowboys on the trail. Cookie of yesteryear was king of camp, and he earned his crown; he was charged with keeping a crew of independents functioning as they tended the demanding needs of roving cattle herds.

It took good grub to attract good workers. Cattlemen, recognizing the worth of a skilled cook, paid him well, with wages equal to the top hands'. In Texas in 1890, payment might have amounted to all of $40 to $45 a month, and Cookie deserved every penny.

Besides cooking, Cookie washed, cut hair, settled disputes, and patched broken bones. He pampered, threatened, and coddled a rough and tough breed who had barely earned respectability. *Cowboy* and *cattle rustler* were almost synonymous until after the Civil War, when *vaquero*, the accepted Spanish name for cattle herder, bit the dust in favor of *cowboy*.

THE CHUCKWAGON: A PORTABLE KITCHEN

Another change took place after the Civil War: in 1867, the railroad reached Abilene, Kansas. Texas ranchers, eager to profit from a beef-hungry nation, made long drives to the railroad to ship cattle to Eastern markets.

Outfitting chuck for this lengthy trek became crucial. In anticipation, Texas cattleman Charles Goodnight came up with an ingenious solution a year before the railroad was due to arrive in Abilene. Starting with a government supply wagon, he put together a portable kitchen—the original chuckwagon. On the end of the wagon was a compart-

Guidetti's Round-Up Barbecue

IN EARLY SPRING, JOE GUIDETTI CALLS FELLOW RANCHERS AND friends to help him round up calves for branding and vaccinations at his ranch in San Luis Obispo, California. As a big thank-you, Guidetti, a master at his open-pit barbecue, feeds the crew a hearty lunch.

While the team drives the calves into the corral for work, Guidetti prepares the meats with his blend of salt, pepper, and garlic salt. Then he expertly grills them to succulent perfection: slow-grilled pork spareribs, 3-inch-thick sirloin steaks, and double-cut pork chops.

Pass-around appetizers of crisp grilled sweetbreads and sausages start the meal. Another choice is marinated beef tongue, contributed by Guidetti's sidekick, George ("Whitey") Whiting, a chuckwagon cook. Guidetti's daughter, Jonell Price, provides salsa (from her mother's recipe), beans, and pies for this handsome spread.

Grilled Sweetbreads and Sausages
Whitey's Pickled Beef Tongue
Grilled Spareribs, Sirloin Steaks, and Pork Chops
Ranch Beans   Jan´s Salsa
(recipes on pages 108–109)
Mixed Green Salad   Garlic Bread
Homemade Apple Pie
Cowboy Coffee   Beer

PETER CHRISTIANSEN

"COME AND GET IT!" *Joe Guidetti grills sausages, steaks, chops, and ribs on his bunk-size barbecue. Cowboys load plates with sizzling meats, beans, salsa, and bread.*

ment-filled box to securely hold cooking utensils, food staples, dishes, and medicine. The hinged lid flipped out to make a convenient worktable. Later models had running water: a barrel with a spigot hitched to the wagon side.

CHUCKWAGON ETIQUETTE

Cookie worked long hours. Rising before the crew, he had the breakfast fire blazing and coffee on by 3 or 4 in the morning. As soon as the meal was cleared, he packed and rode on ahead to make evening camp and had supper ready when bone-weary cowboys straggled in.

The chuckwagon was Cookie's domain and the heart of a cowboy's home on the trail. Cookie set strict rules for activities around the chuckwagon. Cowboys did not disturb the cook's work area; it was forbidden to eat on the chuckwagon table. Buckaroos dined, squatting or seated on a log, a rock, or the ground, with plates in laps.

An unwritten procotol persists. Lela Joslin, of Spanish Springs Ranch in California and Nevada, enlarges upon the code of manners: "There is definitely cowboy etiquette around the chuckwagon. You never ride your horse through the kitchen; you don't tie your horse to the chuckwagon; you ride past the chuckwagon downwind so as to not send dust through the kitchen. The cowboy always waits to be invited to eat (no picking at the food!)."

CHUCKWAGON TOOLS

Basic equipment for camp cooking hasn't changed much since the earliest days. The well-outfitted kitchen includes a big coffee pot; long-handled spatulas, forks, and spoons; a trusty knife; and an assortment of cured, cast-iron pans—frying pans, pots, and particularly the Dutch oven, indispensable for baking.

The Dutch oven has a rimmed lid to hold coals for baking; usually it has legs so it can stand over hot coals.

Wyoming Camp Supper

WHEN HELEN VACEK CAME BACK HOME TO MONTANA IN 1987, she discovered a new career—camp cook. Now she works enthusiastically as a vagabond ranch and trail cook. "I like cooking, people, and the outdoors."

At the Brush Creek Ranch near Saratoga, Wyoming, Vacek rises before the sun, stoking the fire for breakfast. After the meal, she heads out on a 3- to 4-hour ride to set up camp and start the supper stew simmering.

Son-of-a-Son-of-a-Bitch Stew   Green Salad
Helen's Whole-wheat Beer Biscuits
(recipes on pages 108–109)
Cornbread   Butter   Jam
Peach Cobbler   Cowboy Coffee

Pans without legs sit on a portable grate or hang on hooks from an iron horse, a bar that spans the fire with supports at each end.

COWBOY GRUB AND THE CHUCKWAGON LARDER

According to trail cook Lela Joslin, "The old chuckwagons usually had flour, sugar, dried fruit, dried beef, salt pork, coffee beans, pinto beans, salt, lard, baking soda, vinegar, molasses—and whiskey. Some had the luxury of canned milk and canned tomatoes. Everything that was cooked on the trail used these ingredients, along with fresh beef or wild game."

"The most important aspect of cowboy cooking, even now, is that it is filling," ex-plains ranch cook Sunie Lou Thompson of Whitlash, Montana. "Cowboy work was, and still is, physically demanding, so they need food that will stick to the belly and keep their strength up until the next meal. Lots of meat, potatoes, baked or boiled beans, bread or biscuits is typical cowboy fare with, of course, coffee."

Joslin says the appetites of working cowboys and greenhorn guests don't compare. "Pan-fried steak and biscuits and gravy were the standard breakfast one hundred years ago. Nowadays, guests ask for granola in the morning and eschew the high-cholesterol diet that the cowboys do chew. Of course, cowboys figure maybe you aren't working

Blitzen Gorge Supper

HAVE PAN WILL TRAVEL. LEROY PRUITT, TEACHER OF CAMPFIRE cooking, travels with his portable cast-iron kitchen ready to cook on the trail or the river. One of his favorite destinations lies in the Blitzen Gorge of the Steens Mountain Range in southeast Oregon.

Pruitt invented his rhubarb-peach cobbler here, when he harvested the remains of an abandoned garden. As he tells it, "Back about 1900, or soon after, two women staked out homesteads in this beautiful, unique canyon. Their boundaries had one common border on purpose so they could be neighbors in this very remote region. One lady put in a rhubarb patch. She planted the rhubarb right next to the cabin on the west side to take advantage of the afternoon sun to warm the ground."

Rhubarb cobbler became tradition until the patch began to give out. Pruitt combined the last survivors with canned peaches for "a dandy first-time peach-rhubarb cobbler."

Buckaroo Spanish Rice (recipe on page 109)
Green Salad   Leroy's Campfire Biscuits
Blitzen River Cobbler (recipe on page 109)
Cowboy Coffee

hard enough if you can get by on birdseed."

COWBOY COFFEE

The first thing a cowboy demands in the morning is a cup of hot coffee. The same is true when he rides back into camp. He might even down a cup or two before hitting the hay—caffeine jitters are for city slickers.

"When you pour yourself coffee, you always pour for everyone around the fire also," says Joslin, "but you never crowd the cook out when standing around the cooking fire. When the coffee pot is empty, you bring the empty pot to the cook and help refill it."

Cowboys make their coffee plain and simple—no battery-operated grinders or filter paper on the range.

"The cowboy likes his coffee strong and black, and it tastes better made outdoors over an open fire," Sunie Lou Thompson advises. "To make real cowboy coffee, add about a half-cup of coffee grounds to a quart of cold water and boil it for several minutes over the fire. Then throw in a little more cold water to settle the grounds, and keep the coffee warm over the coals. Tip: if it tries to keep boiling, cut a green willow stick and lay it over the top of the pot so it won't boil over."

There may be fewer cowboys today—some are even women—and their duties are more diverse, but the lifestyle is equally demanding. Bert Prindle, a fourth-generation cowhand from Wyoming, observes, "A real cowboy is a jack of all trades. He has a little grease on his hands from fixing equipment, he is a fencer, a veterinarian, and a philosopher. You have to love it because you'll never get rich." Prindle says he wouldn't do anything else in the world. "We are still out in all kinds of weather taking care of the cattle. And we are still awfully independent."

And they still demand good chuck and plenty of hot coffee. Just ask Cookie. ■

GARY MOSS

LEROY PRUITT PRESIDES *over his outdoor kitchen. In banjo-size frying pan set and peaches to make cobbler. Accompanied by biscuits and cornbread, the*

on a grate over a fire, he cooks Buckaroo Spanish Rice. For dessert, he arranges biscuit dough in a lattice pattern over rhubarb Spanish rice and cobbler make a fine meal eaten outdoors in the grandeur of Oregon's Steens Mountain Range.

Good chuck, real cowboy food

Hearty trail fare to cook over a crackling fire, between blankets of hot coals, or in your own kitchen

CHUCK—RIB-STICKING, honest food—that's what real cowboys eat. Menus on pages 101 through 107 describe the meals; here are the recipes.

We tested them at sea level. At higher elevations, you'll have to make adjustments. As elevation increases, water boils at lower temperatures—193° at 10,000 feet compared with 212° at sea level, for example. Foods cooked in water, like dried beans, take longer to cook when the boiling temperature decreases. At 5,000 feet and up, baked goods puff more and are inclined to fall unless you use less leavening and, usually, a little more liquid.

DUTCH OVEN BAKING

ON THE TRAIL, COWBOY cooks bake with professional expertise in cast-iron Dutch ovens with rimmed lids, using hot coals for fuel. The pan may stand on legs or hang from a bail; coals go under and on top of the pan to create even heat.

New pans and scoured pans tend to stick; to minimize sticking, rub pan and lid all over with salad oil. Heat lid and pan in a 325° oven for 1 hour; let cool and wipe clean.

SETTING UP

Make a double layer of foil that is 3 to 4 inches wider than Dutch oven; trace around lid on foil. Lay foil flat on a fire-safe, firm, level surface in a draft-free spot. Or block drafts with a wind barricade that is taller than pan; place 4 to 6 inches from pan.

About 15 to 30 minutes before you're ready to bake, ignite the number of charcoal briquets specified in recipe, plus a few extras so you can add more heat, if needed. Coals are ready when they are just evenly coated with a thin layer of ash.

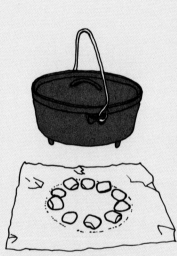

SET FOOD-FILLED *Dutch oven with legs over a ring of hot coals arranged on foil.*

LUCY I. SARGEANT

LIPPED LID HOLDS *more coals. Windguard (from hardware store) shields coals, pan.*

Sourdough Pancakes

Overnight starter (directions follow)
2 tablespoons sugar
1 teaspoon salt
1 teaspoon baking powder
3 tablespoons salad oil
2 large eggs
½ teaspoon baking soda
Butter or margarine
Maple syrup or powdered sugar

To overnight starter, add sugar, salt, baking powder, and oil; mix well. Add eggs and beat to blend. Mix baking soda with 1 teaspoon water; stir into batter.

Place griddle or 10- to 12-inch frying pan over medium heat; when hot, oil lightly. Pour batter in ⅓-cup portions onto griddle or pan, spacing about 1½ inches apart. Cook until bubbles form on top of pancakes and bottoms are browned, about 1 minute. Turn with a wide spatula; cook until brown on bottom, about 1 minute longer. Serve hot with butter and syrup. Makes 10 or 11 pancakes, 3 or 4 servings.—*Jennifer Roeser, McGee Creek Pack Station, Mammoth Lakes, California*

Per serving: 434 cal. (29 percent from fat); 12 g protein; 14 g fat (2.2 g sat.); 65 g carbo.; 807 mg sodium; 107 mg chol.

Overnight starter. In a large bowl, mix 2 cups **all-purpose flour**, 1¼ cups warm (110°) **water,** and ½ cup **sourdough starter.** (If you do not have a starter, see page 156 for recipe source.) Cover with plastic wrap and let stand in a warm place at least 8 or up to 24 hours. Mix ½ cup overnight starter with your sourdough starter to replenish it for future use. Use remaining overnight starter to make pancakes; cover sourdough starter and store it in refrigerator.

Ranch Beans

1 pound (about 2⅔ cups) dried pinto beans
¼ pound bacon, diced
1 small (about 6-oz.) onion, chopped
2 cloves garlic, pressed or minced
2 tablespoons chili powder
⅛ teaspoon pepper
1 can (8 oz.) tomato sauce
Salt

Sort beans and discard debris. Rinse and drain beans; put them in a 3- to 4-quart pan or Dutch oven with 2 quarts water. Bring to a boil on high heat; boil 3 minutes. Remove from heat, cover, and let stand at least 1 or up to 4 hours; drain beans and pour into a bowl.

In pan, stir bacon over medium heat until lightly browned, about 5 minutes. Discard fat. Add onion and garlic; stir until onion is limp, about 5 minutes. Stir in chili powder. Add beans, 3½ cups water, and pepper. Cover and simmer until beans are tender to bite, about 1 hour.

Add tomato sauce. If beans are soupier than you like, boil, uncovered, over high heat until liquid evaporates to suit your taste; stir occasionally and reduce heat as mixture thickens. Add salt to taste. Serves 6.—*Jonell Price, Fresno, California*

Per serving: 359 cal. (21 percent from fat); 19 g protein; 8.4 g fat (2.7 g sat.); 55 g carbo.; 374 mg sodium; 8.9 mg chol.

Helen's Whole-wheat Beer Biscuits

2 cups all-purpose flour
1 cup whole-wheat flour
2 tablespoons sugar
4½ teaspoons baking powder
1 teaspoon salt
¾ teaspoon cream of tartar
¾ cup (⅜ lb.) butter or margarine
1 large egg
1 cup beer

In a bowl, combine all-purpose flour, whole-wheat flour, sugar, baking powder, salt, and cream of tartar. With a pastry blender or knives, cut in butter until mixture forms coarse crumbs.

Beat egg to blend; add to flour mixture along with beer. Stir with a fork just until dough holds together.

On a well-floured board,

gently knead dough 2 or 3 turns until smooth. Pat dough 1 inch thick. Cut with a floured 2½- to 2¾-inch-diameter biscuit or round cookie cutter. Gently pat scraps together; cut out remaining biscuits.

To bake in a Dutch oven, see box on page 108; have 24 ignited charcoal briquets ready to use.

Oil interior of a 12-inch cast-iron Dutch oven with legs; arrange biscuits in a single layer. Put rimmed lid on pan.

When briquets are lightly covered with gray ash, evenly space 8 coals in a circle about ½ inch inside traced ring. Set pan over coals. Arrange remaining coals evenly over lid.

Ignite another 7 to 9 briquets. After about 20 minutes, add 5 of the freshly ignited coals to lid. Bake another 15 minutes. Lift lid and check; if biscuits have not started to brown, add 2 to 4 more remaining coals to lid. Continue baking until biscuits are browned, 10 to 15 minutes longer.

To bake in a conventional oven. Arrange biscuits slightly apart on a greased 12- by 15-inch baking sheet. Bake in a 425° oven until browned, 18 to 20 minutes.

Serve biscuits warm or cool. Makes 8 or 9.—*Helen Vacek, Brush Creek Ranch, Saratoga, Wyoming*

Per biscuit: 307 cal. (47 percent from fat); 5.6 g protein; 16 g fat (9.8 g sat.); 35 g carbo.; 623 mg sodium; 65 mg chol.

Buckaroo Spanish Rice

1 tablespoon butter or margarine

2 large (about 1 lb. total) onions, chopped

2 pounds ground lean (18 percent fat) beef

1 box (14 oz.) instant-cooking white rice

2 cans (16 oz. each) marinara sauce

1 can (11 oz.) whole-kernel corn

1 can (16 oz.) French-cut green beans, drained

1 to 2 tablespoons minced fresh or canned jalapeño chilies

Salt

In a 6- to 8-quart pan or Dutch oven or 12- to 14-inch frying pan over medium-high heat, combine butter and onions. Stir mixture often until onions are limp, 6 to 8 minutes.

Add beef, breaking apart with a spoon; stir until crumbly and browned, 10 to 12 minutes.

Stir in rice and 4½ cups water. Cover and cook over low heat until rice absorbs most of the liquid, about 5 minutes. Stir in marinara sauce, corn, beans, and chilies and salt to taste. Cover and simmer until hot; stir occasionally. Serves 8 or 9.—*Leroy Pruitt, Vida, Oregon*

Per serving: 536 cal. (37 percent from fat); 26 g protein; 22 g fat (8.2 g sat.); 60 g carbo.; 888 mg sodium; 73 mg chol.

Jan's Salsa

1 can (4 or 7 oz.) diced green chilies

1 can (26 oz.) tomatoes, drained and chopped (reserve liquid for other uses)

½ cup chopped onion

1 clove garlic, crushed or minced

1 tablespoon olive oil

1 tablespoon wine vinegar or cider vinegar

1 teaspoon liquid hot pepper seasoning

1 teaspoon pepper

Salt and sugar

Mix the chilies, tomatoes, onion, garlic, oil, vinegar, liquid hot pepper, pepper, and salt and sugar to taste. Serve, or cover and chill up to 4 hours. Makes about 3 cups.—*Jonell Price*

Per ¼ cup: 28 cal. (42 percent from fat); 0.7 g protein; 1.3 g fat (0.2 g sat.); 4 g carbo.; 169 mg sodium; 0 mg chol.

Son-of-a-Son-of-a-Bitch Stew

3 pounds boneless beef stew meat, such as chuck or round, fat trimmed

2 large (about 1 lb. total) onions, chopped

2 cloves garlic, pressed or minced

1 tablespoon Worcestershire

⅓ cup dry red wine

⅓ cup all-purpose flour

2 tablespoons sugar

1 teaspoon dried thyme leaves

¼ teaspoon pepper

1 quart regular-strength beef broth

1 bottle or can (12 oz.) beer

2 large (about 1 lb. total) russet potatoes, peeled and cut into 1½-inch chunks

4 large (about 1¼ lb. total) carrots, sliced ½ inch thick

2 cups coarsely chopped cabbage

1 cup coarsely chopped celery

2 dried bay leaves

Salt

In a 6- to 8-quart pan or Dutch oven, combine beef, onions, garlic, and Worcestershire. Cover and cook over medium-high heat for 30 minutes.

Uncover and stir often until liquid evaporates and its residue turns dark brown. Add wine and stir to release browned bits.

In a small bowl, stir together flour, sugar, thyme, and pepper. Gradually stir in 1 cup broth until mixture is smooth. Add to beef along with remaining broth. Add beer, potatoes, carrots, cabbage, celery, and bay. Adjust heat to maintain a simmer. Cover and simmer until meat is very tender when pierced, 1½ to 2 hours. Season to taste with salt. Serves 6.—*Helen Vacek*

Per serving: 537 cal. (28 percent from fat); 49 g protein; 17 g fat (6.4 g sat.); 45 g carbo.; 273 mg sodium; 148 mg chol.

Blitzen River Cobbler

1 quart ¾-inch rhubarb chunks, or thawed frozen rhubarb pieces

1 quart ¾-inch peeled peach chunks, or drained canned peach slices

¾ cup sugar

Topping (recipe follows)

Whipped cream, vanilla frozen yogurt, or vanilla ice cream (optional)

Spread rhubarb evenly in bottom of a buttered 12-inch cast-iron Dutch oven with legs (for coal baking) or a shallow 3-quart casserole (for oven baking).

Distribute peaches over rhubarb. Pour ¼ cup water around edges of fruit mixture. Sprinkle sugar over the fruit. On a floured board, pat topping into a ½-inch-thick round. Cut into ½-inch-wide strips. Lay strips over fruit, spacing them about 1 inch apart and crisscrossing to make a lattice pattern.

If using a Dutch oven, put lid on pan.

To bake in a Dutch oven, see box on page 108; have 24 ignited charcoal briquets ready to use. Arrange 8 briquets on the foil, spacing them evenly in a circle about ½ inch inside traced ring. Set Dutch oven over coals. Set remaining coals evenly all over lid.

Ignite another 7 to 9 briquets. After about 25 minutes, add 5 freshly ignited coals to lid. Bake 15 minutes longer. Lift lid and check; if topping has not started to brown, add 2 to 4 more remaining coals to lid. Continue baking until top is browned and fruit is bubbly, 10 to 15 minutes longer.

To bake in a conventional oven, set heat at 375°. Place casserole with cobbler, uncovered, in oven. Bake until fruit is bubbly and top is browned, about 45 minutes.

Scoop cobbler, hot or warm, into bowls. Add whipped cream to taste, if desired. Serves 9 or 10.—*Leroy Pruitt*

Per serving: 281 cal. (24 percent from fat); 4.8 g protein; 7.6 g fat (4.5 g sat.); 51 g carbo.; 263 mg sodium; 19 mg chol.

Topping. In a large bowl mix 2 cups **unbleached all-purpose flour,** ⅔ cup **unprocessed bran,** 3 tablespoons **sugar,** and 4 teaspoons **baking powder.** With a pastry blender or knives, cut in 6 tablespoons **butter** or margarine until coarse crumbs form.

Add ¾ cup **buttermilk** and stir just enough to moisten dough; gather dough into a ball. ■

By Linda Lau Anusasananan

NORMAN A. PLATE

FEAST ON ARTICHOKES *boiled with spicy seeds. Leaves are delicious plain or with curry yogurt, mustard dip, mayonnaise, and butter. Complete menu with bread and cheese.*

It's time to feast on artichokes

They're a bargain in May. All sizes are plentiful. Boil, bake, even grill them

L EAF AFTER LEAF, bite after succulent bite, the magnificent thistle—the artichoke—lures you to its inner recesses. Rip away the prickly, pointed, tender leaf crown, scoop out the fuzzy choke, and there, awaiting your pleasure, is the thick, smoky-sweet, meaty bottom.

Observe this ritual now. Artichokes are at peak season, with lowest prices. You might find really big ones for as little as three for $1. And tiny, mature (even though called babies or hearts) artichokes are often a bargain by the bag.

The source for these fleshy, usually thorn-tipped buds is the fog-shrouded coast of central California, from Half Moon Bay, through Santa Cruz and Castroville, to Santa Barbara and San Luis Obispo. Spanish explorers get credit for first bringing the artichoke from the Mediterranean basin to the West, where it has made itself perfectly at home.

Boil a batch of artichokes in spicy broth for a fondue feast; trim really big artichokes and bake, stuffed with lamb; or trim tiny artichokes down to total edibility and grill on skewers.

Artichoke Fondue

⅓ cup vinegar

3 tablespoons Worcestershire

2 dried bay leaves

2 tablespoons black peppercorns

2 tablespoons mustard seed

2 tablespoons cumin seed

1 teaspoon crushed dried hot red chilies

1 tablespoon olive oil

1 dozen medium-size (3- to 3½-in.-wide, 8 to 10 oz. each) artichokes

  Curry yogurt (recipe follows)

  Mustard vinaigrette (recipe follows)

  Melted butter (optional)

  Mayonnaise (optional)

In a 12- to 14-quart pan, combine 5 quarts water, vinegar, Worcestershire, bay leaves, peppercorns, mustard seed, cumin seed, chilies, and oil. Cover and bring to a boil over high heat.

Meanwhile, remove coarse outer leaves from artichokes. Trim stems even with bases. With a sharp knife, cut off thorny top third of each artichoke. With scissors, trim thorny tips off remaining leaves. Immerse artichokes in cool water and swish to rinse; shake out water.

Plunge artichokes into

BAKED JUMBO ARTICHOKE *forms a savory bowl for minted lamb filling moistened with pan juices of wine and broth.*

boiling liquid. Reduce heat, cover, and boil gently until bottoms are tender when pierced, 25 to 35 minutes.

Lift out artichokes and drain. Pour liquid through a fine strainer; reserve seeds for curry yogurt. Discard bay. (If making ahead, cool, cover, and chill artichokes and seeds up to 1 day.)

Serve the artichokes hot, cool, or cold. Offer curry yogurt, mustard vinaigrette, butter, and mayonnaise in individual bowls. Dip artichoke leaves and pieces of the bottom into sauces to eat. Serves 4 as a main course, 12 as a vegetable accompaniment or appetizer.

Per entrée serving without sauces: 146 cal. (13 percent from fat); 9 g protein; 2.1 g fat (0.3 g sat.); 29 g carbo.; 277 mg sodium; 0 mg chol.

Curry yogurt. Mix ¾ cup **unflavored nonfat yogurt,** ¾ cup **reduced-calorie** or regular **mayonnaise,** the **reserved seed mixture** from cooked artichokes (preceding), 1½ teaspoons **curry powder,** and **salt** to taste. (If making ahead, cover and chill up to 2 days.) Makes about 1½ cups.

Per tablespoon: 32 cal. (68 percent from fat); 0.8 g protein; 2.4 g fat (0.5 g sat.); 2 g carbo.; 47 mg sodium; 2.6 mg chol.

Mustard vinaigrette. Whisk together ⅓ cup **olive oil,** ⅓ cup **water,** ¼ cup **white wine vinegar,** 2 tablespoons **Dijon mustard,** 2 tablespoons minced **shallots,** ¼ teaspoon **dried tarragon leaves,** and 2 cloves **garlic,** pressed or minced. (If making ahead, cover and chill up to 1 day.) Makes about 1¼ cups.

Per tablespoon: 35 cal. (95 percent from fat); 0 g protein; 3.7 g fat (0.5 g sat.); 0.5 g carbo.; 45 mg sodium; 0 mg chol.

Baked Artichoke Bottoms with Lamb

1⅓ cups dry white wine

1⅓ cups regular-strength chicken broth

4 large (3½- to 4-in.-wide, about 1 lb. each) artichokes

1 pound ground lean lamb

¼ cup fine dried bread crumbs

1 large egg

¾ cup finely chopped onion

2 cloves garlic, pressed or minced

¼ cup chopped fresh or 1 tablespoon dried mint leaves

½ teaspoon salt (optional)

¼ teaspoon pepper

1 tablespoon cornstarch mixed with 2 tablespoons water

2 tablespoons chopped parsley (if using dried mint)

In a 9- by 13-inch pan, combine wine and broth.

Trim stems flush with artichoke bottoms. About 2 inches above base, cut each artichoke crosswise to remove leaf tops. With scissors, trim remaining thorny tips. Immerse artichokes in cool water and swish to rinse; shake out water.

Coat artichoke bottoms with wine mixture in pan, then set artichokes, bases up, in pan; cover tightly. Bake in a 350° oven until bases are barely tender when pierced, about 50 minutes.

Meanwhile, mix lamb, crumbs, ⅓ cup water, egg, onion, garlic, 2 tablespoons fresh or 1 tablespoon dried mint, salt, and pepper.

With a slotted spoon, lift artichokes from dish. Turn artichokes with leaves up; pull out and discard tiny thorn-tipped leaves in centers. With a small spoon, scoop and discard fuzzy centers from artichokes.

Mound meat mixture firmly into centers and over tops of artichokes. Bake, uncovered, in a 350° oven until meat is well browned and firm to touch, about 45 minutes. With a slotted spoon, transfer artichokes to a platter; keep warm.

Measure pan juices. If needed, add water to make 1 cup; or boil, uncovered, to reduce to 1 cup. Stir cornstarch mixture into liquid in pan. Stir over high heat until boiling; mix in remaining fresh mint (or parsley). Pour sauce over artichokes. Serves 4.

Per serving: 484 cal. (54 percent from fat); 28 g protein; 29 g fat (12 g sat.); 30 g carbo.; 322 mg sodium; 136 mg chol.

Grilled Artichoke Kebabs

2 tablespoons lemon juice

2 tablespoons olive oil

1 teaspoon minced fresh or ½ teaspoon dried thyme leaves

18 small (1½- to 2-in.-wide, about 2¼ lb. total) artichokes

Salt and pepper

CROSSED SWORDS *hold marinated and grilled tiny artichokes; they're trimmed so you can eat every bit. Serve with grilled fish or poultry.*

NORMAN A. PLATE

In a bowl, combine lemon juice, oil, thyme, and 2 tablespoons water.

Trim stems flush with artichoke bottoms. Break off leaves down to pale, tender ones. Cut off the top ⅓ or ½ of each artichoke to remove thorny tips. With a small, sharp knife, smoothly trim fibrous portions from bottoms. If trimmed artichokes are wider than 1½ inches, cut in half lengthwise. As trimmed, coat in lemon marinade. Thread hearts onto metal flat-blade skewers; reserve remaining marinade.

Place artichokes on a grill 4 to 6 inches above solid bed of medium-hot coals (you can hold your hand at grill level only 3 to 4 seconds). Turn often until artichoke bottoms are tender when pierced, and artichokes are lightly browned all over, 12 to 15 minutes. Place skewered artichokes on a platter; drizzle with remaining marinade. Add salt and pepper to taste. Serves 4 to 6.

Per serving: 73 cal. (57 percent from fat); 2.3 g protein; 4.6 g fat (0.6 g sat.); 7.5 g carbo.; 65 mg sodium; 0 mg chol. ∎

By Linda Lau Anusasananan

Armenian peda

Portuguese sweet bread

Scandinavian rye bread

Whole-wheat poppy seed bagels

1993 sourdough parmesan-pepper bread

Nine decades
of great
Western breads

SINCE 1901, WHEN SUNSET'S FIRST BREAD RECIPE WAS published, the West's rich heritage of breads has been duly recorded on our pages, reflecting changing attitudes, ingredients, ethnic mix, and technology—from prethermostat ovens to bread machines.

Whole-grain breads, in favor now, slowly emerged from days when *Sunset* rated baking white bread in camp (at right) an achievement. Hints of shifting tastes appeared in the flapper era with a story called "Breads Blonde and Brunette." Through the years, certain breads that reflect the history and diversity of the West have become much-requested favorites. Here are nine that have become classics.

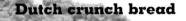

Dutch crunch bread

Pocket bread

BREAD PHOTOGRAPHY: PETER CHRISTIANSEN

Armenian bakers in the Los Angeles Basin shared this recipe for quilted-top peda with us in 1976.

Armenian Peda

- 1 package active dry yeast
- 1 cup warm (110°) water
- 1 tablespoon sugar
- ½ teaspoon salt
- 1½ tablespoons melted and cooled butter or margarine
- 1⅓ cups whole-wheat flour
- 1¼ to 1¾ cups all-purpose flour
- 2 teaspoons sesame seed
   Glaze (recipe follows)

Choose mixing and kneading method (see page 115). Sprinkle yeast over water and sugar; let stand until yeast is softened, about 5 minutes. Add salt, butter, whole-wheat flour, and all-purpose flour as method specifies; knead. Let rise (see page 115) for about 1 hour; knead to expel air bubbles and form a smooth ball.

Set dough, smooth side up, on an oiled and floured 12-by 15-inch baking sheet; cover lightly with plastic wrap. Let stand 30 minutes at room temperature. Uncover dough; pat into an evenly thick 11-by 14-inch oval. Cover with plastic wrap and let stand in a warm place until puffy, 25 to 30 minutes.

Gently brush dough with water. Dip fingertips in water; hold fingers parallel and push through dough to pan 1 inch from edge all around oval. Within oval, impress dough to make lines about 2 inches apart lengthwise and crosswise. Moisten fingers as needed to prevent sticking. Let oval stand, uncovered, in a warm place until puffy, 10 to 15 minutes.

Bake in a 450° oven until golden brown, about 15 minutes. Meanwhile, stir sesame seed in a 6- to 8-inch pan over medium heat until golden. Pour from pan.

When bread is baked, immediately brush with glaze and sprinkle with sesame seed. Serve warm or cool. For storage instructions, see page 115. Makes 1 loaf, about 1 pound 2 ounces.

Per ounce: 74 cal. (15 percent from fat); 2.3 g protein; 1.2 g fat (0.6 g sat.); 14 g carbo.; 71 mg sodium; 2.6 mg chol.

Glaze. Smoothly blend ¼ cup **water** and 1 teaspoon **all-purpose flour** in a 1- to 1½-quart pan. Stir on medium heat until boiling; use or cover up to 2 hours.

Hawaiians adopted the tender, egg-rich bread that Portuguese brought to the Islands in the late 19th century. This is our 1980 version.

Portuguese Sweet Bread

- 1 package active dry yeast
- ¼ cup warm (110°) water
- 2 large eggs
- ½ teaspoon salt
- ½ teaspoon grated lemon peel
- ¼ teaspoon vanilla
   Potatoes (recipe follows)
- 2¼ to 2⅔ cups all-purpose flour

CAMP COOK, *circa 1901, kneads white flour dough for Sunset's first bread recipe.*

Le CONTE

Choose mixing and kneading method (see facing page). Sprinkle yeast over water; let stand until yeast is softened, about 5 minutes. Beat eggs to blend; add all but 1 tablespoon of the eggs to yeast mixture along with salt, lemon peel, vanilla, potatoes, and flour as method specifies; knead. Cover and chill the 1 tablespoon egg. Let dough rise (see facing page) until doubled, 1¼ to 1½ hours; mix or knead to expel air bubbles.

On an unfloured board, gently roll dough with your fingers to form a 30-inch-long rope. Coil rope, twisting slightly as you go, into an oiled 9-inch pie pan, starting at the outside edge of pan and ending in center.

Cover lightly with plastic wrap and let rise in a warm place until puffy, about 30 minutes.

Uncover and brush dough with reserved egg. Bake in a 350° oven until deep golden brown, about 25 minutes. Slip a wide spatula under bread and lift onto a rack. Serve warm or cool; to store, see facing page. Makes 1 loaf, about 1⅓ pounds.

Per ounce: 93 cal. (29 percent from fat); 2.3 g protein; 3 g fat (1.6 g sat.); 14 g carbo.; 84 mg sodium; 27 mg chol.

Potatoes. In a 1- to 1½-quart pan over medium-high heat, stir ⅓ cup **milk** until boiling.

Remove from heat and at once stir in 2 tablespoons **instant mashed potatoes mix,** ⅓ cup **sugar,** and ¼ cup (⅛ lb., in small pieces) **butter** or margarine. Let cool (butter need not melt completely).

"SHAKIN' UP *the sourdough" illustrated a 1944 Sunset item on sourdough baking.*

DARROW M. WATT

FROM PUEBLO INDIAN *horno (adobe oven), bread came indoors for our 1965 report.*

In the Southwest, Pueblo Indians bake slashed basic white loaves in dome-shaped adobe ovens. Over the years, *Sunset* has given directions for many ways to make both the bread and the oven. This recipe, from 1965, is for a conventional oven.

Pueblo Bread

1 package active dry yeast

¾ cup warm (110°) water

1 teaspoon sugar

½ teaspoon salt

1 tablespoon melted and cooled butter or margarine

2 to 2½ cups all-purpose flour

Choose mixing and kneading method (see facing page). Sprinkle yeast over water and sugar; let stand until yeast is softened, about 5 minutes. Add salt, butter, and flour as method specifies; knead. Let dough rise (see facing page) 45 minutes to 1 hour; mix or knead on a lightly floured board to expel air bubbles and form a smooth ball.

Pat ball to flatten slightly. Roll into an 8-inch-wide round. Dust top lightly with flour; fold about ½ the round onto other side, leaving about 1 inch of bottom rim exposed at center of curve.

With a floured knife, make 2 equidistant cuts about ⅔ of the way across loaf from curved side and down through dough.

Lift loaf into an oiled 9-inch pie pan; spread cuts apart so ends of loaf are flush with pan rim. Lightly cover with plastic wrap. Let rise in a warm place until puffy, 20 to 30 minutes.

Remove wrap. Bake in a 375° oven until bread is deep golden brown, about 50 minutes. Serve hot or cool; to cool, transfer from pan to a rack. To store, see facing page. Makes 1 loaf, about 14 ounces.

Per ounce: 75 cal. (12 percent from fat); 2 g protein; 1 g fat (0.5 g sat.); 14 g carbo.; 87 mg sodium; 2.2 mg chol.

The crisp topping, Dutch crunch, enjoyed a heyday in the '60s and '70s on white bread loaves. If your market doesn't sell white rice flour, try a health food store.

Dutch Crunch Bread

Pueblo bread dough (preceding)

2 teaspoons sugar

2 packages active dry yeast

¼ teaspoon salt

6 tablespoons white rice flour

1 teaspoon salad oil

⅓ cup warm (110°) water

While dough is rising, smoothly mix in a bowl the sugar, yeast, salt, rice flour, oil, and water for the topping. Cover with plastic wrap and let rise in a warm place until doubled, 35 to 45 minutes. Stir well. (Topping can stand, covered, another 15 minutes; stir before using.)

Knead dough on a lightly floured board to expel air and make a smooth ball; shape into a smooth 7½-inch-long log. Set smooth side up in a well-oiled 4½- by 8½-inch loaf pan. Spread topping evenly over dough. Let dough rise, uncovered, in a warm place until it fills about ¾ of the pan, 20 to 25 minutes. Bake as directed for Pueblo bread until deep golden brown, 50 to 60 minutes. Run a knife between pan sides and bread; tip loaf out onto a rack and let cool. Serve or store (see facing page).

Makes 1 loaf, about 1 pound 2 ounces.

Per ounce: 76 cal. (13 percent from fat); 2 g protein; 1.1 g fat (0.5 g sat.); 14 g carbo.; 98 mg sodium; 1.7 mg chol.

Pocket bread, now commonplace, was a novelty when we first published a recipe for it back in 1963. Steam makes the hollow in the middle of this Middle Eastern bread.

Pocket Bread

1 package active dry yeast

1½ cups warm (110°) water

½ teaspoon salt

2 tablespoons olive oil

1 cup whole-wheat flour

3 to 3½ cups all-purpose flour

Choose mixing and kneading method (see facing page). Sprinkle yeast over water; let stand until yeast is softened, about 5 minutes. Add salt, oil, whole-wheat flour, and all-purpose flour, as method specifies; knead. Let dough rise (see facing page), about 1 hour; mix or knead to expel air bubbles.

Divide into 12 equal pieces. On a lightly floured board, roll 1 piece into an ⅛-inch-thick round; repeat with 2 more pieces. Lay rounds well apart on an oiled 12- by 15-inch baking sheet.

Bake in a 500°oven on lowest rack until rounds are puffed and speckled brown, 5 to 6 minutes. Transfer to a rack; cool 1 minute, then seal in a plastic bag to soften. Repeat to make remaining rounds. Serve warm or cool. To store, see facing page. Makes 12, each about 2½ ounces.

Per piece: 169 cal. (14 percent from fat); 4.8 g protein; 2.7 g fat (0.4 g sat.); 31 g carbo.; 93 mg sodium; 0 mg chol.

BREAD BASICS: MIXING AND KNEADING (BY HAND OR MACHINE), RISING, AND STORING

Hand-kneading stimulates poetry, but time-crunch reality gives tools appeal. Pick a routine that suits your schedule.

To mix and knead by hand. Prepare dough in a large bowl according to recipe, adding whole-wheat flour (if used) and enough all-purpose flour to make a soft, easy-to-beat dough (usually a little more than ½ the total flour). Beat with a heavy spoon until dough is thoroughly moistened and stretchy, about 5 minutes. Add remainder of minimum amount of flour; stir until dough is evenly moistened.

To knead, scrape dough onto a floured board, using some of the remaining flour; coat dough lightly with flour. Knead briskly but gently enough to avoid breaking the smooth surface that forms on dough, until the dough is no longer sticky and feels satin smooth, 8 to 10 minutes; add just enough flour to keep dough from sticking as you knead.

To beat in a mixer and knead by hand. Prepare dough in a large bowl according to recipe, adding whole-wheat flour (if used) and enough all-purpose flour to make a dough soft enough to beat with an electric mixer (usually a little more than ½ the total flour). With mixer on low speed, stir in flour. On high speed, beat until dough is stretchy, 3 to 5 minutes. Add remaining minimum amount of flour; stir with a spoon (or with mixer) until dough is evenly moistened. Follow directions for kneading by hand.

To beat in a mixer and knead with a dough hook. Prepare dough in mixer bowl, preceding, beating until stretchy.

Switch to a dough hook. Add remaining minimum

amount of flour; mix on low speed until flour is incorporated. Beat on high speed for about 8 minutes. Dough should pull cleanly from bowl sides and no longer feel sticky. If dough still sticks, add flour, 1 tablespoon at a time, until dough pulls free and no longer feels sticky.

To mix and knead in a food processor. In a measuring cup with a lip (or in a small pitcher), soften yeast in water as recipe directs. Add any fat.

In the processor bowl, mix flavorings, any whole-wheat flour, and the minimum amount of all-purpose flour.

With the motor running, stir yeast mixture, then pour it quickly into feed tube. Whirl for about 1 minute total; dough should pull from container sides and no longer feel sticky. If it still sticks, add flour, 1 tablespoon at a time, whirling just until incorporated (overprocessed dough loses its ability to rise).

RISING

If kneading by hand or in a food processor, transfer dough to an oiled bowl; turn it over to oil top. If kneading with a dough hook, remove hook and leave dough in bowl. Cover bowl with plastic wrap; let dough rise in a warm place until doubled (if a hole poked in dough doesn't spring back, dough has risen enough). Knead dough briefly on a lightly floured board or with dough hook to release air bubbles.

STORING

Let bread cool on a rack; package cool bread airtight and hold at room temperature up to 1 day. Freeze to store longer. To recrisp crusty breads (thaw if frozen), place on a rack in a 350° oven until warm, 5 to 10 minutes.

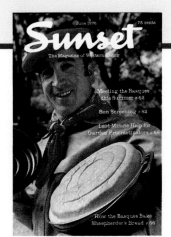

GLENN CHRISTIANSEN

BASQUE SHEEPHERDER *shared this bread with Sunset in 1976; it's still a favorite.*

We continue to receive requests for Basque sheepherder bread, a recipe featured on *Sunset*'s June 1976 cover. You need a 5-quart Dutch oven to bake it in.

Basque Sheepherder's Bread

2 packages active dry yeast

3 cups warm (110°) water

⅓ cup sugar

2 teaspoons salt

½ cup (¼ lb.) melted and cooled butter or margarine

8½ to 9¾ cups all-purpose flour

In a large bowl, sprinkle yeast over water and sugar; let stand until yeast is softened, about 5 minutes. Add salt, butter, and flour. Mix and knead by hand (see above). Let rise (see above) 1 to 1¼ hours; knead on a lightly floured board to expel air bubbles and form a smooth ball.

Line bottom of a 5-quart cast-iron or cast-aluminum Dutch oven with foil cut to fit. Rub foil, pan sides, and underside of lid with oil.

Place dough, smooth side up, in pan; cover with lid. Let rise in a warm place until dough just begins to push against lid, 30 to 40 minutes; watch closely.

Bake, covered with lid, in a 375° oven for 12 minutes; uncover. Bake until bread is deep golden brown, 30 to 35 minutes longer. Slide a knife

between pan sides and bread; tip onto a rack and peel off foil. Turn loaf upright; let cool at least 45 minutes. Serve warm or cool. To store, see above. Makes 1 loaf, about 4¼ pounds.

Per ounce: 73 cal. (18 percent from fat); 1.7 g protein; 1.5 g fat (0.9 g sat.); 13 g carbo.; 79 mg sodium; 3 mg chol.

Sourdough—a forty-niners' staple and the bread woven into Western history—has been the subject of dozens of *Sunset* features since 1933. Early *Sunset* stories were long on lore and short on specifics for capturing the sourdough starter essence.

In 1973, with a little help from science, we introduced a starter that produced consistent results. For a copy of our most recent directions—on

page 138 of the May 1988 *Sunset*—send a business-size, self-addressed, stamped envelope and $1 for handling to Starter, *Sunset Magazine*, 80 Willow Rd., Menlo Park, Calif. 94025.

The following bread came from the 1988 story. We've married it with techniques used by baker Joe Ortiz (May 1991, page 188) to create chewy Italian-style loaves.

1993 Sourdough Parmesan-Pepper Bread

¾ to 1 cup water

½ cup sourdough starter

About 2½ cups all-purpose flour

1 package active dry yeast

1 teaspoon sugar

½ teaspoon salt

¾ teaspoon freshly ground pepper

½ cup grated parmesan cheese

In a bowl, stir together ½ cup warm (90°) water, sourdough starter, and ½ cup flour. Use, or for the sourest flavor, cover mixture tightly with plastic wrap and let stand in a warm place until bubbly and sour smelling, up to 24 hours.

In a container with a spout, sprinkle yeast onto ¼ cup warm (110°) water; let stand until softened, about 5 minutes. Stir in sugar and sourdough mixture (if sourdough has stood more than 12 hours, add ¼ cup more water). Nest container steadily in a bowl of ice; stir often until starter mixture is ice cold, 15 to 20 minutes.

To complete dough in a food processor, mix 1¾ cups flour, salt, pepper, and cheese in container. With motor running, quickly pour in cold yeast mixture and process until dough is elastic (see text following), 1 to 1½ minutes.

To complete dough with a dough hook or by hand, combine 1¾ cups flour, salt, pepper, and cheese in a large bowl. Add yeast mixture and beat on medium speed with an electric mixer or with a heavy spoon until well blended. Using dough hook or heavy spoon, beat dough until it tests as elastic (see text following), about 5 minutes with hook, about 20 minutes with spoon (you may need a helper).

To test for elasticity, pinch off a small piece of the soupy dough and gently pull; if it stretches to form a thin skin you can see through, the dough is ready. Sprinkle the dough with 2 tablespoons flour and scrape it into a large bowl.

Cover bowl with plastic wrap and let dough rise in a warm place until doubled, 2 to 2¼ hours.

To shape loaves, sprinkle 2 tablespoons flour over dough; scrape dough onto a well-floured board and divide in ½. With floured hands, lightly pat each ½ into a 7- by 8-inch rectangle. Starting on a 7-inch side, roll dough jelly-roll fashion; with each turn, press rolled edge against unrolled portion with heel of hand (just firmly enough to make stick). Press dough edge against roll.

Place loaves, seam side down, well apart on a generously floured board. Pat each to make an 8-inch-long log. Sprinkle lightly with flour. Lightly cover logs with plastic wrap; let stand at room temperature for 30 minutes. Ease fingers under 1 log (scrape free with a spatula if it sticks) and lift, allowing it to stretch to 14 inches as you transfer it to an oiled 12- by 15-inch baking sheet. Repeat to put remaining log on another oiled baking sheet.

Let rise, uncovered, in a warm place until slightly puffy, 15 to 20 minutes. Place in a 475° oven; immediately reduce temperature to 425°. Bake until golden brown, about 20 minutes; after 10 minutes, alternate the pan positions.

For crispest crust, turn heat off, prop door slightly ajar, and leave loaves in oven for about 10 minutes. Serve hot or cool. Makes 2 loaves, each about 11 ounces.

Per ounce: 66 cal. (9.6 percent from fat); 2.6 g protein; 0.7 g fat (0.4 g sat.); 12 g carbo.; 87 mg sodium; 1.6 mg chol.

DARROW M. WATT

SUNSET EXPLORED *different flavors of bagels in a 1971 article.*

Sunset's first recipe for bagels, in 1956, described them as "an unusual snack to serve with coffee, beer, or other drinks." Nowadays, bagels are mainstream, coming on strong as a low-fat alternative to breakfast muffins. This recipe, based on one we published in the '70s, has less sugar and salt, in keeping with today's tastes.

Whole-wheat Poppy Seed Bagels

2 packages active dry yeast

2 cups warm (110°) water

2 tablespoons sugar

1 teaspoon salt

2½ cups whole-wheat flour

3 to 3½ cups all-purpose flour

1 large egg, beaten to blend

¼ cup poppy seed

Choose mixing and kneading method (see page 115). Sprinkle yeast over water and 1 tablespoon sugar; let stand until yeast is softened, about 5 minutes. Add salt, whole-wheat flour, and all-purpose flour as method specifies; knead. Let dough rise (see page 115) about 45 minutes; mix or knead to expel air bubbles.

Divide dough into 12 equal pieces. To shape, knead 1 piece at a time into a smooth ball. Hold ball with both hands, and press through center with thumbs to make a hole. With thumbs in the hole, pull dough gently to shape an evenly thick ring that is 3 to 3½ inches wide. Set shaped dough on a lightly floured board; cover with plastic wrap and let stand at room temperature until puffy, 20 to 25 minutes.

Meanwhile, in a 5- to 6-quart pan over high heat, bring 2½ quarts water with remaining 1 tablespoon sugar to boiling. Adjust heat to maintain a gentle boil.

Lightly oil 2 baking sheets, each 12 by 15 inches.

As bagels get puffy, lift with fingers and drop gently into boiling water, up to 4 at a time. Cook, turning often, for 5 minutes. Transfer with a slotted spoon to a cloth towel to drain briefly. Place bagels slightly apart on baking sheets. Brush with egg and sprinkle with poppy seed.

Bake in a 400° oven until bagels are well browned, 30 to 35 minutes; after 15 minutes, switch pan positions. Serve warm or cool. To store, see page 115. Makes 12, each 3 to 3¼ ounces.

Per bagel: 232 cal. (9.7 percent from fat); 8.1 g protein; 2.5 g fat (0.4 g sat.); 45 g carbo.; 192 mg sodium; 18 mg chol.

Scandinavians brought rye breads to the Northwest. We published a version similar to this one in 1983.

Scandinavian Rye Bread

1½ tablespoons melted and cooled butter or margarine

¾ teaspoon salt

Sour rye sponge (directions follow)

2¼ to 2½ cups all-purpose flour

1 tablespoon beaten egg

Choose mixing and kneading method, except food processor (see page 115); add butter and salt to rye sponge. Add all-purpose flour as specified; knead. Let dough rise (see page 115) 45 minutes to 1 hour.

Mix or knead to expel air bubbles; shape into a 10-inch-long log. Set smooth side up on an oiled 12- by 15-inch baking sheet. Dust with 1 teaspoon flour; cover lightly with plastic wrap and let rise in a warm place until puffy, 15 to 20 minutes.

Uncover. With a sharp knife, cut 4 diagonal slashes equally apart and ½ inch deep across loaf. Brush loaf with egg. Bake in a 400° oven until deep brown, about 40 minutes. Serve warm or cool. To store, see page 115. Makes 1 loaf, 1½ pounds.

Per ounce: 70 cal. (13 percent from fat); 1.9 g protein; 1 g fat (0.5 g sat.); 13 g carbo.; 77 mg sodium; 4.6 mg chol.

Sour rye sponge. In a large bowl, mix ¾ cup **coarsely ground** or regular **rye** flour, 1 package **active dry yeast,** and 1¼ cups warm (110°) **water.** Cover with plastic wrap and let stand at room temperature 6 to 24 hours; maximum time gives sourest flavor. Add another ¾ cup rye flour; 1 teaspoon *each* crushed **caraway, cumin,** and **fennel seed;** and 2 teaspoons grated **orange peel.** ∎

By Elaine Johnson

PETER CHRISTIANSEN

SCOOP OF LEMON *pudding cake is firm on top, saucy beneath. Serve with berries.*

Lemon cake is still a surprise

OLD-FASHIONED RECIPES that seem timeless endure because they adapt to lifestyle changes. Lemon pudding cake is a perfect example: it's simple, quick, and reasonably low in fat. The pudding that forms still surprises and mystifies, and, with berries, the dessert's as pleasing as ever.

Lemon Pudding Cake with Berries

About 2 tablespoons butter or margarine

3 large eggs, separated

¾ cup sugar

1 tablespoon grated lemon peel

1 cup buttermilk

⅓ cup lemon juice

¼ cup all-purpose flour

Berry sauce (recipe follows)

3 cups raspberries, blueberries, or hulled strawberries, or a combination, rinsed and drained

Place a buttered 5- to 6-cup soufflé or other straight-sided baking dish in a larger baking pan (at least 2 in. deep); set aside.

In a deep bowl, whip egg whites on high speed until foamy. Continue to beat, gradually adding ¼ cup sugar, until whites hold short, distinct peaks; set aside.

In another bowl, beat (no need to wash beaters) remaining ½ cup sugar, 2 tablespoons butter, peel, and egg yolks on high speed until mixture is thick and lighter in color. Stir in buttermilk, lemon juice, and flour. Add about ¼ of whites to batter; stir to mix well. Gently but thoroughly fold in remaining whites.

Pour batter into soufflé dish. Set dish in pan on center rack of a 350° oven. Pour boiling water into pan up to level of batter. Bake until pudding is a rich brown on top and feels firm in center when lightly touched, about 1 hour.

Serve pudding hot or cool, scooping portions from bottom of dish to get the sauce that forms. Accompany with berry sauce and fruit. Serves 6.

Per serving: 285 cal. (23 percent from fat); 6 g protein; 7.2 g fat (3.4 g sat.); 52 g carbo.; 117 mg sodium; 118 mg chol.

Berry sauce. In a blender or food processor, smoothly purée 2 cups rinsed and drained **raspberries** (or 1 package, 10 oz., thawed frozen raspberries in syrup) with 3 tablespoons **sugar** (or to taste) and 1 tablespoon **berry-flavor liqueur** (optional) such as Chambord or framboise. To remove seeds, rub purée through a fine strainer into a bowl. If making ahead, cover and chill up to 2 days. ■

By Karyn I. Lipman

A Canadian winner

NANAIMO, ON VANCOUVER Island, has a special distinction—a lavishly layered cookie bears its name. British Columbians who dote on this sweet say make it rich or don't bother. Kathy Sobba of Winnipeg, Manitoba, took the advice.

Nanaimo Bars

1 cup (½ lb.) butter or margarine

2¼ cups powdered sugar

¼ cup unsweetened cocoa

1 large egg

1¾ cups graham cracker crumbs

1 cup sweetened flaked dried coconut

½ cup chopped pecans or walnuts

2 tablespoons milk

1 tablespoon vanilla

3 ounces unsweetened chocolate

In a 2- to 3-quart pan, combine 6 tablespoons butter, ¼ cup sugar, and cocoa. Stir over low heat until butter melts. Off heat, beat in egg; mix in crumbs, coconut, and nuts. Press mixture in bottom of an 8-inch-square pan. Bake in a 350° oven until slightly darker, about 20 minutes. Let cool.

Beat ½ cup butter with remaining sugar, milk, and vanilla until fluffy. Spread over crust. In a bowl, combine 2 tablespoons butter and chocolate; set bowl in hot water. Stir often until chocolate is smooth; spread over filling. Cover and chill 1 hour or up to 2 days. Cut into 25 squares.

Per piece: 194 cal. (60 percent from fat); 1.6 g protein; 13 g fat (6.8 g sat.); 20 g carbo.; 137 mg sodium; 29 mg chol. ■

By Christine B. Weber

NORMAN A. PLATE

THE PRIDE *of Nanaimo: creamy filling between coconut crust and chocolate.*

BROAD

Crab cossets with handily assembled ingredients

While pork tenderloins are tamed by Thai seasonings

LOOKING FOR SOMETHING simple and savory for lunch or hot hors d'oeuvres? Seek no further. Dan Golling's seafood toppers are the reward for your search. They are handily assembled out of easily obtained ingredients and, according to Golling, are especially cosseting when the evenings still have a bit of chill and the creeks are running high, particularly if served with a good Sonoma County wine.

Seafood Topper

½ cup reduced-calorie or regular mayonnaise

¼ cup thinly sliced green onions, including tops

2 tablespoons diced red bell pepper

1 tablespoon white wine vinegar

1 tablespoon Dijon mustard

1½ cups (6 oz.) shredded Swiss cheese

½ pound cooked, shelled crab

4 English muffins, split and toasted

Paprika

In a bowl, mix mayonnaise, onion, bell pepper, vinegar, and mustard. Gently stir in cheese and crab. Evenly mound crab mixture on muffin halves and set

in a 10- by 15-inch pan; dust crab with paprika. Bake in a 350° oven until mixture is hot in center, about 25 minutes. Makes 4 or 8 servings.

Per serving: 218 cal. (45 percent from fat); 14 g protein; 11 g fat (4.8 g sat.); 15 g carbo.; 377 mg sodium; 53 mg chol.

DFGolling

Healdsburg, California

IS IT TAME OR IS IT WILD? Harold Merkow calls his barbecued pork Tame Thai Tenderloin so, presumably, our rational universe also has a Wild Thai Tenderloin—which must be very spicy indeed, because the relatively modest amounts of garlic, pepper, chili paste, and cayenne in Merkow's recipe are enough to call most palates to attention. The coconut milk has an emollient effect on the marinade, softening the assertive spices with its sweet, mild nature.

Tame Thai Tenderloin

2 pork tenderloins (¾ to 1 lb. each)

¾ cup (half of a 14-oz. can) coconut milk

¼ cup soy sauce

2 cloves garlic, minced or pressed

1¼ teaspoons ground coriander

½ teaspoon white pepper

¼ teaspoon Asian red chili paste (or liquid hot pepper seasoning)

1 tablespoon lemon juice

¼ teaspoon cayenne

½ teaspoon sugar

Rinse meat and pat dry. Trim fat and silvery membrane from tenderloins. Fold under thin ends of tenderloins to make each piece evenly thick; tie to secure. Put meat in a zip-lock heavy plastic bag (about 2-qt. size). In a small bowl, mix coconut milk, 3 tablespoons soy sauce, garlic, 1 teaspoon coriander, white pepper, and chili paste; pour over meat. Seal bag and rotate to coat meat with sauce; chill 3 to 6 hours. Turn meat over several times.

Lift meat from marinade and drain briefly; discard marinade. Place meat on a lightly greased grill 4 to 6 inches above a solid bed of medium coals (you can hold your hand at grill level only 4 to 5 seconds). Cook, turning often to brown evenly, until meat is no longer pink in thickest part (cut to test), 18 to 22 minutes, or until a thermometer inserted in center of meat (not folded end) registers 155°.

In a small microwave-safe bowl, combine lemon juice, remaining 1 tablespoon soy sauce, remaining ¼ teaspoon coriander, cayenne, and sugar. Heat in a microwave oven on full power (100 percent) until mixture is hot, about 30 seconds.

Cut meat across the grain into thin, slanting slices. Spoon sauce onto meat to taste. Makes 4 servings.

Per serving: 265 cal. (37 percent from fat); 38 g protein; 11 g fat (6.1 g sat.); 2.7 g carbo.; 737 mg sodium; 119 mg chol.

Phoenix

A LIGHTER, FRESHER alternative" is the banner Leslie Des Georges waves for her wild rice salad, comparing it with those made of pasta or potatoes with a mayonnaise dressing. Her claim is substantiated in the nutrition information.

In this instance, less proves

A COMMANDING *hand domesticates wild rice for salad.*

to be more as rice and wild rice contribute substantial body, jicama adds texture, and mandarin orange sections with cilantro add excitement. A light, fruity vinaigrette enhances the whole.

Wild rice, the seed of a native North American aquatic grass (*Zizania aquatica*), although it is still more expensive than true rice, has come down in price since the plant that bears it has been domesticated.

Wild Rice Salad with Raspberry Vinaigrette

1 cup (about 6 oz.) wild rice, rinsed and drained

1 cup long-grain white rice

¾ cup chopped fresh cilantro (coriander)

2 cups julienne strips peeled jicama

½ cup thinly sliced green onions, including tops

2 cans (11 oz. each) mandarin oranges

Raspberry vinaigrette (recipe follows)

Salt and pepper

In a 3- to 4-quart pan, bring 5 cups water to a boil over high heat; stir in wild rice. Cover, reduce heat, and simmer for 30 minutes; stir in white rice. Cover and simmer until both of the grains are tender to bite, 15 to 20 minutes longer. Uncover, drain and discard any liquid, and let rice cool.

Pour rice into a salad bowl and mix with cilantro, jicama, and onions. Drain mandarins, reserving juice.

Add ½ cup juice to raspberry vinaigrette, then mix dressing with salad. Scatter fruit over rice. If making ahead, cover and chill up to 6 hours. Season to taste with salt and pepper. Makes 10 servings.

Per serving: 178 cal. (2 percent from fat); 4.5 g protein; 0.4 g fat (0.1 g sat.); 40 g carbo.; 7.8 mg sodium; 0 mg chol.

Raspberry vinaigrette. Stir together 3 tablespoons **unflavored nonfat yogurt** or sour cream, ¼ cup **raspberry vinegar,** ½ teaspoon grated **orange peel,** and 2 tablespoons **salad oil.**

Sacramento, California

By Joan Griffiths, Richard Dunmire

It's loquat season— time for chutney

F RESH LOQUATS ARE plentiful during their short, early-summer season. The refreshing fruit has a faint apricot flavor; it also has big seeds surrounded by a thin wall of flesh. Getting enough fruit to cook is a bit of a hassle; this slim reward is one reason loquats rarely make it to the market.

However, the loquat tree is decorative and popular in gardens (where freezes are rare), and if you have a tree, or access to one, enjoy loquats fresh and also try them in this sweet-tart chutney.

Loquat juice stains; wear rubber gloves as you work.

By Christine W. Hale

Loquat Chutney

10 pounds (about 1 gal.) loquats, rinsed well and drained

3½ cups firmly packed brown sugar

2 cups cider vinegar

2 tablespoons minced fresh ginger

2 tablespoons grated orange peel

Cut loquats in half. Discard stems, seeds, and inner membranes. Coarsely chop fruit; it will darken.

In a 10- to 12-quart pan, combine loquats, sugar, vinegar, ginger, and peel. Bring to a boil over high heat. Boil gently, uncovered, until mixture is thick and syrupy, about 45 minutes; stir occasionally—oftener as mixture thickens to prevent scorching. Serve warm or cool.

Cool chutney, package airtight, and chill up to 2 weeks; or seal in 1- to 2-cup containers and freeze up to 1 year. Makes about 11 cups.

Per tablespoon: 24 cal. (0 percent from fat); 0.1 g protein; 0 g fat; 6.3 g carbo.; 1.5 mg sodium; 0 mg chol. ■

NORMAN A. PLATE

USE GOLDEN LOQUATS *in chutney that goes well with meats.*

SUNSET'S KITCHEN CABINET

Creative ways with everyday foods—submitted by *Sunset* readers,
tested in *Sunset* kitchens, approved by *Sunset* taste panels

PIZZA FLAVORS *season tender muffins;*
serve for breakfast or as a snack.

Pizza Snack Muffins

Geri Hupp, Brookeland, Texas

2 cups all-purpose flour

2 teaspoons baking powder

1 teaspoon *each* crumbled dried
   basil and dried oregano leaves

¾ cup nonfat milk

1 large egg

   About 2 tablespoons salad oil

½ cup chopped tomatoes

½ cup (2 oz.) finely chopped
   pepperoni

1 can (2¼ oz.) sliced ripe black
   olives, drained

¾ cup shredded mozzarella cheese

In a bowl, mix flour, baking powder, basil, and oregano. Add milk, egg, and 2 tablespoons oil; stir to moisten. Add tomatoes, pepperoni, olives, and ½ the cheese; mix well. Divide batter equally among 10 oiled muffin cups (2 to 2½ in. wide); top with remaining cheese.

Bake in a 350° oven until muffins are well browned, 30 to 35 minutes. Let stand about 5 minutes, then remove from pan. Serve warm or cool. If making ahead, let cool; store airtight at room temperature up to 1 day. Makes 10.

Per muffin: 200 cal. (42 percent from fat); 6.8 g protein; 9.4 g fat (2.8 g sat.); 21 g carbo.; 306 mg sodium; 33 mg chol.

SEASON SPINACH *Indian-style with*
ginger, aromatic spices, and chilies.

Spiced Spinach

Goolcher Wadia, San Anselmo, California

1 large (about ½-lb.) onion, thinly
   sliced

1 teaspoon salad oil

2 garlic cloves, minced or pressed

1 tablespoon minced fresh ginger

½ teaspoon ground cumin

½ teaspoon ground coriander

¼ teaspoon ground turmeric

¼ teaspoon crushed dried hot
   chilies

2 pounds spinach

   Lemon wedges

   Salt

In a 5- to 6-quart pan over medium heat, combine onion, oil, 2 tablespoons water, garlic, ginger, cumin, coriander, turmeric, and chilies. Stir often until onion is golden brown, about 15 minutes.

Meanwhile, rinse spinach well, discarding roots and wilted leaves; drain. Fill pan with as much spinach as it will hold. Stir often until leaves wilt; add remaining leaves as space permits. When all the spinach is in the pan, turn heat to high and stir spinach until wilted and most of the accumulating liquid evaporates, 7 to 10 minutes. Pour into a bowl. Add lemon and salt to taste. Serves 4.

Per serving: 73 cal. (23 percent from fat); 5.5 g protein; 1.9 g fat (0.2 g sat.); 12 g carbo.; 132 mg sodium; 0 mg chol.

Bavarian Crunch Potato Salad

Sally Vog, Springfield, Oregon

2 pounds thin-skinned potatoes,
   scrubbed

½ cup unflavored nonfat yogurt or
   reduced-calorie mayonnaise

½ cup cider vinegar

1 teaspoon caraway seed

2 large (about 1¼ lb. total) red
   apples

½ pound bacon, cooked, drained,
   and crumbled

2 cups shredded green cabbage

½ cup chopped green onions

   Whole green onions, ends
   trimmed (optional)

   Salt

In a 5- to 6-quart pan, combine potatoes with water to cover. Cover pan and bring water to boil on high heat; simmer until potatoes are tender when pierced, 30 to 40 minutes, depending upon size. Drain potatoes; let stand until cool, then cut into 1-inch cubes.

Meanwhile, in a large bowl, combine yogurt, vinegar, and caraway. Core apples and cut into ½-inch chunks into bowl; mix. Add potatoes, all but 2 tablespoons of the bacon, cabbage, and chopped onions; mix gently. Mound salad onto a platter, top with remaining bacon and whole green onions; add salt to taste. Makes about 11 cups, 9 to 11 servings.

Per serving: 140 cal. (21 percent from fat); 4.3 g protein; 3.2 g fat (1 g sat.); 25 g carbo.; 109 mg sodium; 5.1 mg chol.

CRISP APPLES, *cabbage, and bacon go*
with potatoes in a refreshing salad.

Grilled Tuna Steaks

Jane Ingraham, Durango, Colorado

If you want to enjoy the moist flavor of rare tuna and the fish has not been frozen, freeze steaks at 0° for at least 7 days to destroy any potentially harmful organisms. Thaw in the refrigerator.

4 tuna (ahi) steaks, each 1 inch thick (about 1¾ lb. total)

3 tablespoons lime juice

2 tablespoons reduced-sodium soy sauce

1 tablespoon minced fresh ginger

1 tablespoon minced garlic
   Lime wedges
   Oriental sesame oil (optional)

Rinse tuna, pat dry, and lay in a 9- by 13-inch pan. Mix lime juice with soy sauce, ginger, and garlic; pour over fish. Cover airtight and chill at least 1 hour or up to 1 day; turn fish over occasionally.

Lay fish on a lightly oiled grill 4 to 6 inches above a bed of hot coals (you can hold your hand at grill level only 1 to 2 seconds). Cook, turning once, until fish is browned but still pink in center (cut to test), 6 to 7 minutes total. Accompany with lime and sesame oil to add to taste. Makes 4 servings.

Per serving: 207 cal. (7.8 percent from fat); 43 g protein; 1.8 g fat (0.4 g sat.); 2.6 g carbo.; 369 mg sodium; 81 mg chol.

GRILLED TUNA *steaks are marinated; as a final touch, add sesame oil.*

Greek Chicken Pockets

Dorothy Head Krogh, Portland

4 to 6 pocket bread rounds (6 to 7 in. wide)

3 small (about ¾ lb. total) firm ripe tomatoes, cored

2 small (about ¾ lb. total) green bell peppers, stemmed and seeded

3 cups skinned, shredded cooked chicken

¼ cup feta cheese, crumbled
   Herb dressing (recipe follows)

Cut bread rounds in half crosswise. Thinly slice tomatoes and peppers crosswise. Gently open bread pockets and fill them equally with sliced tomatoes, peppers, chicken, and feta cheese. Spoon dressing equally into each portion. Makes 4 to 6 servings.

Per serving: 369 cal. (18 percent from fat); 30 g protein; 7.2 g fat (2.3 g sat.); 46 g carbo.; 521 mg sodium; 68 mg chol.

Herb dressing. Mix together 1 cup **unflavored nonfat yogurt**, ½ cup minced peeled **cucumber**, 1 tablespoon minced **fresh** or 1 teaspoon crumbled dried **dill**, and 1 tablespoon minced **fresh** or 1 teaspoon crumbled dried **mint leaves.**

ADD HERBED YOGURT *to pocket bread with chicken, vegetables, and feta.*

Mexican Chocolate Cream Pie

Judy Hoffman, Lewiston, Idaho

1 tablet (3 oz.) Mexican chocolate flavored with cinnamon (available in Latino markets or well-stocked markets), or 3 ounces semisweet chocolate

⅓ cup sugar

1 tablespoon cornstarch

2 teaspoons (1 envelope) unflavored gelatin

½ teaspoon ground cinnamon

2½ cups 1-percent-fat milk

½ cup half-and-half (light cream)

2 large eggs

1 baked pastry shell for a single-crust 9-inch pie
   Sweetened whipped cream (optional)
   Cinnamon stick (optional)

Chop chocolate and place in a 3- to 4-quart pan. Add sugar, cornstarch, gelatin, and cinnamon; mix well. Stir in milk and half-and-half. Place pan over medium heat; stir often until mixture is bubbling and chocolate is smoothly melted. Stir a little hot liquid into eggs; whisk mixture back into pan. Stir over medium heat for 2 to 3 minutes.

Set pan in ice water to cool chocolate filling quickly, stirring often until mixture begins to thicken, then pour into pastry shell. Cover pie airtight and chill until firm enough to cut, at least 4 hours or up to 1 day. Spoon whipped cream in puffs onto pie; top with a cinnamon stick. Makes 8 to 10 servings.

Per serving: 217 cal. (50 percent from fat); 5.4 g protein; 12 g fat (4.5 g sat.); 24 g carbo.; 160 mg sodium; 49 mg chol.

Compiled by Christine B. Weber

CINNAMON STICK *decorates creamy smooth chocolate-cinnamon pie.*

June Menus

he long, bright days of June make the outdoors appealing for many hours. Match the sun's leisurely pace with casual, easy-to-cook alfresco meals that merit lingering attention.

On the deck of a houseboat—or in the garden—offer a portable salad buffet based on cold noodles and a spicy Thai dressing. On the terrace, imagine viewing the Mediterranean Sea as you sip cool wine and lazily peel salt-grilled shrimp, Italian-style, from their shells. For another simple escape, carry a casserole and crisp salad to a shady patio.

KLONG-STYLE THAI SALAD (at right)
From a waterside buffet, guests build salad from a platter with noodles, chicken, condiments.

AN ITALIAN LUNCH (page 124)
Linger more than labor over an almost no-cook meal with salt-grilled shrimp and cold bean salad.

CALIFORNIA CASSEROLE (page 125)
Savory mix of vegetables bakes with a cheese topping to make an easy, homey casserole.

THE DETAILS

Bean Sprouter

Use jar with cheesecloth lid to sprout beans as directed on page 124.

Noodle Coils

Use golden angel hair pasta or white rice noodles (top) for coils.

Leaf Liners

Line platters or baskets with banana, ti, or Japanese aralia leaves.

Pineapple Blossoms

Cut out pineapple eyes in diagonal rows; slice. Or buy peeled fruit.

KLONG-STYLE THAI SALAD

Thai Noodle Salad Buffet

Beer or Iced Tea

Pineapple Blossoms

Whether you serve this meal on a boat, as along the canals of Thailand, or in the garden, the salad buffet is easy to transport on a big tray. Guests assemble their own salads, seasoning with the flavors of Thailand. Conclude with fresh pineapple.

Prepare the chicken, noodles, and dressing in advance. The rice noodles can be found in Asian markets and many supermarkets. Or use the more widely available dried angel hair pasta. Assemble salad ingredients and condiments up to 4 hours ahead (even earlier for some elements).

For a unique addition, grow your own mung bean sprouts. Look for the small green beans at health food stores or Asian markets.

To grow bean sprouts. Place ½ cup **dried mung beans** in a 1-quart wide-mouth jar. Half-fill jar with **water.** Cover with cheesecloth; secure with jar ring or a rubber band. Let soak overnight. Drain water through the cheesecloth top. Place jar on its side in a dark, warm (68° or above) place. Several times a day, rinse seeds with water and drain through cheesecloth. Grow until sprouts are 1 to 2 inches long, 2 to 3 days. Use, or store in a plastic bag up to 2 days. Makes about 4 cups (about ¾ lb.).

Thai Noodle Salad Buffet

4 chicken breast halves (2 to 2½ lb. total), skinned

1 pound dried angel hair (capellini) pasta or thin rice noodles (mai fun)

1 tablespoon Oriental sesame oil or salad oil

1 large (1-lb.) European cucumber, cut into thin slivers

½ to ¾ pound bean sprouts, rinsed and drained

PETER CHRISTIANSEN

HANDS-ON MEAL FEATURES *salt-grilled shrimp to peel, lettuce leaves, and cherry tomatoes. Dip in olive oil and vinegar.*

¾ cup thinly sliced green onions

¾ cup chopped fresh cilantro (coriander)

½ cup chopped fresh basil leaves

¾ cup finely chopped salted roasted peanuts

Lemon wedges (optional)

Chili dressing (recipe follows)

In a 5- to 6-quart pan, bring 2½ to 3 quarts water to a boil on high heat. Add chicken and return to a boil. Cover pan tightly; remove from heat. Let stand until meat is white in thickest part (cut to test), 20 minutes. If still pink, return to water, cover pan, and let stand; check for doneness at 2- or 3-minute intervals. Remove chicken from water; cool.

Meanwhile, return water to a boil on high heat. Add pasta and cook, uncovered, until barely tender to bite, about 3 minutes for angel hair, 2 to 3 minutes for rice noodles. Drain and immerse noodles in cold water. Add oil to water.

When noodles are cool, lift small handfuls of noodles out of water, draining briefly. Loosely coil each handful of noodles and set on a wide platter, stacking if needed. (If making ahead, cover and let stand at room temperature up to 4 hours.)

Tear chicken into shreds; discard bones. (If making ahead, cover meat and chill up to 1 day.) Arrange chicken, cucumber, sprouts, onions, cilantro, basil, peanuts, lemon, and noodles in individual bowls or mound in separate piles on a platter.

To assemble salad, place a few noodle coils on a plate. Add chicken, cucumber, onions, cilantro, basil, peanuts, lemon, and chili dressing to taste. Serves 6.
—*Mary Robins, Menlo Park, California*

Per serving: 597 cal. (23 percent from fat); 50 g protein; 15 g fat (2.2 g sat.); 67 g carbo.; 255 mg sodium; 84 mg chol.

Chili dressing. In a small bowl, mix ¾ cup **rice** or wine **vinegar,** ½ cup **soy sauce,** 3 tablespoons **sugar,** 2 tablespoons **Oriental sesame oil,** 2 tablespoons minced **fresh ginger,** 1 to 2 teaspoons **crushed dried hot red chilies,** and 2 cloves **garlic,** pressed or minced. Makes about 1⅔ cups.

Per tablespoon: 20 cal. (50 percent from fat); 0.3 g protein; 1.1 g fat (0.1 g sat.); 2.3 g carbo.; 318 mg sodium; 0 mg chol.

AN ITALIAN LUNCH

Taleggio, Mozzarella Fresca, or Italian Fontina Cheese

Crusty Bread

White Bean Salad

Etrusca Salt-Grilled Shrimp with Vegetables

Pinot Grigio or Dry Sauvignon Blanc

Biscotti

Vin Santo–Peach Splashes

It's more work to shop for this Italian lunch than to cook it. For best choices on cheese, wine, olive oil and biscotti, visit a good deli or well-supplied supermarket.

This grazing-style menu fits perfectly into a lazy Sunday afternoon. Set the whole menu on the table and let diners proceed at their own pace. Have them start with Italian cheeses and bread as appetizers, then move on to the main course of salt-grilled shrimp to peel and dip in olive oil and vinegar.

For dessert, pair ripe fragrant peaches with sherry-like Italian Vin Santo or a lightly sweet late-harvest dessert wine, such as Johannisberg Riesling. Serve biscotti to dunk into the wine.

White Bean Salad

2 cans (15 oz. each) cannellini (white kidney) beans or pinto beans

2 to 3 tablespoons balsamic or red wine vinegar

1 to 2 tablespoons extra-virgin olive oil

Salt and pepper

2 tablespoons chopped fresh basil leaves or parsley

Drain beans. In a bowl, mix with vinegar, oil, salt,

and pepper to taste. Sprinkle with basil. If making ahead, cover and chill up to 1 day. Serves 4 or 5.

Per serving: 120 cal. (27 percent from fat); 6.3 g protein; 3.6 g fat (0.5 g sat.); 16 g carbo.; 276 mg sodium; 0 mg chol.

Etrusca Salt-Grilled Shrimp with Vegetables

1½ pounds extra-jumbo (16 to 20 per lb.) shrimp

Extra-virgin olive oil

About 2 tablespoons sea salt or kosher salt

About ¼ pound Belgian endive, rinsed and crisped

½ pound small romaine lettuce leaves, rinsed and crisped

½ to ¾ pound red and/or yellow cherry tomatoes, rinsed and stemmed

Balsamic or red wine vinegar

Freshly ground pepper

Insert a toothpick under the back of the shrimp between shell segments and gently pull up to remove vein. If vein breaks, repeat in another place. Rinse shrimp and pat dry. Mix shrimp with 1 tablespoon oil, then roll in salt to coat lightly.

Arrange endive, lettuce, and tomatoes in bowl.

Place shrimp on a grill 4 to 6 inches above a solid bed of hot coals (you can hold your hand at grill level only 2 to 3 seconds). Cook, turning once, until shrimp are opaque in thickest part (cut to test), about 8 minutes total. Transfer to plates. Serve hot or warm, accompanied by cruets or bottles of oil and vinegar. Individually, in small bowls at the table, blend a little oil in vinegar to make a dressing. To eat, peel shrimp and season foods with dressing and pepper. Serves 4 or 5.

—*Ruggero Gadaldi, Etrusca, San Francisco*

Per serving: 162 cal. (28 percent from fat); 24 g protein; 5 g fat (0.8 g sat.); 4.9 g carbo.; 1,939 mg sodium; 168 mg chol.

Vin Santo–Peach Splashes

1 medium-size (about ½-lb.) ripe peach, peeled and sliced

UNDER GOLDEN CHEESE CRUST LIES *savory all-vegetable combination of eggplant, bell peppers, olives, and tomato sauce. Serve with salad and breadsticks.*

1 to 1½ cups chilled Vin Santo, late-harvest Gewürztraminer, or late-harvest Johannisberg Riesling

Place the peach slices equally in 4 or 5 wineglasses. Fill glasses with wine. Sip wine and eat fruit with a spoon. Serves 4 or 5.

Per serving: 47 cal. (0 percent from fat); 0.3 g protein; 0 g fat; 4.2 g carbo.; 2.4 mg sodium; 0 mg chol.

CALIFORNIA CASSEROLE

Eggplant–Cheese Casserole

Breadsticks

Mixed Green Salad

Apricots   Grapes

Merlot   Milk

An all-vegetable casserole fortified with ricotta and cheddar cheese makes an easy meal for the family; you can start it up to 2 days ahead. While the casserole bakes, mix salad greens with your favorite dressing.

Eggplant–Cheese Casserole

3 small eggplants (about 3 lb. total), stemmed

1 large (about 10-oz.) onion, chopped

1 large (about ½-lb.) green bell pepper, stemmed, seeded, and chopped

¾ cup fine dried bread crumbs

1 large (3.8-oz.) can sliced ripe olives, drained

1 can (15 oz.) tomato sauce

1 cup (½ lb.) ricotta cheese

2 cups (½ lb.) shredded sharp cheddar cheese

Salt and pepper

Cut eggplants into ¾-inch cubes. In a deep 4-quart casserole, mix eggplants, onion, bell pepper, crumbs, olives, and tomato sauce; cover tightly. Bake in a 400° oven until vegetables are soft when pressed, about 1½ hours; stir after 45 minutes, re-covering tightly. (If mak-

ing ahead, let cool and chill, covered, up to 2 days. Reheat, covered, in a 400° oven until hot, about 30 minutes.)

Spoon ricotta in dollops onto hot vegetables; sprinkle with cheddar. Bake, uncovered, until cheddar melts, 10 to 15 minutes longer. Add salt and pepper to taste. Makes 8 servings.

—*Eleanor Ritter Reynolds, Sacramento*

Per serving: 303 cal. (48 percent from fat); 15 g protein; 16 g fat (8.9 g sat.); 28 g carbo.; 736 mg sodium; 45 mg chol. ■

By Linda Lau Anusasananan, Betsy Reynolds Bateson

Curried Rice and Zucchini Salad

This salad goes together quickly for a picnic.

⅓ cup mayonnaise

¼ cup unflavored yogurt

1 teaspoon soy sauce

½ teaspoon curry powder

¼ teaspoon garlic salt

Liquid hot pepper seasoning

2 cups cold cooked rice

1 small jar (2 oz.) chopped pimientos, drained

1 jar (6 oz.) marinated artichoke hearts, drained

1 medium-size zucchini (about 6 oz.), ends trimmed

In a large bowl, blend mayonnaise, yogurt, soy sauce, curry powder, and garlic salt. Add liquid hot pepper seasoning to taste. Add rice, pimientos, and artichoke hearts; mix lightly to coat with dressing. If made ahead, cover and refrigerate for up to one day.

Cut zucchini lengthwise into quarters; slice thinly. Mix zucchini lightly into salad. Makes 4 to 6 servings.

Per serving: 189 cal. (58 percent from fat); 3 g protein; 12 g fat (2 g sat.); 18 g carbo.; 342 mg sodium; 8 mg chol.

Breakfast, Portland-style

Is Portland the breakfast capital of the West? You can sure get a hearty, tasty meal there. Or you can try these regional specialties at home

PULL UP A chair: breakfast is served. In settings that range from elegant to funky, Portlanders are lifting their forks to the Northwest's bounty of seafood and seasonal fruits. Add hearty breads, a bottomless cup of coffee, and a friendly "good morning", and you're set for breakfast, Portland-style.

We've gathered these recipes from Rose City restaurants for you to enjoy at home—but try them at the source if you can.

Zell's Strawberry German Pancake

  3 tablespoons butter or margarine

  ¾ cup all-purpose flour

  ¾ cup milk

  3 large eggs

  2 teaspoons sugar

  3 cups sliced strawberries

     Strawberry sauce (recipe follows)

     Powdered sugar

     Lemon wedges

Divide butter equally between 2 ovenproof frying pans, each 8 to 10 inches. Set pans in a 425° oven until butter melts, 3 to 4 minutes; tilt to coat pan.

Meanwhile, in a blender or food processor whirl flour, milk, eggs, and sugar until smoothly mixed.

Pour batter equally into

JOHN RIZZO

WAKE UP *with Tom Zell's German pancake with strawberries and berry sauce, a specialty at Zell's: An American Cafe.*

hot pans; bake until deep golden brown, 18 to 20 minutes. Serve from pans, or loosen with a spatula and slide onto plates. Accompany with sliced strawberries, strawberry sauce, powdered sugar, and lemon wedges. Makes 2 generous or 4 regular servings.

Per regular serving: 324 cal. (42 percent from fat); 9.6 g protein; 15 g fat (7.5 g sat.); 40 g carbo.; 160 mg sodium; 189 mg chol.

Strawberry sauce. In a blender or food processor, purée 1 cup rinsed, hulled **strawberries,** 2 tablespoons **sugar,** and 2 teaspoons **lemon juice.**

B. Moloch's Coffee-Bran Muffins

  1½ cups unprocessed wheat bran

  1⅓ cups all-purpose flour

  1 teaspoon baking soda

  ½ cup sugar

  ¼ cup (⅛ lb.) butter or margarine

  1 cup buttermilk

  ½ cup cold strong coffee

  ¼ cup dark corn syrup

  1 large egg

  ¾ cup raisins

In a bowl, combine bran, flour, and soda.

In a large bowl, beat

sugar and butter until
smoothly mixed. Add buttermilk, coffee, corn syrup, and
egg; beat to blend. Stir in
flour mixture and raisins just
until evenly moistened.

Equally fill 12 greased or
paper-lined muffin cups (2½-
in. diameter); cups will be
full. Bake in a 375° oven until
tops spring back when firmly
pressed, about 25 minutes.
Makes 12.

*Per muffin: 203 cal. (26 percent
from fat); 4.1 g protein; 5.8 g fat
(3.3 g sat.); 37 g carbo.; 195 mg
sodium; 31 mg chol.*

B. Moloch's Raisin Scones

1¾ cups all-purpose flour

⅓ cup sugar

1 teaspoon baking
   powder

½ teaspoon baking soda

⅔ cup buttermilk

⅓ cup (⅙ lb.) melted butter
   or margarine

⅓ cup raisins

Combine flour, sugar, baking powder, and soda. Stir in
buttermilk, butter, and raisins
just until evenly moistened.

On an oiled 12- by 15-inch
baking sheet, spoon dough
into 6 to 8 equal mounds,
slightly apart. Bake in a 400°
oven until well browned, 18
to 20 minutes; serve hot or
cool. Makes 6 to 8.

*Per scone: 230 cal. (34 percent
from fat); 3.8 g protein; 8.6 g fat
(4.9 g sat.); 35 g carbo.; 240 mg
sodium; 21 mg chol.*

Papa Haydn's Astoria Omelet

6 large eggs

1 to 1½ tablespoons butter
   or margarine

⅓ cup sliced green onions
   Rouille (recipe follows)

½ cup (¼ lb.) shelled
   cooked crab

½ cup (¼ lb.) shelled
   cooked tiny shrimp
   Sour cream (optional)
   Edible flowers (optional)

In a bowl, beat eggs to
blend. For each omelet,

CRAB AND SHRIMP *spill from Papa Haydn's Astoria omelet, made with a hot and spicy red pepper and saffron rouille sauce and topped with a squiggle of sour cream.*

place ½ tablespoon butter in an 8-inch frying pan (preferably nonstick). Melt butter over medium-high heat, tilting pan to coat. Add ⅓ or ½ of eggs and onions, and 1½ tablespoons rouille.

As eggs on pan bottom begin to set, with a spatula push cooked portion toward center, tilting pan so liquid flows to bottom. Repeat until eggs are cooked as you like, 2 to 3 minutes total for moist-looking eggs. Remove pan from heat.

Set aside a few large crab pieces. Scatter omelet with ⅓ or ½ of remaining crab and shrimp. Loosen omelet with a wide spatula; slide onto a warm plate, flipping pan to fold half of omelet over other half. Keep warm while making remaining omelets. Garnish with remaining crab, rouille, sour cream, and flowers. Serves 2 or 3.

Per serving: 363 cal. (64 percent from fat); 26 g protein; 26 g fat (8.1 g sat.); 5.3 g carbo.; 364 mg sodium; 540 mg chol.

Rouille. In a blender, whirl ¼ cup **soft bread crumbs,** ¼ cup chopped **canned roasted red peppers** or pimientos, 2 tablespoons **water** or bottled clam juice, 1 large clove **garlic,** 1 teaspoon **red wine vinegar,** ¼ teaspoon **crushed dried hot red chilies,** and ⅛ teaspoon **powdered saffron.** Whirl until smoothly puréed. With motor running, add 2 tablespoons **olive oil.** Season sauce with **salt** and **pepper** to taste. If making ahead, chill airtight up to 3 days. Makes ½ cup.

Papa Haydn's Lemon–Poppy Seed Waffles with Blueberries

1½ cups all-purpose flour

2 tablespoons sugar

1 tablespoon baking powder

2 teaspoons poppy seed

1 large egg, separated

1½ cups milk

3 tablespoons melted butter or margarine

1 tablespoon grated lemon peel

1½ teaspoons vanilla

About 1½ cups sweetened whipped cream (optional)

2 cups blueberries, rinsed and drained

Maple syrup

In a large bowl, mix flour, sugar, baking powder, and poppy seed. In another bowl, mix egg yolk, milk, butter, lemon peel, and vanilla.

With an electric mixer on high speed, beat egg white until soft peaks form. Add milk mixture to flour mixture and whisk until smooth. Gently fold in egg white.

Preheat a waffle iron as manufacturer directs. Oil lightly; pour in enough batter to fill ⅔ full. Bake until deep golden, about 5 minutes. Top waffles with cream, berries, and syrup to taste. Makes 4, each 8 inches square.

Per waffle: 422 cal. (36 percent from fat); 10 g protein; 17 g fat (8 g sat.); 59 g carbo.; 520 mg sodium; 89 mg chol.

The Heathman Hotel's Smoked Salmon Hash

One type of smoked salmon is moist, the other drier and firmer. Here you need the drier type (hard- or hot-smoked). Buy in a fish market or supermarket, or order from Seaport Fisheries, Inc., at (800) 525-3474. One pound costs $12.95 plus shipping.

If you like, top hash with poached eggs.

½ pound firm-textured smoked salmon or smoked trout

At least ⅓ cup regular or light (reduced-fat) sour cream

3 tablespoons drained canned capers

2 tablespoons prepared horseradish

2 tablespoons minced parsley

1 tablespoon lemon juice

1 small (¼-lb.) red onion, finely chopped

1 teaspoon minced garlic

¼ cup (⅛ lb.) butter or margarine

3 cups frozen hash brown potatoes

2 tablespoons sliced green onions

Freshly ground pepper

Remove skin and bone from salmon; discard. Tear fish into shreds; in a large bowl, gently mix with ⅓ cup sour cream, capers, horseradish, parsley, and juice.

In a 10- to 12-inch nonstick frying pan over medium heat, stir red onion and garlic in 1 tablespoon butter until onion is limp, about 5 minutes; add to salmon.

Melt remaining butter in pan over medium heat; add potatoes. Cover and cook until tender to bite and brown on bottom, 12 to 15 minutes; stir. Cook, uncovered, over medium-high heat, stirring occasionally, until deep golden brown, about 5 minutes longer. Remove from heat. Scrape salmon mixture onto potatoes. Mix gently; pat into even layer. Return to heat; occasionally turn portions over with a spatula until well browned and crusty, about 10 minutes.

Spoon hash onto plates; garnish with green onions and add sour cream and pepper to taste. Serves 4 or 5.

Per serving: 285 cal. (47 percent from fat); 12 g protein; 15 g fat (8.3 g sat.); 26 g carbo.; 627 mg sodium; 42 mg chol. ■

By Elaine Johnson

PETER CHRISTIANSEN

SUMMER JEWELS: *golden raspberries, tiny red currants, black raspberries, crisp green gooseberries, fat boysenberries. Splash with lemon-berry syrup.*

The fleeting berries of summer

A great way to enjoy them is with light syrups

SOME OF THE season's finest domestically grown berries make brief, often sporadic, summer appearances in Western markets and at farm stands. Now through early August—with an occasional last hurrah in early fall—is the best time to seek them out.

Here's what to look for:

Blackberry family. Two true blackberries are *Marion*—tender with rich, tangy-sweet flavor—and *Olallie*—long, slender, and sweetest when deep purple. *Logan* and *Tay*, both blackberry-raspberry crosses, are long and red with a rather musky flavor. *Boysen*, likely a logan-blackberry cross, is large, luscious, sweet, and aromatic.

Raspberry family. In this group, *black raspberries*, or black caps, have a musky, deep berry flavor and seem seedier than their red counterparts. *Golden raspberries*, patterned like honeycombs, are delicately flavored.

Gooseberries. These green, crunchy berries are tart or sweet, depending on the variety. *Josta*, a gooseberry–black currant cross that looks like a purple gooseberry, is sweet-tart in flavor.

Red currants. Brilliantly colored, translucent, tart-sweet berries grow in clusters with lots of little stems; seeds are chewy.

To appreciate any of these berries, serve them simply with one of these light syrups.

For a serving, allow about 1 cup berries (mixed, or 1 kind) and ¼ cup syrup.

Lemon-Berry Syrup

About 2 lemons

1 cup sugar

⅔ cup water

About ⅓ cup berry-flavor liqueur such as raspberry, black raspberry, or strawberry

With a vegetable peeler, cut all the yellow part from 1 lemon. Squeeze enough lemon juice to make ¼ cup. Combine peel, sugar, and water in a 1- to 1½-quart pan. Cover, bring to a boil over high heat, and simmer for 5 minutes.

Discard peel. To syrup add lemon juice and berry liqueur to taste. Use warm, cool, or reheated. If making ahead, let cool; chill airtight up to 1 week. Makes about 1½ cups.

Per ¼ cup: 167 cal. (0 percent from fat); 0 g protein; 0 g fat; 38 g carbo.; 0.5 mg sodium; 0 mg chol.

Lemon-mint syrup. Follow directions for **lemon-berry syrup** (preceding) adding to pan with peel ½ cup rinsed and drained **mint sprigs.** Discard mint with peel, pressing to extract liquid; omit liqueur. Makes 1 cup.

Per ¼ cup: 197 cal. (0 percent from fat); 0.1 g protein; 0 g fat; 51 g carbo.; 0.7 mg sodium; 0 mg chol.

Red Wine Syrup

2 cups dry red wine

⅔ cup sugar

2 tablespoons thinly pared orange peel (colored part only)

¼ teaspoon black peppercorns

1 dried bay leaf

1 tablespoon lemon juice

In a 1½- to 2-quart pan over high heat, boil wine, sugar, orange peel, pepper, and bay until reduced to 1½ cups, about 6 minutes. Pour through a fine strainer into a bowl; discard seasonings. Add lemon juice to syrup. Use warm, cool, or reheated. If making ahead, let cool; chill airtight up to 1 week. Makes 1½ cups.

Per ¼ cup: 132 cal. (0 percent from fat); 0.2 g protein; 0 g fat; 24 g carbo.; 4.7 mg sodium; 0 mg chol. ∎

By Elaine Johnson

Balsamic vinegar without the mystery

So expensive, so many choices. Here's how to shop for it . . . and how to use it

BALSAMIC VINEGAR *brings its unique tang to strawberries.*

SALADS *love balsamic vinegar.*
NORMAN A. PLATE

THE DARLING OF vinegars is a classy Italian—balsamic—whose origins date back to the early 11th century. But only in recent years have so many producers made so many balsamic vinegars—with prices that range from as little as $4 for a utility-size 12-ounce bottle to hundreds of dollars for a perfume-scale vial.

Concurrently, the term *balsamic vinegar* has been splashed across thousands of Western menus. Why all the hoopla? Because well-made balsamic vinegar is like no other vinegar. At its best, it tastes like a fine aged port with a cleansing tang—complex, sweet, mellow, intense, and fragrant. Its exceptional flavor, however, requires a lengthy, carefully monitored production process.

TRADITIONAL STYLE, WORTH A KING'S RANSOM

Balsamic vinegar that's made following the ancient artisanal process is called *aceto balsamico tradizionale.* It begins with the fall harvest of wine grapes in Italy's Modena and Reggio Emilia provinces. The juice of the pressed grapes (called must) is cooked slowly in big kettles until it's reduced by half.

The newly concentrated must and a bit of old vinegar go into a container to ferment and acidify for about a year. Then the mixture moves through a series of progressively smaller casks. As the vinegar travels in this maturation process, it becomes more complex in flavor, mellower, and sweeter. It's also evaporating, developing a shiny brown color, and getting syrupy. When the vinegar reaches the desired stage in the last cask, a portion is drawn off. Younger vinegar is added to the first cask to replenish the old, and the steps begin again.

The series of casks (usually three to seven) is called a *batteria*. Each cask is made of a different wood: acacia, ash, cherry, chestnut, mulberry, oak, or sometimes juniper. Each wood imparts a particular flavor and character.

The batteria is stored in a sunny, airy attic, which provides the necessary temperature swings of hot summers (for fermentation and evaporation) and cold winters (for long rests and settling).

POPULARITY PRESSURES

The popularity of balsamic vinegars has led to shortcut methods that don't produce comparable results.

For quality control, a government-approved consortium of balsamic vinegar producers instituted a DOC (denomination of origin control) for balsamic vinegars made in the traditional way in the provinces of Modena and Reggio Emilia. To be classified as traditional and receive the consortium seal, the classically produced vinegar must be made within either of these two provinces using grapes grown there, then be aged a minimum of 12 years. Vinegars with the consortium seal cannot contain caramel or wine vinegar.

Vinegars that meet these specifications are then rated by experts, and, if accepted by the consortium, the liquid goes into distinctively molded bottles. For those from Reggio Emilia, the color on the label indicates the rating: gold for highest quality, followed by silver and red. Pricing is the judgment of the producer.

The supply of traditional aged vinegars is limited; they are usually found in good Italian delicatessens or specialty food stores and com-

mand a high price—a 100-ml bottle can go for $50 to $700.

Because the flavor of these pricey vinegars is so concentrated, it takes only a few drops to add magic to foods. In Italy, traditional balsamic is used as a condiment (suggestions follow).

Connoisseurs sip tiny glasses of well-aged balsamic like a fine liqueur or digestive.

COMMERCIAL BALSAMIC

Most balsamic vinegars in Western markets from these provinces belong in another, less costly category. These vinegars, called *industriale* in Italy, are often made by producers of traditional balsamic; the labels on ones from Modena read API MO. Industriale, or commercial, vinegars are not subject to controls, and they range widely in method of production, quality, and price (35 cents to $4 per ounce).

The best of these vinegars are a blend of high-quality wine vinegar, young traditionally made balsamic vinegar, reduced must, and caramel.

The smoothest versions are barrel-aged up to 10 years. Age may be indicated on the label. Generally, but not always, a higher price reflects longer aging and/or a higher proportion of traditional balsamic vinegar in the product.

The poorest versions are raw-tasting wine vinegar with caramel and herbs.

Commercial balsamic vinegar is more overtly acidic than the traditional type. It suits salad dressings and marinades and works well in cooking, as for sauces. The smoother, longer-aged commercial vinegars are also pleasing as flavor accents.

What about vinegars labeled balsamic but not produced in Modena and Reggio Emilia? Copycats elsewhere, seeking a share of the booming balsamic trade, are also not required to meet any standards. Quality is uneven; you often get wine vinegar

blended with some commercial balsamic.

HOW TO CHOOSE?

In a fine foods store, you may be overwhelmed by the number of balsamic vinegars. Choosing is confusing. Use the preceding discussion to help you interpret labels, then let taste be your guide.

You might stage a balsamic vinegar tasting party. Ask each guest to bring a different kind. Offer water as a palate cleanser between tiny sips of vinegar. Afterward, use favorites to season a meal of salad, hot meats and vegetables, and fruit.

At *Sunset,* we sampled eight brands of commercial balsamic vinegars, priced from $4 to $20, and compared them with a traditional balsamic, Cavalli cav. Ferdinando. The vinegars we liked best most resembled the traditional balsamic. Some of the costliest—Carandini Emilio & C., Fini, and a commercial Cavalli—were smooth and slightly sweet, with complex flavor. Less expensive ones, such as those produced by Monari Federzori and Adriano Grosoli, are perfectly suitable for everyday use in salads and cooking.

WAYS TO USE

Carlo Middione, chef-owner of Vivande in San Francisco, suggests these uses for balsamic vinegar.

Avocado first course. Fill cavities of **avocado** halves with **balsamic vinegar.** Sprinkle with **fresh oregano leaves.**

Radish appetizer. Dip radishes in **balsamic vinegar.**

Green salads. Dress mixed **salad greens** with **extra-virgin olive oil** and **balsamic vinegar** to taste. If desired, add thin shards of **parmigiano reggiano** (parmesan cheese) and/or **orange segments,** with **salt** and **pepper** to taste.

Stuffed tomatoes. Trim off tops and scoop centers from large ripe **tomatoes.** Save shells and chop centers. Combine chopped tomatoes with drained **canned cannellini** (white kidney) **beans, balsamic vinegar, extra-virgin olive oil,** chopped **fresh basil leaves,** and **salt** and **pepper** to taste. Serve in tomato shells.

Meats and seafood. Drizzle **balsamic vinegar** over hot grilled, roasted, or sautéed **meat,** fish, or poultry.

Mix **balsamic vinegar, fresh herbs,** chopped **shallots,** and **olive oil;** spoon onto poached **chicken,** fish, or meat.

Vegetables. Cook sliced **mushrooms,** zucchini, eggplant, or spinach in **olive oil** and **garlic** until lightly browned. Add **salt, pepper,** and **balsamic vinegar** to taste.

Melon dessert or appetizer. Drizzle **balsamic vinegar** over **cantaloupe** or honeydew wedges or cubes.

Strawberry dessert. Drizzle **balsamic vinegar** over sliced ripe **strawberries.** Dust with freshly ground **pepper.** ∎

By Linda Lau Anusasananan

FRAGRANT BALSAMIC VINEGAR *adds finesse to simple foods: grilled fish, melon wedges, avocado halves, and tomatoes filled with bean salad.*

USE LEMON GRASS *to brush oil onto meat.*

USE SKEWER *to spear onion, rice cube to go with grilled satay. Nibble from the stick.*

PETER CHRISTIANSEN

Malaysia's national snack?

It's satay

THE UNOFFICIAL DISH of Malaysia, satay—barbecued meat on a skewer—is often served from sidewalk stalls. One reason for its vast popularity in a region of habitual snackers is its adaptability: the bamboo skewer it's cooked on doubles as an eating utensil.

To eat, pull the meat from the skewer with your teeth, one bite at a time. Use the same skewer to dip meat into

spicy peanut gravy and to spear bite-size cubes of cold, cooked rice and cool slices of cucumber and onion. Dip them into the gravy, too.

Accompany satay with iced lime juice and water, iced lemon tea, or beer. End the meal with fresh fruits such as pineapple, mangoes, and watermelon.

To simplify preparation, marinate and skewer the meat, cook the gravy, and make the rice cubes in advance. About

DIP SATAY MEAT *skewer into spicy peanut gravy. Use the same dip for cucumber slices and pressed rice cubes.*

a half-hour before serving, ignite the briquets for the barbecue, then slice the cucumbers and onions. When the coals are ready, you might ask guests to help grill the satay.

Look for fresh lemon grass, the tamarind soup base, and coarsely ground dried red chilies in Southeast Asian markets. Or use the suggested alternatives, readily available at supermarkets.

MALAYSIAN SATAY PARTY

Malaysian Satay

Satay Gravy

Pressed Rice Cubes

Iced Lime Juice and Water

Platter of Tropical Fruits

Malaysian Satay

2 pounds lean beef sirloin or leg of lamb

Spice mixture (recipe follows)

1 stalk fresh lemon grass, bruised, or 1 green onion

¼ cup salad oil

1 large (about ½-lb.) red onion, sliced ½ inch thick

1 medium-size (about 1-lb.) European cucumber, thinly sliced

Cut beef into ¼-inch-thick slices about 1½ inches long and ½ inch wide. Mix with spice mixture; cover and chill at least 1 hour or up to 4 hours. Stir occasionally.

Using thin bamboo skewers (about 8 in. long), thread 3 or 4 slices marinated meat on each, weaving skewer in and out of each slice. (If making ahead, cover and chill up to a day.)

Place skewers on a grill 4 to 6 inches above a solid bed of medium-hot coals (you can hold your hand at grill level only 3 to 4 seconds). Using lemon grass with slivered base or a brush, baste meat with oil. Cook meat, turning often, until evenly brown on both sides, about 4 minutes total. (Be careful not to burn the skewers.) Put on a large platter, along with onion and cucumber. Makes about 40 skewers, about 8 servings.

Per serving: 249 cal. (47 percent from fat); 26 g protein; 13 g fat (2.6 g sat.); 8.6 g carbo.; 71 mg sodium; 70 mg chol.

Spice mixture. Mix 2 cloves **garlic,** minced or pressed; 1 large (about ½-lb.) **onion,** finely chopped; 2 tablespoons **ground cumin;** 2 tablespoons **ground coriander;** 1 tablespoon **sugar;** and 1 teaspoon **ground turmeric.**

Satay Gravy

1½ tablespoons ground dried medium-hot Asian chilies (called chili powder), or cayenne

2 tablespoons salad oil

Spice mixture (recipe follows)

2 tablespoons dried tamarind soup base or lemon juice

1 cup canned coconut milk

¼ cup chunk peanut butter

1 tablespoon sugar

Salt

In a 5- to 6-quart pan, stir chilies (or add cayenne later, as directed) in oil on medium-high heat until oil turns red, about 2 minutes. Add spice mixture; stir over high heat until bubbling, about 2 minutes.

Mix tamarind base with 1 cup water; add to spice mixture. Add coconut milk, peanut butter, and sugar.

Cook, uncovered, on medium heat (do not boil), stirring occasionally until sauce thickens to a gravy-like consistency, 30 to 40 minutes. Add salt (and cayenne) to taste. (If making ahead, cool, cover, and let stand at room temperature up to 4 hours. Or chill up to a day; reheat.) Serve warm or at room temperature in shallow dishes. Makes about 2½ cups.

Per tablespoon: 34 cal. (74 percent from fat); 0.7 g protein; 2.8 g fat (1.3 g sat.); 2 g carbo.; 9.4 mg sodium; 0 mg chol.

Spice mixture. Remove tough, dry outer layers from 1 large (about 12-in.) stalk **fresh lemon grass.** Trim off stem ends. Finely chop tender inner portion of stalk. (Or substitute 1 teaspoon grated lemon peel.)

In a food processor or blender, mince lemon grass; 2 large (about 1 lb. total) **onions,** coarsely chopped; and 3 cloves **garlic.** Add 2 teaspoons **ground coriander,** 1 teaspoon **ground cumin,** ½ teaspoon **ground turmeric.** Whirl until smoothly puréed.

Pressed Rice Cubes

2 cups long-grain white rice

3½ cups water

In a 2- to 3-quart pan, combine rice and water. Cover and bring to a boil on high heat, then cook over low heat just until water is absorbed, about 25 minutes.

Spoon hot rice into a 9-inch-square pan. With the back of a spoon or spatula, press rice very firmly to form an even layer; rinse spoon with water to prevent sticking. Cool. (If making ahead, cover and store at room temperature up to 4 hours.)

Run a knife around pan edge, then turn rice out onto a board. Cut into 1-inch squares, frequently rinsing knife. Arrange on platter. Makes 8 servings.

Per serving: 169 cal. (2 percent from fat); 3.3 g protein; 0.3 g fat (0.1 g sat.); 37 g carbo.; 2.3 mg sodium; 0 mg chol.■

By Kaan Gwee

END THE MEAL *with a platter of cut mangoes, watermelon, and pineapple; serve with cool glasses of iced lime juice and water.*

SEE-THROUGH LEAVES *(bottom row) are fried counterparts of fresh herbs (top row). Left to right: basil, sage, mint, cilantro, watercress. Hot oil almost instantly transforms fresh leaves to crisp translucence.*

DARROW M. WATT

For snacks or garnishes, they're "shatter" leaves

FIREWORKS COME to the kitchen when summer herbs and greens burst into brilliant color and brittle crispness in hot oil.

In recent years, chefs have rediscovered this old Asian culinary trick, using pretty, translucent fried leaves to garnish contemporary dishes.

The technique is simple, although somewhat messy. You drop dry, clean leaves into hot oil; in seconds, the oil intensifies their green color and drives off moisture, making the leaves paper-brittle. They retain their fresh flavor.

If you want to avoid aromas of frying when serving these leaves, you can cook them up to three days ahead. However, the leaves must be stored airtight or, within minutes of cooking, they will absorb moisture from the air and get limp.

Fried Shatter Leaves

About 4 cups (2 oz.) fresh, unwilted green leaves (no stems) of arugula, basil, cilantro (coriander), mint, sage, sorrel, or watercress

Salad oil

Rinse leaves, drain well, and pat with towels to dry thoroughly.

In a deep 3- or 4-quart pan, heat about 1 inch oil to 370°. Add about ½ cup greens at a time to oil—stand back, oil may spatter. Turn leaves until they become brighter green and are at least partly translucent, 5 to 20 seconds. With a slotted spoon, quickly lift out leaves before they darken or scorch.

Drain leaves on towels. Repeat until all the leaves are cooked. Serve, or cool completely and store in a towel-lined, airtight container up to 3 days at room temperature. Makes about 2½ cups.

Per ¼ cup cilantro (all these leaves are similar nutritionally): 16 cal. (96 percent from fat); 0.1 g protein; 1.7 g fat (0.2 g sat.); 0.2 g carbo.; 1.9 mg sodium; 0 mg chol.

Showing off with shatter leaves

Eat fried shatter leaves sprinkled with salt as a snack or use to dramatically garnish the following foods. Add leaves just at serving to preserve crispness.

Arugula. Mound onto individual cheese soufflés or open-faced broiled Swiss or cheddar cheese sandwiches.

Basil. Sprinkle onto hot pesto-seasoned pasta or hot baked brie cheese served with toasted baguette slices.

Cilantro. Mound onto curried chicken salad or black bean soup; sprinkle over cooked corn kernels.

Mint. Pile on a cool tabbouleh (cracked wheat) salad or shrimp salad.

Sage. Scatter leaves and shaved parmesan cheese over ravioli mixed with cream or butter.

Sorrel. Moisten cool soft tofu or cold poached salmon lightly with extra-virgin olive oil and top with leaves. Season to taste with lemon juice and salt to taste.

Watercress. Sprinkle over risotto or omelets. ∎

By Karyn I. Lipman

CRISP-FRIED SAGE *leaves add their textural contrast, color, and flavor to tender ravioli in cream sauce.*

the strawberries and set aside. Add half of remaining berries to blender and whirl until smooth; pour into a wide-mouth pitcher or a bowl (at least 2½-qt. size). Smoothly purée lemon juice and remaining whole berries in blender; add to pitcher. Stir in sliced berries and remaining water. Add sugar to taste, if desired, stirring until dissolved.

Cover and chill the punch at least 3 hours or up to 2 days. To serve, stir punch and ladle into glasses. Makes 2 quarts, 8 servings.

Per cup: 134 cal. (3.9 percent from fat); 1 g protein; 0.6 g fat (0 g sat.); 34 g carbo.; 7.4 mg sodium; 0 mg chol.

Fruit Salad Drink

To simplify preparation, you can use larger quantities of fewer kinds of fruit.

- 6   cups water
- ½   cup orange juice
- ¼   cup lemon juice
- 1½ cups finely diced pineapple
- 1   medium-size (about ¾-lb.) firm-ripe mango, peeled, pitted, and finely diced
- 1   medium-size (about 5-oz.) tart green apple, such as Granny Smith, cored and finely diced
- ¾   cup finely chopped iceberg lettuce, rinsed, and crisped
- ½   to ¾ cup sugar
- ¾   cup thinly sliced hulled strawberries

In a bowl, wide-mouth pitcher, or jar (at least 3½-qt. size), stir water with orange juice, lemon juice, pineapple, mango, apple, and lettuce. Add sugar to taste and stir until dissolved. Cover and chill until very cold, at least 3 hours or up to 2 days.

To serve, gently mix strawberries with the punch, then ladle into glasses. Offer with straws for sipping and spoons for eating the fruit. Makes about 3 quarts, 12 servings.—*Monique Jerreda, West Covina, California*

Per cup: 70 cal. (2.7 percent from fat); 0.4 g protein; 0.2 g fat (0 g sat.); 18 g carbo.; 2.2 mg sodium; 0 mg chol. ∎

By Elaine Johnson

PETER CHRISTIANSEN

ROSY STRAWBERRY-MINT *lemonade contains thinly sliced berries to nibble.*

Fresh fruit coolers to sip and spoon

Smooth or chunky, these beverages refresh

CHUNKY PUNCH OR liquid salad? Either way, these refreshing drinks, with their spoonfuls of chopped fruit, will quench your thirst on a hot day. Try them with brunch, as a light dessert, or as coolers anytime.

The first drink blends familiar summer flavors—lemon, mint, and strawberry. Salvadorans call the second beverage, a tropical-tasting combination of fruits and crisp lettuce, *fresco de ensalada.* It's rather like a sweet gazpacho.

Strawberry-Mint Lemonade

- 4   cups water
    About 1¼ cups sugar
- 5   cups lightly packed fresh mint sprigs
- 1   quart hulled strawberries
- 1   cup lemon juice

Place 2 cups water, 1 cup sugar, and mint in a 3- to 4-quart pan. Bring to a boil over high heat; cover and simmer for 10 minutes. Pour through a fine strainer into a blender; press to extract liquid. Discard mint.

Thinly slice about 1 cup of

INGREDIENTS FOR SALVADORAN *fruit salad drink include six fruits and iceberg lettuce. Finely chop components, mix with juice and water, and chill to blend flavors. Serve beverage with a spoon to scoop up fruit salad.*

BRUAD

It's summer and the tomatoes are jumping

Try them in Chef Hensinger's swampy tomato salad

IN SUMMERTIME THE LIVING is easy, and not just because fish are jumpin' an' the cotton is high. Summertime is also the season when tomatoes look, smell, and taste great, and when every gardener's meal includes a platter of sliced tomatoes. If you should ever tire of just plain tomatoes, try James Hensinger's Summer Salad.

This dish is reminiscent of the Mexican *sopa seca*—dry soup. These soups are neither liquid nor solid, but might be described (without prejudice) as swampy. Hensinger's salad could be likened to a gazpacho seco.

Summer Salad

2 slices bacon
½ cup bottled ponzu sauce
2 tablespoons reduced-sodium soy sauce
2 tablespoons minced chives
2 tablespoons finely chopped fresh cilantro (coriander)

1 teaspoon prepared wasabi
⅛ teaspoon ground ginger
1 clove garlic, minced or pressed
2 teaspoons sugar
4 large (about 2 lb. total) ripe tomatoes
1 large (about ½-lb.) firm-ripe avocado
1 can (2¼ oz.) sliced ripe olives, drained

In a 6- to 8-inch frying pan over medium heat, brown bacon (or cook in a microwave oven). Drain bacon well on towels; let cool, then crumble.

In a small bowl, mix ponzu sauce, soy, chives, cilantro, wasabi, ginger, garlic, sugar, and bacon.

Core tomatoes; cut tomatoes into ¾-inch cubes into a wide bowl. Peel and pit avocado. Cut into ½-inch cubes; add to tomatoes. Scatter olives over avocado, then pour dressing over salad. Mix gently. Serves 6 to 8.

Per serving: 88 cal. (53 percent from fat); 2.5 g protein; 5.2 g fat

(0.9 g sat.); 9.7 g carbo.; 643 mg sodium; 1.3 mg chol.

Jam Fred Hensinger

Aurora, Colorado

A national obsession with physical fitness paired with a vestigal puritanism has drawn us to speak of desserts as if they were matters of right and wrong. Desserts are sinfully rich: chocolate decadence is an outstanding example of this moralization. Ice cream, which by law contains a significant quantity of butterfat, is particularly a subject of suspicion.

Bill Robbins of Bolinas, California, sends us absolution from the sin of dessert in the form of a nonfat frozen coffee ice, or sorbet. It's much more delicious than its spartan ingredient list would suggest, and the three familiar ingredients are nearly always at hand.

STUFF YOUR TURKEY *with apricots before roasting.*

Nonfat Coffee Freeze Dessert

3 tablespoons instant coffee powder

6 tablespoons sugar

2 cups nonfat milk

In a 1- to 1½-quart pan, mix coffee powder, sugar, and ⅓ cup milk. Stir over medium heat just until coffee and sugar dissolve. Remove from heat and pour into a shallow 1- to 2-quart metal pan. Mix in remaining milk. Freeze, airtight, until firm, at least 6 hours or up to 1 week.

Let stand at room temperature until you can break frozen mixture into large chunks with a heavy spoon, 5 to 10 minutes.

Whirl chunks in a food processor or beat with a mixer to a smooth slush; serve at once. Serves 4.

Per serving: 120 cal. (1.5 percent from fat); 4.4 g protein; 0.2 g fat (0.1 g sat.); 25 g carbo.; 65 mg sodium; 2.5 mg chol.

Bill Roberts

Bolinas, California

POULTRY OR MEAT AND fruit have been good companions through the years; consider duck with orange, turkey with cranberries, and ham with pineapple. It's no surprise, then, that Gary Kerns was inspired to expand the concept. He stuffs a turkey breast with dried apricots. The availability of turkey in parts makes this white meat roast possible.

Apricot-stuffed Turkey Roast

½ turkey breast (about 3½ lb.), boned and skinned

3 tablespoons Dijon mustard

1 teaspoon dried rosemary leaves

10 to 12 dried apricots

1 tablespoon olive oil

1 teaspoon minced or pressed garlic

Freshly ground pepper

Rinse turkey and pat dry. Cut lengthwise down middle, but not quite through the thickest part of breast. Push cut open and press meat to make it lie as flat as possible.

Spread breast with mustard, sprinkle with ½ teaspoon rosemary, and distribute apricots evenly over meat. From a long side, roll meat to enclose filling. Tie roll snugly with cotton string at 2- to 3-inch intervals. Rub roll with oil, then garlic; pat remaining rosemary onto meat and sprinkle generously with pepper.

Place roast on a rack in a 9- by 13-inch pan. Bake in a 375° oven until a meat thermometer inserted in thickest part registers 160° to 165° and meat is white in center (cut to test), 1 hour and 15 to 20 minutes. Let stand about 10 minutes. Remove string and cut roll crosswise into thick slices. Serves 6 to 8.

Per serving: 208 cal. (13 percent from fat); 39 g protein; 3.1 g fat (0.6 g sat.); 3.7 g carbo.; 246 mg sodium; 97 mg chol.

Gary Kerns

Sacramento, California

By Joan Griffiths, Richard Dunmire

Watermelon sorbet, red or yellow

COCONUT MILK ADDS tropical overtones to these frosty watermelon sorbets. Start with either red or yellow watermelon, then flavor with lemon or lime juice.

Watermelon Sorbet

1 can (15 oz.) coconut milk

½ cup sugar

1 piece (5 to 6 lb.) red or yellow watermelon

¼ cup lemon juice (for red melon) or lime juice (for yellow melon)

In a 1- to 2-quart pan on medium-high heat, stir coconut milk and sugar until sugar dissolves; cover and refrigerate until cold (at least 45 minutes).

Cut flesh from melon; discard seeds. Purée flesh in a blender or food processor; pour through a fine strainer into a bowl. You need 6 cups. Combine purée, coconut mixture, and lemon or lime juice. Pour into 1 or 2 (for faster freezing) metal pans, 9 by 13 inches. Cover airtight; freeze until solid, 6 to 8 hours, or up to 2 weeks.

Let stand at room temperature to soften slightly, 20 to 30 minutes. With a heavy spoon, break into chunks. Beat with an electric mixer or in a food processor until a smooth slush. Return to 1 pan, cover, and freeze until firm, about 2 hours; or store up to 1 week. Scoop into bowls (if sorbet is hard, hold at room temperature 15 to 20 minutes). Makes 2 quarts.

Per cup: 201 cal. (54 percent from fat); 2 g protein; 12 g fat (10 g sat.); 25 g carbo.; 12 mg sodium; 0 mg chol. ■

By Betsy Reynolds Bateson

PETER CHRISTIANSEN

TWISTS OF CITRUS PEEL *adorn frozen desserts of watermelon purées and coconut milk.*

SUNSET'S KITCHEN CABINET

Creative ways with everyday foods—submitted by *Sunset* readers,
tested in *Sunset* kitchens, approved by *Sunset* taste panels

Tarragon Chicken Salad

Susan Ross, Redmond, Washington

Steeping chicken breasts instead of simmering them produces exceptionally moist meat for this refreshing salad.

5 skinned and boned chicken breast halves (about 1½ lb. total)

3 cups thinly sliced celery

½ cup (3-oz. jar) drained pimiento-stuffed Spanish-style olives

Tarragon dressing (recipe follows)

Salt and pepper

Lettuce leaves, rinsed and crisped

In a 5- to 6-quart pan, bring about 3 quarts water to a boil. Add chicken; return water to a boil. Cover tightly and remove from heat; let stand until chicken is white in thickest part (cut to test), 10 to 12 minutes. Lift out and cool. Tear chicken into shreds.

Mix shredded chicken with celery, olives, and tarragon dressing. Add salt and pepper to taste. Spoon onto a lettuce-lined platter or salad plates. Makes 5 or 6 servings.

Per serving: 196 cal. (36 percent from fat); 27 g protein; 7.8 g fat (1.2 g sat.); 4 g carbo.; 471 mg sodium; 66 mg chol.

Tarragon dressing. Mix ½ cup **lemon juice,** 2 tablespoons **olive oil,** 1½ tablespoons minced **fresh** or 1 teaspoon dried **tarragon leaves,** and 1 clove **garlic,** pressed or minced.

COMBINE CHICKEN, *celery, olives, and tarragon-lemon dressing for cool salad.*

White Bean Pâté

Paulette Rossi, Portland

Piquant braised-deglazed onions enrich this mixture.

1 large (about ½-lb.) onion, finely chopped

2 cloves garlic, pressed or minced

About ½ cup regular-strength vegetable or chicken broth

¼ cup sherry vinegar or 3 tablespoons white wine vinegar

1 can (15 oz.) cannellini (white kidney) beans, drained

Salt and pepper

Red bell pepper strips and diagonal carrot slices

In a 10- to 12-inch frying pan, combine onion, garlic, and ¼ cup broth. Stir often over medium-high heat until a brown film forms on pan bottom, 6 to 8 minutes. Deglaze pan by adding vinegar; stir to release brown film. Repeat browning and deglazing once or twice, using 2 tablespoons broth at a time, until vegetables are richly browned.

Add beans to onion mixture and coarsely mash. If needed, add a little more broth to give beans the texture of creamy mashed potatoes. Add salt and pepper to taste. Mound in a bowl or on a plate. If making ahead, cover and chill up to 3 days.

Serve pâté warm or cool; scoop onto red pepper strips and sliced carrots. Makes about 1½ cups, 6 to 8 appetizer servings.

Per serving, pâté only: 52 cal. (6.9 percent from fat); 3.2 g protein; 0.4 g fat (0 g sat.); 8.9 g carbo.; 70 mg sodium; 0 mg chol.

OFFER LOW-FAT BEAN PÂTÉ *to spread on bell pepper strips and crisp carrots.*

Turkey Tortilla Roll-ups

Judy Burk, Oakland, California

Tortillas must be very fresh and not cold to roll. Otherwise they may crack.

4 very fresh flour tortillas (9 to 10 in.)

¼ cup reduced-calorie or regular mayonnaise

¼ cup Dijon mustard

½ pound mozzarella cheese, very thinly sliced

1 package (8 oz.) very thinly sliced roast turkey or cooked ham

4 large leaves butter lettuce, rinsed and crisped; stiff ribs removed

If tortillas are cold, warm to room temperature. Spread each tortilla to the edge with ¼ of the mayonnaise and mustard. Layer cheese, turkey, and lettuce onto tortilla to within about 2 inches of 1 side. Tightly roll up, starting from side opposite unfilled area. If making ahead, seal rolls individually in plastic wrap and chill up to 1 day.

Unwrap and eat out of hand or cut crosswise in 1½- to 2-inch pieces and stand pieces upright. Makes 4 sandwiches or about 20 appetizer pieces.

Per sandwich: 460 cal. (45 percent from fat); 26 g protein; 23 g fat (9.5 g sat.); 37 g carbo.; 1,660 mg sodium; 71 mg chol.

CUT TORTILLA ROLLS FILLED *with turkey, cheese, and lettuce into slices.*

Penne all'Arrabbiata

Tullia Barbanti, Spokane, Washington

1 tablespoon olive oil

6 ounces cooked ham, chopped

1 large (about 8-oz.) onion, finely chopped

½ cup finely chopped carrot

½ cup finely chopped celery

½ teaspoon crushed dried hot red chilies

1 can (28 oz.) ready-cut Italian tomatoes

1 pound dried penne or ziti pasta

¼ cup grated parmesan cheese

Salt and pepper

In a 3- to 4-quart pan, combine oil and ham. Stir often over medium-high heat until lightly browned, about 5 minutes. Add onion, carrot, celery, and chilies; stir often over medium heat until vegetables are limp, about 15 minutes.

Add the tomatoes (including liquid). Simmer uncovered, stirring often, until sauce is reduced to about 3½ cups, 25 to 30 minutes.

In a 5- to 6-quart pan, bring about 2½ quarts water to a boil. Add pasta and cook until barely tender to bite, 10 to 12 minutes. Drain.

In a large bowl, mix pasta, sauce, and cheese. Add salt and pepper to taste. Makes 4 or 5 servings.

Per serving: 496 cal. (16 percent from fat); 23 g protein; 8.9 g fat (2.5 g sat.); 80 g carbo.; 866 mg sodium; 23 mg chol.

SERVE QUILL-SHAPED PASTA *with spicy tomato sauce for Italian supper.*

Wild Rice–Mushroom Pilaf

Camille Thorson, Tucson

A generous portion of mushrooms and toasted nuts lace this wild rice and white rice pilaf.

⅓ cup pine nuts or slivered almonds

1 tablespoon butter or margarine

½ pound mushrooms, thinly sliced

1 cup dry sherry or regular-strength chicken broth

2 cups regular-strength chicken broth

½ cup wild rice, rinsed and drained

1 cup long-grain white rice

Chopped parsley

Salt

In a 2- to 3-quart pan over medium heat, stir or shake nuts often until golden, 6 to 8 minutes. Pour out of pan and set aside.

To pan, add butter and mushrooms. Stir occasionally over high heat until mushrooms are lightly browned, 10 to 12 minutes.

Mix sherry, broth, and wild rice with mushrooms; bring to a boil. Cover and simmer 25 minutes. Stir in white rice; cover and simmer until both grains are tender to bite, about 20 minutes longer. Stir in nuts. Pour rice pilaf into a warm serving dish and sprinkle with the chopped parsley. Add salt to taste. Makes 5 or 6 servings.

Per serving: 257 cal. (24 percent from fat); 7.7 g protein; 6.9 g fat (2 g sat.); 43 g carbo.; 45 mg sodium; 5.2 mg chol.

SHERRY-SCENTED RICE *and mushroom pilaf accompanies fish elegantly.*

Strawberry Slush or Ice Milk

Sarah Thurston, Pollock Pines, California

Use fresh berries to make a slushy-thick drink. Freeze fresh berries or use unsweetened frozen berries to make an ice cream–thick dessert.

1½ cups strawberries

About 1 cup coarsely crushed ice or small ice cubes

2 to 4 tablespoons sugar

1 cup low-fat (1 or 2 percent) milk or buttermilk

3 to 5 strawberries, rinsed and hulled (optional)

Rinse and hull the 1½ cups fresh strawberries.

To make slush, in a blender or food processor combine ice, 2 tablespoons sugar, 1½ cups strawberries, and milk. Whirl until smoothly blended. Taste, and mix in more sugar if desired. Pour slush into glasses.

For ice milk, set 1½ cups strawberries slightly apart on a pan and freeze solid, about 45 minutes. Whirl berries, ice, 2 tablespoons sugar, and milk until smooth and the consistency of soft ice cream. Spoon into bowls.

Garnish with remaining berries. Makes 3 or 4 slushes, 4 or 5 desserts.

Per serving: 53 cal. (12 percent from fat); 1.9 g protein; 0.7 g fat (0.3 g sat.); 11 g carbo.; 25 mg sodium; 2 mg chol.

Compiled by Linda Lau Anusasananan

WHIRL STRAWBERRIES, *ice, and milk for slushy drink or frozen dessert.*

July Menus

QUICK, SEASONAL,
BUDGET-WISE—
FOR FAMILY AND
FRIENDS

otlucks and the Fourth of July have a proven track record as good partners. Make-ahead foods and shared contributions produce this easily paced meal that frees up the day for other important activities, such as games and competitions and visiting with family and friends.

As the thermometer marches higher on July's bona fide summer days, tame the heat's impact with cool meals. Try France's niçoise salad for a light supper, and toast, Italian-style, for brunch.

JULY FOURTH POTLUCK FOR 12 (at right)
Firecracker salad earns its name with a chili bite. Guests bring condiments and dogs of choice (including sausages) to grill.

SUPPER SALAD FROM NICE (page 142)
French, fresh, and quick. Niçoise salad combines canned tuna, cooked vegetables, leafy greens, and toast.

BRUSCHETTA BRUNCH (page 143)
Rich-tasting, faux-mascarpone cheese (made with nonfat yogurt), tomatoes, and basil top toast. Serve with sweet melon.

THE DETAILS

Patriotic Fanfare

Red, white, and blue ribbons, star confetti make inexpensive table trimmings.

Condiment Bar

Invite guests to bring favorite topping for hot dogs, sausages; set condiments out to share.

Cake Options

Dessert starts with angel food cake: purchase, use a mix, or bake from scratch.

Dessert Dazzler

Serve berry-cream cake on white plates drizzled with purée of blueberries, strawberries.

Get the party under way the day before, if you like. The salad keeps well for two days. For neat, easy cutting and serving, the berry- and cream-filled cake needs to stand at least 4 hours beforehand, or it can be chilled up to a day.

To please all appetites, invite guests to bring their own sausages and a condiment they like; expect variety to range from salsa to chutneys, cheeses to mustards. Provide a grill with hot coals when it's time to warm or cook the sausages. Provide plenty of buns; extras can be frozen.

Firecracker Rice Salad with Avocados and Tomatoes

- 9 cups regular-strength chicken broth
- 5 cups long-grain white rice
- 1 cup lime juice
- ½ cup minced fresh cilantro (coriander)
- 2 small (about 1 oz. total) jalapeño chilies, stemmed, seeded, and minced
- ¾ pound jack cheese, shredded
- 2 large (about 1¾ lb. total) firm-ripe avocados
- 6 medium-size (about 3 lb. total) firm-ripe tomatoes, cored and sliced

In a 3- to 4-quart pan over high heat, bring 8 cups broth to a boil. Add rice, cover, and simmer until rice is just tender to bite, about 15 minutes. Drain rice, reserving any liquid. Pour rice into a large bowl and let cool to room

PETER CHRISTIANSEN

NEW TWISTS *for niçoise salad include purchased mixed greens and light dressing, but earthy appeal of the dish shines through.*

temperature.

Mix rice with reserved broth, remaining 1 cup broth, ¾ cup lime juice, cilantro, and chilies. If making ahead, cover and chill up to 2 days.

Spoon salad onto a large platter; sprinkle cheese over and around salad.

Pit, peel, and slice avocados lengthwise; moisten slices with remaining lime juice. Arrange avocado and tomato slices on platter with rice. Makes 12 to 16 servings.

Per serving: 387 cal. (33 percent from fat); 12 g protein; 14 g fat (1.3 g sat.); 55 g carbo.; 160 mg sodium; 19 mg chol.

Star-Spangled Banner Cake

If you want to decorate dessert plates, rinse, drain, and purée separately 1 to 1½ cups each blueberries and hulled strawberries. Sweeten purées to taste and dribble onto plates from a spoon shortly before serving cake.

- 1 angel food cake (9-inch size, about 14 oz.)
- 3 cups strawberries, rinsed and drained

- 3 cups whipping cream
- ⅓ cup sugar
- 1 teaspoon vanilla
- 1 cup blueberries (or frozen unsweetened blueberries), rinsed and drained

With a long, serrated knife, cut a 1-inch-thick horizontal slice from the top of the cake. With knife and your fingers, hollow out a trench in cake, leaving ½-inch-thick walls and bottom. Reserve cake pieces and top.

Hull 1½ cups of the strawberries; reserve remaining berries. Purée hulled berries in a blender or food processor; pour into a bowl.

In a large, deep bowl, whip cream until it holds soft peaks; mix in sugar and vanilla. Spoon 2 cups of the whipped cream into the strawberry purée. Tear reserved cake pieces into about ½-inch chunks and drop into the strawberry mixture. Gently fold mixture together and spoon into the hollowed trench in cake; use all the filling, pressing down gently to fill corners.

Set cake top in place; frost

top and sides of cake with remaining cream. Cover cake without touching (under a large inverted bowl) and chill at least 4 hours or up to 1 day. Decorate cake with remaining strawberries and blueberries. Serves 12 to 16.

Per serving: 225 cal. (56 percent from fat); 2.7 g protein; 14 g fat (8.7 g sat.); 23 g carbo.; 202 mg sodium; 50 mg chol.

If there's time, have the salad makings ready and waiting in the refrigerator a day ahead. Cut a few slices of bread from a crusty baguette to use with the salad.

For dessert, slice sweet, ripe apricots into small bowls, pour orange muscat wine over the fruit, then top with scoops of frozen yogurt.

'90s Niçoise Salad

Add caper dressing to taste.

- 1¼ pounds (about 2½-in.-wide) thin-skinned potatoes, scrubbed
- ½ pound small, tender green beans
- 4 hard-cooked eggs
- 1 jar (12 oz.) roasted red peppers, drained
- 1 can (12 to 13 oz.) water-packed albacore tuna
- ½ pound rinsed and crisped mesclun or bite-size pieces mixed salad greens
- ¾ cup niçoise olives
  Aïoli crusts (recipe follows)
  Salt and pepper

In a 4- to 5-quart pan, combine potatoes and 3 quarts of water. Cover and bring to a boil over high heat; simmer until potatoes are tender when pierced, 25 to 35 minutes. Remove potatoes from water with a slotted spoon; set aside to cool.

Meanwhile, trim ends from green beans. Bring water in pan back to a boil on high heat and add beans. Cook, uncovered, until beans are just barely tender when pierced, about 2 minutes. Drain beans and immediately immerse in ice water. When cold, drain.

If cooking potatoes and beans ahead, wrap airtight and chill up to 1 day.

Shell eggs and cut in half lengthwise. Cut potatoes into 1½-inch chunks. Cut peppers into thin strips. Drain tuna and break into chunks.

To assemble salads, divide mesclun evenly among 4 dinner plates. Arrange eggs, potatoes, beans, peppers, tuna, and olives equally on plates. Accompany each salad with 2 crusts. Add salt and pepper to taste. Serves 4.

Per serving: 379 cal. (26 percent from fat); 34 g protein; 11 g fat (2.6 g sat.); 37 g carbo.; 637 mg sodium; 247 mg chol.

Aïoli crusts. Cut 8 crosswise slices about ½ inch thick from 1 (8-oz.) **baguette.** Reserve remainder of loaf to serve with meal.

In a small bowl, mix ½ cup **reduced-calorie mayonnaise,** 2 cloves minced or pressed **garlic,** and 3 tablespoons shredded **parmesan cheese.** Spread mixture evenly onto 1 side of bread slices; place coated side up in a 10- by 15-inch pan. Sprinkle slices with 1 more tablespoon shredded parmesan cheese.

Broil crusts 4 to 6 inches from heat until tops brown lightly, about 4 minutes. Makes 8.

Per piece: 91 cal. (50 percent from fat); 2.3 g protein; 5.1 g fat (1.4 g sat.); 9.1 g carbo.; 207 mg sodium; 6.4 g chol.

Caper Dressing

¾ cup cider vinegar

2 tablespoons extra-virgin olive or salad oil

2 tablespoons drained canned capers

1 tablespoon Dijon mustard

2 teaspoons minced fresh or 1 teaspoon dried thyme leaves

BRUSCHETTA *to start the day is wholesome, refreshing knife-and-fork toast topped with tomatoes, basil, and thick, cool drained yogurt.*

½ teaspoon sugar

In a small bowl, mix vinegar, oil, capers, mustard, thyme, and sugar. Makes about 1 cup.

Per tablespoon: 18 cal. (90 percent from fat); 0 g protein; 1.8 g fat (0.3 g sat.); 1 g carbo.; 56 mg sodium; 0 mg chol.

True mascarpone is like rich, super-thick, and delicately tart sour cream. Nonfat yogurt, drained at least 12 hours, makes a lavish-tasting imposter.

For a refreshing beverage, mix equal parts frozen orange juice concentrate and frozen raspberry concentrate; dilute with chilled sparkling water.

Bruschetta with Tomato, Basil, and Fresh Mascarpone

4 slices (about ½ in. thick) crusty bread

1¼ pounds ripe Roma-type tomatoes, cored and finely chopped

1 cup (about ½ oz.) loosely packed whole fresh basil leaves, rinsed

Herbed nonfat mascarpone (recipe follows)

Basil sprigs (optional)

Salt

Lay bread slices slightly apart in a 10- by 15-inch pan. Broil about 6 inches from heat until toasted; turn once. Use toast warm or let cool on a rack.

Top each slice with equal portions of tomato and basil leaves, and 3 tablespoons mascarpone. Garnish with basil sprigs, accompany with remaining mascarpone and add salt to taste. Eat with knife and fork . Serves 4.

Per serving: 176 cal. (8.4 percent from fat); 9.3 g protein; 1.6 g fat (0.3 g sat.); 31 g carbo.; 266 mg sodium; 0 mg chol.

Herbed nonfat mascarpone. Line a fine strainer with a double layer of cheesecloth. Set strainer over a deep bowl (bottom of strainer should sit at least 2 in. above bottom of bowl).

Mix together 1 quart **unflavored nonfat yogurt** and ¼ cup minced **fresh basil leaves.** Scrape mixture into cloth. Cover airtight; chill and let drain until yogurt is the consistency of whipped cream cheese, at least 12 hours or up to 2 days; drain off accumulating liquid occasionally. Makes about 1½ cups.

Per tablespoon: 14 cal. (0 percent from fat); 1.5 g protein; 0 g fat; 1.5 g carbo.; 13 mg sodium; 0 mg chol. ∎

By Christine Weber Hale

Hip-pocket Sandwiches

Chicken, cheese, and ham strips, crisp shredded lettuce, and a nippy dressing make a chef's salad sandwich within crescents of warm pocket bread.

4 whole-wheat pocket bread rounds (6 to 7 inches), cut in half

½ cup mayonaisse

2 tablespoons purchased medium-hot red or green chili salsa

1 cup shredded cocked chicken

1 cup (5 to 6 oz.) each julienne strips cooked ham and jalapeño jack cheese

1 to ½ cups shredded romaine lettuce

Wrap pocket bread in foil; heat in 350° oven until warm, about 10 minutes.

In a medium size bowl, blend mayonaise and salsa. Stir in chicken, ham, and cheese.

Tuck equal portions lettuce and chicken filling into worm pocket bread halves. Makes 4 servings, 2 sandwiches each.

Per serving: 639 cal. (57 percent from fat); 34 g protein; 41 g fat (12 g sat.); 38 g carbo.; 1,342 mg sodium; 106 mg chol.

LAMBERT—*sweet, tender Bing look-alike.*

BING—*firm, plump favorite.*

RAINIER—*extra-sweet, fragile.*

Sweet cherry surprises

Dark and plump or golden and blushed, sweet cherries love the West, and Westerners love them. Feast on them now— in stunning, simple dishes

RENEE LYNN

BLUSHING RAINIERS *shine through jam-glazed tart.*

IF LIFE REALLY WERE a bowl of cherries, how delectable it would be. The next best alternative is fresh cherries, and now is the time to savor them. They are at peak supply in June and July—and Westerners are in sweet cherry country. The majority of the nation's sweet cherries grow in California, Idaho, Oregon, Montana, Utah, and Washington. Three varieties—Bing, Lambert, and Rainier—make up 95 percent of them.

Bing dominates in volume and popularity. This cross, developed in 1875 by Hender-son Lewelling in Oregon (and named for an employee), has consistently opulent flavor and is tender, sweet, and crunchy. Lambert is as sweet and richly colored, but less

THE ULTIMATE CHERRY PIE, *beneath a lattice pastry, is full of succulent Bings with a few seasonings; tapioca captures the dark juices.*

PETER CHRISTIANSEN

intensely flavored and softer. Rainier, a golden cherry with a pretty rosy blush, has a higher sugar content than the dark cherries and is much more limited in supply. It's more costly and fragile, bruising and blemishing easily.

Select plump, firm cherries to eat or use in these showstopping recipes; 1 pound of cherries is about 4 cups.

Gingered Cherries on Honeydew Melon

⅓ cup preserved ginger in syrup

1 tablespoon lemon juice

4 cups light or dark sweet cherries with stems

1 large (4 lb.) honeydew melon

Chop ginger and mix with lemon juice. Rinse and drain

CHERRIES STAR *(clockwise from left) on melon with candied ginger, over cheese-filled tart, in a spirited dessert soup, and warmed for a sauce with meat.*

PETER CHRISTIANSEN

cherries. Cut melon into 6 wedges; seed and place on plates. Scatter cherries on fruit; spoon ginger mixture over melon and cherries. Serves 6.

Per serving: 132 cal. (7.5 percent from fat); 1.9 g protein; 1.1 g fat (0.2 g sat.); 32 g carbo.; 20 mg sodium; 0 mg chol.

Cherry Meat Sauce

Ladle this lively sauce over portions of lamb, beef, pork, or poultry; the sauce is especially good with roasted or grilled meats.

⅓ cup currant jelly

¼ cup raspberry vinegar

2 tablespoons orange juice

½ teaspoon dried tarragon leaves

¾ cup rinsed, drained, pitted dark sweet cherries

In a 1½- to 2-quart pan over high heat, stir jelly, vinegar, orange juice, and tarragon until steaming.

Add cherries to the hot liquid. Mix gently and remove from heat.

Spoon warm fruit and juice over meat, as suggested above. Makes about ¾ cup sauce, 3 or 4 servings.

Per serving: 93 cal. (2.9 percent from fat); 0.4 g protein; 0.3 g fat (0.1 g sat.); 23 g carbo.; 4.4 mg sodium; 0 mg chol.

Spirited Cherry Soup

4 cups rinsed, drained, pitted light or dark sweet cherries

3½ cups white grape juice

2 teaspoons grated lemon peel

2 tablespoons lemon juice

3 tablespoons orange-flavor liqueur or 1½ teaspoons grated orange peel

Mint sprigs and finely cut strands of orange peel (optional)

Divide cherries among 4 soup bowls.

In a 2- to 3-quart pan over high heat, bring grape juice and lemon peel to boiling. Add lemon juice and liqueur. Pour over cherries. Garnish with mint sprigs and orange peel. Serves 4.

Per serving: 278 cal. (4.5 percent from fat); 1.8 g protein; 1.4 g fat (0.3 g sat.); 63 g carbo.; 19 mg sodium; 0 mg chol.

WEAVE PASTRY *strips over cherries, sprinkle with sugar, and bake until bubbling.*

Cherry and Cream Cheese Tart

Pastry for a single-crust 9-inch pie

1 large package (8 oz.) light cream cheese

3 tablespoons sugar

1 tablespoon kirsch

5 cups rinsed, drained, pitted light or dark sweet cherries

⅔ cup apricot jam

Roll pastry into a 13-inch-diameter round; fit into an 11-inch tart pan with removable rim. Fold excess pastry down and flush with rim; press to secure. Prick pastry all over with a fork. Bake in a 375° oven until golden brown, about 18 minutes (pastry shrinks). Let cool.

Mix cream cheese with

sugar and kirsch. Spread over bottom of crust. Arrange cherries on cheese filling.

In a 1- to 1½-quart pan over medium heat, stir jam until bubbling. Rub through a strainer, then brush over cherries. If making ahead, chill airtight up to 2 hours. Serves 8 or 9.

Per serving: 297 cal. (36 percent from fat); 5 g protein; 12 g fat (4.5 g sat.); 45 g carbo.; 268 mg sodium; 13 mg chol.

Lattice Cherry Pie

8 cups pitted dark or light sweet cherries

About ½ cup sugar

2 tablespoons quick-cooking tapioca

1½ tablespoons lemon juice

¼ teaspoon almond extract

Pastry for a double-crust 9-inch pie

In a large bowl, combine cherries, ½ cup sugar, tapioca, lemon juice, and extract. Let stand at least 30 minutes or up to 1 hour to soften tapioca; mix occasionally.

On a lightly floured board, roll ⅔ of pastry into a 12-inch-diameter round; ease into a 9-inch pie pan. Fill with cherry mixture. On a floured board, roll remaining pastry into a 6- by 10-inch rectangle. Trim off ragged edges and cut rectangle lengthwise into 6 equal strips. Arrange strips in lattice pattern over pie; trim off strips that lap over rim. Fold edge of bottom crust over lattice, flush with pan rim; flute to seal. Sprinkle lattice with about 1 teaspoon sugar.

Set pie in a foil-lined 10- by 15-inch pan (pie bubbles as it cooks). Bake in a 375° oven on the lowest rack until pastry is golden brown and filling is bubbly, 1 hour and 15 to 30 minutes.

Serve warm or at room temperature. If making ahead, let cool, cover loosely, and store at room temperature up to 1 day. Cut into wedges. Serves 8 or 9.
—*Helen A. Knowlton, Eugene, Oregon*

Per serving: 327 cal. (39 percent from fat); 3.7 g protein; 14 g fat (3.5 g sat.); 48 g carbo.; 246 mg sodium; 0 mg chol. ∎

By Linda Lau Anusasananan, Elaine Johnson

Why?

Why do egg whites act so weird?

Light, puffy whipped egg whites are an important ingredient in many dishes—and essential for soufflés, tender meringue–topped pies, and crisp meringue shells. How egg whites are whipped affects the volume and texture of these foods; the secret is all in the air bubbles.

When egg whites are beaten briskly with a whisk, a rotary beater, or even a fork, the whites stretch and trap air as bubbles. The smaller and more even-size the bubbles, the more stable (long-lasting) the foam. Large bubbles are inclined to break faster. The tools you use and what you add to whites give you considerable control over the size and strength of the bubbles.

A large whisk with many fine wires (or a balloon beater in a mixer) moved at high speed does the best job of introducing air into whites for even-size bubbles. Acid and sugar also affect bubble size and strength (see "What makes egg white foam stronger?" following). Whites foam best when whipped at a cool room temperature (high 60s to low 70s). Whites from the refrigerator warm quickly from incorporated air.

Why does the foam sometimes not achieve maximum volume?

Optimally, whites increase at least nine times in volume when whipped and hold short, distinct peaks. Underbeaten whites haven't firmed enough to hold bubbles. Overbeaten whites are stretched so much that they pop easily; you will see cottony bits of solidified (coagulated) white.

What makes egg white foam stronger?

Plain whipped whites make a fragile, short-lived foam; on standing, their own weight causes bubbles to burst, and the whites become liquid (and won't whip up again).

If cream of tartar (or similar acid) is added to whites as they are whipped, the egg white proteins become stronger: acid coagulates, or stiffens, them slightly. You can add cream of tartar to any recipe that uses plain whipped whites, such as a soufflé, but it's still important to incorporate whites and cook the mixture right away. You need ⅛ teaspoon cream of tartar for each 2 tablespoons (1 large) egg white.

Sugar also strengthens egg white protein, keeps bubbles small, and keeps the foam pliable. In recipes that call for sweetened whipped egg whites, it's still a good idea to add cream of tartar as well, for increased stability.

How much sugar you add and how you add it affect the texture and behavior of the foam dramatically. Once a foam is established (no liquid white remains in bowl), sugar added at a steady rate (about 1 tablespoon every 30 to 45 seconds) dissolves uniformly and forces whites to make small bubbles by slowly increasing osmotic pressure. When whites are stiff enough to retain soft or rigid peaks, they're still pliable enough to mix with other ingredients.

If sugar is added before a foam is established, the whites become so plastic or stretchy that they can't incorporate enough air to make a stiff foam. If sugar is added too rapidly, the beating action won't dissolve it, and bubbles will be uneven.

Why do whites sometimes never get foamy, or collapse?

Fat keeps whites from foaming; it lowers the surface tension of the whites, and bubbles can't form. The culprit is usually a bit of egg yolk or a greasy bowl.

Foam will collapse if the bowl is so small that foam covers the top of a mixer beater—air gets beaten out instead of in. Expect 1 large egg white (2 tablespoons) to take up 1 cup of space.

What does a copper bowl do for egg whites?

A bowl made of copper has two advantages. One is its fine heat conductivity; the second is its metal ions.

As whites are beaten, the friction of the beaters quickly warms whites above the optimum temperature and bubbles get bigger. A copper bowl transfers heat rapidly from the whites, keeping them cooler than they would be in a bowl of glass or another metal. Copper ions, which are released during beating, fortify whites much as cream of tartar does and give the foam a creamy color.

More questions?

If you encounter other cooking mysteries and would like to know why they happen, send your questions to Why?, *Sunset Magazine,* 80 Willow Rd., Menlo Park, Calif. 94025. With the help of Dr. George K. York, extension food technologist at UC Davis, *Sunset* food editors will find the solutions.■

By Linda Lau Anusasananan

NORMAN A. PLATE

BUBBLES *make a difference. Plain whipped whites (top and bottom left) have big, uneven bubbles, which burst readily. Whites whipped with cream of tartar and sugar (right) have tiny, strong bubbles, which hold volume longer.*

MOST OF THIS FARE came from the market ready to eat. Choices include (clockwise from wine) cured meats, bread, melon, sweet peppers, cheese, marinated zucchini, pinto bean salad, green and black olives, marinated onions and mushrooms.

Antipasto is the answer

for a last-minute party

We photographed this quick meal in Rome. You can start at your neighborhood deli or supermarket

W ANT TO ENTERTAIN on a moment's notice? You can stage an antipasto party like the Italian one shown on these pages using imported or local foods from a delicatessen or supermarket. All the makings are there, and you'll be surprised by the variety of choices.

In Rome, the Passagrillis buy ready-to-eat foods from their neighborhood *salumeria* (delicatessen), make a couple of salads, then invite friends over for a feast.

You'll find many of the same foods or suitable substitutes in your own market. If you have time, supplement them with zucchini in vinegar, pinto bean salad, and sweet homemade ricotta cheese; they're all relatively simple to prepare.

To make the party more affordable, you might ask each guest to bring sliced meat, a wedge of cheese, or a bottle of wine.

ITALIAN ANTIPASTO PARTY

Good-quality cold cuts, cheeses, and marinated vegetables make up most of the meal. You can serve almost any number of guests; just make selections from each of the following groups.

Cheese. Allow 2 to 3 ounces per serving. Present cheese in a wedge or chunk, letting guests cut off pieces.

Choices may include sweet or aged sardo, blue-veined gorgonzola, homemade ricotta (recipe follows on facing page) or purchased ricotta, piquant pecorino, aged nutty Parmigiano-Reggiano, smooth taleggio, and moist fresh *bufalo* mozzarella.

Cold cured or cooked meats. Allow 2 to 3 ounces per serving. Buy meats in thin slices, or present small sausages whole for guests to cut on a small board.

Offer salami, prosciutto, coppa, cacciatore (a small pork and beef salami), pistachio-studded mortadella, and galantina (a head cheese—

IN ROME, *guests enjoy feast of deli offerings. You can plan a similar party at home.*

cooked meat and gelatin).

Salads and pickles. You'll want to allow ¾ to 1 cup bean, grain, or pasta salad and ¼ to ½ cup marinated or pickled vegetables per serving.

Widely available choices include olives (green ripe, black ripe, brined, or oil-cured), marinated artichoke hearts or mushrooms, pickled onions, and roasted red or yellow peppers (if peppers are packed in brine, drain and drizzle with extra-virgin olive oil). Recipes follow for zucchini and bean salads.

Fruit. Allow about ½ pound untrimmed fruit per serving. For a bountiful presentation, offer extra fruit and leave some of it whole. Choices may include grapes, peaches, and melons.

Breads. You'll need about ¼ pound bread per serving. Breads to consider include focaccia, crusty rolls or loaves, and breadsticks.

Wines. Offer a selection of wines; allow 8 ounces per serving. Italian wines include Chianti, Orvieto, Pinot Grigio, Rosso Cònero, Soave, and sparkling Asti Spumante. Or consider domestic dry Sauvignon Blanc, Merlot, Gamay or Gamay Beaujolais, or Pinot Noir. Also provide a pitcher of ice water or bottles of mineral water.

Zucchini with Vinegar

2 pounds (8 to 10 medium-size) zucchini, ends trimmed

1 teaspoon salt

2 tablespoons olive oil

2 tablespoons balsamic vinegar or red wine vinegar

Slice zucchini crosswise ⅛ inch thick. Mix with salt; let stand about 30 minutes. Rinse zucchini and drain; pat dry. Pour 1 tablespoon oil into each of 2 baking pans (10- by 15-in. size). Mix ½ the zucchini in each pan; spread into a single layer.

Bake in a 450° oven. If pieces on pan sides brown first, remove from pan and continue cooking the remaining pieces until most are dry and lightly browned, 20 to 25 minutes (if using 1 oven, change pan positions halfway through baking). Combine zucchini in 1 pan; mix gently with vinegar. Serve warm or at room temperature. If making ahead, cover when cool and chill up to a day. Serves 8 to 10.

Per serving: 45 cal. (70 percent from fat); 1.3 g protein; 3.5 g fat (0.5 g sat.); 3.2 g carbo.; 140 mg sodium; 0 mg chol.

Pinto Bean Salad

⅓ cup extra-virgin olive oil

1 large (½ lb.) onion, minced

3 cloves garlic, pressed or minced

2 cups thin slices celery

4 cans (about 1 lb. each) pinto beans, drained

Salt and pepper

In a 10- to 12-inch frying pan, mix 2 tablespoons oil, onion, garlic, and celery; stir often over medium heat until onion is soft, about 6 minutes. Stir in beans. Serve warm or at room temperature. If making ahead, cover when cool and chill up to a day. Add remaining oil and salt and pepper to taste. Makes 8 to 10 servings.

Per serving: 177 cal. (42 percent from fat); 7.2 g protein; 8.3 g fat (1.1 g sat.); 19 g carbo.; 315 mg sodium; 0 mg chol.

Fresh Ricotta Cheese

2 quarts whole milk

2 cups buttermilk

Salt, pepper, extra-virgin olive oil

To cook in a microwave. In a 3- to 4-quart microwave-safe bowl, mix milk and buttermilk. Heat (do not stir) on full power (100 percent) until milk reaches 195° in center of bowl, 15 to 20 minutes. Continue heating, holding the 195° temperature until at least half of the milk clot that forms on top feels like baked custard when gently pressed, 10 to 15 minutes.

To cook on direct heat. In a 5- to 6-quart heavy pan, mix milk and buttermilk to blend. Warm milk mixture (do not stir) over medium heat until 180° in center of pan, 25 to 30 minutes. Reduce heat to low and keep milk temperature between 185° and 200° until at least half of the milk clot that forms on top feels like baked custard when gently pressed, 10 to 15 minutes.

Line a large colander with 4 layers of damp, clean cheesecloth; set in a sink with open drain. Pour milk clot into colander; do not scrape pan bottom if scorched. Drain. When most of the whey (liquid) has drained off, scrape cheese from cloth sides. Gather cloth edges; twist gently to squeeze out excess whey. Continue to drain until firm, at least 45 minutes. Serve or, if making ahead, cool, cover, and chill up to 2 days.

Unwrap cheese and set on a serving plate. Offer with salt, pepper, and olive oil. Makes about 1 pound, 8 to 10 servings.

Per serving: 114 cal. (67 percent from fat); 8.2 g protein; 8.5 g fat (5.3 g sat.); 1.6 g carbo.; 65 mg sodium; 37 mg chol. ∎

By Linda Lau Anusasananan

PETER CHRISTIANSEN

Lean pasta sauces

They rely on fresh vegetables and herbs . . . not butter and oil

PLAIN PASTA HAS the virtue of being low in calories and fat. But the lavish sauces and generous amounts of cheese that often accompany it can send waist-watchers running for the scales.

Good alternatives are sauces that rely on flavors developed with vegetables and herbs, but no butter or oil.

Try curly pasta with a sauce of bell peppers, herbs, and capers; garbanzos boost the protein. Lima beans do the same for spaghetti; seasoned spaghetti squash is the foundation of its sauce.

If you want to add a little parmesan, sprinkle it on pasta at serving time to get the full effect of its flavor.

SCARLET PEPPERS, *handfuls of fresh basil and tarragon, and garbanzos go into lean pasta sauce. It's richly flavored without any added fat.*

Slim Red and Green Pasta

 About 2½ pounds (8 medium-size) red bell peppers or fresh pimientos; or jars or cans (20 to 21 oz. total) roasted red peppers or whole or sliced pimientos

1 cup thinly sliced green onions

1 can (about 1 lb.) reduced-sodium garbanzos, drained

¾ cup chopped fresh or ¼ cup dried basil leaves

1½ tablespoons chopped fresh or 1½ teaspoons dried tarragon leaves

3 tablespoons drained canned capers

1 pound dried curly pasta such as armoniche or rotelle

 Salt and pepper

 Place fresh bell peppers in a 10- by 15-inch pan. Broil about 3 inches below heat, turning until skins are blackened all over, 15 to 17 minutes. Let cool, then pull off skins, remove stems, and rinse off seeds. (Drain and seed canned peppers.)

 Finely chop peppers in a food processor or with a knife. Place in a 3- to 4-quart pan over medium-high heat with onions, garbanzos, basil, tarragon, and capers; stir often until steaming, 5 to 7 minutes.

 Meanwhile, fill a 5- to 6-quart pan ¾ full of water; cover and bring to a boil over high heat. Add pasta and cook, uncovered, until barely tender to bite, 7 to 8 minutes. Drain pasta and pour into a wide, shallow bowl. Spoon pepper mixture onto pasta. Mix to serve; season to taste with salt and pepper. Serves 8.

Per serving: 299 cal. (6 percent from fat); 12 g protein; 2 g fat (0.2 g sat.); 60 g carbo.; 198 mg sodium; 0 mg chol.

Svelte Spaghetti with Spaghetti Squash

1 spaghetti squash, about 2½ pounds

1½ cups regular-strength chicken broth

1 package (10 oz.) frozen baby lima beans

2 tablespoons fresh or 2 teaspoons dried thyme leaves

1½ teaspoons grated lemon peel

2 quarts lightly packed rinsed and drained spinach leaves, sliced into ⅓-inch-wide strips

12 ounces dried spaghetti

 Salt and pepper

 Pierce squash shell in several places. Place in a shallow pan slightly larger than squash. Bake, uncovered, in a 350° oven until shell gives readily when pressed, 1¼ to 1½ hours.

 (Or, to cook in a microwave oven, halve squash lengthwise; remove seeds. Line oven with microwave-safe plastic wrap; lay squash cut side down on plastic. Cook, uncovered, at full power—100 percent—for 5 minutes; rotate pieces ½ turn. Continue cooking, rotating every 5 minutes, until squash gives to fingertip pressure, 10 to 15 minutes longer.)

 Halve squash lengthwise and scoop out seeds. Scrape squash from shell, using a fork to loosen strands; put in a 3- to 4-quart pan. Stir in broth, limas, thyme, and peel. Cover and bring to a boil over high heat. Reduce heat and simmer until limas are tender to bite, about 5 minutes; stir often. Add spinach; cover and cook until leaves wilt, 1 to 2 minutes.

 Meanwhile, fill a 5- to 6-quart pan ¾ full of water. Cover; bring to a boil over high heat. Add spaghetti and cook, uncovered, until barely tender to bite, 7 to 8 minutes. Drain; return to pan. Gently mix in squash mixture. Pour into a bowl. Add salt, pepper to taste. Serves 8 to 10.

Per serving: 207 cal. (6.5 percent from fat); 8.8 g protein; 1.5 g fat (0.3 g sat.); 40 g carbo.; 79 mg sodium; 0 mg chol. ∎

By Elaine Johnson

APRICOT-ROSEMARY *sauce coats succulent veal shanks.*

Summer ways with shanks

What really helps is cooking the meat ahead and grilling later

IN HOT WEATHER, people often forsake the pleasure of eating moist, fork-tender braised shanks because they take a long time to cook.

But if you oven-braise the meat early in the morning or the night before, you can keep a cool house and have meat ready to heat and brown on the grill for dinner.

To prepare grill. Ignite about 60 charcoal briquets on firegrate in a barbecue with a lid. When coals are well spotted with gray ash (about 20 minutes), push half the briquets to each side of the firegrate. Lay a drip pan between coals. Set grill 4 to 6 inches above coals; let coals burn until medium-hot (you can hold your hand at grill level over coals only 3 to 4 seconds). Lightly oil grill.

Grilled Veal Shanks with Apricot Glaze

4 slender veal shanks, each about 6 inches long (about 4 lb. total)

3 cups regular-strength chicken broth

1 cup (about 6 oz.) dried apricots

2 tablespoons lemon juice

1 tablespoon minced fresh or 1 teaspoon crumbled dried rosemary leaves

1 tablespoon grated orange peel

Fresh rosemary sprigs (optional)

4 cups hot cooked couscous

Salt and pepper

Lay shanks in a single layer in a metal 9- by 13-inch pan. Add broth, apricots, lemon juice, minced rosemary, and orange peel; be sure apricots are covered with broth. Cover pan very tightly with foil.

Bake shanks in a 400° oven for 45 minutes. Turn meat over, cover pan tightly with foil, and bake until meat is tender when pierced but not falling off the bone, 45 to 50 minutes longer. If making ahead, let shanks cool; cover and chill up to a day.

Transfer shanks to a platter. Skim and discard any fat from pan juices. Pour juices and apricots into blender or food processor; whirl until smoothly puréed. Return mixture to baking pan and boil over high heat, stirring often, until reduced to 2 cups, about 12 minutes. Pour 1 cup sauce into a small bowl; keep warm or reheat. Use remaining sauce as a baste.

Brush shanks with about half the basting sauce. Lay shanks in center (not over coals) of prepared grill (see preceding). Cover barbecue, open vents, and cook until shanks are lightly browned on bottom, about 10 minutes.

With a wide spatula, gently loosen meat from grill and, using tongs, turn shanks over; meat is inclined to fall off bones. Brush with remaining basting sauce. Cover barbecue; cook until shanks are evenly browned all over, 10 to 12 minutes longer.

Transfer shanks to platter. Garnish with rosemary sprigs. Serve with hot couscous; season to taste with the 1 cup warm sauce and salt and pepper. Serves 4.

Per serving: 528 cal. (12 percent from fat); 46 g protein; 6.9 g fat (2.4 g sat.); 70 g carbo.; 162 mg sodium; 133 mg chol.

Grilled Beef Shanks with Mustard Glaze

4 beef shanks, each 1½ to 2 inches thick (about 4½ lb. total)

2½ cups regular-strength beef broth

1 large (about 10 oz.) onion, chopped

⅓ cup balsamic vinegar (or red wine vinegar plus 2 teaspoons sugar)

2 tablespoons Dijon mustard

1 tablespoon minced fresh or 1 teaspoon crumbled dried tarragon leaves

Fresh tarragon sprigs (optional)

Salt and pepper

Lay shanks in a single layer in a metal 9- by 13-inch pan. Add broth, onion, vinegar, mustard, and minced tarragon. Cover pan very tightly with foil.

Bake shanks in a 400° oven for 45 minutes. Turn shanks over, cover pan tightly, and bake until meat is very tender when pierced but not falling off the bone, 45 minutes to 1 hour longer. If making ahead, let shanks cool, cover, then chill up to a day.

Transfer shanks to a platter. Skim and discard any fat from pan juices. Pour juices into a food processor or blender and whirl until smoothly puréed. Return mixture to pan and boil over high heat, stirring often, until reduced to 2 cups, about 15 minutes. Reserve 1 cup sauce; keep it warm or reheat. Use remaining sauce as a baste.

Brush shanks evenly with about half the basting sauce. Lay shanks in center (not over coals) of prepared grill (see preceding). Cover barbecue, open vents, and cook until shank bottoms are browned, about 10 minutes.

With a wide spatula, gently loosen shanks from grill and carefully turn them over. (If meat falls from bone; turn pieces over). Brush with remaining basting sauce. Cover barbecue and cook until shanks are browned all over, about 10 minutes more.

Transfer shanks to a platter; garnish with tarragon sprigs. Season to taste with the 1 cup warm sauce and salt and pepper. Serves 4. ■

Per serving: 403 cal. (47 percent from fat); 44 g protein; 21 g fat (7.9 g sat.); 6.8 g carbo.; 239 mg sodium; 112 mg chol. ■

By Christine Weber Hale

BROAD

Atomic sauce gives smoked ribs a real blast

And salsa gets a cool-down

IT IS SWEET AND FITTING that every chef should feel that his barbecued ribs are the best in the world. It is not surprising, therefore, that a 1991 *Sunset* article on the "last word on ribs" should stir Bruce Macler to a reaction. The result is Reactionary Ribs, his homage to Oakland-style ribs, which uses a dry marinade (or paste or rub, as you wish), a fair dose of smoke, and an application of a sauce after the meat leaves the smoker.

The sauce, appropriately called Atomic Balm, is hot, but it can be rendered even more glowing with a supplement of cayenne.

Reactionary Ribs

1 slab (about 4 lb.) pork spareribs

4 cloves garlic, minced or pressed

1 tablespoon chili powder

1 teaspoon ground cumin

1 teaspoon pepper

2 cups hickory or other wood chips

Atomic balm (recipe follows)

Trim excess fat from ribs. Mash garlic with chili powder, cumin, and pepper to make a paste. Spread paste over ribs; cover and chill 1 hour to 6 hours.

Combine chips with about 2 cups water and let stand at least 30 minutes.

Meanwhile, on firegrate in a barbecue with a lid, mound and ignite 50 charcoal briquets. When coals are dotted with ash, about 30 minutes, push ½ to opposite sides of grate and set a metal drip pan between mounds. Drain chips and put about ½ cup on each mound of coals. Add 5 briquets to each mound now and 5 more each 30 minutes during cooking.

Position grill 4 to 6 inches above grate. Set ribs on grill over drip pan. Put lid on barbecue and open vents. After 30 minutes, put remaining chips on hot coals. Cook ribs until meat in thickest section is no longer pink at bone (cut to test), 1 to 1½ hours. Cut ribs apart and serve sloshed with atomic balm. Makes 4 servings.

Per serving: 847 cal. (58 percent from fat); 53 g protein; 55 g fat (21 g sat.); 36 g carbo.; 923 mg sodium; 214 mg chol.

Atomic balm. In a 2- to 3-quart pan, combine 1 cup **catsup;** ¼ cup *each* **molasses** and **lemon juice;** 2 tablespoons **sherry vinegar** or red wine vinegar; 2 cloves **garlic,** minced or pressed; 2 tablespoons finely chopped **onion;** 1 tablespoon **chili powder;** and 2 teaspoons **pepper.** Stir often over medium-high heat until just boiling. Reduce heat and simmer gently, uncovered, for about 15 minutes to blend flavors. Use hot or warm; if making ahead, let cool, cover, and chill up to 2 weeks.

Bruce Alan Macler

Albany, California

CAMARILLO FRIENDS OF Randy Richardson's have tongues too tender for the conventional Southwestern salsas. For them, he devised a black bean and corn salsa that stimulates the taste buds without searing them.

The concept of salsa has gone far beyond the original *salsa cruda,* the tomato and green chili dip familiar to lovers of Mexican food. Salsa now embraces any number of fruit or vegetable and spice combinations.

This black bean and corn salsa may be used as a dip or rolled in a tortilla. The salsa also makes a fine companion for meats. You could even add some modest heat with green chilies.

Black Bean and Corn Salsa

1 can (1 lb.) black beans, rinsed and drained

¾ cup corn kernels, fresh and cooked, canned, or thawed frozen

2 medium-size (about ¾ lb. total) firm-ripe tomatoes, cored, seeded, and diced

2 tablespoons finely chopped fresh cilantro (coriander)

4 green onions, ends trimmed, thinly sliced

1 tablespoon red wine vinegar

½ teaspoon *each* sugar and ground cumin

⅛ teaspoon freshly ground pepper

Salt

12 corn tortillas (6 to 7 in., optional)

In a bowl, mix black beans with corn, tomatoes, cilantro, green onions, vinegar, sugar, cumin, pepper, and salt to taste. Serve, or cover and chill up to 1 day.

Lightly rub each tortilla

with water-moistened palms; stack tortillas. To heat in a microwave oven, set stack on a plate and lightly cover with plastic wrap; warm on full power (100 percent) until tortillas are hot in center, about 1½ minutes. To heat in the oven, seal stack in foil. Bake in a 350° oven until hot in center, about 15 minutes.

Eat salsa as a relish or in tortillas. Makes 4 cups.

Per ¼ cup salsa: 28 cal. (9.6 percent from fat); 1.5 g protein; 0.3 g fat (0 g sat.); 5.3 g carbo.; 49 mg sodium; 0 mg chol.

Camarillo, California

"SIMPLIFY, SIMPLIFY," SAID Thoreau, who found his life frittered away by details. If he took his own advice, he probably lived on sandwiches. Although our Chefs of the West tend to ig-

SPECTACULAR giardiniera emerges as a great sandwich filling.

nore Thoreau (their cry is "Enrich, enrich!"), we do occasionally get a quick and easy sandwich recipe. Charles Van Dyke sends this Mediterranean delight with a mystery ingredient—*giardiniera.*

You may have seen giardiniera in an Italian delicatessen or among the pickles in a supermarket without learning its name. Layered sliced vegetables in glass jars (sometimes of spectacular height) make a colorful spectacle.

These constitute giardiniera: carrots, celery, pickles, and peppers (the usual ingredients, although others may be added). They take a mildly hot flavor from their pickling liquid. Van Dyke chops these vegetables to make a relish for his salami and cream cheese sandwiches.

A Different Sandwich

1 cup drained giardiniera (Italian pickled vegetables)

1 small package (3 oz.) neufchâtel (light cream) cheese

8 slices whole-wheat bread, toasted

⅓ pound thinly sliced Genoa-style salami

In a food processor or with a knife, finely chop the giardiniera.

Spread cream cheese evenly on 1 side of each toast slice. Spoon giardiniera equally onto cheese on 4 slices; spread level. Top each giardiniera layer equally with salami and a remaining piece of toast, cheese down. Makes 4 sandwiches.

Per sandwich: 348 cal. (57 percent from fat); 15 g protein; 22 g fat (8.5 g sat.); 24 g carbo.; 1,199 mg sodium; 56 mg chol.

Kalispell, Montana

By Joan Griffiths, Richard Dunmire

CHOCOLATE CHUNKS *peek out from cheesecake.*

NORMAN A. PLATE

This cheesecake has a secret

Cookie dough lumps hide beneath its cool surface

SOFT, CREAMY LUMPS of chocolate chip cookie dough, made without egg, are a tantalizing surprise in this smooth cheesecake. It's a dessert that indulges those addicted to nibbling cookies before they bake.

Chocolate Chip Cookie Dough Cheesecake

1½ cups finely crushed chocolate wafer cookie crumbs (about 30 cookies)

1 cup sugar

¼ cup (⅛ lb.) melted butter or margarine

2 large packages (8 oz. each) cream cheese or neufchâtel (light cream) cheese, cut into chunks

1 cup regular or light (reduced-fat) sour cream

3 large eggs

1 teaspoon vanilla

Cookie dough (recipe follows)

Topping (recipe follows)

Mix crumbs, 2 tablespoons sugar, and butter; press firmly over bottom and ½ inch up sides of a 9-inch cheesecake pan with removable rim. Bake in a 350° oven until slightly darker color, about 8 minutes.

In a food processor or with a mixer, whirl or beat remaining sugar with cheese. Add cream, eggs, and vanilla; mix well. Pour into crust. Drop cookie dough in 2-tablespoon portions evenly over cake; push dough beneath surface.

Bake in 350° oven until cake jiggles only slightly in center when gently shaken, about 40 minutes. Spread topping over hot cake. Let cake cool, then chill until cold, at least 4 hours; serve or wrap airtight up to 2 days. Serves 12 to 16.

Per serving: 417 cal. (58 percent from fat); 5.8 g protein; 27 g fat (16 g sat.); 40 g carbo.; 281 mg sodium; 100 mg chol.

Cookie dough. In a bowl, beat to blend ¼ cup (⅛ lb.) **butter** or margarine, ¼ cup firmly packed **brown sugar,** and ¼ cup **granulated sugar.** Stir in 2 tablespoons **water** and 1 teaspoon **vanilla.** Beat in ½ cup **all-purpose flour** and 1 cup (6 oz.) **semisweet chocolate baking chips** or chopped pieces.

Topping. Mix 1 cup regular or light (reduced-fat) **sour cream,** 2 teaspoons **sugar,** and 1 teaspoon **vanilla.** ∎

By Karyn I. Lipman

SUNSET'S KITCHEN CABINET

Creative ways with everyday foods—submitted by *Sunset* readers,
tested in *Sunset* kitchens, approved by *Sunset* taste panels

Almond-Zucchini Stir-steam

Sarah Pratt, Altadena, California

ZUCCHINI STICKS *stir-steam in liquid instead of stir-frying in oil.*

6 large (about 2 lb. total) zucchini

½ cup slivered almonds

2 cloves garlic, minced or pressed

About 2 tablespoons soy sauce

3 cups hot cooked rice

Trim and discard zucchini ends. Cut zucchini into sticks about 2 inches long and ¼ inch thick; set aside.

In a 10- to 12-inch frying pan over medium heat, stir or shake almonds often until a deep gold, 4 to 5 minutes.

Pour from pan and set aside.

To pan, add zucchini, garlic, and 2 tablespoons water. Place on high heat; turn zucchini frequently with a wide spatula until tender-crisp to bite and liquid evaporates, about 8 minutes. Add 2 tablespoons soy sauce; mix. Put rice in a bowl and pour zucchini over it; sprinkle with almonds. Add soy sauce to taste. Makes 6 servings.

Per serving: 224 cal. (26 percent from fat); 7.1 g protein; 6.4 g fat (0.7 g sat.); 36 g carbo.; 351 mg sodium; 0 mg chol.

Chunky Summer Gazpacho

Cristine M. Cashatt, Spokane, Washington

SUMMER-RIPE *vegetables, puréed and chopped, make cool, fresh gazpacho.*

6 large (about 3¾ lb. total) firm-ripe tomatoes, cored

3 medium-size (about 1½ lb. total) cucumbers, peeled

Tomato juice base (recipe follows)

2 large (each about 10 oz.) bell peppers, 1 yellow and 1 green, stemmed and seeded

½ cup diced red onion

1 large (about ¾-lb.) firm-ripe avocado

1 tablespoon lemon juice

1 cup unflavored nonfat yogurt

Extra-virgin olive oil (optional)

Salt

Chop 3 tomatoes and 1 cucumber. Fill a blender or food processor with vegetables; with motor running add enough of the tomato juice base to smoothly purée mixture. Pour mixture into a large bowl or tureen. If needed, purée any remaining chopped vegetables. Add to tureen with any remaining tomato base.

Cut remaining tomatoes, cucumbers, and bell peppers into about ⅜-inch cubes. Add to bowl along with onion; mix, cover, and chill until cold, about 2 hours, or up to 1 day.

Peel, pit, and slice avocado into 10 to 12 wedges; coat wedges with lemon juice. Stir gazpacho and ladle into wide soup bowls; top with avocado slices and spoonfuls of yogurt. Offer olive oil to drizzle into portions to taste; season to taste with salt. Makes 9 or 10 servings.

Per serving: 119 cal. (35 percent from fat); 4.3 g protein; 4.6 g fat (0.7 g sat.); 19 g carbo.; 303 mg sodium; 0.5 mg chol.

Tomato juice base. Combine 3 cups **tomato juice,** ¾ cup **red wine vinegar,** and ½ teaspoon **pepper.**

Soy-Honey Barbecued Flank Steak

Beth Ann Hite, Peoria, Arizona

BARBECUED FLANK STEAK *is flavored by soy, garlic, and generous dose of ginger.*

½ cup red wine vinegar

About ¼ cup soy sauce

3 tablespoons honey

¼ cup minced fresh ginger

1 tablespoon olive or salad oil

4 large cloves garlic, minced or pressed

About 1 teaspoon pepper

1 flank steak (about 2 lb.), fat trimmed

Lime wedges (optional)

In a 9- by 13-inch pan, mix vinegar, ¼ cup soy sauce, honey, ginger, oil, garlic, and 1 teaspoon pepper. Turn steak over in marinade. Cover and chill at least 30 minutes or up to 1 day; turn meat over 3 or 4 times.

Drain steak; discard marinade. Lay meat on a grill 4 to 6 inches above a solid bed of hot coals (you can hold your hand at grill level only 2 to 3 seconds). Cook, turning to brown evenly, until meat is medium-rare, pink in thickest part (cut to test), 10 to 12 minutes. Transfer to a board; garnish with lime wedges. Thinly slice steak across grain. Season to taste with soy and pepper. Serves 6.

Per serving: 269 cal. (43 percent from fat); 31g protein; 13 g fat (5.1 g sat.); 6 g carbo.; 452 mg sodium; 76 mg chol.

Beverly's Tuna Spread

Beverly Zegarski, Montara, California

2 large eggs

1 can (12 oz.) albacore tuna in water, drained

1 large (about ¼-lb.) carrot, peeled and grated

1 medium-size (10-oz.) red bell pepper, stemmed, seeded, and diced

¾ cup diced celery

½ cup unflavored nonfat yogurt

2 tablespoons sweet pickle relish

Salt and pepper

8 tiny (about 4-in.-wide) pocket breads, cut in half crosswise, or unsalted crackers

In a 1½- to 2-quart pan, cover eggs with 1 inch cool water. Place over high heat until water just begins to simmer; turn heat to low and cook 15 minutes. Drain and immerse eggs in cold water; when cool, shell and dice eggs.

In a bowl, stir tuna with a fork to break into bite-size pieces. Add eggs, carrot, bell pepper, celery, yogurt, and sweet pickle relish; mix. Add salt and pepper to taste. Serve, or cover and chill up to 1 day.

Arrange pocket breads slightly apart in a 10- by 15-inch pan. Bake in a 400° oven until toasted, about 10 minutes; turn over after 5 minutes. Spoon tuna mixture onto bread. Makes 16.

Per piece: 89 cal. (13 percent from fat); 8 g protein; 1.3 g fat (0.3 g sat.); 11 g carbo.; 188 mg sodium; 35 mg chol.

CELERY, *red bell pepper, and carrot add crunch to tuna-egg spread.*

Cool Spaghetti Salad

Jane Ingraham, Durango, Colorado

½ pound dried spaghetti

1 medium-size (about ¾-lb.) cucumber, peeled and chopped

1 cup *each* thinly sliced carrot and celery

½ cup thinly sliced green onions

½ cup minced fresh cilantro (coriander) leaves

Dill sauce (recipe follows)

Fresh cilantro sprigs

2 green onions, ends trimmed (optional)

Salt and pepper

In a 4- to 5-quart pan, bring about 2 quarts water to boiling over high heat. Break spaghetti into thirds; add to water. Cook, uncovered, just until tender to bite, about 8 minutes. Drain pasta, immerse in cold water until cool, then drain well and pour into a wide bowl.

To bowl, add cucumber, carrot, celery, sliced onions, minced cilantro, and dill sauce; mix gently. Garnish with cilantro sprigs and whole onions. Serve, or cover and chill up to 4 hours. Add salt and pepper to taste. Serves 6.

Per serving: 215 cal. (14 percent from fat); 8.7 g protein; 3.4 g fat (1.5 g sat.); 38 g carbo.; 384 mg sodium; 7.2 mg chol.

Dill sauce. Combine 1 cup finely chopped **dill pickles,** ¾ cup **unflavored nonfat yogurt,** and ½ cup **light** (reduced-fat) **sour cream.**

SPAGHETTI, *cooked and chilled, mixes with raw vegetables, pickles in salad.*

Raspberry-Cornmeal Tea Muffins

Susan McGrath, Portland

1 cup all-purpose flour

⅔ cup yellow cornmeal

⅓ cup sugar

2 teaspoons baking powder

½ teaspoon *each* baking soda and salt

2 large eggs

1 cup vanilla-flavor lowfat yogurt

¼ cup salad oil

1 cup raspberries, rinsed and drained

In a large bowl, mix all-purpose flour, cornmeal, sugar, baking powder, soda, and salt.

In another bowl, beat to blend eggs, yogurt, and oil; add to flour mixture. Stir to moisten evenly; gently fold in berries.

Divide batter equally among 10 oiled or paper-lined muffin cups (2½-in. size). Bake in a 375° oven until golden and tops spring back when touched in center, 20 to 25 minutes. Cool on a rack; serve warm. If making ahead, cool, wrap airtight, and hold up to 1 day. Freeze to store longer. Makes 10.

Per muffin: 204 cal. (36 percent from fat); 4.5 g protein; 8.2 g fat (1.4 g sat.); 28 g carbo.; 276 mg sodium; 44 mg chol.

Compiled by Betsy Reynolds Bateson

RASPBERRIES AND CORNMEAL *make good partners in these sweet tea muffins.*

August Menus

Abundance of fruit is the driving force behind our August menus. To take advantage of the various berries and stone fruit available now, the classic fruit shortcake provides an ideal foundation. But, for a change, try it as the main course for a refreshing brunch or supper.

Mountains of melons inspire you to use them with abandon. An appetizing way to enjoy their sweet succulence is to cut small ones in half to use as bowls for other foods—such as chicken salad.

SHORTCAKE SPREE (at right)
Bountiful peaches, blueberries, and strawberries debut with wedges of tender shortcake and whipped cream for this garden party.

CHICKEN SALAD BRUNCH (page 158)
Served in a cantaloupe half, this chicken salad comes with an edible bowl; offer with wholesome oatmeal muffins.

THE DETAILS

Speedy Decor

Gather flowers in small cartons and place in an inexpensive enamel pot.

Simple Shortcake

To save time, pat dough into one giant round and score into 8 wedges.

Spearmint Tea

Steep fresh spearmint sprigs with your favorite loose tea; tea ball contains leaves.

Sugar Shakers

Powdered sugar disburses evenly from shakers with large holes or a wire cover.

Begin the meal with bloody or virgin Marys to sip as you nibble tiny tacos dipped in purchased salsa. You'll find miniature tacos in supermarket freezers.

Fruit shortcake functions as main course and dessert. Guests fill their own according to preferences.

To make spearmint tea, pour hot water over spearmint sprigs (allow 2 sprigs for each serving) and loose or bagged tea (if using loose tea, allow about 1 teaspoon for each cup, or use 1 bag for every 2 cups). Let tea and mint steep about 15 minutes. Pour over ice. Any tea will work; choose one of your favorites.

Summer Fruit
Shortcakes

About 6 pounds firm-ripe freestone peaches (yellow or white flesh)

2 tablespoons lemon juice

5 cups strawberries, rinsed, hulled, and halved

2 cups blueberries, rinsed and drained

Garden shortcake wedges (recipe follows)

2 to 3 cups softly whipped cream

Powdered sugar (optional)

In a 3- to 4-quart pan, bring about 2 quarts water to a boil. Immerse peaches, 2 or 3 at a time, just until skin pulls free easily (to test, make a nick in skin and pull), 15 to 60 seconds. Lift out with a slotted spoon. Let cool slightly, then pull off skin and slice peaches; discard skin and pits. Gently mix slices with lemon juice. If making ahead, cover and chill up to 2 hours.

PETER CHRISTIANSEN

CHICKEN, *bell pepper, and fruit join to make a lean entrée.*

To serve, present peaches, strawberries, and blueberries, together or in separate bowls. Also offer shortcake wedges, whipped cream, and powdered sugar. Let guests assemble their own shortcakes, spooning fruits and cream between split wedges of shortcake. Sprinkle with powdered sugar to taste. Serves 8.—*Barbara Lewis, San Mateo, California*

Per wedge with 2 cups fruit and ¼ cup whipped cream: 557 cal. (37 percent from fat); 9.5 g protein; 23 g fat (14 g sat.); 83 g carbo.; 528 mg sodium; 70 mg chol.

Garden shortcake wedges. Combine 3 cups **all-purpose flour,** 2 tablespoons **sugar,** 4½ teaspoons **baking powder,** and ½ teaspoon **salt.** With a pastry blender or knife, cut in ½ cup (¼ lb.) **butter** or margarine until mixture resembles coarse crumbs. (If making ahead, cover and chill up to 1 day.) Add 1¼ cups **milk;** stir just until dough sticks together.

Lightly oil and flour a 10-inch round on a 12- by 15-inch baking sheet. Spoon dough into center of floured area and press into a 9-inch round. Cut dough into 8 wedges, leaving wedges in place. Bake in a 450° oven until golden brown, about 15 minutes. Transfer to a rack; pull wedges apart, slice horizontally into halves, and serve warm or cool.

For cantaloupe bowls that are steady, slice off a little of the rounded bottom of each melon half.

Chicken Salad in
Cantaloupe Halves

1 small (about 6-oz.) yellow bell pepper

1 medium-size (about 1-lb.) firm-ripe papaya

3 cups (about ¾ lb.) shredded cooked chicken

¼ cup minced fresh cilantro (coriander) leaves

2 tablespoons drained canned capers

2 teaspoons grated lime peel

¼ cup *each* lime juice and orange juice

2 small cantaloupes (each about 2¼ lb.), cut into halves and seeded

Lime wedges (optional)

Salt and pepper

Stem and seed bell pep-

per; finely dice pepper. Cut papaya into halves and discard seed; peel fruit and cut into about ⅜-inch cubes.

Combine bell pepper, papaya, chicken, cilantro, and capers. (If making ahead, cover and chill up to 4 hours.) Stir together lime peel, lime juice, and orange juice. Pour citrus juices over chicken mixture; stir to mix. Spoon chicken equally into melon halves; garnish with lime. Add salt and pepper to taste. Serves 4.

Per serving: 301 cal. (22 percent from fat); 28 g protein; 7.2 g fat (1.8 g sat.); 34 g carbo.; 212 mg sodium; 76 mg chol. ∎

By Betsy Reynolds Bateson

Dutch Baby
Pancake

Long a favorite with *Sunset* readers, this giant pancake wins applause for showstopping looks, great taste, and ease of preparation. Serve it with fruit or syrup for brunch, or filled with chili or other savory mixture for a supper main dish.

3 tablespoons butter or margarine

4 large eggs

1 cup milk

1 cup all-purpose flour

Powdered sugar

Lemon wedges

Put butter in a 10- to 12-inch-diameter shallow casserole or ovenproof frying pan. Set in a 425° oven until butter is lightly browned, 7 to 8 minutes.

Meanwhile, combine eggs, milk, and flour in a blender or food processor. Whirl until very smooth.

Pour batter into hot pan in oven. Bake until pancake is a rich brown and sides have puffed, 25 to 30 minutes. Sift powdered sugar liberally over pancake; cut pancake into wedges. Serve at once with lemon to taste. Serves 6.

Per serving: 201 cal. (49 percent from fat); 7.7g protein; 11g fat (5.5 g sat.); 18g carbo.; 121 mg sodium; 163 mg chol.

By Christine B. Weber

WATER-SOAKED POPCORN *swells enough above rim of cup to knock lid off.*

PETER CHRISTIANSEN

Popcorn does push-ups

An edible lesson in science and history

L ET'S MAKE CORN do a push-up. With this enticement, Janice McCormick shows her young children and their friends the scientific principle of the power of expansion. To keep their attention, she uses a food they all like: popcorn.

First, she fills a measuring cup to the rim with unpopped popcorn and adds water. Then she sets a lightweight lid on top. By the next day, the corn has swollen above the cup rim, spilling over onto the plate, and has either lifted up the lid or tipped it off.

The soaked popcorn, simmered with seasonings, tastes like the pozole Southwest Indians cook, bringing in a historical angle. McCormick seasons the corn with an oil and vinegar dressing and calls it Indian salad. The flavor is simple but intriguing—like comfort food. Spoon into lettuce leaves and roll up to make lettuce tacos.

Popcorn Push-up

Fill a 1-cup dry measure (flat on top) level to the rim with unpopped **popcorn.** Set on a plate. Carefully pour in **water** (about ⅓ cup) to fill cup to rim. Set the bottom of a lightweight removable pie or cake pan on top of cup.

Let stand at least 8 hours or up to a day.

Indian Corn Push-up Salad

Popcorn push-up (preceding) or 1 cup unpopped popcorn

1 teaspoon cumin seed

1 teaspoon coriander seed

1 tablespoon olive oil

¼ cup balsamic vinegar (or red wine vinegar plus 1 tablespoon sugar)

¼ cup chopped green onion

¼ cup chopped red onion

1 cup cherry tomatoes, stemmed and halved

Salt and pepper

About 3 dozen (about 1⅓ lb.) butter lettuce leaves, rinsed and crisped

In a 2- to 3-quart pan, combine popcorn push-up, 3 cups water, cumin, and coriander. Bring to a boil, cover, and simmer until corn is tender to bite, about 2½ hours (unsoaked corn takes about 3 hours). Drain corn and let cool.

Mix corn with oil, balsamic vinegar, green onion, red onion, and tomato halves. Season to taste with salt and pepper. Spoon corn onto lettuce leaves and roll up to eat. Serves 6 to 8.—*Janice McCormick, Ojai, California*

Per serving: 132 cal. (22 percent from fat); 4.3 g protein; 3.2 g fat (0.4 g sat.); 24 g carbo.; 7.2 mg sodium; 0 mg chol. ■

By Linda Lau Anusasananan

BOILED POPCORN, *dressed with vinaigrette, makes a chewy salad to eat in lettuce.*

Secrets of Wine Country Cooks

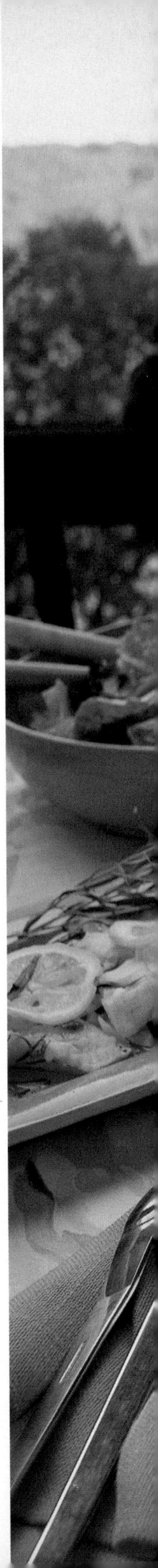

Entertaining is a way of life for winemakers. Here's how they do it

by Linda Lau Anusasananan

ROM GRAPE TO GLASS, EVERY STAGE OF WINEMAKING IS AIMED AT THE HAPPY PROSPECT of teaming wine with food. In the Napa Valley, wine and food together are a way of life for many winemakers who—short on time but long on creativity—have turned entertaining into an efficient, elegant art. What are their secrets? On these pages, two winemaking families, and a group of young winemakers who grew up together in the valley, share some exceptionally simple, effective ways to pair the products of their vineyards and their kitchens.

For a romantic start, Guenoc Estate Vineyards and Winery is perfect. Lillie Langtry, the famous British actress, once owned part of the property, and her face graces the winery's label. In the late 1800s, Langtry resided in the valley, awaiting settlement of a headline divorce. The respectable part of her time was devoted to making quite decent wines—about 50 tons of grapes' worth each year.

Orville Magoon dusted off history when he began to replant the vineyards in 1963. While he tends grapes and makes wine, his wife, Karen Melander-Magoon, manages the winery's public relations and marketing. They have restored Langtry's home to use for wine industry and community events.

However, on weeknights, the Magoons often entertain casually in their own nearby home—with its expansive view of their 30-square-mile estate. "Wine demands a whole different tempo—it slows the dining experience to a relaxed pace and helps bring family and friends

PETER CHRISTIANSEN

AT GUENOC WINERY, *with guests as company, Karen Melander-Magoon uses garden herbs to season bass her husband, Orville, caught in the morning. She also serves Chinese pea pods and salad greens from her garden.*

160

Midweek Supper with Guenoc Winery Wines

Yerba Santa Alpine Chèvre with Crackers

1991 Sauvignon Blanc Estate Bottled

1991 Langtry Meritage White Wine Estate Bottled

Fish with Herbs (recipe on page 168)

Chinese Pea Pods

Toasted Rice

Garden Greens with Sesame Dressing

1991 Chardonnay Estate Bottled

1991 Chardonnay Genevieve Magoon Vineyard Reserve Estate Bottled

Brownies with Bittersweet Chocolate Chunks

1990 Petite Sirah

together," says Mrs. Magoon. With both Magoons at work, cooking ahead is impossible, so cooking with company becomes part of entertaining.

To show off their wines, the Magoons usually serve lightly seasoned dishes with ingredients from the garden—and, on a lucky day, largemouth bass from the property's lake.

The evening we joined them, Mrs. Magoon scattered chopped shallots, tarragon, thyme, and sage over the day's catch, poured a light white wine over it, and put it in to bake while we nibbled cheese and sipped the house's dry Sauvignon Blanc.

PETER CHRISTIANSEN

GUENOC PETITE SIRAH *tastes especially smooth with chocolate brownies.*

In what seemed like much less than the hour it was, the table was laden with fish, rice pilaf, peas, and salad dressed with balsamic vinegar and Oriental sesame oil. Chardonnay accompanied the meal.

As we pulled up our chairs, chocolate brownies went into the oven. With the warm dessert came Petite Sirah, and music trilled into the dusky night. Mrs. Magoon, an opera singer, burst into an impromptu aria.

DOLORES AND JACK CAKEBREAD WORK AS A TEAM, but within well-established territories. While he and their sons planted the first vineyard more than 20 years ago, she started her flower and vegetable gardens. Now, he runs Cakebread Cellars and she still oversees a garden that enriches their table year-round. She also

plans and prepares, or directs, meals to go with the wines he selects. Mrs. Cakebread's longtime approach to food emphasizes wholesome, good-tasting dishes with minimum fat and cholesterol. "Our theory is to cook tastefully and healthfully so you can enjoy a good glass of wine and, following the 'French Paradox,' remain healthy," she explains.

Entertaining is frequent, and groups are often large. As a result, the winery's kitchen is professional in scale. A resident chef and an assistant free up Mrs. Cakebread's time to act as hostess for the basic business of making and selling wine.

When our party of six arrived in early afternoon, Mr. Cakebread had red wines open and whites chilling. That morning, Mrs. Cakebread had harvested fresh, perfect ingredients for lunch from the garden. Some of these were mounded as a still life in a big, well-used basket.

With a fragrant ratatouille simmering on the range, cheese ravioli assembled and ready to boil, and dessert in the refrigera-

Harvest Lunch with Cakebread Cellar Wines

Goat Cheese Ravioli with Cilantro Pesto (recipe page 168)

1991 Sauvignon Blanc Napa Valley

Chicken with Ratatouille (recipe page 168)

Crusty Bread

1991 Chardonnay Napa Valley

Cherry and Chocolate Trifle (recipe page169)

1989 Cabernet Sauvignon Napa Valley

TERI SANDISON

DOLORES CAKEBREAD HARVESTS *bell peppers, tomatoes, eggplant, and herbs to make a ratatouille bed for sliced chicken breast. Chardonnay accompanies the dish.*

163

tor, the Cakebreads led us outside to a table draped in colors of the summer harvest. Vegetables and flowers provided decorations, and an impressive array of glasses, ready for the wines, flanked place settings.

Mrs. Cakebread plans her menus to enhance the wines. The tang of cilantro pesto and goat cheese ravioli goes with dry Sauvignon Blanc's fresh, crisp taste. The mellow ratatouille topped with grilled chicken is at ease with rich Chardonnay. And the cherry trifle brings out the cherry overtones in their lush Cabernet Sauvignon.

GROWING UP IN THE wine business—some have several generations of winemaking behind them—Rollie Heitz, Paula Kornell, Peter Mondavi, Jr., and Katie Wetzel Murphy developed close friendships and well-educated palates.

Today, their enthusiasm for food and wine has moved into the professional arena, but their pleasure in celebrating wine and food together in a relaxed environment hasn't declined. It's just more difficult.

Many of them travel in their jobs, so times when everyone is in the area are limited. Parties need to come together easily. The favorite solution is potluck. Each cooks a favorite dish scaled to serve the whole group, and often the dish is completed at the host's house, with getting-caught-up conversations buzzing. Along with the dish, each person brings one or more wines. Some wine is sipped while they cook, and all are available with the meal—served buffet-style.

Our invitation came for the night the group gathered at Paula Kornell's home. We were struck by the fearless way they paired wine and food. It was good fun; the more daring the combination, the more relaxed the mood. Everyone jumped in to argue for favorites.

Heitz championed Chardonnay with his spicy shrimp-filled artichokes; Murphy crowed about the Zinfandel with the pork; Mondavi pleaded a good case for the Grignolino with the meat. We tried them all; a bite of bread soothed less successful choices.

With this meal, as with the ones with the Magoons and Cakebreads, the message came through clearly: wine fits in easily. It's equally at home with a weekday supper, low-fat lunch, potluck—or formal dinner.

Young Winemakers' Potluck

Half-shell Oysters with Tangy Sauces (recipe page 169)

Artichokes with Smoldering Shrimp (recipe page 169)

Mixed Salad Greens

Salsa di Pomodori (recipe page 169)

Grilled Pork with Cumin (recipe page 169)

Berries with Herbs and Champagne (recipe page 167)

1992 Charles Krug Napa Valley Sauvignon Blanc

1991 Alexander Valley Vineyards Chardonnay

1988 Heitz Cellars Zinfandel

1988 Heitz Cellars Grignolino

1987 Hanns Kornell Sparkling Blanc de Noirs

Hanns Kornell Brut Champagne

YOUNG WINEMAKERS COOK AS A TEAM—*Peter Mondavi, Jr., boils pasta; Paula Kornell grills pork; Katie Wetzel Murphy shucks oysters; and Rollie Heitz fills artichokes. For dessert, sparkling wine goes over berries with basil and mint.*

PETER CHRISTIANSEN

TASTE ANY WINE *with any food in this four-cook feast, and discover good partners, traditional or heretical.*

Putting wine to work throughout the meal

PETER CHRISTIANSEN

A GENEROUS splash of wine introduces an appetizing array of flavors. Use wine to baste chicken (above), in sauces and soups, as a cooking liquid, or just as it is.

WHAT DO WINEMAKERS do with all those open bottles left from tastings? Much of the wine is used for cooking. Splashed as freely as water into or over foods, wine brings interesting complexity and flavors in return for a minimum commitment of ingredients and technique.

Even if you don't have extra wine, the delicious impact of using wine in the simple combinations that follow, from roasted meats to cooling ices, makes pulling a cork all the more rewarding.

WHICH WINE?

To use odds and ends of wines, it's handy to know which kinds you can mix without confusing their effect on foods. This brief list describes what pools well. If you start from scratch, use wines suggested with the recipes or an equivalent type.

Dry red wines include Cabernet Sauvignon, Gamay Beaujolais, Merlot, Petite Sirah, Pinot Noir, Zinfandel, and any dry red wine blend.

Dry white wines include Chardonnay, Sauvignon Blanc, Chenin Blanc, and any dry white blend.

Slightly sweet, fruity wines include some Sauvignon Blancs, most Chenin Blancs, Gewürztraminer, Johannisberg Riesling, and white Zinfandels.

Sweet, fruity wines are late-harvest wines made from Johannisberg Riesling, Gewürztraminer, and even Zinfandel, as well as dessert wines like Moscato di Canelli.

Sparkling wines range from sweet to dry; if a dish is sweet and the wine is dry, you can compensate by adding sugar.

Wine-roasted Chicken and Onions

Rinse and pat dry a 3- to 4-pound **chicken;** pull off and discard fat. Set chicken, breast down, on a rack in an 11- by 17-inch pan. Cut 3 or 4 **onions** (about 6 oz. each) in half vertically and lay cut side down in pan. Pour 1 cup **slightly sweet, fruity** or dry **white wine** (choices precede) over chicken. Sprinkle chick-

en with 1 teaspoon **fresh** or ½ teaspoon dried **rosemary leaves.**

Bake in a 400° oven 30 minutes. Turn chicken over and bake, basting often with ½ cup more white wine until chicken is very well browned, 1 to 1¼ hours. If onions at pan edges begin to scorch, pour a little more wine or water around them.

Drain juice from chicken into pan; transfer chicken and onions to a platter. Skim fat from pan juices. Add ½ cup each **regular-strength chicken broth** and white wine. Scrape browned bits free. Mix 1 tablespoon **cornstarch** and 2 tablespoons **water,** mix into juices, and stir over high heat until sauce boils. Serve with chicken and onions; season with **salt** to taste. Serves 4.

Per serving: 451 cal. (48 percent from fat); 43 g protein; 24 g fat (6.7 g sat.); 14 g carbo.; 138 mg sodium; 135 mg chol.

Wine-roasted Lamb and Onions

Follow directions for chicken, preceding, except use a 5- to 6-pound **leg of lamb** instead of the chicken and dry red wine instead of white wine. Trim fat from lamb. Bake in a 325° oven, without turning, until thermometer inserted through the thickest part to the bone reads 135° for medium-rare, 1¾ to 2 hours. Serves 6 to 8.

Per serving: 310 cal. (38 percent from fat); 40 g protein; 13 g fat (4.6 g sat.); 7.3 g carbo.; 100 mg sodium; 123 mg chol.

Steeped Salmon in Chardonnay Broth

In a 3- to 4-quart pan, combine 2½ cups **dry white wine** (choices precede), 2½ cups **regular-strength chicken broth,** 1 teaspoon **white peppercorns,** ½ teaspoon **fresh** or ¼ teaspoon dried **thyme leaves,** ½ teaspoon **coriander seed,** ¼ teaspoon **whole allspice,** and 4 strips **lemon peel** (yellow part only, each 4 in. long). Cover and simmer 20 to 30 minutes.

Add 4 pieces (about ¼ lb. each) rinsed **salmon fillet.** Bring to a boil, cover pan, and remove from heat. Steep until fish is barely opaque and still moist-looking in thickest part (cut to test), 8 to 10 minutes. Transfer fish to wide shallow bowls. Ladle broth over fish. Garnish with sliced **chives.** Serves 4.

Per serving: 189 cal. (39 percent from fat); 24 g protein; 8.2 g fat (1.4 g sat.); 2.8 g carbo.; 91 mg sodium; 62 mg chol.

Wine-poached Carrots

Peel 1½ pounds small **carrots** (each about 5 in. long). In a 10- to 12-inch frying pan, combine 1¼ cups **slightly sweet, fruity wine** (choices precede), ¾ cup **regular-strength chicken broth,** and 1 teaspoon **butter** or margarine. Add carrots, cover, and simmer, shaking pan occasionally, until carrots are tender when pierced, 10 to 15 minutes.

Uncover and boil over high heat until liquid evaporates and carrots begin to brown, about 10 minutes; shake pan

CARROTS COOKED with sweet white wine are topped with chervil.

often. Serve with fresh **chervil sprigs** (optional) and **salt** to taste. Serves 6.

Per serving: 70 cal. (13 percent from fat); 1.4 g protein; 1 g fat (0.5 g sat.); 12 g carbo.; 52 mg sodium; 1.7 mg chol.

Pears with Red Wine Syrup

In a 1½- to 2-quart pan, mix 1 cup **dry red wine** (choices precede), ½ cup **water,** ½ cup **sugar,** ¼ cup **lemon juice,** 1 tablespoon chopped **fresh** or ½ teaspoon dried **mint leaves,** 1 teaspoon **black peppercorns,** and 1 teaspoon **fresh** or ¼ teaspoon dried **tarragon leaves.** Boil over high heat, uncovered, until reduced to ½ cup, 12 to 15 minutes. Pour through a fine strainer into a bowl. Use warm or cool.

Slice 3 large (about ½ lb. each) firm-ripe **Bartlett** or Comice **pears** in half lengthwise; core.

Starting at blossom end, make lengthwise cuts about ¼ inch apart to within about ½ inch of stem end. Place on a dessert plate and press down gently to fan out slices. Pour wine syrup equally over pears. Garnish with **fresh tarragon** or mint **sprigs.** Serves 6.

Per serving: 132 cal. (2.7 percent from fat); 0.6 g protein; 0.4 g fat (0 g sat.); 34 g carbo.; 4.4 mg sodium; 0 mg chol.

Wine Slush

Pour 1½ cups chilled **sweet, fruity wine** (choices precede) into a 2-cup or larger container of an ice cream maker (frozen cylinder, self-refrigerated, or ice- and salt-cooled). Process according to manufacturer's directions until softly frozen. Spoon into chilled bowls or onto **melon** or peach slices. Serves 4 or 5.

Per serving without fruit: 69 cal. (0 percent from fat); 0 g protein; 0 g fat; 3.2 g carbo.; 4.5 mg sodium; 0 mg chol.

Berries with Herbs and Champagne

Rinse and drain 1 quart **berries** (raspberries, blueberries, blackberries, or strawberries; hull and thinly slice the strawberries).

Place equal portions of berries in 8 stemmed glasses.

Finely chop 1 tablespoon each **fresh mint** and **fresh basil leaves;** scatter over fruit. Serve, or cover and chill up to 4 hours.

Pour 1 bottle (750 ml.) chilled **sparkling wine** (sweet or dry) over fruit. If desired, add a small scoop of **vanilla ice cream** to each portion. Serves 8.—*Paula Kornell, Hanns Kornell family, St. Helena, California*

Per serving: 97 cal. (2.8 percent from fat); 0.6 g protein; 0.3 g fat (0 g sat.); 8.9 g carbo.; 6 mg sodium; 0 mg chol. ∎

CHARDONNAY makes a delicate backdrop for steeped salmon with herbs and spices.

QUICK DESSERTS with wine: refreshing slush is frozen sweet wine; red wine syrup enhances fresh pears.

PETER CHRISTIANSEN

WEEKNIGHTS, *the Magoons cook quick dishes like fresh-caught fish baked with herbs.*

Wine country recipes for successful entertaining

Fresh flavors, simple methods produce memorable meals

RELIABLE RECIPES make entertaining easy. These are favorites that the busy winemakers pictured on pages 160 through 164 turn to.

Fish with Herbs

2   pounds skinned and boned striped bass or sole fillets

½   cup dry white wine
    About ½ cup regular-strength chicken broth

⅓   cup minced shallots

1   tablespoon chopped fresh tarragon, thyme, or sage leaves

6   to 8 thin lemon slices
    Fresh tarragon, thyme, or sage sprigs

2   teaspoons cornstarch
    Salt and pepper

Rinse fish, pat dry, and arrange, overlapping slightly, in a shallow 9- by 13-inch casserole. Pour wine and broth over fish; sprinkle with shallots and chopped herbs. Lay lemon slices and herb sprigs on fish.

Bake, uncovered, in a 375° oven until fish is opaque but still moist-looking in thickest part (cut to test), about 15 minutes.

Tilt dish, and ladle or siphon pan juices into a 1- to 2-quart pan; keep fish warm.

Boil juices over high heat, uncovered, until reduced to ¾ cup, about 5 minutes. Mix cornstarch with 1 tablespoon water, and stir into pan juices. Stir over high heat until sauce boils. Pour a little sauce over fish; pour remainder into a small bowl. Season portions with sauce, salt, and pepper to taste. Serves 6. —*Karen Melander-Magoon, Guenoc Winery, Middletown, California*

Per serving: 163 cal. (20 percent from fat); 27 g protein; 3.7 g fat (0.8 g sat.); 3.9 g carbo.; 111 mg sodium; 121 mg chol.

Chicken with Ratatouille

2   teaspoons olive oil

1   large (about ½-lb.) onion, thinly sliced

1   medium-size (about 1¼-lb.) eggplant, stemmed and cut into ¾-inch cubes

3   large (about 1½ lb. total) bell peppers (use 1 color or a mixture of red, yellow, and green), stemmed, seeded, and cut into ¾-inch cubes

5   medium-size (about 1¼ lb. total) zucchini, ends trimmed and cut into ¾-inch cubes

4   medium-size (about 2 lb. total) firm-ripe tomatoes, peeled, cored, seeded, and chopped

2   cloves garlic, pressed or minced

1   teaspoon minced fresh or ½ teaspoon dried thyme leaves

1   teaspoon minced fresh or ½ teaspoon dried rosemary leaves

1   tablespoon chopped fresh or 1 teaspoon dried basil leaves

6   boned and skinned chicken breast halves (about 5 oz. each)
    Salt and pepper

In a 6- to 8-quart pan, stir 1 teaspoon oil and onion over medium heat until onion is limp, about 10 minutes. Add eggplant, bell peppers, zucchini, and tomatoes. Cover and simmer, stirring occasionally, until eggplant is very soft when pressed, about 30 minutes. Add garlic,

thyme, rosemary, and basil. Boil, uncovered, over high heat until all the liquid evaporates, about 15 minutes; stir often. Keep ratatouille warm.

Meanwhile, in a 10- to 12-inch nonstick frying pan over medium-high heat, cook chicken in 1 teaspoon oil, turning once, until meat is white in center (cut to test), 8 to 10 minutes total.

Spoon ratatouille equally on dinner plates. Slice chicken, lay equally on ratatouille. Add salt and pepper to taste. Serves 6.—*Dolores Cakebread, Cakebread Cellars, Rutherford, California*

Per serving: 278 cal. (14 percent from fat); 37 g protein; 4.2 g fat (0.8 g sat.); 25 g carbo.; 114 mg sodium; 82 mg chol.

Goat Cheese Ravioli with Cilantro Pesto

½   pound unripened goat cheese

1½ tablespoons chopped parsley

¾   teaspoon minced lemon peel (yellow part only)
    Ground white pepper
    36 won ton skins
    Cilantro pesto (recipe follows)

2   tablespoons drained oil-packed dried tomatoes, cut in slivers

2   tablespoons toasted pine nuts (see cilantro pesto recipe, following)

Mix cheese, parsley, and lemon peel with pepper to taste. Place about 2½ teaspoons cheese mixture in center of 1 won ton skin (keep remaining skins covered with plastic wrap). Brush skin around filling with water. Lay another skin on top of filling; with a 2½- to 3-inch-wide biscuit cutter, cut to make ravioli round; discard scraps. To seal, press skins close to filling with fingers.

As ravioli are cut, place on a floured 10- by 15-inch pan and cover with plastic wrap. Repeat to fill remaining won ton. (If making ahead, chill, covered, up to 6 hours.)

Equally spoon pesto onto 6 salad plates; spread slightly.

Meanwhile, bring 2½ to 3 quarts water to boiling in a 5- to 6-quart pan on high heat. Add ravioli; cook, uncovered, until skins are tender to bite,

2 to 3 minutes. With a slotted spoon, lift out ravioli, drain briefly, and place 3 on each plate. Garnish with tomatoes and nuts. Makes 6 first-course servings.—*Dolores Cakebread*

Per serving: 343 cal. (47 percent from fat); 16 g protein; 18 g fat (8.8 g sat.); 32 g carbo.; 592 mg sodium; 34 mg chol.

Cilantro pesto. In a 6- to 8-inch frying pan, shake 6 tablespoons **pine nuts** over medium heat until golden. Pour from pan.

In a 3- to 4-quart pan, bring about 2 quarts **water** to a boil over high heat. Immerse 2 cups (about 3 oz.) lightly packed coarsely chopped **spinach** and 1 cup (about 2 oz.) lightly packed coarsely chopped **fresh cilantro** (coriander) into water; cook just until they turn bright green, about 30 seconds. Drain and let cool. Press out excess water.

In a food processor or blender, smoothly purée spinach, cilantro, ⅓ cup water, ¼ cup of the pine nuts, and 1 clove **garlic** (optional). Add 1 or 2 tablespoons of **lemon juice,** and **salt** and **pepper** to taste. (If making ahead, cover and chill up to 6 hours.) Save extra nuts to garnish ravioli.

Cherry and Chocolate Trifle

1   cup chopped dried sweet cherries

¾   cup Cabernet Sauvignon

3   cups ½-inch cubes angel food cake (about ¼ lb. total)

6   tablespoons medium-dry sherry

     Custard sauce (recipe follows)

     Fresh mint sprigs

     Chocolate cabernet sauce (recipe follows)

In a 1- to 1½-quart pan, combine cherries and Cabernet Sauvignon. Cover and simmer over low heat until cherries are soft, about 5 minutes.

In each of 6 wine glasses or dessert bowls, layer 2 to 3 tablespoons cake, 1 teaspoon sherry, about 1½ tablespoons custard, and 1 tablespoon cherries; repeat layers 2

more times to use all ingredients. Cover and chill at least 2 hours or up to 1 day. Garnish with mint. Add chocolate sauce to taste. Serves 6.—*Dolores Cakebread*

Per serving: 299 cal. (23 percent from fat); 6.1 g protein; 7.8 g fat (4.3 g sat.); 46 g carbo.; 199 mg sodium; 1.2 mg chol.

Custard sauce. In a 1- to 1½-quart pan, mix 1½ tablespoons **sugar** and 4 teaspoons **cornstarch**. Stir in 6 tablespoons **liquid egg substitute** or 2 **large eggs**; add 1½ cups **nonfat milk**. Stir with a whisk over medium heat just until sauce boils, about 8 minutes; stir in 1½ teaspoons **vanilla**. Use warm or cool. Makes about 2 cups.

Chocolate cabernet sauce. In a 1- to 1½-quart pan over low heat, stir ¾ cup (4 oz.) chopped **bittersweet** or semisweet **chocolate** with ⅓ cup **Cabernet Sauvignon** until smooth, 3 to 5 minutes. Serve warm. Makes ½ cup.

Half-shell Oysters with Tangy Sauces

2   dozen chilled small to medium-size oysters, scrubbed and shucked

     Vinegar-soy sauce (recipe follows) and cocktail sauce

Serve oysters cold or on ice with sauces to add to taste. Makes 8 servings. —*Katie Wetzel Murphy, Alexander Valley Vineyards, Healdsburg, California*

Per plain oyster: 9.8 cal. (37 percent from fat); 1 g protein; 0.4 g fat (0.1 g sat.); 0.6 g carbo.; 16 mg sodium; 7.8 mg chol.

Vinegar-soy sauce. Mix ⅓ cup **balsamic vinegar,** ⅓ cup **soy sauce,** and 2 tablespoons thinly sliced **green onion.** Makes ⅔ cup.

Per tablespoon: 2.5 cal. (0 percent from fat); 0.2 g protein; 0 g fat; 0.5 g carbo.; 170 mg sodium; 0 mg chol.

Salsa di Pomodori

4   pounds firm-ripe Roma-type tomatoes, peeled and cored

½   cup extra-virgin olive oil

1   pound dried vermicelli

⅔   cup freshly grated Parmigiano-Reggiano or regular parmesan cheese

⅔   cup freshly grated romano cheese

¼   cup finely slivered fresh basil leaves

Cut tomatoes in half crosswise; squeeze out seeds. Thinly slice tomatoes. In a 10- to 12-inch frying pan, combine tomatoes and oil. Simmer, uncovered, until tomatoes disintegrate into a purée and oil separates when sauce is stirred, 45 to 60 minutes; stir often.

In a 5- to 6-quart pan, bring 2½ to 3 quarts water to a boil on high heat. Add pasta; cook, uncovered, until tender to bite, about 9 minutes; drain. Mix pasta, sauce, cheeses, and basil. Serves 8.—*Peter Mondavi, Jr., Charles Krug Winery, St. Helena, California*

Per serving: 434 cal. (42 percent from fat); 15 g protein; 20 g fat (3.7 g sat.); 52 g carbo.; 253 mg sodium; 13 mg chol.

Artichokes with Smoldering Shrimp

2   small (about ¾ lb. total) red bell peppers

1½   teaspoons olive oil

½   cup minced onion

¼   cup chopped celery

4   cloves garlic, minced or pressed

2   teaspoons minced fresh or ¾ teaspoon dried thyme leaves

2   teaspoons minced fresh or ¾ teaspoon dried oregano leaves

2   large packages (8 oz. each) neufchâtel (light cream) cheese

3   tablespoons mayonnaise

1   tablespoon vinegar

¼   to ½ teaspoon cayenne

1½   pounds shelled cooked tiny shrimp, drained and rinsed

8   large (3½- to 4-in.-wide) artichokes, cooked and chilled

2   tablespoons minced parsley

Cut bell peppers in half lengthwise. Lay cut side down in a 9-inch-wide pan. Broil about 4 inches from heat until charred, about 10 minutes. Let cool. Pull off and discard stems, seeds, and

skin. Set peppers aside.

In a 6- to 8-inch frying pan over medium-high heat, combine oil, onion, celery, garlic, thyme, and oregano; stir often until onion is limp, about 5 minutes.

In a food processor or blender, whirl roasted peppers, cheese, mayonnaise, vinegar, and cayenne until smooth. Transfer to a bowl; stir in onion mixture and shrimp.

Pull out center leaves of artichokes and scrape out fuzzy centers with a spoon. Fill artichokes equally with shrimp mixture. (If making ahead, chill airtight up to 1 day.) Sprinkle with parsley. Serves 8.—*Rollie Heitz, Heitz Wine Cellars, St. Helena*

Per serving: 375 cal. (48 percent from fat); 28 g protein; 20 g fat (9.4 g sat.); 25 g carbo.; 581 mg sodium; 212 mg chol.

Grilled Pork with Cumin

3   tablespoons soy sauce

3   tablespoons olive oil

3   tablespoons balsamic vinegar

¾   cup dry red wine

2   teaspoons ground cumin

2   teaspoons crushed dried hot red chilies

3   pork tenderloins (about 2½ lb. total), fat trimmed

In a large plastic food bag set in a large bowl, combine soy, oil, vinegar, wine, cumin, and chilies; mix well. Add pork; seal bag. Chill, turning occasionally, at least 2 hours or up to 1 day.

Lift pork from marinade and place on a grill 4 to 6 inches above a solid bed of medium-hot coals (you can hold your hand at grill level only 3 to 4 seconds); or use a gas grill, following manufacturer's directions.

Cook pork, turning to brown, until a thermometer inserted in thickest part reads 155°, a total of 20 to 35 minutes. Let meat rest about 5 minutes. Thinly slice across the grain. Serves 8.—*Paula Kornell, Hanns Kornell Family, St. Helena*

Per serving: 221 cal. (33 percent from fat); 33 g protein; 8 g fat (2.2 g sat.); 0.9 g carbo.; 269 mg sodium; 104 mg chol. ∎

By Linda Lau Anusasananan

NORMAN A. PLATE

USE A KETTLE-STYLE COVERED BARBECUE *to smoke-cook a Texas mixed grill of beef brisket, chicken, and spareribs.*

Where there's smoke, there's Texas barbecue

For aromatic, succulent meat, you need a covered barbecue and patience

O N A RECENT TREK to the Dallas–Fort Worth area, we found several barbecue masters who appeased our hankering for the local version of Texas barbecue. Among them, Sam Higgins—author and former caterer from Arlington—was very articulate about how to create succulent slow-cooked, smoked meats. Here he shares his acclaimed technique. As a bonus, he's tossed

SPRINKLE SOAKED *mesquite or hickory chips in small amounts onto coals for slow, steady smoke.*

in his recipe for an authoritative tomato-based barbecue sauce to serve with the meats.

With a covered barbecue and patience, you can duplicate his professional barbecue smoker-oven results at home.

WHEN THE CHIPS ARE DOWN

At the heart of most debates about which barbecue tastes best is the kind of wood used to smoke it. Most Texans favor mesquite or hickory, which home cooks can buy in chip form. Mesquite provides a mild, clean smokiness; hickory smoke is heavier and sweeter. The smoke flavor of choice is so essential to the formula of a barbecue that restaurants keep their wood supplies under lock and key.

Commercially smoked meats cook in specially constructed ovens, some of which are big enough to walk into. At one end of the oven, wood is burned down to coals. The meat goes into the oven, well away from direct heat of coals, and cooks for hours at carefully maintained (with regular addition of coals) low temperatures. When the meat emerges, it has the deep, rich color of mahogany.

THE BEEF COMES FIRST

In this state, where cattle reign, beef brisket sets the standard for good barbecue. When cooked long and slow, this fibrous, chewy cut becomes tender and moist. And when sliced across the grain, it's downright delicious. Serve it plain or tucked into soft buns with Sam Higgins's lively barbecue sauce.

While the beef cooks, other meats such as chicken, spareribs, sausages, and ham usually share grill and smoke, achieving equal succulence.

Higgins has reduced his massive recipe so it will work

on a standard covered (kettle) barbecue using charcoal briquets and wood chips. In this unit, you can smoke a beef brisket, a rack of pork spareribs, and a chicken—enough to serve 20 to 24 people.

The technique is easy. First, rub meats with a blend of salt, pepper, paprika, and chilies, then sear them briefly over hot coals to brown. Push the coals to one side of the firegrate; sprinkle them with a few soaked wood chips for slow, steady smoke, and place meats on the grill—but not over coals. Cover the barbecue and regulate vents to maintain a low temperature for at least 3 hours.

THE TEXAS TWO-STEP

After the brisket smoke-cooks, it needs 3 hours of slow oven-baking. This turns making Texas barbecue at home into a two-step process.

Higgins's recipe takes one rather long day; alternatives that follow split the cooking time between two days.

Texas Two-step Mixed Grill Barbecue

4 to 6 cups hickory or mesquite wood chips

1 broiler-fryer chicken (about 3½ lb.)

1 beef brisket (4 to 5 lb.)

1 rack (3 to 4 lb.) pork spareribs

   Pepper rub (recipe follows)

   Sam Higgins's sauce (recipe follows)

In a bowl, pour water over chips to cover; soak them at least 30 minutes. Split chicken in half lengthwise, rinse, and pat dry. Rub chicken, beef, and pork with pepper rub, using all.

Ignite 55 charcoal briquets on firegrate in a barbecue (about 22-in. diameter) with a lid. When coals are well dotted with gray ash, 30 to 40 minutes, spread in a single solid layer (coals must touch). Place grill 4 to 6 inches above coals. Cook chicken, beef, and ribs over coals on grill until browned, 3 to 5 minutes a side.

Lift off grill; mound coals against one side of firegrate. Put 3 briquets on coals; scatter 2 cups drained, soaked wood chips on coals. Replace grill and set all meats on grill, not over any coals.

Cover barbecue and open or close vents to maintain temperature between 200° and 225° for 1 hour. To measure temperature, insert a long-stemmed instant-read thermometer through vent in lid (if thermometer is left in place, smoke may discolor stem). For more heat, open vents; for less heat, partially close vents. If temperature drops so low that you are unable to increase it by opening vents, add 1 or 2 briquets to coals and open all vents until coals ignite.

After 1 hour, remove lid; using tongs or thick hot pads,

tilt up grill to expose coal mound; add 2 more briquets and 1 to 2 cups drained soaked chips (use smaller amount for milder smoke flavor). Replace grill and lid; continue smoking 1 hour, maintaining 200° to 225° temperature by adjusting vents. Repeat step, adding 2 more briquets and 1 to 2 cups soaked chips; cook until meat at thigh bone of chicken is no longer dark pink (cut to test) and meat pulls easily from sparerib bones, 1 to 1½ hours longer. (Smoke causes meat just under skin or at surface to turn bright pink.)

Remove meat from grill; chicken and ribs are ready to serve, but the beef takes more cooking. Seal beef in foil and set in a 9- by 13-inch pan. Bake in a 200° oven until meat is very tender when pierced, 2½ to 3 hours.

About 30 minutes before beef is done, seal chicken and ribs separately in foil and put in oven.

Drain and save beef juices; skim and discard fat. Reserve juices for barbecue sauce (recipe follows).

Serve the meats hot. (If making ahead, see two-step cooking options that follow.) Slice beef, cut ribs between bones, and cut chicken apart. Add barbecue sauce to taste. Serves 20 to 24.

Per serving: 377 cal. (67 percent from fat); 28 g protein; 28 g fat (11 g sat.); 1.2 g carbo.; 500 mg sodium; 104 mg chol.

Pepper rub. Mix 3 tablespoons **California** or New Mexico **ground chilies,** 3 tablespoons **paprika,** 1½ tablespoons **salt,** and 1½ tablespoons **pepper.**

Sam Higgins's sauce. In a 1½- to 2-quart pan, combine 1½ cups **catsup,** the reserved **beef juices** (from beef brisket, preceding) and enough water (or regular-strength beef broth) to make ¾ cup, ¾ cup **Worcestershire sauce,** ½ cup **lemon juice,** 6 tablespoons firmly packed **brown sugar,** ½ cup chopped **onion,** and 2

teaspoons **liquid hot pepper seasoning.**

Simmer, uncovered, until reduced to 3 cups, 35 to 40 minutes. Serve warm or cool; add more liquid hot pepper to taste. If making ahead, cover and chill up to 2 weeks. Makes 3 cups.

Per tablespoon: 19 cal.; 0.3 g protein; 0 g fat; 4.8 g carbo.; 137 mg sodium; 0 mg chol.

Two-day barbecue two-step. The first day, cook beef and finish it in the oven. Let cool and chill overnight. Next day, smoke-cook chicken and ribs; as they cook, heat beef packet in a close-fitting pan on grill.

Two-day oven two-step. Seal cool cooked meats in foil. Chill up to a day. To reheat, set wrapped beef in a close-fitting pan and other meats in packets, on oven racks or baking sheets; bake in a 200° oven until meats are hot in thickest part, about 2 hours for the beef and ribs, 1½ hours for the chicken. ■

By Linda Lau Anusasananan

Locals share favorite barbecue spots in the Dallas–Fort Worth area

Cowboy-booted ranchers, high-heeled fashion plates, and business-suited professionals rub shoulders as they devour Texas barbecue in the following restaurants—all of which get consistently high ratings locally. The mix of barbecue choices varies, but smoked beef brisket (sliced or chopped) is basic. Other likely options include pork spareribs, chicken, sausage, or ham, plus the inevitable side orders of coleslaw, beans, potato salad, corn on the cob, and onion rings. Prices for barbecue served as dinner range from $6.50 to $10; sandwiches cost around $3. Smoked meats can also be purchased to take home for around $8 to $9.50 per pound.

LINDA LAU ANUSASANANAN

TEXAS BARBECUE
restaurants attract loyal followings; these two are among the favorites in the Dallas area.

Angelo's, 2533 White Settlement Road, Fort Worth; (817) 332-0357. Open 11 to 10 Mondays through Saturdays. This local institution excels in juicy pork spareribs and well-spiced beef.

Baker's Ribs, 2724 Commerce Road, Dallas; (214) 748-5433. Open 11 to 7 Mondays through Thursdays, 11 to 9 Fridays and Saturdays. Customers line up for hickory-smoked pork spareribs rubbed with four kinds of pepper, and the tangy sauce.

Gaylen's Nationally Famous Barbecue, 826 N. Collins, Arlington; (817) 277-1945. Open 11 to 10 Mondays through Saturdays. This restaurant serves big, meaty pork spareribs. Help yourself to mild or spicy sauce to lavish onto smoked meats.

Mac's Bar-B-Que, 3933 Main Street, Dallas; (214)

823-0731. Open 11 to 2:30 weekdays. Since 1946, this family-owned operation has served fine barbecue in a crowded 50-seat restaurant. Customers vigorously endorse the stuffed baked potato topped with smoked beef and sauce.

N. Main Street B-B-Q, 406 N. Main Street, Euless; (817) 283-0884. Open 11:30 to 2 and 6 to 9 Fridays and Saturdays. This restaurant offers all-you-can-eat barbecue for only $10. It has twice won the title of "Rib Champion of the World." Bring your own beer.

Smokey John's Barbecue Depot, 6412 Lemmon Avenue, Dallas; (214) 352-2752. Open 11 to 7 Mondays through Saturdays, to 8 on Fridays. Well-seasoned meats make robust, succulent barbecue; the beef

gets raves.

Sonny Bryan's Smokehouse, 2202 Inwood Road, Dallas; (214) 357-7120. Open 10 to 4 weekdays, 10 to 3 Saturdays, 11 to 2 Sundays. Also at 302 N. Market Street; 744-1610. Open 11 to 10 Mondays through Thursdays, 11 to 11 Fridays and Saturdays, noon to 9 Sundays. And at 325 N. St. Paul Street; 979-0102. Open 10:30 to 2:30 weekdays. This old-timer, in operation since 1910, cooks a beef brisket that melts in your mouth. The oldest smokehouse, on Inwood, is small, crowded, and hot. Sit at old-fashioned school chairs with armrest tables and eat beef sandwiches off plastic plates. The Market Street location boasts air-conditioning, tables, and chairs.

The zucchini avalanche starts again

Don't be overwhelmed. There's more than one way to reveal or conceal the king of summer squash

Z UCCHINI JUST doesn't know when to stop. This fertile resident of the garden keeps growers and cooks busy trying to keep up with its unrelenting production.

Fortunately, this summer squash's mild flavor gives it versatility few other vegetables are known for; you can eat it almost every day in a different guise. For those who are skeptical, here's proof.

Zucchini Spaghetti

6 large (about 2½ lb. total) zucchini

2 or 3 cloves garlic, pressed or minced

3 cups spaghetti sauce (homemade or purchased), heated until hot

Grated parmesan cheese

Salt and pepper

Trim ends off zucchini. Push zucchini lengthwise over a shredder horizontally positioned, with cutting side up, to make long thin strands.

In 10- to 12-inch frying pan over high heat, stir garlic and zucchini until zucchini is hot, about 3 minutes. Pour

Zucchini Steam-sauté

1 small (about ¼-lb.) onion, thinly sliced
2 teaspoons chili powder
1 teaspoon cumin seed
1 teaspoon mustard seed
1 large (about 6-oz.) carrot, cut in matchstick-size slivers
3 large (about 1¼ lb. total) zucchini, ends trimmed, cut in matchstick-size slivers

Salt and pepper

In a 10- to 12-inch frying pan, combine 3 tablespoons water and onion. Stir often over medium heat until onion is limp, about 5 minutes. Stir in chili powder, cumin, and mustard until blended.

Add carrot and zucchini; stir often until tender-crisp to bite, about 3 minutes. Pour onto plates. Add salt and pepper to taste. Serves 6.

Per serving; 39 cal. (14 percent from fat); 1.9 g protein; 0.6 g fat (0 g sat.); 8 g carbo.; 22 mg sodium; 0 mg chol.

(Continued on page 174)

SUMMER'S NUMBER ONE SQUASH, *zucchini makes good eating from infancy to tender maturity. Start harvesting while flower is still attached (left), quit when the skin of club-size squash is tough to pierce. Mild golden or green varieties adapt to many flavors and presentations. Split and fill oversize ones with a Mexican seasoned beef and vegetable mixture (below), then bake for a hearty entrée.*

NORMAN A. PLATE

zucchini into a colander in sink; let drain 2 to 3 minutes. Transfer zucchini to a platter or wide bowl. Pour hot spaghetti sauce over zucchini noodles. Sprinkle with cheese. Mix well and serve at once, adding more cheese and salt and pepper to taste. Zucchini continues to drain if allowed to stand. Makes 4 servings.—*Shirley Blumberg, Mammoth Lakes, California*

Per serving: 246 cal. (34 percent from fat); 6.8 g protein; 9.3 g fat (1.4 g sat.); 38 g carbo.; 935 mg sodium; 0 mg chol.

Zucchini Polenta

1 cup polenta or yellow cornmeal
3 cups regular-strength chicken broth
2 cups shredded zucchini
½ cup shredded jack cheese (optional)

In a 3- to 4-quart pan, stir together polenta and broth. Continue stirring over high heat until boiling.

Mix in zucchini; simmer over low heat, stirring often, until polenta tastes smooth, about 10 minutes. Stir in cheese. Pour into serving bowl. Serves 4.

Per serving: 158 cal. (10 percent from fat); 5.4 g protein; 1.8 g fat (0.4 g sat.); 30 g carbo.; 43 mg sodium; 0 mg chol.

ZUCCHINI SHREDS DISAPPEAR *into chocolate cake as it bakes. The cake's moist texture is the only clue to the vegetable's presence.*

NORMAN A. PLATE

Zucchini Grande Olé

First, test texture of zucchini; if skin and flesh pierce easily with the tip of a sharp knife, it's good for cooking.

1 large (2- to 2½-lb., 13- to 14-in.-long, and fairly straight) zucchini, tested for cooking, preceding

½ pound ground lean beef

1 small (6-oz.) onion, chopped

1 small (about 6-oz.) red bell pepper, stemmed, seeded, and chopped

1 tablespoon chili powder

½ teaspoon ground cumin

1 can (4 oz.) diced green chilies

1 can (8 oz.) corn, drained

1 can (8 oz.) Mexican-style stewed tomatoes

¼ cup chopped fresh cilantro (coriander)

¼ cup fine dry bread crumbs

½ cup shredded jack cheese

Cilantro sprigs

Cut zucchini in half lengthwise. Scoop out and discard soft, seedy center. Scoop out enough flesh to make a ½-inch-thick zucchini shell. Coarsely chop flesh and reserve. Place squash, cut side up, in a 10- by 15-inch baking pan.

Meanwhile, in a 10- to 12-inch frying pan over high heat, frequently stir beef, onion, and bell pepper until meat is crumbled and browned, 8 to 10 minutes. Drain off and discard fat. Mix into pan the chili powder,

cumin, chilies, corn, tomatoes, and reserved chopped zucchini. Boil on high heat, uncovered, until most of the liquid evaporates, about 5 minutes; stir often. Mix in chopped cilantro, bread crumbs, and half the cheese. Spoon all filling equally into zucchini shells in pan.

Bake in a 350° oven until zucchini is soft when pierced and filling is hot in center, 30 to 40 minutes. Sprinkle filling with remaining cheese; bake until cheese browns lightly, 10 to 15 minutes longer. With wide spatulas, put zucchini on a platter. Garnish with cilantro sprigs. Cut into wide slices. Makes 4 to 6 servings.—*Catharine McNair, Stockton, California*

Per serving: 209 cal. (40 percent from fat); 13 g protein; 9 g fat (2.2

g sat.); 22 g carbo.; 491 mg sodium; 31 mg chol.

Chocolate Zucchini Rum Cake

About ¾ cup (⅜ lb.) butter or margarine, at room temperature

2 cups sugar

3 large eggs

2 cups lightly packed shredded zucchini

⅓ cup rum, brandy, or water

2½ cups all-purpose flour

1 cup chopped walnuts

1 cup semisweet-chocolate baking bits

½ cup unsweetened cocoa

2½ teaspoons baking powder

1½ teaspoons baking soda

1 teaspoon salt

¾ teaspoon ground cinnamon

¼ cup milk

Rum glaze (recipe follows, optional)

In a large bowl with an electric mixer, beat ¾ cup butter and sugar until smoothly blended. Beat in eggs, 1 at a time, until fluffy. With a spoon, stir in zucchini and rum.

Mix flour with nuts, chocolate, cocoa, baking powder, soda, salt, and cinnamon. Stir flour mixture and milk into egg mixture until well blended. Spread batter into a well-buttered and flour-dusted nonstick 10-inch plain or fluted tube pan.

Bake in a 350° oven until cake begins to pull from pan sides and springs back when firmly pressed in center, 50 to 55 minutes. Let cool in pan on a rack about 15 minutes. Invert from pan onto rack; let cool. Drizzle glaze over cake. Serve or store airtight up to 1 day. Makes 16 to 20 servings.—*Andee Zetterbaum, Modesto, California*

Per serving: 299 cal. (45 percent from fat); 4.5 g protein; 15 g fat (6.7 g sat.); 41 g carbo.; 352 mg sodium; 52 mg chol.

Rum glaze. Mix together until smooth 1⅔ cups **powdered sugar** and 3 tablespoons **rum** or water. Use within 1 hour. ∎

By Linda Lau Anusasananan

Pulses pulsate with microwaves

And dinner salad follows the news

MANY PEOPLE THINK of protein solely in terms of meat, milk, and eggs, but the vegetable world yields many proteins, too. The pulses (beans, peas, lentils, and such) are especially valuable because they contain lysine, one of the essential amino acids. Pulse and grain together are protein-rich and favored in many cuisines—like lentils and rice in India and hopping John in the Southern states.

Lawrence Stukel's Pinto Beans and Rice is an elegant version of hopping John. The elegance comes from the seasonings; convenience comes from canned beans and a microwave oven.

Pinto Beans and Rice

1 cup cooked long-grain brown rice

1 can (about 15 oz.) pinto beans, rinsed and drained

1 cup shredded rinsed and crisped iceberg lettuce

1 cup coarsely chopped tomato

1 small (about 3 oz.) red or green bell pepper, stemmed, seeded, and coarsely chopped

1 small (about ¼-lb.) onion, chopped

¼ cup chopped fresh cilantro (coriander) leaves

Prepared salsa

Unflavored nonfat yogurt

Salt

In a 2- to 3-quart bowl (microwave-safe), mix rice, beans, ½ cup lettuce, ½ cup tomato, ½ of the bell pepper, ½ of the onion, and ½ of the cilantro. Cover and cook in a microwave oven on full power (100 percent) for 3 minutes. Stir, cover, and cook until hot throughout, 1 to 2 minutes longer.

Stir in remaining lettuce, tomato, bell pepper, onion, and cilantro; spoon into individual bowls. Add salsa, yogurt, and salt to taste. Makes 5 cups; 2 or 3 servings.

Per serving: 187 cal. (7.7 percent from fat); 8.3 g protein; 1.6 g fat (0.2 g sat.); 36 g carbo.; 241 mg sodium; 0 mg chol.

Fountain Hills, Arizona

AS JANE McCREARY tells us, it's sometimes difficult for a person alone to figure out what to eat when the appetite lags.

One solution is this easy one-dish meal. She tosses romaine, avocado, mango, blue cheese, and thin-sliced red onions into a bowl, then watches the evening news.

When she decides that it's time to eat, she drizzles her salad with a simple dressing.

Jane's Salad

1½ to 2 cups bite-size pieces rinsed and crisped romaine leaves

1 tablespoon crumbled blue cheese

½ small (about ½ lb. whole) ripe mango, peeled and cut into bite-size pieces

½ large (about ½ lb. whole) ripe avocado, peeled, pitted, and diced

4 or 5 thin red onion slices

1 tablespoon salad oil

1 tablespoon cider vinegar

Pepper

TOSS SALAD *into a bowl to make a one-dish meal.*

In a wide soup bowl, combine romaine, blue cheese, mango, avocado, and onion. Combine oil and vinegar; pour over salad and mix well. Season to taste with pepper. Serves 1.

Per serving: 563 cal. (67 percent from fat); 8.2 g protein; 42 g fat (7.5 g sat.); 48 g carbo.; 151 mg sodium; 6.3 mg chol.

Glendale, California

By Joan Griffiths, Richard Dunmire

SUGAR-DUSTED NAPOLEON *pastry is filled with juicy, sliced peaches and buttery caramel sauce resting on a pillow of whipped cream.*

PETER CHRISTIANSEN

Peach pastry or peach ice cream

Aren't you glad it's summertime?

F RAGRANT, ROSY-hued peaches are among summer's most delightful treasures. Enjoy this juicy fruit in its prime as the stellar ingredient in these two show-off desserts.

Napoleons of split puff pastry layers, filled to the brim with peaches, almond-flavored cream, and lush caramel sauce, are the first appealing choice. In the second recipe, peaches, brown sugar, and sour cream are masterfully merged into a smooth ice cream.

To peel peaches, immerse fruit in boiling water to cover for 2 to 3 seconds. Lift out, cool briefly, and pull off skin.

Caramel Peach Napoleons

½ pound (half of a 17¼-oz. box) frozen puff pastry, thawed

1 tablespoon milk

¾ cup whipping cream

½ cup powdered sugar

½ teaspoon almond extract

3 medium-size (about 1 lb. total) firm-ripe peaches

1 tablespoon lemon juice

Caramel sauce (recipe follows)

On a lightly floured board, roll out pastry to form a 9- by 12-inch rectangle. Cut pastry into 6 rectangles, each 3 by 6 inches. With a spatula, transfer rectangles to a lightly oiled 12- by 15-inch baking sheet. Pierce the pastry all over with a fork, then brush evenly with milk.

Bake rectangles in a 350° oven until golden brown, about 20 minutes. With a spatula, carefully slide pastry onto a rack to cool. If making ahead, cool, wrap airtight, and hold at room temperature up to 1 day.

In a bowl, beat the cream, all but 1 tablespoon sugar,

and the almond extract on high speed until the cream holds soft peaks. If making in advance, cover and chill up to 2 hours.

Peel peaches (see preceding directions), pit, and cut into thin slices; mix slices with the lemon juice.

With a small, sharp knife, carefully split each pastry rectangle into 2 layers. Spread ⅙ of the cream mixture over base layer of each rectangle. Pile peach slices equally onto cream; drizzle each portion with about 1½ tablespoons caramel sauce. Set pastry tops on fruit. Dust napoleons with remaining sugar. Offer remaining caramel to add to taste. Serves 6.

Per serving: 302 cal. (57 percent from fat); 2.9 g protein; 19 g fat (6.7 g sat); 29 g carbo.; 192 mg sodium; 53 mg chol.

Caramel sauce. In a 1½- to 2-quart pan, melt 2 tablespoons **butter** or margarine over high heat. Add ¾ cup

sugar and ½ teaspoon **vanilla;** stir until sugar is melted and amber-colored, about 5 minutes.

Remove mixture from heat and slowly stir in ½ cup **whipping cream.** Let stand until room temperature. If making ahead, cover and chill up to 1 week. Bring sauce to room temperature before using. Makes 1 cup.

Per tablespoon: 71 cal. (47 percent from fat); 0.2 g protein; 3.7 g fat (2.3 g sat.); 9.6 g carbo.; 17 mg sodium; 12 mg chol.

Sour Cream–Brown Sugar Peach Ice Cream

1½   cups low-fat milk
1   cup half-and-half (light cream)
1   cup firmly packed light brown sugar
3   large egg yolks
1   teaspoon vanilla
9   medium-size (about 3 lb. total) ripe peaches
½   cup sour cream
2   tablespoons lemon juice

In a 3- to 4-quart pan over medium heat, combine milk, half-and-half, and sugar. Stir often until sugar dissolves.

In a bowl, beat yolks to blend. Whisk some milk mixture into yolks, then stir mixture back into pan. Stir over medium heat until mixture is thick enough to coat a metal spoon in a smooth layer, about 20 minutes. At once, set pan in ice water. Add vanilla; stir often until mixture is cool. Lift from water, cover, and chill until cold, at least 4 hours or up to 1 day.

Peel peaches (see directions, facing page), pit, and slice. Whirl fruit in a blender or food processor with sour cream and lemon juice until smoothly puréed; add to milk mixture. Freeze according to manufacturer's directions in a self-refrigerated ice cream maker, or in an electric or manual ice cream maker with 1 part salt to 6 parts ice, until the dasher is hard to turn. Serve, or freeze in an airtight container up to 1 week. Makes about 2 quarts.

Per ½ cup: 136 cal. (30 percent from fat); 2.4 g protein; 4.5 g fat (2.4 g sat); 23 g carbo.; 27 mg sodium; 49 mg chol. ■

By Christine Weber Hale

PETER CHRISTIANSEN

CILANTRO LEAVES *are a bold color and flavor element in main-dish shredded chicken salad.*

An Asian touch for lunch

EVERYDAY ASIAN FLAVORS IN A refreshing dressing make this dish reminiscent of the popular Chinese chicken salad, but much leaner. Instead of fried noodles as the base, you get lettuce.

Lean Chinese Chicken Salad

6   tablespoons seasoned rice vinegar (or rice vinegar and 1 tablespoon sugar)
2   teaspoons sugar
2   teaspoons Oriental sesame oil
    About 1 tablespoon soy sauce
2½   cups shredded cooked chicken
8   cups (about 1½ lb.) finely shredded rinsed and crisped iceberg lettuce
1   cup cherry tomatoes, rinsed and cut in half
½   cup thinly sliced green onions
½   cup fresh cilantro (coriander) leaves
6   to 8 large iceberg lettuce leaves, rinsed and crisped

In a large bowl, combine vinegar, sugar, oil, 1 tablespoon soy, and chicken. Add shredded lettuce, tomatoes, onions, and cilantro; mix. Mound salad equally onto leaves on 4 to 6 plates. Add soy to taste. Makes 4 to 6 servings.

Per serving: 177 cal. (32 percent from fat); 19 g protein; 6.3 g fat (1.4 g sat.); 11 g carbo.; 533 mg sodium; 52 mg chol. ■

By Karyn I. Lipman

Poached swordfish, Pacific-style

FISH AND COCONUT, STAPLES of South Pacific dishes, inspired this simple entrée. Coconut extract replaces richer coconut milk.

South Seas Swordfish

1½   cups regular-strength chicken broth
2   tablespoons minced fresh ginger
½   teaspoon coconut extract
1   to ¼ pounds swordfish, cut ¾ inch thick
1   pound rinsed and drained spinach leaves
3   cups hot cooked rice
1   tablespoon cornstarch blended with 1 tablespoon water
¼   cup lemon juice
    Salt

In a 10-to 12-inch frying pan over high heat, bring broth, ginger, and coconut extract to boiling. Add fish; cover and simmer until opaque but still moist-looking in thickest part (cut to test), about 10 minutes. Transfer fish to a platter; keep warm.

Add spinach to pan and stir on high heat until wilted, about 3 minutes. With a slotted spoon, put spinach on platter with rice. Add cornstarch mixture to pan; stir until boiling. Add lemon juice; pour over fish. Add salt to taste. Serves 4.

Per serving: 386 cal. (14 percent from fat); 31 g protein; 6 g fat (1.6 g sat.); 51 g carbo.; 219 mg sodium; 44 mg chol. ■

By Betsy Reynolds Bateson

NORMAN A. PLATE

CILANTRO *and lemon enhance fish.*

Creative ways with everyday foods—submitted by *Sunset* readers,
tested in *Sunset* kitchens, approved by *Sunset* taste panels

Overnight Fiery Oven Strata

Audrey Thibodeau, Fountain Hills, Arizona

- 9 or 10 slices (10 to 11 oz. total) firm-texture whole-wheat bread
- 2 cups thinly sliced mushrooms
- 1 cup sliced green onions, including tops
- 1 large can (7 oz.) diced green chilies
- 3 cups (¾ lb.) shredded sharp cheddar cheese
- 4 large eggs
- 2 large egg whites
- 2½ cups nonfat milk
- 1 tablespoon *each* dried ground mustard and liquid hot pepper seasoning
- 1 cup coarsely crushed tortilla chips
  Salt and prepared salsa

Line bottom of an 8- by 12-inch baking dish with 1 layer of bread (about ½); trim to fit and reserve scraps. Top bread with ½ the mushrooms, onions, chilies, and cheddar; repeat layers, starting with bread and scraps and ending with cheese.

Beat eggs and whites to blend with milk, mustard, and hot pepper seasoning; pour over mixture in casserole. Cover; chill at least 8 or up to 24 hours. Uncover and scatter chips over casserole. Bake in a 350° oven until golden, about 55 minutes; let stand for 15 minutes. Spoon out portions and season to taste with salt and salsa. Makes 8 to 10 servings.

Per serving: 319 cal. (48 percent from fat); 18 g protein; 17 g fat (8.5 g sat.); 25 g carbo.; 667 mg sodium; 123 mg chol.

STRATA *combines bread, cheese, eggs, and seasonings arranged in layers.*

Pasta, Spanish-style

Catherine Long, Santa Rosa, California

- ½ pound dried linguine
- 1 jar (6 oz.) marinated artichokes, quartered
- 2 cloves garlic, minced or pressed
- 1 tablespoon anchovy paste
- 1 can (2¼ oz.) sliced black ripe olives, drained
- ½ cup chopped parsley
  Parsley sprigs
  Freshly ground pepper
  Grated parmesan cheese

Half-fill a 5- to 6-quart pan with water; bring to a boil over high heat. Add linguine; cook, uncovered, until barely tender to bite, 8 to 9 minutes. Drain; return pasta to pan.

Meanwhile, drain marinade from artichokes into a 1- to 2-quart pan over medium heat; add garlic and stir often until pale gold, about 3 minutes. Add anchovy paste, ripe olives, and marinated artichokes; stir gently until hot, about 2 minutes.

Pour artichoke mixture over pasta. Add chopped parsley; mix and serve onto warm plates. Garnish with parsley sprigs. Add pepper and parmesan to taste. Makes 4 to 6 servings.

Per serving: 189 cal. (20 percent from fat); 6.6 g protein; 4.2 g fat (0.6 g sat.); 32 g carbo.; 353 mg sodium; 1.7 mg chol.

LINGUINE *with artichokes and olives goes with meats or makes a first course.*

Quick Pickled Vegetables

T. B., Lake Oswego, Oregon

- 1 cup diagonally sliced carrots
- 2 cups cauliflowerets
- ¾ pound slender green beans, ends trimmed
- 2 cups thin red bell pepper strips
- 1 medium-size (5-oz.) red onion, thinly sliced
- 1 small (about ½-lb.) cucumber, peeled and diagonally sliced
  Pickling mixture (recipe follows)

Pour ½ inch water into a 5- to 6-quart pan. Bring to a boil over high heat and add carrots, cauliflowerets, green beans, and pepper strips. Simmer, covered, until carrots are barely tender-crisp to bite, 2 to 4 minutes. Drain; put vegetables in a large noncorrodible bowl, and add onion and cucumber. Pour boiling pickling mixture over vegetables and let cool; stir occasionally. Cover and chill pickled vegetables until cold, at least 6 hours, or up to 2 weeks. Makes 1 quart.

Per ½ cup: 81 cal. (3.3 percent from fat); 2 g protein; 0.3 g fat (0 g sat.); 20 g carbo.; 15 mg sodium; 0 mg chol.

Pickling mixture. In a 2- to 3-quart pan over high heat, bring 2 cups **distilled white vinegar**, 2 cups **water**, 1½ cups **sugar**, 1 tablespoon **mustard seed**, 2 teaspoons **pickling spice**, and 1 **stick cinnamon** (about 3 in. long) to a boil, stirring. If making ahead, reheat to use.

VEGETABLES, *raw and cooked, soak in marinade. Serve, or chill up to 2 weeks.*

Grilled Salmon and Pineapple

J. Hill, Sacramento, California

- 3 tablespoons lime juice
- 3 tablespoons Oriental sesame oil
- 1 tablespoon *each* minced fresh ginger, brown sugar, and soy sauce
- 1 salmon fillet (2 lb. and about 1 in. thick in thickest part)
- 1 medium-size (3 to 3½ lb.) pineapple, peeled, cut into 6 slices, and cored
- 1 teaspoon sesame seed
- 1 tablespoon sliced green onion
  Lime wedges and salt

In large bowl, combine lime juice, oil, ginger, sugar, soy, salmon, and pineapple. Mix, cover, and chill for 30 to 45 minutes; mix occasionally. Drain.

In a 6- to 8-inch frying pan, shake sesame seed over medium heat until golden, about 4 minutes. Pour from pan and save.

Set fish, skin down, on foil cut to fit. In a barbecue with a lid, place fruit, and fish with foil, on a grill 4 to 6 inches above a solid bed of low-heat coals (you can hold your hand at grill level 5 to 6 seconds). Cover, open vents, and cook until fish is opaque but moist-looking in center, 10 to 12 minutes. Turn fruit to brown, about 10 minutes total. On a platter, top fish and fruit with sesame and onion. Add lime and salt to taste. Serves 6.

Per serving: 312 cal. (40 percent from fat); 31 g protein; 14 g fat (2 g sat.); 16 g carbo.; 155 mg sodium; 83 mg chol.

GRILLED SALMON *and pineapple have subtle Asian-style seasonings.*

Golden Potato Salad

Karen Mathieson, Seattle

- ½ pound slender green beans, ends trimmed
- 3½ pounds (about 2-in.-wide) red thin-skinned potatoes, scrubbed
- ¾ cup chopped yellow bell pepper
  About ⅓ cup regular-strength chicken broth
- 3 tablespoons red wine vinegar
- 1 tablespoon balsamic vinegar
- 1 tablespoon olive oil
- 1 teaspoon *each* ground turmeric, crushed anise seed, and dried tarragon leaves
  Salt and pepper

Bring about 3 inches water to a boil in a 5- to 6-quart pan on high heat. Add beans and cook, uncovered, until barely tender when pierced, about 3 minutes. Drain and at once immerse beans in ice water. Meanwhile, put potatoes in pan and barely cover with water; cover pan. Bring to a boil; simmer until potatoes are tender when pierced, 25 to 30 minutes. Drain and let cool; drain beans. Slice potatoes ½ inch thick; cut beans into 1-inch lengths.

In a large bowl, combine bell pepper, ⅓ cup broth, red wine and balsamic vinegars, oil, turmeric, anise, and tarragon. Add potatoes and beans; mix gently. Add a little more broth if you want a moister salad. Season to taste with salt and pepper. Serves 8.

Per serving: 190 cal. (10 percent from fat); 4.5 g protein; 2.2 g fat (0.2 g sat.); 39 g carbo.; 19 mg sodium; 0 mg chol.

POTATO SALAD *with green beans is tinted by turmeric; it's light for summer.*

Tri-City Brownie Ice Cream Cake

K. T. Fingerson, Richland, Washington

- 2½ cups vanilla ice cream
  Brownie (recipe follows)
- 1 cup purchased fudge sauce
- ⅓ cup pecan halves

Let ice cream stand in refrigerator until easy to scoop, about 10 minutes; spread smoothly over brownie. Cover and freeze until firm, about 2 hours. Spread fudge sauce over ice cream; arrange pecans on fudge. Wrap airtight and freeze until firm, 2 hours or up to 1 week. Let stand at room temperature for 15 minutes. Remove pan rim. Cut into wedges. Serves 10.

Per serving: 400 cal. (45 percent from fat); 5.5 g protein; 20 g fat (9.7 g sat.); 55 g carbo.; 140 mg sodium; 71 mg chol.

Brownie. In a 2- to 3-quart pan over medium-low heat, stir ¼ cup (⅛ lb.) **butter** or margarine and 2 ounces **unsweetened chocolate** until melted. Off the heat, add 1 cup **sugar, 2 large eggs,** 1 teaspoon **vanilla,** ½ cup **all-purpose flour,** and ½ **cup chopped pecans** (optional); stir to mix well.

Scrape batter into a buttered, floured 8-inch-diameter cake pan with removable rim. Bake in a 350° oven until brownie just begins to pull from pan side, about 22 minutes; let cool. Remove rim, slide a spatula beneath brownie to separate from pan bottom but leave on pan. Set brownie back in rim.

Compiled by Elaine Johnson

ICE CREAM *and fudge sauce top brownie base; pecans decorate this dessert.*

September Menus

QUICK, SEASONAL,
BUDGET-WISE . . .
FOR FAMILY AND
FRIENDS

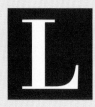

Lazy cooks have it easy this month. Wonderful produce is overwhelming gardens and markets; take advantage of nature's generosity and focus on single, wholesome foods for fabulously simple meals. Here we zero in on two—at their ripest and best value—and put them center stage.

Some warm evening, eat your fill of sweet corn; for a quick, any-day lunch, savor a salad of really ripe tomatoes with a fresh cheese.

Because corn and tomatoes are favorites as motifs in serving pieces (see top right), check your shelves; you might have such dishes hidden away.

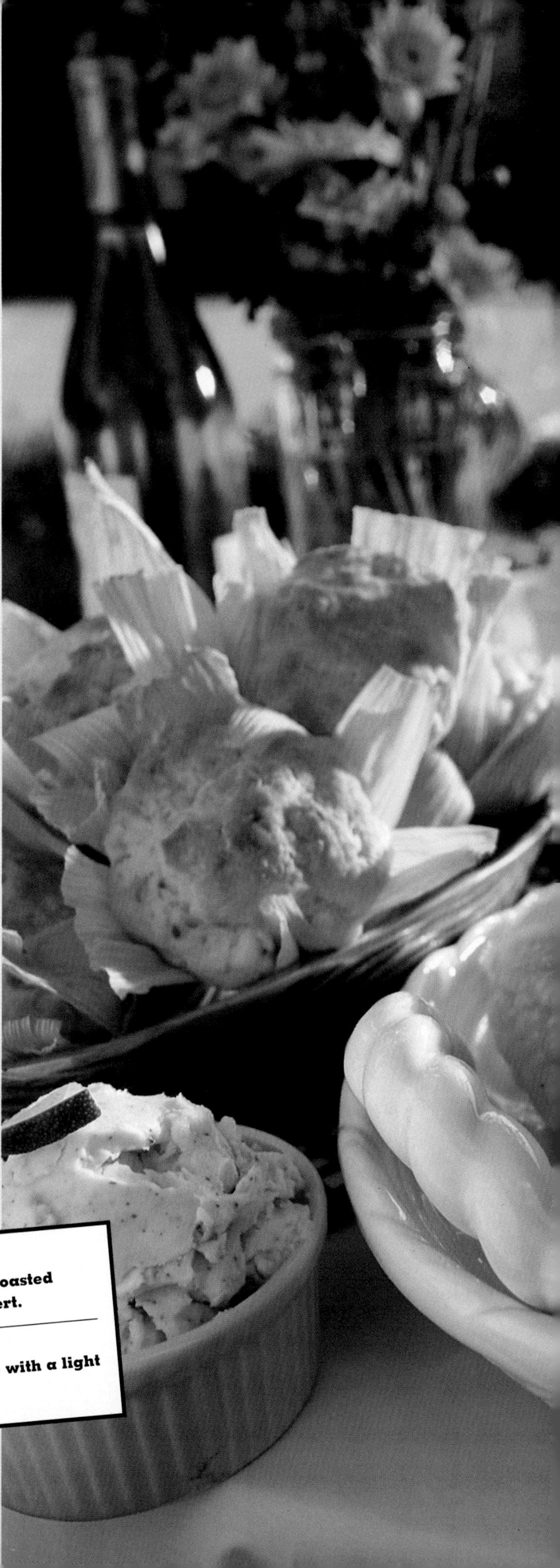

PETER CHRISTIANSEN

CORN FEAST (at right)
Slather hot corn with various spreads; serve with roasted sausage chunks and muffins. Have melon for dessert.

TOMATO LUNCH (page 182)
Really ripe tomatoes and fresh mozzarella cheese with a light dressing make a grand summer classic.

THE DETAILS

Corn Fun

For a corn menu, corn design in serving pieces is an amusing accent.

Pan Liners

Dry cornhusk strips make decorative liners for muffins as they bake.

Hot Ears, Cool Fingers

Impale ends of hot corn with corn holders to protect fingers.

Fruit Splash

Use fruit syrup, fruit liqueur, or lemon juice to moisten melon wedges.

To reduce last-minute activities, start up to a day ahead by organizing the butters and cheese for the corn, roasting chunks of Italian sausage, and measuring dry ingredients for the muffins. Then, while water for corn comes to a boil, make the muffins.

Plain melon is fine, or dress it up with a splash of fruit syrup or liqueur (black raspberry, cassis, orange).

Boiled Corn with Lime, Butters, and Cheese

16 to 24 medium-size ears of corn, husks and silks removed

Lime wedges

Flavored butters (suggestions follow)

About 1 cup soft cheese such as boursin or rondelé, flavored with herbs (optional)

Salt, pepper, and crushed dried hot red chilies

Rinse and drain corn; if husking ahead, cover corn with damp towels and chill up to 4 hours.

Half-fill a 16- to 20-quart pan (or 2 smaller pans of equal volume) with water. Cover and bring water to a boil over high heat. Carefully drop corn into boiling water; cover, remove from heat, and let stand until kernels look slightly darker in color, about 10 minutes. Serve corn on a platter or from hot water. Have lime wedges, butters, and cheeses in small bowls.

To eat, season corn as desired: rub ears with lime and sprinkle with salt and pepper or chilies, or spread with the flavored butters or cheese. Makes 8 servings, 2 or 3 ears each.

PETER CHRISTIANSEN

SHOW OFF *juicy ripe tomatoes—any color you like—as a main salad with cheese and a crusty loaf of bread.*

Per ear with lime juice: 78 cal. (13 percent from fat); 2.9 g protein; 1.1 g fat (0.2 g sat.); 17 g carbo.; 14 mg sodium; 0 mg chol.

Flavored butters. Choose 1 or several flavors (following); if making ahead, cover and chill up to 2 days. To make each flavor, beat ¼ cup (⅛ lb.) **butter** or margarine, at room temperature, to blend with 1 of the following combinations. Allow about ½ tablespoon flavored butter for each ear of corn.

Hot-sour butter. Add ½ teaspoon grated **lime peel**, 1 tablespoon **lime juice**, and ¼ teaspoon **cayenne.** Makes about ¼ cup.

Per ½ tablespoon: 54 cal. (100 percent from fat); 0.1 g protein; 6 g fat (3.7 g sat.); 0.2 g carbo.; 61 mg sodium; 16 mg chol.

Wasabi butter. Add 1 tablespoon chopped **fresh cilantro** (coriander) and 1 tablespoon **wasabi powder** (Japanese horseradish) or prepared horseradish. Makes about ¼ cup.

Per ½ tablespoon: 54 cal. (100 percent from fat); 0.1 g protein; 6 g fat (3.7 g sat.); 0.2 g carbo.; 63 mg sodium; 16 mg chol.

Bacon butter. Add ¼ cup chopped cooked **bacon.** Makes about ½ cup.

Per ½ tablespoon: 28 cal. (93 percent from fat); 0.4 g protein; 2.9 g fat (1.6 g sat.); 0 g carbo.; 45 mg sodium; 7.3 mg chol.

Cumin Muffins

16 strips dried cornhusks, about 2 inches wide and 6 to 8 inches long (optional)

2¼ cups all-purpose flour

2½ teaspoons baking powder

½ teaspoon baking soda

1 tablespoon sugar

1 teaspoon cumin seed

½ cup (¼ lb.) butter or margarine, cut into chunks

1¼ cups buttermilk

Discard any debris on cornhusks. Place husks in a bowl and pour boiling water over them; soak until pliable, 10 minutes or up to 1 day. Drain husks and pat dry.

In a bowl, combine flour, baking powder, baking soda, sugar, and cumin seed. With 2 knives or a pastry blender, cut butter into flour mixture until coarse crumbs form; add buttermilk and stir until mixture holds together.

Crisscross 2 husk strips over center of each of 8 buttered muffin cups (2½ in. wide); if husks are not used, line cups with paper baking cups. Divide dough equally among cups, pushing husks down. Bake in center of a 375° oven until muffins are browned, about 35 minutes. Serve hot or warm. Makes 8.

Per muffin: 261 cal. (45 percent from fat); 5.1 g protein; 13 g fat (8 g sat.); 31 g carbo.; 399 mg sodium; 35 mg chol.

This meal is so easy and quick that the salad recipe is mostly a shopping guide.

Sliced Tomatoes with Herb Dressing and Fresh Cheese

About 2½ pounds (4 or 5 large) ripe tomatoes, any color, rinsed or peeled, and cored

½ to ⅔ pound fresh (buffalo) or regular mozzarella cheese, or Mexican-style panela

2 tablespoons extra-virgin olive oil

¼ cup red wine vinegar

1 tablespoon chopped fresh basil leaves

1½ teaspoons chopped fresh or ½ teaspoon dried thyme leaves

Fresh basil sprigs

Salt and pepper

Slice tomatoes and cheese, overlapping, on a platter. Mix oil, vinegar, and chopped basil and thyme; pour over salad. Garnish with basil sprigs and add salt and pepper to taste. Serves 4.

Per serving: 278 cal. (65 percent from fat); 12 g protein; 20 g fat (1.1 g sat.); 15 g carbo.; 64 mg sodium; 40 mg chol. ■

By Karyn I. Lipman

Tailgate Traditions

It's kickoff time *for tailgate picnics and college football around the West. Here's a lineup of recipes, plus an insider's guide to some great football towns (page 186).*

TAILGATE CHEFS *grill garlic steak sandwiches for friends as part of annual picnic at Stanford. See recipe on page 185.*

PETER CHRISTIANSEN

All-star tailgates: big on flavor— and tradition

By Christine Weber Hale and Bill Crosby

COLLEGE FOOTBALL IS about tradition, from The Axe to the Apple Cup, from a cross-state rivalry that preceded statehood to shared remembrances of hallowed quarterbacks, coaches, games, and plays.

Part of that tradition is tailgating. It's around bountiful tailgate spreads outside the West's college stadiums that the tales of yesterday's heroes live on and the flames of excitement over today's heroes are fanned like briquets on the hibachi. It's oral tradition: beer, wine, soft drinks, and a regional, seasonal, movable feast. It's Sixkiller and salmon, Brodie and beef, Curly Culp and Chili-Cheese Triangles. It's college football heaven.

Here, we share nine recipes inspired by some of the most ardent tailgaters in the West. These offerings are as likely to win fans among your family and friends as they have among the Cardinal, Husky, and Sun Devil fans who shared them with us.

Cardinal tradition: garlic steak barbecue down on The Farm

Rob Christopher's family grows garlic around Gilroy, California. In fact, they grow more fresh garlic than any other grower in the United States. After Rob (pictured at left) went off to Stanford University in 1972, his dad, Don, decided he'd host an annual tailgate party: for The Big Game versus Cal, when it's played at Stanford, and in alternate years, before the USC game.

But this is no ordinary pregame party, unless you consider a country-folk band, 12 running feet of barbecue grills, and upward of 400 guests typical. Fans who have been lucky enough to sample the Christophers' signature sandwich, featuring the stinking rose, of course, hold it in the same regard they afford John Elway, Jim Plunkett, and Frankie Albert.

Christopher Ranch Garlic Steak Sandwiches

2 large (about 1 lb. total) green bell peppers, stemmed, seeded, and cut into thin strips

2 large (about 1 lb. total) red bell peppers, stemmed, seeded, and cut into thin strips

1 large (about ½-lb.) onion, coarsely chopped

6 cloves garlic, minced
  Garlic butter (recipe follows)

1 flank steak, 1¼ to 1½ pounds

8 crusty sandwich rolls (each about 6 in. long)

(Continued on page 186)

185

In a 5- to 6-quart pan over medium-high heat, combine peppers, onion, garlic, and 2 tablespoons garlic butter. Stir often until vegetables are browned and onions taste sweet, about 30 minutes; keep warm.

Lay flank steak on a grill 4 to 6 inches above a solid bed of hot coals (you can hold your hand at grill level only 2 to 3 seconds). Turn meat to brown evenly until it reaches desired doneness; allow 10 to 14 minutes total for rare.

Meanwhile, cut rolls in half lengthwise and brush cut sides with remaining garlic butter. Lay rolls, buttered side down, on grill, and toast until golden brown, about 1 minute.

On a board, slice steak thinly across the grain. Fill rolls equally with sliced meat, any juices, and the pepper-garlic mixture. Makes 8.

Per sandwich: 350 cal. (31 percent from fat); 20 g protein; 12 g fat (5.1 g sat.); 40 g carbo.; 436 mg sodium; 43 mg chol.

Garlic butter. Mash together ½ cup (¼ lb.) **butter** or margarine, at room temperature, and 4 cloves minced

garlic. If making ahead, cover airtight and chill up to 1 day.

Per tablespoon: 105 cal. (100 percent from fat); 0.2 g protein; 12 g fat (7.2 g sat.); 0.7 g carbo.; 118 mg sodium; 31 mg chol.

Grilled Ratatouille-Cheese Sandwiches

As an alternative to beef, here's a meatless sandwich that's surprisingly hearty. Thread vegetables onto metal skewers at home and carry to your outing to grill. You'll need six to eight skewers, each about 14 inches long.

1   medium-size (about 1 lb.) eggplant, stem trimmed, cut into 1-inch chunks

2   medium-size (⅔ lb. total) zucchini, ends trimmed, each cut diagonally into 8 equal slices

2   large (about 1 lb. total) red bell peppers, stemmed, seeded, and cut into 1½-inch pieces

1   large clove garlic, minced or pressed

⅓   cup olive oil

3   tablespoons lemon juice

SPATHIS & MILLER

TENDER CHUNKS *of vegetables team up in* Grilled Ratatouille-Cheese Sandwiches.

2   tablespoons coarsely chopped fresh or 2 teaspoons dried basil leaves

1   tablespoon chopped fresh or 1 teaspoon dried marjoram leaves

6   medium-size (1 lb. total) Roma-type tomatoes, cut in half lengthwise

1   long loaf (1 lb.) flat

Italian bread (*ciabatta*) or sourdough bread

3   cups (¾ lb.) shredded fontina cheese

Fresh basil sprigs (optional)

Thread eggplant, zucchini, and bell pepper pieces separately onto skewers. Combine garlic, oil, lemon juice, chopped basil, and marjo-

5 College towns that score big

Fresno State University

FSU's 13-year-old Bulldog Stadium was built for tailgating. It's ringed by fenced lawn that's thrown open to rabid red-frocked fans 4 hours before each game. Pickups towing their barbecues are the hub of the most elaborate tailgate parties; since games are played Saturday nights, lanterns, table lamps, and portable generators are de rigueur. Grape prunings from local vineyards give a regional flavor, literally, to some of the grandest barbecues.

Ambience, spirit. All those red shirts are as likely to be emblazoned with the logo of an agricultural supply outfit or church group as with a bulldog. The aura is more local pro team than hometown college, and the Bulldogs are the biggest show in town.

The battlefield. Think of a gimmick, and 41,031-seat Bulldog Stadium has it: skyboxes, big-screen television for instant replays and commercials, even a golf cart shaped like a giant Bulldog helmet. The elite seats (for season ticket holders) are between the 20-yard lines on both sides of the field; they have their own concessions, their own rest rooms, even their names on the seats. Have

a beer to wash down the stadium's signature treat, sunflower seeds.

How about those 'Dogs? This whole setup is clearly meant for something bigger, and the Bulldogs are getting there; just ask USC (victims of the 'Dogs in last year's Freedom Bowl). Why go to Norman, Lincoln, or College Station when there's Fresno?

The 'Dogs are clearly stoked about having switched conferences last season from the Big West to the Western Athletic Conference. They certainly have a wideopen WAC offense; the first play from scrimmage against Utah last year was a halfback option for 92 yards. Junior QB Trent Dilfer is back for '93, and they're talking Heisman Trophy in Fresno. Dilfer, a second-team All-

OTTO GREULE, JR./ALLSPORT

FSU BULLDOG *on the prowl.*

ram. Lightly brush vegetables and tomatoes with some of the oil mixture. If making ahead, place skewers and tomatoes in a 10- by 15-inch pan, wrap airtight, and chill up to 6 hours. Pour remaining oil mixture into a leakproof container and hold at room temperature up to 6 hours.

In a barbecue with a lid, place skewers on a grill 4 to 6 inches above a solid bed of medium coals (you can hold your hand at grill level only 4 to 5 seconds). Cook 12 minutes, turning to brown evenly. Place tomatoes, skin down, on grill. Turn skewers, as needed, until all vegetables are very tender when pressed, about 10 minutes longer. Transfer vegetables to a platter; remove skewers.

Meanwhile, cut bread diagonally into 3 equal pieces, then split each piece horizontally. If needed, trim crust so bread sits steady. Brush cut sides with remaining oil mixture. Place bread, cut side down, on grill until toasted, about 3 minutes. Off the grill, top toasted sides equally with cheese, then vegetables.

Set bread on grill, cheese up; cover barbecue, open vents, and cook until cheese melts, 3 to 4 minutes (be careful not to scorch bottom of bread). Garnish with basil sprigs. Serves 6.—*Elaine Johnson*

Per serving: 595 cal. (47 percent from fat); 24 g protein; 31 g fat (13 g sat.); 57 g carbo.; 911 mg sodium; 67 mg chol.

Husky tradition: fans and salmon arrive by water

Where else will a university's water taxi pick you up from your yacht and ferry you to the dock just outside the stadium? Taking a cue from the remarkable waterside setting of University of Washington's Husky Stadium in Seattle, we present a recipe for grilled salmon that comes to us from a UW alumni barbecue cookoff held at a recent Rose Bowl. We also share a pear salad which uses one of the state's favorite crops, and a hearty apple and pork stew that should satisfy football

PETER CHRISTIANSEN

SALMON FILLET, *marinated in vermouth and lemon juice, is grilled and served with lemon and onion slices.*

American, directed the nation's highest-scoring offense; his 21 TD passes placed him fifth nationally.

Extracurriculars. At the intersection of Shaw and Cedar avenues, the Bulldogmania shop is open game nights for any last-minute sweatshirts, sponge fingers, or pompons fans might need.

Take some delectable local Armenian cuisine to the game: George's Shish Kebob, 4081 Blackstone Avenue (just south of Ashlan Avenue), will pack to go its namesake dish or anything else on the menu.—*Bill Crosby*

Portland State University

Two great things about PSU football are the wonderfully weird stadium where it's played and its downtown location. An easy walk from the campus, the rest of downtown, or the Nob Hill or Northwest neighborhoods, old Civic Stadium is virtually ringed by a prodigious number of fine watering holes, among them the Bullpen, the Driftwood Room, Goose Hollow Inn, The Kingston Saloon, and The Ram's Head. Better to share a pitcher of Henry's, check up on other games in progress, and play a little state-sponsored video poker within the cozy confines of The Kingston than to stand in the cold and the dark for the $3-a-head pregame fete in a parking lot across from the stadium.

Ambience, spirit. This is a serious school; 1992 home-

coming highlights included all sorts of seminars and a lecture by National Public Radio reporter Susan Stamberg. Nevertheless, PSU always ranks among the top-drawing NCAA Division II colleges (12,000 average attendance last year). Why? The team is good (five playoffs in the past six years), and the place is wacky.

Sure, there are the usual cheerleaders and mascots. But the "band" is a combo that plays Led Zeppelin's *Immigrant Song* as the rallying riff; it also does a fine rendition of *Low Rider.* The National Anthem was played as a trumpet solo in fine lounge lizard form.

The battlefield. Make no mistake: this is a baseball stadium, and a fine one at that, despite the plastic turf. It's as though Pacific Coast League baseball lives on through autumn as

PORTLAND STATE UNIVERSITY

PSU VIKING *girds for battle.*

PETER CHRISTIANSEN

fans from schools on both sides of the Cascades.

UW Alumni Grilled Salmon

⅓ cup lemon juice

⅓ cup dry vermouth

1 boned salmon fillet with skin, about 2½ pounds

1 small (about ¼-lb.) onion, very thinly sliced

2 lemons, very thinly sliced and seeds removed

Cucumber sauce (recipe follows)

Salt and pepper

Pour lemon juice and vermouth into a 1-gallon-size plastic food bag. Add salmon, onion, and lemon slices to bag; seal. Rotate bag to mix well. Chill at least 20 minutes or up to 1 day.

Mound 24 charcoal briquets on firegrate of a barbe-cue with a lid. Ignite coals.

Drain and discard marinade from bag. Set salmon, skin side down, on a slightly larger piece of heavy foil; fold or trim foil to fit outline of fish. Lay onion and lemon slices on top of fish.

When coals are dotted with ash, in about 25 minutes, push half of them to each side of the firegrate. Set grill 4 to 6 inches above coals. Set salmon with foil in

FLOATING TAILGATES *are held on boats docked by Husky Stadium (left). Apples from orchards east of the Cascades simmer with pork and sausage in Northwest Apple and Pork Stew.*

PSU football. Summer supporters of the Portland Beavers may well supply the bulk of fall Vikings fans.

The 50-yard-line seats in the left-field bleachers are 60 yards from the sideline. Over the right-field wall (the south end zone), the fitness buffs in the posh Multnomah Athletic Club watch the game through picture windows while working out on treadmills and StairMasters. The 18-foot-long Jantzen lady still swims over the left-field wall, though she looks a tad cold on November nights. Between them on the outfield fences, it's billboards, billboards, billboards. The old stadium really echoes. Sit in the upper deck and you'll stand a fair chance of looking around a post.

How about those Vikings? A perennial Division II powerhouse, PSU looks to make the play-offs again this season, the first as an independent in a decade. Quarterback-of-the-future Bill Matos got early experience at the end of last season, when star John Charles's college ca-

reer ended with a broken wrist. PSU has a rich history of record-setting signal callers; recall Neil Lomax throwing eight TD passes to lead the Vikings to a 105-0 victory over Delaware State in 1980.

Extracurriculars. All of Portland is at your feet, so go wild! The stadium, just off main drag Burnside Street, is just up the hill from the lively downtown.—*B. C.*

Washington State University, Pullman

In the heart of the Palouse wheat fields, Pullman is a true land-grant college town. Its population of about 7,000 swells to 24,000 during the school year, and on Saturdays Martin Stadium hosts a 4-hour population averaging 32,000 (or its 40,000 capacity for big games). Fair-weather teams fear playing the Cougars around Halloween: the "curse of the Palouse"—and the fickle weather—has helped the underdog Cougars triumph (Continued on page 190)

WASHINGTON STATE UNIVERSITY

WSU COUGARS *plot strategy in '92 Apple Cup win.*

center of grill (not over coals). Cover barbecue and open vents. Cook until the thickest part of salmon is opaque but still moist-looking (cut to test), 25 to 30 minutes. Supporting with foil and spatulas, transfer salmon to a large platter. Serve hot or cool. If making ahead, cool, cover, and chill up to 1 day.

To transport cold salmon, wrap airtight and keep it cold in an insulated container. Accompany with cucumber sauce; add salt and pepper to taste. Serves 8.— *Delaware Valley Chapter, University of Washington Alumni Group*

Per serving: 207 cal. (38 percent from fat); 27 g protein; 8.7 g fat (1.3 g sat.); 4.4 g carbo.; 62 mg sodium; 74 mg chol.

Cucumber sauce. Peel, seed, and finely chop 1 large (about ½-lb.) **cucumber.** Mix cucumber with 1 cup **light** (reduced-calorie) or regular **sour cream** and 1 tablespoon chopped **fresh dill.** If making ahead, cover airtight and chill up to 1 day. Transport sauce in an insulated bag. Makes 2 cups.

Per tablespoon: 13 cal. (69 percent from fat); 0.5 g protein; 1 g fat (0.5 g sat.); 0.7 g carbo.; 0.4 mg sodium; 2.5 mg chol.

Washington Pear Salad

⅓ cup hazelnuts

½ cup balsamic or red wine vinegar

3 tablespoons honey

3 tablespoons minced crystallized ginger

8 small or 4 large (about 2 lb. total) firm-ripe Bartlett pears

2 tablespoons lemon juice

Leaf lettuce, rinsed and crisped (optional)

Pour nuts into an 8- to 9-inch pie pan. Bake in a 350° oven until nuts are golden brown under skin, about 20 minutes. Pour nuts from pan onto a clean towel. Rub briskly with towel to remove as much of the nuts' papery husks as possible; discard husks. Coarsely chop nuts. If

making ahead, store airtight up to 2 days.

Mix vinegar, honey, and ginger for dressing. If making ahead, cover and chill up to 2 days.

Cut pears in half, core, and immediately brush cut sides with lemon juice. Arrange pear halves on a platter with lettuce leaves. Spoon dressing and nuts over the fruit. Serves 8.

Per serving: 139 cal. (22 percent from fat); 1.1 g protein; 3.4 g fat (0.2 g sat.); 29 g carbo.; 4.9 mg sodium; 0 mg chol.

Northwest Apple and Pork Stew

1½ pounds fat-trimmed and boned pork shoulder or butt, cut into 1½-inch cubes

¾ pound mild Italian sausage, casings removed, crumbled into bite-sized pieces

1 large (about ½-lb.) onion, chopped

4 cups regular-strength beef broth

1 cup regular or hard cider

¼ cup lemon juice

1 tablespoon grated lemon peel

1 teaspoon caraway seed

2 pounds firm, tart-sweet apples (such as Fuji, Granny Smith, or Golden Delicious), cored, peeled, and cut into ½-inch chunks

2 tablespoons cornstarch mixed with ¼ cup water

Minced parsley

Salt and pepper

In a 5- to 6-quart pan over medium-high heat, combine pork, sausage, and onion. Cover and cook until meat gives off juices, about 15 minutes. Uncover and boil over high heat until juices evaporate and brown bits stick in pan. Add ½ cup broth, stir to free browned bits, and boil until liquid evaporates. If possible, drain off and discard any fat.

To pan, add remaining broth, cider, lemon juice, peel, and caraway. Cover and simmer until pork is very tender when pierced, about 1¼ hours. Add apple chunks; cover and simmer until apples are tender when pierced, 10 to 20 minutes. Stir

TOASTED HAZELNUTS *top Washington Pear Salad, a refreshing starter for a tailgate picnic. The make-ahead honey dressing is accented by balsamic vinegar and crystallized ginger.*

cornstarch mixture into stew; stir until bubbling.

To transport hot stew, cover and carry in an insulated bag, or put into a large (at least 1-gal.) thermos. Serve within 3 hours. Sprinkle with parsley, and add salt and pepper to taste. Serves 8.

Per serving: 328 cal. (41 percent from fat); 24 g protein; 15 g fat (5.2 g sat.); 24 g carbo.; 358 mg sodium; 81 mg chol.

Arizona tradition: rival schools catch tailgate fever

Long before Arizona was a state, Arizona State University (then Tempe Normal School) and the University of Arizona began battling: their first match was in 1899; the Copper State became number 48 in 1912. Given the ancient—and intense—relationship between the two schools, it's remarkable they got together to celebrate one thing they do share: a love of tailgating.

Susan Shaffer, who works

SPATHIS & MILLER

TRIO OF CHILIES *provides firepower for cooked salsa; omit chili seeds for milder taste.*

in the ASU football office, collected recipes from coaches and their wives, serious tailgaters, and other football friends at Arizona schools. These recipes are published in *Tailgate Fever Cookbook* (Golden West

Publishers, Phoenix, 1992; $9.95; to order, call 800/658-5830). The first two recipes we present, "Whip Them Cats" Salsa and Chili-Cheese Triangles, were adapted from the cookbook. The third, Sun Devil Squares, is our own cre-

ation featuring two of Arizona's tasty exports—pecans and oranges.

"Whip Them Cats" Salsa

Remove seeds from jalapeño and serrano chilies

---

inexplicably too many times to ignore.

Ambience, spirit. The atmosphere is idyllic, wholesome, 1950s; you almost expect Ricky Nelson to be playing at the Compton Union Building (CUB) after the game. CUB is right next to the stadium (its balcony looks down into the stadium); it hosts a variety of pre- and postgame events.

The battlefield. Adding 12,500 seats to Martin Stadium back in '79 made it more intimate; workers lowered the playing field 16 feet and removed the track, expanding inward. The enlargement also meant the big games stayed at home instead of moving up the road to Spokane.

How about those Cougs? Drew Bledsoe is a hard act to follow; the first pick in this year's NFL draft leaves his WSU quarterbacking duties in the hands of Mike Pattinson, who has waited four years for his shot in the Pac 10. If the Cougs stay true to their long-standing form, figure on another 4,000-yard season and an average 25 points per game; a little defense and the team should find itself bowl-bound again this year. WSU always seems to surprise someone; the hated Huskies fell 42-23 in a Pullman blizzard during last year's Apple Cup. Will the curse befall UCLA or ASU this fall?

Extracurriculars. Cheese tastings, featuring the cheddar-like Cougar Gold produced by WSU's creamery, are set up near the deli in CUB. A Taste of Washington, held in CUB's Carey Ballroom, offers an elegant pregame sampling of eastern Washington bounty, from wines and produce to

grilled lamb and freshly baked breads ($8 worth of samples should amply fortify an adult).

Ferdinand's, whose name and decor were inspired by the flower-sniffing bull, sits out on the campus fringe in the Food Quality Building, next to the food science and nutrition building. There, you can get a scoop of Cappuccino Crunch or 13 other flavors of student-made ice cream. Or buy a can of Cougar Gold to go. Ferdinand's is about a 5-minute walk from the stadium and is open 3½ hours before kickoff.

After the game, follow the band to Hollingbery Fieldhouse (next to the stadium) for what is always hoped to be a raucous celebration (pregame food and festivities are also offered at this hangout). If it's a chilly day, stop by Lewis Alumni Centre, the converted campus dairy barn, and warm yourself by the roaring fire.—*Jena MacPherson*

Arizona State University, Tempe

Tempe's historic Old Town district, in the shadow of Sun Devil Stadium, becomes one giant party during football season. Most of the action takes place on Mill Avenue between University Drive and First Street, just west of the stadium. In the restaurants, bars, and shops here, fans can warm up before the game and celebrate afterward well into the wee hours.

Ambience, spirit. With a crowd so large, you'll find just about every kind of fan, from the hard-core motorhome conif you want to tone down the fire.

1 can (28 oz.) ready-cut tomatoes

8 fresh medium-size (about 7 oz. total) green jalapeño chilies, stemmed

4 fresh large (about 1 oz. total) serrano chilies, stemmed

2 cloves garlic, minced or pressed

1 small (about 6-oz.) onion, chopped

1 can (4 oz.) diced green chilies

2 tablespoons minced fresh or 2 teaspoons dried oregano leaves

Salt

Drain tomato juices into a blender; whirl with jalapeños, serranos, and garlic until smooth. Pour tomatoes into a 4- to 5-quart pan; add puréed chili mixture, onion, canned chilies, and oregano. Bring to a boil over high heat. Boil rapidly, uncovered, until reduced to 4 cups, 8 to 10 minutes; stir often. Let cool; if making ahead, cover airtight and chill up to 5 days. Season to taste with salt. Makes 4 cups.

Per ¼ cup: 20 cal. (5 percent from fat); 0.8 g protein; 0.1 g fat (0 g sat.); 4.7 g carbo.; 265 mg sodium; 0 mg chol.

Chili-Cheese Triangles

1 cup all-purpose flour

½ cup yellow cornmeal

½ teaspoon chili powder

¼ cup (⅛ lb.) butter or margarine, melted

¼ cup milk

1 large egg

1½ cups (6 oz.) shredded sharp cheddar cheese

1 can (4 oz.) chopped green chilies

¼ cup finely chopped green onion

In a bowl, mix flour, cornmeal, and chili powder. Add butter, milk, and egg; stir just until moistened. Press mixture in an even layer in a buttered 9-inch square pan. Bake in a 350° oven until cornmeal mixture is lightly browned at edges and begins to pull from sides of pan, about 25 minutes.

Mix cheese, chilies, and

PETER CHRISTIANSEN

MELTED CHEDDAR, *chilies, and green onion top spicy cornmeal crust of Chili-Cheese Triangles.*

DAVID G. McINTYRE

TEMPTER IN TEMPE *cheers for ASU Sun Devils.*

tingent who still wish Frank Kush was coach (he left in 1979) to the students who are more interested in passing each other up the bleachers than in who wins. Games begin at 7; starting any earlier would be torture for players and spectators alike.

The battlefield. Literally blasted out of the two buttes it sits between, 73,656-seat Sun Devil Stadium is an imposing edifice about 12 stories high. You enter the stadium from the north or the south; the east and west sides are still solid rock. Upper-deck seats afford a view out the horseshoe-shaped stadium's south end, where you can watch the sun setting over the Valley of the Sun.

For a few years, the stadium was sold out, but not lately. Second-season head coach Bruce Snyder is hoping to change that.

How about those Sun Devils? Luring coach Snyder from Cal put ASU's rebuilding program in motion, and this Pac 10 team got a big boost last year, when the Sun Devils won five of their last seven games and wound up their season by beating favored archrival Arizona 7-6 in Tucson. The Devils may be in the hunt for the roses this year. Heisman candidate Mario Bates was averaging 7.6 yards per carry at tailback last year before he blew out his knee against Nebraska just three games into the season. Fullback-turned-tailback George Montgomery was averaging 6.6 before he blew out *his* knee two weeks later—on the same pitch play. Both are back and, presumably, ambulatory; let's hope that play isn't.

Extracurriculars. Bandersnatch Brew Pub on Fifth Street starts filling up 4 hours before kickoff; patrons spill out from the pub onto the adjacent volleyball court, enjoying kielbasa and ale in the mild night air.

Along Mill Avenue, Stan's Metro Deli is popular for New York–style sandwiches; Balboa Cafe, Mill Landing, and Paradise Bar & Grill offer fuller menus, with entrées green onion; spread over hot cornmeal bread. Bake until cheese melts, 15 to 20 minutes longer. Serve warm or cool. Cut into 6 equal rectangles, then cut each piece diagonally across to make triangles. If making ahead, cool, wrap airtight, and store at room temperature up to 6 hours. Makes 12.

Per piece: 167 cal. (53 percent from fat); 5.9 g protein; 9.8 g fat (5.9 g sat.); 14 g carbo.; 199 mg sodium; 45 mg chol.

Sun Devil Squares

3   cups pecan halves
    Cookie crust (recipe follows)
6   large eggs
2   cups firmly packed brown sugar
1   tablespoon grated orange peel
1   tablespoon vanilla

Place pecans in a 9- to 10-inch pie pan. Bake in a 325° oven until nuts are golden brown, 20 to 25 minutes. Sprinkle nuts evenly over cookie crust.

In a bowl, beat to blend eggs, sugar, orange peel, and vanilla. Pour over

pecans.

Bake on the lowest rack of a 325° oven until filling jiggles only slightly when pan is gently shaken, 30 to 35 minutes. Cool; if making ahead, cover airtight and chill up to 1 day. Cut into 48 squares.

Per piece: 122 cal. (53 percent from fat); 1.9 g protein; 7.2 g fat (1.8 g sat.); 13 g carbo.; 32 mg sodium; 36 mg chol.

Cookie crust. Beat ½ cup (¼ lb.) **butter** or margarine, at room temperature, with ⅓ cup sugar and 1 **large egg** until well mixed. Stir in 1½ cups **all-purpose flour.** Press dough evenly over bottom and ½ inch up sides of a 9- by 13-inch pan. Bake in a 325° oven until pale golden, 20 to 25 minutes. Use warm or cool.

TOASTED PECANS *are glazed by rich orange-brown sugar filling of Sun Devil Squares.*

PETER CHRISTIANSEN

Peach Cobbler with Almond Topping

If you want ice cream for the cobbler, make some before the game, using an old-fashioned ice-and-salt crank freezer; or pack purchased ice cream.

9   medium-size (about 3 lb. total) firm-ripe peaches
2   tablespoons sugar
2   tablespoons lemon juice

2   tablespoons cornstarch
    Almond topping (recipe follows)
    Vanilla ice cream (optional)

Immerse peaches in boiling water to cover for

PATRICK CONE

WASATCH RANGE *looms over Cougar Stadium in Provo.*

ranging from hamburgers to fish and steak.

After the game, many of the shops and smaller restaurants are closed, but Mill Avenue hosts a lively bar scene. Fat Tuesday, with its New Orleans ambience, is popular with the late crowd, as are Bandersnatch and the bar at Balboa Cafe. For a jolt of java, The Coffee Plantation is elbow-to-elbow with a young and colorful crowd. Kelly's Café & Bakery, a bit farther north on Mill, offers espresso and, often, live music on the patio.

Some hotels and restaurants in metro Phoenix offer private buses to and from games; Aunt Chilada's restaurant at The Pointe Hilton Resort at Squaw Peak uses an old English double-decker.—*Nora Burba Trulsson*

Brigham Young University, Provo

It's not your ordinary campus. With 27,000 students, BYU is the largest private university in the country. With 97 percent of those students Latter-day Saints, the school is the Mormon Church's preeminent institution of higher learning. Cougar football is unique, too. BYU boosters regard coach LaVell Edwards as they might regard the Wasatch mountains that loom so spectacularly over Cougar Stadium: a force of nature, magnificent and immutable. After all, in a career where job tenure is frequently measured in nanoseconds, Edwards has served as head coach here for 22 years, winning 15 Western Athletic Conference titles and one national championship, and helping vault

QB Ty Detmer to the 1990 Heisman Trophy.

Ambience, spirit. Sure, "Clean, Sober and Insufferable" was how *Sports Illustrated* once headlined an article on BYU football. But attend a game here and you'll probably be won over. BYU crowds are proof positive that you don't need alcohol to fuel good times. Let the frat boys and sorority girls from less earnest schools throng around beer

2 to 3 seconds. Lift out, cool briefly, then pull off skins with a knife. Pit and slice peaches into a shallow 1½- to 2-quart casserole. Add sugar, lemon juice, and cornstarch to peaches; mix gently. Sprinkle fruit evenly with almond topping.

Bake in a 350° oven until topping is browned and center is bubbling, 45 to 50 minutes.

Serve hot or cool. If making ahead or to transport, lightly cover (so topping won't steam); keep at room temperature and serve within 6 hours. Scoop into bowls and top with ice cream, if desired. Makes 6 to 8 servings.

Per serving: 243 cal. (26 percent from fat); 3.8 g protein; 6.9 g fat (0.7 g sat.); 44 g carbo.; 3.6 mg sodium; 0 mg chol.

Almond topping. Crumble 1 cup (7 oz.) **almond paste** into a bowl. Add ½ cup **sugar** and 2 tablespoons **cornstarch**. Rub with your fingers until well blended. Squeeze mixture together, then break into about ½-inch chunks. ∎

SPATHIS & MILLER

TOTABLE COBBLER *hides sweet, juicy peach slices under crunchy almond topping.*

---

kegs. At BYU, gamegoing students line up for ice cream made right on campus. And when mascot Cosmo Cougar dances across the field, fans' yells seem to echo up Mount Timpanogos and back down again.

The battlefield. First things first: 65,000-seat Cougar Stadium is, by common agreement, one of the world's most beautifully sited stadiums, its mountain backdrop inevitably leading the mind to contemplation of higher things, like Ty Detmer's passing record (15,031 yards from '88 to '91). For the best alpine view, aim to sit way up on

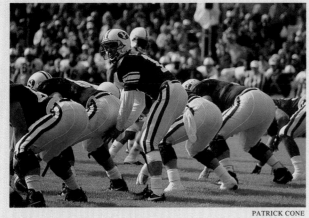

PATRICK CONE

BYU'S ATTACK *almost always achieves aerial artistry.*

the west or south side. Provo lies at 4,500 feet, so autumn afternoons can be crisp: you might think about wrapping yourself in a Cosmo Cougar sweatshirt, because coffee is nowhere to be found.

How about those Cougs? When aren't these guys good offensively? Most backfield players return, including potential All-American Jamal Willis—at running back! John Walsh is the likely starter from a trio of good returning quarterbacks. Cougar fans are near rapture about Notre Dame coming to Provo for the first time on October 16; tickets have been sold out since last winter.

Extracurriculars. Provo (population: 86,000) is probably best known for being headquarters of computer company Novell and for placing number one in *Money Magazine*'s list of best American cities a few years back. But a howling postgame party town it isn't. After the game, you'll find a lot of Cougar fans driving immediately back to that sophisticated, daring metropolis to the north—Salt Lake City. Still, Provo supports a diverse range of restaurants, perhaps because BYU students come from 100 different countries and because many of the native Utahans have served on missions abroad. Try The Torch on University Avenue for Cuban food, or Osaka on W. Center Street for Japanese. For elegant dining, head up scenic Provo Canyon to the Tree Room at Robert Redford's Sundance Resort, where steaks and seafood are served in an atmosphere of woodsy luxury.—*Peter Fish* ∎

CHILE RELLENO *goes new wave at Geronimo in Santa Fe— crusted with tortilla chips, filled with smoked shrimp, and garnished with yellow tomato salsa. Recipe is on page 202.*
LOIS E. FRANK

Chile Crazy in New Mexico

By Linda Lau Anusasananan

PETER CHRISTIANSEN

EDWARD VELARDE GROWS *the same chiles his ancestors grew 400 years ago. He ties them into ristras and sells them at The Fruit Basket in Velarde.*

CHILE PEPPERS POSSESS A MAGICAL spell that captivates hotheads all over the world. Nowhere in the West is this more evident than in Hatch, New Mexico, where, for the last 21 years, chile fanatics have flocked to a small dust-swept airport to eat, smell, and buy chiles at a two-day Labor Day weekend festival.

Festivities start Saturday morning as the parade rolls through downtown. Banners proclaiming "Chile! Gotta have it!" decorate a flatbed float; on board stands a robber caught stealing chiles from the First National Bank. The Ben Archer Health Center entry offers a prescription for the Hatch community, "Rx: Chile. Eat three times daily in generous amounts." The Green and Red Chile Queens, dressed in red and green satin formals, sit upon polished low-riders blowing kisses to the crowd. As the parade ends, spectators pile into cars and follow in a bumper-

A food lover's guide to the state where peppers are king

to-bumper crawl to the airport, where food and more entertainment await.

Like many small county fairs, this is a far cry from Disneyland. In a hot dusty field, carnival rides, game booths, food stalls, and vendors vie for attention. Pungent smells of green chiles roasting in big mesh drums over propane burners draw a crowd. A sign reads: "Chile $10 a sack, $5 roasting." A cowboy-hatted grower empties a gunnysack of shiny long green Sandias into a drum; he turns on the fire, and jets of flame lick the chiles as he spins his wares. In 5 minutes, he opens the door and black blistered roasted peppers tumble out.

Across the path, a blazing display of 3-foot-long ropes of red chiles hangs from the Flores

Farms truck. Other vendors peddle wreaths of slender hot chiles, bags of fresh jalapeños, dried chile and flower arrangements—even pastel silk chile ristras. And at one of the most popular stalls, people wait in line for Hatch chile relleno burritos (chiles rellenos wrapped in warm flour tortillas). For others, the choices are cheeseburgers topped with roasted green chiles, or gorditas (sort of a fried bread with a pocket) filled with green chile beef stew.

The sun gets hotter, and some daring souls cool off with a green chile sundae under the big tent shading the main stage. At one table, a trio of chile cooking judges scoop into more traditional fare, more than 50 entries of salsa, enchiladas, tacos, entrées, and relishes. This year's trophy goes to Eloisa Mendez with her Green and Red Salsa Jalapeño.

Across the stage, several reporters stalk a tall blond man looking at plates of peppers. This is the famous Mr. Chileman, Paul Bosland. His reputation among chile experts and New Mexicans precedes him. And for good reason: as the latest in a long line of chile gurus at New Mexico State University, Bosland in the last seven years has seen chile growing become big business. Last year New Mexico farmers received $59 million for their chile crops, making it the most valuable agricultural commodity in the state.

BREEDING COUNTS

This day, the Chileman's job is to judge the chile-growing contest. The criterion for judging is how well the chiles (the preferred spelling in New Mexico) meet standards for commercial production. He points to a pair of sleek, smooth green

RUSSELL BAMERT

ROOF ABLAZE *with drying red chiles sets hot theme for Hatch Chile Festival as horsemen ride by in opening parade.*

Harvest fiestas

At peak harvest, Santa Fe and Hatch celebrate with big parties, inviting everyone to come and eat.

Hatch Chile Festival, September 4 and 5, 8:30 to 1 A.M. at the Hatch Airport, off State Highway 26 toward Denning. Free admission, charge for parking. Call (505) 267-5050.

Santa Fe Wine & Chile Fiesta, September 21 through 26. Varied menu of events includes chile farm tours, cooking classes, restaurant and wine tastings, and campfire breakfasts. Call 982-8686 for schedule, reservations, and prices.

chiles on a flimsy white paper plate. The New Mexico 6-4 has been the industry standard for 40 years. Fabian Garcia developed its forerunner in the early 1900s; he wanted a milder chile that could be canned and dehydrated. The pod has nice smooth shoulders and a smooth taper; no chance for water to sit in cracks. It is 6 to 7 inches long. Processors will cut 4 inches off the bottom to can as whole chiles; they chop the top to use for diced chiles. Consistency, that's what processors want.

All kinds of chiles grow here: jalapeño, cayenne, even the hottest habanero. But the chiles New Mexico is famous for are generally large and long, mild to medium-hot, and can be appreciated in large quantities. They're valued for their distinctive flavor—robust, pungent, and earthy. People call this breed New Mexico chiles. Grown here at least 400 years, these chiles continue to flourish.

Many cultivated varieties exist within the breed of New Mexico chiles—Sandia, Big Jim, Barker, and even the Anaheim, grown in California, are all the same type of chile (for a guide, see page 200). Yet where they grow makes a big difference in their flavor. "If you grow an Anaheim chile in Santa Maria, California, and another one in Hatch, New Mexico, they won't taste the same. There is something special about New Mexico's high altitude, warm days, cool nights, and intense light that gives ours a distinctive full chile flavor and a nice tolerable heat," explains Bosland.

When New Mexicans talk about green and red, they're referring to chiles of different maturity. Most New Mexico–type chiles are green when ripe, and red at their ripest. They are harvested and eaten at both stages. Most growers start picking the green chiles in late July to mid-August. They might harvest the green pods once or twice before they leave remaining chiles on the plant to ripen to red. Cooks use the green chiles fresh, frozen, or canned and the red chiles dried. Brown, orange, and yellow chiles were developed by Bosland specifically for decorative ristras.

The southern dry valleys around Hatch are best known for their meaty green pods. With their long season and warm weather, chiles quickly put on flesh. Since the green chiles are roasted and peeled before eaten, many cooks find it easier working with these thick-fleshed pods.

North of Santa Fe lies a smaller chile-growing area. The short season and cooler weather produce smaller, thin-fleshed, and often hotter chiles. Because they are thin, they dry quickly, so many are harvested red and then dried.

CHILES ARE HOT. WHY NOW?

The Aztecs and Mayans were chile breeders and made seed selections for the ancho, pasilla, and jalapeño chiles. Some believe that by the time Columbus arrived in the New World, these were here; when he found them, he thought he had discovered Asia's black pepper, and so named them.

In the last few years, chile has been a hot subject throughout America. Last fall the Hatch Chile Festival hit big time with a clip on national 6 o'clock news. Chiles made the cover of *Smithsonian* magazine. Books, catalogs, and stores devote themselves to the subject. Why this sudden frenzy?

Dave DeWitt, editor of *Chile Pepper,* a 7-year-old six-times-a-year magazine devoted solely to spicy world cuisine, has a quick answer: "Americans are finally catching up with what the rest of the world knew for centuries. Chiles are good for you, and they spice up food."

The change in immigration patterns brings here from all over the world people who have eaten chiles all their lives—

AT SANTA FE FARMERS' MARKET, *shoppers buy ristras, wreaths, and fresh chiles from small local growers.*

CHARLES MANN

How to shop &where to go

A T HARVEST TIME, CHILE connoisseurs flock to the state. In Hatch, a customer from Tucson buys 14 bags (40 pounds each) of fresh green chiles to take home to family and friends. Another one from El Paso buys five bags. Buying direct allows customers to choose the varieties that suit their tastes (see page 200 for a guide); outside New Mexico, chile varieties may be limited or unlabeled.

It's best to get fresh chiles home within 24 hours, then chill or roast and freeze them. If you travel by plane, carry them on or check them. Car travelers need to take extra precations. Fresh chiles can soften to mush in a few hours in a hot trunk. Suggestions fol-

PETER CHRISTIANSEN

low for taking them home.

Fresh green chiles. Buy fresh green chiles only if you can get them home within about a 4-hour drive. Keep the chiles cool and slightly moist; pack in a cooler and sprinkle with water. If carried in the back of a pickup, wet the burlap bags they come in and sprinkle with water occasionally. Upon arrival, chill or roast, then freeze.

Roasted green chiles. Most growers will roast green chiles for you in big mesh drums tumbled over hot flames. In less than 5 minutes, 40 pounds shrinks to less than half the original volume. Pack chiles in coolers with ice for a long drive home. Some growers freeze these roasted chiles to sell or ship. They're a good alternative to fresh and preferred to the canned product, which has a mushier texture, contains citric acid, and is so consistently mild that many hotheads find it too bland.

Fresh red ristras. They need sun and air. Hang in the car with windows open. Best for short car trips.

Dried chiles, ristras, whole pods, or ground. Easy to transport over long distances. Store dried chile ristras and loose pods in paper bags to keep dry. At home, hang ristras in a dry place to avoid mildew. To preserve nondecorative pods' flavor and color over a long pe-

riod, store in the refrigerator or freezer.

For cooks who can't get to New Mexico, the easiest way to buy fresh, frozen, or dried chiles is to order them direct from one of these sources. Shipping is extra. The area code is 505.

Coyote Cafe General Store, 132 W. Water St., Santa Fe; 982-2454. Open 10 to 9 daily. This store sells breads, dried chiles, and other Southwest ingredients. Offers frozen roasted green chiles from the southern Mesilla Valley for shipping. Catalog available; call (800) 866-4695.

Flor Del Rio Decorations Rio Grande Fruit Stand, on State Highway 68, Velarde; 852-4457. Open 9 to 7 daily. Owner Anna Mae Salazar makes beautiful decorative wreaths and arrangements with chiles, and sells edible ristras of dried red Hatch chiles. Mail order available.

Flores Farms, 616 Franklin Ave., Hatch; 267-4994. Open 8 to 6 daily. Sells fresh Hatch chiles, Big Jims, and jalapeños. Also offers ristras and other handcrafts made with chiles, and ships fresh and dried chiles.

Hatch Chile Express, 622 Franklin, Hatch; 267-3226. Open 8 to 5 daily, 2 to 3 hours longer during chile season. Stock ranges from chile collectibles to edible fresh and dried chiles. Will ship fresh and frozen roasted green chiles; order frozen ones by February to ensure availability. To order, call (800) 292-4454.

Herman Valdez Fruit Stand, on State 68, Velarde;

852-2129. Open 9 to 6 or 8 daily. Sells chile ristras and wreaths. Mail order available.

Jackalope Pottery, 2820 Cerrillos Rd., Santa Fe; 471-8539. Open 8:30 to 6:30 daily, 9:30 to 6 Sundays. In the back, look for fresh green chiles from Hatch. To order fresh chiles, call (800) 753-7757.

Santa Fe Area Farmers' Market, Sanbusco Market Center, 500 Montezuma Ave., Santa Fe; 983-4098. Open 7 to 11:30 A.M. Tuesdays and Saturdays. Many farmers gather in the parking lot to sell produce and farm crafts. Look for fresh and dried chiles, ristras, and wreaths. Chile roaster is also on site during chile season. Some farmers will ship your purchases.

Santa Fe School of Cooking and Market, 116 W. San Francisco St., Santa Fe; 983-4511. Open 9:30 to 5:30 Mondays through Fridays, 9 to 5 Saturdays, 11 to 4 Sundays. Ships fresh green chiles from Hatch. Catalog available.

The Chile Shop, 109 E. Water St., Santa Fe; 983-6080. Open 9:30 to 6 Mondays through Saturdays, noon to 4 Sundays. The best seller is a red chile powder from Dixon that has a rich, slightly sweet flavor. Catalog available.

The Fruit Basket, on State 68, in Velarde; 852-2310. Open 9 to 5 daily, September through November. The Velarde family hand-ties the lighter-colored native chiles into ristras; prices start at $5.50 for a 1-foot strand. The Velardes also sell fresh green and red chiles and local apples. Mail order available.

Southeast Asians, Caribbeans, Latin Americans. As they open restaurants and people taste their hot and spicy food, they get hooked. Add the role of regional cuisines such as Southwest and Cajun, and spicy food has swept across the country. "We rarely hear anyone say, 'I used to eat hot and spicy food; now I like bland food.' That just doesn't happen," notes DeWitt.

If DeWitt's explanation isn't concrete enough, Jeanne Croft, organizer of International Connoisseurs of Green and Red Chile, headquartered in Las Cruces, has her theory. "People who love chiles are fanatics. They become crazed and have to share it with people."

In New Mexico, the popularity of chiles is more than a new-found fad. DeWitt explains: "It's a part of our lives—a very familiar part. It forms the base of all our traditional dishes. In Tex-Mex they mix chile with a lot of other ingredients; they don't have that intense flavor we get. We use it pure; that's unusual."

Which might explain why during the short harvest so many people rush around buying 40-pound sacks of green chiles—it's their year's supply, much of which will be stashed in the freezer to use next summer. Forty pounds might sound like a lot, but here some people eat chiles three times a day. They are good for you—high in vitamins A and C and low in calories and fat.

A NATURAL HIGH

A couple of weeks later, Mr. Chileman is at it again. This time it's the Santa Fe Wine & Chile Fiesta. The scene changes from dusty country to classy urban. On a chic hotel patio, amid tables promoting every specialty from red chile peach ice cream to Chardonnay, stands Dr. Chile with his chile display. Curious chile-ites come to ask the expert questions.

"I get a real high when I eat chiles. Why?" Bosland answers: "It's not your imagination. When the brain senses pain, the body produces endorphins to block the pain signals. Eating chiles sets off your body's alarm and floods your system with these natural painkillers, which make you high, much like you feel after drinking a strong cup of coffee. That may be part of the explanation of the addiction some fanatics have for chile."

"Which is hotter, a red or a green chile?" "You never know because of varietal differences. My advice is to ask the waiter which is the hottest of the day."

And, on a more personal level, how does the Chileman prefer his pepper? "In my wife's chiles rellenos. The 'NuMex Joe E. Parker' makes a great relleno. It has a nice flavor and thick wall. It's just the right size for stuffing. When you bite into it, you get a lot of flavor with it. It's a new cultivated variety you might see next year."

Finding your way through Chile Country

RUSSELL BAMERT
AROUND HATCH, *chile plants blanket fields supplying much of the country with chiles.*

Chiles grow all over the state but major production is concentrated in the dry valleys in the south and the cooler regions of the north.

In southern New Mexico, from Hatch to Las Cruces, you're in the heart of the largest chile-growing region in the state, where more than 38,000 acres of chiles were grown in 1992. Here they produce the highly esteemed thick-fleshed long green chiles as well as other varieties for processing. To catch a glimpse of chile production, drive north from Las Cruces to Hatch, on State Highway 185. Chile fields flank the road, and pickers may be at work. Most of these chiles go to processing plants, so don't expect roadside stands or tourist amenities. The season runs from late July to mid-October.

Las Cruces is the commercial center of this area and home of New Mexico State University. The small historic town of Mesilla, just southwest of Las Cruces, offers a charming although somewhat touristy experience of an old Spanish colonial town.

Up north, you'll find the second major growing area. Just a short drive above Santa Fe, in the farming towns of Velarde, Dixon, Chimayo, and Española, grows a smaller, thin-fleshed, lighter-colored native chile (an old-time pepper not subject to a lot of breeding as many of the cultivated varieties are). On State 68, produce stands draped with drying ristras beckon you to stop. The dried red chiles are highly valued for their rich, intense flavor and medium-hot bite. The season spans August through mid-October.

After stopping at the chile stands on State 68, drive north to Taos. Or, to return to Santa Fe, go east on State 75 and south on State 76 for a loop through mountains and small towns such as Truchas and Chimayo.

Eating
the
& green

DINERS ENJOY *contemporary Southwest cuisine at Geronimo.*

IN ALMOST EVERY RESTAURANT serving traditional New Mexican food, you'll find many dishes served with one of two basic sauces, green or red. Green sauce has a lively, slightly herbaceous, spicy, robust flavor. Red sauce made with dried red chiles takes on a deeper, richer, mellower flavor. Both sauces unabashedly scream chile, since few other ingredients are added. If you want to try both sauces, ask for Christmas.

Area code is 505.

Santa Fe area

Cafe Pasqual's, 121 Don Gaspar Cafe Pasqual's Ave., Santa Fe; 983-9340. Open 7 to 3 and 6 to 10 Mondays through Saturdays, 8 to 2 and 6 to 10 Sundays. Small lively restaurant serves eclectic menu of traditional and nouvelle New Mexican dishes. Especially popular for breakfast ($4 to $9.50); try to arrive before 8 to avoid waiting. Reservations for dinner only.

Coyote Cafe, 132 W. Water St., Santa Fe; 983-1615. Open 5:30 to 10 P.M. daily, plus 11 to 2 on weekends. Nationally known upscale restaurant attracts more tourists than locals but presents interesting chile dishes; the red chile onion rings and mashed potatoes are famous side dishes. Three-course

dinner costs $37.

Geronimo, 724 Canyon Rd., Santa Fe; 982-1500. Open at 6 P.M. daily, plus 11:30 to 2:30 Tuesdays through Sundays. Seasonal menu features international dishes with Southwestern flavor. The chile relleno is a favorite. Entrées range from $5.75 to $9.50 for lunch, $15.50 to $22 for dinner. Dinner reservations advised.

Josie's Casa De Comida, 225 E. Marcy St., Santa Fe; 983-5311. Open 11 to 4 weekdays only. Owner Josie Gallegos cooks and serves no-frills lunch in a funky old house. Some locals love her green chile; great homemade desserts. No reservations; arrive at 11:15 or 2:30, or prepare for a long wait and slow service. Take-out window available. The most expensive meal is the complete Mexican dinner for $6.

Maria Ysabel Restaurant, 409 W. Water, Santa Fe; 986-1662. Open 11 to 3 and 5 to 9:30 weekdays, 11 to 10 weekends. With six or more guests, order the eight-course family-style New Mexican dinner, which includes a celebrated carne adovada (recipe on page 112). Meals run $9 to $15.

Rancho De Chimayó, on State Highway 520, Chimayo (about 32 miles north of Santa Fe); 984-2100 or 351-4444. Open noon to 9 daily. Dine on

traditional northern New Mexican family recipes in a ristra-draped adobe hacienda. Carne adovada (pork in red chile sauce) and Chimayó cocktail (apple juice and tequila) are house specials. Prices range from $6 to $13. Reservations are essential.

Rincon del Oso, 639 Old Santa Fe Trail, Santa Fe; 983-5337. Open 11 to 2:30 weekdays and 6 to 9 Fridays only. This restaurant is favored by locals for traditional food. Lunch averages $5.50 to $7.95. No reservations for lunch, advised for Friday dinner.

Santacafe, 231 Washington Ave., Santa Fe; 984-1788. Open 11:30 to 2 Mondays through Saturdays and after 6 P.M. daily. Innovative use of chiles results in dishes such as chile relleno filled with crab and cheese with red and yellow pepper sauces. Entrées range from $18.50 to $23. Reservations suggested.

Tecolote Cafe, 1203 Cerrillos Rd., Santa Fe; 988-1362. Open 7 to 2 Tuesdays through Sundays. The cafe serves the best breakfasts in town. Try the egg and chile burritos, atole piñon hotcakes, and shirred eggs. Wonderful thin, crisp potatoes and homemade

PETER CHRISTIANSEN

FLAT ENCHILADA *epitomizes tradition at Rancho De Chimayó (recipe on page 203).*

breads often come with breakfast orders. Portions are big, so you might want to split an order: $1 for extra plate. Average cost per order is about $5. No reservations.

The Shed, 113½ E. Palace Ave., Santa Fe; 982-9030. Open 11 to 2:30 Mondays

through Saturdays. The specialty at this old-time favorite lunch spot in an adobe hacienda is red chile blue corn enchiladas. Lunch averages about $5. No reservations.

Tomasita's Santa Fe Station, 500 S. Guadalupe St., Santa Fe; 983-5721. Open 11 to 10 Mondays through Saturdays. The menu warns guests, "We serve it hot." Favorites include chiles rellenos and blue corn red chile cheese enchiladas. Meals for $5 to $10. Very popular; order a margarita while you wait. No reservations.

Las Cruces area

Chope's Town Cafe, on State 28 in La Mesa, 16 miles south of Las Cruces; 233-9976. Open noon to 1:30 and 6 to 8:30 Tuesdays through Saturdays. More than 50 years old, this legendary family-run institution draws customers with its great chile dishes; the chiles rellenos are popular. The place is packed on weekends; leave your name on the waiting list in the dining room, then go wait in their bar next door. Great home-cooked food at giveaway prices; you can eat for less than $5.

Dora's Chile Capital Café, 401 E. Hall St., Hatch; 267-9294. Open 6 A.M. to 8 P.M. weekdays, until 7 on Saturdays and 2 on Sundays. Local growers gather at this historic hole-in-the-wall cafe to eat chile. Many like the red enchiladas. Most lunches priced from $5 to $6. Reservations not necessary.

La Posta de Mesilla, ½ block off State 28 (look for sign), Mesilla; 524-3524. Open 11 to 9 Sundays through Thursdays, to 9:30 Fridays and Saturdays. Eat a typical New Mexican meal in a 175-year-old adobe weigh station. Chile is geared to mild tourist tastes. Most entrées from $4 to $7. Reservations advised.

Nellie's Cafe, 1226 W. Hadley Ave., Las Cruces; 524-9982. Open 8 to 8 Mondays through Saturdays. Hole-in-the-wall cafe serves best food representative of area. Meals start with a scorching salsa. Try the bañados (hefty burritos smothered with chiles.) Nothing over $6. Reservations accepted.

The Chile Guide

from long, mild greens to tiny firebombs

IN THE DUSTY SHED, HATCH chile grower Jim Lytle tries to explain what makes chiles hot. He slits open a Big Jim and slices off a piece of the plain green flesh. "Taste it." It's sweet and mild like a green pepper. "Now take a look at the rest of this chile. See these yellow threads running down the side veins? Touch your tongue on one of those veins." I lick the tip of my tongue across the yellow threads. Instantly I feel the burn: sharp and persistent. "Capsaicin," he says. "Makes them hot. It's found in the placenta of the chile, the part just under the stem where the seeds attach, and down the ribs or veins. People think the seeds are hot; they just taste hot because they rub against the parts that hold the fire. When you roast the chiles, the capsaicin tends to spread throughout the flesh." To tone down the heat, remove veins and seeds from chile.

Can you tell if one chile is hotter than another just by looking at them? Sometimes.

Variety makes a difference. Some varieties are naturally hotter than others; it's in their genes. Big Jims generally are milder than Españolas and 6-4s are milder than Jims. But varietal differences really apply only to pure breeds. Lots of home gardeners plant different varieties side by side; they cross-pollinate and you get an unknown mixed-up hybrid.

Often, but not always, size indicates heat. Generally, smaller varieties are hotter than larger ones, because they have less flesh in proportion to the amount of veins. If you make a green chile sauce with mild 6-4s and find it disappointingly mild, try adding a few smaller hotter pepper varieties such as jalapeño or serrano.

Where the chiles are grown also affects heat level. Those produced in cooler, wetter climates tend to be milder than ones grown in hot, dry conditions. So most experts agree hotness really results from a combination of factors—genetics, size, and growing conditions.

Yet old-time farmers will throw in another theory. They claim the chile's heat reflects the mood of the person who

New Mexico 6-4. *Long, with thick flesh; used for commercial canning. Heat scale 3, Scoville rating 1,000 to 1,200.*

Big Jim. *Smooth and long; often favored for rellenos. Heat scale 4, Scoville rating 1,500.*

Sandia. *Thin flesh; often used red and dried. Heat scale 5, Scoville rating 2,000.*

Española Improved. *Thin flesh, slightly curved; often harvested red and dried for ristras and chile powder. Heat scale 6, Scoville rating 3,000.*

Güero. *Yellow wax type; often pickled. Heat scale 5, Scoville rating 2,000.*

The veins tell all

Hot blood runs through chile veins. Yellow veins down sides of chiles hold capsaicin, compounds that make chile hot.

Shape can influence heat in some varieties. Long green New Mexico chiles have a vein running down the center of each side. Cross section shows flatter pepper on left has two sides, two capsaicin veins; three-sided pepper on right has an additional vein. The pod with more capsaicin is likely to be hotter.

planted it. If he was angry on that day, the peppers will be fiery hot; if in a happier mood, the chiles will be mild. It is just another theory to explain the mystery of chile heat.

As I depart, Lytle's mother rides by on her scooter. She stops and hands me a piece of dried greenish leathery pulp. I chew on the tough slab—spicy, slightly hot, and surprisingly sweet. "It's a dried peeled roasted green chile. It's next best to fresh or frozen green chiles. Just soak it in water until it swells three to four times its size, then use like a roasted green chile. Transplanted New Mexicans love it, and we can even send it to Saudi Arabia. It costs more; takes 3,200 pounds of fresh green chiles to make 100 pounds dried." Another gift to chile fanatics—maybe they ought to call it green chile jerky? ∎

Jalapeño.
Thick walls, conical; used in salsa, pickled, canned. Heat scale 7, Scoville rating 10,000.

Chile de Arbol.
Slender, tapered; dried and used in wreaths and powder. Heat scale 7, Scoville rating 20,000.

Serrano.
Slender, cylindrical, with medium-thin walls; used fresh to make salsa verde and pico de gallo. Heat scale 8, Scoville rating 35,000.

Pequin.
Small, oval; heat dissipates rapidly; green are pickled, red are dried and ground. Heat scale 9, Scoville rating 50,000 to 70,000.

Habanero.
Hottest chile in the world turns golden orange, puffy, and wrinkled when ripe. Heat scale 10, Scoville rating 150,000 to 200,000.

Measuring the heat

Back in 1902, pharmacologist Wilbur Scoville from the Parke Davis Pharmaceutical Company developed a method to measure the power of capsaicin. He needed a way to measure the heat of the peppers used in making the muscle salve Heet. In the original test, Scoville mixed ground chiles, sugar, alcohol, and water, then a panel of five tasted it and gave it a value. The number was based on how much you had to dilute the chile before you could taste no heat. Now computerized technology replaces human tasters. The scale ranges from zero for bell peppers to 150,000 to 200,000 for the hottest habaneros. Pure capsaicin rates 15,000,000.

What's mild, what's hot?

Based on Scoville ratings, a simplified scale of 1 (mildest) to 10 (hottest) is also often used to assign general heat levels to different pepper varieties. On this page, you'll find Paul Bosland's heat scale and Scoville ratings for chiles grown in New Mexico; grown in another area, they can be hotter or milder. Keep in mind the scale is only a general guideline; a wet or dry year, hot or cool weather, and cross-pollinating can modify the rating.

In this chart we subjectively describe what these numbers mean. Your own tolerance for heat might judge them much differently.

10 - nuclear meltdown

9 - explosive, blistering

8 - sweat inducing, searing

7 - combustion, nose runs

6 - slight sizzle, body warms up

5 - glowing embers, some singe

4 - toasty, tinged with light burn

3 - mellow gentle tingle

2 - lukewarm, faint warmth

1 - heat barely noticeable

0 - no heat, bell pepper cool

CHILE CLASSES *help many tourists who are novices.*

Cooking with chiles

In New Mexico, learn how to cook with chiles in a class. For directions and recipes on how to cook with New Mexico chiles, see page 202.

Santa Fe School of Cooking and Market, 116 W. San Francisco St., Santa Fe; 983-4511. Offers 2½ hour demonstration classes in traditional and contemporary New Mexican cuisine lunch is included. In a farmer's market class, students go to the market to buy fresh produce, then return to the school to cook it. Reservations advised for all classes; prices start at $25.

Cooking with chiles

*Green and red, fresh and dried . . .
they're the spark that kindles the fires
of traditional New Mexican cooking*

MOST TRADITIONAL New Mexican dishes start with locally grown chiles (see page 197 for sources). Green chiles, roasted and peeled, are used whole or chopped. Dried red chile pods are made into sauces or ground for seasoning. Green and red chile sauces are splendid spooned onto many foods—from eggs to steaks. As an ingredient, the sauces are basic to many dishes including enchiladas, burritos, and braised meats; they keep well. Try the sauces as suggested, or improvise.

When working with a large quantity of chiles, especially hot kinds, protect your hands from chile burn with rubber gloves. To extinguish chile fire in the mouth, eat dairy products, starches, or sweets.

Roasted Green Chiles

Rinse and dry fresh **New Mexico green chiles;** place in a single layer in a shallow pan. Broil about 4 inches from heat, turning as needed until chiles are blistered and charred on all sides, 10 to 15 minutes; cool. If making ahead, freeze unpeeled chiles in easy-to-use amounts.

To use freshly roasted or thawed chiles, pull off and discard skin and seeds. One pound fresh chiles makes ¾ to 1 cup peeled, seeded, and chopped roasted chiles.

Per ¼ cup: 33 cal. (5.5 percent from fat); 1.7 g protein; 0.2 g fat (0

g sat.); 7.8 g carbo.; 5.8 mg sodium; 0 mg chol.

Green Chile Sauce

- ½ cup chopped onion
- 2 cloves garlic, pressed or minced
- 1 tablespoon salad oil
- 2 tablespoons all-purpose flour
- 1½ cups regular-strength chicken or vegetable broth
- 1½ cups chopped roasted green chiles (directions precede)
  Salt

In a 2- to 3-quart pan, stir onion and garlic in oil over medium heat until limp, about 5 minutes; stir in flour. Smoothly mix in broth; add chiles and stir until boiling. Add salt to taste. Use hot; or, if making ahead, cool, cover, and chill up to 3 days or freeze. Makes 2⅔ cups.

Per ½ cup: 92 cal. (33 percent from fat); 3.2 g protein; 3.4 g fat (0.5 g sat.); 14 g carbo.; 24 mg sodium; 0 mg chol.

Red Chile Sauce

- 1 teaspoon salad oil
- 1 cup chopped onion
- 2 to 4 cloves garlic, pressed or minced
- 3 ounces (10 to 14 about 6-in.-long) dried New Mexico chiles
  Salt

In a 3- to 4-quart pan over medium heat, stir oil, onion, and garlic frequently until onion is limp, about 5 minutes. Remove onion from

pan and set aside.

Place chiles in a single layer in a 10- by 15-inch baking pan. Bake in a 300° oven until chiles smell slightly toasted (watch closely; chiles scorch easily and develop a bitter taste if burned), about 5 minutes; cool. Remove and discard chile stems and seeds. Rinse chiles; drain and break into pieces into pan used for onion. Add 3 cups water. Cover and simmer until chiles are soft, about 15 minutes; drain, reserving water.

Whirl chiles and onion in a blender or food processor, gradually adding 1½ cups reserved water. When smoothly puréed, pour mixture into pan. Cover, bring to a boil on high heat, and simmer 15 minutes; stir often. Add salt to taste. Use hot; or, if making ahead, cool, cover, and chill up to 3 days or freeze. Makes 2½ cups.

Per ½ cup: 61 cal. (46 percent from fat); 1.9 g protein; 3.1 g fat (0.5 g sat.); 10 g carbo.; 4.9 mg sodium; 0 mg chol.

Quick red chile sauce. For a speedier version of **red chile sauce,** preceding, use ground New Mexico chiles (made from the dried chiles and often labeled red chile powder; don't confuse it with seasoned chile powder mixtures).

Cook **onions** and **garlic** in **oil** as directed, using a 1½- to 2-quart pan. Add 2 tablespoons **all-purpose flour** and ½ cup **ground New Mexico chiles;** stir 1 to 2 minutes. Smoothly mix in 2 cups **regular-strength chicken** or vegetable **broth;** stir until boiling. Add **salt** to taste.

Store as directed. Sauce thickens on standing; if desired, reheat, then thin to desired consistency with water. Makes about 2¼ cups.

Per ½ cup: 105 cal. (39 percent from fat); 3.9 g protein; 4.6 g fat (0.8 g sat.); 16 g carbo; 33 mg sodium; 0 mg chol.

Chiles Rellenos with Smoked Shrimp

Teriyaki marinade (recipe follows)

- ¾ pound large (31- to 35-per-lb.) shrimp, peeled and deveined
- 2 cups hickory chips

- 1½ cups (6 oz.) shredded white cheddar cheese
- ¼ cup thinly sliced green onions
- ¼ cup chopped fresh cilantro (coriander)
- 8 roasted and peeled green chiles, each 5 to 6 inches long (recipe precedes)
- ½ cup finely crushed tortilla chips
  Yellow tomato salsa (recipe follows) or red or green chile sauce (recipes precede)
  Cilantro sprigs and sour cream

Reserve 2 tablespoons teriyaki marinade. Mix remaining marinade with shrimp; cover and chill 30 minutes to 1 hour.

Soak hickory chips at least 30 minutes in water to cover. Thread shrimp onto metal skewers. Drain wood chips.

In a barbecue with lid, scatter chips over a solid bed of medium-low coals (you can hold your hand at grill level only 4 to 5 seconds). Lay shrimp on grill; cover barbecue and open vents. Cook until shrimp are opaque in center (cut to test), 5 to 6 minutes; turn several times. Coarsely chop shrimp; mix with reserved 2 tablespoons marinade, cheese, onions, and chopped cilantro.

Cut a lengthwise slit down 1 side of each chile; discard seeds and stuff chiles equally with shrimp mixture. Set chiles, slits up, in a 10- by 15-inch pan. (If making ahead, cover and chill up to 1 day.) Sprinkle tortilla chips onto the chiles.

Bake, uncovered, in a 350° oven until filling is hot in center, 8 to 10 minutes. Top chiles with salsa, cilantro sprigs, and sour cream. Makes 8 appetizer or 4 entrée servings.

Per appetizer serving: 180 cal. (46 percent from fat); 14 g protein; 9.1 g fat (4.9 g sat.); 11 g carbo.; 648 mg sodium; 75 mg chol.

Teriyaki marinade. Mix ⅓ cup **soy sauce,** 2 tablespoons firmly packed **brown sugar,** 1 tablespoon minced **fresh ginger,** 1½ teaspoons grated **orange peel,** 1½ teaspoons minced **garlic,** and ¼ teaspoon **dried thyme leaves.**

Yellow tomato salsa. Core and chop 1 large (about ½-lb.) **yellow tomato;** mix with 3 tablespoons chopped **red onion,** 2 tablespoons chopped **fresh cilantro,** 2 tablespoons **lime juice,** 1 tablespoon chopped **fresh jalapeño chile,** and **salt** to taste. Makes about 1 cup.

Per 2 tablespoons: 8.3 cal. (11 percent from fat); 0.3 g protein; 0.1 g fat (0 g sat.); 1.9 g carbo.; 3.5 mg sodium; 0 mg chol.

Flash-fried chiles rellenos with smoked shrimp. Follow directions for **chiles rellenos with smoked shrimp** (preceding); fill slit chiles but do not bake.

Beat 1 **large egg** with 1 tablespoon **water.** Dip filled chiles in egg mixture, then coat with finely crushed **tortilla chips** (about ⅔ cup total).

In a 10- to 12-inch frying pan, heat about 1 inch **salad oil** to 350°. Add chiles, 2 or 3 at a time, and turn until lightly browned on all sides, 2 to 3 minutes. Drain on towels. Keep warm; serve hot as directed.—*Gina Ziluca, Geronimo, Santa Fe*

Per serving: 265 cal. (54 percent from fat); 15 g protein; 16 g fat (6 g sat.); 16 g carbo.; 693 mg sodium; 101 mg chol.

Flat Cheese or Chicken Enchiladas

About ½ cup regular-strength chicken or vegetable broth

3 corn tortillas (6 in. wide)

2 tablespoons minced onion

⅓ cup shredded cooked chicken (or an additional ⅓ cup cheddar cheese)

¾ cup green or red chile sauce (recipes precede), warmed

½ cup shredded cheddar or jack cheese

1 softly fried egg (optional)

Sour cream (optional)

Pour broth into a 6- to 8-inch frying pan; place over medium-high heat. When broth simmers, immerse 1 tortilla at a time until limp, about 5 seconds. Drain in a single layer on towels.

Set 1 tortilla on a plate; top with ½ the onion, ⅓ the chicken, ⅓ the chile sauce, and ⅓ the cheese. Repeat layers with cheese on top. Place in a 350° oven until cheese melts, about 5 minutes. Top with fried egg, and add sour cream to taste. Serves 1.—*Laura Jaramillo Swendson, Rancho de Chimayó, Chimayo, New Mexico*

Per serving: 631 cal. (41 percent from fat); 37 g protein; 29 g fat (14 g sat.); 59 g carbo.; 552 mg sodium; 101 mg chol.

Carne Adovada

4 pounds boned pork shoulder or butt, fat trimmed, cut into 1-inch slices

2½ cups red chile sauce (recipe precedes)

1 tablespoon dried oregano leaves

Salt

Mix pork slices, red chile sauce, and oregano in a 9-by 13-inch pan; cover tightly with foil.

Bake in a 350° oven until meat is very tender when pierced, about 3 hours. Skim and discard fat. Add salt to taste. Serves 8 to 10.—*Bell Mondragón, Maria Ysabel Restaurant, Santa Fe*

Per serving: 312 cal. (46 percent from fat); 36 g protein; 16 g fat (5.2 g sat.); 5.4 g carbo.; 141 mg sodium; 122 mg chol. ∎

By Linda Lau Anusasananan

Sunset readers applaud two ageless recipes

Party favorites, both dessert and appetizer are easy to put together and bake in a jiffy

THROUGH THE YEARS *Sunset* readers have requested certain recipes again and again. Here are two favorites, a dessert and an appetizer. Both can be assembled easily from ingredients that are available in any season.

Pear or Apple Crisp

This recipe appeared in a 1949 issue of *Sunset.* Pears or apples are lightly spiced, then baked beneath a crust of sweet, buttery crumbs.

4 medium-size (about 2¼ lb. total) Anjou pears, Bartlett pears, or Golden Delicious apples, peeled, cored, and sliced

1 teaspoon ground cinnamon

¼ teaspoon ground nutmeg

1 teaspoon lemon juice

½ cup water

1 cup sugar

¾ cup all-purpose flour

½ cup (¼ lb.) butter or margarine

Whipping cream (optional)

Place pears in a greased 8-inch-square baking pan. Sprinkle with cinnamon, nut-meg, lemon juice, and water; mix lightly.

In a medium-size bowl, mix sugar and flour. Using a pastry blender or 2 knives, cut in butter until mixture resembles coarse crumbs; evenly scatter crumbs over pear mixture. Bake in a 350° oven until fruit is tender when pierced and crust is lightly browned, about 1 hour. Offer cream to pour over individual portions. Serves 4.

Per serving: 622 cal. (35 percent from fat); 4 g protein; 24 g fat (14 g sat.); 104 g carbo.; 236 mg sodium; 62 mg chol.

Artichoke Nibbles

This popular appetizer is also a favorite at *Sunset.*

2 jars (about 6 oz. each) marinated artichoke hearts

1 small onion, finely chopped

1 clove garlic, minced or pressed

4 large eggs

¼ cup fine dried bread crumbs

¼ teaspoon salt

⅛ teaspoon *each* pepper, dried oregano, and liquid hot pepper seasoning

2 cups (about 8 oz.) shredded sharp cheddar cheese

2 tablespoons minced parsley

Drain marinade from 1 jar of artichokes into a small frying pan. Drain remaining jar; reserve marinade for other uses. Chop all artichokes; set aside. Over medium heat, cook onion and garlic in pan, stirring often, until onion is soft when pressed, about 5 minutes.

In a bowl, beat eggs to blend. Stir in crumbs, salt, pepper, oregano, hot pepper seasoning, cheese, parsley, artichokes, and onion mixture. Pour into a greased 7-by 11-inch baking pan.

Bake in a 325° oven until custard feels set when lightly touched, about 30 minutes. Let cool slightly in pan, then cut into 1-inch squares. Serve warm or at room temperature; or cover and refrigerate to serve cold. To reheat, bake, uncovered, in a 325° oven until heated through, 10 to 12 minutes. Makes about 6½ dozen appetizers.

Per appetizer: 22 cal. (82 percent from fat); 1 g protein; 2 g fat (0.7 g sat.); 0.7 g carbo.; 54 mg sodium; 14 mg chol. ∎

By Christine Weber Hale

ANY RIPE TOMATO *can go into this lively, simmered sauce, putting odds and ends of fruit to good use; freeze some sauce for the winter.*

Too many tomatoes?
Make pasta sauces

Three easy recipes capture the full flavor of ripe tomatoes

TOMATO SEASON IS peaking, with end-of-summer heat quickly ripening fruit still on the vine. If you have a bumper crop of home-grown tomatoes or want to take advantage of good-quality, good-value tomatoes from the market, one of the best ways to use them in quantity is for pasta sauces.

Here we offer three distinctly different recipes designed to accentuate different attributes of the tomato. Each sauce will accommodate any ripe tomato—red, yellow, or green (yes, some varieties are green when ripe, as you can see above), big or small.

For best flavor, start sauces with fully ripe tomatoes; they should feel slightly soft, but not squishy, when gently pressed. If they have bruised spots or splits, trim generously around damaged areas. If tomatoes need to ripen, let them stand at room temperature out of direct sunlight for several days. Enclosed in a paper bag, they ripen faster.

The first recipe is for a big batch of a classic, slow-simmered spaghetti sauce. Its rich flavor base combines onions, carrots, garlic, herbs, and chilies. You can use the sauce as soon as it's cooked, or freeze some in convenient-size portions.

By contrast, the next sauce comes together in a flash. You stir-fry tomato chunks with chili oil just until the mixture is hot, add basil, then mix with hot cooked pasta—in any shape you like.

The last sauce is roasted. It develops a complex, smoky-sweet intensity and thick consistency that mingles well with either a plain pasta or a filled one like ravioli.

Be sure to accompany these pasta and sauce combinations with grated or shredded parmesan cheese; the cheese helps the sauce to cling.

All-purpose Spaghetti Sauce

Use this sauce as is, or, for variety, convert it to a meat sauce. To make a meat sauce, brown ground meat (beef, pork, veal, lamb, chicken, or turkey; allow ½ to 1 lb. meat for each quart of sauce), then add the sauce and simmer 10 to 15 minutes to blend flavors. Allow ¾ to 1 cup sauce for each cup of hot cooked pasta, and serve with grated parmesan cheese.

4 cloves garlic, minced or pressed

2 large (about 1¼ lb. total) onions, finely chopped

2 large (about ¾ lb. total) carrots, finely chopped

¾ cup regular-strength chicken broth

10 pounds (about 6 qt.) ripe tomatoes, stems removed, peeled (if desired), rinsed, cored, and chopped

1¼ cups balsamic or red wine vinegar

1 cup minced parsley

1 cup minced fresh or ¼ cup crumbled dried basil leaves

3 tablespoons minced fresh or 1 tablespoon crumbled dried oregano leaves

1 tablespoon crushed dried hot red chilies
Salt

In an 8- to 10-quart pan over high heat, combine garlic, onions, carrots, and ¼ cup broth. Stir occasionally until liquid evaporates and vegetables start to brown and stick, 12 to 15 minutes. Stir browned bits free with ¼ cup broth; boil until liquid evaporates and vegetables stick; stir occasionally. Repeat step using another ¼ cup broth.

Add tomatoes, vinegar, parsley, basil, oregano, and chilies. Bring to boiling. Reduce heat and boil gently, uncovered, until sauce is reduced to 9 to 10 cups, about 1 hour and 10 minutes; stir occasionally. Use sauce hot, seasoned to taste with salt. (If you did not peel tomatoes and want a smoother sauce, whirl mixture in a blender until puréed.)

To store, let sauce cool, package airtight, and chill up to 5 days or freeze in easy-to-use amounts up to 1 year. Makes 2 to 2¼ quarts.

Per 1 cup: 156 cal. (12 percent from fat); 5.8 g protein; 2 g fat (0.3 g sat.); 35 g carbo.; 65 mg sodium; 0 mg chol.

Stir-fry Tomato Sauce

Make this simple sauce with any variety or size of ripe tomato.

2 pounds ripe tomatoes, rinsed and stems removed

1 large (about ½-lb.) onion, chopped

2 cloves garlic, minced or pressed

About 2 tablespoons hot chili oil (or olive oil and ½ teaspoon crushed dried hot red chilies)

¾ pound dried linguine or fettuccine

2 cups (about 2 oz. total) firmly packed fresh basil leaves, slivered

1 to 2 cups (¼ to ½ lb.) shredded or grated parmesan cheese
Basil sprigs (optional)
Salt

Core regular tomatoes; if a less juicy sauce is desired, cut tomatoes in half crosswise and squeeze out and discard seeds. Coarsely chop regular or cherry tomatoes. You should have 4 to 6 cups (varies with size of tomato pieces).

In 10- to 12-inch frying pan over medium-high heat, combine onion, garlic, and 2 tablespoons chili oil; stir often until onion is golden, about 15 minutes.

Meanwhile, bring 3 quarts water to boiling in a covered 5- to 6-quart pan over high heat. Add pasta and cook, uncovered, until tender to bite, 10 to 12 minutes. Drain pasta well; pour into a wide serving bowl.

As pasta cooks, add tomatoes to onion; turn heat to high and stir just until tomatoes are hot, 2 to 3 minutes. Remove from heat, stir in slivered basil, and pour sauce over pasta. Sprinkle with ½ to 1 cup cheese; mix and garnish with basil sprigs. Season pasta with more chili oil, cheese, and salt to taste. Serves 4 to 6.
—Richard Eastes, Long Beach, California

Per serving: 385 cal. (26 percent from fat); 17 g protein; 11 g fat (3.9 g sat.); 57 g carbo.; 323 mg sodium; 13 mg chol.

Roasted Tomato Sauce

6 pounds (about 4 qt.) ripe tomatoes, stemmed, rinsed, cored, and cut into large chunks

6 cloves garlic, minced or pressed

3 large (about 2 lb. total) onions, chopped

½ cup dry red wine

1 cup regular-strength beef broth

¾ pound dried spaghetti or cappellini

1 to 2 cups (¼ to ½ lb.) shredded or grated parmesan cheese
Salt and pepper

Combine tomatoes, garlic, and onions in an 11- by 17-inch roasting pan. Bake, uncovered, in a 450° oven until liquid evaporates and vegetables begin to stick and brown around edge of pan, about 1¾ hours; stir often. Add wine and ½ cup broth; stir to scrape browned bits free. Bake until vegetables at edge of pan brown again, 15 to 20 minutes; stir free with remaining broth. Keep warm, or, if making ahead, cool, cover, and chill up to 3 days; reheat to use.

Bring about 3 quarts water to boiling in a covered 5- to 6-quart pan over high heat. Add pasta and cook, uncovered, until tender to bite, 10 to 12 minutes. Drain pasta well; pour into a wide serving bowl, top with sauce, and sprinkle with 1 cup cheese. Mix pasta and serve; add cheese and salt and pepper to taste. Serves 5 or 6.

Per serving: 450 cal. (15 percent from fat); 20 g protein; 7.4 g fat (3.5 g sat.); 77 g carbo.; 351 mg sodium; 13 mg chol. ■

By Christine Weber Hale

TOMATO STIR-FRY *with fresh basil makes a quick sauce. Golden tomatoes give a new look to pasta, but tomatoes of other colors are good, too.*

NORMAN A. PLATE

NORMAN A. PLATE

TEAR CHUNKS *from warm, tender loaf of challah; enjoy with butter and honey. Try the bread sliced and toasted, too.*

A delicate twist on classic challah

This golden crown has honey and raisins

FAT, ROUND, AND coiled to symbolize wholeness—this is the shape challah takes in honor of the Jewish high holidays, including Rosh Hashana, the day on which kings were crowned.

There are many recipes for challah, but this golden egg bread, from Lorraine Shapiro's recipe, is exceptionally tender and fine textured. Offer it with butter and honey for Rosh Hashana, or bake it throughout the year, as a coil or in the form of a braid.

You can mix and knead the dough by hand, or use a dough hook.

The bread freezes well if you want to bake ahead.

Holiday Challah

1 package active dry yeast
¼ cup honey
⅓ cup golden raisins
2 large eggs
   About 3½ cups all-purpose flour
½ teaspoon salt
2 tablespoons salad oil

In a large bowl, combine yeast, ¾ cup warm (110°) water, and honey; let stand 5 minutes to soften yeast.

In a small bowl, pour 1 cup hot water over raisins; set aside. In another small bowl, beat eggs to blend; spoon out 1 tablespoon and chill, covered.

To yeast mixture, add balance of egg, 1½ cups flour, salt, and oil; beat with a spoon or mixer until batter is stretchy. Add 2 cups flour and drained raisins; stir with spoon until dough is well moistened.

To knead by hand. Scrape dough onto a lightly floured board and knead until smooth and elastic, about 10 minutes; add flour to prevent sticking. Rinse, dry, and oil bowl; turn dough over in bowl to oil top.

To knead with a dough hook. Beat on high speed until dough pulls from bowl sides, 5 to 8 minutes. If dough clings to bowl or is sticky to touch, mix in flour, 1 tablespoon at a time.

Cover dough (kneaded by either method) with plastic wrap; let rise in a warm place until doubled, about 1 hour. Knead on a lightly floured board by hand or with dough hook to expel air. On the floured board, shape dough into a rope 32 inches long and tapered at 1 end. If dough is so elastic it shrinks back, let rest a few minutes, then continue.

In a 9- to 10-inch oiled cheesecake pan with removable rim, place thick end of dough in center, then form a coil to pan rim, and tuck any extra under the loaf. Cover with plastic wrap and let stand until puffy, 20 to 30 minutes. Uncover and gently brush dough with reserved beaten egg.

Bake bread in a 325° oven, on rack about ⅓ from bottom, until a dark golden brown, 30 to 35 minutes. Check at 20 minutes; if top is dark, drape with foil and continue to bake until loaf is evenly colored. Let cool in pan about 10 minutes, then remove rim. Serve warm or cool. If making ahead, wrap airtight when cool. Store at room temperature up to 1 day; freeze to store longer (thaw wrapped). To reheat (thaw, if frozen), set on a sheet of foil in a 300° oven until warm in center, 25 to 35 minutes. Makes 1 loaf, about 1¾ pounds.—*Lorraine Shapiro, Los Angeles*

Per ounce: 86 cal. (16 percent from fat); 2.2 g protein; 1.5 g fat (0.3 g sat.); 16 g carbo.; 44 mg sodium; 15 mg chol. ∎

By Karyn I. Lipman

DAVE BROAD

Salad is well tuned

By ingredients that harmonize

THIS PEAR-ENDIVE SALAD owes its subtlety to a combination of unusual greens and an unusual dressing.

The greens include chopped cilantro and thinly sliced broccoli flowerets along with familiar curly endive and green onions. A well-balanced dressing combines walnut oil with a fruit-flavor vinegar that emphasizes the pear. The famous affinity of pears with blue cheese and walnuts is another harmony in the composition.

This salad is thoughtfully conceived as well as delicious.

Pear-Endive Salad

1 small (about ½-lb.) head curly endive

½ cup chopped fresh cilantro (coriander)

⅓ cup thinly sliced green onions, including tops

1 cup thinly sliced broccoli flowerets

2 tablespoons crumbled blue-veined cheese

1 large (about ½-lb.) ripe pear

1½ tablespoons fruit-flavor vinegar, such as blueberry, raspberry, or tangerine

1 tablespoon walnut oil or salad oil

   Salt and freshly ground pepper

Separate endive leaves; rinse and drain. To crisp, if desired, wrap in towels and enclose in a plastic bag. Refrigerate 30 minutes to 2 days.

Stack endive leaves and thinly slice crosswise.

In a bowl, combine sliced endive, cilantro, onions, broccoli, and blue cheese.

Core and thinly slice pear onto salad. Sprinkle with vinegar and oil; mix gently. Season to taste with salt and pepper. Serves 4 to 6.

Per serving: 64 cal. (46 percent from fat); 1.9 g protein; 3.3 g fat (0.7 g sat.); 8 g carbo.; 51 mg sodium; 2.1 mg chol.

Kirkland, Washington

ACCORDING TO Larousse Gastronomique, it is customary to serve a variety of hors d'oeuvres at the beginning of a meal. That was then; now we are more inclined to do chips and dips. So cunningly devised and richly prepared are these preliminary temptations that diners must sometimes be prodded to the table for the main event. Indeed, some very successful informal parties have been built around dips, chips, and beverages.

Although most are served cold (notably the ubiquitous sour cream and onion soup mix), many others are brought forth hot or warm. Here is one of the latter. Based on cheeses, spinach, and tomato, it picks up a little steam from green chilies. Cumin enhances the Mexican element in the dish, as do tortilla chips.

For a leaner and more nutrient-packed choice, spoon the molten cheese onto crisp raw vegetable slices.

Bake-it-easy Dip

   About ¾ pound spinach rinsed, drained, and chopped (stems and wilted leaves discarded)

1 teaspoon salad oil

1 small (¼-lb.) onion, finely chopped

4 cloves garlic, minced or pressed

2 or 3 Anaheim (New Mexico or California) green chilies (each 6 to 7 in. long), stemmed, seeded, and chopped; or 1 can (4 oz.) diced green chilies

1 large (about ½-lb.) firm-ripe tomato, cored, seeded, and chopped

2 packages (3 oz. each, ½ cup total) neufchâtel (light cream) cheese

½ cup nonfat milk

½ teaspoon ground cumin

1¼ cups (6 oz.) shredded mozzarella or jack cheese

1 can (2¼ oz.) sliced ripe olives, drained

   Tortilla chips or 4 to 6 cups thin slices of raw vegetables such as carrot, cucumber, or turnip (optional)

Place spinach in a 10- to 12-inch frying pan over medium-high heat and stir until spinach wilts, 2 to 3 minutes. Pour into a fine strainer and press to squeeze out as much liquid as possible; set spinach aside.

To pan, add oil, onion, garlic, and fresh chilies. Stir often over medium-high heat until vegetables are limp, 8 to 10 minutes. Add tomato (and canned chilies). Stir until hot; set aside.

In a bowl, combine neufchâtel cheese, milk, and cumin; stir, then beat until smoothly mixed. Add all but 2 tablespoons of the mozzarella, and all the spinach and cooked vegetables; mix well. Spread evenly in a shallow 1-quart baking dish. Sprinkle with olives and remaining mozzarella.

Bake in a 450° oven until hot in center and bubbly, 15 to 20 minutes. Let cool 10 minutes. Serve warm to scoop onto tortilla chips. Makes 8 to 10 servings.

Per serving: 126 cal. (64 percent from fat); 6.6 g protein; 9 g fat (4.9 g sat.); 5.6 g carbo.; 216 mg sodium; 26 mg chol.

Sandy Szwarc

Albuquerque

By Joan Griffiths, Richard Dunmire

SUNSET'S KITCHEN CABINET

Creative ways with everyday foods—submitted by *Sunset* readers,
tested in *Sunset* kitchens, approved by *Sunset* taste panels

Brunch Paella

Barbara Cummings, Everett, Washington

RICE AND LEAN TURKEY SAUSAGE *simmer to make paella for a morning meal.*

1 pound Italian (turkey or pork) sausages, cut into ½-inch-thick slices

1 cup long-grain white rice

2 cups regular-strength chicken broth

1 can (about 14½ oz.) cut stewed tomatoes, or 1½ cups chopped fresh tomato

1 teaspoon caraway seed

Condiments (suggestions follow)

Stir sausage slices frequently in a 10- to 12-inch pan over medium-high heat until browned, about 10 minutes; discard fat.

Add rice to pan and stir until grains are slightly opaque, about 2 minutes. Add broth, tomatoes and their liquid, and caraway seed; bring to a boil on high heat. Reduce heat, cover, and simmer paella until liquid is absorbed and rice is tender to bite, about 20 minutes; stir occasionally. Spoon portions of the paella onto warm dinner plates and top with condiments, adding them to taste. Makes 4 to 6 servings.

Per serving without condiments: 263 cal. (29 percent from fat); 16 g protein; 8.5 g fat (3.2 g sat.); 30 g carbo.; 658 mg sodium; 45 mg chol.

Condiments: Shredded **fontina cheese, unflavored nonfat yogurt,** chopped **fresh cilantro** (coriander) **leaves,** and **lime wedges.**

Beer Quick Bread

Lucien Pagerie, Spanaway, Washington

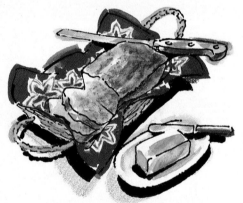

FLAVOR OF CRUSTY *quick bread reflects the taste of the beer you use to make it.*

2¼ cups all-purpose flour

3 tablespoons sugar

1 tablespoon baking powder

½ teaspoon baking soda

¼ teaspoon salt

1 bottle (12 oz.) beer

Butter or margarine (optional)

Honey (optional)

In a large bowl, mix flour, sugar, baking powder, baking soda, and salt. Add beer; mix just until evenly moistened. Spread batter to make level in an oiled 4½- by 8½-inch loaf pan.

Bake in a 400° oven until loaf is well browned and just begins to pull from pan sides, about 45 minutes. Invert onto a rack.

Serve beer bread warm or cool. If making ahead, wrap when cool and hold at room temperature up to 1 day; freeze to store. Cut in thin slices. Serve with butter and honey. Makes 1 loaf, about 1 pound 6 ounces.

Per ounce: 58 cal. (4.7 percent from fat); 1.4 g protein; 0.3 g fat (0 g sat.); 12 g carbo.; 121 mg sodium; 0 mg chol.

Golden Couscous Salad

Sally Vog, Springfield, Oregon

ORANGES, ALMONDS, *candied ginger, and raisins join up in couscous salad.*

1¼ cups regular-strength chicken broth

1 cup couscous

½ cup golden raisins

2 tablespoons finely chopped crystallized ginger

1 teaspoon grated orange peel

½ teaspoon ground cumin

3 tablespoons seasoned rice vinegar (or rice vinegar and ½ teaspoon sugar)

3 tablespoons orange juice

½ cup finely chopped cucumber

¼ cup thinly sliced green onion

4 large (about ½ lb. each) oranges

1 or 2 tablespoons chopped roasted, salted almonds

In a covered 3- to 4-quart pan over high heat, bring broth to a boil. Stir in couscous, raisins, ginger, orange peel, and cumin; cover pan and remove from heat. Let stand until couscous absorbs liquid, about 5 minutes. With a fork, stir couscous to fluff slightly, then stir in vinegar, orange juice, cucumber, and onion; if making ahead, let stand up to 4 hours. Stir before using.

Cut peel and white membrane from oranges and thinly slice fruit crosswise. Arrange orange slices in a ring around edge of a rimmed platter; mound couscous in center of oranges and sprinkle salad with the salted almonds. Makes 4 or 5 servings.

Per serving: 307 cal. (7.9 percent from fat); 7.5 g protein; 2.7 g fat (0.4 g sat.); 66 g carbo.; 225 mg sodium; 0 mg chol.

Litchi Chicken Salad

Lisa Doyen, El Cerrito, California

1 can (about 1 lb. 4 oz.) litchis
½ cup unflavored nonfat yogurt
½ cup finely diced celery
½ teaspoon grated lemon peel
1 tablespoon lemon juice
1 teaspoon dried thyme leaves
3 cups bite-size pieces cooked chicken or turkey
8 large butter lettuce leaves, rinsed and crisped
¼ cup chopped chives or green onions with tops
Salt and pepper

Drain litchis and save 2 tablespoons of the syrup; set fruit aside. In a bowl, mix the 2 tablespoons litchi syrup, yogurt, celery, lemon peel, lemon juice, thyme, and chicken pieces; if making ahead, cover salad and litchis and chill up to 4 hours.

Arrange lettuce leaves on 4 dinner plates and spoon chicken salad equally onto leaves. Top each salad with an equal portion of the litchis; sprinkle with chives. Add salt and pepper to taste. Makes 4 servings.

Per serving: 324 cal. (23 percent from fat); 33 g protein; 8.2 g fat (2.2 g sat.); 31 g carbo.; 175 mg sodium; 94 mg chol.

SWEET LITCHIS *are refreshing with chicken in a yogurt dressing.*

Coriander-Curry Shrimp

Aron Green, Los Angeles

1 large (8-oz.) onion, thinly sliced
1 clove garlic, minced or pressed
1 teaspoon salad oil
1 tablespoon curry powder
1 tablespoon ground coriander
¼ teaspoon cayenne
⅔ cup pineapple-coconut juice (or ⅔ cup pineapple juice and ¼ cup shredded, sweetened, dried coconut)
2 teaspoons cornstarch
1½ pounds large shrimp (31 to 35 per lb.), shelled and deveined
2 tablespoons minced parsley
6 cups hot cooked pasta
Salt
Lime wedges

In a 10- to 12-inch frying pan over high heat, frequently stir onion, garlic, oil, and 2 tablespoons water until water evaporates and onions are limp and start to brown slightly, about 5 minutes. Add curry powder, coriander, and cayenne; stir to blend.

Blend pineapple-coconut juice smoothly with cornstarch. Add shrimp to pan and stir over high heat for about 2 minutes. Pour in pineapple juice mixture and stir until mixture is boiling and shrimp turn pink and are opaque in center (cut to test), about 3 minutes longer. Add parsley and mix. Mound hot pasta on a platter or plates and spoon the shrimp mixture onto the pasta. Season individual portions with salt and lime to taste. Makes 5 or 6 servings.

Per serving: 354 cal. (11 percent from fat); 26 g protein; 4.5 g fat (1.4 g sat.); 51 g carbo.; 149 mg sodium; 140 mg chol.

PINEAPPLE AND COCONUT, *in juice form, season shrimp served on pasta.*

Lemon Frozen Yogurt

Christina McCarroll, Los Altos, California

4 cups vanilla-flavor low-fat yogurt
4 teaspoons grated lemon peel
¼ cup lemon juice
¼ cup light corn syrup
Thin lemon slices
Gingersnap cookies (optional)

In a 9- to 10-inch square metal pan, mix yogurt, lemon peel, lemon juice, and corn syrup. Cover airtight and freeze until firm, at least 6 hours or up to 3 weeks.

Break frozen mixture into large chunks; if too hard, let stand a few minutes at room temperature to soften. Whirl chunks in a food processor or beat with a mixer until a smooth-textured slush forms. Return slush mixture to pan. Cover and freeze until firmed slightly, 30 minutes to 3 hours. Scoop frozen yogurt into chilled bowls, decorate with lemon slices, and accompany with gingersnap cookies. Makes 6 to 8 servings.

Per serving: 128 cal. (9.8 percent from fat); 5.6 g protein; 1.4 g fat (0.9 g sat.); 24 g carbo.; 89 mg sodium; 5.7 mg chol.

Compiled by Karyn I. Lipman

LOW-FAT FROZEN YOGURT *has best texture if served slightly soft.*

October Menus

QUICK, SEASONAL,
BUDGET-WISE...
FOR FAMILY AND
FRIENDS

ones to chew on, bones with crisp browned edges and succulent meaty chunks, bones with creamy marrow centers. If you love bones, cooler days make this a good time for two substantial bone meals with veal shanks or pork ribs. Both menus let you sit back and relax as the oven roasts the meats and their companions to tenderness.

Fall produce wearing nature's palette of red, orange, yellow, and green lends its colors and flavors to the first two menus and the quick golden fruit soup-and-sandwich lunch.

AN AUTUMN SUPPER (at right)
The tart snap of shiny pomegranates accents Italian-style veal shanks, mushrooms, wild rice, and spinach salad.

BEER FOOD (page 212)
Use your favorite beer to flavor spareribs in sticky sauce; serve with low-fat baked onion rings, roasted vegetables.

RAINY DAY LUNCH (page 213)
Curried persimmon soup gives a new style to the traditional lunchtime soup-and-sandwich pairing.

Seasonal Decor

Brighten the table with produce and foliage such as lady apples and liquidambar leaves and pods.

Mushrooms to Roast

From the produce market. buy woodsy chanterelles, milder common mushrooms, or both.

Stain Control

Immerse pomegranates in water to catch spatters as you break seeds free. Pat seeds dry.

Marrow Tools

Extract shank marrow with long marrow spoons, lobster picks, or similar slender tools.

PETER CHRISTIANSEN

This grand meal takes some time to prepare, but you have many make-ahead opportunities, starting the day before.

For salad, dress spinach, Belgian endive, and sliced lady apples with balsamic vinegar, olive oil, and grated orange peel.

Up to 3 hours before dinner, you can rinse and slice mushrooms; seed pomegranates; and rinse wild rice. About 1 hour ahead, reheat shanks, then add mushrooms.

Roasted Veal Shanks and Mushrooms with Wild Rice and Pomegranates

- 6 pounds veal shanks, cut into 1½-inch lengths
- 3 tablespoons minced garlic
- ⅓ cup chopped fresh or 2 tablespoons dried marjoram leaves
- ¾ or 1½ cups dry white wine
- 2 cups regular-strength chicken broth
- 2¼ pounds mushrooms (common, chanterelle, or a combination), rinsed and sliced lengthwise ¾ inch thick

  Wild rice (recipe follows)

  About 1¼ cups pomegranate seeds

  Fresh marjoram or parsley sprigs

  Salt

Rinse shanks and lay, cut side down, in an 11- by 17-inch roasting pan at least 2 inches deep; add 2 tablespoons water. Bake, uncovered, in a 425° oven for 30 minutes. Turn shanks over and bake until meat is lightly browned, about 45 minutes longer. Combine garlic,

PETER CHRISTIANSEN

SHINY GLAZE *on baked spareribs comes from beer, molasses, and spices. Potatoes and onions roast with meat.*

chopped marjoram, ¾ cup wine, and broth. Pour over shanks and stir to release browned bits in pan; cover pan very tightly with foil. Bake 1½ hours more. (If cooking ahead, let covered shanks cool; chill up to 1 day. Add ¾ cup wine, cover tightly, and reheat in a 425° oven for 30 minutes.)

Push shanks into ½ of the pan; baste with pan juices. Put mushrooms in empty space and mix with pan juices. (If more than ½ the mushrooms are chanterelles, tightly cover pan; otherwise, do not cover.) Bake until meat pulls apart easily and mushrooms are limp, 25 to 40 minutes longer. Stir mushrooms occasionally. With a slotted spoon, transfer shanks and mushrooms to a platter. Add wild rice to platter; sprinkle foods with pomegranate seeds and garnish with marjoram sprigs. Accompany with pan juices and salt to taste. Serves 6.

Per serving: 428 cal. (15 percent from fat); 46 g protein; 7.2 g fat (2 g sat.); 48 g carbo.; 894 mg sodium; 124 mg chol.

Wild rice. Rinse 1½ cups **wild rice** in a fine strainer. In a 3- to 4-quart pan over high heat, bring rice and 2¾ cups **regular-strength chicken broth** to a boil. Cover and

simmer until rice is tender to bite, 50 to 60 minutes; drain and serve hot.

Fennel-Apple Tart

- ¾ cup plus 2 teaspoons all-purpose flour
- ½ cup regular rolled oats
- ¼ cup (⅛ lb.) butter or margarine
- 1 large egg white
- ⅓ cup granulated sugar
- 1 teaspoon ground cinnamon
- 2 tablespoons dried currants
- 2 cups peeled, cored, ¼-inch-thick slices apples such as Empire or Newtown Pippin
- 1½ cups crosswise-sliced fennel (about ¼ in. thick)
- 2 teaspoons lemon juice

  Powdered sugar

In a food processor or a bowl, whirl or rub ¾ cup flour, oats, and butter until fine crumbs form. Whirl or stir in egg white until dough holds together. Press dough evenly over bottom and side of an 8-inch-wide tart pan with a removable rim.

In a bowl, mix remaining 2 teaspoons flour, granulated sugar, cinnamon, and currants. Add apples, fennel,

and lemon juice; mix well. Pour into pan; pat fruit mixture to make level.

Bake on lowest rack in a 425° oven until top of filling starts to brown, about 45 minutes. Drape with foil and bake until juices begin to bubble, about 30 minutes more. Remove pan rim and slide a wide spatula under hot tart to release crust; leave tart in place. Serve warm or cool; dust tart with powdered sugar. Serves 6.

Per serving: 237 cal. (33 percent from fat); 4 g protein; 8.7 g fat (5.1 g sat.); 37 g carbo.; 119 mg sodium; 22 mg chol.

Get into the spirit of the West's Oktoberfest celebrations with beer food: ribs, potatoes, and roasted onions (they're reminiscent of onion rings but don't have the fat that comes with frying). Although the meat, potatoes, and onions take about 2 hours to cook, all you have to do is stir now and then.

Spareribs with Beer-Molasses Sauce and Roasted Vegetables

- 4 pounds pork spareribs
- 1 large (about ½-lb.) red bell pepper
- 3 large (about 1⅔ lb. total) onions
- ½ teaspoon *each* pepper and cayenne
- 2 tablespoons salad oil

  Beer-molasses sauce (recipe follows)

- 2¼ pounds small (2-in.-diameter) thin-skinned potatoes, scrubbed
- 3 tablespoons fine dried bread crumbs

  Chopped parsley

  About ½ cup regular-strength chicken broth

  Salt

Trim and discard excess fat from ribs. Rinse ribs and place in an 11- by 17-inch roasting pan at least 2 inches deep. Add ¾ cup water ; cover pan tightly with foil. Bake ribs on lowest rack in a 425° oven until meat is tender when pierced, 1 hour to 1 hour and 20 minutes.

Meanwhile, stem, seed, and coarsely chop bell pepper. Cut onions crosswise into ½-inch slices; separate into rings. In a 12- by 15-inch broiler pan (or another pan, the same size as used for ribs), evenly mix vegetables with pepper, cayenne, and salad oil.

Remove ribs from oven; turn oven temperature to 500°. Pour out and save juices from ribs; skim and discard the fat.

Pour beer-molasses sauce over ribs in pan, turning meat to coat well. Arrange ribs in a single layer. Return, uncovered, to a rack positioned in lower ½ of oven.

Pierce each potato with a fork and place directly on rack above ribs (take care to avoid touching oven sides); set pan of mixed vegetables beside potatoes.

Bake, turning over ribs and stirring vegetables occasionally, until ribs and onion mixture are browned and potatoes give readily when pressed, about 35 minutes; after 15 minutes alternate pan positions. To prevent the sweet rib sauce from scorching, stir in some of the reserved pan juices when sauce begins to stick.

Sprinkle bread crumbs over vegetables in pan and mix slightly; bake 5 minutes more. Transfer foods to a large platter and sprinkle with parsley. To pan, add remaining pan juices and enough broth to make 1 cup. Stir over high heat to loosen browned bits, pour the sauce into a bowl, and offer to spoon onto food. Cut ribs apart into individual serving portions. Add salt to taste. Makes 6 servings.

Per serving: 772 cal. (47 percent from fat); 40 g protein; 41 g fat (15 g sat.); 58 g carbo.; 269 mg sodium; 143 mg chol.

Beer-molasses sauce. In a small bowl, combine ½ cup **beer** or ale, ⅓ cup **dark molasses**, ⅓ cup **lemon juice**, 2

GOLDEN CURRIED SOUP *starts with persimmons. Enjoy with hearty tea-style cheese and chutney sandwiches.*

large cloves **garlic** (minced), 2 teaspoons **dried ground mustard,** ¼ teaspoon **ground allspice,** and ¼ teaspoon **ground cinnamon.**

RAINY DAY LUNCH

Curried Persimmon Soup

Cheddar-Chutney Sandwiches

Milk

Butter Cookies

Red or Green Seedless Grapes

Although quite simple, the flavors and look of this meal make it a nice choice to serve to guests. For this soup you can use either Fuyu-type or Hachiya-type persimmons. Flat-bottom Fuyus are ready to eat when crisp and as they begin to soften. Pointed-tip Hachiyas must be soft-ripe to use; otherwise they are very astringent. Hachiyas will gel the soup if it stands, so stir before serving.

Make classic teatime sandwiches with thinly sliced bread, cheddar cheese, chutney, and watercress.

For an easy dessert, offer grapes with homemade or purchased cookies.

Curried Persimmon Soup

- 3¼ pounds (6 to 8 medium-size) firm-ripe or soft-ripe Fuyu-type persimmons or 2⅔ pounds (4 or 5 medium-size) soft-ripe Hachiya-type persimmons
- ½ cup minced onion
- 1½ tablespoons minced fresh ginger
- 1 quart regular-strength chicken broth
- 1½ teaspoons curry powder
  Fresh cilantro (coriander) leaves (optional)
  Lemon wedges
  Salt and pepper

Cut and discard stems from persimmons. Peel Fuyus and slice fruit, or scoop Hachiya fruit from peel. Discard peel.

Combine onion, ginger, and ¼ cup broth in a 3- to 4-quart pan. Boil over high heat, stirring occasionally, until liquid evaporates and vegetables brown and start to stick, about 5 minutes. Add ¼ cup broth; repeat step until vegetables are slightly browned again. Add ¼ cup broth and repeat step. Add curry and stir for 30 seconds.

Stir remaining broth into pan and bring to a boil over high heat.

If using Fuyus, add to pan,

cover, and simmer until slices are tender when pierced, 5 to 8 minutes; whirl smooth, a portion at a time, in a blender.

If using Hachiyas, whirl pulp in a blender until smooth; stir into hot broth (Hachiyas will thicken soup; stir to thin).

Ladle soup into bowls; garnish with cilantro, and season to taste with lemon, salt, and pepper. Makes 7 to 8 cups, 4 servings.

Per serving: 424 cal. (5.7 percent from fat); 5.7 g protein; 2.7 g fat (0 g sat.); 105 g carbo.; 991 mg sodium; 0 mg chol. ■

By Elaine Johnson

Fudgy Brownies with Peanut Butter Chips

Tuck these brownies into the corner of a lunch box or bag.

- ½ cup (¼ lb.) butter or margarine, cut into chunks
- 3 ounces unsweetened chocolate
- ⅔ cup each granulated sugar and firmly packed brown sugar
- 2 large eggs
- 1 teaspoon vanilla
- ½ cup all-purpose flour
- ½ cup peanut butter–flavor baking chips

In a 2- to 3-quart pan over low heat, combine butter and chocolate; when ingredients begin to soften, stir until melted and blended. Remove from heat.

To chocolate mixture add granulated and brown sugars, eggs, and vanilla, then beat until smooth. Beat in flour.

Spread batter in a greased, flour-dusted 8-inch-square baking pan. Sprinkle with baking chips. Bake in a 350° oven until brownie feels firm at edges and springs back in center when gently pressed, about 25 minutes. Let cool in pan on a rack. Cut into bars or squares. Makes 1 dozen.

Per serving: 269 cal. (50 percent from fat); 4 g protein; 15 g fat (8 g sat.); 33 g carbo.; 113 mg sodium; 57 mg chol.

It's center stage for vegetable casseroles

You don't have to be a vegetarian to enjoy these hearty combinations

THIS MAY COME AS A shock to staunch meat and potato lovers, but vegetarian main dishes have moved into the menu mainstream. The basic ingredients of these entrées—vegetables and grains or grain products—are naturally low in fat, and, when their flavor potential is exploited, the deceptively rich-tasting results have very broad appeal. Making this point most effectively are the three following recipes—a stew with dumplings, and two handsome pies.

These casseroles join the ranks of many all-vegetable

dishes that *Sunset Magazine* has published through the years. To serve your growing interest in the subject, we gathered our best past dishes and added to them other favorite recipes, modified to omit meat products, in a just-released, 160-page *Complete Vegetarian Cookbook* (Sunset Publishing Corporation, Menlo Park, Calif., 1993; $14.99). The lentil pie is a sampler from the book; the other two recipes are new.

Double Squash Stew with Cornmeal Dumplings

1½ cups regular-strength vegetable or chicken broth

5 cloves garlic, minced or pressed

1 large (about ½-lb.) onion, chopped

1 can (4 oz.) diced green chilies

2½ pounds Roma-type tomatoes, cored and chopped

3 pounds butternut or banana squash, peeled and cut into 1-inch pieces

1½ teaspoons ground cumin

1 teaspoon ground cinnamon

1½ pounds zucchini, ends trimmed, cut into ¼-inch-thick slices

⅓ cup minced fresh or 2 tablespoons dried basil leaves

Cornmeal dumplings (recipe follows)

Salt and pepper

In a shallow 10- by 15-inch casserole (at least 4½ qt.) combine ½ cup broth, garlic, and onion. Bake, uncovered, in a 400° oven until vegetables are browned and stick to pan, about 35 minutes. Add another ½ cup broth, scrape browned bits free, and bake until liquid evaporates and vegetables stick again.

Add remaining broth; stir browned bits free, then mix in chilies, tomatoes, butternut squash, cumin, and cinnamon. Cover tightly with foil. Bake in a 400° oven until butternut squash is tender when

pierced, 45 to 50 minutes. (If making ahead, let cool, cover, and chill airtight up to 1 day. Bake, covered, in a 400° oven until hot, about 20 minutes.) Mix zucchini and basil into hot vegetables. Spoon dumplings in 6 to 8 equal mounds onto vegetables, or in dollops around edge of casserole. Cover with foil (don't touch dumplings). Bake until dumplings are firm and dry to touch, about 20 minutes. Add salt and pepper to taste. Serves 6 to 8.—*Lori Matthew, Eugene, Oregon*

Per serving: 313 cal. (19 percent from fat); 9.3 g protein; 6.6 g fat (3.1 g sat.); 59 g carbo.; 275 mg sodium; 39 mg chol.

Cornmeal dumplings. In a bowl, mix together 1½ cups **yellow cornmeal,** ½ cup **all-purpose flour,** 1½ teaspoons **baking powder,** and 1½ teaspoons **sugar.** Add 1 **large egg,** ¾ cup **nonfat** or low-fat **milk,** and 3 tablespoons melted **butter** or margarine. Mix well. Let stand until batter is thick enough to hold its shape, at least 5 minutes.

Mushroom and Barley Casserole with Fila Crust

Mushroom duxelles (recipe follows)

Barley filling (recipe follows)

Cheese filling (recipe follows)

4 sheets fila dough (each about 12 by 16 in.)

3 tablespoons melted butter or margarine

Nonfat or regular sour cream, or unflavored yogurt (optional)

Prepared horseradish with beets

Salt

Spread duxelles evenly in a 2½- to 3-quart casserole (6 by 11 in. and 2 in. deep, to 8 by 11 in. and 1½ in. deep). Cover evenly with barley filling, then cheese filling. Lay 1 fila sheet flat and brush lightly with about 1½ teaspoons butter. (Keep fila covered with plastic wrap, except when using, to prevent drying.) Top with remaining fila sheets, buttering each, including the top. Fold stack

PETER CHRISTIANSEN

BUTTERY LAYERS *of fila dough bake crisply to make a melt-in-the-mouth topping for layers of mushroom duxelles, barley, and lemon-spiked cheese in this novel vegetable pie. Add sour cream or rosy horseradish for a bright accent.*

in half, bringing short ends together. Lay fila stack on top of filling, centering in casserole; fold ends of fila under to fit flush with casserole rim. Brush top of fila with remaining butter. With a sharp knife, cut diagonally through fila every 1½ to 2 inches to make a diamond pattern. If making ahead, cover airtight and chill up to 1 day.

Bake, uncovered, in a 350° oven until fila is a deep golden brown and filling is hot in center, about 45 minutes (50 to 55 minutes, if chilled). Spoon portions onto plates and accompany with sour cream, horseradish, and salt to taste. Serves 6 to 8.

Per serving: 262 cal. (22 percent from fat); 15 g protein; 6.4 g fat (3.1 g sat.); 38 g carbo.; 341 mg sodium; 17 mg chol.

Mushroom duxelles.
Rinse, drain, and mince 2½ pounds **mushrooms.** In a 5- to 6-quart pan over high heat, combine mushrooms, ½ cup minced **shallots** or red onions, and ½ teaspoon **ground nutmeg.** Stir often until juices evaporate and mixture browns and sticks, about 30 minutes. Add ⅓ cup **reserved barley liquid** (following); stir to scrape browned bits free. Stir often until liquid evaporates. Use

warm or cold. If making ahead, cool, cover, and chill up to 1 day.

Barley filling. Rinse 1 cup **pearl barley.** Combine barley in a 5- to 6-quart pan with 3 cups **regular-strength vegetable** or chicken **broth.** Cover, bring to a boil over high heat, and simmer until barley is tender to bite, about 30 minutes. Drain, reserving liquid for mushroom duxelles, preceding. To barley, add 1 tablespoon **tomato paste** and ¼ cup **nonfat,** reduced-fat, or regular **sour cream.** Use, or, if making ahead, cover and chill up to 1 day.

Cheese filling. Pour 2 cups **nonfat** or low-fat **cottage cheese** into a fine strainer. Let drain at least 10 minutes or up to 1 hour. Transfer drained cheese to a bowl and mix with 1 tablespoon **grated lemon peel** and ½ teaspoon **pepper.** If making ahead, cover airtight and chill up to 1 day.

Lentil and Golden Squash Pot Pie

2 large (about 1 lb. total) onions, chopped

2 cloves garlic, pressed or minced

2 tablespoons minced fresh ginger

2 teaspoons coriander seed

1 teaspoon cumin seed

1 teaspoon cardamom seed (without pods)

½ teaspoon crushed dried hot red chilies

2 cups (about 12 oz.) lentils

1½ quarts regular-strength vegetable or chicken broth

About 2¾ pounds banana, hubbard, or butternut squash

Salt and pepper

Pastry for a double-crust 9-inch pie

About 1 tablespoon beaten egg

Yogurt sauce (recipe follows)

In a 5- to 6-quart pan, mix onions, garlic, and ginger.

With a mortar and pestle, coarsely crush coriander, cumin, and cardamom seed (or whirl in a blender to make a coarse powder). Add to onion mixture along with chilies and ½ cup water. Cook, stirring occasionally over medium-high heat, until liquid evaporates and a brown film forms in pan, 10 to 12 minutes.

Deglaze pan by adding ¼ cup water and stir to loosen brown film. Repeat step,

cooking mixture dry and deglazing with ¼ cup water, until vegetables are richly browned, about 2 more times.

Sort lentils, discarding debris. Rinse and drain lentils; add to pan along with broth. Bring to a boil; reduce heat, cover, and simmer 10 minutes.

Meanwhile, cut off and discard peel and scoop seeds from squash. Cut squash into ¾-inch cubes, enough to make about 2 quarts.

Add squash to pan; cover and simmer until lentils and squash are soft when pressed, 15 to 20 minutes. Season to taste with salt and pepper. Drain liquid from lentils and measure; return no more than 1½ cups liquid to lentils (reserve any extra liquid to use when making soup). Pour mixture into a shallow 3-quart casserole (about 9 by 13 in.). If making ahead, cover and chill up to 1 day.

On a lightly floured board, roll pastry dough to match dimensions of casserole plus 1 inch on all sides. Lay pastry rectangle over vegetable mixture. Fold excess pastry under and press dough firmly against casserole rim, then pinch dough to flute edge; brush evenly with beaten egg. Decoratively slash top. (If making ahead, cover and chill up to 1 day; uncover.)

Bake in a 400° oven until crust is richly browned and filling hot, 25 to 30 minutes (increase baking time to about 45 minutes, if chilled). If pastry rim begins to darken excessively before center is brown, drape dark areas with foil. Scoop through crust and down into filling to serve; accompany with yogurt sauce to add to taste. Serves 8 to 10.

Per serving: 410 cal. (31 percent from fat); 17 g protein; 14 g fat (3.3 g sat.); 57 g carbo.; 263 mg sodium; 0.9 mg chol.

Yogurt sauce. In a medium-size bowl, combine 2 cups **unflavored nonfat yogurt,** ¼ cup chopped **fresh** or 2 tablespoons dried **mint leaves,** and ¼ cup chopped **fresh cilantro** (coriander); stir until blended. ∎

By Christine Weber Hale

PETER CHRISTIANSEN

MACHINE-MADE WHOLE-WHEAT BREAD *is delicious—and practically effortless.*

How to make bread machines work for you

"I fell in love at first bite."
—*Linda J. Wilson,*
Grants Pass, Oregon

I HAVE TO CONFESS I'M NOT A charter member of the new generation of breadmakers, a group that makes bread by machine. I only joined (and rather hesitantly) when the *Sunset* test kitchen began getting calls about the machine. The calls convinced me that we needed to investigate this latest kitchen gadget.

My research began with a query in *Sunset* asking readers for their opinions about the machines. More than 200 letters brought words of praise, recipes, and questions on how to fix problem loaves. Armed with these questions, and lots of advice from readers and bread machine converts, I began to bake bread in four machines that I felt were representative of the dozen or so available models: the 1-pound-capacity Panasonic Bread Bakery and Welbilt Bread Oven; and the 1½-pound-capacity Zojirushi Home Bakery and DAK Turbo Baker IV. Four months later, here's what I found.

WHAT BREAD MACHINES OFFER

You get fresh, good-tasting bread by convenience—a no-mess, no-fuss proposition—anytime you want from ingredients you choose. The machine mixes ingredients, warms the dough so it will rise, kneads it, then bakes the bread. You never touch the dough; all you do is measure the ingredients into the machine's bread pan, pick a baking cycle, and push the start button. The bread will be ready in 2½ to 4 hours, depending on the cycle and the particular machine.

The downside? Funny-looking loaves by traditional standards, reduced counter space, and the cost of the machine. The price can range from as little as $99 (for a basic 1-pound capacity) to $400 (top of the line, 1½-pound capacity). Many readers didn't let cost, space, or loaf shape considerations affect their view of the machine.

Says Tom Walton, of Seattle, "It's the next best thing since—you guessed it—sliced bread! I haven't bought bread at the store since I got it."

SOME THINGS TO CONSIDER BEFORE YOU BUY

Machine size and bread shape. Choices include machines with 1-, 1½-, and 2-pound loaf capacities (determine how much bread you eat in one or two days). Loaf shapes may be round, square, or rectangular.

Cycle options. Consider a *100 percent whole wheat cycle* (loaves may rise higher than with a regular cycle); a *dough cycle,* good for making dough for pizza and rolls you intend to shape and bake in a conventional oven; a *delayed cycle* (a timer sees to it that you have fresh-baked bread when you wake or return from work); or a *programmable cycle* (you can develop your own program for recipes, good for heavier and nonwheat bread recipes).

Other features. A *window* allows easy viewing for checking dough consistency (you can lift the lid of windowless machines to check dough, but only quickly and occasionally, to avoid heat loss). A *yeast dispenser* keeps yeast away from liquid—especially important in delayed cycles (however, carefully layering ingredients avoids this problem). Consider *cleaning:* most machines are easy to clean, but those with removable bread pans keep spills out of the machine. And check *noise level* before you choose a machine. Some machines are louder than others; if your kitchen is near the bedroom and you want to use the delayed cycle for overnight bread, you'll want a quieter machine.
(Continued on next page)

COMMON PROBLEMS—
AND THEIR SOLUTIONS

Attempt solutions one at a time, in descending order

PROBLEM	SOLUTIONS
1. Overrises, then sinks (*Too much leavening action*) 	1. Decrease liquid 2. Decrease sugar by 50% 3. Decrease yeast by 25% 4. Increase fat by 50%
2. Too dense (*Inadequate gluten structure or insufficient leavening*) 	1. Add wheat gluten (1½ teaspoons per cup of whole-grain flours) 2. Substitute bread flour for some of whole-grain flour 3. Increase yeast and/or sugar
3. Gnarled (*Too much flour*) 	1. Reduce flour 2. Increase yeast 3. Increase liquid (but not so much that recipe becomes too large for machine)
4. Large, uneven holes (*Leavening action is too fast for rise cycle*) 	1. Decrease liquid 2. Decrease yeast 3. Use regular active dry yeast, rather than rapid or quick yeast 4. Increase salt by 50%
5. Sinks before baking (*Improper flour-liquid ratio, resulting in weak gluten structure*) 	1. Increase flour 2. Decrease sugar

PETER CHRISTIANSEN

WHAT WE LEARNED IN OUR TEST KITCHEN

Do your initial baking with manufacturers' recipes. Recipes that come with your bread machine have been developed specifically for its programmed cycles, so they tend to work best. If you wish to use other recipe sources—or adapt regular bread recipes—you'll need to be ready for some trial-and-error loaves. Recipes from general bread machine cookbooks are not usually developed for a particular machine, and may work better in some machines than others. In our test kitchen, no single recipe performed the same way in all machines. However, almost all loaves were edible, and most were delicious.

For a good start, follow directions. All manufacturers recommend using bread flour (which has more gluten—a tough, elastic protein—and provides a stronger framework than all-purpose flour). And, most manufacturers suggest using room-temperature ingredients—some, liquids heated to between 75° and 110°—to maximize the yeast's leavening potential. (If you use cold ingredients, the loaf is likely to be dense with less height.) A few machines have a heat-up period before ingredients are mixed together, so you needn't worry about temperature.

Once ingredients are in the pan, you choose a cycle. Each recipe states which cycle to use. Cycles vary in rise time and baking heat (important for sweet doughs—they need lower heat). You can choose rapid or turbo cycles to reduce cycle time by about an hour, but loaves will be lower.

Check dough consistency. Ideally, once the machine is loaded and the cycle is in progress, you can walk away; however, until you have a failproof recipe and know your machine, you'll need to check the dough's consistency—which determines the success or failure of a loaf—before you go about other business.

It's important to watch the dough for about 10 minutes of the first mix-knead cycle. The proper balance between liquid and flour is essential for a good loaf. You want a soft ball that pulls clean from the sides of the pan. (If dough is too stiff, the machine can't knead effectively; if too soft, the machine can't add extra flour.)

Machines can't compensate for variations in humidity, heat, altitude, and ingredients. That's why they sometimes produce overproofed loaves, loaves that don't rise properly, and loaves that are doughy—and why a recipe that's successful in spring and fall may not work as well in summer.

Size and appearance don't necessarily indicate success or failure. Since all loaves from a machine are similarly shaped, the machine's loaf gets character from the ingredients, not the shape. However, some loaves may be high with domed tops, others only half as high as the pan. And others may sport bumpy tops.

Don't let appearance dictate your opinion. A loaf that doesn't rise as high as the pan isn't necessarily a failure. Loaves made from whole-grain flours won't rise as high as those made with 100 percent bread flour (although they'll gain height with the addition of wheat gluten—add 1½ teaspoons to each cup of whole-grain flour). You may prefer to forgo a perfectly domed white loaf for a stubbier, dense loaf with great whole-grain flavor.

Interesting results from our baking. Some machine manuals recommend rapid-rise yeast. We tested with both regular and rapid-rise yeast and found the results comparable in most machines. We also used a whole package of yeast (2¼ teaspoons) when a recipe called for 2 teaspoons without encountering any problems.

Many machine recipes were too salty for our taste-testers. Cutting the salt in half didn't affect the loaves (½ teaspoon worked well for both 1- and 1½-pound-capacity machines). Loaves without any salt, however, were squat and coarse textured.

ADAPTING RECIPES SUCCESSFULLY

If, as we did, you alter a recipe to achieve better results—higher loaf, finer texture—keep track of the changes you make, so that you have an accurate account when you develop the perfect recipe. You may need to re-make and readjust a recipe several times before you're satisfied.

When you adapt a traditional bread recipe, first determine your machine's flour capacity; then adjust the recipe's flour to this amount, and other ingredients proportionally. One ingredient you don't need to change significantly is yeast—machine baking tends to require more yeast than traditional bread baking. Use the amount recommended in your machine's recipes (most machines specify a similar amount for all recipes). If your machine customarily calls for 1 package of yeast, use 1 package in the recipe you're adapting, even if the proportional amount would be 1½ teaspoons.

If a loaf fails to work after you've experimented with the liquid and flour, you can change (one at a time) the other ingredients that affect rising properties: yeast, salt, sugar, and fat.

But first, check to see that you've used the proper amount of yeast and that the package expiration date hasn't passed. Make sure that the yeast does not contact hot liquids (over 120° will kill yeast); conversely, liquid that is below 75° slows yeast's leavening action (your manual gives the correct liquid temperature for your machine).

Salt retards yeast's action, so you may want to decrease it by half. Or, there might not be enough sugar to feed the yeast (sugar speeds up yeast's action); try increasing the sugar by 50 percent. If that doesn't work, reduce the fat—it also slows yeast's action.

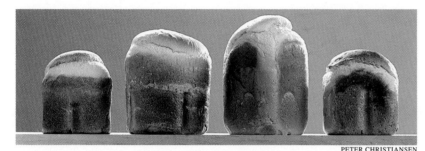

PETER CHRISTIANSEN

SOURDOUGH LOAVES *made in four machines have different shapes and sizes, but share the classic sour taste and chewy texture.*

Sunset's Sourdough Recipe for Bread Machines

Ingredients	1-lb. machine	1½-lb. machine
Water	½ c. + 2 tbsp.	1 c.
Sourdough starter (room temperature)	¾ c.	1 c.
Bread flour	2½ c.	3½ c.
Sugar	2 tsp.	1 tbsp.
Salt	¾ tsp.	1 tsp.
Active dry yeast	1 pkg.	1 pkg.

Fill machine's bread pan according to manufacturer's directions; select white bread cycle. Observe dough during first mixing; it should form a soft ball. If dough won't hold together in a ball and machine labors, add more water, 1 tablespoon at a time, until dough holds together. Or, if dough is too soft to form a ball, add more bread flour, 1 tablespoon at a time, until soft ball forms (flour must be completely absorbed before you add more; wait at least 30 seconds between additions). At end of baking cycle, remove loaf promptly; cool on rack before slicing. Makes 1 loaf: about 1 pound 6 ounces in 1-pound machine, 1 pound 14 ounces in 1½-pound machine.

Per ounce: 74 cal. (3.6 percent from fat); 2.7 g protein; 0.3 g fat (0 g sat.); 15 g carbo.; 79 mg sodium; 0.2 mg chol.

Sourdough starter. In a 1- to 1½-quart pan over medium heat, or in a nonmetal container in a microwave oven, heat 1 cup **nonfat** or low-fat **milk** to 90° to 100°. Remove from heat and stir in 3 tablespoons **unflavored yogurt.** Pour into a warm 3- to 6-cup glass, ceramic, plastic, or stainless steel container with a tight lid. Cover and let stand in a warm place (80° to 90°) until mixture is the consistency of yogurt, a curd has formed, and mixture doesn't flow readily when container is tilted (it may also form smaller curds suspended in clear liquid); process takes 18 to 24 hours. If some clear liquid rises to top of milk during this time, stir to mix with curds. If the liquid turns light pink, discard and start again. Once curd has formed, stir in 1 cup **bread flour** until smooth. Cover tightly and let stand in a warm place (80° to 90°) until mixture is full of bubbles and has a good sour smell (2 to 5 days). Again, if clear liquid forms, stir it back into starter; if pink, discard and start over. To store, cover and refrigerate. Makes about 1⅓ cups.

To feed starter and maintain a supply, add **nonfat** or low-fat **milk** and **bread flour** in equal amounts to starter you'll be using. (For example, if recipe calls for 1 cup starter, add 1 cup milk and 1 cup flour.) Cover tightly; let stand in a warm place until it bubbles, smells sour, and forms a clear liquid on top, 12 to 24 hours. Use, or cover and chill. Stir to use.

REFERENCE HELP

Owner's manuals have trouble-shooting sections. Use this first. A bimonthly newsletter is also available. To order, write to Donna R. German, 976 Houston Northcutt Blvd., Suite 3, Mount Pleasant, S.C. 29464; fax (803) 849-0530. A one-year subscription costs $14.95.

Fleischmann's Yeast's *Best-Ever Breads* recipe book has a thorough section on bread machines and helpful tips for adjusting recipes. To order, send a $2.95 check or money order to *Best-Ever Breads*, Box 5970, Department PR, Stacy, Minn. 55078; allow four to six weeks for shipment.

Welbilt/Red Star Yeast has a recipe club. Membership costs $14.99; for details, call (800) 445-4746 between 8 and 5 CST.

Three on-line computer services offer weekly forums where machine bakers can share recipes, tips, and problems. Call America Online, (800) 827-6364; CompuServe, (800) 848-8199; or Prodigy, (800) 776-3552. ∎

By Betsy Reynolds Bateson

READER TIPS

"I was bemoaning the fact that I'd burned my fingers trying to lift the pan handle, when I thought of my large metal crochet hook. It's perfect for the job; then I use a pot holder to remove the pan."—*Joan Dickey, Moss Beach, California*

"If you are not going to bake in the unit, you can double the batch of dough and just let the machine knead and rise."—*Karen Jensen, Garrison, Utah*

"The handiest trick I've learned is 'double kneading'… to make breads using lower-gluten flours (whole-wheat, rye) lighter in consistency…. I just stop it, then start the machine again after the first knead cycle."—*Marjorie Geiser, Running Springs, California*

"For crunch, I replace some of the flour with ¼ to ⅓ cup cornmeal or polenta."—*Ann Swanson, Menlo Park, California*

"We (yes, we—my husband makes bread more often than I do) often mix up several batches of dry ingredients at one time. We just need to add the wet ingredients and yeast each time we bake."—*Julie Sessions, Bellingham, Washington*

NORMAN A. PLATE

MANY INGREDIENTS *give jerk seasoning its intriguing complexity. Peppery bite of jerk-coated pork (above) is tamed by sweet papaya wedges, vinegar-tart pasta, and sweet-sour chutney.*

Jamaican jerk puts the bite in chicken, pork

It's a blend of tastes you won't forget

J AMAICANS FAVOR AN aromatic seasoning mix on grilled meat and fish that has such a kick you might think that's why it's called jerk. In reality, jerk seasonings were originally used to help preserve smoked meats. Although this role for jerk has declined, it's still popular for everyday use.

Jerk is interpreted many ways, but at its heart are black pepper, hot chilies, and fragrant spices and herbs ground to a paste. Foods are spread with the paste and grilled.

To balance the flavor impact, temper the jerk foods with pasta, fruit, and sweet-tart mixtures.

Jamaican Jerk Chicken with Spiced Fettuccine

   Jerk seasoning paste (recipe follows)

4 boned and skinned chicken breast halves (about 1½ lb. total), rinsed and patted dry

2 cups regular-strength chicken broth

¼ cup whipping cream

12 ounces dried fettuccine

   Fresh cilantro sprigs

   Lime wedges

   Salt

Cover and chill 1 tablespoon jerk seasoning. Coat chicken breasts with remaining mixture. Cover and chill at least 20 minutes or up to 1 day.

In a 10- to 12-inch frying pan, mix reserved jerk seasoning, broth, and cream. Boil on high heat until reduced to 1½ cups, about 10 minutes. If making ahead, reheat to use.

Place chicken on an oiled grill 4 to 6 inches above a solid bed of medium-hot coals (you can hold your hand at grill level only 3 to 4 seconds). Turn meat often until it is no longer pink in center of thickest part (cut to test), about 10 minutes.

Meanwhile, bring about 3 quarts water to a boil in a 5- to 6-quart covered pan over high heat.

When chicken is done, transfer to a platter and keep warm. At once, add fettuccine to boiling water and cook, uncovered, until tender to bite, about 8 minutes. Drain well; return to pan and add jerk-seasoned broth. Mix pasta with 2 forks over medium heat until most of the broth is absorbed; also add juices drained from chicken. Spoon pasta onto plates and top with chicken. Garnish with cilantro; offer lime and salt to add to taste. Serves 4.

Per serving: 602 cal. (16 percent from fat); 53 g protein; 11 g fat (4.5 g sat.); 70 g carbo.; 165 mg sodium; 196 mg chol.

Jerk seasoning paste. In a blender or food processor, combine ¼ cup firmly packed **fresh cilantro,** 3 tablespoons **water,** 3 tablespoons minced **fresh ginger,** 2 tablespoons **black peppercorns,** 1 tablespoon **ground allspice,** 1 tablespoon firmly packed **brown sugar,** 2 cloves **garlic,** ½ teaspoon **crushed dried hot red chilies,** ¼ teaspoon **ground coriander,** and ¼ teaspoon **ground nutmeg.** Whirl to make a smooth paste. If making ahead, cover and chill up to 5 days.

Jerk Pork with Pasta and Mango-Banana Chutney

1 large (about ½-lb.) firm-ripe banana

   About ¾ cup Major Grey (or other mango) chutney

¼ cup lime juice

3 tablespoons sweetened flaked dried coconut

2 pork tenderloins (each about ⅔ lb.), fat trimmed

   Jerk seasoning paste (see preceding recipe)

1 pound dried angel hair (capellini) pasta

¾ cup regular-strength chicken broth

¼ cup seasoned rice vinegar (or ¼ cup rice vinegar and 1 teaspoon sugar)

¼ cup minced fresh cilantro (coriander)

2 teaspoons sugar

2 medium-size (about 1¾ lb. total) firm-ripe papayas, peeled, seeded, and cut into ½-inch-thick slices

   Fresh cilantro sprigs

   Salt

Peel and coarsely chop banana. In a small bowl, mix banana with ¾ cup chutney, 1 tablespoon lime juice, and coconut. If making ahead, cover and chill up to 1 day.

Coat meat with jerk seasoning, wrap airtight, and chill at least 20 minutes or up to 1 day.

Ignite 60 charcoal briquets on firegrate in a barbecue with a lid. When coals are coated with ash, in about 30 minutes, push to sides of grate. Set grill 4 to 6 inches above coals. When coals are medium-hot (you can hold your hand at grill level only 3 to 4 seconds), oil grill and lay pork in center (not over coals). Cover barbecue, open vents, and cook until a thermometer inserted into the thickest part of the tenderloins registers 155°, about 20 minutes.

Meanwhile, bring 3 quarts water to a boil in a 5- to 6-quart covered pan over high heat.

When meat is done, put on a platter and keep warm. At once, add pasta to boiling water and cook, uncovered, until tender to bite, about 5 minutes. Drain pasta; return to pan over medium heat and mix with chicken broth until most of the liquid is absorbed, then mix in remaining lime juice, vinegar, minced cilantro, and sugar.

Cut pork into ½-inch slices; serve with pasta and papayas. Garnish with cilantro sprigs; offer chutney and salt to add to taste. Serves 6.

Per serving: 577 cal. (7.8 percent from fat); 32 g protein; 5 g fat (1.8 g sat.); 102 g carbo.; 137 mg sodium; 65 mg chol. ∎

By Christine Weber Hale

Sprinkle it on freely... sprightly sumac

IN THE MIDDLE EAST, ONE species of sumac plant (*Rhus coriaria*) serves a multitude of purposes. It's used for fabric dyes, in medications, and for tanning. The tart red berries, dried, are used as a food seasoning.

This useful plant is not to be confused with three sumacs that grow wild in North America, all of which can cause severe dermatitis: poison oak, poison ivy, and poison sumac.

As edible sumac's red berries dry, they turn brick red or purplish in color; they are then ground into powders of varying fineness. We found that the finer grinds had the most intense sour tang and subtle fruity overtones. As is true of most spices and herbs, sumac's flavor fades over time. When you shop for the seasoning, a busy Middle Eastern market is likely to have the freshest, most fragrant choices. Store sumac airtight in a cool, dark place.

Use the spice freely, sprinkled on everyday foods like salads, soups, meats, and fish.

Shish Kebabs with Sumac

About ⅓ cup ground sumac

2 teaspoons minced fresh ginger

½ teaspoon ground allspice

½ teaspoon crushed dried hot red chilies

2 pounds boned and fat-trimmed lamb leg or sirloin (in 1-in. cubes)

2 cloves garlic, minced or pressed

About 1 cup unflavored low-fat yogurt

Salt and pepper

In a bowl, mix together ⅓ cup sumac, ginger, allspice, and chilies. Add lamb and garlic; mix well. Cover and chill at least 30 minutes or up to 1 day. Thread meat onto skewers, keeping the pieces slightly apart.

Lay lamb on a grill 4 to 6 inches above a solid bed of medium coals (you can hold your hand at grill level for only 4 to 5 seconds). Turn frequently to brown evenly, and cook until meat is still pink in thickest part (cut to test), about 10 minutes.

Serve with yogurt and additional sumac, salt, and pepper to add to taste. Makes 6 servings.

Per serving: 238 cal. (31 percent from fat); 33 g protein; 8.3 g fat (3.1 g sat.); 5.6 g carbo.; 124 mg sodium; 102 mg chol.

Sumac-crusted Chicken

1 broiler-fryer chicken (3½ to 4 lb.), quartered, skin and fat removed

About ⅓ cup ground sumac

1 tablespoon dried oregano leaves

½ teaspoon *each* pepper, salt, and ground cinnamon

2 tablespoons olive or salad oil

1 tablespoon water

About 1 cup unflavored nonfat yogurt (optional)

Rinse chicken and pat dry; set aside. In a small bowl, stir together ⅓ cup sumac, oregano, pepper, salt, and cinnamon; mix with oil and water. Rub herb mixture onto the meatiest side of each chicken piece.

Lay chicken pieces in a single layer, spiced side up, in a 10- by 15-inch pan. Bake in a 425° oven until well-browned and meat at thigh is no longer pink (cut to test), about 30 minutes. Accompany chicken with yogurt and additional sumac to add to taste. Makes 4 servings.

Per serving: 348 cal. (44 percent from fat); 41 g protein; 17 g fat (3.8 g sat.); 4.7 g carbo.; 396 mg sodium; 127 mg chol.

Sumac and Lentil Salad

1 package (12 oz., about 1¾ cups) lentils

4 cups regular-strength chicken broth

1 large (about 1-lb.) cucumber, peeled and chopped

1 large (about 8-oz.) red or yellow bell pepper, stemmed, seeded, and thinly sliced

½ cup fresh cilantro (coriander) leaves (optional)

Dressing (recipe follows)

Ground sumac

Salt and pepper

Sort lentils to remove debris; rinse and drain. In a 3- to 4-quart pan over high heat, bring broth to boiling; add lentils. Cover and simmer until lentils are tender, about 25 minutes. Drain; save broth for other uses. Let lentils cool. If cooking ahead, cover and chill lentils and broth up to 1 day.

Mix lentils, cucumber, bell pepper, cilantro, and dressing. Serve with ground sumac, salt, and pepper to add to taste. Serves 8.

Per serving: 220 cal. (20 percent from fat); 14 g protein; 4.8 g fat (0.8 g sat.); 32 g carbo.; 37 mg sodium; 0 mg chol.

Dressing. Combine ½ cup **orange juice**, ½ cup minced **red onion**, ¼ cup **lemon juice**, 3 tablespoons grated **orange peel**, 3 tablespoons **ground sumac**, and 2 tablespoons **extra-virgin olive oil** or salad oil. ∎

By Betsy Reynolds Bateson

PETER CHRISTIANSEN

CRUSTED *with sumac, lamb grills to a deep purple-brown.*

PETER CHRISTIANSEN

TENDER STALKS *of Chinese leek flower accompany ginger- and sherry-flavored chicken with rice.*

Cooking with onion bulbs, leaves, buds and stalks

Plant perennial onions in the fall and harvest them for years to come

OTATO ONIONS, Egyptian onions, and Chinese leek flowers are seldom featured prominently on supermarkets' produce counters, nor will you find them in most home gardens.

These cousins of the ordinary bulbing onion are part of a diverse group in the *Allium* family known as perennial onions. Once you plant them, they'll provide many crops.

Potato onions are related to common single-bulb onions and shallots, which grow by dividing. Egyptian onions belong to the type called topset onions, which produce many leafy green stalks; small bulblets form on their tops. Chinese leeks (also called Oriental garlic chives) and Chinese leek flowers are related to common chives.

The more unusual perennial onions must be ordered by mail. Here are four sources.

Nichols Garden Nursery, 1190 N. Pacific Highway, Albany, OR 97321; (503) 928-9280 (free catalog). Chives, Oriental garlic chives, and onions (bunching, Egyptian).

Seeds Blüm, Idaho City Stage, Boise, ID 83706 (catalog $3). Welsh onions and potato onions.

Southern Exposure Seed Exchange, Box 158, North Garden, VA 22959; (804) 973-4703 (catalog $3). Shallots, and bunching, Egyptian, and potato onions.

Sunrise Enterprises, Box 330058, West Hartford, CT 06133; (203) 666-8071 (catalog $2). Bunching onions, and broad-leafed, common, and Chinese leek flowers.

Chive Mayonnaise

Serve as a dip for vegetables or as a sandwich spread.

1 cup thinly sliced chives, Chinese leeks, or Chinese leek flower leaves

½ cup unflavored nonfat yogurt

½ cup reduced-calorie or regular mayonnaise

Salt

In a blender or food processor, combine the chives, yogurt, and mayonnaise; whirl until smoothly blended. Add salt to taste. Serve, or cover and chill up to 1 day. Makes 1¼ cups.

Per tablespoon: 20 cal. (72 percent from fat); 0.4 g protein; 1.6 g fat (0.4 g sat.); 0.9 g carbo.; 37 mg sodium; 2 mg chol.

Pickled Egyptian Onions

1 cup Egyptian onion bulblets (about ½ in. wide)

⅔ cup seasoned rice vinegar (or ½ cup rice vinegar plus 3 tablespoons sugar and salt to taste)

Separate bulblets, trim ends, peel, rinse, and drain. In a 1- to 2-quart pan, combine bulblets and vinegar. Bring to a boil over high heat; boil, uncovered, for 1 minute. Pour into a wide-mouthed jar; cover. Cool, and chill at least 1 day or up to 1 month. Makes 1 cup.

Per ¼ cup: 49 cal. (0 percent from fat); 0.4 g protein; 0 g fat; 12 g carbo.; 800 mg sodium; 0 mg chol.

Gingered Chicken with Leek Flowers

When using the Chinese leek flowers, pick young tender stalks with tightly closed buds. As the flowers open and plant matures, the stalks become woody and tough.

To determine where the tender part begins, gently bend stalk, working up from the tough end; the stalk will snap where tender, much like asparagus.

1 tablespoon butter or margarine

2 skinned and boned chicken breast halves (about 6 oz. each)

⅓ cup dry sherry

⅓ cup regular-strength chicken broth

1 teaspoon finely shredded fresh ginger

4 to 6 ounces tightly closed Chinese leek flowers with stalks, or 6 bunching (or green) onions

1 teaspoon cornstarch mixed with 1 tablespoon water

In a 10- to 12-inch frying pan, melt butter over medium-high heat. Add chicken; brown on all sides, 2 to 3 minutes total. Add sherry, broth, and ginger. Reduce heat to low, cover, and simmer 3 minutes.

Meanwhile, snap off tough ends from leek flower stalks (see preceding; or trim ends and tops of bunching or green onions); rinse. Add leek flower stalks (or onions) to chicken; simmer, covered, until breast halves are no longer pink in thickest part (cut to test) and leeks are tender when pierced, 4 to 6 minutes. With a slotted spoon, transfer chicken and leek flowers to a warm platter; keep warm.

Measure pan juices. If needed, add water to make ½ cup; stir in cornstarch mixture. Return mixture to pan and stir over high heat until boiling. Pour sauce over chicken. Makes 2 servings.

Per serving: 346 cal. (22 percent from fat); 41 g protein; 8.3 g fat (4.2 g sat.); 15 g carbo.; 193 mg sodium; 114 mg chol. ■

By Lauren Bonar Swezey, Linda Lau Anusasananan

BOUNTIFUL PERSIMMON HARVEST dries suspended from strings so air can circulate and moisture evaporates.

Pucker up, it's persimmon time

Beautiful burnished copper orbs dry sweet as candy

THERE'S SOMETHING almost sinful about persimmons. They taste like temptation," says Howard Statham, of Fresno, California. He and his wife, Yolanda, are so fond of dried persimmons that each year they preserve their tree's bountiful harvest to enjoy for months beyond the fruit's short season.

The dried persimmons become a natural confection; their dense, chewy flavor is much like that of dates' but not as cloying. Dried persimmons are a long-standing delicacy in countries in the Orient and are found in many Asian markets.

The fruit drying process is simple. The Stathams clip bright orange but still-firm Hachiya-type persimmons from the tree, leaving about 1½ inches of the stem, "a T for hanging." (If you start with stem-trimmed store fruit, refer to the following instructions for an alternative procedure.) Then they peel the fruit, tie string onto the stems, and hang the persimmons from nails in the ceiling beams and a rack they've devised.

As the persimmons hang, moisture evaporates (unpeeled fruit softens and ripens instead of drying).

For a chewy texture, the Stathams dry the fruit just un-til it's leathery but still pliable. Then they snap off stems and store the persimmons airtight in the freezer. Whenever they want a persimmon, they just pull one out.

The Stathams dry the Hachiya-type persimmons because this is what their tree produces, but crisp, flat-bottomed Fuyu-type fruit dries equally well.

You can also dry persimmon slices. A dehydrator works best, but you can use your oven.

Oven-dried persimmon slices may darken or turn black where they touch the metal racks (a harmless heat-activated reaction).

Dried Whole Persimmons

Hachiya-type persimmons are good to eat fresh only when the fruit is very soft. But for drying, they must be fully colored (no green) and firm enough to peel; the fruit loses its astringency as it dries.

Fuyu-type persimmons are good to eat crisp and firm, and they can be dried at this stage. The fruit should be a bright orange.

To dry whole persimmons with stems. Clip persimmons from tree, keeping a short T of stem. Break or trim off the calyxes (green ruffled tops) without loosening the stems, then peel persimmons with a vegetable peeler. Tie a 10- to 12-inch length of cotton string securely around each stem.

To dry whole persimmons without stems. Keep calyxes intact and peel persimmons. Slip a 10- to 12-inch length of cotton string under each calyx and tie snugly.

Hang persimmons from string so the fruit is free on all sides and air can circulate. Let persimmons hang until they feel leathery but are still pliable, about 1 month. Remove string.

Eat dried persimmons whole or cut into slices; to store, package airtight and chill up to 6 months, or freeze to store longer.

During storage, dried persimmons often develop a sugary surface that looks like white powder and is quite natural.

Dried Persimmon Slices

Peel firm-ripe Hachiya- or Fuyu-type persimmons and cut crosswise into ¼-inch-thick slices.

To avoid harmless discoloration, line metal racks with cheesecloth.

Dehydrator method. Arrange slices slightly apart on dehydrator racks. Dry slices at 100°, turning occasionally, until edges are nearly crisp and centers are leathery but still pliable, about 24 hours.

Oven method. Arrange persimmon slices slightly apart on metal cooling racks set on 12- by 15-inch pans. Bake in a 150° oven, turning occasionally, until edges are nearly crisp and centers are leathery but still pliable, about 8 hours. If the oven gets too hot, occasionally prop the door open to cool.

Let slices cool, then eat or store as directed for dried whole persimmons. ∎

By Christine Weber Hale, Elaine Johnson

PETER CHRISTIANSEN

PEEL FIRM HACHIYA-TYPE *persimmons; they lose their moisture, astringency, and puckery effect as they dry, becoming very sweet and dense—almost like candy.*

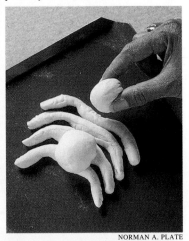

FIRST GRADERS DISPLAY
*baby spider breads; teacher
holds the big mom. All were
shaped from thawed frozen
dough, then baked. The
realistic results (bottom) were
proudly toted home.*

Return
of spider
bread

*Thirty-five first
graders create
baby spiders*

S EVERAL OCTOBERS
ago, we published a
recipe for a big
black widow spider
bread. Ann Straw, a teacher at
St. Simon School in Los Altos, California, created the se-
quel to our recipe as a hands-
on class project for 5- and
6-year-olds. The results were
delightful baby spider rolls,
an idea to try at home.

Straw adapted the recipe to
purchased yeast roll dough so
each child could make his or
her own spider. The dough
comes in conveniently cut,
easy-to-use portions. Two
portions make a spider roll;
one part is used for body and
head, the other for legs.

With scissors to divide the
dough, young bakers easily
assembled spiders for baking
with little supervision.

Baby Spider Rolls

1   package (1 lb. 9 oz.)
    frozen Parker House roll
    dough, thawed

1   large egg, beaten to
    blend

¼   cup black sesame seed
    or poppy seed

To make each spider, use
2 rolls. Dip scissors in flour,
then cut 1 roll into 4 equal
strips. With floured hands or
on a floured board, roll or

stretch each strip into a log
about 4½ inches long. On a
greased 12- by 15-inch baking sheet, set logs parallel to
each other, about ¼ inch
apart. Bend each log slightly
on both ends to resemble spider legs.

Cut remaining roll apart,
making 1 piece about twice
as large as the other. Shape
each piece into a smooth
ball. Set balls, touching each
other, on top of the legs,
forming body and head (see
photo at top right). Gently
press body and head, sticking them onto the legs.

Repeat to make remaining
spiders, spacing them about

2 inches apart on pan. Cover
lightly with plastic wrap. Let
rise in a warm place until
puffy, 10 to 15 minutes. Brush
dough lightly with beaten
egg and sprinkle evenly with
sesame seed.

Bake in a 350° oven until
golden brown, about 20 minutes. Transfer to racks; let
cool. Serve warm or cool. (If
making ahead, store cool
rolls airtight up to 1 day. To
store, freeze up to 2 weeks.)
Makes 12.

*Per roll: 153 cal. (21 percent from
fat); 6 g protein; 3.6 g fat (0.3 g
sat.); 24 g carbo.; 5.6 mg sodium;
18 mg chol.* ■

By Linda Lau Anusasananan

From tart to sweet and back

Don't dismiss the worth of persimmons

LIKE SLEEPING BEAUTY, the Hachiya persimmon was given all the graces but a wicked fairy laid a curse on it: the unripe fruit is so astringent that many people, once victimized by its puckery harshness, are unwilling to taste it again even after its ripeness is attested to by its softness. (Ripe fruits have the feel of water balloons that sportive college students drop from their dorm windows.) At the proper stage, these beautiful bags of sweetness not only are delicious when spooned up or slurped directly from their skins, but also make prime ingredients in baked goods like this splendid persimmon pudding.

Persimmon Pudding

1½ cups ripe Hachiya-type persimmon pulp (about 3 large persimmons)
1 tablespoon baking soda
3 large eggs
1 cup firmly packed brown sugar
About ½ cup (¼ lb.) butter or margarine, melted
1 cup milk
2 teaspoons vanilla
¾ cup *each* all-purpose flour and whole-wheat flour
1½ teaspoons baking powder
2 teaspoons ground cinnamon
1 teaspoon ground ginger
½ teaspoon ground nutmeg
¼ cup bulgur (cracked wheat)
1 cup chopped walnuts or almonds
Whipped cream (optional)

Whirl pulp smooth in a blender, or rub through a strainer into a small bowl. Stir baking soda into persimmon pulp; set aside (mixture gets firm and thickens as it stands; whirl or beat with a whisk to use).

In a large bowl, beat eggs with a mixer on high speed until foamy, then stir in persimmon mixture, sugar, ½ cup butter, milk, and vanilla; stir to blend. Mix all-purpose flour, whole-wheat flour, baking powder, cinnamon, ginger, and nutmeg; add to batter along with bulgur and nuts; mix well.

Scrape batter into a buttered 8-inch-diameter 2½- or 3-quart soufflé dish or casserole. Bake in a 325° oven until center springs back when firmly pressed, about 1 hour and 10 minutes. Serve warm or at room temperature, scooped into bowls. Add whipped cream to taste. Makes 10 to 12 servings.

Per serving: 330 cal. (44 percent from fat); 6.1 g protein; 16 g fat (6.4 g sat.); 42 g carbo.; 491 mg sodium; 78 mg chol.

Louise Galen

Los Angeles

COLESLAW IS OFTEN thought of as a ho-hum kind of dish, the sort of thing offered as a dieter's substitute for french fries on the blue plate special.

No more: Janet Wood gives us Thai coleslaw, which brings the mystery of the East to the humble cabbage. (Not so humble at that; the cabbage is curly Savoy, supplemented by crunchy bok choy and rosy radicchio.) The hot, spicy, tart, and lean dressing has a truly Oriental complexity.

Thai Coleslaw

⅓ cup rice vinegar
⅓ cup lime juice
¼ cup drained, red-color slivered pickled ginger
2 small fresh serrano or jalapeño chilies, stemmed, seeded, and finely chopped
1 tablespoon Oriental sesame oil
1 tablespoon sugar
1 tablespoon fish sauce (*nam pla* or *nuoc mam*)
½ teaspoon wasabi (green horseradish) powder
2 teaspoons sesame seed
About 1 pound bok choy
2 medium-size (about 6 oz. total) carrots
1 small (about ¼-lb.) red onion
8 cups finely slivered Savoy or green cabbage
1 small (about 3-oz.) radicchio, finely slivered

In a small bowl, stir together vinegar, lime juice, pickled ginger, chilies, sesame oil, sugar, fish sauce, and wasabi powder; set aside.

In a 6- to 8-inch frying pan, shake sesame seed over medium heat until golden, about 3 minutes. Pour from pan and save.

Rinse and drain bok choy; discard bruised or wilted leaves. Thinly slice bok choy and carrots. Cut onion in half; thinly slice vertically.

In a large bowl, mix bok choy, carrots, onion, cabbage, radicchio, and vinegar mixture; sprinkle with sesame seed. Makes about 16 cups, 8 to 12 servings.

Per cup: 54 cal. (28 percent from fat); 2.2 g protein; 1.7 g fat (0.2 g sat.); 8.8 g carbo.; 57 mg sodium; 0 mg chol.

Eugene, Oregon

By Joan Griffiths, Richard Dunmire

SUNSET'S KITCHEN CABINET

Creative ways with everyday foods—submitted by *Sunset* readers,
tested in *Sunset* kitchens, approved by *Sunset* taste panels

DRIED PEACH *chunks stud these wholesome oat bran muffins.*

Bran-Peach Muffins

Laura Waguespack, Dallas

- 1 cup all-purpose flour
- ½ cup whole-wheat flour
- ½ cup oat bran
- 2 teaspoons baking powder
- ¾ cup firmly packed brown sugar
- 1 teaspoon ground cinnamon
- 1½ cups (about 10 oz.) firmly packed dried peaches, coarsely chopped
- 1¼ cups milk
- 1 large egg white
- About 2 tablespoons salad oil

In a bowl, mix all-purpose flour, whole-wheat flour, oat bran, baking powder, sugar, and cinnamon. Add peaches, milk, egg white, and 2 tablespoons oil; stir to moisten evenly. Divide equally among 12 oiled or paper-lined muffin cups (2 to 2½ in. wide).

Bake in a 350° oven until muffins are well browned, about 30 minutes. Serve warm or cool. If making ahead, let cool; store airtight at room temperature up to 1 day. Makes 12.

Per muffin: 221 cal. (20 percent from fat); 4.4 g protein; 4.9 g fat (1 g sat.); 44 g carbo.; 106 mg sodium; 3.6 mg chol.

Spinach-Ricotta Burritos

Linda Strader, Amado, Arizona

BAKED BURRITOS *enclose ricotta-spinach filling in flour tortillas.*

- ½ pound spinach
- 2 tablespoons all-purpose flour
- ¾ teaspoon chili powder
- ½ teaspoon ground cumin
- ½ teaspoon crushed dried hot red chilies
- About 2 cups (15-oz. carton) ricotta cheese
- 4 flour tortillas (9- or 10-in. size)
- 6 ounces part-skim mozzarella cheese, thinly sliced
- 2 teaspoons melted butter or margarine
- Prepared tomato or tomatillo salsa
- Salt

Discard wilted spinach leaves and roots; rinse leaves well and drain.

Coarsely shred ½ the spinach. Wrap remaining spinach in towels, seal in a plastic bag, and chill.

In a bowl, mix flour, chili powder, cumin, and crushed chilies; mix in ricotta. Lay 1 tortilla flat; layer in center ¼ each of mozzarella, shredded spinach, and ricotta mixture. Fold opposite sides over filling, then roll tortilla over and tuck open ends under it. Lay seam down in an oiled 9- by 13-inch casserole. Repeat to fill remaining tortillas. Brush tops of burritos with the melted butter.

Bake, uncovered, in a 400° oven until golden brown, about 25 minutes. Present burritos on spinach leaves; add salsa and salt to taste. Serves 4.

Per serving: 515 cal. (47 percent from fat); 29 g protein; 27 g fat (15 g sat.); 40 g carbo.; 607 mg sodium; 84 mg chol.

Sunni's Gazpacho with Shrimp

Sunni Moland-McNary, Spokane, Washington

AVOCADO SLICES *top chilled tomato soup with tiny shrimp and cream cheese.*

- 6 cups clam-flavored tomato juice
- 2 medium-size (about 1½ lb. total) cucumbers, peeled, seeded, and diced
- ¼ cup minced fresh or 2 tablespoons crumbled dried basil leaves
- 2 tablespoons red wine vinegar
- 2 teaspoons pepper
- ½ pound shelled cooked tiny shrimp
- 1 large (about 10-oz.) firm-ripe avocado
- 1 tablespoon lemon juice
- 1 small package (3 oz.) cream cheese, cut into ¼- to ½-inch cubes
- Salt

Combine 3 cups flavored tomato juice and ½ the cucumbers in a blender or food processor; whirl until smooth. Pour mixture into a large bowl, and stir in remaining tomato juice, remaining cucumbers, basil, vinegar, and pepper. Cover and chill until soup is cold, at least 1 hour or up to 1 day.

Rinse shrimp with cool water; drain. Peel, pit, and thinly slice avocado lengthwise; coat slices with lemon juice. Ladle soup into 4 to 6 wide bowls. Add to each bowl equal portions shrimp, avocado, and cheese. Season to taste with salt. Serves 4 to 6.

Per serving: 291 cal. (34 percent from fat); 12 g protein; 11 g fat (4.1 g sat.); 38 g carbo.; 1,224 mg sodium; 89 mg chol.

Bok Choy Salad with Mint

Maggie Morgan, Sun City West, Arizona

8 cups finely slivered bok choy

½ cup thinly sliced red onion

¼ cup minced fresh mint leaves

2 tablespoons minced fresh cilantro (coriander)

Dijon dressing (recipe follows)

Large bok choy leaves, rinsed and drained (optional)

Salt and pepper

In a bowl, combine slivered bok choy, onion, mint leaves, cilantro, and Dijon dressing. Gently mix.

Lay bok choy leaves in a serving bowl, stalks toward the center; mound salad onto leaves. Season portions to taste with salt and pepper. Makes 4 to 6 servings.

Per serving: 41 cal. (11 percent from fat); 1.7 g protein; 0.5 g fat (0 g sat.); 8.2 g carbo.; 608 mg sodium; 0 mg chol.

Dijon dressing. Mix together ½ cup **seasoned rice vinegar** (or ½ cup rice vinegar mixed with 1 teaspoon sugar), 2 tablespoons **Dijon mustard,** and 1 clove minced or pressed **garlic.**

CRISP BOK CHOY *is base of vegetable salad with Dijon mustard dressing.*

Johnny Appleseed Burgers

J. Hill, Sacramento

1 pound ground turkey

¼ pound bulk pork sausage

1 large egg white

¼ cup fine dried bread crumbs

½ cup peeled and finely chopped tart apple

¼ cup minced onion

1 tablespoon minced fresh ginger

4 toasted hamburger buns

Apple cabbage slaw (recipe follows)

Salt

Mix together turkey, sausage, egg white, bread crumbs, apple, onion, and ginger. Shape into 4 equal-size patties, each about ¾ inch thick. Lay patties on a lightly oiled grill 4 to 6 inches above a solid bed of medium-hot coals (you can hold your hand at grill level for only 3 to 4 seconds). Cook, turning as needed, until patties are no longer pink in the center (cut to test), 15 to 20 minutes.

Place patties in hamburger buns; top with equal amounts of slaw and add salt to taste. Serves 4.

Per serving: 404 cal. (33 percent from fat); 28 g protein; 15 g fat (4.3 g sat.); 36 g carbo.; 596 mg sodium; 94 mg chol.

Apple cabbage slaw. Mix together 1 cup finely shredded **red cabbage,** 1 cup very thinly sliced unpeeled **tart green apple,** 3 tablespoons **orange juice,** and 1 tablespoon **balsamic** or red wine **vinegar.**

APPLE CABBAGE SLAW *goes with moist turkey burgers; offer tomatoes, too.*

Apple Cobbler with Oatmeal Cookie Crust

Marjorie Mitchell, Brighton, Colorado

5 tablespoons butter or margarine

1 cup sugar

1 large egg white

1 teaspoon vanilla

1 cup all-purpose flour

¾ cup regular rolled oats

¾ teaspoon ground cardamom or ground cinnamon

Apple filling (recipe follows)

Vanilla ice cream or frozen yogurt (optional)

In a large bowl, beat butter and sugar with an electric mixer or spoon until creamy. Add egg white and vanilla; beat until blended.

Stir in flour, oats, and cardamom. If making ahead, wrap crust mixture air-tight and refrigerate up to 1 day.

Crumble crust mixture over apple filling. Bake, uncovered, in a 350° oven until topping is richly browned, about 1 hour. Spoon dessert, hot or cool, into bowls and top with ice cream. Makes 8 servings.

Per serving: 466 cal. (17 percent from fat); 3.7 g protein; 8.6 g fat (4.7 g sat.); 98 g carbo.; 81 mg sodium; 19 mg chol.

Apple filling. Core, peel, and slice 10 large (about 5 lb. total) **tart apples** (such as Gravenstein or Granny Smith) into a shallow 3- to 3½-quart casserole. Mix slices with ¾ cup **sugar,** 1 tablespoon **cornstarch,** 1½ teaspoons **ground cinnamon,** and ½ teaspoon **ground allspice;** use within 10 to 15 minutes.

Compiled by Christine Weber Hale

AROMATIC SPICES *flavor oatmeal cookie crust that bakes on top of sliced apples.*

A grand Thanksgiving of choices

WE HAVEN'T THROWN OUT
THE TURKEY OR STUFFING,
BUT EVERYTHING ON
THE TABLE SHOULD
SURPRISE YOUR FAMILY

I n most families, planning Thanksgiving dinner is ticklish business. The challenge is always the same—to preserve traditions your family considers essential while introducing innovative food experiences. As well, you need to make allowances for busy schedules, be sensitive (if only slightly, because this is a

SAVOR *warm pear focaccia and pickled vegetables before sitting down at autumn-decorated holiday table.*

228

NORMAN A. PLATE

THREE GENERATIONS *of the Skov family watch as patriarch, John, presents barbecued turkey with chili-orange glaze.*

feast) to nutritional concerns, and still present a memorable meal. Such demands strain the creativity of even the most experienced cooks.

A good launching pad for a meal to meet these needs is our Thanksgiving master menu on page 230. Use it as a guide, selecting dishes with a fresh approach to traditional flavors, and drop in your family favorites where appropriate. The 26 recipes you can choose from all include make-ahead steps, minimize

last-minute touches, travel well (if sharing the labor is part of your scheme), and provide a range of richness—some are startlingly low-fat, others forthrightly indulgent. Each recipe is designed to serve eight; if your gathering is larger, make duplicate dishes or add some others, as you like.

With our menu as a guide, the Skov family of San Francisco tailored the holiday meal shown here for six adults and four small children

(recipes for eight made just the right amounts). First, they chose chili-orange glaze for the barbecued turkey. The meal was rounded out with a wilt-resistant salad—Belgian endive with tangelos and cranberry dressing; chilled sugar snap peas with mint and bacon dressing, and garlic mashed potatoes; red pepper relish to go with the turkey; brown giblet gravy; and polenta, Swiss chard, and sausage dressing. A cashew caramel tart was selected to

COLORFUL *fruit and endive salad is waiting at the table.*

The Thanksgiving Dinner checklist

Appetizers *(Pick one or both)*

☐ Pear and Pepper Focaccia *(page 232)*   ☐ Italian Pickled Vegetables*** *(page 233)*

Salads *(Choose one)*

☐ Belgian Endive, Tangelo, and Cranberry Salad*** *(page 233)*   ☐ Poached Leeks with Caper-Lemon Dressing *(page 233)*   ☐ Hazelnut, Avocado, and Mesclun Salad *(page 234)*

The Bird *(Decide on the finishing touch)*

☐ Barbecued Turkey Glazed or Basted, *(page 231)*   ☐ Chili-Orange Glaze*** *(page 231)*   ☐ Brown Sugar Crackle Glaze*** *(page 231)*   ☐ Sage Butter Baste *(page 231)*

The Gravy *(To go with everything)*

☐ Rich Brown Giblet Gravy** *(page 237)*

Vegetables *(Make at least two, maybe more)*

☐ Chilled Sugar Snap Peas with Mint and Bacon Dressing* *(page 234)*   ☐ Garlic Mashed Potatoes* *(page 235)*   ☐ Baked Fennel with Gorgonzola *(page 235)*

☐ Creamed Spinach in a Squash Shell* *(page 234)*   ☐ Double-Ginger Sweet Potatoes with Port*** *(page 235)*   ☐ Sweet Mustard Carrots with Pistachios *(page 235)*

Dressing *(One is enough)*

☐ Polenta, Swiss Chard, and Sausage Dressing *(page 236)*   ☐ Wild Rice and Porcini Mushroom Dressing*** *(page 236)*   ☐ Old-fashioned or Lean** Multigrain Bread Dressing *(page 236)*

Relishes *(Offer one or both)*

☐ Red Pepper Relish with Aromatics*** *(page 237)*   ☐ Cranberry-Grapefruit Relish*** *(page 237)*

Dessert *(To diet or not to diet)*

☐ Chocolate Twig Cake *(page 239)*   ☐ Spiced Pumpkin Roll*** *(page 239)*   ☐ Ruby Grapefruit Sorbet*** *(page 240)*

☐ Chestnut Tiramisù* *(page 240)*   ☐ Cashew Caramel Tart *(page 240)*

Wines *(For selections, see page 241)*

***10 percent, **20 percent, or *30 percent or fewer calories from fat

---

fill the dessert spot.

Wondering what wines to serve with such a diverse selection of foods and flavors? On page 241, Bob Thompson, *Sunset*'s wine consultant, provides a list of wines that easily accommodate your holiday menu no matter what your budget is. He also advises on serving the wines and what glasses to use.

Finally, in trying a fresh approach to traditional Thanksgiving fare, you may have some concerns about pleasing pickier palates among family and friends. Here's a hint from the Skov family's most discriminating personalities—the grandchildren. When confronted with the pear and pepper focaccia, they were reluctant to try it until they realized the fruit-topped slices looked similar to the squares of a pizza they had seen advertised on television. Upon that discovery, they dug right in. ■

By Christine Weber Hale

PACE SLOWS *with dessert—rich cashew tart and coffee.*

When turkey meets grill

Three glazes that work on the barbecue or in the oven

THE BENEFITS OF barbecuing your turkey are twofold. First, it frees up the oven and kitchen space. Second, it browns the bird magnificently. But barbecued or oven roasted, the Thanksgiving bird benefits from these glazes. Choose the tangy orange with mild chili heat, the crunchy brown sugar glaze, or the more traditional sage butter.

Barbecued Turkey

To prepare turkey, remove and discard leg truss. Pull off and discard lumps of fat and remove giblets. Rinse bird inside and out, then pat dry. Rinse giblets, drain, and reserve for rich brown giblet gravy (recipe page 237). Insert thermometer straight down through the thickest part of the breast to the bone.

In a charcoal-fueled barbecue with a lid, mound and ignite 40 charcoal briquets on firegrate. When briquets are dotted with gray ash, about 30 minutes, divide in half and push to opposite side of firegrate. Place a metal drip pan between coals. Add 5 briquets (10

NORMAN A. PLATE

GENEROUSLY BRUSH *chili-orange glaze on turkey when it is almost cooked; sweet finish darkens quickly.*

total) to each mound of coals now and every 30 minutes while cooking. Set grill 4 to 6 inches above coals.

In a gas barbecue, adjust controls for indirect heat, set a drip pan between heat sources (if manufacturer recommends), and turn heat to high; allow 5 to 10 minutes to reach temperature.

Rub grill lightly with oil. Set turkey, breast up, on grill over drip pan. Cover with lid; open vents on charcoal-fueled barbecue. Cook turkey for time suggested in chart below, but, because temperature, heat control, and size and shape of the bird can all vary, start checking doneness at least 30 minutes before minimum cooking time.

If parts of the turkey begin to get dark before the bird is done, drape those areas with foil.

Per ¼ pound boneless cooked turkey, based on percentages of white and dark meat found in average turkey (including skin): 229 cal. (39 percent from fat); 32 g protein; 10 g fat (3 g sat.); 0 g carbo.; 82 mg sodium; 93 mg chol.

Chili-Orange Glaze

3   tablespoons ground dried New Mexico or California chilies, or 3 tablespoons chili powder

1   large container (12 oz., or 1½ cups) frozen orange juice concentrate, thawed

2   tablespoons grated orange peel

1   teaspoon ground cumin

Mix ground chilies (or chili powder), orange juice concentrate, orange peel, and cumin. *If making ahead, cover and chill up to 3 days.*

The last 20 minutes the turkey cooks (at bone, temperature in the breast will be about 150° for birds up to 18 lb., 155° for birds over 18 lb.), spread turkey generously with the glaze.

Continue to cook until a thermometer inserted into the thickest part of turkey breast to the bone registers

160°; if glaze starts to get very dark, drape dark areas with foil. Makes enough to glaze a 12- to 24-pound turkey.

Per tablespoon: 32 cal. (6 percent from fat); 0.6 g protein; 0.2 g fat (0 g sat.); 7.4 g carbo.; 10 mg sodium; 0 mg chol.

Brown Sugar Crackle Glaze

2   cups firmly packed brown sugar

5   tablespoons Dijon mustard

2   teaspoons coarse-ground pepper

Mix together sugar, mustard, and pepper. *If making ahead, cover and chill up to 3 days.* The last 45 minutes the turkey cooks (at bone, temperature in the breast will be about 135° for birds up to 18 lb., about 145° for birds over 18 lb.), spread turkey with half the glaze. Cook 20 minutes; brush with remaining glaze. Continue to cook until a thermometer inserted into the thickest part of turkey breast to the bone registers 160°. If sections of the glaze start to darken excessively before turkey is done, drape with foil. Makes enough to glaze a 12- to 24-pound turkey.

Per tablespoon: 49 cal. (2 percent from fat); 0 g protein; 0.1 g fat (0 g sat.); 12 g carbo.; 67 mg sodium; 0 mg chol.

Sage Butter Baste

¼   cup (⅛ lb.) butter or margarine, melted

¼   tablespoon minced fresh or 1 tablespoon crumbled dried sage leaves

2   tablespoons lemon juice

Mix together butter, sage, and lemon juice. The last 45 minutes the turkey cooks (at bone, temperature in the breast will be about 135° for birds up to 18 lb., about 145° for birds over 18 lb.), baste often with the butter. Continue to cook until a thermometer inserted into thickest part of breast to the bone registers 160°. Makes enough to baste a 12- to 24-pound turkey.

Per tablespoon: 73 cal. (99 percent from fat); 0.1 g protein; 8 g fat (5 g sat.); 0.5 g carbo.; 82 mg sodium; 22 mg chol. ■

By Christine Weber Hale

Barbecued* or Oven-roasted Turkey

Turkey weight with giblets	Oven temp.*	Internal temp.**	Cooking time
10 to 13 lb.	350°	160°	1½ to 2¼ hr.
14 to 23 lb.	325°	160°	2 to 3 hr.
24 to 26 lb.	325°	160°	3 to 3¾ hr.
28 to 30 lb.	325°	160°	3½ to 4½ hr.

* See barbecued turkey, above, for heat controls for charcoal or gas barbecues.
** Insert thermometer through thickest part of breast to bone.

COLD LEEKS *with capers is a salad that waits well.*

The full plate

To accompany the turkey, the choice is yours: complement family traditions or try a whole new feast

S EASONAL INGREDIENTS and holiday flavors overlap deliciously in this varied collection of recipes. Start your menu plan with dishes your family won't do without, then supplement it with these fresh ideas. If you want to be ready when guests arrive, or want to make the dinner a cooperative effort, take advantage of the make-ahead steps. If dishes will be transported, store them in insulated bags or chests or wrap the covered dishes in several thick layers of newspaper.

Each of these recipes serves eight.

RED PEPPERS *make a relish.*

POACHED FENNEL, *baked with gorgonzola and crumb topping, has*

STARTERS

Pear and Pepper Focaccia

1 loaf (1 lb.) frozen white bread dough, thawed

2 tablespoons lemon juice

2 medium-size (about ¾ lb. total) firm-ripe pears

Parsley pesto (recipe follows)

1½ tablespoons sugar

1 teaspoon coarse-ground pepper

¾ cup shredded parmesan cheese

Parsley leaves (optional)

Place dough in a lightly oiled 10- by 15-inch rimmed pan; press and push to cover pan evenly. If dough is too elastic, let it rest a few min-

utes, then press again. Cover dough lightly with plastic wrap and let stand in a warm place until puffy, about 1 hour.

Meanwhile, put lemon juice in a bowl. Core and thinly slice pears into bowl, mixing fruit with juice.

With your fingertips, gently press dough to cover it with dimpled impressions;

also press dough gently into pan corners. Spread parsley pesto evenly over dough. Arrange pear slices on dough and press in gently. Mix sugar and pepper and sprinkle over the focaccia.

Bake in a 400° oven until focaccia is well browned on edges and underside, 30 to 35 minutes; after 20 minutes, sprinkle with parmesan

NORMAN A. PLATE
garnish of tender fennel leaves.

cheese. Cut while hot, warm, or cool. *If making ahead, cool, cover, and hold at room temperature up to 6 hours. To reheat, lightly cover pan with foil and bake in a 350° oven until warm to touch, 10 to 15 minutes.* Serves 12.

Per serving: 180 cal. (35 percent from fat); 5.2 g protein; 6.9 g fat (1.8 g sat.); 25 g carbo.; 280 mg sodium; 5.8 mg chol.

TINY CARROTS, *simmered in mustard broth, are seasoned with reduced broth, then sprinkled with pistachios.*

Parsley pesto. In a blender or food processor, combine 1½ cups firmly packed **parsley,** 3 tablespoons **olive** or salad **oil,** and 1 tablespoon grated **lemon peel.** Whirl until smoothly puréed; scrape container sides often. Use. Or, *if making ahead, cover and chill up to 1 day.*

Italian Pickled Vegetables

½ pound small (4- to 5-in.-long) carrots, peeled

1 package (10 oz.) frozen petite onions, thawed

1 large (about ½-lb.) red bell pepper, stemmed, seeded, and cut into ½-inch-wide strips

1 package (9 oz.) frozen artichoke hearts, thawed

2 cups white wine vinegar

¾ cup sugar

2 tablespoons drained canned capers

2 whole dried hot red chilies

2 cloves garlic, crushed

In a 2- to 3-quart pan, bring 1 quart water to a boil. Add carrots and cook, covered, until barely tender when pierced, about 3 minutes; drain. In a wide mouthed 1½- to 2-quart jar, layer carrots, onions, pepper, and artichoke hearts.

In the same pan, mix vinegar, sugar, capers, chilies, and garlic. Bring to a boil, stirring until sugar dissolves. Pour hot mixture over vegetables. Cover and chill at least 1 day or up to 2 weeks. Ladle vegetables from marinade to serve. Makes about 1½ quarts.

Per ¼ cup: 28 cal. (3.2 percent from fat); 0.5 g protein; 0.1 g fat (0 g sat.); 6.8 g carbo.; 19 mg sodium; 0 mg chol.

SIT DOWN TO SALADS

Belgian Endive, Tangelo, and Cranberry Salad

3 large (1 lb. total) Belgian endive

6 small (about 1⅓ lb. total) tangelos or medium-size tangerines

½ cup raspberry jelly

¼ cup white wine vinegar

1½ cups fresh or frozen cranberries

Salt and pepper

Trim ends from endive; rinse, and separate into leaves. Trim leaves to make them approximately equal length, 3 to 4 inches. Reserve trimmed portions and tiny leaves for other salads. *To crisp leaves, wrap separately in towels, enclose in plastic bags, and chill at least 30 minutes or up to 1 day.*

Grate enough peel from tangelos to make 2 tablespoons; set aside. Cut off and discard remaining peel and white membranes from all the tangelos. Separate into segments.

In a 1- to 2-quart pan over medium-high heat, stir peel, jelly, vinegar, and cranberries until berries begin to pop, about 5 minutes. Use lukewarm or cold. *If making ahead, chill tangelos and jelly dressing separately, airtight, up to 1 day.*

Arrange endive spoke-fashion on 8 salad plates; put tangelos in the center. Spoon dressing over salads. Add salt and pepper to taste. Serves 8.

Per serving: 96 cal. (1.9 percent from fat); 1 g protein; 0.2 g fat (0 g sat.); 24 g carbo.; 11 mg sodium; 0 mg chol.

Poached Leeks with Caper-Lemon Dressing

8 leeks (about 1½-in. diameter, 3½ lb. total)

1 tablespoon liquid from canned capers

2 tablespoons drained canned capers, slightly crushed

3 tablespoons lemon juice

3 tablespoons olive oil

⅓ cup long, fine shreds parmesan cheese

Italian parsley sprigs

NORMAN A. PLATE

MULTIGRAIN *bread dressing can be made rich or lean.*

Thin lemon slices

Salt and pepper

Trim roots (but not bases) and tough dark green tops from leeks. Halve leeks lengthwise; hold under cool running water and rinse well between layers. Tie each piece in the middle with cotton string.

In a covered 5- to 6-quart pan over high heat, bring about 3 quarts water to boiling. Drop leeks into water and simmer, uncovered, until tender when pierced, about 8 minutes. Drain and immerse in ice water until cold; drain and remove strings.

Combine caper liquid, capers, lemon juice, and olive oil. *If making ahead, chill leeks and dressing separately, airtight, up to 1 day; use at room temperature.*

Arrange leeks on 8 salad plates. Stir dressing and spoon over leeks; top with parmesan and garnish with parsley and lemon slices. Add salt and pepper to taste. Serves 8.

Per serving: 118 cal. (50 percent from fat); 3 g protein; 6.5 g fat (1.5 g sat.); 13 g carbo.; 163 mg sodium; 3.20 mg chol.

Hazelnut, Avocado, and Mesclun Salad

1 cup hazelnuts

5 tablespoons lime juice

3 tablespoons water

2 tablespoons hazelnut oil

¾ teaspoon sugar

3 quarts (about ½ lb.) mesclun or other mix of tender salad greens, rinsed and crisped

2 medium-size (½ lb. each) firm-ripe avocados

Salt and pepper

Place nuts in an 8- to 9-inch-wide pan. Bake in a 350° oven until deep golden brown beneath skins, 15 to 20 minutes; shake occasionally. Rub nuts in a towel to remove loose brown skin; discard skins. *If making ahead, let nuts cool, then store airtight up to 1 week.*

Combine lime juice, water, oil, and sugar. *If making ahead, chill the mixture airtight up to 2 days; use at room temperature.*

In a large bowl, combine mesclun with most of the dressing; spoon onto 8 plates. Pit, peel, and quarter avocados and place on plate; spoon remaining dressing onto avocados. Place nuts on plates. Season with salt and pepper. Serves 8.

Per serving: 197 cal. (87 percent from fat); 3.1 g protein; 19 g fat (1.9 g sat.); 7.3 g carbo.; 8.7 mg sodium; 0 mg chol.

MAKE-AHEAD VEGETABLES

Chilled Sugar Snap Peas with Mint and Bacon Dressing

1½ to 2 pounds sugar snap peas or Chinese pea pods, rinsed

1 tablespoon sugar

2 teaspoons cornstarch

½ cup *each* regular-strength chicken broth and rice vinegar

2 tablespoons minced fresh mint leaves

4 or 5 thick slices (about ¼ lb.) bacon, cooked crisp, drained, and crumbled

Break ends off peas and pull off strings. In a 4- to 5-

quart covered pan, bring about 2 quarts water to a boil over high heat. Add peas; cook, uncovered, until tender-crisp to bite, about 1 minute. Drain and, at once, immerse peas in ice water until cold. Drain. *If making ahead, wrap airtight and chill up to 1 day.*

In a 1½- to 2-quart pan, mix sugar and cornstarch, then stir in broth and vinegar. Bring to boil over high heat, stirring. Let cool. *If making ahead, cover and chill up to 1 day; let come to room temperature and stir well.* Arrange peas in a bowl; stir mint into sauce and pour over peas. Sprinkle with bacon. Serves 8.

Per serving: 69 cal. (29 percent from fat); 3.7 g protein; 2.2 g fat (0.7 g sat.); 8.7 g carbo.; 70 mg sodium; 3.4 mg chol.

Creamed Spinach in a Squash Shell

1 squat, round (7- to 8-in.-wide, about 4-lb.) hard-shell red kuri squash (orange color) or kabocha (green color)

Creamed spinach (directions follow)

Long, thin strands of lemon peel (optional)

Rinse squash and pierce through top to center in 2 or 3 places, using a metal skewer. For easy handling, set squash on a piece of cheesecloth large enough to enclose it. Tie cheesecloth loosely on top of squash (leaving some access to vegetable for testing). Set squash on a rack above ¾ to 1 inch water in a 5- to 6-quart pan at least 1 inch wider than squash; water should not touch squash. Cover and bring to a boil on high heat; steam over medium heat until very tender when pierced,

LARGE, *sweet-fleshed kuri squash, steamed, holds creamed spinach.*

about 30 minutes.

Protecting your hands, use cheesecloth to lift squash from pan; untie cloth. Neatly slice off top quarter of squash to make a lid. With a small spoon, gently scoop out seeds and discard; take care not to tear or poke a hole in shell (some kinds are more fragile, so handle carefully). *If making ahead, put lid on squash, wrap airtight, and chill up to 1 day. To reheat, place unwrapped squash on a microwave-safe plate in a microwave oven on full power (100 percent) for 4-minute intervals until hot, about 12 minutes. Or seal in foil and place in a 375° oven until hot, about 45 minutes; unwrap on a serving plate.*

Fill squash with creamed spinach, sprinkle with lemon peel, and, if desired, set lid in place. To serve, lift lid and scoop squash from the shell as you spoon out spinach. Serves 8.

Per serving: 189 cal. (23 percent from fat); 8 g protein; 4.9 g fat (2.2 g sat.); 34 g carbo.; 96 mg sodium; 10 mg chol.

Creamed spinach. Thaw 3 packages (10 oz. each) **frozen chopped spinach;** squeeze spinach dry and set aside.

In a 10- to 12-inch frying pan over high heat, combine 1 large (8- to 10-oz.) finely chopped **onion** and ¼ cup **water.** Stir often until liquid evaporates and onion starts to brown. Add ¼ cup **regular-strength chicken broth** and stir to release browned bits in pan; boil and stir often until pan is dry and onions begin to brown. Remove from heat and mix 3 tablespoons **all-purpose flour** thoroughly with the onions. Gradually, smoothly mix in 1 cup regular-strength chicken broth and ½ cup **reduced-fat** or regular **sour cream;** add 1

234

NORMAN A. PLATE

SWEET POTATOES *bake with port and two kinds of ginger.*

teaspoon **freshly grated nut-meg** and 1 teaspoon grated **lemon peel.** Stir over high heat until boiling vigorously. Stir and boil about 3 minutes; remove from heat and stir in spinach. For creamier spinach, purée ¼ to ½ the spinach mixture in a blender or food processor; stop and start motor frequently, and push mixture down onto cutting blade. Return puréed spinach to pan. Add another ½ cup **reduced-fat** or regular **sour cream** and **salt** and **pepper** to taste. *If making ahead, cover and chill up to 1 day.* Stir creamed spinach over medium-high heat until hot. Use hot.

Garlic Mashed Potatoes

For a quick version, omit garlic and neufchâtel cheese; mash potatoes and add 2 packages (each 4 to 5 oz.) garlic-flavor boursin or rondelé cheese (regular or reduced-fat).

1 to 2 tablespoons olive oil
3 or 4 heads garlic
4 pounds golden or white russet potatoes
1 large package (8 oz.) neufchâtel (light cream) cheese or cream cheese
¾ to 1 cup regular-strength chicken broth or milk
Salt and pepper

Pour olive oil into a 9- to 10-inch square pan. Cut garlic heads in half crosswise through cloves, and lay cut sides down on pan. Bake, uncovered, in a 375° oven until garlic is golden brown on bottom, about 35 minutes.

Slip a thin spatula under garlic to release from pan. Use. Or, *if making ahead, cool, cover airtight, and let stand up to 1 day.* Reserve 1 or 2 half-heads of garlic; pluck or squeeze cloves from remaining garlic.

Peel potatoes and cut into about 2-inch chunks. Set on a rack over ¾ to 1 inch water in a 5- to 6-quart pan. Cover pan, bring water to boil over high heat, and boil gently until potatoes mash very easily when pressed, about 40 minutes. Transfer potatoes to a large bowl. Add loose garlic cloves and cheese. Mash potatoes, using a masher or a mixer. Add broth to potatoes as you mash, making them as soft and creamy as you like. (If you plan to serve the potatoes as soon as they are mashed, heat broth before adding.) Season to taste with salt and swirl into a shallow 2- to 2½-quart casserole. Serve, garnished with reserved roasted garlic. Or, *if making ahead, let cool, cover airtight, and chill up to 1 day. To reheat, place potatoes, uncovered, in a 375° oven until hot in center, about 30 minutes; after 15 minutes, garnish with reserved garlic.* Sprinkle with pepper. Makes 8 servings.

Per serving: 297 cal. (27 percent from fat); 8.7 g protein; 9 g fat (4.5 g sat.); 47 g carbo.; 138 mg sodium; 22 mg chol.

Double-Ginger Sweet Potatoes with Port

4 pounds (about 6 medium-size) sweet potatoes or yams, peeled and thinly sliced

About 1¼ cups regular-strength chicken broth
1¼ cups port or broth
2 tablespoons minced fresh ginger
3 tablespoons minced crystallized ginger
2 tablespoons sugar
¼ to ½ cup pomegranate seeds (optional)
Salt

Spread potato slices level in a shallow casserole about 9 by 13 inches. Mix 1¼ cups broth, port, and fresh ginger. Pour over potatoes and cover tightly with foil. Bake, covered, in a 375° oven until potatoes are very tender when pierced, about 1¼ hours. *If making ahead, let cool and chill up to 1 day; to continue, add 2 tablespoons broth or water to casserole.*

Sprinkle potatoes evenly with crystallized ginger and sugar. Bake, uncovered, in a 375° oven until potatoes are glazed with brown, about 30 minutes longer (*about 40 minutes, if chilled*). Scatter pomegranate seeds on top; add salt to taste. Serves 8.

Per serving: 228 cal. (2.8 percent from fat); 3.1 g protein; 0.7 g fat (0.2 g sat.); 53 g carbo.; 37 mg sodium; 0 mg chol.

Baked Fennel with Gorgonzola

4 fennel heads, each about 3½ inches wide, with some green tops
1¾ cups regular-strength chicken broth
¼ pound (½ cup packed) gorgonzola or cambozola cheese
2 tablespoons fine dried bread crumbs
Salt

Rinse fennel; trim off stems and reserve about 1 cup of the tender green leaves. Trim

any bruises or dry-looking areas from fennel, then cut in half from stem through root end. Lay fennel in a 10- to 12-inch frying pan; add broth. Cover and bring to a boil on high heat; simmer until fennel is tender when pierced, 20 to 25 minutes. With a slotted spoon, transfer fennel to a shallow casserole, 9 to 10 inches wide; lay cut side up.

Boil broth, uncovered, on high heat until reduced to about ⅓ cup; stir in about half the fennel leaves. Spoon mixture evenly over fennel.

Mash cheese with bread crumbs, then dot evenly over fennel. *If making ahead, cover and chill up to 1 day; also wrap remaining fennel leaves in a towel, seal in a plastic bag, and chill.* Bake casserole, uncovered, in a 375° oven until cheese begins to brown and fennel is hot, about 20 minutes (*25 minutes, if chilled*). Tuck remaining leaves around fennel; season to taste with salt. Makes 8 servings.

Per serving: 76 cal. (54 percent from fat); 4.7 g protein; 4.6 g fat (2.8 g sat.); 4.1 g carbo.; 301 mg sodium; 11 mg chol.

Sweet Mustard Carrots with Pistachios

2 to 2¼ pounds small (¼-to ½-inch thick) carrots
1 cup regular-strength chicken broth or water
¼ cup Dijon mustard
3 tablespoons firmly packed brown sugar
1 tablespoon butter or margarine
⅓ cup coarsely chopped roasted and salted pistachios
Italian parsley sprigs (optional)

Peel or scrub carrots. In a 12-inch frying pan or 5- to 6-quart pan, combine carrots, broth, mustard, sugar, and butter. Bring to a boil over high heat; cover and simmer until carrots are just barely tender when pierced, 5 to 12 minutes, depending on thickness. Uncover and boil over high heat, shaking pan frequently, until sauce forms thick, shiny bubbles; take care not to scorch. Serve. Or, *if made ahead, cover and chill up to a day. To warm,* add 2 tablespoons water; shake often over medium heat until hot. Pour carrots and sauce onto a platter, top with pistachios, and garnish with parsley. Serves 8.

Per serving: 117 cal. (37 percent from fat); 2.3 g protein; 4.8 g fat (1.3 g sat.); 18 g carbo.; 303 mg sodium; 3.9 mg chol.

THE DRESSINGS

Polenta, Swiss Chard, and Sausage Dressing

For soft polenta, make and serve; for firm polenta, make ahead and reheat.

- 1 pound Swiss chard (or 1 package, 10 oz., frozen chopped Swiss chard, thawed and drained)
- 1 pound mild Italian sausages, skins removed
- 1 cup finely chopped celery
- 1 large (about-½ lb.) onion, finely chopped

- 8 cups regular-strength chicken broth
- 2 cups polenta or yellow cornmeal
- 1 cup chopped parsley
  Celery leaves

Rinse Swiss chard well and trim off discolored stem bases and any bruised parts of the leaves. Cut white ribs from leaves; finely chop ribs and leaves separately.

Break sausages into small pieces in a 5- to 6-quart pan; stir often over medium-high heat until meat begins to brown, about 10 minutes. Spoon out and discard fat. To pan add the chopped chard ribs, celery, onion, and ½ cup water. Stir to release browned bits and stir often over high heat until vegetables are limp and begin to brown. Stir browned bits free with ¼ cup water and continue stirring until browning resumes. Stir in broth and polenta; stir often on medium-high heat until boiling (mixture spatters). Stir chard leaves (or frozen chard) and parsley into polenta; pour into a shallow 3- to 4-quart casserole. Bake, uncovered, in a 375° oven until polenta is very thick and tastes creamy (not gritty), about 1 hour and 15 minutes; stir occasionally. Let stand 10 to 15 minutes, then serve. *If making ahead, let cool, cover, and chill up to 1 day. To reheat, bake, uncovered, in a 375° oven for 30 minutes.* Garnish with celery leaves. Spoon soft polenta from casserole. *If made*

ahead, polenta is firmer and can be cut into pieces to serve. Makes 8 servings.

Per serving: 316 cal. (37 percent from fat); 15 g protein; 13 g fat (4.2 g sat.); 34 g carbo.; 565 mg sodium; 32 mg chol.

Wild Rice and Porcini Mushroom Dressing

- 2 large (about ½ lb. each) onions, finely chopped
  Soaked porcini mushrooms (directions follow)
- ¾ teaspoon dried thyme leaves
- ¼ teaspoon freshly grated or ground nutmeg
- 6 cups regular-strength chicken broth
- 2 cups wild rice, rinsed and drained
- 2 tablespoons dry sherry (optional)
  Fresh thyme sprigs (optional)

In a 5- to 6-quart pan, combine onions, ½ cup of the soaking liquid from mushrooms, thyme, and nutmeg. Boil over high heat, uncovered, stirring often until liquid evaporates and onions begin to stick. Add remaining soaking liquid, mushrooms, broth, wild rice, and sherry; stir to free browned bits. Cover and bring to a boil; simmer gently until rice is tender to bite and grains begin to split open, about 1 hour. Drain, reserving liquid. Serve rice hot. *If making ahead, let cool, cover, and chill up to 2 days. Combine with reserved liquid and heat until boiling; drain and serve (use liquid for soups).* Garnish with thyme sprigs. Serves 8.

Per serving: 193 cal. (7.9 percent from fat); 8.4 g protein; 1.7 g fat (0.4 g sat.); 37 g carbo.; 45 mg sodium; 0 mg chol.

Soaked porcini. In a 1- to 1½-quart pan over high heat, combine 1½ cups **water** and ½ cup (about ½ oz.) **dried porcini mushrooms.** Cover and bring to a boil; remove from heat and let stand until cool. Squeeze mushrooms gently to release grit, then lift from water. Finely chop mushrooms. Carefully pour soaking liquid into another container and save; discard gritty residue.

Old-fashioned or Lean Multigrain Bread Dressing

Whether to add butter is your choice in this moist, traditional dressing.

- 1½ pounds firm-textured multigrain bread
- 2 cups chopped onion
- 2 cups thinly sliced celery, including leaves
- ½ cup chopped parsley
- ¼ cup chopped fresh or 2 tablespoons dried rubbed sage leaves
- 1½ tablespoons minced fresh or 1½ teaspoons dried rosemary leaves
- 1½ tablespoons minced fresh or 1½ teaspoons dried thyme leaves
- ¾ teaspoon pepper
- ⅓ cup (⅙ lb.) butter or margarine (optional)
- 3½ cups regular-strength chicken broth
  Salt

Tear bread into 1-inch chunks; place in large bowl.

In a 10- to 12-inch frying pan, combine onion, celery, parsley, sage, rosemary, thyme, and pepper. For the traditional version, add butter and stir often over medium heat until vegetables are limp and slightly browned, about 10 minutes.

For the lean version, add ⅔ cup water to vegetables and stir often over high heat until liquid evaporates and vegetables begin to brown, about 10 minutes. Repeat this step 3 more times, adding ⅓ cup water each round, or as needed, until vegetables are richly browned, about 8 minutes total.

For either version, add broth and stir to loosen browned bits. Pour over bread and mix gently to coat.

Spoon dressing into a 2½- to 3-quart shallow baking dish about 9 by 15 inches. Cover tightly with foil. *If making ahead, chill up to 2 days.* Bake, covered, in a 325° oven until hot in center, about 45 minutes (*1 hour, if chilled*). For a crusty top, uncover and broil 3 inches from heat until brown, about 5 minutes. Add salt to taste. Makes about 3 quarts, 12 servings.

Per serving with butter: 212 cal. (33 percent from fat); 6.9 g pro-

NORMAN A. PLATE

WILD RICE *with porcini mushrooms is an exceptionally low-fat turkey dressing.*

ACCOMPANIMENTS TO *the sit-down banquet include chilled sugar snap peas with mint and bacon dressing, garlic mashed potatoes, rich brown giblet gravey, and red pepper relish with aromatic spices.*

tein; 7.8 g fat (3.7 g sat.); 30 g carbo.; 363 mg sodium; 14 mg chol.

Per serving without butter: 167 cal. (15 percent from fat); 6.9 g protein; 2.7 g fat (0.6 g sat.); 30 g carbo.; 311 mg sodium; 0 mg chol.

ACCOMPANIMENTS

Rich Brown Giblet Gravy

For more gravy to go with birds 18 pounds or larger, increase broth to 7 cups, wine to 1 cup, and cornstarch to 7 tablespoons. Adjust final measure of broth to make 6 cups, adding water if needed. These changes yield 6 to 6½ cups gravy.

 Giblets from a 12- to 24-pound turkey
2 medium-size (about ¾ lb. total) onions, quartered
2 large (about ½ lb. total) carrots, cut into chunks
¾ cup sliced celery
5 cups regular-strength chicken broth
½ cup dry white wine
½ teaspoon pepper
⅓ cup cornstarch
 Salt

Rinse giblets and cut neck into 3 or 4 sections; chill liver airtight. Combine remaining giblets, neck pieces, onions, carrots, celery, and ½ cup broth in a 5- to 6-quart pan over high heat.

Boil, uncovered, stirring often as liquid evaporates; cook until giblets and vegetables are browned and browned bits stick to the pan, 15 to 20 minutes.

Add another ½ cup broth and stir to loosen browned bits; boil and brown, uncovered, as directed in the preceding step.

Add remaining broth, wine, and pepper to pan; stir to scrape browned bits free. Cover pan and simmer gently until gizzard is tender when pierced, about 1½ hours. Add liver and cook 10 minutes.

Pour broth through a fine strainer into a bowl and reserve; discard vegetables. Save giblets for gravy or other uses. If using giblets, pull meat off neck and finely chop neck meat and giblets.

Measure reserved broth; if needed, add water to make 4 cups liquid. *If making ahead, cover and chill liquid and giblets up to 1 day.*

In the pan, mix cornstarch with ¼ cup water until smooth; add broth and chopped giblets. Stir over high heat until boiling, about 5 minutes. Season gravy to taste with salt. Makes 4 to 5 cups.

Per ½ cup: 51 cal. (18 percent from fat); 2.6 g protein; 1 g fat (0.3 g sat.); 7.7 g carbo.; 41 mg sodium; 16 mg chol.

Red Pepper Relish with Aromatics

1 to 1¼ pounds red bell peppers, stemmed, seeded, and thinly sliced
1 lemon, ends trimmed, thinly sliced
1 cup *each* rice vinegar and water
1 cup sugar
 Aromatic spice mix (following)

Cut pepper slices into 1- to 1½-inch lengths; cut lemon slices in quarters, discarding seeds. In a 4- to 5-quart pan, combine peppers, lemon, vinegar, water, sugar, and aromatic spice mix. Bring to a boil over high heat and boil rapidly, stirring often, until liquid is almost evaporated, about 20 minutes; take care not to scorch. Serve warm or cold. *If making ahead, let cool, cover airtight, and chill up to 1 week. Stir before serving.* Makes about 1½ cups.

Per 2 tablespoons: 71 cal. (3.8 percent from fat); 0.5 g protein; 0.3 g fat (0 g sat.); 18 g carbo.; 3.9 mg sodium; 0 mg chol.

Aromatic spice mix. Combine 1 tablespoon **mustard seed,** 1 teaspoon **coriander seed,** ¼ teaspoon **fennel seed,** ⅛ teaspoon hulled **cardamom seed,** ⅛ teaspoon **ground nutmeg,** and 3 or 4 whole cloves.

Cranberry-Grapefruit Relish

2 large (1 lb. each) grapefruit
1 can (16 oz.) whole cranberry sauce or cranberry jelly

With a knife, cut peel and white membrane from grapefruit. Holding fruit over a bowl, cut between membranes to release fruit segments; squeeze juice from membrane into bowl.

In a 1- to 2-quart pan, stir cranberry sauce over medium-high heat until melted. Drain grapefruit well, reserving juice for other uses. Place grapefruit in a 3- to 4-cup bowl, pour in cranberry sauce, and mix gently. Cover and chill until cold, 2 hours or up to 1 day. Makes about 3 cups.

Per 2 tablespoons: 35 cal. (0 percent from fat); 0.1 g protein; 0 g fat; 8.9 g carbo.; 5.5 mg sodium; 0 mg chol. ∎

By Linda Lau Anusasananan, Betsy Reynolds Bateson, Jerry Anne Di Vecchio, Christine Weber Hale, Elaine Johnson

CRISP COCOA MERINGUE *twigs conceal meringue-and-chocolate-cream layer cake.*

DELICATE TEXTURE *of chestnut tiramisù contrasts with crunchy chocolate curls.*

CREAMY FILLING *spirals through spiced pumpkin cake roll.*

JUICY GRAPEFRUIT *segments top lively ruby grapefruit sorbet.*

Beyond the pumpkin pie

Sweet secrets are hidden behind the sophisticated good looks and holiday flavors in these five desserts

CLASSIC CONCEPTS restructured give these desserts unexpected virtues. None of them are difficult to make, all are handsome—and two look like the work of a pastry chef. Some are sinfully rich. Some are amazingly lean, but flavor hides the fact. For the time-pressured cook, each of these holiday desserts can be made at least a day ahead of time.

Chocolate Twig Cake

- 6 large egg whites
- 1 teaspoon cream of tartar
- 1½ cups granulated sugar
- 6 tablespoons unsweetened cocoa

  Chocolate mousse frosting (recipe follows)

- 1 tablespoon powdered sugar mixed with 2 teaspoons unsweetened cocoa

To make chocolate meringue, line 2 baking sheets, each 14 by 17 inches, with cooking parchment, or butter sheets and dust with flour. On 1 sheet, draw 2 circles, each 7½ inches in diameter (use knife tip on floured sheets).

In large bowl of a mixer, beat 4 egg whites and ¾ teaspoon cream of tartar at high speed until foamy. Gradually add ¾ cup sugar, about 1 tablespoon every 30 to 45 seconds; scrape bowl occasionally. Mix another ¼ cup sugar with 4 tablespoons cocoa; beat into whites at the same rate. Whites should hold very stiff peaks; beat until they do.

Fit a pastry bag with a ½-inch plain or fluted tip. Add meringue to bag, filling no more than ⅔. Twisting bag top, squeeze bag to pipe meringue about 1 inch thick over each circle, covering evenly and using all the meringue.

Bake meringues in a 250° oven until they feel firm and dry to touch, about 1 hour.

Meanwhile, in the same bowl (using unwashed beaters), beat remaining 2 egg whites, remaining ¼ teaspoon cream of tartar, and 6 tablespoons sugar as directed for the meringue disks, preceding. Mix remaining 2 tablespoons cocoa with the remaining 2 tablespoons sugar, and whip into whites, as directed.

Pipe remaining meringue in ½-inch-thick long ropes about 1 inch apart on the remaining baking sheet. Add to oven with meringue disks, moving disks to another rack. Bake ropes until they feel firm and dry to touch, at least 50 minutes; if disks are dry first, remove from oven until ropes are dry. Then, with both pans in oven, turn off heat and let meringues stand in closed oven 2 hours.

Slip a spatula carefully under pieces to release. *If making ahead, store airtight up to 1 week.* If pieces crack, patch together with frosting when finishing cake.

To assemble cake, set 1 meringue disk on a flat plate. Spread about ⅓ the chocolate mousse frosting level over top of disk. Set second meringue disk on top of the first and gently press to secure to frosting. Spread remaining frosting over top and sides of cake. Break meringue ropes into 1- to 2-inch lengths and press gently but firmly into frosting on top

and sides of cake. Serve. Or, *if making ahead (and for easier cutting), cover and chill up to 1 day.* Dust with powdered sugar mixed with cocoa. Serves 12 to 16.

Per serving: 219 cal. (45 percent from fat); 2.8 g protein; 11 g fat (7 g sat.); 30 g carbo.; 30 mg sodium; 25 mg chol.

Chocolate mousse frosting. In a 1- to 1½-quart pan, combine 8 ounces **bittersweet chocolate** and ½ cup **whipping cream.** Stir over medium heat just until chocolate is smoothly melted. Chill, covered, until cool but not solid, about 20 minutes. Stir in 1 more cup **whipping cream** and 2 to 3 tablespoons **coffee-flavor liqueur** (optional); beat cream until it holds distinct peaks.

Spiced Pumpkin Roll

  About ¾ cup all-purpose flour

- 2 teaspoons ground cinnamon
- 1 teaspoon *each* baking powder and ground ginger
- ½ teaspoon *each* ground allspice and ground nutmeg
- ¼ teaspoon salt
- 3 large eggs
- 1 cup granulated sugar
- ⅔ cup canned pumpkin

  About 5 tablespoons powdered sugar

  Vanilla yogurt filling (recipe follows)

  Rinsed and dried nontoxic fall leaves, or paper stencils cut like leaves

  Marmalade topping (recipe follows)

(Continued on page 240)

NORMAN A. PLATE

Lightly oil a 10- by 15-inch baking pan; line pan bottom with waxed paper cut to fit. Oil paper and dust with flour.

Mix ¾ cup all-purpose flour with cinnamon, baking powder, ginger, allspice, nutmeg, and salt.

In a mixer bowl, beat eggs at high speed until thick and foamy, gradually adding sugar, about 5 minutes. Add flour mixture and pumpkin; mix on low speed or stir until evenly moistened.

Evenly spread batter in prepared pan. Bake in a 375° oven until top springs back when touched, about 15 minutes. With a knife, cut between cake and pan rim; immediately invert cake onto a towel sprinkled with 3 tablespoons powdered sugar. Gently peel waxed paper from cake, and roll cake from a narrow end with towel (to keep sections of cake apart) into a cylinder; set on a rack until cool.

Gently unroll cake and leave on towel; spread cake to the rim evenly with yogurt filling; reroll, using towel to guide. Set roll on a flat plate; wrap airtight. *Chill at least 4 hours or up to 1 day.* Unwrap, lay leaves on top of cake, and dust with remaining powdered sugar. Carefully lift off leaves. Slice roll into portions and accompany with marmalade topping to add to taste. Makes 10 to 12 servings.

Per serving: 268 cal. (10 percent from fat); 7.1 g protein; 3.1 g fat (0.4 g sat.); 54 g carbo.; 154 mg sodium; 56 mg chol.

Vanilla yogurt filling.
Line a fine strainer with a double layer of cheesecloth. Set strainer over a deep bowl (bottom of strainer should sit at least 2 in. above bottom of bowl).

Spoon 6 cups **vanilla-flavor low-fat yogurt** into cloth. Cover airtight. *Chill and let drain until yogurt is the consistency of whipped cream cheese, at least 24 hours or up to 3 days.*

Discard accumulated liquid. Stir 2 to 3 tablespoons **powdered sugar,** to taste, into the yogurt. Makes about 2 cups.

Marmalade topping.
Stir together ¾ cup **orange marmalade,** ½ cup **pow-dered sugar,** and ¼ cup **orange juice.**

Ruby Grapefruit Sorbet

- 1 envelope gelatin
- 1½ cups sugar
- 2 cups water
- 4 cups unstrained ruby grapefruit juice (takes about 4 lb. of fruit)
- 2 tablespoons sweet vermouth (or grapefruit juice)
- 2 tablespoons grenadine syrup (or grapefruit juice)

  Grapefruit segments and rinsed citrus or mint leaves (optional)

In a 2- to 3-quart pan, stir together gelatin and sugar; add water and bring to a boil over high heat. Stir until sugar dissolves. Let cool. Add grapefruit juice, vermouth, and grenadine syrup.

Freeze in a 1-quart or larger ice cream freezer container (self-refrigerated, frozen cylinder, or with ice and salt), following the manufacturer's directions.

Or pour mixture into a metal pan (about 9 by 13 in.); cover. *Freeze until solid, at least 6 hours or up to 1 month.* Break into small chunks and whirl in a food processor or beat with a mixer until a smooth slush forms. Return to freezer for 20 to 30 minutes.

Serve sorbet softly frozen. If stored, sorbet gets very hard; just beat again for smooth texture.

Spoon into chilled dishes and garnish with grapefruit segments and leaves. Makes 2 quarts, 10 to 12 servings. —*Mrs. L. K. Ross, Elk Grove, California*

Per serving: 140 cal. (0.6 percent from fat); 0.9 g protein; 0.1 g fat (0 g sat.); 34 g carbo.; 2.3 mg sodium; 0 mg chol.

Chestnut Tiramisù

- 12 ounces ladyfinger cookies or pound cake
- 1 can (17½ oz.) or 1½ cups sweetened chestnut spread
- 2 tablespoons rum or orange juice

  Orange syrup (recipe follows)

- 1 cup whipping cream
- 2 cups unflavored nonfat yogurt or regular sour cream
- 3 to 4 ounces semisweet chocolate
- 3 or 4 thin crosswise slices peeled orange, Clementine, or tangerine (optional)

Separate ladyfingers (or thinly slice cake) and lay pieces side by side (or overlap, as needed) to cover a rimmed patter or very shallow bowl 14 to 15 inches wide; leave a 1-inch-wide bare area between cookies and dish rim.

Mix chestnut spread with rum and 2 tablespoons of the orange syrup. Pour remaining syrup over ladyfingers to moisten evenly. Gently spread chestnut mixture over ladyfingers, leaving a 1-inch rim uncovered.

Beat the whipping cream until it holds distinct peaks; whisk in the yogurt. Swirl over chestnut spread and most of the exposed ladyfinger rim.

Pare chocolate with a vegetable peeler to make curls, or finely chop with a knife or in a food processor. Scatter chocolate over tiramisù; top chocolate with orange slices. Serve. *Or cover airtight without touching topping and chill up to 1 day.* Scoop out portions. Serves 10 to 12.

Per serving: 469 cal. (23 percent from fat); 7.8 g protein; 12 g fat (6.2 g sat.); 80 g carbo.; 92 mg sodium; 126 mg chol.

Orange syrup. In a 1- to 1½-quart pan, boil on high heat, uncovered, 1 cup **water,** ½ cup **sugar,** and 2 teaspoons finely shredded **orange peel** until reduced to ¾ cup. Let cool slightly and add ¼ cup **rum** or orange juice. Use hot or cool.

Cashew Caramel Tart

- 10 sheets (each 12 by 16 in., about 5 oz. total) fila

  About ¼ cup butter or margarine, melted

- 2 cups (1 or 2 jars, about 20 oz. total) purchased caramel sauce
- 2 large eggs
- 1 tablespoon *each* grated orange peel and lemon peel

- 2 tablespoons lemon juice
- 2 cups salted, roasted whole cashews

  About 1 tablespoon powdered sugar

Stack fila sheets; cut in half crosswise to make 20 pieces. Cover fila with plastic wrap to prevent drying when not using.

Lightly brush butter onto an 11-inch plain or fluted tart pan with removable bottom. Brush 1 fila piece lightly with butter; cover about ⅔ of the pan bottom with the sheet and drape extra fila over pan rim; rub fila to attach it lightly to pan bottom. Gently fold extended edge of fila down into pan to make a rim that is slightly higher than the side of the pan.

Repeat step with another buttered fila piece, covering pan bottom from the opposite direction. Repeat step with 2 more pieces of fila, but position them to form a cross over the first layer.

With 4 more fila pieces, make another cross on top of the first, but rotate cross to cover corners of first layer. Repeat this pattern, alternating cross positions, using all but 4 fila pieces.

Lightly butter each remaining fila piece and fold in half lengthwise. Arrange pieces around the inside of the fila rim to make a puffy border.

Stir caramel sauce in a 1- to 1½-quart pan over high heat until barely warm. In a bowl, beat eggs to blend with orange peel, lemon peel, and lemon juice; stir in caramel sauce. Pour caramel mixture into fila-lined pan and sprinkle evenly with cashews. Bake in a 325° oven until fila is a rich golden brown and caramel bubbles, 40 to 45 minutes. Let cool until caramel firms, at least 1½ hours. *If making ahead, wrap airtight up to 1 day.* Remove pan rim, and dust tart with powdered sugar. Cut into wedges. Makes 10 to 12 servings.

Per serving: 329 cal. (44 percent from fat); 6.1 g protein; 16 g fat (4.8 g sat.); 45 g carbo.; 408 mg sodium; 46 mg chol. ∎

By Betsy Reynolds Bateson, Jerry Anne Di Vecchio

All the right wines

Here's how to complete the Thanksgiving table with confidence

NORMAN A. PLATE

CHOOSE A GLASS *that gives space to the wine; any of these can work well for white, red, or rosé.*

C ONSIDER THE FRENCH when you plan what wine to pour this Thanksgiving. Faced with a wide array of flavors, they may opt to serve an understated wine that goes with many foods; or, if the group is a large one, they may offer several strikingly different wines all at once, leaving each diner to choose a favorite or two. Glassware can be as extensive as your space and budget permit. Even one glass will do. A pitcher of water and a small dump bucket allow reds and whites to alternate in the same glass. Sparkling wines do best in narrow, deeper flutes.

The selections for our Thanksgiving dinner follow the French preference for the understated and the agreeable. All are widely available in the West, many at less than $10 a bottle. Prices vary from store to store. As a buying guide, allow at least one bottle (total) to serve two. ■

By Bob Thompson

WHITE WINES

Chenin Blanc has undemanding flavors, and most producers work to keep the wine that way. The first wine listed is dry and shows flavors of aging in oak; the rest put fruit foremost, and are progressively less dry ($6 to $7.50).
- **1991 Chappellet Napa Valley Chenin Blanc**
- **1992 Dry Creek Vineyard California Dry Chenin Blanc**
- **1992 The Hogue Cellars Columbia Valley Chenin Blanc**
- **1992 Mirassou Monterey Dry Chenin Blanc**

Riesling (or Johannisberg Riesling) has perfumes that are a little more specific than Chenin Blanc's, but it is still a wine of many uses. Both of these are round in texture, pointedly fruity in flavor ($6 to $7.50).
- **1991 The Firestone Vineyard Santa Ynez Valley Riesling**
- **1992 Chateau Ste. Michelle Johannisberg Riesling Columbia Valley**

Chardonnay has acquired a deserved reputation as being difficult to match with food because oak and other flavors from winemaking can be strong. However, these true-to-the-grape examples are versatile indeed ($8 to $11).
- **1991 Buena Vista Carneros Chardonnay**
- **1991 Callaway Calla-Lees Chardonnay**
- **1991 Louis M. Martini Napa Valley Chardonnay**

SPARKLING WINES

What is a festive dinner without something bubbly? The Thanksgiving table is not a place for halfway measures. Either go dry on behalf of the food, or pick the last wine in the list and go dessert-sweet ($5 to $16).
- **Domaine Chandon Carneros Blanc de Noirs (nonvintage)**
- **1990 Mirassou Monterey Blanc de Noir**
- **Mumm Cuvée Napa Valley Brut Prestige (nonvintage)**
- **Gran Spumante Ballatore**

REDS AND ROSÉS

Rosés struggle for identity in the United States. More's the pity, for well-made ones capture some of the best qualities of both red and white when foods of contrasting flavors must be met by one wine. The first wine is frankly sweet, the second just as dry ($5 to $9).
- **1992 Glen Ellen Proprietor's Reserve California White Zinfandel**
- **1992 Joseph Phelps Vineyards Vin du Mistral Napa Valley Grenache Rosé**

Beaujolais-style, in which grape variety is much less important than technique, means light-hearted reds made to be drunk almost as soon as they come from the fermenting tanks. These progress from off-dry to faintly sweet ($5.50 to $7.50).
- **1992 Beringer Vineyards North Coast Gamay Beaujolais**
- **1992 Geyser Peak North Coast Gamay Beaujolais**
- **1992 Mirassou Vineyards Monterey Cru Gamay**
- **1991 Louis M. Martini Fresco Rosso California Red Table Wine**

Pinot Noir is always versatile, but those with forthrightly light-hearted grape flavors seem especially suited to a Thanksgiving table ($7 to $10).
- **1991 Buena Vista Carneros Pinot Noir**
- **1991 Carneros Creek Pinot Noir Fleur de Carneros**
- **1992 Saintsbury Carneros Pinot Noir Garnet**

Zinfandel, the eternal chameleon of California wine, can be titanic or modest. The modest ones offer a winier alternative to such grapes as Gamay for those who insist on real red wine. This sequence goes from easiest to most complex ($5.75 to $10).
- **1991 Robert Mondavi Woodbridge California Zinfandel**
- **1991 Franciscan Oakville Estate Zinfandel**
- **1991 Gundlach-Bundschu Sonoma Valley Zinfandel**

Merlot in the United States was initially styled to echo Cabernet Sauvignon's flavors but not its tannic firmness. Not all have kept the original thought; those that have produce a roundly agreeable red. The first example is briskly refreshing, the second easy-chair soft ($7 to $12).
- **1991 Columbia Crest Columbia Valley Merlot**
- **1991 Sebastiani Sonoma County Merlot**

Wild reminiscences of first Thanksgivings

Have you ever seen pumpkin rind cake or turkey in a flaming bag?

EMEMBER THE FIRST Thanksgiving dinner you made all on your own, without Mom at your side—or rather, without you at her side? If you're like the following group of 20th-century Pilgrims, chances are you could tell a tale or two. Their Thanksgiving adventures are sure to bring memories—and smiles.

NOVICE COOK *probes mysteries of the holiday bird.*

WHICH END IS UP?

"Cookbooks tell you to put the turkey in the oven, but they don't say which *way* to put it in the oven," remarks self-proclaimed novice cook Sara Reynolds Davi of Chico, California. "So last year, when I roasted my first turkey, I just tied the legs together and put it in there.

"The recipe said to test the temperature in the breast. Well, I didn't know what the breast was, so I kept sticking a thermometer in the part that was up—which was *awfully* bony. Finally, I decided that the turkey had been

in the oven for 4 hours and that it just had to be done. When my husband went to carve it, he looked at it strangely, then ventured, 'Did you know this turkey's the wrong way up?'

"He flipped the bird over. It was white and ugly! My friends still laugh at me—but at least now I can recognize which is the breast and which is the back."

THE ADVENTURES OF PATRICK, CLIFF, AND THE BONELESS TURKEY

Boning a turkey isn't a project that most cooks take lightly, but Patrick McEvoy of Palo Alto, California, is not easily daunted. When *Sunset* ran a recipe in 1986 for an "easy-carve" turkey, he knew what to make for his 60 Thanksgiving guests. Two weeks ahead, he held a trial run dinner to practice boning out the carcass, stuffing, and reshaping the bird. His friend Cliff Jenkins attended, and admired the neat, boneless slices of meat and stuffing.

TIDAL DECOR *adds bite to seafoam salad.*

On Thanksgiving, Patrick woke at 6 A.M. to bone two 30-pound turkeys to feed this large group, deploying each on its own barbecue. He then cooked a third turkey that a friend had won in a raffle the night before, but he didn't have time to bone it.

At serving time, pandemonium reigned in the kitchen. Across a sea of people, Patrick yelled to Cliff to please unstuff and carve the turkey on the table. All went well, as this was the raffle bird. But Cliff, being a very helpful sort of guy, proceeded to the next—boneless—turkey.

It wasn't long before Patrick heard Cliff talking to himself. "Hmm. This is strange. What the hell? Pat, there's something wrong with this turkey!"

Like the infamous birds in cartoonist Gary Larson's Boneless Chicken Ranch, the turkey had been reduced to an inelegant floppy mess. The third turkey, saved from Cliff's helpful hands, was most thoroughly admired.

A '50s FAMILY FAVORITE DRESSED UP FOR THE '90s

Sunset senior editor David Mahoney remembers well the first time he and his siblings had Thanksgiving on their own. "My youngest brother, Dan, volunteered to prepare seafoam salad, a pale green gelatin concoction made in a ring mold, and a staple at our family Thanksgivings. But he

'improved' on the basic recipe of lime gelatin, cream cheese, and canned pears by collecting crab claws, seaweed, and other tidal detritus at the beach, then artfully arranging them on top."

A PUMPKIN CAKE WITH FIBER

One novice Thanksgiving host, not liking traditional pumpkin pie but wanting to keep the holiday spirit, decided to make a pumpkin cake. He used a recipe for carrot cake but substituted shredded pumpkin for shredded carrots—not a bad idea, until guests discovered he'd used shredded pumpkin *rind* instead of flesh. Talk about fiber!

DAVE BROAD

TRIUMPH FADES *when guests try pumpkin rind cake.*

EVEN WILD ANIMALS WOULDN'T EAT THE STUFFING

"One year when I was growing up, we spent our first camping Thanksgiving on some friends' property out in the middle of nowhere," recalls Allison Zarem, photo coordinator in *Sunset*'s Los Angeles office.

"Mom made a traditional Thanksgiving meal, including a new stuffing recipe that she'd received from a neighbor. Everything was delicious—except for the stuffing, which was disgusting.

"After dinner, we took the turkey carcass and stuffing into the woods, thinking the animals might eat them. The next day, my brother and I crept back to the spot to see what had happened to the leftover food. Not a scrap of turkey was left—not even a bone. But the animals—raccoons, wolves, whatever they were—weren't fooled. They hadn't touched the horrible stuffing!

"We really gave our mom a hard time. Later, when our neighbor asked how we liked the stuffing, we told her about the animals' sensitive taste buds. 'That's funny,' she said. 'All *our* guests ate it.'"

JUST BAG THE THANKSGIVING BIRD

Chef Monique Barbeau of Fullers restaurant in Seattle isn't likely to forget her first attempt at Thanksgiving dinner, which she cooked for a group of friends during her freshman year at college.

"Mom used to wrap the turkey in a brown paper sack to help keep it moist and crisp.

"What I didn't know was that I was supposed to get the bag wet first. It burst into flames, filling the kitchen with smoke! Everyone thought I'd burned the turkey and that we'd have to order Chinese food, but I was able to remove the paper sack and save the bird, which was dry

but edible. I eventually got over my embarrassment and continued in the cooking profession. But now I make ham for Thanksgiving."

HIDE-AND-SEEK WITH THE GIBLET BAG

Several first-time turkey cooks recall learning the mystery of "that funny little bag" inside the bird. "I didn't even know it was in there," confessed one woman. "You should have seen my look of embarrassment when my new father-in-law discovered it as he was carving!"

SWEET POTATO PIE WITH CRUNCH

"I've always been ambitious, but at 16 I thought I knew a heck of a lot more than I did," says chef Leonard Cohen of the Olde Port Inn in Avila Beach, California. "I volunteered to cook Thanksgiving dinner, and my dad said I could prepare whatever I wanted, so I made a really elaborate meal. Everything came out pretty well except for the sweet potato pie. It *looked* great—the marshmallows were all melted and gooey.

"But my little sister took one bite and said, 'There's a problem with this!' I didn't know I was supposed to preboil the sweet potatoes. We scooped the marshmallows off the top and ate those."

BUT WAIT, THE TURKEY SKIN!

For *Sunset* CEO Robin Wolaner, the best part of the turkey has always been the crunchy skin. You can imagine her interest at her first Thanksgiving with her "almost-in-laws" when from across a counter she watched the family patriarch carefully carve the turkey, then lift off the skin (to another platter, she assumed).

Later, her interest turned to dismay when she realized that he had deposited the skin in

WORTH ITS SALT? *Not when a typo enters the mix.*

the garbage disposal! She might have been healthier for the skinless bird, but definitely wasn't happier.

A RECIPE TO TAKE WITH A GRAIN OF SALT

Mary Etta Moose, coowner of Moose's restaurant in San Francisco, shares a story of Thanksgiving in the days before she learned to cook.

"Imagine my surprise when my gregarious husband, Ed, with an 'Oh, by the way…' visited my debut as a hostesscook upon me. So green a cook was I that the authors in the bookstore cookbook section meant nothing to me. But I recognized the name of Michael Field, whose piano concerts I had so enjoyed, and figured that anyone who could play like that could cook.

"His Truffled Roast Turkey with Sausage and Chestnut Stuffing, with black truffle slices slipped under the skin before roasting (described by the French as *dindonneau en demi-deuil,* or young turkey in half-mourning), looked good. I couldn't have guessed there'd be a typo in such an extravagant recipe. But proofreaders hadn't caught the typesetter's substitution of 1 tablespoon for 1 teaspoon of salt in the stuffing.

"'Twas I who was in halfmourning—sitting at the din-

ing table watching our guests politely push their salt-pickled bird and stuffing around their plates, digging the truffle slices from under the turkey skin to eat with their vegetables. Perhaps my story will save another novice cook from the same embarrassment."

HOW NOT TO IMPRESS A DATE

A reader we'll call John had a big crush on a woman with whom he worked. Finally, he mustered enough courage to ask her to dinner. Since it was the Saturday before Thanksgiving, he decided to impress her by preparing a turkey dinner—complete with a 24-pound bird!

But he had never cooked anything other than frozen dinners and didn't know that a large turkey needs more than the hour it takes to cook a chicken.

Thinking he would allow about 30 minutes for appetizers and conversation before dinner, he popped the turkey into the oven shortly before his date arrived. Conversation dragged on for an interminable 3 hours until the bird was done. It was their first and last date. ∎

By Elaine Johnson.
Betsy Reynolds Bateson and
Christine Weber Hale
contributed to this report.

PUSH A THERMOMETER *through thickest part of turkey breast until it touches bone. When it reads 160°, the bird is perfectly cooked.*

Why?

The do's and don'ts of cooking turkey

A gloriously golden brown turkey, the cornerstone of Thanksgiving dinner, brings sighs of satisfaction when it's juicy and succulent, and disappointment when it's not. Even though cooking a turkey is a simple process, a dry bird is a common frustration, and stuffing safety is always a concern.

Why does turkey taste dry?

Overcooking is the culprit. As turkey cooks, heat makes the meat tighten, firm, and release flavorful juices. If cooked beyond optimum doneness, the meat continues to tighten and squeeze out juices until it is hard and dry.

Why is overcooking so common?

If you cook turkey the way your grandmother did, from the crack of dawn until dinner, you are headed for big trouble. Today's turkeys are much younger, meatier, and tenderer than those of years ago, and they cook more quickly. A 10-pound bird may be ready to eat in as little as 1½ hours, and a 30-pound bird is usually done in less than 5 hours (see chart on page 136 for temperature guides and barbecue and roasting times). Unfortunately, old ways die hard. You may still rely on an old favorite cookbook. Also, directions on some turkey wrappers still give out-of-date cooking times, and meat thermometers are marked for turkey doneness at a temperature higher than desirable. Nonetheless, a thermometer is essential if you want a perfectly cooked bird.

Why use a thermometer?

The best way to judge when your turkey is done is with an accurate meat or instant-read thermometer.

A turkey is not the same temperature throughout when cooked because the meat is different thicknesses on the carcass. We find the most reliable place to put the thermometer is through the thickest part of the breast to the bone. When the breast is perfectly cooked, the thermometer is at 160°; if you pull the thermometer up into the breast's thick center part, it will read about 10° hotter—170°—but that center is more difficult to locate than the breast bone.

When the breast is done, thigh meat at the hip joint may still be too pink (although safe) for most tastes. As the turkey rests for carving (10 to 30 minutes), the juices settle back into the meat, the heat in the bird equalizes, and sometimes the joint will lose the pink color. If not, when you carve off thighs, return them to a 450° oven until meat fibers at joint pull apart easily, 10 to 15 minutes longer. Meanwhile, carve breast and drumsticks.

Why do I need to thaw a frozen turkey in the refrigerator?

Safety is the reason. Bacteria multiply rapidly on food left unrefrigerated for several hours. With the turkey's large mass, it takes too long for the bird to thaw completely at room temperature without risk of spoilage. When you rush the process by defrosting a turkey at room temperature or in warm water, the outside of the bird thaws first and quickly reaches the temperature conducive to bacterial growth while the interior remains frozen for hours longer.

At refrigerator temperatures, the bird can thaw more evenly, with minimum bacterial growth. Set the turkey, sealed in its plastic bag, on a pan to collect juices; allow two to four days in the refrigerator, depending on bird size.

If you need to speed the process or you don't have room in the refrigerator, you can immerse the turkey in the sealed bag in cool water for 12 to 48 hours, changing the water often. Another way is to set the wrapped turkey in a pan inside a double set of sealed paper bags. The air between the bags acts as insulation to keep the cold from dissipating, so the exterior of the bird remains cool. Allow 14 to 24 hours.

Can I stuff the turkey the night before?

No. If you want to stuff the turkey, do so just before you cook it. There is real danger if the dressing stands in the bird for a long period. Because both the dressing and bird are moist, and either may contain harmful bacteria (typically, *Staphylococcus aureus*), the bacteria can grow to dangerous levels if held at 60° to 120° for 2 to 3 hours.

As a turkey cooks, the dressing heats slowly. Harmful bacteria aren't killed until the temperature in the center of the dressing registers 140° for at least 3 minutes (or 160° for instant-kill). If the dressing does not get this hot, scoop it from the turkey into a casserole and bake, covered, until it reaches the safe temperature.

However, for convenience, you can make the dressing ahead and store it, covered, in the refrigerator. Another safe alternative is to cook the dressing and bird separately from the start.

As soon as a stuffed bird is cooked, spoon out the dressing. Store leftovers separately in the refrigerator.

More questions?

If you come across other cooking mysteries and would like to know why they happen, send your questions to Why?, *Sunset Magazine*, 80 Willow Rd., Menlo Park, Calif. 94025. With the help of Dr. George K. York, extension food technologist at UC Davis, *Sunset* food editors will find the solutions. ∎

By Linda Lau Anusasananan

FOLD WARM TORTILLAS *around chili-seasoned turkey and beans topped with crisp red cabbage salsa.*

NORMAN A. PLATE

Burritos and Thai salad cure those leftover turkey blues

They're good enough to merit cooking an extra bird

EVEN IF COMPETITION for cold turkey sandwiches is intense the day after Thanksgiving, by the second or third day a little window dressing may be needed to arouse enthusiasm for yet another bird-based entrée.

Fortunately, turkey's basic neutrality makes it a good foundation for the flavorful mantles that dress up these bean burritos topped with red cabbage salsa and a lively Thai-inspired salad.

Both dishes travel well, if you believe a change of scenery will further dissociate turkey from its second-day status. Consider a cool-weather picnic.

Bean and Turkey Burritos

1 pound (2¼ cups) dried red beans

1 large (about ¾-lb.) onion, chopped

5 cups regular-strength chicken broth

½ cup chili powder

½ cup firmly packed brown sugar

2 whole star anise or 1 teaspoon anise seed

About 4 cups bite-size pieces skinned cooked turkey

12 large (9- to 10-in.-wide) warm flour tortillas

Red cabbage salsa (recipe follows)

Unflavored nonfat yogurt

Salt

Sort beans for debris. Rinse beans and put in a 6- to 8-quart pan with 2 quarts water. Cover and bring to a boil on high heat; remove from heat and let stand 1 hour or up to 1 day. Drain and discard water; set beans aside.

To pan, add onion, 5 cups water, broth, chili powder, brown sugar, and star anise; cover and bring to a boil over high heat. Add beans to pan and simmer gently until very tender to bite, about 1½ hours. Drain beans, saving liquid. *If making ahead, let cool, cover beans and liquid separately, and chill up to 2 days.* In pan, boil cooking liquid over high heat until reduced to 3 cups. Add beans and mash to make the mixture thick. Add turkey. Stir gently until mixture is hot.

Spoon onto warm tortillas; add salsa, yogurt, and salt to taste; roll to enclose filling. Relishes can include olives and raw vegetables. Makes 12 servings.

Per serving: 469 cal. (16 percent from fat); 29 g protein; 8.1 g fat (1.5 g sat.); 71 g carbo.; 384 mg sodium; 36 mg chol.

Red cabbage salsa. Combine 4 cups thinly shredded **red cabbage,** 1 cup sliced **green onion,** ⅓ cup minced **fresh cilantro** (coriander), ¼ cup **lime juice,** and ½ teaspoon **pepper.**

Sesame Thai Turkey Salad

About 4 cups bite-size pieces skinned cooked turkey

2 large (about ½ lb. total) carrots, shredded

1 large (about ½-lb.) red or green bell pepper, stemmed, seeded, and thinly sliced

½ cup thinly sliced green onions

¼ cup roasted, salted peanuts

¼ cup thinly sliced dried apricots

Thai dressing (recipe follows)

Napa cabbage leaves, rinsed and crisped

Whole green onions, ends trimmed (optional)

Peeled orange slices (optional)

In a large bowl, combine turkey, carrots, bell pepper, sliced green onions, peanuts, apricots, and Thai dressing; mix well.

On 4 to 6 salad plates or 1 platter, arrange cabbage leaves, then spoon turkey salad equally onto leaves; garnish with whole green onions and orange slices. Makes 4 to 6 servings.
—*Maryellen Weber, Casa de los Niños Garden Restaurant, Sacramento*

Per serving: 291 cal. (37 percent from fat); 30 g protein; 12 g fat (2.5 g sat.); 15 g carbo.; 336 mg sodium; 72 mg chol.

Thai dressing. Stir together ¼ cup **rice vinegar,** 2 tablespoons *each* **reduced-sodium** or regular **soy sauce** and **Oriental sesame oil,** 1 tablespoon **honey,** and 2 teaspoons *each* **crushed dried red hot chilies** and grated **orange peel.** ∎

By Betsy Reynolds Bateson

Give gifts of the season

Turn shiny persimmons, glossy chestnuts, and exotic mushrooms into arrangements to admire first and eat later

FURLED MUSHROOMS *tucked into a handsome basket look great for a day, then can be sautéed for seasoning on the second day.*

NORMAN A. PLATE

THREE GREAT EDIBLES of fall—Fuyu persimmons, chestnuts, and wild and cultivated mushrooms—make elegant, original gifts when presented in handsome containers with lavish bows. Not only are they delightful to look at, but if you include some simple instructions for cooking, the presentations can be converted to good eating.

PERSIMMON FIXINGS

Present flat-bottomed, firm Fuyu-type persimmons and a few almonds in the shell in an attractive shallow baking dish. Include a bag of homemade streusel mix (directions follow). Instruct the recipient to refrigerate the mix while enjoying the beauty of the fall arrangement.

The fruit can be eaten anytime, but when it begins to soften (in 1 to 2 weeks), it's time to slice it into the baking dish, top with the streusel, and bake persimmon crisp for breakfast or dessert.

Persimmon Crisp

Thinly slice enough **Fuyu-type persimmons** into a shallow 1- to 1½-quart baking dish to fill the dish to the rim. (If you have more than 4 cups fruit, mix in **sugar** to taste.) Squeeze **streusel topping** (recipe follows) to form lumps and scatter over fruit. Bake in a 375° oven until topping is well browned, 45 to 50 minutes. Serve hot or cool; scoop into bowls and top with **eggnog** or sweetened softly whipped cream.

Streusel topping. Mix ¾ cup **all-purpose flour**, ½ cup firmly packed **brown sugar**, ½ teaspoon **ground cinnamon**, and ¼ teaspoon **ground nutmeg**. With your fingers or a pastry cutter, rub or cut 6 tablespoons firm **butter** or margarine into flour mixture until it resembles coarse crumbs. Stir in ⅓ cup chopped **almonds** or walnuts. Seal in a plastic bag; store in refrigerator up to 1 month.

CHESTNUTS AND MORE

Package chestnuts, a bottle of madeira (malmsey, dry or sweet), and perhaps a chestnut knife or other short-bladed knife in a good-looking shallow pan.

Roasted Chestnuts with Madeira

With a small, sharp knife, cut an X through the shell on the flat side of each **chestnut.** Place nuts in a single layer in a shallow pan. Roast in a 400° oven until nuts are mealy in center when broken open, 20 to 30 minutes.

Using thick napkins as protection, crack roasted nuts 1 at a time between your hands; pull off the shell and thin skin inside. Eat chestnuts while sipping madeira.

A MUSHROOM BOUQUET

Select whole, fresh-looking mushrooms such as hedgehog, matsutake, portabella, oyster, chanterelle, and shiitake. Arrange unrinsed mushrooms in a towel-lined basket; garnish with greenery such as fresh rosemary or thyme sprigs. Let stand at room temperature up to 24 hours.

Or enclose the mushrooms in towels, seal in plastic bags, and store in the refrigerator 2 or 3 days.

Forest Mushroom Sauté

Brush or trim off caked-on debris from **mushrooms.** Quickly immerse a few mushrooms at a time in cool water, shaking them gently to help dislodge any debris or insects. Lift out, shake gently, and drain on towels. Cut off and discard woody or tough stems and damaged areas. Check mushrooms for tiny holes and cut into them to trim out any insects. Leave small mushrooms whole, or slice or chop them all.

In a 10- to 12-inch frying pan, melt 2 tablespoons **butter** or margarine. Add enough cleaned whole or cut mushrooms to fill pan to a depth of 1½ inches. Cook over medium-high heat, stirring occasionally, until lightly browned (most mushrooms exude liquid; cook until it evaporates). Add **salt, pepper,** and **fresh rosemary** to taste. Serve as a vegetable or add to any dish desired. If made ahead, seal sautéed mushrooms airtight and refrigerate up to 2 days; freeze to store longer. ∎

By Linda Lau Anusasananan

MOUND FUYU PERSIMMONS in a shallow baking dish with a bag of streusel mix and directions for persimmon crisp. The fruit can be displayed for many days, then baked for dessert.

NESTLE MADEIRA with chestnuts in a shallow pan. Include directions for roasting the nuts to munch as the wine is sipped.

COOL SEAFOOD, *presented on lemon-seasoned linguine, gets additional flavor from spinach pesto.*

NORMAN A. PLATE

Dinner is ready

The secret to surviving the holiday feeding frenzy: make-ahead, one-dish entrées

SAVVY COOKS, FACED with the challenge of hungry house-guests or yet one more holiday gathering, have a secret: keep it simple, preferably one grand dish, and do some of the work ahead of time.

This holiday season, go hot or cold, light or hearty. Choose a cool Italian seafood salad, a Thai curry casserole, or a meaty French lentil cassoulet. Their robust flavors hide a bonus: most are low in fat.

To round out the party, start with a simple appetizer (perhaps purchased), offer salad and bread with the entrées, and conclude with a spectacular dessert (for

some make-ahead choices, see page 238). Each main dish serves 8 to 10.

Italian Fisherman's Salad

3 cups regular-strength chicken broth

1½ cups dry white wine

2 pounds large (31- to 35-per-lb.) shrimp, shelled, deveined, and rinsed

1 pound bay scallops, rinsed

3 to 4 dozen small mussels or clams in shells (or a combination), suitable for steaming, scrubbed

Lemon dressing (recipe follows)

2 pounds dried linguine

3 tablespoons chopped parsley

Thin lemon slices

Spinach pesto dressing (recipe follows)

In a 6- to 8-quart pan, combine broth, wine, and 2 cups water. Bring to a boil over high heat. Stir in shrimp; cover pan tightly, remove from heat, and let stand just until shrimp are pink and opaque but moist-looking in center of thickest part (cut to test), about 3 minutes. With a slotted spoon, put shrimp in a large bowl.

Return broth to a boil; stir in scallops. Cover pan tightly, remove from heat, and let stand until scallops are opaque in thickest part (cut to test), about 2 minutes. With a slotted spoon, transfer scallops to bowl with shrimp.

Return broth to a boil. Discard any gaping mussels or

clams that do not close when tapped. Add mussels or clams to boiling broth, cover, and simmer until shells pop open, 5 to 10 minutes. With a slotted spoon, transfer them as they open to bowl with other seafood (discard unopened ones).

Pour broth from pan into a bowl, holding back gritty sediment; discard sediment and rinse pan. Also, drain off and collect accumulated broth in bowl of seafood. Let broth cool; reserve 3¾ cups for dressings (following). Save remaining broth for other uses (chill, covered, up to 1 day; freeze to store longer).

Mix cooked seafood with 1 cup lemon dressing.

To pan, add about 4 quarts water; cover and bring to a boil over high heat. Add linguine and cook, uncovered, just until barely tender to bite, 7 to 9 minutes. Drain, rinse well with cold water until cool, and drain again. Pour pasta into a large shallow bowl or rimmed platter (at least 15 by 21 in., or 16-in. diameter). Mix pasta with remaining lemon dressing.

Mound marinated seafood over pasta; drizzle any excess lemon dressing over salad. *If making ahead, cover and chill up to 1 day.*

Garnish with parsley and lemon slices. Offer spinach pesto dressing to add to individual servings. Serves 8 to 10.

Per serving: 541 cal. (15 percent from fat); 38 g protein; 9.3 g fat (1.3 g sat.); 74 g carbo.; 274 mg sodium; 134 mg chol.

Lemon dressing. Mix 1 tablespoon finely shredded **lemon peel**, ¾ cup **lemon juice**, 1¾ cups **broth from seafood** (see preceding), ½ cup minced **shallots**, ¼ cup **olive oil**, 1½ teaspoons **coarse-ground pepper**, and 2 or 3 cloves **garlic**, pressed or minced. Makes 2¾ cups.

Spinach pesto dressing. In a 1½- to 2-quart pan, bring about 1 quart **water** to a boil. Plunge 3 cups (about 5 oz.) lightly packed, coarsely chopped **spinach** leaves into water just until they turn bright green, about 30 seconds. Drain; let cool and squeeze dry. In a blender or food processor, smoothly purée spinach, ½ cup **re-**duced-fat mayonnaise, ½ cup **pine nuts** or slivered almonds, 3 tablespoons **dried basil leaves,** and 1 clove **garlic.** Gradually add 2 cups **broth from seafood** (see preceding); blend until smooth. *If making ahead, cover and chill up to 1 day.* Just before serving, stir in 3 tablespoons **lemon juice.** Makes about 2½ cups.

Per ¼ cup: 83 cal. (78 percent from fat); 2.8 g protein; 7.2 g fat (1.4 g sat.); 3.9 g carbo.; 87 mg sodium; 4 mg chol.

Thai Curry Casserole

3½ pounds banana or butternut squash, seeded and cut into large chunks

1 pound lean ground chicken or turkey

4 cloves garlic, minced or pressed

1 large onion, finely chopped

½ cup minced fresh or 2 tablespoons crumbled dried basil leaves

½ cup minced fresh or 2 tablespoons crumbled dried mint leaves

¼ cup minced fresh cilantro (coriander)

2 tablespoons minced fresh ginger

½ teaspoon crushed dried hot red chilies

1 tablespoon all-purpose flour

½ cup regular-strength chicken broth

4 tablespoons seasoned rice vinegar (or 4 tablespoons rice vinegar and ½ teaspoon sugar)

2 tablespoons Thai fish sauce (*nuoc mam* or *nam pla*) or soy sauce

2 to 2¼ pounds russet potatoes, peeled and diced

Coconut-citrus topping (recipe follows)

2 cups finely shredded carrots

1 or 2 fresh small chilies (optional)

Sprigs of basil, mint, and cilantro (optional)

Salt

Place squash, cut side down, in a 4½- to 5-quart casserole (about 10 by 15 in.). Add about ½ inch water and cover tightly. Bake in a 350° oven until squash is tender when pierced, about 1 hour. Let squash stand until cool enough for you to handle; cut off and discard skin. Cut squash into ½- to ¾-inch chunks. Drain casserole and return squash to it.

Meanwhile, combine chicken, garlic, onion, basil, mint, cilantro, ginger, and chilies in a 10- to 12-inch frying pan. Stir often over medium-high heat until meat and onion are lightly browned, about 10 minutes. Stir flour into meat mixture, then mix in broth, 3 tablespoons vinegar, and fish sauce. Stir until bubbling and thick; remove from heat.

Tuck potatoes around squash pieces; spoon chicken mixture over vegetables and spread to make level. *If making ahead, cover and chill up to 1 day.*

Pour or spread coconut-citrus topping evenly over chicken mixture. Bake casserole, uncovered, in a 375° oven until topping is browned at casserole edges and juices are bubbling, 50 to 60 minutes.

In a bowl, gently mix

SPICY THAI CURRY *sparks flavor of squash, potato, and ground meat casserole.*

NORMAN A. PLATE

NORMAN A. PLATE

STREAMLINED CASSOULET *replaces beans with lentils as basic ingredient.*

carrots with remaining rice vinegar.

Serve carrots from a small bowl to accompany the curry casserole, or use carrots or chilies and herb sprigs to decorate it. Scoop out portions and add salt to taste. Serves 8.

Per serving: 327 cal. (19 percent from fat); 18 g protein; 6.8 g fat (1.8 g sat.); 51 g carbo.; 251 mg sodium; 49 mg chol.

Coconut-citrus topping. In a 4- to 5-quart pan, smoothly blend 2 cups **regular-strength chicken broth** with ¼ cup **all-purpose flour.** Add 1½ cups **low-fat** or extra-light **milk,** 1 tablespoon *each* grated **lemon peel** and **lime peel,** and 2 teaspoons **coconut extract.**

Stir mixture often over medium-high heat until sauce boils; simmer gently, stirring often, for 5 minutes. Use sauce hot or cool. *If making ahead, let cool, cover, and chill up to 1 day. Stir sauce vigorously to smooth before using.*

Lentil Cassoulet

3½ to 4½ pounds country-style pork ribs

2 tablespoons salt

2 tablespoons sugar

1 teaspoon pepper

1 pound turkey Polish sausage

About 10 cups regular-strength chicken broth

2 large (about 1 lb. total) onions, chopped

3 cloves garlic, pressed or minced

2 teaspoons dried thyme

2 teaspoons coriander seed

1 dried bay leaf

2 pounds (5⅔ cups) lentils

3 large (about ¾ lb. total) carrots, chopped

1 cup coarse soft bread crumbs

1 tablespoon olive oil

2 tablespoons chopped parsley

Trim and discard fat from pork; cut ribs apart between bones. Mix salt, sugar, and pepper; rub all over pork. Seal meat in a plastic food bag. *Chill, turning occasionally, at least 6 hours or up to 1 day.* Rinse meat well and pat dry.

Place pork and sausage in a single layer in 2 pans, each 10 by 15 inches. Bake in a 450° oven until meat is browned, 30 minutes. When sausage is cool, diagonally cut into ¼-inch-thick slices.

In a 6- to 8-quart pan, combine 1 cup broth with onions, garlic, thyme, coriander, and bay. Stir often over high heat until liquid evaporates and a brown film forms in pan, about 10 minutes. Deglaze by stirring brown film free with ⅓ cup broth. Boil until liquid evaporates and brown film forms again; stir often. Repeat deglazing 1 or 2 times until onion is well browned; use ⅓ cup broth each time.

Meanwhile, sort and discard debris from lentils; rinse lentils. Add lentils, pork, 8

cups broth, and coarsely chopped carrots to pan; cover and simmer until lentils are tender to bite, 30 to 40 minutes.

With a slotted spoon, set aside pork. Pour lentil mixture into a shallow 5- to 6-quart casserole (about 12 by 16 in.); nestle pork and sausage slices into lentils. *If making ahead, cool, cover, and chill up to 1 day.*

Tightly cover casserole with foil. Bake, covered, in a 350° oven until hot in center, about 35 minutes (about 1 hour and 30 minutes, if chilled).

Mix crumbs and oil; uncover casserole and sprinkle with crumbs. Bake, uncovered, until crumbs are golden, 20 to 25 minutes longer. Sprinkle with parsley. Serves 8 to 10.

Per serving: 631 cal. (26 percent from fat); 54 g protein; 18 g fat (5.5 g sat.); 65 g carbo.; 739 mg sodium; 94 mg chol. ■

By Linda Anusasananan, Christine Weber Hale

PETER CHRISTIANSEN

THE CHILDREN *pour wheat berries into a grain-grinding mill attached to an electric mixer. (A blender also works well.) The result is fine whole wheat flour (below right).*

From seed to bread

Kids gain hands-on experience with the staff of life

ASK A KID WHERE bread comes from and "the grocery store" is the probable answer. Unlike children of earlier generations, whose parents most likely lived on a farm, grew much of their food for the table, and baked bread every week from grain they had raised in the fields, children today don't usually make a connection between what they eat and where it came from.

Landscape designer and author Rosalind Creasy started growing grain as an experiment to see if fresh grain would make a difference in the flavor of homemade bread. She found that a patch of soil of about 100 square feet (hers is 4 feet by 24 feet) provides flour for about 20 loaves. Growing and harvesting the wheat berries turned out to be so much fun, she got the neighborhood kids involved.

For information on growing and harvesting your own wheat, write to Reader Service, Sunset Magazine, 80 Willow Road, Menlo Park CA 94025.

Where to get seeds

Buy wheat berries at natural-food and farm supply stores. Or order by mail from Bountiful Gardens, 18001 Shafer Ranch Rd., Willits, CA 95490; (707) 459-6410 (catalog free).

Grow-Your-Own Whole-wheat Bread

Enjoy the aroma of bread made with freshly ground flour. Use home-grown hard spring or winter wheat or buy it at a natural-food store.

- 1 package active dry yeast
- 2¾ cups warm water (110° to 115°)
- ½ cup firmly packed dark brown sugar
- ¼ cup (⅛ lb.) butter or margarine, at room temperature
- 2 teaspoons salt
- 4 cups bread flour
  About 3½ cups freshly ground whole-wheat flour (directions follow)

In a large bowl, soften yeast in ¼ cup of the water, about 5 minutes. Blend in remaining 2½ cups water, sugar, butter, and salt. Stir in all the bread flour until moistened. Beat with an electric mixer or a heavy spoon until dough is stretchy, 10 to 15 minutes. Add 3½ cups whole-wheat flour.

If using a dough hook, beat on low speed until flour is moistened. Then beat at high speed until dough pulls cleanly from sides of bowl, 5 to 7 minutes. If dough still sticks, add whole-wheat flour 1 tablespoon at a time until it pulls free.

If mixing by hand, with a heavy spoon stir flour into dough until moist. Scrape dough onto a lightly floured board. Knead until smooth and elastic, adding as little flour as possible to prevent sticking, about 15 minutes. Place dough in a large bowl.

Cover dough with plastic wrap; place in a warm, draft-free place. Let dough rise until almost doubled, 1 to 1½ hours.

Knead with dough hook or on a lightly floured board to expel air bubbles. On a floured board, divide dough in half and shape each portion into a loaf. Place each loaf in a greased 4- by 8-inch loaf pan. Cover lightly with plastic wrap and place in a warm, draft-free place. Let rise until almost doubled, about 45 minutes.

Uncover and bake in a 375° oven until richly browned, 40 to 50 minutes. Turn loaves onto a wire rack to cool. Makes 2 loaves (each about 1¾ lb.).

Per ounce: 76 cal. (14 percent from fat); 2.2 g protein; 1.2 g fat (0.6 g sat.); 14 g carbo.; 89 mg sodium; 2.3 mg chol.

Freshly ground whole-wheat flour. Sort through 3 cups (about 1⅓ lb.) **hard spring** or winter **wheat;** remove any grit or dirt (some chaff is all right). Grind wheat in a grain grinder or whirl 1-cup portions in a blender until finely ground. Makes about 4 cups flour. If flour isn't used at once store in airtight freezer. ∎

By Lauren Bonar Swezey with Linda Lau Anusasananan

WHOLE WHEAT BERRIES *(left) are ground into powdery whole wheat flour right.*

CREAMY *pumpkin mousse is spiked with a hint of hazelnut liqueur.*

DARROW M. WATT

Pumpkin makes the difference

Mousse, risotto, or soup . . . start with canned pumpkin

CANNED PUMPKIN, A staple for the holiday pantry, need not be limited to use in the traditional pie. Its mellow flavor, smooth texture, and golden color can bring a rich-tasting dimension to many dishes.

Pumpkin-Hazelnut Mousse

1 cup sugar

1 envelope (2 teaspoons) unflavored gelatin

½ teaspoon ground cinnamon

½ teaspoon ground ginger

1¼ cups lowfat milk

2 cups light (reduced-fat) sour cream

1 can (16 oz.) pumpkin

⅓ cup hazelnut-flavor liqueur (optional)

¾ cup whipping cream

6 to 8 hazelnuts

Reserve 2 tablespoons sugar. In a 2- to 3-quart pan, mix remaining sugar, gelatin, cinnamon, and ginger. Add ½ cup milk; stir often over medium-high heat until milk is steaming. Add remaining ¾ cup milk, sour cream, pumpkin, and liqueur. Set pan in ice water and stir often until mixture just begins to set, about 20 minutes (if mixture gets too stiff, stir over heat to soften).

Whip cream with reserved 2 tablespoons sugar on high speed until soft peaks form; cover and chill ⅓ cup of the cream until serving. Gently fold remaining cream into pumpkin mixture.

Divide mousse evenly among 6 to 8 glasses or ramekins (about 1-cup size). Lightly cover; chill until mousse is set, at least 4 hours or up to 1 day. Garnish with reserved cream and hazelnuts. Serves 6 to 8.

Per serving: 307 cal. (47 percent from fat); 7.2 g protein; 16 g fat (8.7 g sat.); 36 g carbo.; 31 mg sodium; 46 mg chol.

Oven Pumpkin Risotto

5 cups regular-strength chicken broth

2 cups medium- or short-grain (pearl) white rice

1 can (16 oz.) pumpkin

1 tablespoon grated lemon peel

¼ teaspoon ground nutmeg

⅓ cup shredded parmesan cheese

Parmesan cheese curls, cut with a vegetable peeler

Freshly grated nutmeg (optional)

In a 3- to 4-quart shallow casserole, mix broth, rice, pumpkin, peel, and ground nutmeg.

Bake, uncovered, in a 400° oven until liquid begins to be absorbed, about 20 minutes. Stir well, then continue baking, stirring often, until rice is tender to bite and mixture is creamy, about 25 minutes longer. Stir in shredded cheese. Transfer to serving dish. Scatter parmesan curls and freshly grated nutmeg onto risotto. Serves 6.

Per serving: 311 cal. (9.3 percent from fat); 8.9 g protein; 3.2 g fat (1.4 g sat.); 60 g carbo.; 131 mg sodium; 3.5 mg chol.

Curried Pumpkin Soup

1 large (about 10-oz.) onion, finely chopped

1 tablespoon minced fresh ginger

1 clove garlic, minced or pressed

1 teaspoon curry powder

3½ cups regular-strength chicken broth

1 cup milk

1 can (16 oz.) pumpkin

¼ cup light (reduced-fat) sour cream

2 tablespoons roasted pumpkin seeds

Combine onion, ginger, garlic, curry, and ½ cup broth in a 3- to 4-quart pan. Cook over high heat, stirring occasionally, until liquid evaporates and browned bits stick in pan. Deglaze pan, adding ¼ cup water. Scrape free browned bits. Stir often until pan is dry and browned bits form again. Repeat deglazing step until onion is richly browned and pan is dry, about 20 minutes.

Add remaining broth, milk, and pumpkin; stir to scrape browned bits free. Bring to a boil, stirring over high heat. Ladle into bowls; garnish with sour cream and seeds. Serves 4 to 6.

Per serving: 110 cal. (34 percent from fat); 5 g protein; 4.2 g fat (1.9 g sat.); 14 g carbo.; 56 mg sodium; 9 mg chol. ∎

By Christine Weber Hale

RICH HUE *of creamy, lemon-accented risotto and curried soup comes from canned pumpkin; both go together in less than an hour.*

CRISP PASTRIES *start with won ton skins. Fry them briefly, then shake hot pastries in cinnamon sugar mixture.*

PETER CHRISTIANSEN

Central American dessert saga

Rich flan and crisp pastries have a touch of history

THESE DESSERTS TELL a tale of how recipes evolve as they move from country to country, and from cook to cook. The story starts in Spain with two classics: caramel-coated flan and crisp fried buñuelos.

When the Spanish came to Central America, they brought these traditional dessert recipes. In Guatemala, a soft cheese was added to flan, giving it the delicate density of cheesecake. In Costa Rica, buñuelos acquired a local name: *prestiños.*

When two cooks from Central America moved to new homes in California, they modified their own versions of these recipes. Marta Troche switched to cream cheese for preparation of her flan. Marlen Campain took a more daring step—her prestiños, made with fried won ton

skins, are as tasty and crisp as those made with homemade dough, but they're faster to make.

Cream Cheese Flan (Flan con Queso)

½ cup sugar

8 large eggs

1 can (14 oz.) sweetened condensed milk

½ teaspoon ground cinnamon

2 large packages (8 oz. each) cream cheese, cut into chunks

Fresh pineapple slices (optional)

Place sugar in a deep 1½- to 2-quart metal mold (plain or fluted) or bowl (not tin-lined; heat will damage). Over medium-high heat, shake mold frequently (protect hands with pot holders) until sugar melts and turns amber color.

At once, rotate to coat bottom and sides of mold with the very hot melted sugar; set aside until cool and caramel hardens.

In a blender or food processor, whirl until smooth the eggs, milk, cinnamon, and cheese. Pour flan mixture into mold; cover tightly with foil.

Place a ¼- to 1-inch-high rack in an 8- to 10-quart pan. Set covered mold on rack; top of mold needs to be below pan rim. Add water to pan halfway up sides of flan. Cover pan. On high heat, bring water to simmering; simmer until flan feels firm when lightly pressed in center (lift foil to check), about 1 hour.

Lift flan from water, uncover, and let cool at least 2 hours. Serve, or, if making ahead, cover and chill up to 2 days.

To release flan, run a thin knife between mold side and flan. Cover mold with an inverted rimmed plate; hold containers together and invert. Lift off mold; melting caramel helps flan slip free. Spoon onto plates; serve with pineapple. Cover and chill leftovers up to 3 days. Serves 12 to 14.—*Marta Troche, San Francisco*

Per serving: 274 cal. (56 percent from fat); 8.2 g protein; 17 g fat (9.5 g sat.); 24 g carbo.; 168 mg sodium; 167 mg chol.

Cinnamon Pastries (Prestiños)

½ cup sugar

2 teaspoons ground cinnamon

About 2½ cups salad oil

30 won ton skins (each 3¼ in. square)

In a small paper bag, mix sugar and cinnamon.

In a deep 2- to 3-quart pan over medium heat, bring 1 inch oil to 375° on a thermometer.

Cook 1 won ton at a time, turning until golden, about 25 seconds. With a slotted spoon, transfer won ton to towels to drain.

Shake warm pastries in cinnamon-sugar mixture. Serve, or store pastries airtight up to 1 week. Makes 30; serves 6 to 8. —*Marlen Campain, Los Angeles*

Per piece: 47 cal. (48 percent from fat); 0.8 g protein; 2.5 g fat (0.3 g sat.); 5.7 g carbo.; 1.8 mg sodium; 0 mg chol. ∎

By Elaine Johnson

DARROW M. WATT

CARAMEL *soaks into velvety, dense cream cheese flan; fresh pineapple offsets the rich cheesecake texture.*

BRADED BREAD *has speckled crust of anise, sesame, and nigella seeds. Pull loaf apart to enjoy with feta cheese and salty, wrinkled olives.*

Crunch comes easily with whole seeds

Use sesame, anise, pumpkin, and more

E XPERIMENT WITH WHOLE seeds in these easy recipes for Greek bread, Indian fish, and Mexican chicken.

Nigella (also called *kalonji* and, incorrectly, black onion seed) is sold in Indian and Middle Eastern groceries. The small black seeds taste slightly sweet, like anise, and somewhat bitter. Hulled pumpkin seed is often available in bulk or jars at supermarkets.

Fragrant Greek Seed Bread

2 loaves (2 lb. total) frozen whole-wheat bread dough, thawed

1 tablespoon beaten egg

1½ tablespoons sesame seed

1½ teaspoons nigella (kalonji), optional

¾ teaspoon anise seed

On a floured board, knead dough to combine loaves into a smooth ball. Cut dough into 3 equal pieces. Roll

each piece into an 18-inch rope; transfer ropes to an oiled 10- by 15-inch pan. Pinch 3 rope ends together, then braid them to form a loaf diagonally across pan; pinch remaining ends to secure. Brush with egg.

Combine sesame, nigella, and anise; sprinkle over braid. Cover dough loosely with plastic wrap. Let rise in a warm place until puffy, 40 to 45 minutes; remove plastic. Bake loaf in a 375° oven until deep golden, about 30 minutes. Serve warm; or let cool on a rack and store airtight up to 2 days or freeze. Makes 1 loaf, 2 pounds.

Per ounce: 79 cal. (19 percent from fat); 2.2 g protein; 1.7 g fat (0.4 g sat.); 14 g carbo.; 137 mg sodium; 3.4 mg chol.

Seed-crusted Fish, Indian-style

½ teaspoon coarsely ground pepper

½ teaspoon *each* cumin seed and fennel seed

1 teaspoon *each* coriander seed and mustard seed

1 pound skinned and boned lingcod, rockfish, or orange roughy fillets, ½ to 1 inch thick

2 teaspoons salad oil
Fresh cilantro (coriander) sprigs
Salt

Mix pepper and cumin, fennel, coriander, and mustard seed; set aside.

Rinse fish and cut into 4 equal pieces. Brush with oil and place in a 12- by 14-inch broiler pan. Broil about 3 inches from heat for 3 minutes. Turn fish over and sprinkle with seed mixture. Broil until fish is opaque but still moist-looking in thickest part (cut to test), 2 to 4 minutes longer. Top with cilantro; add salt to taste. Serves 4.

Per serving: 125 cal. (28 percent from fat); 20 g protein; 3.9 g fat (0.5 g sat.); 0.9 g carbo.; 68 mg sodium; 59 mg chol.

Chicken with Pumpkin Seed

Squeeze lime wedges over chicken.

4 chicken breast halves (about 1¾ lb. total), skinned

⅓ cup hulled roasted pumpkin seed

1 can (4 oz.) diced green chilies

½ cup shredded jack cheese

Place chicken in a 9- by 13-inch baking dish. Mix seed, chilies, and cheese; pat evenly onto chicken. Bake in a 450° oven until thickest part of breast is no longer pink at the bone (cut to test), 20 to 25 minutes. Serves 4.

Per serving: 226 cal. (27 percent from fat); 35 g protein; 6.9 g fat (0.6 g sat.); 4.6 g carbo.; 334 mg sodium; 87 mg chol. ∎

By Elaine Johnson

SEASONING SEEDS *include (from top) fennel, anise, sesame, pumpkin, cumin, mustard, coriander, nigella.*

OUR NATIONAL OLEOPHOBIA (fear of fat) has decreed that gravies and rich sauces are out. What do we substitute as adornment for fish, flesh, or fowl?

One answer is a chutney, which might be described as a complex hybrid of a fruit preserve and a pickle. Originally from India, and best known with a base of mango, chutneys are now made from almost any fruit.

Peg Roberts sends us a chutney based on lemons. She tells us that her inspiration comes from a prize-winning New Zealand recipe.

Lemon Chutney

    2 to 2 ¼ pounds (6 to 8 medium-size) lemons
    2 large (about 1 lb. total) onions, chopped
    3 tablespoons salt
    2 cups distilled white vinegar
    4 cups sugar
    1 cup raisins
    ¼ cup mustard seed
    2 teaspoons ground ginger
    ¼ to ½ teaspoon cayenne

Trim off and discard the lemon ends. Then thinly slice the lemons and discard the seeds. Cut the lemon slices in half and place in a large bowl with the onions and the salt. Cover and let the lemon mixture stand at room temperature for at least 4 hours or up to 1 day.

Drain the lemon mixture in a colander and rinse well under cold water. In a 5- to 6-quart pan, combine the lemon mixture and 2 cups water. Bring to a boil over high heat; reduce heat and boil gently, uncovered, until the lemon peel is very tender when pierced, about 15 minutes.

Mix in the vinegar, sugar, raisins, mustard seed, ginger, and ¼ teaspoon cayenne (more for hotter flavor). Stir over low heat until the sugar dissolves; bring to boiling over high heat. Simmer, uncovered, until reduced to 2 quarts, about 1 hour; stir occasionally. Let cool, then spoon the chutney into small jars. Serve, or store airtight in the refrigerator up to 3 months. Makes 8 cups.

Per tablespoon: 32 cal. (2.8 percent from fat); 0.2 g protein; 0.1 g fat (0 g sat.); 8.4 g carbo.; 18 mg sodium; 0 mg chol.

Peg Roberts

Santa Barbara, California

By Joan Griffiths, Richard Dunmire

Chicken with vinegar means adobo

ADOBO, A CLASSIC FILIPINO TYPE of meat cookery, can be a casserole, a stew, a barbecue, a sauté, or some mixture of the above. Scott Skougard's formula begins with marinating the meat as for barbecuing, then browning it in oil, simmering it in the marinade, and then reducing the marinade to a sauce. He makes his adobo heart-friendly by removing the skin from the chicken and pouring off the fat at two stages during cooking. As he says, adobo is easy to prepare, keeps well for days in the refrigerator, and reheats appetizingly in the microwave. He recommends serving it with stir-fried vegetables, steamed white rice, and fresh fruit, with iced tea or beer as a beverage.

Adobos may contain other ingredients than those listed below; coconut milk and hot peppers are two of many possibilities. What is essential to any adobo is vinegar.

Filipino Adobo

    6 chicken thighs (about 1¾ lb. total)
       About 1½ pounds pork back ribs
    ¾ cup rice vinegar
    ⅓ cup reduced-sodium soy sauce
    2 tablespoons minced garlic
    1 teaspoon Oriental sesame oil
    ¼ teaspoon pepper
    2 teaspoons salad oil
       Thinly sliced green onion (including top)

Remove skin from chicken and discard; rinse thighs.

Trim and discard excess fat from ribs; cut ribs into 2-rib pieces. In a deep bowl, combine vinegar, soy, garlic, sesame oil, pepper, and ¼ cup water. Add meats and mix well. Cover and chill at least 15 minutes or up to 6 hours; mix occasionally.

Lift meat from marinade; drain and pat dry. Save marinade.

Pour salad oil into a 5- to 6-quart pan over medium-high heat. When oil is hot, add chicken and turn to brown well, about 12 minutes total. Remove from pan and drain on towels. Add ribs to pan; turn to brown well, about 10 minutes total. Drain ribs on towels. Drain fat from pan; add reserved marinade and scrape browned bits in pan free. Add chicken and pork. Bring to a boil on high heat; cover and simmer until meat at bones is no longer pink (cut to test), 25 to 30 minutes longer.

With a slotted spoon, transfer meats to a platter; keep warm. Skim and discard fat from cooking liquid; boil liquid, uncovered, over high heat until reduced to about ¾ cup. Pour over meats and garnish with green onion. Makes 6 servings.

Per serving: 304 cal. (56 percent from fat); 29 g protein; 19 g fat (6.2 g sat.); 3.6 g carbo.; 640 mg sodium; 116 mg chol.

Burnsville, Minnesota

SUNSET'S KITCHEN CABINET

Creative ways with everyday foods—submitted by *Sunset* readers,
tested in *Sunset* kitchens, approved by *Sunset* taste panels

Quick Broccoli-Sausage Pizza

Janet Schott, Livermore, California

1 package (10 oz.) frozen reduced-fat, brown-and-serve pork link sausages, sliced

1 cup chopped onion

2 cloves garlic, pressed or minced

2 cups (½ lb.) chopped fresh broccoli, or 1 package (10 oz.) frozen chopped broccoli or flowerets

1 teaspoon fennel seed

¼ teaspoon crushed dried hot red chilies

1 package (16 oz., about 12 in. wide) baked Italian bread shell

½ pound (2 cups) shredded mozzarella cheese

In an 8- to 10-inch frying pan, frequently stir sausages, onion, and garlic over medium-high heat until onion is limp, about 5 minutes.

Add broccoli, fennel, and chilies to frying pan; stir until broccoli is tender-crisp, 2 to 3 minutes.

Place bread shell on a 12-inch pizza pan or 12- by 15-inch baking sheet. Sprinkle cheese evenly over crust. Distribute broccoli mixture evenly over cheese. Bake in a 450° oven until browned, about 15 minutes. Cut into wedges. Serves 4.

Per serving: 674 cal. (49 percent from fat); 38 g protein; 37 g fat (no data, sat.); 58 g carbo.; 1,207 mg sodium; 104 mg chol.

CHEESE, SAUSAGE, *and broccoli top purchased crust for quick supper pizza.*

Orange Pumpkin Soup

Roxanne Chan, Albany, California

1 teaspoon salad oil

1 large (about ½-lb.) onion, chopped

1 teaspoon ground coriander

1 can (16 oz.) pumpkin

1 quart regular-strength chicken broth

1½ cups orange juice

½ cup dry white wine or more broth

1 small package (3 oz.) cream cheese

Chives or thinly sliced green onions

Salt and pepper

In a 3- to 4-quart pan, stir oil, onion, coriander, and ¼ cup water over high heat until liquid evaporates and onion is very limp, 5 to 7 minutes. Add pumpkin, broth, juice, and wine; stir until blended.

Bring to a boil; reduce heat to low, cover, and simmer 20 minutes. Cut cheese into ½-inch chunks into a blender or food processor. Whirl, adding about 1 cup soup, until smooth. Return to soup in pan. Stir until hot. Serve hot or cold. If making ahead, cool, cover, and chill up to 1 day; reheat, if desired. Ladle into bowls, garnish with chives, and add salt and pepper to taste. Serves 8.

Per serving: 119 cal. (39 percent from fat); 3.2 g protein; 5.2 g fat (2.7 g sat.); 13 g carbo.; 63 mg sodium; 12 mg chol.

ORANGE JUICE, *chicken broth, and canned pumpkin make colorful soup.*

Ojai Waldorf Salad

Sally Hoover, Ojai, California

1 piece or 1 small (about 1-lb.) jicama

2 large (about 1 lb. total) Granny Smith or Newtown Pippin apples

1 cup thinly sliced celery

½ cup golden raisins

½ cup dry-roasted, salted peanuts

⅓ cup pitted dates, coarsely chopped

Ginger dressing (recipe follows)

Large butter lettuce leaves, rinsed and crisped

Peel jicama and cut enough into ½-inch cubes to make about 3 cups. Core apples and cut into ½-inch cubes. In a bowl, combine jicama, apples, celery, raisins, peanuts, dates, and dressing. Spoon onto lettuce leaves. Serves 8.

Per serving: 203 cal. (40 percent from fat); 4.4 g protein; 9 g fat (1.7 g sat.); 29 g carbo.; 184 mg sodium; 5.2 mg chol.

Ginger dressing. Mix ½ cup **reduced-fat** or regular **mayonnaise,** ½ cup **unflavored nonfat yogurt,** 2 tablespoons **lemon juice,** 2 teaspoons grated **fresh ginger,** ½ teaspoon **grated lemon peel,** ⅛ teaspoon each ground **cinnamon** and **nutmeg.**

COMBINE JICAMA *and apple with peanuts, dates, and raisins for salad.*

Steamed Clams with Garlic

Susie Wyshak, San Francisco

1 teaspoon butter or margarine

2 medium-size (about ¾ lb. total) onions, thinly sliced

¼ to ½ cup chopped garlic

2 medium-size (about ¾ lb. total) firm-ripe tomatoes, cored and chopped

1 teaspoon paprika

1 teaspoon dried thyme leaves

1 teaspoon pepper

⅛ teaspoon cayenne

1 cup dry white wine

3 dozen clams in shells, suitable for steaming, scrubbed

In a 5- to 6-quart pan, combine butter, onions, garlic, and ¼ cup water. Stir often over medium heat until liquid evaporates and onions are limp, about 10 minutes. Add tomatoes, paprika, thyme, pepper, and cayenne to pan; stir. Cook, uncovered, 5 minutes. Add wine; bring to a boil.

Discard gaping clams that do not close when tapped. Add clams to pan, cover, and simmer until they pop open, 10 to 15 minutes. Ladle into wide bowls; discard clams that don't open. Makes 3 or 4 servings.

Per serving: 216 cal. (12 percent from fat); 20 g protein; 2.8 g fat (0.8 g sat.); 19 g carbo.; 100 mg sodium; 48 mg chol.

STEAM CLAMS *in a tomato and onion wine sauce, intense with garlic.*

Simple Sukiyaki

Mary Perrott Smith, Golden, Colorado

1 tablespoon salad oil

½ pound thinly sliced boned and fat-trimmed beef rib eye or sirloin

1 tablespoon minced fresh ginger

1 medium-size (about 6-oz.) onion, thinly sliced

4 large (2¼-in.-wide, about 6 oz. total) mushrooms, rinsed and thinly sliced

1 cup thinly sliced celery

4 green onions, ends trimmed, cut into 3-inch lengths

¼ pound spinach, stems trimmed and wilted leaves removed, rinsed, and drained

Cooking sauce (recipe follows)

Hot cooked rice

Pour oil into a 10- to 12-inch frying pan over high heat. When oil is hot, add beef and ginger; stir often until beef loses its pinkness, about 2 minutes. With a slotted spoon, transfer beef to a bowl.

Add onion, mushrooms, and celery to pan; stir 2 minutes. Add green onions and spinach; stir until spinach wilts, about 1 minute. Add cooking sauce and beef; stir until boiling. Serve with rice. Makes 2 servings.

Per serving: 430 cal. (36 percent from fat); 32 g protein; 17 g fat (4.8 g sat.); 31 g carbo.; 1,692 mg sodium; 67 mg chol.

Cooking sauce. Mix ½ cup **canned condensed consommé,** ¼ cup **dry sherry** or more consommé, ¼ cup **reduced-sodium soy sauce,** and 1 tablespoon **sugar.**

STREAMLINED SUKIYAKI: *Vegetables and beef in broth make a speedy main dish.*

Cranberry-Mandarin Sauce

Jean Mangan, Spokane, Washington

This pretty, easy-to-make cranberry sauce, packed in decorative jars, is an attractive hostess gift. Serve the sweet-tart sauce as a relish with turkey or ham; or spoon it over vanilla ice cream, crêpes, or slices of pound or angel food cake for dessert.

1 quart fresh or frozen cranberries

1 cup light corn syrup

½ cup orange-flavor liqueur or orange juice

2 cans (11 oz. each) mandarin orange segments, drained

In a 3- to 4-quart pan, combine cranberries and corn syrup. Cook, covered, over medium heat, until most berries have popped, about 10 minutes. Gently stir in orange-flavor liqueur and mandarin orange segments. Ladle into widemouthed jars. Let cool.

Serve cool; if making ahead, cover and chill up to 1 month. Makes about 4½ cups.

Per ¼ cup: 185 cal. (0.5 percent from fat); 0.5 g protein; 0.1 g fat (0 g sat.); 44 g carbo.; 44 mg sodium; 0 mg chol.

Compiled by Linda Lau Anusasananan

SPOON CRANBERRY-MANDARIN *sauce over ice cream and cake for dessert.*

December Menus

QUICK, SEASONAL,
BUDGET-WISE...
FOR FAMILY AND
FRIENDS

e savor December: the tree trimmings, the rounds of car- ols, the gatherings with family and friends—and, of course, the voluptuous foods. But December is a month that calls for the easiest menus when the most is going on.

For an elegant Christmas dinner that lets you sit back and enjoy the day, crown your table with maple-cherry glazed ham, artichokes, and sweet potato spoon bread. Later on, give leftover ham new life in fla- vorful calzones. And for a warming start to a winter morning, curl up in front of the fire with fresh-from-the-oven scones.

CHRISTMAS DINNER FOR 8 TO 10 (at right)
Celebrate with baked ham with maple-cherry glaze, sweet potato spoon bread, artichokes, and a showy citrus tart.

NEW LIFE FOR LEFTOVERS (page 261)
Calzones filled with surplus Christmas ham enhanced with mushrooms and cheese are quick and hearty.

WARMING WINTER BREAKFAST (page 261)
Family and holiday houseguests wake to the aroma of freshly baked apricot-ginger scones.

THE DETAILS

Elegant First Course

Dress mixed greens with cider vinegar, olive oil, and honey to taste; arrange with sliced apples and chèvre; add toasted pecans.

Ham Options

Bone-in, boned, and presliced hams work equally well with a tangy maple-cherry glaze.

Show-off Citrus Tart

A chocolate-lined crust boasts a cream cheese–marmalade filling and an orange and chocolate garnish.

Tiramisù Coffee

Stir key flavors from the popular Italian dessert (rum and orange liqueurs, whipped cream, and chocolate curls) into coffee.

DAVID DUNCAN LIVINGSTON

259

The day before, prepare the maple-cherry glaze and the chocolate citrus tart (except for the orange and chocolate garnish). For the lemon mayonnaise, stir lemon juice to taste into mayonnaise; chill. Cook 1 small or ½ large artichoke per person; chill until serving time, or rewarm in a steamer or in simmering water.

On Christmas Day, bake the ham, prepare and bake the spoon bread, and assemble the salad (allow about 2 cups rinsed and crisped salad mix—mesclun—per person). Garnish the tart, reserving a few chocolate curls to add along with whipped cream, rum, and orange liqueur to brewed coffee or espresso.

Baked Ham with Maple-Cherry Glaze

2 cups dried cherries

1¼ cups port

¾ cup maple syrup

2 tablespoons balsamic or red wine vinegar

1 tablespoon grated orange peel

1 teaspoon ground cinnamon

1 bone-in, boned, or presliced cooked ham (6 to 7 lb.)

2 cups regular-strength beef broth

1½ tablespoons cornstarch mixed with ¼ cup water

In a 2- to 3-quart pan, combine cherries, port, syrup, vinegar, peel, and cinnamon. Bring to a boil over high heat; cover and simmer until cherries are plump, about 10 minutes. If making ahead, cover and chill up to 1 day. Whirl half in a food processor or blender until smooth; reserve remaining glaze.

Place ham in a 10- by 15-inch roasting pan. Bake in a 325° oven, basting frequently with pan juices, until a meat thermometer inserted in thickest part (not touching the bone) registers 140°; allow about 20 minutes per pound, or 2 to 2¼ hours total. If ham begins to look dry, cover with foil and bake until glaze is added.

When ham has about 40 minutes left to bake (internal temperature will be 130° to 135°), uncover ham and brush puréed glaze over top and sides. Continue baking until internal temperature is 140° and glaze is well browned and bubbling, about 40 minutes longer.

Meanwhile, combine reserved whole-cherry glaze and beef broth in a 3- to 4-quart pan over medium-high heat. Stir often until mixture boils; briskly stir in cornstarch mixture until sauce boils again. Transfer ham to a platter, sauce to a serving container. Cut ham into thin slices; offer with sauce. Serves 8 to 10 with leftovers.

Per 4-oz. serving with sauce: 354 cal. (25 percent from fat); 26 g protein; 10 g fat (3.5 g sat.); 40 g carbo.; 1,708 mg sodium; 70 mg chol.

DAVID DUNCAN LIVINGSTON

CUT INTO *hearty calzones to discover a savory mixture of ham, onion, mushrooms, and fontina cheese.*

Sweet Potato Spoon Bread

1¼ cups yellow cornmeal

1 cup all-purpose flour

2½ teaspoons baking powder

1 teaspoon baking soda

1½ cups buttermilk

3 large eggs

⅓ cup butter or margarine, melted

1 pound sweet potatoes or yams, peeled and coarsely grated

1 small onion, minced

1 cup (4 oz.) shredded jack cheese

⅓ cup grated parmesan cheese

Italian parsley (optional)

In a large bowl, stir together cornmeal, flour, baking powder, and baking soda. Add buttermilk, eggs, and butter; mix until evenly blended. Stir in potatoes, onion, and jack cheese. Pour mixture into a lightly buttered 3- to 3½-quart casserole or 9- by 13-inch baking pan. Sprinkle with parmesan.

Bake in a 400° oven until golden and puffed, about 25 minutes; serve hot or warm. Garnish with parsley. Serves 8 to 10.

Per serving: 298 cal. (39 percent from fat); 10 g protein; 13 g fat (7.2 g sat.); 35 g carbo.; 487 mg sodium; 97 mg chol.

Chocolate Citrus Tart

1½ large packages (8 oz. each) neufchâtel (light cream) cheese, softened

¾ cup orange marmalade

2 tablespoons orange-flavor liqueur (optional)

Chocolate-lined pastry shell (recipe follows)

3 large (about 2 lb. total) oranges

Chocolate curls (optional)

Beat together cheese, marmalade, and liqueur until well blended. Pour mixture into prepared pastry shell. Chill until filling thickens slightly, at least 1 hour or up to 1 day. Cut peel and outer white membrane from oranges, then cut between inner membranes to release sections; discard seeds. Lay orange sections decoratively over filling. Chill up to 4 hours. Sprinkle with chocolate curls. Serves 8 to 10.

Per serving: 311 cal. (41 percent from fat); 5 g protein; 14 g fat (7.3 g sat.); 42 g carbo.; 227 mg sodium; 26 mg chol.

Chocolate-lined pastry shell. Press **pastry for a single-crust 9-inch pie** (purchased or homemade) over bottom and sides of a 9-inch tart pan with removable rim. Bake in a 350° oven until golden brown, 25 to 35 minutes.

Remove from oven; immediately sprinkle crust with ½ cup (3 oz.) chopped **semisweet chocolate.** When it has melted, spread over bottom and sides of crust. Cool crust completely; wrap airtight and chill until chocolate hardens, at least 30 minutes or up to 1 day.

Prepare the salad while the calzones bake; buy assorted pickled and roasted peppers to serve with the meal.

Ham, Cheese, and Mushroom Calzones

⅓ pound mushrooms, sliced

1 large (about 10 oz.) onion, thinly sliced

2 cloves garlic, minced or pressed

2 tablespoons minced fresh or 2 teaspoons crumbled dried basil leaves

½ cup regular-strength chicken broth

1 tablespoon all-purpose flour

2 cups chopped cooked ham

1 loaf (1 lb.) frozen white or whole-wheat bread dough, thawed

¾ cup (3 oz.) shredded fontina cheese

1 large egg yolk beaten with 1 tablespoon water

Combine mushrooms, onion, garlic, and basil with half the broth in a 10- to 12-inch frying pan over medium-high heat. Stir often until vegetables are browned and begin to stick to pan, about 8 minutes. Add remaining broth. Stir to scrape browned bits from pan; cook until liquid evaporates. Stir in flour and ham; remove from heat.

On a lightly floured board, divide dough into 4 equal pieces; shape each into a ball. Roll out each ball into a 5- to 6-inch round. With your hands, flatten one dough round until it is 7 to 8 inches wide. Spoon ¼ of ham mixture over half the round to

within ½ inch of the edge. Sprinkle filling with ¼ of the fontina. Brush perimeter of round with water. Fold plain half over filling, pressing edges firmly together to seal. With a fork, prick top several times. Repeat, using remaining dough, filling, and cheese.

Place calzones on a lightly oiled 12- by 15-inch baking sheet. Brush with yolk mixture. Bake in a 425° oven until richly browned, about 20 minutes. Makes 4.

Per calzone: 578 cal. (31 percent from fat); 33 g protein; 20 g fat (8 g sat.); 65 g carbo.; 1,780 mg sodium; 125 mg chol.

To save time in the morning, measure out the scones' dry ingredients and chop the

apricots and ginger the night before. Brew herbal tea while scones are baking.

Apricot-Ginger Scones

3¼ cups all-purpose flour

⅓ cup sugar

2½ teaspoons baking powder

½ teaspoon *each* baking soda and salt

¾ cup (⅜ lb.) butter or margarine, cut into small pieces

¾ cup (4 oz.) diced dried apricots

⅓ cup (2 oz.) diced crystallized ginger

1 teaspoon grated lemon peel

1 cup buttermilk

In a food processor or large bowl, whirl or mix together flour, sugar, baking powder, soda, and salt. Add butter; whirl or rub with fingers until coarse crumbs form. If using a food processor, add apricots, ginger, and peel; pulse until just blended. Otherwise, stir them into flour mixture. Add buttermilk, and whirl or stir just until evenly moistened.

Scrape dough onto a

floured board and knead about 6 turns or until dough holds together. On a 12- by 15-inch lightly greased baking sheet, pat dough into an oval about 7 by 12 inches. With a floured knife, cut diagonal lines through dough, forming 8 or 9 triangles (see photo below).

Bake in a 400° oven until golden brown, about 25 minutes. Break along scores to serve. Makes 8 or 9.

Per serving: 393 cal. (37 percent from fat); 6.2 g protein; 16 g fat (9.9 g sat.); 57 g carbo.; 520 mg sodium; 43 mg chol. ∎

By Christine Weber Hale, Betsy Reynolds Bateson

Microwave Brittle

Nutty brittle cooks in minutes in the microwave oven. To avoid boilovers, cook in a large bowl.

About 1½ tablespoons butter or margarine

1 cup coarsely chopped hazelnuts or almonds

1 cup sugar

½ cup light corn syrup

¼ teaspoon salt (optional)

1 teaspoon vanilla

1 teaspoon baking soda

Butter a 12- by 15-inch baking sheet. Put a candy thermometer in a bowl of very hot water. In a 2- to 3-quart microwave-safe bowl, mix nuts, sugar, syrup, and salt. Cook, uncovered, in a microwave oven at full power (100 percent) for 7 minutes; stir every 2 minutes. Add 1 tablespoon butter; cook until thermometer put in candy (not while oven runs) reads 300°, 1½ to 5½ minutes longer.

Stir in vanilla and soda (mixture foams). Scrape onto baking sheet; spread fairly thin. When just cool enough to touch, butter hands and stretch candy thinner. When cool, break into chunks. Serve, or store airtight up to 1 week. Makes 15 ounces.

Per ounce: 143 cal. (37 percent from fat); 1 g protein; 5.9 g fat (1.1 g sat.); 22 g carbo.; 83 mg sodium; 3.1 mg chol. ∎

By Elaine Johnson

PETER CHRISTIANSEN

DRIED APRICOTS *and crystallized ginger stud fragrant, freshly baked scones; offer soft cream cheese as a spread.*

Three basic recipes, more than two dozen holiday treats

Start with recipes for cookies, sweet bread, and cake. Make simple variations in shapes and flavors

BETWEEN THE LAST-MINUTE SHOPPING, WRAPPING GIFTS, and entertaining, where can a busy cook fit in some good, old-fashioned holiday baking?

Consider this easy approach to making lots of different cookies, breads, and cakes: start with basic recipes and make quick and simple changes in flavors, shapes, sizes, and decorations. These three fine recipes, tweaked slightly, give you more than two dozen elegant products—more than enough choices for gift packages, family treats, and ever-ready refreshments for guests.

1. The Ultimate Christmas Cookie Dough

1 cup (½ lb.) butter or margarine

¾ cup sugar

1 large egg

Flavor and shape variations (choices follow)

2½ cups all-purpose flour

In a large bowl or food processor, beat butter and sugar with a mixer, or whirl until fluffy. Add egg and flavoring; beat or whirl to blend well. Stir in flour, then beat or whirl until well mixed. For easiest handling, chill dough airtight at least 1 hour or up to 5 days. (If chilled dough is too hard to work with, let stand at room temperature until soft enough to roll or shape.)

Flavor, shape, and bake, using the choices that follow. Cool cookies on racks. When cool, serve or immediately package airtight. Chill up to 3 days; freeze to store longer.

FLAVOR AND SHAPE VARIATIONS

Cutout cookies. Make **the ultimate Christmas cookie dough,** preceding. Roll dough until ¼ inch thick, a portion at a time, on a board generously coated with **all-purpose flour.** Cut dough with cookie cutters.

Using a wide spatula, place cookies slightly apart on ungreased 12- by 15-inch baking sheets. As sheets are filled, bake cookies in a 350° oven until golden brown, 15 to 20 minutes.

Reroll scraps with remaining dough and repeat rolling and cutting until all the dough is used.

With spatula, gently transfer baked

cookies to racks. Serve, or store as directed. Makes 4 to 5 dozen, each 2 to 3 inches in diameter.

Per cookie: 57 cal. (51 percent from fat); 0.7 g protein; 3.2 g fat (1.9 g sat.); 6.5 g carbo.; 32 mg sodium; 12 mg chol.

Spice cutouts. Make **the ultimate Christmas cookie dough,** preceding, mixing 2 teaspoons **ground cinnamon,** 1 teaspoon **ground ginger,** and ½ teaspoon **ground nutmeg** with the flour. Continue as directed for cutout cookies.

Per cookie: same as cutout cookies.

Chocolate cutouts. Make **the ultimate Christmas cookie dough,** preceding, reducing **all-purpose flour** to 2 cups and increasing **sugar** to 1 cup. To flour, add 3 tablespoons **unsweetened cocoa powder.** Continue as directed for cutout cookies.

Per cookie: 57 cal. (51 percent from fat); 0.6 g protein; 3.2 g fat (2 g sat.); 6.7 g carbo.; 32 mg sodium; 12 mg chol.

Button cookies. Make **the ultimate Christmas cookie dough,** preceding, in any flavor for rolled and cut variations. Follow directions for cutout cookies, cutting

Spice cutout

dough into 3-inch rounds. Place rounds on baking sheets. With a round cookie cutter (or the rim of a small glass) slightly less than 3 inches in diameter, gently press each cookie to form rim of "button"; do not cut through dough. Use a skewer or the tip of a small sharp knife to make 4 holes in the center of each cookie to form "thread holes." Continue as directed. Makes 48.

Per cookie: 71 cal. (51 percent from fat); 0.8 g protein; 4 g fat (2.4 g sat.); 8.1 g carbo.; 41 mg sodium; 15 mg chol.

Chocolate half-dips. Make **cutout cookies,** preceding. Melt 16 ounces **semisweet chocolate chips** or chunks (for directions, see marble cookies, following). Dip each cookie halfway into chocolate (or spread chocolate over half of each cookie). Let excess

NORMAN A. PLATE

chocolate drip off, then lay cookies on a rack. Let stand until chocolate is firm, about 1 hour. Serve, or package airtight up to 3 days; freeze to store longer.

Per cookie: 92 cal. (52 percent from fat); 1 g protein; 5.3 g fat (3.1 g sat.); 11 g carbo.; 33 mg sodium; 12 mg chol.

Almond-topped cookies. Make **the ultimate Christmas cookie dough,** preceding, and shape into 48 equal balls. Pour ⅔ cup **sliced almonds** into

a small bowl. Press each cookie ball into nuts to coat 1 side. Place balls on baking sheets, almonds up; press cookies with fingertips to flatten slightly. Bake, cool, and store as directed for cutout cookies.

If desired, seal 2 ounces **semisweet chocolate chips** or chunks in a small, unpleated zip-lock plastic bag. Set bag in top of double boiler over simmering water; heat until chocolate melts. Trim a corner from the bag to make a ⅛-inch hole. Pipe chocolate from bag over cookies to decorate. Let stand until chocolate is firm. Store as directed. Makes 48.

Per cookie: 79 cal. (54 percent from fat); 1.1 g protein; 4.7 g fat (2.5 g sat.); 8.4 g carbo.; 41 mg sodium; 15 mg chol.

Chocolate-tipped logs. Make **the ultimate Christmas cookie dough,** preceding. Shape into 48 logs, each about 3 inches long. Bake as directed for cutout cookies. Cool.

Melt 6 ounces **semisweet chocolate chips** or chunks (for directions,

see marble cookies, at right). Dip both ends of logs into chocolate to coat, then roll ends in ½ cup finely chopped **walnuts** or pecans. Set on racks until chocolate is firm. Store as directed. Makes 48.

Per cookie: 96 cal. (53 percent from fat); 1.2 g protein; 5.7 g fat (3.1 g sat.); 11 g carbo.; 41 mg sodium; 15 mg chol.

Brown sugar trees. Make **the ultimate Christmas cookie dough,** preceding, omitting **egg** and **granulated sugar;** add 1 cup firmly packed **brown sugar.** If necessary, squeeze dough between your hands until it sticks together.

Pat or roll dough on a 12- by 15-inch baking sheet into a 5- by 14-inch rectangle. On a 14-inch side, mark edge of dough at 2-inch intervals. On the opposite side, make the first mark at 1 inch, then every 2 inches. With a knife, score across dough from the 1-inch mark to the top opposite corner, then score from the 1-inch mark to the first 2-inch mark; repeat until you have 13 triangles plus 2 narrow end pieces. Cut off the end pieces; press the dough together, and divide it into 13 equal pieces. Press each piece onto a wide end of each triangle, shaping it like a tree trunk.

Bake in a 300° oven until cookies are golden brown, about 40 minutes. While cookies are still warm, cut through score marks. Let cookies cool on the baking sheet.

To decorate, use 2 ounces **semisweet chocolate chips** or chunks as directed for almond-topped cookies, at left, and pipe over the triangle portion of each tree. Or smoothly mix 1 cup **powdered sugar** and 2 tablespoons **milk;** spoon into a small, unpleated zip-lock plastic bag. Trim a corner of the bag to make a ⅛-inch hole, and pipe over trees. Store as directed. Makes 13.

Per cookie: 314 cal. (39 percent from fat); 2.7 g protein; 15 g fat (8.9 g sat.); 43 g carbo.; 152 mg sodium; 39 mg chol.

Marble cookies. Make **the ultimate Christmas cookie dough,** preceding. Put dough in a bowl. Melt 1½ ounces **semisweet chocolate chips** or chunks in a bowl over hot (not simmering) water; stir until smooth. Pour chocolate over dough; with a knife or spatula, swirl chocolate partially through dough. Do not overmix or marbling effect will be lost. Shape into 48 equal balls, or chill dough to roll and cut as directed for cutout cookies. Bake, cool, and store as directed.

Per ball: 75 cal. (50 percent from fat); 0.9 g protein; 4.2 g fat (2.6 g sat.); 8.7 g carbo.; 41 mg sodium; 15 mg chol.

Caramel, hazelnut, and chocolate chunks. Make **the ultimate Christmas cookie dough,** preceding, using

2 **large eggs** and increasing **all-purpose flour** to 3 cups.

Pour 2½ cups **hazelnuts** into a 10- by 15-inch pan. Bake in a 350° oven until nuts are lightly browned under skins, 15 to 20 minutes. Pour nuts onto a towel; rub with towel to remove as much of the loose brown skins as possible. Lift nuts from towel; discard skins. Coarsely chop nuts.

Let pan cool, wipe clean, and add cookie dough; press evenly over bottom and up sides of pan. Bake crust in a 325° oven until golden brown, 20 to 25 minutes.

Meanwhile, in a bowl, beat to blend 5 **large eggs,** 1¾ cups firmly packed **brown sugar,** 1 tablespoon **all-purpose flour,** and 1 teaspoon **vanilla.** Sprinkle nuts and 8 ounces **coarsely chopped semisweet chocolate** over crust; pour egg mixture over nuts and chocolate.

Bake on the lowest rack of a 325° oven until filling is set when gently shaken, about 25 minutes. Cool, then chill until cold, about 2 hours. Cut into 1½-inch squares. If making ahead, wrap airtight and chill up to 3 days; freeze to store longer. Makes about 5½ dozen.

Per cookie: 129 cal. (50 percent from fat); 2 g protein; 7.1 g fat (2.7 g sat.); 15 g carbo.; 38 mg sodium; 30 mg chol.

Christmas mazarin tarts. Make **the ultimate Christmas cookie dough,** preceding, using 2 **large eggs** and increasing **all-purpose flour** to 3 cups. Divide dough equally among 72 miniature (1- to 1½-in. diameter) tart pans; press dough evenly over bottom and sides of pans. (If you don't have 72 pans, make tarts in sequence; keep unused dough and filling chilled.) Set pans close together on 12- by 15-inch baking sheets.

In a food processor or bowl, whirl or beat 10 ounces (about 1 cup) **almond paste,** 3 tablespoons **all-purpose flour,** and 3 tablespoons **granulated sugar** until fine crumbs form. Add 2 **large eggs,** 1 at a time, 2 **large egg whites,** and ½ teaspoon **al-**

mond extract; whirl or beat until smooth.

Spoon 1 teaspoon filling into each tart pan. Bake in a 325° oven until tops are golden brown, about 30 minutes. Cool 5 minutes.

Smoothly mix 1 cup **powdered sugar** and 2 tablespoons **milk;** spoon about ¼ teaspoon of the mixture on top of each warm tart.

If icing stands while you bake tarts in batches, stir to make smooth and, if needed, add a few drops of milk to maintain a smooth consistency.

When tarts are cool, remove from pans; use the tip of a small, sharp knife, if needed, to help loosen pastry. Serve, or chill airtight up to 2 days; freeze to store longer. Makes 6 dozen.

Per tart: 82 cal. (43 percent from fat); 1.5 g protein; 3.9 g fat (1.8 g sat.); 10 g carbo.; 32 mg sodium; 19 mg chol.

2. Golden Bread Dough

1 package (¼ oz.) active dry yeast

¼ cup warm (110°) water

¾ cup (⅜ lb.) butter or margarine, cut into chunks

⅓ cup milk

5 large eggs

¾ cup sugar

About 4¾ cups all-purpose flour

1 large egg yolk mixed with 1 tablespoon water

In a large bowl, sprinkle yeast on water; let soften about 5 minutes. In a 1- to 1½-quart pan, combine butter and milk. Warm over medium heat just until milk is 110°; butter does not need to melt. (Or heat butter and milk in a microwave-safe bowl in a microwave oven until milk is 110°.)

Add milk mixture, whole eggs, sugar, and 2 cups flour to yeast mixture. Beat with a mixer at medium speed until dough is well moistened. Stir in 2¾ cups flour.

To knead with a dough hook, beat at high speed until dough is smooth, shiny, and stretchy, 10 to 15 minutes; dough will be sticky.

To knead by hand, scrape dough onto a lightly floured board; dust lightly with flour. Knead until very smooth and elastic, adding just enough flour to keep dough from sticking, at least 10 to 15 minutes. Return dough to bowl.

Cover bowl with plastic wrap. Let dough rise in a warm place until doubled, 1 to 1½ hours. Beat with dough hook (if dough sticks to bowl, add flour, 1 tablespoon at a time, until it pulls free) or knead dough on a floured board to expel air. Use as suggested, following.

Golden star bread. Make **golden bread dough,** preceding. Divide dough into 4 equal pieces; roll each between lightly floured palms or on a board to shape a rope about 25 inches long. Lay 1 rope across center of a lightly oiled 14- by 17-inch baking sheet. Leaving an 8-inch straight section in the center, coil rope ends equally, but in opposite directions. Center another rope perpendicularly across the first and coil ends as directed. Repeat with remaining ropes, positioning them over center of coiled ropes, like spokes of a wheel. Cover dough lightly with plastic wrap and set in a warm place until it is puffy, about 30 minutes. Remove wrap and brush loaf gently and evenly with egg yolk mixture.

Bake in a 350° oven until golden brown, about 25 minutes. Let cool on pan about 5 minutes, then carefully slide loaf from pan onto a large rack (or 2 smaller racks put together) to cool. Serve warm or cool. If making ahead, wrap cool loaf airtight and store at room temperature up to 1 day; freeze to store longer (thaw wrapped). To reheat, place bread (thawed, if frozen) on a baking sheet, cover lightly with foil, and bake in a 325° oven until warm, about 15 minutes. Makes 1 loaf, about 3 pounds. Makes 12 to 14 servings.

Per ounce: 94 cal. (36 percent from fat); 2.1 g protein; 3.8 g fat (2.1 g sat.); 13 g carbo.; 38 mg sodium; 35 mg chol.

Spiced star bread. Make **golden bread dough,** preceding, adding 1 teaspoon **ground cinnamon,** ½ teaspoon **ground allspice,** and ¼ teaspoon **ground nutmeg** to milk mixture. Finish as directed for golden star bread.

Per ounce: same as golden star bread.

Golden or spiced buns. Make **golden bread dough,** preceding; if desired, add seasonings for spiced star bread. Divide dough into 15 equal pieces and shape each into a smooth ball. Set balls, smoothest side up and edges touching, on baking sheet. Let rise, brush with egg yolk mixture, and bake as directed for golden star bread until golden brown, about 25 minutes. Serve, or store and reheat as directed. Makes 15.

Per bun: 301 cal. (36 percent from fat); 6.8 g protein; 12 g fat (6.6 g sat.); 41 g carbo.; 120 mg sodium; 111 mg chol.

Fruited golden or spiced bread or buns. Make **golden bread dough,** preceding, adding 1 tablespoon grated **orange peel** to milk mixture. If desired, add seasonings for spiced star bread. When dough is kneaded, add 1 cup (6 oz.) chopped **dried apricots** and 1 cup (6 oz.) **golden raisins.** Continue to knead until fruit is incorporated. Let rise, shape, bake, and serve or store as directed for golden or spiced star bread or buns.

Per ounce: 113 cal. (30 percent from fat); 2.3 g protein; 3.8 g fat (2.1 g sat.); 18 g carbo.; 38 mg sodium; 35 mg chol.

Cinnamon rolls. Make **golden bread dough,** preceding; add seasonings for spiced star bread. After dough has risen and air is expelled, roll out on a floured board into a 16- by 24-inch rectangle.

Mix together 1¾ cups firmly packed **brown sugar,** 2 cups **raisins,** and 1 cup chopped **pecans** or walnuts; sprinkle evenly over dough, leaving a ½-inch bare border along 1 long side. Starting at the long side opposite bare edge, roll dough jelly roll–style. Pinch dough at seam to seal. With a floured knife, cut roll crosswise into 15 equal slices. Lay slices on a cut side, touching, in a lightly oiled 10- by 15-inch pan. Let rise as directed. Omit **egg yolk mixture.** Bake until golden brown, 25 to 30 minutes. Serve warm; if making ahead, let cool in pan, then store and reheat as directed for golden star bread.

While rolls are warm, smoothly mix 2 cups **powdered sugar** and ¼ cup **milk;** drizzle evenly over rolls. Serve warm or at room temperature. Makes 15.

Per roll: 565 cal. (27 percent from fat); 7.9 g protein; 17 g fat (7 g sat.); 99 g carbo.; 134 mg sodium; 97 mg chol.

3. Cranberry-Tangerine Cake Batter

2¼ cups all-purpose flour

1 cup sugar

1 teaspoon baking powder

1 teaspoon baking soda

2 cups fresh or frozen cranberries, rinsed and drained

1 cup raisins

2 large eggs

1¼ cups buttermilk

About ½ cup (¼ lb.) butter or margarine, melted

In a large bowl, mix together flour, sugar, baking powder, soda, cranberries, and raisins.

In another bowl, beat to blend eggs, buttermilk, and ½ cup melted butter. Add to flour mixture; stir just until evenly moistened. Use to make tea cake, loaves, or trifle, following.

Cranberry-tangerine tea cake. Make **cranberry-tangerine cake batter,** preceding. Pour batter into a buttered 10-cup plain or fluted tube cake pan.

Bake in a 325° oven until cake is richly browned and begins to pull from pan sides, about 1 hour. Invert rack over pan; holding rack and pan together, invert cake onto rack to release from pan, then tip back into pan. With a slender skewer, poke holes about 1 inch apart through cake to pan. Slowly spoon hot **tangerine syrup** (choices follow) over cake, letting syrup soak in gradually. Let stand at least 6 hours, or cover and chill up to 2 weeks. Invert cake onto a plate and cut into slices. Makes 1 cake (3½ lb.), 12 to 14 servings.

Tangerine syrup. In a 1- to 1½-quart pan over medium-high heat, combine 1 teaspoon grated **tangerine peel,** ⅔ cup **tangerine juice,** 3 tablespoons **lime juice,** and ¾ cup **sugar.** Stir often until sugar dissolves and syrup boils rapidly, about 5 minutes. Use hot; if making ahead, let stand up to 6 hours and reheat to boiling.

Per serving with tangerine syrup: 295 cal. (24 percent from fat); 4.2 g protein; 8 g fat (4.6 g sat.); 53 g carbo.; 229 mg sodium; 50 mg chol.

Tangerine-rum syrup. Make **tangerine syrup,** reducing **tangerine juice** to ½ cup and omitting **lime juice.** After boiling, add ½ cup **rum** and use.

Per serving with tangerine-rum syrup: 311 cal. (23 percent from fat); 4.2 g protein; 8 g fat (4.6 g sat.); 53 g carbo.; 229 mg sodium; 50 mg chol.

Tangerine-Cointreau syrup. Make **tangerine syrup,** reducing **tangerine juice** to ½ cup and omitting **lime juice.** After boiling, add ½ cup **orange-flavor liqueur** (such as Cointreau or Grand Marnier) and use.

Per serving with tangerine-Cointreau syrup: 316 cal. (23 percent from fat); 4.2 g protein; 8 g fat (4.6 g sat.); 55 g carbo.; 229 mg sodium; 50 mg chol.

Cranberry-tangerine loaf cakes—big, medium, or small. Make **cranberry-tangerine cake batter,** preceding, and spoon batter into a large buttered loaf pan (5½ by 9½ in., 7-cup size). Or divide batter between 2 medium-size buttered loaf pans (4 by 7½ in., 3-cup size), or among 4 small buttered loaf pans (3½ by 6 in., 2-cup size).

Bake in a 325° oven until cakes are browned and begin to pull from pan sides, about 1 hour for a large loaf, 50 to 55 minutes for medium-size loaves, and 45 to 50 minutes for small

NORMAN A. PLATE

loaves. Release and return to pans, as directed for cranberry-tangerine tea cake. Moisten evenly with hot **tangerine syrup** of your choice. Serve or store as directed. Makes 1 large cake (3½ lb.), 2 medium-size cakes (1¾ lb. each), or 4 small cakes (about 14 oz. each).

Per ounce with tangerine syrup: 74 cal. (24 percent from fat); 1 g protein; 2 g fat (1.1 g sat.); 13 g carbo.; 57 mg sodium; 12 mg chol.

Cranberry-Tangerine Trifle

1 cup whipping cream, softly whipped and sweetened to taste

1 cup low-fat or nonfat vanilla yogurt

14 ounces to 1 pound cranberry-tangerine tea cake with tangerine syrup (recipe precedes), coarsely crumbled

¼ cup raspberry jam

Fresh mint sprigs (optional)

Fresh or frozen cranberries (optional)

In a bowl, fold together the whipped cream and vanilla yogurt.

Divide ½ the cake crumbs evenly among 6 tall glasses or goblets (1- to 1½-cup size). Dot crumbs equally with ½ the jam and ½ the yogurt mixture. Repeat layers of crumbs, jam, and yogurt mixture.

Cover glasses and chill at least 4 hours or up to 1 day. Uncover desserts and garnish with mint sprigs and cranberries. Makes 6 servings. ∎

Per serving: 373 cal. (48 percent from fat); 5.3 g protein; 20 g fat (12 g sat.); 46 g carbo.; 179 mg sodium; 85 mg chol.

By Christine Weber Hale

ANDY FREEBERG

AGUSTÍN GAYTÁN'S *salad for Las Posadas includes a rainbow of fruits, vegetables, and nuts.*

Heritage dishes

Four cooks from different cultures share their special holiday foods

I N THE WEST'S RICH melting pot, December is a festive time of year for many cultures—for sharing gifts, good times, and, especially, good food.

Here, four cooks with different heritages share dishes that make their holidays memorable. Because the recipes focus on vegetables or fruits, they're easily added to any seasonal meal.

Las Posadas is a big celebration that runs the nine days before Christmas in Agustín Gaytán's native town of San Miguel de Allende, Mexico. During that period, townspeople dressed as Mary, Joseph, and the Wise Men go door-to-door, singing songs asking for shelter—which they receive in the form of food and good cheer. When Gaytán moved to Berkeley, California, he kept his favorite part of the celebration, the party. Friends gather at his home for special dishes, in-

DENA HURST SEMMONS
prepares a light version of Southern greens for Kwanzaa.

cluding this colorful salad made with a refreshing mix of fruit and vegetables and a tequila dressing. You can buy the *piloncillo* (semiprocessed sugar) at a Mexican market, or use regular brown sugar.

Ensalada de Navidad
(Mexican Christmas Salad)

2 large beets, peeled and sliced

⅓ pound piloncillo (about ⅔ cup small pieces) or ¾ cup firmly packed dark brown sugar

6 whole cloves

¼ cup lemon juice

1 medium-size tart green apple, cored and sliced

Romaine lettuce leaves, rinsed and crisped

2 cups peeled, shredded jicama

1 medium-size red apple, cored and sliced

2 medium-size oranges, peel and membrane cut off, quartered and thinly sliced

½ small pineapple, peeled, cored, halved, and thinly sliced

1 large banana, sliced

3 tablespoons pomegranate seeds

3 tablespoons roasted unsalted peanuts

2 tablespoons toasted pine nuts

Tequila dressing (recipe follows)

In a 2- to 3-quart pan, place beets, piloncillo, cloves, lemon juice, and 3 cups water. Bring to a boil over high heat; reduce heat, cover, and simmer until beets are tender when pierced, 12 to 15 minutes. Drain, reserving liquid; let beets and liquid cool.

Let green apple slices stand in beet juice until pink; drain and discard juice. Cover a large platter with romaine. Arrange beets, jicama, red and green apples, oranges, pineapple, and banana on top. Sprinkle with pomegranate seeds, peanuts, and pine nuts, and add dressing. Serves 6.

Per serving: 272 cal. (30 percent from fat); 4.1 g protein; 9 g fat (1.2 g sat.); 46 g carbo.; 44 mg sodium; 0 mg chol.

Tequila dressing. In a small pitcher, combine ⅓ cup each **orange juice** and **white wine vinegar,** 2 tablespoons each **olive oil** and **tequila,** 4 teaspoons **sugar,** and **salt** and **pepper** to taste.

Kwanzaa, meaning "first fruits of the harvest" in Swahili, is a seven-day celebration of African-American culture. On December 31, the last day of Kwanzaa, Dena Hurst Semmons of Oakland, California, invites friends over for the feast called *karamu.*

Though the food for karamu can express aspects of black heritage from many corners of the globe, Semmons likes to incorporate soul food from the American South, such as her Mississippi mother's recipe for greens, Semmon's version contains no meat and very little fat. She likes to augment the natural flavor of the mixed greens with colorful red bell pepper and vegetable broth, plus a little sugar and vinegar.

Ellena's Greens for Kwanzaa

1 pound *each* mustard greens, turnip greens, and collard greens or spinach

1 large onion, chopped

1 large red bell pepper, chopped

1 tablespoon salad oil

1 quart vegetable broth

1 tablespoon sugar

1 tablespoon distilled white vinegar

Salt and pepper

Discard tough stems and yellowed leaves from greens. Rinse well (if using spinach, keep it separate) and drain. In a 6- to 8-quart pan over medium-high heat, cook onion and bell pepper in oil, stirring often, until limp, 8 to 10 minutes. Stir in broth, sugar, and vinegar, then add greens (except spinach).

Cover; bring to boil over high heat. Simmer, stirring occasionally, until greens are tender when pierced, about 45 minutes (if using spinach, stir in after 20 minutes). Offer greens and pot liquor in bowls. Season with salt and pepper. Serves 6 to 8.

Per serving: 85 cal. (30 percent from fat); 3.7 g protein; 2.8 g fat (0.2 g sat.); 13 g carbo.; 90 mg sodium; 0 mg chol.

For Joanne Miksis of Eugene, Oregon, who married into a Lithuanian family, Christmas is a time to celebrate Lithuanian heritage with traditional foods such as kugelis. Delicious in its simplicity, kugelis reminds us of extra-good scalloped potatoes. Miksis usually incorporates the full amount of butter, but you can use less.

Lithuanian Kugelis
(Potato Pudding)

4 large eggs

1½ cups milk or half-and-half (light cream)

1 tablespoon lemon juice

1 teaspoon freshly ground pepper

4 to 8 tablespoons butter or margarine, melted

1 medium-size (about 6 oz.) onion, finely chopped

SPATHIS & MILLER

JOANNE MIKSIS *peels and shreds potatoes for kugelis (pictured above).*

MICHAEL THOMPSON

2¾ pounds thin-skinned potatoes

Sour cream (optional)

Snipped chives and whole chives

Salt

In a large bowl, beat eggs until well blended. Stir in milk, juice, pepper, butter, and onion. Peel potatoes, then coarsely shred, using a food processor or grater. Quickly stir into milk mixture to prevent discoloring.

Pour mixture into a well-buttered 2½- to 3-quart shallow baking dish. Bake, uncovered, in a 375° oven until well browned and crisp, about 1½ hours. Garnish with sour cream and snipped and whole chives. Season with salt. Serves 6.

Per serving: 318 cal. (37 percent from fat); 10 g protein; 13 g fat (7.1 g sat.); 40 g carbo; 166 mg sodium; 171 mg chol.

Lorraine Shapiro of Los Angeles is always looking for new food ideas that fit within established Jewish dietary patterns—both for her family and in her work as a food writer specializing in Jewish cooking. Her potato waffles are a twist on latkes (potato pancakes), traditional for Hanukkah because of the oil used. (Two millennia ago, only enough oil existed to keep the flame in the Holy Temple burning for one day, yet it miraculously burned for eight.)

Shapiro kept the traditional oil and the good flavor and crisp texture of latkes, but eliminated the mess of frying. Although she generally serves them on their own as a party dish, she also likes them as a savory accompaniment to other foods.

Hanukkah Potato Waffles

3 pounds russet potatoes, peeled

4 large eggs

½ cup chopped onion

½ cup salad oil

2 tablespoons lemon juice

⅔ cup all-purpose flour

4 teaspoons baking powder

1 teaspoon salt

½ teaspoon *each* pepper and sugar

Sour cream (optional)

Red wine applesauce (recipe follows)

In a food processor, coarsely shred potatoes (or finely shred with a grater). Remove from processor and squeeze dry. In processor or a large bowl, whirl or stir eggs with onion until combined. Add oil, lemon juice, flour, baking powder, salt, pepper, and sugar; whirl or stir until well combined, then mix in potatoes just to blend.

Heat waffle iron according to manufacturer's directions. Oil grids; fill ⅔ full with batter, spreading evenly. Cook until deep golden, about 10 minutes. Place directly on a rack in a 250° oven while cooking remaining waffles. Serve with sour cream and applesauce. Makes 5 waffles, each 8 inches square.

Per waffle: 706 cal. (34 percent from fat); 12 g protein; 27 g fat (4.1 g sat.); 98 g carbo.; 906 mg sodium; 170 mg chol.

Red wine applesauce. In a 2- to 3-quart pan, combine 1¾ pounds (about 4 large) peeled, quartered **Rome Beauty apples**; ¾ cup **sweet Concord grape wine**; ⅓ cup **sugar**; and ¼ teaspoon **ground cinnamon.** Simmer, covered, stirring occasionally, until apples are tender when pierced, about 20 minutes. With a mixer, beat just to form a chunky sauce. ∎

By Elaine Johnson

LORRAINE SHAPIRO *likes latke-style waffles with red wine applesauce.*

CHAD SLATTERY

The fast bites party primer

Nothing takes more than 20 minutes to put together. And you don't have to make everything yourself

THE HEART SAYS party, but the schedule says panic! Yes, it really is possible to have friends over during the holidays and keep one's sanity. Here's how some of us *really* entertain.

• **6:30 P.M.** Set down grocery bags. Put white wine in the freezer. Race around the house hiding junk and cleaning. Feed the cat.

• **6:45** Grab some serving dishes. Open grocery bags. Start throwing together a couple of simple recipes, and slightly pricey but inviting takeout food from the fancy grocery store, creating combinations and arrangements that will impress friends. Don't chop, peel, or slice anything you don't have to.

• **7:30** Set food on table with napkins. Rescue wine from freezer and pour a glass. Pause for air.

• **7:40** Put glasses and opened wine bottle on table, with more bottles and a corkscrew.

• **7:45** First guests arrive—early. Make partner greet them. Jump in the shower and change clothes.

• **8** Say hello to guests. Make a couple of warm appetizers.

• **11:20** Continue to accept compliments on the wonderful time and fabulous food as the last guests depart. Leave dishes for the next day.

ANDY FREEBERG

Cherry Pepper Shooters
Prep time: 20 minutes. *Cooking time:* 0 minutes.

Drain 2 jars (16 oz. each) **mild cherry peppers.** Slice off and discard stems; with a small spoon, scoop out and discard seeds. Cut 2 ounces thinly sliced **prosciutto** into 1- to 2-inch squares. Drain 1 can (8 oz.) **pineapple chunks.** Cut each chunk in half, wrap in prosciutto, and stuff into a pepper. Serves 12.

Per serving: 41 cal. (15 percent from fat); 1.4 g protein; 0.7 g fat (0.2 g sat.); 7.6 g carbo; mg sodium unavailable; 3.8 mg chol.

Caponata Pizza
Prep time: 4 minutes.
Cooking time: 8 minutes.

Heat oven to 500°. Place 2 **prebaked packaged bread shell crusts** (6 in. size, 8 oz. total) on a 12- by 15-inch baking sheet and bake until crisp to touch, 3 to 5 minutes. Spread crusts equally with 1 can (7½ oz.) **caponata** (eggplant relish). Scatter 1½ tablespoons **pine nuts** on top. Bake until nuts are golden, 3 to 4 minutes. Garnish with whole **fresh chives** or green onions. Place on a board with scissors; cut into wedges to eat. Serves 12.

Per serving: 73 cal. (33 percent from fat); 3 g protein; 2.7 g fat (0.3 g sat.); 9.3 g carbo; 169 mg sodium; 1 mg chol.

Quick Cheese Fondue
Prep time: 4 minutes.
Cooking time: 5 minutes.

Heat oven to 500°. In a 2- to 3-cup shallow baking dish, place an 8-ounce piece of **brie,** cambozola, Saint-Nectaire, or Taleggio **cheese.** Bake until melted, 4 to 5 minutes. Coarsely grind **pepper** on top.

Set dish on a heatproof surface and serve with whole **apples** or pears, and **walnut** or other **bread** for guests to cut and use to scoop up fondue. Serves 12.

Per serving fondue only: 63 cal. (74 percent from fat); 3.9 g protein; 5.2 g fat (0 g sat.); 0.1 g carbo; 119 mg sodium; 19 mg chol.

Chili Popcorn
Prep time: 1 minute.
Cooking time: 5 minutes

Pour 3 quarts warm **popcorn** (about ⅔ unpopped corn, made in an air popper, or in a pan with salad oil) into a large bowl. Mix well with 1 to 4 tablespoons melted **butter** or margarine. Then sprinkle and mix thoroughly with 2 teaspoons **chili powder** and **salt** to taste. Serves 12.

Per serving (with air-popped corn and 1 tablespoon butter): 40 cal. (29 percent from fat); 1 g protein; 1.3 g fat (0.6 g sat.); 6.4 g carbo; 14 mg sodium; 2.6 mg chol.

Hasty Hots for the '90s

Prep time: 8 minutes.
Cooking time: 5 minutes.

Heat broiler. Split 1 **slender baguette** (8 oz.), halve pieces crosswise, and place cut side up on a 12- by 15-inch baking sheet. Broil about 3 inches from heat until toasted, 2 to 3 minutes.

Meanwhile, mix ½ cup sliced **green onions,** ½ cup **reduced-fat mayonnaise,** and ½ cup grated **parmesan cheese.** Spread mixture on bread. Broil until lightly browned, about 1½ minutes. Let cool about 2 minutes to crisp. Present uncut on a board, with a knife. Serves 12.

Per serving: 95 cal. (41 percent from fat); 3.2 g protein; 4.3 g fat (1.4 g sat.); 11 g carbo; 232 mg sodium; 5.9 mg chol.

Sausage Mushroom Caps

Prep time: 8 minutes.
Cooking time: 5 minutes.

Heat broiler. Rinse 24 medium-size (about 1 in. wide, 1 lb. total) **mushrooms.** Scoop out stems with a small spoon and save for other uses. Mix ⅓ pound **seasoned bulk pork sausage** and 3 tablespoons **seasoned dried bread crumbs.** Mound meat mixture in caps, then place meat side up in a rimmed 10- by 15-inch baking pan. Broil 6 to 7 inches from heat until meat is well browned, about 5 minutes. Lift mushrooms onto a platter. Scatter with **Italian parsley leaves.** Serves 12.

Per serving: 66 cal. (71 percent from fat); 2.3 g protein; 5.2 g fat (1.8 g sat.); 2.8 g carbo; 134 mg sodium; 8.5 mg chol.

Shrimp and Papaya with Asian Dunk Sauce

Prep time: 16 minutes.
Cooking time: 0 minutes.

Peel and seed 1 large (1 lb.) ripe **papaya;** cut into ¾-inch chunks. Mix with 1 tablespoon chopped **fresh cilantro** (coriander), and mound on a platter. Beside it arrange 24 (¾ lb. total) **peeled cooked large shrimp.**

In a bowl, stir ¼ cup **lime juice,** 2 teaspoons **fish sauce** (*nam pla* or *nuoc mam*) or soy sauce, 2 teaspoons **sugar,** and ¼ teaspoon **crushed dried hot red chilies.** Spear fruit and shrimp with tiny forks to dip into sauce. Serves 12.

Per serving: 44 cal. (8 percent from fat); 6.2 g protein; 0.4 g fat (0.1 g sat.); 3.8 g carbo; 64 mg sodium; 55 mg chol.

Apricots with Goat Cheese

Prep time: 4 minutes. *Cooking time:* 0 minutes.

Arrange ½ pound **dried apricots,** 6 ounces plain or decorative **soft unripened goat cheese,** and ¼ cup shelled **roasted, salted pistachios** on a tray. To eat, spread fruit with cheese and top with a few nuts. Serves 12.

Per serving: 98 cal. (40 percent from fat); 3.9 g protein; 4.4 g fat (2.2 g sat.); 12 g carbo; 66 mg sodium; 6.5 mg chol. ∎

By Elaine Johnson

ANDY FREEBERG

Buy-and-serve appetizers

• *Antipasti* such as cornichons, roasted peppers, baby corn, pickled onions or green beans, peperoncini, marinated artichoke hearts, jalapeño- or anchovy-stuffed olives: drain and arrange on a platter. Also try sliced salami and rinsed, prepeeled, raw baby carrots.

• *Aegean meze.* Choose a combination: cheeses such as feta, manouri, and mizithra; dolmas (stuffed grape leaves); seasoned olives; pocket bread; prepared hummus (garbanzo spread).

• *Vegetable pâté* from the deli, with crackers.

• *Smoked salmon* or trout, with bagel chips or thin pumpernickel bread, capers, and lemon.

• *Grand blue cheeses* such as Stilton, Roquefort, Maytag Blue, cambozola, bleu d'Auvergne: buy 2 or 3. Serve with fruit, bread, red wine.

• *Caviar.* Go fancy, with imported or domestic sturgeon roe; or inexpensive, with lumpfish, whitefish, salmon, or flying fish roe (*tobiko*). Offer 1 or several kinds with melba toast, sour cream, and lemon wedges. Serve sturgeon caviar from the container; rinse other kinds in a fine strainer, then place in small dishes.

Gingerbread masterpieces

Castles, cottages, and other architectural wonders on exhibit in the West—many to benefit good causes

By Elaine Johnson

Onion domes rise above a Russian palace.

FRED KIHARA

KEVIN CANDLAND

New Museum of Modern Art in San Francisco gets a gingerbread finish.

If Hansel and Gretel could choose among the season's marvels in gingerbread, would the witch's little bungalow get a second glance? Clever take-offs on the classic gingerbread house are bringing the craft to new levels of sophistication. And they're baked with far better intentions than the old witch had.

To raise money for a host of good causes, pastry chefs, architects, and amateurs are turning their talents to gingerbread. You can admire the results at events in many Western cities, and perhaps bid to bring home your own mansion. Events are free to $35; call for prices.

Arizona. Phoenix, December 4 through 8. Gingerbread creations are for sale at the Phoenix Art Museum League's Festival of Trees & Marketplace. Hours: 10 to 6 daily, except noon to 6 Sunday and 10 to 9 Wednesday. Phoenix Art Museum, 1625 N. Central Avenue; (602) 257-1222.

Peoria, December 11 through 23. Home bakers compete. Hours: noon to 6:30 at December 11 Festival of Lights; then 8 to 5 weekdays. Peoria City Hall and Peoria Public Library, 8401 W. Monroe Street; (602) 412-7137.

California. San Francisco, December 6 through 10. Architects and pastry chefs team up. Auction at 6 P.M. on December 6; viewing from 7 A.M. to 11 P.M. December 7 through 10. Rincon Center, 101 Spear Street; (415) 292-5453.

PROVIDENCE MEDICAL FOUNDATION

Pittock Mansion was an imposing exhibit at a recent Festival of the Trees, in Portland.

Hello, Hawaii. Miniature Aloha Tower greeted past visitors to the Big Island's Gingerbread Wonderland.

San Mateo, December 4 through 15. Houses by nearly 100 amateurs and professionals. Hours: 10 to 5 Tuesdays through Saturdays, noon to 5 Sundays. Coyote Point Museum, 1651 Coyote Point Drive; (415) 342-7755.

Colorado. Denver, November 19 through 28. ArtReach Festival of Trees is sponsoring the exhibit. Hours: 10 to 9 Fridays and Saturdays, 10

Frosting snow and broccoli trees completed Ernst Meissner's winner in the 1992 San Mateo, California, event.

to 5 Sundays through Wednesdays (closed Thanksgiving). Radisson Hotel Denver, 1550 Court Place; (303) 777-2209, ext. 231.

Hawaii. Kohala Coast, Island of Hawaii, December 9 through 25. Pastry chefs and amateurs build the Gingerbread Wonderland; silent auction during event. On view 24 hours daily. The Mauna Lani Bay Hotel and Bungalows,

1 Mauna Lani Drive; (800) 367-2323.

Idaho. *Boise, November 24 through 28.* Many houses for sale at Festival of Trees. Hours: 10 to 9 daily, except 2 to 9 on Thanksgiving. Boise Centre on-the-Grove, 850 Front Street; (208) 378-2797.

New Mexico. *Albuquerque, December 3, 4, and 5.* About 200 participants enter works to be sold. Hours: noon to 9 Friday, 10 to 7 Saturday, noon to 6 Sunday. Coronado Mall, 6600 Menaul Boulevard N.E.; (505) 842-7108.

Oregon. *Portland, December 2 through 5.* The Festival of the Trees has buildings of the Northwest created by local architects, plus traditional houses. Hours: 10 to 6 Thursday and Sunday, 10 to 9 Friday and Saturday. Oregon Convention Center, 777 N.E. Martin Luther King Jr. Boulevard; (503) 230-6020.

Utah. *Salt Lake City, December 1 through 4.* About 80,000 attend the Festival of Trees. Many houses are for sale. Hours: 10 to 10 daily. Salt Palace, 100 S. West Temple Street; (801) 588-3675.

Washington. *Orcas Island, November 26 and December 3.* Eastsounders bake a gingerbread village for the Holi-day Fair. Hours: 10 to 7 on November 26. Orcas Island School cafeteria. Gala Dinner and auction from 6 to 10 on December 3 at Orcas Center; (206) 376-4827.

Seattle, November 26 through December 24. Employee efforts on view in the lobby. Visitors vote for favorites. Sheraton Seattle Hotel and Towers, 1400 Sixth Avenue; (206) 621-9000. ■

WEST MEETS EAST *in a multicultural dried legume mix with curry seasonings. The mix needs only a few additional ingredients to cook up into a mouth-watering soup. Southwestern beans dominate in a second mix.*

It's in the bag

Beans and spices are almost all you need for satisfying, inexpensive gifts

THE HUMBLE DRIED bean has acquired new status. Dressed up with seasonings and an accompanying soup recipe, dried bean combinations have found their way onto shelves in supermarkets, fancy food stores, and health food markets, usually at gourmet prices.

But you can assemble your own bean mixes to keep at the ready on a pantry shelf or to give as gifts for half the price. Each of our bean soup combinations makes up into 12 mixes costing less than $2 apiece, including ingredients and packaging. Furthermore, once you've bought the ingredients, it takes less than an hour to package 12 mixes.

Our two bean combinations yield soups of highly differing flavors. One mixes beans commonly used in the West with seasonings and legumes associated with the Far East. The colorful bean assortment in the Four Corners mix reflects the Southwestern landscape where the states of Arizona, Colorado, New Mexico, and Utah meet.

9 POUNDS OF BEANS YIELDS 12 GIFTS

Rounding up the beans and seasonings can take a little time (shopping is easiest, and the selection most varied, at stores that sell in bulk). But packaging the mixes is simple and makes a great group project. Just stir together a pound each of nine different dried legumes. Divide evenly into 12 plastic bags (or other containers). To each, add a seasoning packet. Close or tie shut, then attach a recipe and bow or other finishing touch. You can package the beans in plastic, cellophane, or paper bags; glass containers; Chinese food boxes; or gift containers of your own design. Good sources for packaging materials are supermarkets, craft stores, and specialty gift wrap shops.

The lucky people on your gift list need add only a few vegetables and broth to the soaked beans and seasonings to reap a richly flavored soup.

If you have trouble finding a particular dried bean, pea, or lentil at your supermarket, check at specialty or health food markets. Or, you can order any of the beans by mail from The Bean Bag, 818 Jefferson St., Oakland, Calif. 94607; call (800) 845-2326 or fax (510) 791-0705. Allow 2 weeks for delivery.

WEST MEETS EAST SOUP MIX

Dried beans. In a large bowl, combine 1 pound *each* **dried baby lima beans, dried black-eyed peas, dried garbanzo beans** (chickpeas), **dried mung beans, dried small red beans, dried green split peas, dried yellow split peas, dried soy-** **beans,** and **dried Appaloosa beans** or small white beans. Mix to distribute evenly. Divide bean mixture equally among 12 pint plastic bags or other containers; each should contain about 1¾ cups mixed dried beans.

Seasonings. Combine ¾ cup (1 oz.) **dried lemon grass** (or 3 tablespoons dried lemon peel, plus 1 tablespoon lemon pepper), ½ cup (2 oz.) **hot** or regular **curry powder,** ½ cup (2 oz.) **ground ginger,** ¼ cup (¾ oz.) **dried fennel seed,** 2 tablespoons **garlic powder,** and 1 tablespoon **black pepper.** Mix ingredients until well blended. Divide seasonings equally among 12 small plastic or cellophane bags (available in craft stores, in specialty gift wrap shops, or in stores that sell in bulk); each will contain about 2 tablespoons seasonings.

West Meets East Soup

1 package (about 13 oz.) soup mix

2 large (about 1¼ lb. total) onions, chopped

About 8 cups regular-strength chicken broth

1 large (about 8 oz.) russet potato, peeled and diced

1 cup thinly sliced celery

Optional ingredient (choices follow)

About ½ cup fresh cilantro (coriander) leaves

About 1 cup thawed frozen peas

Salt and pepper

Set aside seasonings from soup mix. Sort and discard foreign matter from beans. Rinse beans and place in a 5- to 6-quart pan; add 2½ quarts water. Let stand at least 8 hours or overnight; drain and rinse.

To speed the process, bring beans and water to a boil; boil 2 to 3 minutes. Cover; cool at least 1 hour or up to 4 hours. Drain and rinse beans.

Meanwhile, in a 6- to 8-quart pan, add onions and ½ cup broth. Stir often over high heat until liquid evaporates and onions brown and start to stick, about 10 minutes. Add potato and ½ cup broth; stir to release browned bits. Cook until liquid evaporates, as in preceding step. Repeat adding and evaporating liquid until the vegetables are moderately browned, 2 or 3 more times.

Add celery, seasonings, beans, and 6 cups broth. Bring to a boil; simmer, covered, until beans are tender to bite, about 1¾ hours. Add optional ingredient if desired. Serve, offering cilantro and peas as accompaniments to sprinkle over the soup. If desired, add salt and pepper to taste. Makes 13 cups, 6 to 8 servings.

Per serving: 249 cal. (13 percent from fat); 15 g protein; 3.5 g fat (0.7 g sat.); 41 g carbo.; 124 mg sodium; 0 mg chol.

Optional ingredient. When soup is ready to serve, add 1 pound (about 2⅔ cups) **shelled cooked crab** or 1 pound (about 2¼ cups) **cooked chicken,** cut into bite-size pieces. Stir into soup and heat just until meat is hot, about 3 minutes.

FOUR CORNERS

SOUP MIX

Dried beans. In a large bowl, combine 1 pound *each* **dried adzuki beans, dried Anasazi beans, dried black beans, dried cranberry** or pink **beans, dried large lima beans, dried pinto beans, dried red kidney beans, dried Red Chief lentils,** and **barley.** Mix to distribute the beans evenly. Divide the mixture equally among 12 pint plastic bags or other containers; each should contain about 1¾ cups mixed dried beans.

Seasonings. Combine ¾ cup (3 oz.) **paprika,** ¾ cup (¾ oz.) **dried oregano leaves,** ½ cup (2 oz.) **Creole** or Cajun **spice blend** (or ¼ cup [1 oz.] onion powder, plus 3 tablespoons *each* red and black pepper), ½ cup (4 oz.) firmly packed **brown sugar,** 2 tablespoons **garlic powder,** and 2 tablespoons **ground allspice.** Mix ingredients until well blended. Divide seasonings equally among 12 small plastic or cellophane bags (available in craft stores, in specialty gift wrap shops, or in stores that sell in bulk); each will contain about 3 tablespoons seasonings.

Four Corners Soup

1 package (about 13 oz.) soup mix

2 large (about 1¼ lb. total) onions, cut into thin wedges

2 large (about ½ lb. total) carrots, thinly sliced

About 8 cups regular-strength chicken broth

Optional ingredient (choices follow)

1 package (10 oz.) thawed frozen whole-leaf spinach

Set aside seasonings from soup mix. Sort and discard foreign matter from beans. Rinse beans and place in a 5- to 6-quart pan; add 2½ quarts water. Let stand at least 8 hours or overnight; drain and rinse beans.

To speed the process, bring beans and water to a boil; boil 2 to 3 minutes. Cover; cool at least 1 hour or up to 4 hours. Drain and rinse beans.

Meanwhile, in a 6- to 8-quart pan, add onions, carrots, and ½ cup broth. Stir often over high heat until liquid evaporates and vegetables brown and begin to stick, about 8 to 12 minutes. Add another ½ cup broth; stir to release browned bits. Cook until liquid evaporates, as in preceding step. Add optional ingredient if desired. Repeat adding and evaporating liquid until the vegetables are moderately browned, 2 or 3 more times.

Add seasonings, beans, and 6 cups broth. Bring to a boil; simmer, covered, until beans are tender to bite, about 1½ hours. Just before serving, stir in spinach; heat just until spinach is hot, about 3 minutes. Makes 12 cups, 6 to 8 servings.

Per serving: 234 cal. (9 percent from fat); 14 g protein; 2.5 g fat (0.6 g sat.); 42 g carbo.; 191 mg sodium; 0 mg chol.

Optional ingredient. While browning vegetables, add 1 pound **poultry sausage,** sliced or broken into bite-size pieces (consider smoked chicken-apple sausage, broccoli-apple-turkey sausage, and other choices available at specialty supermarkets and butcher shops), or 1 pound **ground turkey** or **chicken.** ∎

By Betsy Reynolds Bateson

CHAD SLATTERY

COVER JARS of dressed-up preserves with fabric rounds; tie on snugly with ribbons.

Shortcuts for sweet gifts

F OR SPEEDY HOLIDAY gifts, dress up spreads. Start with purchased cranberry sauce or fruit preserves, jams, or jellies. To convert the sauce to an old-fashioned curd to eat on muffins or in tarts, cook it with eggs, sugar, butter, and lime. Customize preserves by adding complementary ingredients such as chocolate or liqueurs.

Cranberry-Lime Curd

1 can (16 oz.) whole cranberry sauce

4 large eggs

2 teaspoons grated lime peel (green part only)

½ cup lime juice

½ cup sugar

½ cup (¼ lb.) butter or margarine, in chunks

In a blender or food processor, whirl to smoothly mix the cranberry sauce, eggs, lime peel, lime juice, sugar, and butter.

Pour mixture into a 10- to 12-inch frying pan. Stir often on low heat until mixture begins to thicken, then stir until curd coats the back of a metal spoon in a smooth, velvety layer, about 20 minutes total. Pour into small, clean decorative jars and let cool. Cover airtight and chill until cold, at least 2 hours or up to 3 weeks. Makes about 3 cups.

Per tablespoon: 46 cal. (45 percent from fat); 0.6 g protein; 2.3 g fat (1.3 g sat.); 6 g carbo.; 28 mg sodium; 23 mg chol.

Preserves with Chocolate Chunks

1 jar (18 oz.) or 2 jars (10 oz. each), or 1½ to 1¾ cups preserves (choices follow)

¼ cup chopped chocolate (choices follow)

Mix preserves with chocolate to blend. Spoon into clean decorative jars. Serve, or cover and store in refrigerator up to 2 months. Makes 1¾ to 2 cups.

Per tablespoon: 57 cal. (9.5 percent from fat); 0.2 g protein; 0.6 g fat (0.3 g sat.); 13 g carbo.; 2.2 mg sodium; 0 mg chol.

Choices: orange marmalade and **bittersweet** or semisweet **chocolate; currant jelly** and **white chocolate.**

Spirited Preserves

1 jar (18 to 20 oz.) or 2 jars (10 oz. each), or 1½ to 1¾ cups jam, jelly, or preserves (choices follow)

3 to 4 tablespoons liqueur or wine (choices follow)

Mix the jam and liqueur to taste until well blended. Spoon into clean decorative jars. Serve, or cover and store in the refrigerator up to 2 months. Makes 1⅔ to 1¾ cups.

Per tablespoon: 58 cal. (0 percent from fat); 0.1 g protein; 0 g fat; 14 g carbo.; 2.4 mg sodium; 0 mg chol.

Choices: raspberry jam and **raspberry-flavor liqueur; apricot jam** and **orange-flavor liqueur; apple butter** and **port.** ∎

By Linda Lau Anusasananan, Betsy Reynolds Bateson

Wine gadgets the pros prefer

Gift ideas for any wine buff

By Linda Lau Anusasananan

IS THERE A WINE GADGET YOU JUST COULDN'T LIVE without?" we asked people in the wine business. In the course of uncovering their preferences, we discovered some inexpensive stocking-stuffers—as well as an extravagance or two.

Look for these gadgets and other accessories in wine and cookware stores. Three sources offer a wide selection by mail.

IWA, Inc., 11020 Audelia Rd., Suite B-113, Dallas 75243; (800) 527-4072.

The Wine Appreciation Guild, 155 Connecticut St., San Francisco 94107; (800) 231-9463.

The Wine Enthusiast, Box 39, Pleasantville, N.Y. 10570; (800) 356-8466. ∎

NORMAN A. PLATE

Keep it chilled.

"When we relax," explains Deborah Cahn of Navarro Vineyards, "we like to get away and take a picnic with cold champagne." She slips an insulated jacket around the bottle to keep it cold. The Quick Chill, above (about $12, from Sierra Housewares), is one of several freezable jackets that chill a room-temperature bottle in 10 to 15 minutes.

Keep it sparkling. Can't finish that bottle of bubbly? John Scharffenberger of Scharffenberger Cellars caps his bottles with a stopper (above, about $5 from Le Bouchon) that screws down onto the top. "I love it because wine won't leak even if you put the bottle on its side," he says. A similar model (about $6 from A. Zanger Co.) comes from Spain. For still wines, use an all-purpose stopper (below, $1.50 from Ghidini-FGB) that clamps down tightly.

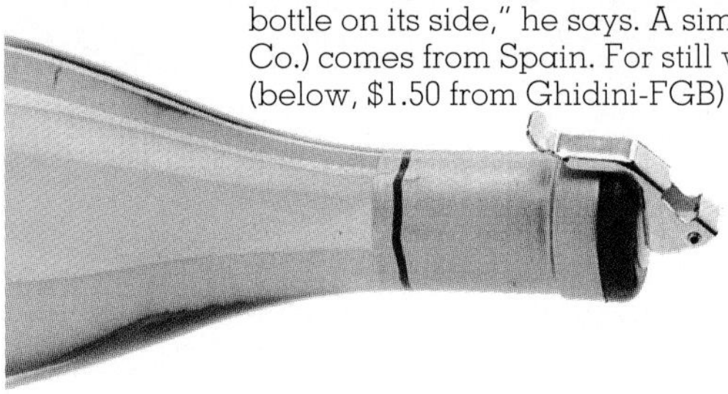

Open it easily. "Once you get good with any opener, you swear by it," declares Donna Bottrell, president of The Wine Appreciation Guild. Nan Campbell of Carneros Quality Alliance, like many who work in wine-tasting rooms, touts the top-of-the-line Screwpull Lever Model by Le Creuset (below right, $100 to $120) as being fast and easy. "When I had to do big tastings," she explains, "I'd borrow one from the wineries. They got so tired of me asking, they gave me one as a gift." Many pros like the waiter's corkscrew (below left, about $5), the twin-pronged cork puller ($3 to $12), and Screwpull's pocket and table models (both about $20).

Keep it fresh.

Wineries have long used nitrogen and other gases to keep wine fresh. Now, gases come canned for home use. "Private Preserve is great," exclaims Darlene Zandanel, wine steward at Elka, in San Francisco. "It lays a blanket of gas on the wine, which keeps it really fresh." A ½-ounce can (enough for 80 uses) costs about $10.

Guard against drips. Spouts keep wine from dripping and staining labels and tablecloths. This silver-plated model (about $20, from Mema) has a cork stopper. Other choices include drip collars that fit onto a bottle's neck (about $10) and flexible disks that fit into a bottle's neck to form a spout (three for about $4).

SUGAR-TRIMMED *cranberry margarita sports whole berries as garnish; dip glass rim in cranberry juice, then sugar, for festive pink hue.*

Merry cranberry margaritas

I F YOU THOUGHT FROZEN margaritas were at their best as hot-weather sippers, this winter variation might change your mind. Try it at your next holiday party for a refreshing twist.

Cranberry Margaritas

1¼ cups cranberry juice cocktail

½ cup sugar

1½ cups (6 oz.) fresh or frozen cranberries, rinsed

¾ cup lime juice

¾ cup tequila

½ cup orange-flavor liqueur

3 cups coarsely crushed ice

Pour ¼ cup of the cranberry juice into a shallow bowl. Pour 3 tablespoons sugar onto a flat plate. Dip the rims of 4 to 6 widemouthed glasses (6- to 8-oz. size, suitable for margaritas) into juice, then into sugar. Set the glasses aside.

Reserve 12 cranberries. In a blender, whirl until smooth and slushy the remaining cranberries, cranberry juice, sugar, lime juice, tequila, orange liqueur, and ice. If necessary, blend in 2 batches, then mix. Fill glasses; garnish with reserved berries. Serves 4 to 6.

Per serving: 239 cal. (0.8 percent from fat); 0.2 g protein; 0.2 g fat (0 g sat.); 36 g carbo; 6.7 mg sodium; 0 mg chol. ∎

By Christine Weber Hale

Smoky, fast low-fat appetizer

I N ABOUT 10 MINUTES, THIS low-fat appetizer can be ready to serve; it's made with canned albacore tuna and other ingredients that you can keep on hand. The smoke taste comes from liquid smoke; you'll find this product in supermarkets near the barbecue sauces or in the fancy foods section.

Quick-Smoke Tuna Spread

1 can (9¼ oz.) albacore tuna packed in water, drained

⅓ cup low-fat cottage cheese

3 tablespoons lemon juice

½ teaspoon liquid smoke

Freshly ground pepper

About 1 tablespoon drained canned capers

Parsley sprig

Thin strip of lemon peel

In a food processor or with an electric mixer, whirl or beat tuna, cottage cheese, lemon juice, and liquid smoke until very smooth. Add pepper to taste.

Spoon spread into a small bowl; garnish with capers, parsley, and the lemon peel, twisted. Use, or, if making ahead, cover and chill up to 1 day. Makes 1⅓ cups.—*Mary Brock, Grass Valley, California*

Per tablespoon: 19 cal. (14 percent from fat); 3.5 g protein; 0.3 g fat (0.1 g sat.); 0.2 g carbo.; 71 mg sodium; 5 mg chol. ∎

By Elaine Johnson

CAPER-DOTTED *smoked fish spread goes well on toasted baguette slices.*

TANGY *eggplant relish suits lamb.*

This marmalade is for meats

R OASTING EGGPLANT CHUNKS soak up sweet-tart seasonings and become creamy soft to make the mellow foundation for this refreshing meat condiment. For an appetizer, spread it on toast.

Roasted Eggplant Marmalade

4 small (about 4 lb. total) eggplants, stems trimmed

¼ cup minced garlic

¼ cup minced fresh ginger

⅓ cup firmly packed brown sugar

¼ cup red wine vinegar

2 tablespoons Oriental sesame oil

2 tablespoons chopped fresh or 2 teaspoons dried tarragon

2 teaspoons fennel seed

1 cup regular-strength chicken broth

Cut eggplants into ½-inch cubes. In a 10- by 15-inch pan (2 in. deep), mix cubes, garlic, ginger, sugar, vinegar, oil, tarragon, and fennel.

Bake in a 400° oven; stir occasionally until liquid evaporates and browned bits form in pan, about 1½ hours. Add ½ cup broth; scrape browned bits free. Bake until liquid evaporates, about 20 minutes. Add remaining broth and repeat step. Serve marmalade warm or cool. If making ahead, cover and chill up to 10 days; freeze to store longer. Makes about 4 cups.—*Gary J. Danko, The Ritz-Carlton, San Francisco*

Per tablespoon: 17 cal. (26 percent from fat); 0.4 g protein; 0.5 g fat (0.1 g sat.); 3.2 g carbo.; 2.5 mg sodium; 0 mg chol. ∎

By Christine W. Hale

SUNSET'S KITCHEN CABINET

Creative ways with everyday foods—submitted by *Sunset* readers,
tested in *Sunset* kitchens, approved by *Sunset* taste panels

VIBRANT MAGENTA BEETS *are the base of this dip for crisp vegetables.*

Ruby Vegetable Dip

Paulette Rossi, Portland

This beautifully colored dip has great flavor but practically no fat—and it's easy to make.

1 can (8¼ oz.) diced, julienne, or sliced pickled beets

½ cup minced red onion

½ cup unflavored nonfat yogurt
   Salt and pepper
   About 1 cup *each* broccoli flowerets and carrot, cucumber, and thin jicama slices

Drain beets, reserving ¼ cup liquid. In a food processor or blender, whirl beets and reserved liquid until very smoothly puréed. In a small bowl, mix with onion and yogurt; add salt and pepper to taste. If making ahead, cover and chill up to 4 hours.

Set ruby dip on a tray and surround with broccoli, carrot, cucumber, and jicama, to scoop into sauce as eaten. Makes 1½ cups, about 12 servings.

Per serving: 33 cal. (2.7 percent from fat); 1.4 g protein; 0.1 g fat (0 g sat.); 7 g carbo.; 66 mg sodium; 0.2 mg chol.

Gingerbread-Apple Coffee Cake

Louise Galen, Los Angeles

CARAMELIZED APPLES *top moist gingerbread. Cut into squares.*

3 tablespoons butter or margarine

6 cups peeled and sliced tart apples (about 2 lb.)

¼ cup sugar

¼ cup bourbon or apple juice
   Gingerbread batter (directions follow)
   Whipped cream (optional)

In a 10- to 12-inch frying pan over medium-high heat, melt butter. Add apples; turn often with a spatula until just tender when pierced, about 5 minutes. Stir in sugar and bourbon; cook until liquid evaporates and apples begin to brown, about 6 minutes. Spoon apples into a well-buttered 9- by 13-inch pan; top with gingerbread batter.

Bake in a 350° oven until cake starts to pull from pan sides and center springs back when lightly pressed, about 40 minutes. Run a knife around pan sides; invert cake onto a platter. Serve warm or cold with whipped cream. Serves 12.

Per serving: 382 cal. (28 percent from fat); 3.4 g protein; 12 g fat (6.9 g sat.); 65 g carbo.; 368 mg sodium; 64 mg chol.

Gingerbread batter. In a 1- to 2-quart pan, bring 1 cup **dark molasses** and 1 cup **water** to a boil. Stir in 1 teaspoon **baking soda** and let cool.

In a bowl, beat 1 cup firmly packed **brown sugar** and ½ cup (¼ lb.) **butter** or margarine until smoothly mixed. Add 2 **large eggs** and beat until well blended. Mix 2 cups **all-purpose flour,** 1 tablespoon **baking powder,** 2 teaspoons *each* **ground cinnamon** and **ground ginger,** and ¼ teaspoon **ground cloves.** Alternating, stir ½ the flour and molasses mixtures at a time into sugar and butter until well mixed.

Beat-the-holiday-rush Beans

Pam Mulkey, Tonopah, Nevada

CANNED BEANS *and garbanzos give staying powder to quick, hearty soup.*

1 pound ground turkey

1 large (10 oz.) onion, chopped

4 cloves garlic, minced or pressed
   About 4 cups regular-strength chicken broth

1 can (about 15 oz.) *each* kidney beans, lima beans, pinto beans, and garbanzos, drained and rinsed

¾ cup catsup

⅓ cup firmly packed brown sugar

2 tablespoons red wine vinegar

4 teaspoons ground dried mustard

In a 5- to 6-inch quart pan, break turkey into chunks; add onion, garlic, and ½ cup chicken broth. Stir often over medium-high heat until liquid evaporates and meat and onion start to brown. Add another ½ cup broth; stir to release browned bits. Boil dry as in preceding step. Repeat, adding liquid and boiling dry until meat and onion are well browned, 2 or 3 more times.

Stir in 1½ cups broth; kidney, lima, and pinto beans; garbanzos; catsup; sugar; vinegar; and mustard. Cover and simmer gently until flavors are blended, about 1 hour; stir often. If making ahead, let cool, cover, and chill up to 3 days; reheat to serve. Serves 6.

Per serving: 371 cal. (21 percent from fat); 25 g protein; 8.6 g fat (1.8 g sat.); 50 g carbo.; 740 mg sodium; 55 mg chol.

Shrimp and Capers

Audrey Thibodeau, Fountain Hills, Arizona

- 1 bottle or can (12 oz.) beer
- ½ cup minced onion
- ¾ teaspoon celery seed
- 1 dried bay leaf
- 1 pound large (31 to 35 per lb.) shrimp, shelled and deveined
- ½ cup tomato-based chili sauce
- 1 tablespoon honey-flavor mustard
  Spinach leaves, stems removed, rinsed and crisped
- 2 tablespoons drained canned capers
  Lemon wedges

To a 10- to 12-inch frying pan, add beer, onion, celery seed, and bay leaf. Bring to a boil over high heat and boil 2 minutes. Add shrimp; cover and simmer until shrimp turn pink and are opaque but still moist-looking in thickest part (cut to test), about 3 minutes; stir occasionally. With a slotted spoon, lift out shrimp; cover and chill until cool, at least 1 hour or up to 1 day.

Boil beer mixture, uncovered, on high heat until reduced to ⅓ cup; discard bay leaf. Mix liquid with chili sauce and honey mustard. Cover and chill up to 1 day.

Arrange spinach on 6 plates, top with shrimp and beer dressing, sprinkle with capers, and garnish with lemon. Makes 6 first-course servings.

Per serving: 110 cal. (9.8 percent from fat); 13 g protein; 1.2 g fat (0.2 g sat.); 11 g carbo.; 472 mg sodium; 93 mg chol.

SHRIMP SALAD *on spinach leaves has beer-flavored dressing.*

Sweet Potato Stir-fry

Holly Kaslewicz, Stanford, California

- 2 tablespoons salad oil
- 2 pounds sweet potatoes or yams, peeled and cut into ½-inch cubes
- ½ cup golden raisins
- ½ cup orange juice
- 1 tablespoon honey
  About 1 cup regular-strength chicken broth
- ¼ teaspoon *each* ground cloves and ground nutmeg
- ½ cup sweetened, shredded dried coconut
  About ¼ cup roasted, salted almonds

To a 10- to 12-inch frying pan over medium-high heat, add oil. When oil is hot, add sweet potato cubes; stir often until tender-crisp to bite, about 7 minutes. Stir in raisins, orange juice, honey, ½ cup broth, cloves, and nutmeg. Cover and simmer gently 10 minutes. Add remaining ½ cup broth; cover and simmer until potatoes are tender to bite and most of the liquid is absorbed, about 25 minutes total. Stir in shredded coconut, and pour the sweet potato mixture into a bowl. Sprinkle with almonds. Serves 8.

Per serving: 215 cal. (34 percent from fat); 3.2 g protein; 8.2 g fat (2.1 g sat.); 34 g carbo.; 69 mg sodium; 0 mg chol.

AFRICAN FLAVORS *go into sweet potato stir-fry. Garnish with Italian parsley.*

Nana's Crunchy Anise Cookies

Edith S. Beccaria, South San Francisco, California

- 4 large eggs
- 1¼ cups sugar
- ½ cup (¼ lb.) butter or margarine, melted
- ½ cup half-and-half (light cream)
- 1 tablespoon vanilla
- 5 cups all-purpose flour
- 5 teaspoons baking powder
- 2 teaspoons anise seed, crushed

In a large bowl, beat to blend eggs, sugar, and butter. Beat in half-and-half and vanilla. Stir together flour, baking powder, and anise seed; add to egg mixture and beat to mix well (dough is thick and sticky). Cover and chill until firm enough to handle.

Divide dough into quarters. On a lightly floured board, shape 1 quarter at a time into a 1-inch-diameter rope. Cut into 1-inch pieces and place about 2 inches apart on lightly oiled 12- by 15-inch baking sheets (2 sheets, used repeatedly, are adequate).

Bake in a 350° oven until cookies are pale ivory and feel firm when touched, about 15 minutes. On pans, cut each piece in half diagonally. Place cut sides down. Switch pan positions in oven, and bake cookies until golden, about 10 minutes longer. Cool on racks. Serve, or store airtight up to 2 weeks; freeze to store longer. Makes about 16 dozen.

Per cookie: 24 cal. (26 percent from fat); 0.5 g protein; 0.7 g fat (0.4 g sat.); 3.9 g carbo.; 19 mg sodium; 5.9 mg chol.

Compiled by Betsy Reynolds Bateson

TINY, SHINY *cookies are baked twice to become crunchy like biscotti.*

Articles Index

Index of Recipe Titles

General Index

A

Add-on chili with beans, Gloria's, 8
Adobo, Filipino, 255
All-apple jelly, 68
All-purpose spaghetti sauce, 204
Almond
  meringue stars with berries and champagne sabayon, 69
  -topped cookies, 263
  topping, peach cobbler with, 192
  -zucchini stir-steam, 154
Alsatian beef brisket with broth, 31
Angel pie, rhubarb, 73
Angel wings, spiced, 35
Anise cookies, Nana's crunchy, 277
Antipasto party, 148–149
Antipasto salad, celery root, 72
Appetizers
  apricots with goat cheese, 269
  artichoke fondue, 110
  artichoke nibbles, 203
  bake-it-easy dip, 207
  Beverly's tuna spread, 155
  buy-and-serve, 269
  caponata pizza, 268
  celery root antipasto salad, 72
  cherry pepper shooters, 268
  chili popcorn, 268
  dried tomato tapenade, 71
  hasty hots for the '90s, 269
  quick cheese fondue, 268
  quick-smoke tuna spread, 275
  roasted eggplant marmalade, 275
  ruby vegetable dip, 276
  sausage mushroom caps, 269
  shrimp and papaya with Asian dunk sauce, 269
  spiced angel wings, 35
  turkey tortilla roll-ups, 138
  white bean pâté, 138
Apple(s)
  -blueberry jam, 68
  breakfast cobbler, 17
  cabbage slaw, 227
  cobbler with oatmeal cookie crust, 227
  coffee cake, gingerbread-, 276
  crisp, 203
  grilled pork with greens and, 87
  jelly, all-, 68
  -mint jelly, 68
  pie, praline, 71
  and pork stew, Northwest, 189
  -raspberry jelly, 68
  salad, sweet potato and, 21
  tart, fennel-, 212
Applesauce, red wine, 267
Apricot(s)
  -ginger scones, 261
  glaze, grilled veal shanks with, 151
  with goat cheese, 269

Apricot(s) (cont'd.)
  -stuffed turkey roast, 137
Armenian peda, 113
Aromatics, red pepper relish with, 237
Artichoke(s)
  bottoms, baked, with lamb, 111
  -celery salad, 45
  cream soup, 92
  fondue, 110
  kebabs, grilled, 111
  nibbles, 203
  with smoldering shrimp, 169
Asian chicken salad, sweet and spicy, 99
Asian dunk sauce, shrimp and papaya with, 269
Asparagus
  and pasta stir-fry, 95
  stir-fried pork and, 73
Astoria omelet, Papa Haydn's, 127
Avocado, mesclun, and hazelnut salad, 234
Avocados and tomatoes, firecracker rice salad with, 142

B

Baby spider rolls, 224
Bacon dressing, chilled sugar snap peas with mint and, 234
Bacon, white bean, and chicken salad, 64
Bagels, whole-wheat poppy seed, 116
Baked artichoke bottoms with lamb, 111
Baked fennel with gorgonzola, 235
Baked fish-and-chips, 8
Baked ham with maple-cherry glaze, 260
Baked lentils with honey and chutney, 73
Bake-it-easy dip, 207
Balsamic vinegar, information about, 130–131
Banana chutney, mango-, jerk pork with pasta and, 220
Barbecued chicken, lemon-rosemary, 37
Barbecued flank steak, soy-honey, 154
Barbecued pork crown roast, 92
Barbecued turkey, 231
Barbecue, Texas two-step mixed grill, 170
Barley
  casserole, mushroom and, with fila crust, 215
  pilaf, wild rice and, 32
  salad, grilled lamb chops with, 86
  soup, sausage-, with Swiss chard, 25
Basel seeded wheat twists, 9
Basil, fresh mascarpone, and tomato, bruschetta with, 143
Basil leaves, transparent, 35
Basque sheepherder's bread, 115
Bastes for turkey, 231
Batter bread, onion herb, 20
Bavarian crunch potato salad, 120
Bean(s)
  beat-the-holiday-rush, 276

Bean(s) (cont'd.)
  black, and corn salsa, 152
  black, chili with oranges, 13
  black, hummus, and carrot slaw sandwiches, 16
  dried, how to cook, 62
  Four Corners soup, 273
  Gloria's add-on chili with, 8
  and hominy stew, 62
  pinto, and rice, 175
  pinto, salad, 149
  ranch, 108
  salad, red pepper flan with, 77
  soft tacos with, 62
  soup, black and white, 64
  and tomato salad, 62
  and turkey burritos, 245
  West meets East soup, 272
  white, chicken, and bacon salad, 64
  white, pâté, 138
  white, salad, 124
Beat-the-holiday-rush beans, 276
Beef
  birria-style brisket, 17
  brisket, Alsatian, with broth, 31
  buckaroo Spanish rice, 109
  Christopher Ranch garlic steak sandwiches, 185
  Gloria's add-on chili with beans, 8
  low-fat spaghetti and meatballs, 18
  Malaysian satay, 133
  shanks, grilled, with mustard glaze, 151
  short rib and vegetable stew, 57
  simple sukiyaki, 257
  son-of-a-son-of-a-bitch stew, 109
  soy-honey barbecued flank steak, 154
  steaks, tequila, 26
  Texas two-step mixed grill barbecue, 170
  zucchini grande olé, 174
Beer
  biscuits, Helen's whole-wheat, 108
  -molasses sauce and roasted vegetables, spareribs with, 212
  quick bread, 208
Belgian endive and radish salad, 94
Belgian endive, tangelo, and cranberry salad, 233
Berries
  and champagne sabayon, almond meringue stars with, 69
  with herbs and champagne, 167
  lemon pudding cake with, 117
  summer, serving ideas for, 129
Berry
  sauce, 117
  syrup, lemon-, 129
Beverages
  chocolate shake, 34
  citrus wine splashes, 13
  classic margarita, 28
  convenience margarita, 28
  cranberry margaritas, 275
  frozen virgin margarita, 28
  fruit salad drink, 135

Beverages (cont'd.)
  mocha au lait, 24
  strawberry-mint lemonade, 135
  tequila or orange sours, 98
Beverly's tuna spread, 155
Birria-style brisket, 17
Biscuits, Helen's whole-wheat beer, 108
Black and white bean soup, 64
Black bean
  chili with oranges, 13
  and corn salsa, 152
  hummus and carrot slaw sandwiches, 16
  and white bean soup, 64
Blitzen River cobbler, 109
Blueberries, Papa Haydn's lemon–poppy seed waffles with, 128
Blueberry jam, apple-, 68
Blue cheese dip, 72
Blue cheese pockets, lamb chops with, 88
B. Moloch's coffee-bran muffins, 126
B. Moloch's raisin scones, 127
Boiled corn with lime, butters, and cheese, 182
Bok choy salad with mint, 227
Bourbon bread pudding, 93
Bow ties, poppy seed, 63
Bran
  muffins, coffee-, B. Moloch's, 126
  oat, whole-wheat muffins, 19
  -peach muffins, 226
Brandy, oranges in, 31
Bread dressing, old-fashioned or lean multigrain, 236
Bread machines, using, 217–219
Bread pudding, bourbon, 93
Breads. See also Muffins; Pancakes
  apricot-ginger scones, 261
  Armenian peda, 113
  baby spider rolls, 224
  Basel seeded wheat twists, 9
  Basque sheepherder's, 115
  beer quick, 208
  B. Moloch's raisin scones, 127
  chili-cheese triangles, 191
  cinnamon rolls, 265
  Dutch crunch, 114
  fougasse, 63
  fragrant Greek seed, 254
  fruited golden or spiced bread or buns, 264
  golden, 264
  golden or spiced buns, 264
  golden star, 264
  grow-your-own whole-wheat, 251
  Helen's whole-wheat beer biscuits, 108
  holiday challah, 206
  kulich with candied orange peel, 76
  mixing and kneading basics, 115
  nineteen ninety-three sourdough parmesan-pepper, 115
  one-hour dinner rolls, 63
  onion herb batter, 20
  pocket, 114
  poppy seed bow ties, 63
  Portuguese sweet, 113
  pueblo, 114

∴ General Index